PLATE I

Kipeles, Chief Medicine Man of the Nandi, surrounded by his advisers (Henderson).

Frontispiece

THE NANDI

THEIR LANGUAGE AND FOLK-LORE

BY

A. C. HOLLIS

WITH INTRODUCTION BY
SIR CHARLES ELIOT

NEGRO UNIVERSITIES PRESS
WESTPORT, CONNECTICUT

Originally published in 1909
by The Clarendon Press, Oxford

Reprinted from an original copy in the collections
of the University of Illinois Library

Reprinted in 1971 by
Negro Universities Press
A Division of Greenwood Press, Inc.
Westport, Connecticut

Library of Congress Catalogue Card Number 71-76481

SBN 8371-1515-9

Printed in the United States of America

PREFACE

ON my return to East Africa in January, 1905, I determined to pursue my studies in the languages, folk-lore, and customs of those tribes inhabiting our Protectorate that form an offshoot of the Nilotic stock, and to write an account of the Nandi-Lumbwa group on somewhat similar lines to those followed in my book on the Masai.[1]

But little is known of the Nandi and allied tribes, notwithstanding the fact that we have administered some of their territories for a decade or more, and the following books and papers are, so far as I am aware, all that have been published on the language and customs of these people.

1. *Notes on the Ethnology of tribes met with during progress of the Juba Expedition*, by Lt.-Col. (now General Sir) J. R. L. Macdonald (Journal of the Anthropological Institute for Great Britain and Ireland, 1899).

2. *Eastern Uganda*, by C. W. Hobley (London, 1902).

3. *The Uganda Protectorate*, by Sir H. H. Johnston, G.C.M.G., K.C.B. (London, 1902).

4. *Anthropological Studies in Kavirondo and Nandi*, by C. W. Hobley (Journal of the Anthropological Institute for Great Britain and Ireland, 1903).

5. *The East Africa Protectorate*, by Sir C. Eliot, K.C.M.G., C.B. (London, 1905).

I have consulted these works freely, and wherever my account differs from them it may be assumed that I have been unable to obtain confirmation of the earlier reports.

My own account, which has been written during my leisure hours miles away from Nandi, is far from exhaustive, and an anthropologist will everywhere feel that the evidence obtained might well be supplemented by further

---

[1] *The Masai, their Language and Folk-Lore* (Oxford, 1905).

inquiry. In fact, the result of my researches will in many instances be only sufficient to whet the appetite for more, and I hope that those living on the spot will endeavour to obtain further information on the various points raised. For example, there is without doubt more cattle magic in East Africa than meets the eye, and many customs, otherwise inexplicable, probably have or had some reference to securing the welfare of, or to pleasing, the cattle.

I had at first some difficulties to contend with. Nandi is situated some distance from Nairobi and Mombasa, and in 1905 but few of these free savages cared about accepting employment with Europeans and leaving their own country. I succeeded, however, in obtaining the services of two small boys, named Oriare and Matang, the former of whom was a Masai-speaking Nandi and the latter a Swahili-speaking Kipsikīs or Lumbwa. These two boys remained with me for some months and then returned to their homes, but not before I had mastered the intricacies of their language. From August to December, 1905, I was stationed in Mombasa, and I was fortunate enough to find interned there a Nandi political prisoner, named Ar-ap-Sirtoi, who gladly relieved the monotony of his existence by spending a few hours with me two or three times a week talking to me of his country and describing the customs and folk-lore of his people. From him and later on from another political prisoner, named Ar-ap-Kuna, who was interned at Machakos, I obtained much useful information. After the close of the Nandi punitive expedition in April, 1906, I secured the services of a warrior named Ar-ap-Chepsiet, who had been wounded. This man remained with me till I left East Africa in April, 1908, and to him I am indebted to a very great extent for the account of the customs, &c., and for the vocabulary.

I have twice travelled through Nandi, and I have also twice been to Lumbwa, but, except for a flying visit to Elgeyo in 1903, I have not seen the countries of any of the other allied tribes. I have, however, had opportunities of meeting and conversing with men from Elgeyo, Kamasia,

Buret, and Sotik, as well as with Dorobo from Mau and Kikuyu. The language spoken by all of these people is, except for dialectic differences, identical with that of the Nandi, and the grammar and vocabulary of the Nandi will serve equally well for the other tribes, who, with the allied peoples on Mount Elgon, and the Dorobo in British and German East Africa, number at least a quarter of a million souls. The customs, religious ideas, and folk-lore of the allied tribes are also very similar to those of the Nandi.

During my second trip to Nandi, made early this year, I had the advantage of meeting influential men and women of all the clans. I was thus in a position to check and amplify my notes, and it was then that I procured most of the proverbs and riddles—the latter from children who entered whole-heartedly into the fun. I was also able in February last to go through some of my notes with the chief medicine man of Lumbwa, Ar-ap-Koileke, who is probably better acquainted with the folk-lore of the Nandi and Lumbwa than any one living. I have myself witnessed the smiths, potters, and medicine men at work; I have been present at many of the dances; I have personally inspected the huts, stock, plantations, traps, and honey-barrels, &c.; and I have seen cattle slaughtered, game killed, food cooked and eaten, corn sown, houses erected, and boys and girls attired in their strange costumes both before and after the circumcision ceremonies.

My thanks are due to the Director of the British Museum for the photographs of the implements and ornaments, &c., and to the following gentlemen for permission to reproduce their photographs: Captain R. Meinertzhagen, Mr. C. W. Hobley, C.M.G., Dr. F. L. Henderson, Captain H. A. Wilson, Captain H. C. Hart, Mr. R. J. Stordy, Captain C. V. Champion de Crespigny, Mr. H. Rayne, and Mr. G. E. Powter. To Mr. E. Battiscombe I am indebted for the identification of the trees given in Appendix I, to Mr. E. L. Waring for the excellent map, to Dr. A. D. Milne for the sketch of the Nandi hut and the description of the operation given on p. 55, and to Mr. W. J. Monson for the free translation of the prayer given on p. 42. I desire to express my gratitude to those Provincial and District Commissioners (notably Messrs. C. S. Hemsted, J. B. Ainsworth, and H. B. Partington) who have assisted me in my work, and to Sir C. Eliot and Mr. R. R. Marett for perusing the proofs and offering suggestions. To Sir C. Eliot I am also deeply grateful for the valuable introduction he has so kindly written. I should further like to acknowledge the help I derived from Professor J. G. Frazer's *Questions on the Customs, Beliefs, and Languages of Savages* (Cambridge, 1907), a copy of which I have now sent to all the stations in the East Africa Protectorate for the use of officials.

The Nandi themselves since the punitive expedition of 1905–6 have settled down quietly, and give promise to become a law-abiding tribe. The land included in their native reserve is some of the best in the Protectorate, and early this year I passed through miles of country made ready for the sowing operations which had just commenced. The suspicious attitude shown by the Nandi towards the Administration and their fear and dislike of the white man have now quite disappeared, and it only rests with those officials who, by sympathetic treatment, have so successfully won their affections to develop the best qualities of these people and make them useful members of the community.

A. C. HOLLIS.

October, 1908.

CONTENTS

	PAGE
INTRODUCTION	xiii

PART I

History	1
Divisions of the Nandi Country and People	4
Sacred Animals	6
Social Divisions	11
Mode of Subsistence	13
Wearing Apparel, Weapons, &c.	27
Industries	35
Religious Beliefs	40
Government	48
Circumcision Festivals	52
Marriage	60
Birth	64
Illness and Death	69
Inheritance	72
Punishment for Crime	73
Miscellaneous Customs	77
Relationship	92
Divisions of Time	94
Myths	97

FOLK-TALES.

The Hare and the Elephant	101
The Hare who acted as Nurse	101
The Hare and the Old Woman	102
The Hyena's Prophecy	103
The Origin of the Leopard and Hyena	104
The Hyenas and their Medicine Man	104
The Tapkōs Bird and the Child	105
How the Masai were first repulsed by the Nandi	106
The Warriors and the Devil	106
The Demon who ate people, and the Child	107
How the Dorobo discovered Poison	107

CONTENTS

	PAGE
The Philosophy of the Dorobo	108
The Sayings of Animals and Birds	109
The Story of the Creation	111
The Story of the Dogs	114
The Story of the Cattle	116
The Story of the Eleusine Grain	120
The New Moon	122
The Nandi *House that Jack Built* or *The Old Woman and her Pig*	123
NANDI PROVERBS	124
NANDI ENIGMAS	133

PART II. NANDI GRAMMAR

Alphabet and Pronunciation	152
Changes of Letters	153
The Accent	156
Gender and Number	158
The Article	160
Cases	164
Substantives	166
Adjectives	180
Numerals	183
Pronouns	184
Personal	184
Possessive	184
Demonstrative	186
Reflexive	187
Relative	187
Indefinite	188
Interrogative	188
Verbs	189
Simple Verbs	193
Derivative Verbs: Verbs denoting motion towards the speaker	208
Verbs denoting motion from the speaker	209
The Dative form	211
The Applied form	213

CONTENTS

	PAGE
The Reflexive form	213
The Reciprocal form	214
Intransitive Verbs	215
Causative Verbs	216
Neuter or Quasi-passive form	216
Neuter Verbs	218
Irregular Verbs	219
Auxiliary Verbs	226
Reduplication	227
Adverbs	227
Conjunctions	229
Prepositions	230
Interjections	230
ENGLISH-NANDI VOCABULARY	232
APPENDIX I: List of Nandi Trees, Grasses, &c.	313
APPENDIX II: The Meanings of the Clan Names	317
INDEX	318

LIST OF ILLUSTRATIONS

PAGE

Kipeles, Chief Medicine Man of the Nandi, surrounded by his advisers (Plate I) . . . . . . *Frontispiece*

Nandi Hills, looking over the Nyando Valley (Plate II) . . *To face Introduction*

Nandi elders (Plate III) . . . . . *To face* p. 1

(*a*) Nandi warriors in battle array. (*b*) The peace conference, December 14, 1905, with the Nandi escarpment in the background (Plate IV) . . . . . *To face* p. 4

(*a*) Entrance to Nandi cattle-kraal. (*b*) Nandi hut (Plate V) . *To face* p. 14

Iron and wooden hoes (Figs. 1–4) 18

Axes and bill-hook (Figs. 5–7) 18

(*a*) Nandi herdsman. (*b*) Stream near Nandi Fort (Plate VI) *To face* p. 20

Nandi shooting with bow and arrow (Plate VII) . *To face* p. 23

Bow and arrows used for bleeding purposes (Figs. 8–13) . . 23

Knife used for tapping palms (Fig. 14) 25

Drinking straw (Fig. 15) 26

(*a*) Pipe, tobacco pouches, snuff-boxes, &c. (*b*) Girls' dresses (Plate VIII) . . . . *To face* p. 26

(*a*) Nandi girl wearing the ingoriet-ap-ko garment and the osiek apron. (*b*) Nandi woman wearing her ear-rings as a necklace (Plate IX) . . . . . . *To face* p. 29

Needle (Fig. 16) 30

Nandi warrior, showing cicatrices raised on shoulder and scars burnt on wrist (Plate X). . . . . *To face* p. 30

Spears (Figs. 17–20) 31

Quiver, scabbard, and swords (Figs. 21–24) 32

(*a*) Ear-rings worn by men, women, and boys. (*b*) Ostrich-feather head-dress and ostrich-feather receptacle (Plate XI) *To face* p. 32

Clubs (Figs. 25–27) 33

Bows (Figs. 28, 29) 34

Arrows with wooden and iron heads, and shaft (Figs. 30–36) . 34

LIST OF ILLUSTRATIONS

	PAGE
Necklaces worn by men, women, and children (Plate XII) . *To face* p.	35
(*a*) Nandi pots and jars. (*b*) Milk gourds and calves' feeding bottle (Plate XIII). . . . . . *To face* p.	36
Smith's pincers or tongs (Fig. 37). Cutting-iron (Fig. 38) .	37
Pestle and mortar (Figs. 39, 40)	38
Nandi stool (Fig. 41)	38
Nandi bellows (Plate XIV) . . . . . *To face* p.	38
Nandi lyre (Fig. 42) ; Lumbwa lyre (Fig. 43) . . .	39
(*a*) Barrel used by old men for putting their garments in. (*b*) Basket. (*c*) Boys' bull-roarer and friction drum (Plate XV) . . . . *To face* p.	40
(1) Water-jar. (2) Girls' friction drum. (3) Drum stick (Plate XVI) . . . . . . *To face* p.	43
Bag in which warriors carry eleusine flour when proceeding on a raid (Fig. 44)	43
(*a*) Nandi warrior blowing a war-horn. (*b*) Nandi warriors' dance (Plate XVII) . . . . . *To face* p.	45
(*a*) Bracelet used by archers for protecting the wrist. (*b*) Armlets (Plate XVIII). . . . . . *To face* p.	46
Kipchomber or Ar-ap-Koileke, the Chief Medicine Man of the Kipsikīs or Lumbwa, with his son, Sonaiet or Ar-ap-Kipchomber, his principal advisers, and the headmen of Buret and Sotik (Plate XIX) . . . . *To face* p.	50
Two specimens of Kimaranguchet head-dress (worn by boys after circumcision) (Plate XX). . . . *To face* p.	53
Boys' circumcision knife (Fig. 45)	53
Tarusiot, or boy recently circumcised, wearing the nyorkit garb and the kimaranguchet head-dress (Plate XXI) *To face* p.	54
Tarusiot, or girl about to be circumcised, wearing warrior's garments (Plate XXII) . . . . . *To face* p.	56
(*a*) Tarusiek, or girls recently circumcised, wearing the nyorkit garb, the soiyuet head-dress, and carrying the motolik sticks. (*b*) Soiyuet head-dress, worn by girls after circumcision (Plate XXIII) . . . . . *To face* p.	59
Girls' circumcision knife (Fig. 46)	59
Nariet head-dress (Plate XXIV) . . . . *To face* p.	60
A Nandi bride (Plate XXV) . . . . . *To face* p.	63
A wife and daughter of Ar-ap-Koileke, the Chief Medicine Man of the Lumbwa (Plate XXVI) . . . . *To face* p.	64
(*a*) Nandi hut. (*b*) Granary and hut (Plate XXVII) *To face* p.	69
(*a*) Nandi elder with two of his daughters. (*b*) A Nandi family (Plate XXVIII) . . . . . . *To face* p.	76

LIST OF ILLUSTRATIONS

	PAGE
Boys' wooden spears (Figs. 47, 48)	82
(a) Warrior's shield (painted). (b) Boys' wooden shields (Plate XXIX).	To face p. 83
Boys' arrows and shaft (Figs. 49–51)	83
(a) Nandi woman and child; (b) Warriors' thigh bell; calves' bell and cows' bell (Plate XXX) . . .	To face p. 87
(a) Stones used by medicine men for divining purposes. (b) Divining boxes (Plate XXXI) . . .	To face p. 88
(a) Nandi boy wearing the kipalpaliot ear-rings, lapuonik necklace, and the seeds of the murguyuet tree in his hair. (b) Nandi women carrying their children (Plate XXXII) .	To face p. 90
Group of Nandi with goats and sheep (Plate XXXIII)	To face p. 94
Nandi elder with his goats and sheep (Plate XXXIV)	To face p. 98
Waterfall in Nandi (Plate XXXV)	To face p. 100
(a) Group of Nandi warriors. (b) Drinking-place for cattle (Plate XXXVI)	To face p. 111
(a) Group of Nandi boys and warriors. (b) Group of Nandi women and children (Plate XXXVII) . .	To face p. 119
Nandi elder—(a) full face; (b) profile (Plate XXXVIII) . .	To face p. 122
Nandi outposts (Plate XXXIX)	To face p. 129
(a) Nandi warriors. (b) Nandi girls (Plate XL) .	To face p. 130
(a) Nandi honey barrel. (b) A Nandi bridge (Plate XLI) .	To face p. 135
(a) Nandi women crushing grain. (b) Nandi women going to market (Plate XLII)	To face p. 138
Small knife (Fig. 52)	142
(a) A salt-lick. (b) River in Nandi (Plate XLIII) .	To face p. 143
Woman's walking-stick (Fig. 53)	144
Two young Nandi warriors—(a) full face; (b) profile (Plate XLIV)	To face p. 144
MAP OF THE DISTRICT	To fold out at end

PLATE II

Nandi Hills, looking over the Nyando Valley (Meinertzhagen).

To face Introduction

INTRODUCTION

In a previous work [1] Mr. Hollis gave an account of the language and customs of the Masai, one of the most important and interesting tribes of Eastern Equatorial Africa. The present volume, which contains a similar study of the Nandi, may be regarded as a continuation of the same researches, for the two tribes are certainly connected, and all information about the physical characters, language, customs, and religion of either sheds light on the origin and affinities of both and of the whole group to which they belong.

The Nandi have obtained a considerable prominence, partly because the Nandi plateau is one of the most beautiful and fertile districts in the East African Protectorate, and partly because they were long an obstacle to the pacification and administration of the country. Ten or twenty years ago they intercepted caravans on their way from the coast to Uganda and killed many traders. Somewhat later they attacked the telegraph line and the Uganda Railway. In 1905 certain sections of them were removed, and the whole tribe has been placed in a reserve a little to the north of the plateau where they formerly dwelt. It would seem, however, that the pre-eminence of the Nandi is simply political, and that for the ethnologist they are merely one section of a large tribe which, though appearing under many and often obscure names, is really one in language and customs, and is disposed in a semicircular belt extending from Mount Elgon to the Southern Mau, but not reaching the shores of Lake Victoria at any point. Among the divisions of this tribe are (1) those inhabiting Mount Elgon, particularly the Kony, less correctly called Elgonyi; (2) those inhabiting the mountains round the Kerio Valley, such as the Elgeyu or Keyu, the Kamasia or Tuken, and the Mutei; (3) those living farther south in the districts called after them Lumbwa, Buret, and Sotik (or Soot). Lumbwa, though now accepted as an official and geographical term, is really an opprobrious Masai word signifying those who have given up the noble art of war and taken to agriculture, and the people known as Lumbwa call themselves Kipsikīs; (4) the Nandi proper, who according to their traditions came partly from Elgon and partly from the Lumbwa country.

[1] *The Masai: Their Language and Folklore*, Clarendon Press, 1904.

In considering the distribution and possible migrations of the Nandi in the past, we must take account of the interesting but somewhat perplexing fact that most of the wild hunting tribes called Dorobo speak a dialect of Nandi. This seems to be certain not only for the Dorobo of the Mau, Lumbwa, &c., but also for those who live on Mount Kenya and in Kikuyu, and near the Natron Lake in German territory. As far as the linguistic evidence goes, the Dorobo might be regarded as an offshoot of the Nandi; but this view is hardly probable, for the traditions of the Masai and Nandi agree in representing the Dorobo as a primitive race who occupied the country before their advent, and the Dorobo, even when they live among the Nandi and speak their language, remain distinct from them. Also the Dorobo dialect contains words which are not Nandi, and a Dorobo colony to the north of Mount Kenya, near the Guaso-Nyiro, is reported to speak a quite different language.[1] It is therefore probable that the Dorobo have borrowed the language of the Nandi. It is common in Africa for an inferior tribe to adopt the speech of a stronger tribe whom they recognize as being in some way their masters, and it is said that another example of the same process may be seen in Kikuyu and near Kilima Njaro, where the Dorobo speak Masai as well as Nandi. But the difficulty is by no means solved by admitting that the Dorobo have borrowed the Nandi language, for there are now no Nandi in Kikuyu or the Rift Valley or anywhere east of Lumbwa and Kamasia. We may suppose either that the Nandi once occupied Kenya, Kikuyu, and the country to the south, and were driven westward by the Masai and others, or that the Dorobo once spread from the Mau to Kikuyu across the Rift Valley. The whole tribe would thus have been in touch with Lumbwa, Nandi, and Kamasia, until a Masai invasion supervened, and by occupying the Rift Valley drove in a wedge of Masai population between Kikuyu and the Mau. This solution is perhaps the simpler of the two, for I think that the balance of probabilities indicates that the Nandi came from the northwest; but a contrary theory, that they came from the northeast, is also tenable, and derives some support from the existence of the Nandi language in Kikuyu and from place names in the Rift Valley.[2] Also there can be little doubt that in the past the Nandi were in contact with Gallas and

---

[1] See the account and short vocabulary in 'Further Notes on the El-Dorobo or Oggiek', by C. W. Hobley, in *Man*, 1905, pp. 43-4.

[2] e. g. the river Morendat (N. *marandut*, footprint) and Mount Suswa (N. *suswo, susua*, grass).

INTRODUCTION

Somalis: their numerals alone show this. Now there is a tradition that these tribes formerly had settlements in Kikuyu and were driven out about seventy years ago, but as far as I know we have no record of their presence on the Mau. Still the most probable hypothesis is that the area where took place the contact and fusion which resulted in the formation of the Masai, Nandi, &c., lay to the north or northwest of the Rift Valley. Sir Samuel Baker states that the Galla once extended, or interpenetrated, as far as the Latuka territory. Many data indicate that in the last century the Galla, as a whole, have receded northwards and eastwards, and it is probable that the Masai and Nandi have moved southwards.

Mr. Hollis thinks that the Nandi had not been for many generations on the Nandi plateau when they were discovered by Europeans. There had probably been much fighting and migration in the previous hundred years. The Nandi have a tradition that they were once expelled from their country by the Sirikwa, a tribe who lived on the Uasin Gishu plateau and built stone kraals. These Sirikwa were driven out by the Masai, and the Masai themselves were subsequently annihilated owing to internal quarrels. An inspection of an ethnographic map (e.g. in Sir H. Johnston's *Uganda Protectorate*, p. 884) suggests that the Nandi retired from the plains and open pasture lands before the Masai and Turkana, but maintained themselves in wooded and mountainous districts.[1] A tradition, which may contain elements of historical value, states that circumcision was introduced by a person called Kipkenyo who came from a country called Do and settled in Nandi at a time when it was called *Chemñgal*. Sir H. Johnston states that none of the Nile races circumcise when free from Mohammedan influence.[2] Now in Turkana the word *ñgaal* (probably borrowed) means camels. Can this tradition contain an allusion to the borrowing, direct or indirect, of the rite of circumcision from camel-riding Mohammedans?

It is generally admitted that the Masai, Turkana, Nandi, and Suk are, to some extent at any rate, hybrids, one element in their composition being the Galla or Somali, two tribes which should probably be regarded as identical for ethnological purposes. This element seems to be stronger in the Nandi and Masai. We know less of the Suk and Turkana, but their features are reported to approach the type of the Nilotic

[1] Lumbwa, though a low district relatively to Nandi, is not a plain like the Rift Valley, and is very uneven.
[2] *Uganda Protectorate*, p. 760.

negroes more closely. It is also admitted that the evidence of language and customs (such as dress or the want of it, the shaven heads of the women, drinking the blood of living animals, &c.) connects all four tribes with the Latuka, Bari, Dinka, and other Nilotic peoples. All the known evidence indicates that a section of these tribes moving eastwards became modified by contact with the Gallas and Somalis. Other authorities, especially Merker[1] and those who accept his statements, are of opinion that the Masai (and presumably with them the Nandi, Turkana, &c.) are the remains of a Semitic race which has wandered southwards from Arabia and been mingled with African elements. The chief objection to this theory is that the undisputed facts which support it are very slight, seeing that in spite of search no confirmation has been found of most of the traditions reported by Merker. On the west we find a clear series of links uniting the Nandi, Masai, &c., to the Nilotic group both by language and by customs. To the east there are no such links: no tribes have been singled out in Abyssinia or Somaliland as specially akin to the Masai or Nandi. There has been contact and influence, and there is a considerable resemblance in religion, but no proof has been brought forward of a migration from the north-east or of more than an infusion of Hamitic (Galla-Somali) blood. It is perhaps well to emphasize this point, since some of the most recent authorities (e.g. Keane, article on Africa in *Encyclopaedia of Religion and Ethics*, 1908) classify the Masai, Turkana, and Wahuma as Eastern Hamites without further qualification.

In language, the Nandi (which term I use in the wider sense to include the Lumbwa, Kamasia, &c.) seem to be most nearly allied to the Bari among the Nilotic tribes. A glance at the map will show that from the territories of this people, who inhabit both banks of the Nile between Nimule and Kero, there extends to the Mau and Rift Valley a continuous linguistic area in which languages of the same class (Latuka, Karamojo, Suk, Turkana, Nandi, Masai) are spoken. But it is not recorded that in other respects the Nandi specially resemble the Bari, and in their customs and manner of life they show more affinity to the Masai. This may be the result not only of common origin and parallel development, but also of direct imitation. The Masai were admired as the most formidable tribe of East Africa, and we find that the Nandi medicine-men are descended from a Masai clan, and

---

[1] *Die Masai*, Berlin, 1904.

that the song which is sung at the Nandi war-dance is in Masai.

The features which distinguish the East African section of Nilotes—that is, the Masai, Turkana, Nandi, and Suk, to whom we ought perhaps to add the little-known Latuka—are that they are more or less nomadic, and that the young men are organized as a special class of warriors. It is clearly as a result of these features, which are perhaps due to the admixture of Galla-Somali blood, that they have spread so widely over East Africa. The other tribes, such as the Bari, Acholi, Aluru on the Nile, and the Ja-luo, who are the neighbours of the Nandi on the shores of Lake Victoria, are stationary cultivators. They fight on occasion and esteem bravery, but they do not consecrate the most active years of their life exclusively to raiding or despise labour. This feature, as well as the nomadic habit, is found most fully developed in the Masai, who disdain agriculture [1] and all occupations except fighting and tending cattle. One section of the Suk are agriculturists: the other section and the Turkana do little in the way of cultivation, but hunt and tend cattle. The various divisions of the Nandi appear to have taken to agriculture in the last few generations, and to practise it in a somewhat desultory fashion. In Lumbwa their methods are so imperfect that the country has recently been more than once threatened by famine owing to the total failure of the crops, and a serious loss of life would have ensued had not the population been able to fall back on their large herds of cattle and goats or on food provided by the Government.

Though the Nandi are thus to a certain extent cultivators, it is clear both from Mr. Hollis's account of their customs and from their conduct in the last decade that, like the Masai, they regard recurring, if not continuous, warfare and raiding as part of the proper business of life. They had not the same power of executing rapid and extensive movements, but the position of their country, which commanded all the old caravan routes to Uganda and subsequently the railway, brought booty to their doors. The circumcision, classification, and life of the warriors is much the same as among the Masai, and a solemn ceremony takes place about every seven and a half years by which the country is committed to the care and protection of the new age, that is to say the warriors who have been circumcised about four years previously. As

[1] The best-known sections of the Masai do not practise agriculture at all, but in a good many places when impoverished by cattle disease or defeat they have settled down as cultivators.

among the Masai, this tendency to recognize no ideal but successful raiding and to place the principal authority in the body of young warriors has prevented the Nandi from forming a state like the kingdom of Uganda or from becoming more than a republic of military herdsmen. The Orkoiyot or medicine man is greatly respected, and has the power of sanctioning or forbidding raids, but his authority seems to depend on his supposed power of predicting the result of these expeditions. Nevertheless, the civil organization of the tribe was somewhat more developed than among the Masai, and we seem to see traces of two administrations, for the Nandi country was divided into districts, each governed by two men, the representative of the Orkoiyot and of the people respectively. As the Orkoiyots come of a Masai family, and their office is precisely equivalent to that of the Masai Laibons, it is probable that the whole system was introduced a few generations ago, and that the Kiruogik, or representatives of the people, are an older institution. The fourth Orkoiyot was killed by the Nandi in 1890, but ultimately this act of rebellion strengthened the position of his successors, for it was held to be the cause of all the disasters which fell on the tribe. It is probable that the institution of Laibons and Orkoiyots is traceable to the Gallas, among whom magicians, who employ similar methods of divination, enjoy great influence, though they have not the same position as military and political advisers.

The Nandi, though no longer even partially nomadic like the Masai, have no villages or towns. The absence of such centres is the more remarkable because their neighbours, both Bantu and Ja-luo, construct well-defined villages surrounded by hedges or mud walls. In Nandi and Lumbwa alike there are no collections of houses, but from any given point one or two huts may usually be seen. The result is that the inhabitants are generally distributed and visible at the waysides to the traveller on his march, a striking contrast to most parts of East Africa, where long stretches of country showing no signs of human habitation are occasionally interrupted by populous villages. This scattering of dwellings evidently implies that the Nandi have little fear of either external invasion or internal robbery, and is a proof that both the national defence and police, or the customs which take their place, must be efficacious.

Mr. Hollis has given a very full and interesting account of the Nandi customs, and I need not recapitulate his statements. Anthropologists will find particularly interesting the lists of totems and the degrees of relationship expressed by special words. These terms show that the Nandi have a system of classificatory relationship which has not hitherto been recorded from this part of Africa. It may, however, be worth while to review what we know of their religious beliefs, for these have an important bearing on their affinities and their possible relationship to Semitic peoples. Mr. Hollis has not been able to discover among the Nandi, any more than among the Masai, traditions resembling those of the Pentateuch, such as Merker states are current in German East Africa. The legends which he reports are meagre and childlike: they do not give any account of the origin and government of the world which can be compared to the creation stories and theogonies of Europe and Asia.

The religious ideas of the Nandi are concerned with the worship of (1) a supreme deity, identified with the sun, and (2) spirits of the departed. The deity is called Asis, or, with the article, Asista. No native derivation is forthcoming for this word,[1] and one might easily suppose it to be borrowed, but no probable origin in any of the neighbouring languages has been suggested. On the other hand, Asis is the ordinary word for 'sun', and we find that the name of God among the Ja-luo[2] (Chieng) and among the people of Taveta[3] (Izuwa) has the same meaning. The language used about Asista has little reference to his special attributes as the sun. We do not hear of his splendour, his rising and setting, &c., but are led to suppose that he is a benevolent and powerful but somewhat vague deity. Though we are told that he created man and beast, and that the world belongs to him, yet when we examine the myths collected by Mr. Hollis, we find instead of this general statement a number of inconsistent legends which have a rude and primitive air. Thus the world was produced by the union of the sky and earth (a very old and widespread idea), and also the sun married the moon. When Asista came to set the earth in order it was inhabited by a Dorobo, an elephant, and the thunder, who, according to a quaint story,[4] retired to the sky because he was afraid of the Dorobo. This, like various Masai traditions, assumes that the Dorobo are an ancient aboriginal race. So, too, we hear that a Dorobo's leg swelled, and that when it burst the first man and woman (that is, apparently, the first Nandi) came out of it.

[1] *Sis* means to be silent, but the connexion in meaning is not clear.
[2] A Nilotic race closely allied to the Acholi, and resident in Kavirondo.
[3] A mixed race of Masai and Bantu elements.
[4] See pp. 111-14. Cf. *The Masai*, p. 266.

Cattle, goats, and sheep are said to have issued from a lake at the bidding of a personage who is given no name but appears to be similar to Naiteru-Kop.[1] Leopards and hyenas are the descendants of a pair of lion cubs who painted themselves. As in the Masai legend, the dead ought to return like the moon, and the present unfortunate arrangement is the result of a misunderstanding. Besides Asista, we hear of a demon called Chemosit, who seems to be a fantastically shaped ogre rather than a spirit, and of two Thunder Gods, exactly as in the Masai legend, called Īlet-ne-mie and Īlet-ne-ya, or the good and the bad God. Īlet (cf. the Suk *Elat*, God) is possibly borrowed from the Somali *Ilahe*, which in its turn appears to be borrowed from the Arabic. It is also probable that the Nandi believe in various nature spirits inhabiting trees, water, &c., for though Mr. Hollis records few definite beliefs of this kind, he tells us that trees and rivers are sanctuaries, and that trees are rarely felled, because it is unlucky if the branches make a noise which is called crying.[2] Both the Nandi and Masai pray to the new moon. But the Thunder Gods and other spirits seem to have little importance in the life of the Nandi, whereas prayers are constantly addressed to Asista. Men are supposed to pray every morning and evening, and additional supplications are offered on special occasions, such as when the warriors are away on a raid, after harvest, or in the time of cattle disease and drought. These prayers are mostly simple requests in the form, ' God (Asis) give us health (offspring, cattle, milk, &c.). Guard our children and cattle.' They certainly imply that, however vague the personality of Asis may be, he takes a benevolent interest in the daily life of the Nandi. Thus he is invoked when a house is built, and by potters when baking pots. ' God give us strength,' they say; 'let us bake them so that men may like them.' The daily prayer is somewhat anthropomorphic. It says, 'I have prayed to thee. Thou sleepest and thou goest. I have prayed to thee. Do not say, "I have become tired."' A somewhat similar idea seems to underlie a ceremony performed after the birth of a child and called *ki-iñget Asis* (that God may be awakened). Spitting as a sign of blessing is a characteristic of the Nilotic tribes, and hence we find that on various occasions the Nandi spit towards the rising sun. The Chagga of Kilimanjaro have a similar observance, and call their deity Ruwa, which also signifies sun. Libations of beer, milk, &c., and offerings of salt are made, and animals are

The Masai, p. 270.   [2] pp. 74, 60.

ceremonially slaughtered. These proceedings are described as sacrifices, but it is not clear that the animal is in any way offered to Asista, or that he is invited to partake of the flesh or blood, or that any portion of the victim is burnt. The entrails are inspected in order to obtain omens, and the flesh after being roasted is eaten by the company. The rite thus appears to be a sacred meal rather than the presentation of an oblation. But at one ceremony the old men take beer and milk into their mouths, which they spit out towards the rising sun, and say, 'Asis ... look at this beer and milk.' And in Taveta, where the religious customs are probably derived from the Nandi or some kindred tribe, it is recorded that the heads, tongues, or viscera of victims are thrown into water or set aside.[1] When a Nandi child is four months old, its face is washed in the undigested food found in the stomach of an animal sacrificed in honour of the occasion, and this stomach is invoked in a prayer together with Asis and the spirits of ancestors. 'Asis, give us health: Asis, protect us: spirits of the departed, protect this child: stomach, protect this child.' There seems to be here a combination of several stages of religious belief.

The cult of the dead is fairly well developed. The spirit is believed to reside in the shadow, and when adults die it survives, though children are supposed to perish entirely. The spirits of the departed, called *oiik*,[2] are supposed to live under the earth, and are rich or poor in this spirit-world just as in their human existence. The widespread story of a man who went to the country of the dead but was sent back because he had arrived before his time, is known to the Nandi. Earthquakes are caused by the *oiik* moving about in their underworld. Hornets' nests in the ground and steam-jets (such as are found in various volcanic districts of East Africa) are their peep-holes, and white ants are said to issue from their cooking-pots. Snakes are sometimes considered to be spirits or the messengers of spirits, perhaps because they live in holes.

These *oiik* are regarded as the cause of sickness, and when a Nandi is ill, it is necessary to discover and propitiate the particular ancestor who has occasioned the disaster. But they cannot be wholly malevolent, for they are invoked to protect children and absent warriors. The daily prayer after

[1] 'Notes on the History and Customs of the People of Taveta,' by A. C. Hollis, *Journ. African Soc.*, 1901, pp. 119-20.
[2] The singular of this word is *oiin*, and it is probably connected with *oin*. old age, and *oo*, great.

addressing Asista continues:—'Our spirits, (be not angry) for you died (naturally), and do not say "a man killed us": protect us who are here above.' The spirits are supposed to be below, and it is evidently implied that the spirit of a murdered man would be malignant and revengeful. Another prayer, accompanied by libations of beer poured on the ground, says, 'Our spirits, we have prayed to you. Look at this beer: give us health.' Still more definite is the offering of beer and corn to a spirit who is supposed to have caused sickness. 'Go away: look at this beer and grain. Beer and grain have been sprinkled on you: enjoy them as you go.' Corpses are exposed so that they may be eaten by hyenas, but the practice, though horrible, is accompanied by ceremonies which show that it must not be ascribed to callousness but is rather comparable to the methods of disposing of the dead practised by Parsees and Tibetans. Old people and young children are buried in cow-dung near the cattle-kraal, and provisions are put in the graves of old men.

Another series of religious—or at least superstitious—beliefs is connected with the Orkoiyots, or principal medicine men, who are Masai by race and have introduced most of the ideas and practices connected with the Masai Laibons, but with some variations of their own. They are said never to pray to Asis but only to the spirits of their ancestors, and to receive miraculous powers from sacred snakes.[1] They divine and predict the future, exactly like the Masai Laibons, and are credited with the same powers of producing rain, children, and success in war. They do not accompany the warriors, but are believed to have the power of detaching their heads and sending them with the expedition to see what is being done. We are not told that they pray to the Masai deity Eng-Aï, but after a successful expedition there is a war-dance and a song of triumph, the refrain of which is 'I pray to Eng-Aï and I pray to Mbatian' (a former Laibon of the Masai). Besides the Orkoiyot, there are minor medicine men of various classes, who pretend to discover wizards and to make rain.

Taking the Nandi beliefs as a whole, we find that they are very similar to the religious notions of the Gallas. Our information about the latter (particularly for the East Africa Protectorate) is not full,[2] but the following points seem

---

[1] Among the Masai the souls of Laibons and influential people are supposed to turn into snakes after death. See *The Masai*, p. 307.

[2] See Paulitschke, *Ethnographie Nord Ost Afrikas*, 1896. Some recent information about the beliefs of the Gallas in the East Africa Protectorate will be

certain: (a) They worship a Supreme Being called Wak or Waka. (b) They pray to him daily and turn to the East when doing so. (c) They fear the souls of the dead, who are called Ekera. A man's spirit is supposed to be in his shadow. When he dies, the spirit goes to a subterranean world but may also return and annoy its relations. (d) Various genii or spirits (distinct apparently from the spirits of the dead) are venerated. (e) Animals are sacrificed, and diviners tell the future by inspecting their entrails. *Wak* seems to mean the sky[1] rather than the sun, but the Deity is also called *adu* (sun) and in one prayer is addressed as 'Sun with thirty rays'. The turning to the east also suggests sun-worship.

It has been said that the Nilotic negroes have no religion. This is probably incorrect, but we may perhaps conclude that they do not, like the Nandi, invoke one God in a public manner. We hear, however, that the Jaluo, who are in contact with the Nandi, and the people of Taveta, who are perhaps a hybrid offshoot from them, worship the sun. It would seem that the religious observances of those Bantu tribes in East Africa who have not been influenced by the Masai, Nandi, or Gallas are concerned almost entirely with ancestor-worship. In Uganda, where a whole pantheon had been developed before Christian times, the deities seem to have been chiefly deified ancestors, but there was a God of the firmament called Kazoba, whose name seems to mean Sun. It is possible that his worship may be due to the Bahima conquerors of Uganda, who are believed to have been a Hamitic tribe. It is not surprising that the Nandi and Galla should combine with this rude monotheism the worship or at least the fear of ancestral spirits. The strange thing rather is that this cult should be almost unknown among the Masai, who believe that ordinary people cease to exist after death, and that only Laibons and persons having many children and cattle live on as snakes. I am inclined to connect the lacuna with the comparatively little influence enjoyed by Masai elders, popular respect being paid to the young warriors and the medicine men.

Those who believe in the Arabian or Semitic origin of these tribes may justly point to many Semitic features in their

---

found in the *Life of Thomas Wakefield* (a missionary among the Galla), by E. S. Wakefield, 1904, pp. 200-17.

[1] In Nandi *Wake* means the month of April, and is possibly borrowed from Galla, though the connexion of meaning is not clear. *Rob*, rain, is also borrowed from Galla.

religious beliefs—the practical monotheism, the sacrifice of animals, and the place of spirits below the earth. But these features are all found among the Gallas,[1] and it seems to me most probable that they have simply passed from them to the Nandi and Masai. How easily religious names and ideas may be transferred in East Africa is shown by the fact that the Kikuyu have adopted the Masai deity Eng-Aï, and Nandi traditions indicate that the rite of circumcision is borrowed. As for the Galla, it may be that they and the Somali came originally from Arabia. At any rate, they have had ample opportunities of being influenced by Semitic ideas, and I think that the Galla prayers, if not due to contact with Moslems or Abyssinian Christians, were at least modified by such contact. But the information (possibly incomplete) which we possess of both the Galla and Nandi religions indicates that they resemble the ideas not only of Semites but also of many Central Asian peoples and the ancient Chinese. These nations have: (a) a vague monotheism, described as the worship of heaven; (b) the worship of equally vague nature-spirits; (c) the worship or veneration of ancestors. The ideas of the tribes which we have been considering are really very similar, and are probably characteristic of a certain stage of culture among half-nomadic races who have no centres tending to develop the cult of local and territorial deities, and little in the way of art or literature to foster mythology.

In its general construction the Nandi language resembles Masai. The inflections of the noun only distinguish the singular and plural: there are no cases and very few prepositions. The article and the relative play a considerable part in the syntax. The verb is well developed and not only indicates person and time, but can assume forms which express such ideas as the direction or object of an action, and thus to some extent compensates for the absence of cases. But the two languages show considerable divergences in detail: they are parallel developments, and neither is borrowed from the other.

Whereas the article in Masai, as in Greek, can express both gender and number in one monosyllable, Nandi denotes gender by prefixes; and the definite article, which is an affix, can only indicate number.[2] The prefixes are *kip* (*ki, kim*) and

---

[1] The Gallas also seem to have the custom of sacrificing the first-born. It is said that they expose and leave to die any children who may be born in the first few years after marriage. See Maud, *Geog. Journ.*, 1904, pp. 567-8.

[2] It is interesting to find that these languages show the same variation in the position of the article that meets us in Aryan and Semitic languages.

INTRODUCTION

chep (*che, chem*) for the masculine and feminine respectively, these terms being understood, as in Masai, to denote not merely sex but degrees of size and strength. Sometimes these prefixes are simply equivalent to masculine and feminine terminations, *ki-miñgat* a deaf man, *che-miñgat* a deaf woman (= *surdus, surda*). But they frequently serve to construct a derivative noun, and signify a person who is connected with the simple noun. Thus, *lakwa*, a child, *chep-lakwa*, not a female child, but a nurse; *kericho*, medicine, *kip-kericho*, a doctor; *ter*, a pot, *chep-ter-e-nio*, potter; *kes*, to cut, *chep-keswai*, knife. They may be added to verbs as well as nouns, and then form a *nomen agentis*; e.g. *kip-uny-i-ke*. Here *unyike* is simply a verb in the third person singular, *he hides himself*, and the whole means 'one who hides himself'. The simple form of the affixed article is *t* in the singular and *k* in the plural, but it not infrequently assumes the form *ta, to*: *da, do*, in the singular, in order, it would seem, to prevent the word from ending in two consonants, e. g. *sese*, dog, *seset*; but *ror*, heifer, *rorta*.[1] Beside the article, demonstrative affixes can be appended to nouns, which with these additions assume a very varied appearance. Thus from *sese* are formed *seset, sesonni, sesenju*; from *tien, tiendo, tieni*, and *tienwagichu*. But the article is a less necessary part of a word than in Masai, and a noun used in a general sense dispenses with it, e. g. *maoitos ma pei*, Fire does not cross water.

The plural is formed by the addition of various affixes, such as *oi, ai*; *s* and *n*, either alone or with vowels; *ua* and *wag*, all of which have analogies in Masai. These affixes are often attached by connecting syllables, and to the whole may be added the plural article, so that we obtain very complicated forms, such as *kepen*, cave, *kepenōsiek*; *kor*, land, *korotinuek*; *ma*, fire, *mostinuek*. As in Masai, many nouns are in their simple form collective, and a suffix must be added to make a true singular, indicating one person. Thus *Nandi* means the Nandi tribe, and with the plural article becomes *Nandiek*. A Nandi man is *Nandiin*, and the same with the definite article becomes *Nandiindet*. Yet with this power of building up complicated forms Nandi has not attempted to indicate

Thus it is prefixed in Masai and Turkana, affixed in Nandi and Bari. Similarly, though prefixed in most European languages, it is affixed in Bulgarian, Roumanian, Albanian, and the Scandinavian languages. It is prefixed in Hebrew and Arabic, but Aramaic uses an affix. In Somali and Galla it is affixed.

[1] Sometimes *e* is inserted before the article, sometimes *a* or *o* is added after it. The cause of this difference in treatment is not plain. Thus *ror*, heifer, *rorta*; but *ror*, stubble, *roret* : *koñg*, eye, *konda*; but *loñg*, shield, *loñget*.

a single case by the use of affixes. The nominative and accusative are distinguished by their position, the normal order being verb, subject, object (*maoitos ma pei* : crosses-not fire water). The vocative is simply a noun with a demonstrative (*korkónni*, this woman, or O woman). Similar instances are quoted from Galla, and we may compare οὗτος σύ in classical Greek. The genitive is expressed by means of a particle which appears most commonly as *ap*, more rarely as *pa* or *po*. It appears to be a simple preposition, and the language possesses only one other, *eñg*, which indicates local relation in the most general sense, its special meaning in any sentence—such as motion to or from or rest in—being defined by the verb.

Though the pronouns show a general resemblance to those of Masai, the divergence in detail is very considerable. The sound *ch* seems characteristic of the plural of these words, and is found in the personal, possessive, demonstrative, and relative pronouns. The demonstratives are affixed, like the article. The relative is a prefix, *ne* in the singular and *che* in the plural. It does not indicate gender, but there is a special form *ye* used with the word *olto*, place (cf. *ne* in Masai, used with the word *e-wēji*).

In verbal forms the third person is not indicated,[1] but the first and second are marked by *a* and *i* in the singular, *ki* and *o* in the plural. These syllables can be prefixed directly to nouns and adjectives : as *a-orkoiyot*, I am the chief ; *a-kararan*, I am beautiful. This predicative use of the adjective assumes a more distinctly verbal shape in the past tense, where we find such forms as *ki-a-kararan-itu*, I was beautiful. Here *ki* is a particle apparently connected with *ki-nye*, formerly, and *itu*[2] seems to have no temporal or personal meaning, but to build up a verbal stem out of the simple adjective. Ordinary verbs are conjugated by prefixing *a*, *i*, &c., directly to the root, and tense signs do not intervene between these syllables and the root. The simple root is used as the imperative. To make the present, *i* or *e* is suffixed to the root, and the pronominal signs are prefixed. The following table will show the resemblance to Masai [3] :—

[1] But sometimes it appears to be represented by *ko*.
[2] It may perhaps be compared with such Masai forms as *A-suj-ita*, I am following ; *ki-ta-gol-ito*, we were strong (where *ki* is first pers. plu., not a tense sign).
[3] The simple present (I follow) in Masai is *a-suj*, but I have selected the progressive present (I am following) because it exhibits the same structure as appears in Nandi : personal prefix + root + verbal affix.

INTRODUCTION xxvii

Nandi. *cham*, to love.	Masai *suj*, to follow.
1. Sing. A-chom-e	A-suj-ita.
2. I-chom-e	I-suj-ita.
3. Chom-e	E-suj-ita.
1. Plu. Ki-chom-e	Ki-suj-ita.
2. O-chom-e	I-suj-ita-ta.
3. Chom-e	E-suj-ita.

The pronominal object of the verb, if of the first or second person, is indicated by affixes, namely (1) *a* or *o*, and (2) *n* or *in* for the singular, (1) *ech* and (2) *ak* or *ok* for the plural. Thus, 'you love us' is *o-chom-ech*, and 'we love thee', *ki-chom-in*. Nandi thus has simple objective affixes, and avoids the Masai construction by which both subject and object are indicated, though somewhat imperfectly, in a single prefix (e. g. *ki-suj*, thou followest me, or, they follow thee).

As in Masai, there are two classes of verbs which differ slightly in conjugation: those beginning with *i*, and those beginning with other letters. This prefix *i* also appears in causatives (*i-cham*, to cause to love) and apparently intensifies the verbal force of a root. The tenses are formed almost without exception [1] simply by prefixing particles, not by further modifications of the root. The past is formed with *ki*, *ka*, *ke*, or *kwo*, apparently signifying formerly; the future with *ip*, go, or *inyo*, come; the conditional with various syllables such as *ingo-nga*, in which a nasal predominates. Thus there is a scarcity of anything that can be called moods and tenses, but in contrast there are a considerable number of derivative conjugations expressing modifications of the meaning of the verb. They are often lengthy and elaborate formations: *al*, to sell, can form *a-ol-to-chi-ni*: *iro*, to see, *a-'aror-chi-ni*. Many of them show a resemblance to the Masai derivatives of equivalent meaning. For instance, (1) forms denoting motion hither: *a-'sup-u*, I follow him hither—Masai, *a-suj-u*; (2) forms with a dative sense: *A-'sup-chi-ni*, I follow him— Masai, *A-suj-aki*; (3) the applied forms: *na-a-tep-e*, that I may sit on it—Masai, *la barn-ye*, or *na-barn-ye*, that I may shave with it; (4) intransitive forms: *mwet-isie*, to wash— Masai, *a-isuj-ish-o*; (5) causatives: cause to wash, *iun-e*— Masai, *A-isuj-ye*.

It would appear from a vocabulary of the Dorobo language (about 150 words) and some grammatical notes which Mr. Hollis has kindly placed at my disposal, that some sections

---

[1] The only exception is the present, in which the root vowel *a* often becomes *o*. Root *cham*, present *a-chom-e*, I love.

of this tribe at any rate speak a language which is little more
than a dialect of Nandi. Mr. Hollis's materials were collected
in German East Africa near the Natron Lake. More than
two-thirds of the vocabulary are practically the same as in
Nandi, and of the words which do not correspond a large pro-
portion are the names of animals and utensils, which might
naturally be local. As peculiarities of the Dorobo dialect
may be mentioned : (1) some pronominal forms, such as *arko*,
he, *tichee* or *ndichee*, they. (2) A prefix *ar* is found in the
conjugation of the verb, both in the past active (*ar-a-mach-a*,
I wanted) and in the passive (*ar-ke-mach-a*, I am wanted).
(3) Many nouns in the singular end in *anda*, though they
reject this affix in the plural. In Nandi we find such forms
as *tiony*, animal, *tiondo*, the animal ; *koñg*, eye, *konda*, the eye ;
and combinations of a substantive with a demonstrative affix,
such as *oriat*, an ash, *oriandanni*, this ash. Apparently this
usage is extended by analogy in Dorobo, for we have *kuyanda*,
bow, where Nandi has *kwanget* ; *pelyandee*, elephant, for *pēliot* ;
puniandee, enemy, for *punyot*. (4) There are some differences in pronunciation. *N* is sometimes omitted, i. e. *muyare*,
salt (N. *munyu*) ; *taamuye*, beard (N. *tamnet*). There seems to
be a preference for the broad *a* sound, *maae*, belly (N. *mo*) ;
kaawe, bone (N. *kowo*). *P* is sometimes replaced by *v* : *Vanda*,
journey (N. *panda*) ; *vaiyaa*, old man (N. *poiyo*). This interchange of *p* and *v* is also found in Nandi.

To the best of my belief nothing is known of the Suk language except the list of words with a few short phrases
published by Sir H. Johnston in his *Uganda Protectorate*,
vol. ii. pp. 903–11, and a vocabulary published by Col. Mac-
Donald.[1] Examined in the light of Mr. Hollis's present researches, these lists show that Suk is closely allied to Nandi,
more closely than Turkana is allied to Masai. More than fifty
per cent. of the words quoted are obviously the same as their
Nandi equivalents. This is a very high percentage, for it does
not include words in which the relationship is obscured by
phonetic change. With regard to the grammar, it seems clear
that Suk has an affix resembling the Nandi article, for we
find *porto*, body (N. *por, porto*) ; *kumat*, honey (N. *kumia,
kumiat*) ; *kainat*, name (N. *kaina, kainet*) ; *Tit, tuit*, ox,
(N. *tany, teta*) ; *diebto*, woman (N. *tie, chepto*). In all these
words, the *t* or *to* clearly corresponds to the Nandi article and
is not part of the stem. But in Suk this suffix appears to be
used much more rarely than in Nandi, and there is no proof

---

[1] *Journ. Anthrop. Instit.*, 1899.

INTRODUCTION   xxix

that it has grammatically the meaning of an article. *Polto* is quoted as meaning sky. In Nandi we find *pol*, clouds, as a collective plural, and in the singular *poldo*, one cloud, or, with the article *poldet*. Here *to* or *do* is clearly not part of the root, but it is hard to say if it should be regarded as an article or not. There is no trace of a prefixed article in the Suk vocabulary unless *k* sometimes has this function; nor is there any clear instance of a plural except *solōwa*, twins (cf. the Nandi forms on p. 174). As far as can be seen, the formation of nouns is much the same as in Nandi. The suffix -*n* denotes the agent in the singular: *pōnin*, a witch, *tsorin*, a thief (N. *ponin* and *chorin*). As for the prefixes, there are some indications that *chep* is used, though its precise significance is not clear: *chep-to* is a woman, but *chep-tenyo* is quoted as meaning both brother and sister.[1] The names of several animals begin with *tyet* or *tyem*. The prefix *kip* is not recorded, but *ki* seems to occur in *kiruotito*, dream (Nandi, *iruotite*, to dream), and *kiruokin*, chief (N. *kiruogin*). The personal pronouns are given as *ane, nyi, chichinō; mū, agwa, puchuno* or *pichuno*. Many of these forms are obscure, but *chichinō* and *pichuno* are perhaps not true pronouns, for they resemble the Nandi expressions *chii-chi*, this man, and *pii-chu*, these men. The demonstrative is affixed in three other examples, prefixed in one. The following verbal forms may be quoted: I come, *ane k-a-nyon*[2] (N. *a-nyo-ne*); you love, *O-cham-inyi* (N. *O-chom-e*); I know, *Oñgetan* (N. *a-ngen* or *a-nget*); I do not know, *m-ongetan-ye* (N. *m-á-ngen*); I do not come, *mōngunanye* (N. *m-á-nyo-ne*).

Mr. Hollis has also kindly supplied me with a vocabulary and grammatical notes on the Turkana language, as well as a few stories. I proceed to give an abstract of this valuable unpublished material.[3]

The following forms are quoted as illustrating the use of the article: *e-takho*,[4] a calf, *ñgi-takh* (rarely *i-takh*), calves, masculine; *a-takho, ñga-takh* (rarely *a-takh*) being the corresponding feminine forms. There is a similar series of forms for the definite article: *nye-takho*, the calf, *ñgi-takh*, the calves; and in the feminine, *nya-takho, ñga-takh*. The vowel of the masculine, but not of the feminine article, falls out before

[1] In Nandi *chep-to* means the girl, *cheptan-nyo*, my girl or daughter.
[2] Nearly all the forms quoted for the first person singular begin with *k*.
[3] In my introduction to *The Masai* I spoke of the Suk-Turkana group, based on the idea that these tribes are similar in physique and manner of life. But linguistically they do not form a group.
[4] *Kh* in Turkana is said to be pronounced as *ch* in German *ach*, *th* as in English *this*.

another vowel. The following forms are also quoted: *nye-kile*, the male, pl. *ñgiliokh*; *nya-khaal*, the camel, pl. *ñgaal*; *nyekileñg*, the sword, pl. *ñgilenya*; *nye-kasgout*, the elder, pl. *ñgasgou*. In these also, the vowel of the article seems to fall out and the resulting combination of consonants is simplified in pronunciation. It thus appears that we have a simple vowel prefix *e*, *a*[1] (cf. *ēpei* one, m.; *āpei* f.) used chiefly in the singular, with which can be combined other more definite prefixes (*ny*, *ñg*) possibly akin to the demonstratives.

Substantives have the same general features as in Masai and Nandi. The following plural affixes are found: *a, ya, o, yo, e, ae, t, k, tha, in, syo, is*. Nouns ending in *an* (all the examples are nouns denoting an agent) change the *n* to *kh* in the plural: *nye-kalepan*, the beggar, *ñgi-kalepakh*. Collective words form the singular by adding to the plural form *i, o*, or *t* (*at, it, et*): *Ñgi turkana*, the Turkana; *e-turkanait*, a Turkana man; *ñgitakh*, the calves; *nye-takho*, the calf. The particle *a* is used to indicate not only the genitive, but also local relation. *Nye-sikirya a nye-tuñgunan*, the-donkey of the-man; but also *A-iboikini a nya-moni*, I-stay in the-wood. As nouns are always quoted with the articles (without which they appear to be unintelligible) they are often polysyllabic, but fewer prefixes and suffixes seem to be used in their formation than in Masai and Nandi. Of prefixes, we find *ki* for certain, e.g. *kile*, male (Masai *ol-lee*, *il-lewa*); *a-ki-mwo-yin*, a finger (Masai *ol-ki-mōjīno*, Nandi and Bari *morin*); and more doubtful prefixes seem to be present in *e-lāp*, moon (Masai *ol-apa*); *alokoinya*, brains[2] (Suk *koinyot*); *ja-mu*, hides (Nandi *mui*); *a-kopiro*, ostrich feathers (Masai *ol-piro*). *T, i* and *ñg* are used as affixes, but their significance is indefinite or uncertain. *N* is affixed in the singular to form nouns which generally signify an agent: *kedalan*, lover; *yokon*, husbandman; *kokolan*, thievish.

Adjectives follow the noun which they qualify and are generally connected with it by the relative and another prefix, *ki* or *ka*: *nye-mukura lo-ki-rion*, the black mountain; *nye-kile la-ka-agongon*, the strong warrior. (Cf. the expression *e-kel ka-nya-tom*, ivory.) When used predicatively, the adjective precedes the substantive: *e-rono nye-tungunan*, the man is short (he is short the man).

The numerals are as follows; they are generally used in combination with the definite article:

---

[1] The imperfect vocabularies of Latuka which we possess indicate that in it the prefixes *a, e* and *n* are articles.

[2] It is not clear what is the relation of this word to the Masai *ol-le-l'-*

INTRODUCTION

	Turkana.	Nandi.	Masai.
1.	m. ēpei, f. āpei	akenge	m. ōbo, f. nabo.
2.	are	aeñg	m. aare, f. are.
3.	uni	somok	m. ōkuni, f. uni.
4.	omwon	añgwan	m. ooñgwan, f. oñgwan.
5.	akhan or ñgan (i.e. ñgi-akhan)	mut	imyet.
6.	akhan ka pei (ñgan)	ịllo	ille.
7.	akhan ka are	tisap	m. oopịshana, f. naapịshana.
8.	akan ka uni	sisiit	isyet.
9.	akhan ka omwan	sokol	m. ōudo, f. naudo.
10.	tomon	taman	tomon.

Whereas Masai and Nandi have borrowed words for the higher numerals from Galla or Somali, Turkana expresses them by multiples of the native numerals as *ñgi tomon are*, twenty (Masai *tigităm*, Nandi *tiptem*, from Galla *digetam*). But a hundred is *pokol* (Somali *boghol*, Nandi *pokol*, Masai *ip*).

The pronouns are as follows :—

Personal.		Possessive.	
Sing.	Plur.	Sing.	Plur.
1. Ayoñg	sua or thua.	khañg or kañg	khosi or iyokh.
2. Iyoñg	Ezi.	khon or kon	kus.
3. nyezi	Ikezi.	keny or keñg	kech.

Among the examples given are: *A-khai khang*, my house; *ñga-khais kus*, your houses.

The principal demonstratives are :

Masc.	Fem.	Used with *neni* place.[1]
lo or en	na or en	ne, this.
lu	nu	ne, these.
ye or ei	ya	inne, that.
ñgul	ñgun	nege, those.

It is noticeable that the demonstratives follow the noun as in Nandi: *A-beru-na*, this woman; *ñgi-tunga-lu*, these men. The relative is the same as the first of the demonstratives cited above (*lo, na*, &c.). As in Masai, it undergoes some changes when combined with a verb. The interrogatives are *ñgae?* who? and *ani?* (sing.); *alu?* (pl. m.), *anu?* (pl. fem.), what? or which?

As in Masai and Nandi, the verbs are divided into two classes, which show some differences in conjugation: those

---

lughunya, the-of-the-head (brain). Such a combination is explicable by Masai but not by Turkana grammar, as known. *Lughunya* itself may be a derivative of the Turkana *kū*, head.

[1] Cf. the corresponding usage in Nandi and Masai with *olto* and *e-wēji*.

beginning with *i*, and those beginning with any other letter. The following is the present tense of the verb *cham*, to love, the object being in the third person :—

Sing.	Plur.
1. A-cham-it, I am loving (him).	Ki-cham-it, We are loving (him).
2. I-cham-it, Thou art loving (him).	I-cham-it, You are loving (him).
3. E-cham-it, He or she is loving (him).	E-cham-it, They are loving (him).

The syllable *-it* here appears to correspond to the *-i* of Nandi and the *-ita* of Masai. When the object is the first or second personal pronoun, the prefix is changed much as in Masai and with the same ambiguities. Thus, *ka-cham-it* means, I am loving thee, *or* he (they) is (are) loving me (cf. Masai *Aasuj*); *ki-cham-it* means, Thou art loving me, *or* he is loving thee (cf. Masai *kisuj*).

There is also an indefinite present tense formed by affixing *i* (*-ri*, *-ni*) to the root: *a-cham-i*, I love; *a-ipena-ri*, I sharpen. The formation of the past is somewhat uncertain, but apparently in *i*-verbs *k* is prefixed to the root, *a-inok-i*, I kindle; *a-k-inok*, I have kindled; while in others the pronominal prefixes are simply added to the root: *a-yeñg*-i, I slaughter; *a-yeñg*, I have slaughtered. The narrative tense is formed by prefixing to *i*-verbs *k*, and to other verbs *t* and a vowel: *K-irimo*, and he remains; *ta-ma*, and he says. Similarly in the imperative we have *k-iwor*, speak, but *ta-ma*, say to him. The particle *ani* is prefixed to the conditional: *ani-a-nyam-i*,[1] if I eat it. The negative is formed by prefixing *ny*: *ny-a-cham-it*; I am not loving him. The derivative conjugations, as far as they are known, resemble those of both Nandi and Masai. There are quoted; (1) a passive: *ka-cham-it-ae*, I am being loved; (2) a form expressing motion hither, with the affix *un*; (3) a dative with the affix *kino*; (4) a causative with the prefix ita: *a-nyun-i*,[2] I see, *a-ita-nyun-i*, I cause to see.

Turkana clearly belongs to the same group as Nandi, Masai, and Suk, and agrees with them in all essential points of grammatical structure. It is peculiar in its articles, its negative, and some pronouns. It shows some resemblance to Nandi in indicating the genitive relation by the particle *a*

---

[1] Cf. Nandi *am*, to eat, but Masai *nya*.
[2] In some parts of the Nandi verb to see, which is irregular, the root appears to be *iony*.

INTRODUCTION xxxiii

and in affixing the demonstrative, but on the whole has greater affinities to Masai, with which it agrees in such points of detail as (1) a prefixed article denoting both number and gender in one syllable; (2) verbal prefixes indicating both the subject and the object; (3) the forms of the relative. These are often formed with *l* in Masai when combined with a verb. The resemblance in vocabulary, though clear on examination, is not very obvious at first sight. In some stories which Mr. Hollis has provided with Masai versions only ten per cent.[1] or less of the words are clearly identical in origin. The superficial resemblance to Nandi is even less, but I have had no difficulty in identifying about twelve roots or simple words, and this number could no doubt be easily increased. Loan-words from Somali seem to be more numerous than in Masai. Turkana agrees with Masai in the numerals two and three, which are *are* and *uni*, whereas Nandi and Suk have *aeñg* (*ōyeñg*) and *somok*, but differs in its word for five (*akhan* or *ñgan*), which also appears in Bari and some Suk forms.

From Sir H. Johnston's vocabularies it would appear that Turkana is closely allied to the dialects spoken in Karamojo.

Mr. Hollis has also made some notes on the language of the Kunōno, or smiths, who live among the Masai in an inferior and almost servile status. It appears to be simply a dialect, and to differ from normal Masai less than Dorobo does from Nandi. More than two-thirds of the vocabulary (150 words) are the same as Masai. Of the remainder, twelve words are Nandi. It is curious to notice that four words which specially concern the trade of a smith are not like either the Masai or the Nandi equivalents: iron, *e-samereita*; knife, *o-siota*; spear, *en-gandiit*; axe, *e-wuyuwuyu*.

All the languages mentioned, including such varieties of Nandi as Lumbwa, Kamasia, &c., and also the little-known Latuka (which appears to be nearly allied to Masai), form a sub-group within the family of Nilotic languages. This family is as yet neither thoroughly investigated nor clearly defined, but it appears to comprise at least Dinka, Shilluk, Bari, Acholi, and Jaluo. The sub-group is characterized by a certain homogeneity of vocabulary and by the length of its words. Monosyllables are rare, and most of them are particles which cannot be used alone; words of five syllables are frequent, whereas in the other languages monosyllables

---

[1] This percentage may not give a just idea of the resemblance, for the translator may have employed the words most idiomatic in Masai, not those most like the Turkana equivalents.

and disyllables appear to be the rule. The greater length of the words is due to a wealth of formative elements, both prefixes and suffixes, by which derivatives are formed from roots.

Within this sub-group, Nandi with its dialects, including Dorobo, is closely allied to Suk: Masai and Turkana are more closely allied to one another than either is to the Nandi-Suk division, but can hardly be classed together as a corresponding subdivision, for Turkana has special features, such as its articles and the use of *ny* as a negative, which seem greater than the peculiarities (as far as our very limited knowledge goes) which separate Suk from Nandi.

The common features of all these languages (perhaps shared by some of those spoken on the Nile) are somewhat as follows. The syntax, or connexion of words in a sentence, is very imperfectly developed. There are no inflectional cases, hardly any prepositions, and nothing corresponding to the categories and prefixes of the Bantu languages. The nominative and accusative are distinguished by their position, the usual order (at least in Nandi, Masai, and Turkana) being verb, subject, object. Otherwise, the part which a substantive plays in a sentence can only be inferred from the general sense: *'Ngi-rep-e lakwa rotua ke-ken-ji ket*. This means, If you take a knife away from a child, give him a piece of wood to play with instead; but translated literally it is, If-you-take-from child knife and-you-coax-with wood. It will be seen that the general plan of this sentence is given in the two verbs. The substantives are left to fit into it as best they can: their place is not indicated either by case, prepositions, or position. The inconvenience of this disconnected character is clear, and an attempt is made to overcome it in two ways. Firstly, prefixes and affixes are multiplied in order to put as much meaning as possible into single nouns and verbs. Secondly, words are connected by the relative in a way which seems to us superfluous and clumsy. Instead of saying 'the beautiful woman' these languages prefer some such form as 'the woman who-beautiful': instead of 'who is at the gate?' 'who who-is gate?'

The distinction between verbs and nouns is slight. It is said that in Dinka the same word can be used without change as a noun, verb, or preposition. In the sub-group pronominal prefixes can be added to nouns and adjectives, which then become neuter verbs. On the other hand, the prefixes used to form derived nouns can be added to verbs: *Kip-uny-i-ke,* the-he-hides-himself, i.e. a man who conceals himself, *Kip-set-*

met, the-go-head, one whose head goes to the wars.[1] Both prefixes and affixes are used in amplifying verbs and nouns, and what is a prefix in one language may be an affix in another. The pronominal subject is always prefixed to a verb; the pronominal object may be either prefixed (Masai, Turkana) or affixed (Nandi). Signs of tense and mood are mostly prefixed (being in fact merely particles), but a few are affixed. The opposite is true of the elements which form the reflexive, reciprocal, dative, and other varieties of derived verbs. They are nearly all affixes: only causatives show a prefix. In nouns the articles and demonstratives are either prefixes or affixes. All the signs known to indicate gender are prefixes. In Nandi these are *kip* and *chep*. The former is perhaps connected with a widely used prefix, *ki* or *gi*. More rarely, simple *k* (perhaps a shortening of *kip*) is found as a prefix, e.g. Nandi *lel*, *ichi-lil*, to err, *kachililo*, error; *imut*, to lead, *kamutin*, a leader; *-iak-e*, to tend sheep, *k-oiok-in*, shepherd. Also *ma*, *m-*: Nandi *karin*, riches, *ma-kori-o*, rich man; *iñgir-te*, to lessen, *m-iniñg*, small; Masai *añgata*, plains, *m-añgat-inda*, an enemy (apparently one who comes from, or sweeps over the plains). *Mishire*, a brand mark, and *amēyu*, hunger, are perhaps derived from the verbal roots *sir*, to write, and *iyo*, to wish. There is also a *t* prefix: Masai *ta-mweiyai*, a sick person, from *mweiyan*, sickness, or *a-mweiy-u*, to be sick. All these forms are perhaps connected with *en-gää*, death, and *a-ā*, to die. So too, in Nandi *man-ach*, to be pregnant; *to-mon-o*, a pregnant woman; and perhaps *tu-lua*, a mountain, from *lany*, to mount. The plural is usually formed by affixes, but in Masai, Nandi, Turkana, and also in Dinka and Bari, some nouns (chiefly those indicating relationship) form it by a prefix which often contains *k* (*ke* in Dinka, *ko* in Bari, *akut* in Nandi, but *ta* in Turkana). *K* is also one of the commonest elements in the many plural affixes, but they are very numerous, even within the limits of a single language, and few of them can be said to have a definitely plural meaning. Their precise significance seems to depend on the use of each word. Similarly, the meaning of the affixes used to form nouns varies greatly. The most consistent is *n* preceded by a vowel (often *i*), which in all the languages of the sub-group denotes the agent in the singular. Its original significance seems to be one person or thing, for it is used to form individualizing

[1] The chief medicine man is supposed to be able to send his head to the wars without his body.

nouns from collectives. Thus, in Nandi, *Masaein* means a Masai person; *Chorin* a steal-person or thief; *ani* or *oni* in Masai is a longer form of the same affix, e.g. *areshōni*, a trap-person or trapper. But other affixes have not so clear a meaning, and very often we find that one language will select one for a definite grammatical purpose, while the others employ it more vaguely. Thus in Nandi *t* and *k* have a definite grammatical function, and represent the singular and plural of the article. But in Masai we find many words ending in *t* in which this affix is neither radical nor an article (since another article is used at the same time). Even in Nandi we find words like *poldo, perto, kwendo* (pl. *pol, per, kwen*) in which *to* or *do* is indistinguishable in form from the article, but is regarded by usage as a mere suffix, since when the article is expressed these words become *poldet*, &c. *K*, which is the plural of the definite article in Nandi, is in Masai and Turkana (*kh*) only an occasional plural termination of nouns. *Nye, nya*, which in Turkana are the singular of the definite article, appear sporadically in Nandi and Masai as prefixes or particles. Masai: *nye-lle ol-tuñgani*, this man here; *nyanna e-ñgorōyōni*, this woman here; Nandi: *nyokorio*,[1] fear (cf. Masai *kuret*, coward).

The thought underlying these languages is so simple and direct that there are few abstract nouns, but in Masai the action of a verb in its general sense is often expressed by a noun formed with the affix *ata, oto*. If the root begins with *i, k* (*g* after *n*) is at the same time added as a prefix.[2] Thus, *iteru*, to begin, *en-giterunoto*, the beginning; *isuj*, to wash, *en-gisujata*, the cleaning; *tem*, to measure, *en-demata*, the measure. This affix has perhaps the same origin as the Nandi article, though it is used in a less specialized sense. In Nandi, *-io* or *-yo* is a common nominal affix, but it is hard to assign to it any special meaning. The form *-eyua* or *-eyuo* seems to denote instruments, as *kanameyuo*, tongs (*nam*, to take in the hand); *roteyua*, a slender pole (*rat*, to bind); *che-sol-eyua*, paint (*sal*, to paint). The formation of the few abstract nouns quoted is various: *ya-itio*, badness; *mie-no*, goodness; *lararin*, beauty (but beautiful, *kararan*, pl. *kororon*); *nyikisin*, thickness (*nyikis*, thick); *kīmnon*, strength (*kīm*, strong).

If a series of formations in one of these languages is

---

[1] These words have also a *k* prefix, for in Masai the verbal root is *ure*. Is this the same as Nandi *iyue*?

[2] I defer to Mr. Hollis's explanation while wondering if we should not write *eng-iterunoto*.

INTRODUCTION

examined, and still more if kindred forms in other languages are included, it soon becomes clear that the common part, or the root in contradistinction to prefixes and affixes which can be detached, is very short. Thus we find in the Nandi vocabulary: old age, *oin*; old, *os*; an old person, *poiyo* or *chepioso*. Here the common part seems to be simply *o* or *oi*. *Oo*, great, is probably akin; *chep* is certainly a prefix, and perhaps the *p* of *p-oiyo* represents the remains of *kip*. Similarly, the verbal root signifying *to pray* is found in the simple form *sa* or *so*, intensified as *sa-ise* or *sai-sai*. This root is apparently amplified to *som*[1], in the sense of to beg or request, *sa-o* or *som-o*, prayer; *som-in*, beggar; *chep-soiso*, beggar; and, with the same meaning, *chem-ñge-susuo*, which appears to be a derivative from the same root. Nandi *ma*, fire; *mat*, the fire; plural *mostinua* (*ek*); Masai *en-gi-ma*, the fire; Turkana, Karamojo, &c., *a-ki-m*; Dinka *mach*, and also *mañge* or *man* in certain combinations; Bari *ki-ma*; Jaluo *maty*. Similarly, Masai *kina*, singular, breast; plural *kī*; Dorobo *iina*, plural *iinosye*; Nandi *kīna*, pl. *kīnaiik*. Masai *ñge-jep*, tongue; Nandi *ñge-lyep*, plural *ñge-lyep-ue-k*; Bari *nye-dep*; Acholi *leb-a*; Jaluo *lep, lew-a*; Aluru *ma-lep*; Dinka *lyep* or *lyeme*. In this example a curious interchange of consonants seems established, namely $j = l$. But the change of *d* to *l* or *r* can be paralleled in other languages, and *j* in Masai seems to be originally *dy*,[2] and in the present case we find the form *nye-dep* in Bari. Compare Masai *en-geju*, the foot; Nandi *kel-do*. Among other remarkable changes of letters it may be mentioned that the syllable *io* or *yo* seems to develop a palatal consonant with great ease, e.g. Nandi *mopcho*, sugar-cane, for *mopio*; Turkana *yokon*, but Masai *chōkut*, a herdsman (Nandi *ko-iokin*). In Masai verbs, initial *i* when preceded by another *i* becomes *m* if it is followed by a labial, and *n* if it is followed by *d, k, g, t,* or *sh*: *imbot* for *i-i-pot*, thou callest; *indim*, for *i-i-dim*, thou art able. The change apparently is purely phonetic and due to a desire to emphasize the syllable.

It would appear from the foregoing that the roots in these languages are short, generally monosyllabic, and often consisting of only a single consonant or vowel. But disyllabic roots are also found; some may be primitive; some are due to reduplication; and many are formed with the prefix -*i*, which seems to intensify their verbal force.

---

[1] It is not clear what, if any, is the relation of the Masai *ōmono*, prayer, to this root.
[2] Hollis, *The Masai*, p. 2.

As it has been suggested that these tribes, especially the Masai, are of Semitic origin, it may be well to give a list of the points in which their languages show some resemblance to the Semitic and Hamitic families:—

(1) The vowels of a word undergo changes which sometimes at any rate have a definite grammatical meaning; (a) they distinguish the singular and plural: Nandi *panan*, poor, plural *ponon*; *kararan*, pl. *kororon*, beautiful. Similarly, *tangoch*, pl. *tongōch*, riddle. This is rarer in Masai, but we find *rok*, pl. *rook*, black; *oti*, pl. *ooti*, small. (b) In Nandi the vowel *a* in a verbal root generally becomes *o* in the present tense: *Cham*, love, present, *achome*, I love; so, *wal*, alter, *awole*; *itany*, forge, *a'tonyi*.

(2) The article plays a prominent part, and often distinguishes both number and gender. In Somali also there is an affixed article which denotes sex, e.g. *nin-ki*, the man; *nag-ti*, the woman.

(3) The affixes used to form the plural are not dissimilar in general character from those found in Galla (*-ō*; *-ōta*, *-n*, *-ōni*, *-oli*) and Somali (*-yal*, *-in*, *-o*, *-ya*). But the commonest method of forming the plural in Galla and Somali seems to be by reduplication, and this process is not much used in the languages which we are considering. Nandi offers one instance, *ñgô*, who? plural *ñgô ñgô*. Reduplication is sometimes employed in the formation of stems, but the only instance in which I have found it as an aid to inflection is the second person plural of the Masai verb, i.e. *i-suj*, thou followest, *i-suj-usuju*, you follow. In Nandi we find *nun-at*, rotten; *nu-nanun*, very rotten. Roots are not infrequently reduplicated.[1]

(4) The simplest forms of the verb bear a certain resemblance to Semitic and some Somali forms. But on examination it seems clear that the chief distinction between the personal signs, that is the pronouns, lies in the vowels (Masai *a-suj*, *i-suj*, *e-suj*). There is no trace of *t* in the second person, nor of *n* in the first, but all the languages associate *ki* with the first person plural. In the second person Nandi indicates the pronominal object by *n* in the singular and *ak* or *ok* in the plural, but *k* in the singular is not recorded.[2] It will thus be seen that the resemblance to the Semitic pronouns and verbs is really very slight. It has been suggested

---

[1] See, for examples, p. 227 below, and *The Masai*, p. 97.
[2] The Masai verbal prefixes in which the pronominal subject and object are combined (*The Masai*, p. 48) are not very clear. *Aa* indicates I—thee, he—me, they—me : *ki* indicates we—thee, him, them; thou—me; you—me; they—thee.

that *isuj* (thou followest) is for *tisuj*, the *t* falling out as in *na-ito*, O girl (for *na-tito*). But *na-ito* is an isolated form in Masai, and neither in Masai nor Nandi is there any objection to beginning a word with *ti*.

(5) The order of words in the sentence is verb, subject, object.

(6) Some vague resemblances may be noted. Both prefixes and affixes are employed to form nouns, and may be used together. Compounds of the type found in Aryan languages are rare, but two words united by the genitive particle *ap* are often used to express a single idea. Thus in Nandi a market is called *kâpwalio* (*ka-ap-walio*), house of exchange. The verb is susceptible of several derivative conjugations, but they are formed chiefly by affixes, whereas in Semitic languages they are formed chiefly by prefixes or changes in the roots.[1] In vocabulary the resemblances are few. There are obvious loan-words from Somali and Galla, but only a few words show a possible and by no means conclusive similarity to the Semitic languages. Such in Nandi are *tukul*, all, *iro*, to see, *me*, to die, *ki-maita*, a dead person.

Just as there is probably a strain of Galla or Somali blood in the Nandi, Masai, &c., so also there is nothing improbable in the idea that Somali influence may be traceable in their language. They certainly owe to it some of their numerals, and it may be that the use of the articles and the order of words are due to the same cause. But in details I see no proof of near kinship. The resemblances mentioned above are mostly of a very general character, and they diminish on closer examination.

Thanks to the researches of Mr. Hollis we have now an account of the language and customs of two tribes, the Masai and Nandi. It would be rash to make any general statements about the whole group until we have similarly full accounts of some of its western members, such as the Bari and Dinka, and of the Gallas of the East African Protectorate, but all our information favours the theory, indicated in the foregoing observations, that its home is on the banks of the Nile, and that the more eastern sections represent an eastern migration which has come into contact with Hamitic tribes, probably Gallas. The influence exercised by these tribes was both

---

[1] Causatives formed by prefixing *i* (N. *cham*, love; *i-cham*, cause to love) might be compared with the Hiphil conjugation in Hebrew, but other Semitic forms indicate that the essential feature of this conjugation is not an *i* prefix.

linguistic and religious. The Galla worship of Wak, though not borrowed from Christianity or Islam, has certainly been modified by intercourse with Abyssinian Christians and Mohammedan Somalis, and in this sense it may be said that some Semitic ideas have penetrated among the Nandi and Masai. But there is no proof that the foundation of either the language or the religious beliefs is Semitic.

Before concluding I should like to draw attention to the valuable results which Mr. Hollis has obtained by training African natives to take down the language of the wilder and more distant tribes. Thus the Turkana vocabulary and stories were collected by a native of Taveta, who had learnt to write in the Mission there, and then spent some months among the Turkana. It would appear that the intelligence of an educated native of East Africa is quite equal to such a task. I do not know if this method has been employed in other parts of Africa, but it has clearly great advantages, besides being a considerable economy of time. A native inspires less mistrust in the wilder tribes than a European; he understands their ideas more readily, and his notes are not likely to be influenced by preconceived theories.

C. ELIOT.

PLATE III

Nandi elder (Wilson).

Nandi elder (Hobley).

PART I

HISTORY.

THE Nandi tribe inhabited, until 1905, the whole of the highlands known as the Nandi plateau. This country was roughly bounded by the Uasin Gishu plateau, extending to Mount Elgon on the north, by the Nyando valley on the south, by the Elgeyo escarpment on the east, and by Kavirondo on the west. Recently, as a result of a punitive expedition, rendered necessary by the continued attacks of the warriors of certain sections of the Nandi on the Uganda Railway and on inoffensive natives, the whole tribe has been placed in a reserve somewhat to the north of the escarpment which bears their name, and away from the immediate neighbourhood of the railway.

The origin of the Nandi people is uncertain. We know that they are allied to the Masai and Turkhana, &c., and that all of these tribes are also allied to the Bari, Latuka, and other peoples living on the Nile; but the Nandi represent doubtless a mixture of many different negro races, and, according to Dr. Shrubsall,[1] they exhibit in their cranial characteristics the incomplete fusion of something like four stocks—the Nile negro, the Masai, the Bantu, and some pigmy element, possibly allied to the Bushmen of South Africa. There may even be, he thinks, a dash of a fifth element—the Galla.[2] In appearance the Nandi

[1] *The Uganda Protectorate* (Johnston), vol. ii, p. 857.

[2] I do not consider that the part which the Galla have played in building up the Masai, Nandi-Lumbwa, and other races, such as perhaps the Bahima of Uganda, has been sufficiently realized or taken into account in the past. The influence of their Galla ancestors is frequently shown in the personal appearance, religion, customs, and, in a lesser degree, in the languages of many of these tribes.

It may be worth mentioning that there are at the present day many Samburu Masai women living amongst the Gallas on the Tana River. These women, who are called Korre (this being the Somali and Galla name for Masai), were formerly kidnapped by the Somalis of Kismayu and kept as slaves, but they have since effected their escape, and live contentedly with the Gallas, whom they regard as friends, and with whom they have intermarried.

Mr. Dundas reports, in an article appearing in *Man*, 1908, pp. 136–9, that according to a tradition of the Kikuyu and Dorobo the Gallas or other allied people had formerly extensive settlements in what is now Kikuyu country, and that they were only driven out some seventy years ago.

sometimes resemble the Masai, *i.e.* there are men of tall stature, with features almost Caucasian; at other times dwarfish types are noticeable with marked prognathism and low foreheads.

The Nandi are closely allied to the Lumbwa[1] (or Kipsikīs), the Buret (or Puret), and the Sotik (or Soot) on the south; to the Kamasia (or Tuken), the Elgeyo (or Keyu), the Mutei and other smaller and less known tribes on the east and north-east; to the Nyangori (or Terik) on the west; and to various tribes inhabiting Mount Elgon, notably the Kony,[2] on the north-west. The tribe of hunters usually known as the Dorobo, Andorobo, or Wandorobo,[3] who live in forests stretching from about 1° north to 5° south of the Equator, are also nearly akin to the Nandi, and generally speak a dialect closely related to the Nandi tongue.

The ancestors of the main body of what constitutes the so-called Nandi-Lumbwa group came, beyond doubt, from the north. There is a distinct tradition to this effect, and it seems probable that the tribes allied to the Nandi who live on or near Mount Elgon[4] (the Lako, Kony, Mbai, Sabaut, Sapin, Pôk, and Kâpkara) are only a section of the migrants, the remainder having pushed on to the south and east, and settled in Nandi, Lumbwa, Buret, Sotik, Elgeyo, and Kamasia. Both Sir H. Johnston[5] and Mr. Hobley[6] date this migration at a fairly remote period owing to the large area over which the group has spread; and I am inclined to agree with them. But I do not consider it at all certain that the Nandi country has been inhabited by the Nandi tribe for more than a few generations, for there exist in Nandi the remains of irrigation canals,[7] which, although of no great age, are the workmanship of other people. The Nandi have a tradition that

---

[1] This name is a misnomer. It is a term of opprobrium applied by the nomadic Masai to all pastoral tribes who have taken to agriculture; but it has been adopted by the Swahili as the name for the *Kipsikīs*, and has, like so many other names, been accepted by Europeans as the correct designation for this tribe. The Kipsikīs are called by the Masai the *Kakesan*.

[2] Commonly but incorrectly called Elgonyi.

[3] The Masai name is *Il-Torobo*. The Dorobo call themselves *Okiek*, which is also the Nandi name for them.

[4] Mr. Hobley reports that the Lako have a tradition that they and the Nandi were at one time settled on Kamalinga Mountain, forty-five miles north-west of Mount Elgon. (*The Journal of the Anthropological Society for Great Britain and Ireland*, 1903, p. 332.)

[5] *The Uganda Protectorate*, p. 796.

[6] *Eastern Uganda*, p. 10.

[7] I am indebted to Mr. Hobley for this information.

HISTORY

they were at one time expelled from their country by the Sirikwa, a tribe about whom very little is known beyond the fact that they inhabited the Uasin Gishu plateau, that they lived in stone kraals, the ruins of which are still to be seen, and that they were eventually exterminated or driven south by the Masai.[1] It is possible that the canals were cut by the Sirikwa; but it is more likely that the work must be ascribed to a former Bantu occupation, which in that case would not be of very ancient date.

The more recent history of Nandi dates back less than twenty years. The country was practically closed to Arab and Swahili traders, for the Nandi, who were hardy mountaineers and skilful fighters, refused to allow strangers to cross the threshold of their country without special permission. It frequently occurred that caravans, after safely passing the plains that were infested with the dreaded Masai, met with a serious check at the hands of the Nandi. On arriving at the frontier the Coast people were usually met by a few old men who told them in course of conversation that there was a large supply of ivory at a place situated two or three days' journey from the camp, but that only a small party consisting of ten or twenty men might go to barter for it. So great was the avidity of the Swahili trader that he often fell into the trap, and a small party would be dispatched laden with cloth, wire, and other trade goods, only to be ambushed by the Nandi and massacred.

The first actual outbreaks of the Nandi were provoked by the aggressions of a Scotch trader who had penetrated into their country. The reprisals which they took included the murder of another white trader, and it was subsequently found necessary to dispatch an expedition against them in 1895. Since then punitive measures have been undertaken against them on two occasions, in 1900 and 1903, but the Nandi were never really subdued, and remained hostile to the Administration and overbearing towards other tribes. Eventually, owing to their truculent behaviour, it was considered necessary in 1905 to deal them a crushing blow, the result of which has been to move them into a reserve and, it is hoped, to settle once and for all a difficult native problem which has long confronted the peaceful administration and settlement of the East Africa Protectorate.

[1] To the present day the Nandi speak of the Masai living near Ikoma in German East Africa as the Sirikwa. It is therefore possible that the Sirikwa were only a branch of the Masai.

DIVISIONS OF THE NANDI COUNTRY AND PEOPLE.

The Nandi country is divided into six counties (*emet*, pl. *emotinuek*) as follows:—

North: Wareñg.
East: Masop.
South: Soiin or Pelkut.
West: Aldai and Chesume.
Central: Em-gwen.

The Nandi people are divided geographically into districts or divisions (*pororiet*, pl. *pororōsiek*), and parishes or subdivisions (*siritiet*, pl. *siritaiik*), and genealogically into clans and families (*oret*, pl. *ortinuek*). Each clan has one or more totem or sacred animal. In the following lists the divisions and the traditional places or tribes of origin of the various clans are given:—

Geographical division.	Meaning.	Counties.
1. Kåmelilo	Leopard	Wareñg, formerly Soiin.[1]
2. Kâpchepkendi	Tapkendi (woman's name)	Wareñg, formerly Soiin and Masop.[1]
3. Kàpkiptalam	Grasshopper	Wareñg and Masop.[1]
4. Koileke	Spotted sheep	Masop.
5. Kåkipoch	Pimples	Aldai and Wareñg.
6. Kåpianga	Tapianga (woman's name)	Aldai.
7. Kåpsile	Tapsile (woman's name)	Aldai.
8. Tipiñgot	Tipiñgot (man's name)	Chesume.
9. Cheptol[2]	Unknown	Chesume.
10. Kimñgoror[2]	Goat	Chesume.
11. Kåkimno	Goat	Chesume.
12. Murk'-ap-Tuk' (Kåpwaren)	Warriors' cows	Chesume.
13. Kåptumoiis	Forest	Em-gwen.
14. Kåpsiondoi	Tapsiondoi (woman's name)	Em-gwen.
15. Tuken	Kamasia country	Soiin.

[1] Moved after the 1905–6 punitive expedition.
[2] Included for administrative purposes in Murk'-ap-Tuk' (Kåpwaren).

PLATE IV

Nandi warriors in battle array. Eastern clans on left, Western clans in centre, Central clans on right (Hart).

The peace conference, December 14, 1905, with the Nandi escarpment in the background (Henderson).

DIVISIONS OF THE COUNTRY AND PEOPLE 5

GENEALOGICAL DIVISIONS.

Principal name of clan (*oret*).	Other names (used by women only).	Totem, or sacred animal (*tiondo*).	Traditional place of origin.
1. Kipoiis [1]	Mende Kerus	(*Leluot*) Jackal (*Solopchot*) Cockroach	Mt. Elgon and Lumbwa.
2. Kipkoiitim	Kâpongen Kiram-gel	(*Peliot*) Elephant (*Nyiritiet*) Chameleon	Mt. Elgon and Segela Masai.
3. Kipamwi	Ñgemwiyo Kipketoi	(*Cheptirgichet*) Duiker	Mt. Elgon, Sotik and Kosowa.
4. Kipkenda	Maiimi Maram-goñg Ram-dolil Kuchwa Kami-pei	(*Segemyat*) Bee (*Mororochet*) Frog	Mt. Elgon and Lumbwa.
5. Kipkōkōs	Kâpsegoi	(*Chepkōkōsiot*) Buzzard	Mt. Elgon.
6. Kipiegen	Ingoke Katamwa Kipwalei	(*Moset*) Baboon (*Muriot*) House rat	Mt. Elgon and Lumbwa.
7. Talai [2]	Kipya-kut Tule-kut Kimapelameo	(*Ñgetundo*) Lion	Segela Masai and Kamasia.
8. Toiyoi	Moriso	(*Pirechet*) Soldier ant (*Robta*) Rain	Segela Masai.
9. Kipsirgoi	Pale-kut Kâpil Malet-kam	(*Toret*) Bush pig	Mt. Elgon and Elgeyo.
10. Sokom	Kâpyupe	(*Chepsiriret*) Hawk	Mt. Elgon and Elgeyo.
11. Moi	Rarewa Kâparit-kisapony Partatukasōs	(*Koñgonyot*) Crested crane (*Soet*) Buffalo	Mt. Elgon, Elgeyo and Marokor.
12. Kiptopke	Tuitokoch	(*Chereret*) Monkey (*Cercopithecus griseoviridis*)	Mt. Elgon and Elgeyo.
13. Kâmwaïke	Kipongoi	(*Taiyuet*) Partridge	Mt. Elgon and Elgeyo.
14. Tungo	Korapor Pale-pēt	(*Kimaketyet*) Hyena	Lumbwa.
15. Kipaa	Koros Kâpcher - Mwamweche	(*Erenet*) Snake (*Koroiityet*) Colobus monkey	Lumbwa.
16. Kipasiso	Kipkōyo Kâparakok	(*Asista*) Sun (*Puñguñgwet*) Mole	Lumbwa.
17. Chemur [3]		(*Kiptuswet*) Wild cat	Lumbwa.

[1] The Kipoiis clan is said to have been the first to inhabit the Nandi country. It will be noticed that they claim to be a mixture of people from Lumbwa (Kipsikīs) and Mt. Elgon (Kony). They are believed to have first settled on Terik Hill (Nyangori).
[2] The medicine men, or *Orkoiik* (equivalent to the Masai *'L-oibonok*) all belong to this clan.
[3] It is uncertain whether this clan is still in existence.

6   THE NANDI

Each clan is subdivided into families, the names of the families being taken from the ancestors who are believed to have been the first to settle in Nandi. Thus, the Kâmarapa family of the Kipiegen clan are descended from one Marapa, and the Kâpkipkech family of the Sokom clan are descended from one Kipkech. Families may often not intermarry though there may be no direct prohibition against the intermarriage of the clans to which the families belong.

A man may not marry a woman of the same family as himself, though there is no objection to his marrying into his own clan. This rule also applies to warriors having sexual intercourse with immature girls before marriage.

SACRED ANIMALS.

In former times the killing of his sacred animal, or totem, by the clansman was strictly forbidden, and any breach of this law was severely dealt with, the offender being either put to death or driven out of his clan and his cattle confiscated. Nowadays custom is less severe, and although it is still considered wrong to kill the sacred animal, if this is done, an apology to the animal is apparently all that is necessary. Thus, a Kipkoiitim once told me that he shot an elephant, his sacred animal, because it had good tusks. When the animal was lying dead on the ground, he went up to it and spoke somewhat as follows: 'So sorry, old fellow, I thought you were a rhino.' He traded the tusks with the Swahili, gave the elders a present, and no notice was taken of his action. Children are, however, taught to respect the totem of their clan, and if a child were to kill or hurt his totem he would be severely beaten.

The following little episode illustrates, I think, a real (not merely a magical) control exercised by a Nandi over his totem. In March, 1908, I was on the point of encamping at the foot of the Nandi escarpment. The porters were pitching the tents, the cook had lit his fire, and I was having lunch. All at once an ominous buzzing warned us that a swarm of bees was near at hand, and in less than a minute we had to leave our loads and fly, hotly pursued by the bees, which, to use a Swahili expression, had made up their minds to wage war on us. During the course of the afternoon we tried two or three times to rescue our loads, but without success, some of the porters being badly stung in the attempt. At four o'clock, when I had just decided to do nothing more till dusk, a Nandi

SACRED ANIMALS 7

strolled into camp and volunteered to quiet the bees. He told us that he was of the bee totem, and that the bees were his. He said we were to blame for the attack, as we had lit a fire under the tree in which their honey-barrel hung. He was practically stark naked, but he started off at once to the spot where the loads were, whistling loudly in much the same way as the Nandi whistle to their cattle. We saw the bees swarm round and on him, but beyond brushing them lightly from his arms he took no notice of them and, still whistling loudly, proceeded to the tree in which was their hive. In a few minutes he returned, none the worse for his venture, and we were able to fetch our loads.

The only animal that all Nandi, like most East African tribes, hold in respect or fear is the hyena, which animal was once aptly described by Sir A. Hardinge as the living mausoleum of their dead. It is true that the Nandi will kill or wound a hyena if it is on nobody's land, but they will not touch him if he prowls round their houses. Should the droppings of a hyena be found in a plantation, the corn is considered unfit for use until the field has been purified by a person from Kamasia, who receives a goat as payment. Nobody dares to imitate the cry of a hyena, under pain of being turned out of the tribe or of being refused a husband or wife in marriage. If a child is guilty of this, he is not allowed to enter a hut until a goat has been slaughtered and the excrement rubbed on to him, after which he is well flogged. When a hyena howls at night time, all Nandi women, except those of the Tungo clan, flick their ox-hide covers until it stops.

The Nandi say that hyenas are hermaphrodites, and that they are the longest sighted and possess the keenest scent of all animals. When they leave their burrows to forage they are supposed to put on spectacles (*merkonget*), and an apparatus for assisting them to smell called *kañgweto*. They are also believed to talk like human beings, and to hold communication with the spirits of the dead. Whenever several children in one family have died, the parents place a newly born babe for a few minutes in a path along which hyenas are known to walk, as it is hoped that they will intercede with the spirits of the dead and that the child's life will be spared. If the child lives, it is called *Chepor* or *Chemaket* (hyena).

Besides holding certain animals sacred, there are various things which the members of the different clans may or may not do. In the following list the several prohibitions and peculiarities are given.

Clan—Kipoiis. *Totems*—Jackal and cockroach.

No man of this clan may take as his first wife a woman who has previously conceived, but if he himself has caused her to conceive he may take her as a junior wife. The Kipoiis may not make traps, though they may hunt; they may not build their huts near a road; and they may not wear the skins of wild animals except the hyrax. The Kipoiis may not intermarry with the Talai clan.

Clan—Kipkoiitim. *Totems*—Elephant and chameleon.

The Kipkoiitim do not as a rule hunt, but they may eat all kinds of game. They may not wear garments made from the skins of any wild animals, except the hyrax, and they may under no circumstances marry a girl who has previously conceived.

Clan—Kipamwi. *Totem*—Duiker.

The Kipamwi are great hunters and live largely by the chase. They may not, however, eat the flesh of the duiker or of the rhinoceros. No Kipamwi may plant millet, nor may they settle in Lumbwa, or have any intercourse whatever with the smiths. They may not even build their huts in the proximity of the smiths, buy their weapons direct from them, or allow their goats to meet the goats belonging to the smiths on the road. The Kipamwi are forbidden to intermarry with the Tungo clan.

Clan—Kipkenda. *Totems*—Bee and frog.

No person of this clan may go to Kavirondo or to Kamasia. The Kipkenda may not hunt, make traps, or dig game pits, but they may eat all kinds of meat and wear the skins of any wild animal except the duiker. Whenever a marriage ceremony is held, a goat must be slaughtered when the bride is fetched. The Kipkenda and Kiptopke may not intermarry.

Clan—Kipkōkōs. *Totem*—Buzzard.

The members of the Kipkōkōs clan are forbidden to settle in Nyangori and in Kavirondo; they may not hunt, but they may eat the flesh of all game except the rhinoceros and the zebra; they may not wear the skins of wild animals except the hyrax; and they may not marry a girl who has previously conceived. The Kipkōkōs are prohibited from intermarrying with the Tungo clan.

Clan—Kipiegen. *Totems*—Baboon and house rat.

No Kipiegen may settle in Lumbwa, eat zebra meat, hunt, dig pits,

PROHIBITIONS AND PECULIARITIES

make traps, or wear the skins of wild animals, except the hyrax. They may not bleed oxen or collect honey during the rains, and they may not marry as first wife a girl who has previously conceived. A Kipiegen may, however, take a girl who has given birth to a child as junior wife, provided that he or one of his brothers has caused her to conceive. Forbidden clans for the purpose of marriage are the Kiptopke and Tungo.

Clan—Talai.   *Totem*—Lion.

The Talai may not eat the meat of an animal killed by a lion, or wear a lion-skin head-dress; they may not settle in Nyangori or Kamasia; they may only fight on the right flank in a battle; they may strike no person on the head; and they may only bleed oxen in the morning. All children of this clan wear a necklace made of pieces of gourd, called *sepetaiik*, and during the circumcision festival boys wear a necklace made of ostrich egg-shell beads, called *kelelik*. The Talai do not perform the *rīkset* ceremony after circumcision, and may not see the bull-roarer or friction drums.[1] A man of this clan may not marry a person who has previously conceived, or intermarry with the Tungo, Kipoiis, or Sokom clans.

Clan—Toiyoi.   *Totems*—Soldier ant and rain.

If soldier ants enter the house of a Toiyoi they are requested to leave, but no steps are taken to drive them away, and the house is vacated if necessary until the ants have passed on. During a heavy thunderstorm, the Toiyoi seize an axe, and, having rubbed it in the ashes of the fire, throw it outside the hut, exclaiming at the same time: *Toiyoi, sis kain-nyo* (Toiyoi, or thunder, be silent in our town). In the event of a hut being struck by lightning a member of this clan is called in to burn the place down, and when an ox is struck it is the duty of a Toiyoi to turn it over on its side.[2]

No Toiyoi may build in or near a forest, wear the skins of wild animals, except hyrax, or settle in Kamasia, Elgeyo, or Lumbwa. They prefer eloping with the girl of their choice to the ordinary form of marriage; and instead of it being considered a disgrace for their daughters to conceive before marriage, they look upon it as a good sign, as they are likely to be prolific. They may not, however, take a girl who has previously conceived as their first wife. No Toiyoi child is named until it is six or seven years of age. The women of this clan generally wear brass instead of iron-wire ornaments.

[1] *Vide* p. 56 sq.   [2] *Vide* also p. 99.

Clan—Kipsirgoi.   *Totem*—Bush pig.

The Kipsirgoi are mainly hunters, but whenever a beast has been wounded by a person belonging to another clan, they may not kill it. They may also not touch a donkey or allow one to graze near their herds. Whenever a Kipsirgoi wishes to marry for the first time, he must select a girl who has previously conceived; if he has difficulty in finding such a one, he must capture his bride and arrange with the parents regarding the purchase-price afterwards.[1]

Clan—Sokom.   *Totem*—Hawk.

The members of this clan may not settle in Kavirondo or Lumbwa; they may not eat the flesh or wear the skin of the duiker, but with this exception they may eat any kind of meat and wear the skin of any wild animal; they must always live apart and build their huts away from the huts of other people; and they must make their own fires by means of fire sticks. The Sokom may not intermarry with the Tungo, Kiptopke, and Talai.

Clan—Moi.   *Totems*—Crested crane and buffalo.

The Moi are not allowed to settle in Kamasia, or raid in Kavirondo; they may not build in or near a forest; they are prohibited from taking small boys prisoners in order to adopt them; they may not wear a garment made from a bush-buck or duiker skin; and their first wife must be a woman who has not had a child. When they move their kraals or break down their huts, they must select a site to the east of their former abode. Three days before a circumcision festival is commenced the members of the Moi clan perform a special ceremony called *kireku leget*. The cattle belonging to the members of the Moi clan are not branded like most Nandi cattle, the distinctive mark being clipping of the ears.

Clan—Kiptopke.   *Totem*—Monkey (*Cercopithecus griseo-viridis*).

The Kiptopke may not dig game pits or make traps, and their cattle may not pass the night outside their own kraal. Intermarriage with the Kipkenda and Sokom clans is prohibited.

Clan—Kâmwaïke.   *Totem*—Partridge.

No person of this clan may settle in Nyangori or marry a girl who has previously conceived. The Kâmwaïke may not intermarry with the Kipaa and Tungo clans.

---

[1] Some Kipsirgoi repudiate this and say that they, like most other Nandi, may not marry as first wife a girl who has previously conceived.

PROHIBITIONS AND PECULIARITIES

Clan—Tungo. *Totem*—Hyena.

The Tungo are held in high esteem, and one of their number is selected as a judge or umpire in all disputes. It also falls to their lot to close the roads against an attacking enemy and to form the rear-guard in case of retreat. No man of this clan may elope with a girl if the parents refuse their consent, and he must not ask for a bride until the girl has performed the *kâpkiyai* ceremony.[1] The marriage price for a Tungo girl is less than for any other clan, being only one ox and five goats.[2] The women do not flick their ox-hide covers when a hyena is heard at night time, as is the case with the other clans,[3] and when a Tungo dies and the corpse is not at once taken by the hyenas, it must not be changed from one side to the other.[4] The Tungo do not intermarry with the Kipamwi, Kipkōkōs, Kipiegen, Talai, Sokom, and Kâmwaïke clans.

Clan—Kipaa. *Totems*—Snake and Colobus monkey.

The Kipaa may not hunt or make traps, and they may wear the skin of no wild animal except the hyrax; they may only bleed their oxen in the morning during the rains; they may not take as first wife a girl who has previously conceived; and they may not intermarry with the Kâmwaïke. Whenever possible a member of this clan is engaged to erect the *korosiot* sticks at weddings.[5]

Clan—Kipasiso. *Totems*—Sun and mole.

The Kipasiso may not catch rain-water in vessels or use it for cooking. If a goat sniffs at their grain or walks over it when it is spread out to dry or ripen, they may not use it except for feeding unnamed children, which ceremony does not take place with them until a child is six or seven years of age. Whenever the Kipasiso prepare porridge, they must first of all sprinkle a little spring water on the fire. The members of this clan may drink milk one day after eating game.[6]

Clan—Chemur. *Totem*—Wild cat.

No prohibition or peculiarity known.

SOCIAL DIVISIONS.

According to the social system of the Nandi the male sex is divided into boys, warriors, and elders, the female sex into girls and married women. The first stage is continued till circumcision, which may be

[1] *Vide* p. 60.   [2] *Vide* p. 61.   [3] *Vide* p. 7.
[4] *Vide* p. 71. [5] *Vide* p. 62 sq. [6] *Vide* p. 24.

performed between the ages of ten and twenty. A boys' circumcision festival takes place about every $7\frac{1}{2}$ years,[1] and lasts for a couple of years. All boys who are circumcised at the same time are said to belong to the same *ipinda*, *i.e.* age or cycle. There are seven ages in all, which gives about fifty-three years. They always bear one of the following names (which are taken by their respective members), and succeed one another in the following order:—

Maina (small children, who will be circumcised about 1915).

Nyonge (boys between 10 and 20, circumcision festival commenced 1907).

Kimnyike (men between 18 and 28, circumcised about 1900).

Káplelach (men between 26 and 36, circumcised about 1892).

Kipkoiimet (men between 34 and 44, circumcised about 1885).

Sowe (men between 42 and 52, circumcised about 1877).

Juma (men between 50 and 60, circumcised about 1870).

In each age or cycle there are three subdivisions, called fires (*mat*, pl. *mostinuek*), probably from the fact that the members of each subdivision associate round their own fires, and do not allow the members of the other subdivisions to join them. The seniors of each age belong to the *Changen-opir* fire, the next ones in point of years are called *Kipal-koñg*,[2] and the youngest are the *Kiptoito* (pl. *Kiptoiinik*, the young bulls).

The Saket-ap-eito ceremony. The ceremony of handing over the country from one age to another is one of the most important in the annals of Nandi history. This takes place about every $7\frac{1}{2}$ years, and some four years after the circumcision festival. The last one took place about 1904, the next one will be held about 1911. All the adult male population that can conveniently do so collect together at a certain spot, but no married warrior may attend, nor may he or his wife leave their houses whilst the ceremony is taking place. The *Orkoiyot*, or chief medicine man, must be present, and the ceremony is started by slaughtering a white bullock, which is purchased by the young warriors for the occasion. After the meat has been eaten by the old men, each of the young men makes a small ring out of the hide, and puts it on one of the fingers of his right hand. A circle is then formed round the chief

[1] Since the removal of the Nandi to their reserve they seem to have altered this custom, and boys are now circumcised every year or so like the girls.

[2] These two expressions are meaningless in Nandi; but they are equivalent to *Big ostrich feathers* and *We tear out the eyes* in Masai.

SOCIAL DIVISIONS 13

medicine man, who stands near a stool, about which is heaped cow dung studded with the fruit of the *lapotuet* shrub.[1] All the old men and the members of the age immediately preceding the one in power stand up, whilst the warriors who are going to receive the control of the country sit down. On a sign from the chief medicine man the members of the preceding age divest themselves of their warriors' skins and put on old men's fur garments. The warriors of the age in power, *i.e.* those who were circumcised some four years previously, are then solemnly informed that the safety of the country and the welfare of the inhabitants are placed in their hands, and they are instructed to guard the land of their fathers.[2]

At the conclusion of the ceremony everybody departs to his own home and nobody may sleep by the wayside.

MODE OF SUBSISTENCE.

Houses. The Nandi, like the Lumbwa and other nearly allied tribes, do not live in villages or towns, but each man has his own hut (*kaita*) or group of huts (*ñganaset*), which he builds in or near his fields of eleusine grain and millet.

The huts (*kápsat*, pl. *korik-ap-sat*) are circular in shape, and are built of wattle and mud mixed with cow dung; the walls are about four feet high, and the grass roofs are conical. There are two rooms in each hut, one occupied by the man, his wife, small children, and a few goats, and the other by the calves, sheep, and the remaining goats. The former is called *Koiimaut*, the latter *Injorut*. The two rooms are separated by a wattle and daub partition called *tōtet*, in which is a small doorway. The *Koiimaut* is used as a kitchen as well as a living-room and a bedroom, and there is a ceiling of wickerwork less than four feet from the floor. In the space above the ceiling, which is reached by a large open skylight (*kutit-ap-taput*), grain, tobacco, gourds, and cooking utensils are stored. A few inches below the ceiling and over the fire a wickerwork tray is slung. This is

[1] *Solanum campylanthum.*
[2] Mr. Hobley in the *Journal of the Anthropological Institute*, 1903, p. 343, writes:—'The use of the solanum fruit with clay, as a charm for good, seems to be rather widespread, for at the close of the Nandi campaign of 1900, when the chiefs were making overtures for peace, they brought to the Government Station a native stool, on which was a conical mass of moist red clay, which rather reminded one of a child's mud pie; this was studded all over with the yellow solanum fruit, and was said to be a great peace medicine.' Were the Nandi handing over the control of their country to the white man?

Diagram of Nandi Hut.

1. Man's bed.
2. Woman's bed.
3. Clay division.
4. Cooking stones.
5. Skylight support.
6. Depression for beer-pot.
7. Urinal gutter.
8. "Eye" of gutter.
9. Thongs for tying up goats.
10. Door posts.
11. Entrance to goat-chamber.
12. Milk compartment.
13. Partition wall.
14. Pegs.
15. Pegs for milk-gourds.
16. Pole supporting roof.
17. Wall of hut.
    Section through A-B
18. Tray for drying grain.
19. Ceiling of living room.
20. Skylight.
21. Finial of central pole.
22. Grass binding.
23. Broken pot.
24. Grass roof

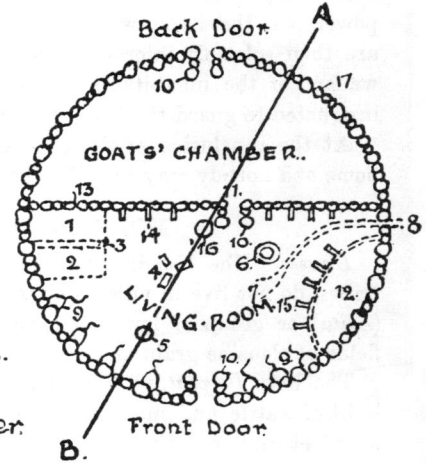

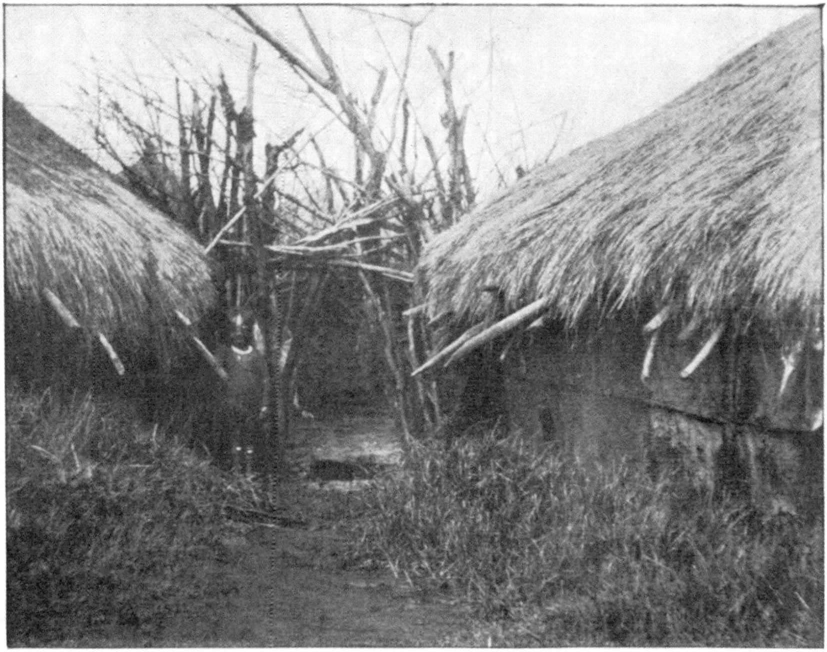

PLATE V

Entrance to Nandi cattle-kraal (Stordy).

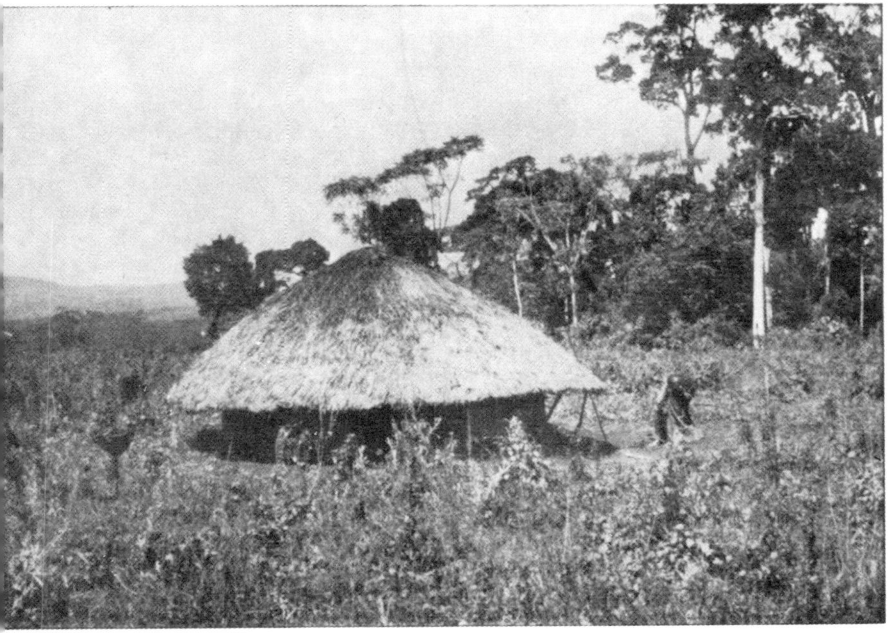

Nandi hut (Meinertzhagen).

MODE OF SUBSISTENCE

called *sainet*, and is used for drying grain. A small compartment is built out of the wall and is set aside for storing milk. It is called *Káplengut*, and the milk gourds are hung round it. A depression in the floor, which is known as *kilonget*, is made near the central pole for the accommodation of a beer pot.

The furniture of the huts consists of cooking utensils, jars, gourds, arms, and stools. The arms and gourds are suspended from the partition by means of pegs (*irēusiek*). There are also two mud beds, which are usually slightly raised at one end, a small mound of earth and sheep's dung doing the duty of pillow. The beds are covered by an ox-hide.

A short inaugural ceremony is performed when the erection of a house is commenced. The elders of the family pour milk and beer and put some salt into the hole which has been prepared for the reception of the central pole (*taloita*), and say :

Asis !	kōn-ech	sapon.		
God !	give-us	health.		
Asis !	kōn-ech	cheko.		
God !	give-us	the-milk.		
Asis !	kōn-ech	uindo.		
God !	give-us	the-power.		
Asis !	kōn-ech	päk.		
God !	give-us	the-eleusine-grain.		
Asis !	kōn-ech	kii	tukul	ne-mie.
God !	give-us	thing	every	which-is-good.
Asis !	tuk-w-ech	lakōk	ak	tuka.
God !	cover-for-us	the-children	and	the-cattle.[1]

All work in connexion with the building of the huts is performed by the men until the skeleton is ready, when the work is taken over by the women, who finish it. The posts and poles are cut by the men during the waning of the moon. When the house is nearing completion a piece of a cooking-pot or a wreath of grass is passed over the apex of the roof, and the top of the central pole is bound round with grass. If, as is frequently the case, the central pole is not tall enough, it is surmounted by a stick, and the erection, which is styled *kimonjōkut*, is frequently almost phallic in appearance.[2] During the first four days after the house has been occupied the owner may not sleep with his wife, and nobody in the house may mention the ground-

---

[1] Guard our children and cattle.
[2] For further particulars *vide* p. 71 sq.

hornbill (*cheptĭbĭt*) by name. Were either of these rules to be broken, it is believed that the house would always be draughty and cold. One month later a few sticks of the *tepesuet* [1] tree are put in the ground in the form of a circle near the front door and are bound round with some cord of the *chemnyelilet* tree. This little charm is called *mabwaita*, and is supposed to bring good luck to the occupants of the house. Those Nandi whose ancestors hail from Lumbwa generally renew the *mabwaita* after it has become dilapidated, whilst others throw the sticks away.

Near the huts are as a rule one or two granaries called *choket*. They are built on poles about two feet from the ground, are circular in shape, and are made of wickerwork or wattle and daub mixed with cow dung with thatched roofs.

A little to the rear is the *sigiroinet*, where the unmarried warriors sleep. As many as ten men sometimes inhabit one hut, which on the outside resembles in appearance the ordinary houses. Inside, however, there is no room for the goats. The unmarried girls are allowed to visit the warriors in these buildings, staying with them for a few days at a time and living with them in a state of free love. No married women may enter the *sigiroinōsiek*, and when the warriors go away for a time or depart for the wars, their 'sweethearts' look after these huts until their return. There is also at times a kind of club house called *kait'-am-murenik* (the warriors' house) in which the warriors meet occasionally, and in which the old men drink beer, depressions for the accommodation of their pots being made round the central pole. No women are allowed access to this house.

Youths and young girls generally live in huts by themselves or with old women. Small boys, who are used by the warriors as servants, frequently sleep in the *sigiroinet*.

The warriors also have small huts in the woods where they go and slaughter oxen from time to time. These places are called *ekoruek*.

A few head of cattle are usually kept near the dwelling huts in a *pēut*, or cattle enclosure, but the bulk of the stock live the greater part of the year on the grazing grounds some distance away. The cattle kraal is called *Kâp-tich*. It is formed of thorny bushes kept in place by poles, and it has two entrances, one for the cows and the other for the calves. In the centre of the kraal is a hut called *chepkimaliot*. This hut, like the ordinary dwelling huts, is divided into two rooms, but instead of a conical grass roof it has a flat roof covered with cow

[1] *Croton sp.*

MODE OF SUBSISTENCE

dung, and the walls, which are of wattle and cow dung, are about five feet high. The herdsmen with two or three warriors and girls sleep in one room, whilst the calves occupy the other. Each morning, when the cattle have left the kraal, the girls, who remain at home, sweep up the enclosure and throw the refuse on one side, where in course of time it forms a large mound.

A small grass hut, known by the name of *keriet*, is sometimes seen in Nandi. It is built in the cornfields and is used when the grain is ripening as a shelter for the people who are engaged in driving away the birds.

A few superstitious customs are observed in regard to the interior of huts. Nobody may stand upright in a hut, or sit at the door or on the threshold. If a person has entered a hut by one door he must leave by the same door, unless he pauses for a time in the hut, when he may go out by the other door. Nobody may peep into a hut and then go away; the threshold must be crossed before a person can proceed on his way. A man may not touch the threshold of his house, or anything in the house except his own bed, if his wife has a child at the breast. No warrior may leave a hut in the dark, and if he wishes to go outside, he says to his mother or to whoever is the owner of the hut, *Ilal mat* (Make up the fire). A *chesorpuchot*, i. e. a woman who gave birth to a child before she married, may never look into a granary for fear of spoiling the grain. When food is scarce in the land and the women have to undertake long journeys to purchase what is required, it is customary for small children during their mothers' absence to embrace the door-posts and say: *A-sa-i, eiyo, ip-u omdit* (I pray, mother, bring food). Other superstitions are mentioned on pages 7, 61, 66, 68 sqq., 74, and 90.

Caves. In former times the Nandi are said to have lived in caves like some of the tribes on Mount Elgon. During the military expeditions which have been undertaken in the Nandi country the inhabitants have invariably found shelter for themselves and their cattle in the vast natural caves which lie hidden in the almost impenetrable forests.

Agriculture. The Nandi were probably originally a tribe of hunters, like the Dorobo at the present day[1]; in fact, they have a tradition to that effect.[2] They have, however, now taken to agriculture, and grow

[1] *Vide* p. 2.   [2] *Vide* p. 120.

large quantities of eleusine grain [1] and millet. Other products are beans, pumpkins, sweet potatoes, and tobacco; and in small quantities

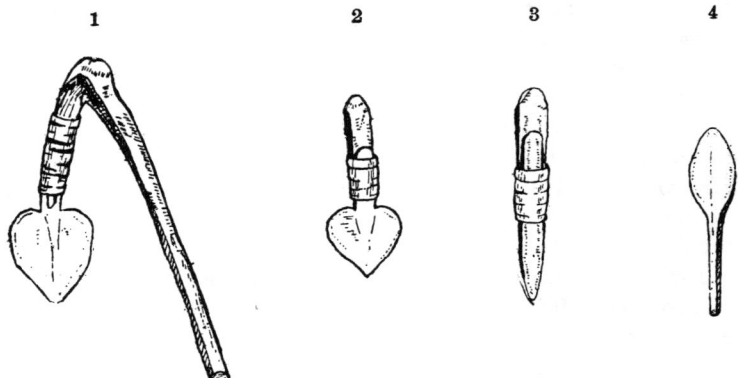

FIGS. 1–4 (scale 1/12). Hoes: (1) Side view. (2) Front view. (3) Wooden hoe. (4) Blade of hoe used by people of the western counties.

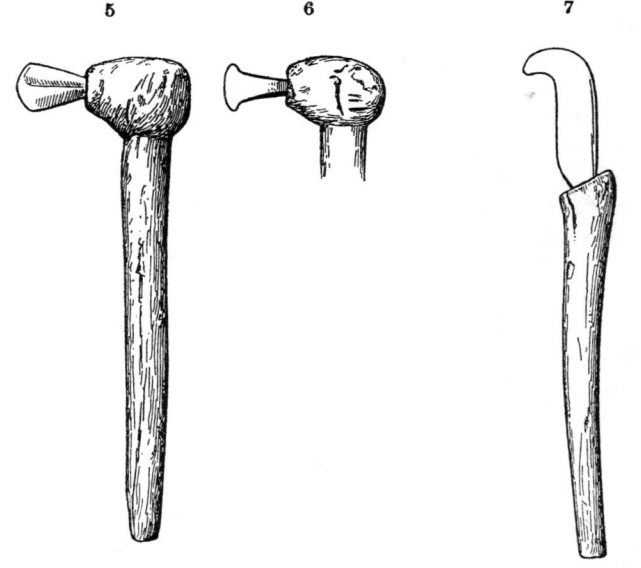

FIGS. 5–7 (scale 1/8). (5) Axe. (6) Axe used in the western counties. (7) Bill-hook.

[1] *Eleusine coracana*, Gaertn.

MODE OF SUBSISTENCE

maize and bananas. The only agricultural implements are the iron hoe, a two-pronged fork, an axe, and a bill-hook. In rocky ground a wooden digging-stick or hoe is used instead of the iron hoe.

The rough work of clearing the bush for plantations is performed by the men, after which nearly all work in connexion with them is done by the women. The men, however, assist in sowing the seed, and in harvesting some of the crops. As a rule trees are not felled, but the bark is stripped off for about four feet from the ground and the trees are then left to die.

The planting is mostly, if not entirely, done during the first half of the *Kiptamo* moon (February), which is the first month of the year, and when the *Iwat-kut* moon rises (March) all seed should be in the ground. The chief medicine man is consulted before the planting operations begin, but the Nandi know by the arrival in the fields of the guinea-fowl, whose song is supposed to be, *O-kol, o-kol ; mi-i tokoch* (Plant, plant ; there is luck in it), that the planting season is at hand.

When the first seed is sown, salt is mixed with it, and the sower sings mournfully : *Ak o-siek-u o-chok-chi* (And grow quickly), as he sows.

After fresh ground has been cleared, eleusine grain is planted. This crop is generally repeated the second year, after which millet is sown, and finally sweet potatoes or some other product. Most fields are allowed to lie fallow every fourth or fifth year. The Nandi manure their plantations with turf ashes.

Great damage to the crops is at times done by moles, rats, and field-mice, but the Nandi are skilled trappers, and place small nooses just inside the holes. As bait they use the root of the *menjeiyuet* plant [1] for moles, and pieces of meat for rats and mice. All plants destroyed by vermin as well as weeds are thrown on the heaps or mounds made by the black ants, one or two of which exist in most plantations. These mounds are called *kâpsagunik*. If the damage is considerable the plants are scattered in the road, the person scattering them walking towards the west.

Charms are put in the fields or hung on the hedges to guard the crops against locusts and birds.[2] Traps are also set for birds.

The eleusine crops are harvested by both men and women. All other crops are reaped by the women only, who are at times assisted by the children.[3]

The corn is pounded and winnowed by the women and girls. When

---
[1] *Indigofera sp.*   [2] *Vide* p. 86.
[3] For further particulars *vide* p. 46.

there is no wind to separate and drive off the chaff from the grain, the girls whistle and say, *Chepusoon! A-tiñg-u-n lakwet* (Wind! I will seize thy child and put it in my lap).

When in the plantations, nobody may carry a spear or put one in the ground; thigh bells must not be worn; a hide may not be dragged along the ground; and nobody may whistle.

After an earthquake or a hail storm,[1] when a death has occurred in the family, if a hoe breaks, or a beast of prey seizes a goat, no work may be performed in the fields for the rest of the day and for twenty-four hours afterwards, as it is believed that any sick person who eats the grain when harvested, or who drinks beer made from the grain, will die, and that pregnant women will abort.

If the owner of a plantation dies whilst his crops are ripening, all the grain must be eaten and none may be reserved for sowing, otherwise it is feared that the grain will rot in the ground.

Stock. Cattle, sheep, and goats are kept and bred. Formerly the Nandi owned enormous herds, but during the late punitive expedition they lost large numbers. As they do not often sell their animals or kill them for food, there is no reason, unless cattle-disease breaks out in the Nandi Reserve, why they should not again become as wealthy as before.

Cattle-herding is the chief occupation of the men and big boys. They love their beasts, as they say themselves, more than anything in the world; they talk to, pet and coax them; and their grief is great when a favourite sickens and dies. A couple of herdsmen can easily manage a herd of two hundred cows; and the animals understand the men so thoroughly that they come and go as directed. The warriors who accompany the herds are generally fully armed, as it is their duty to protect the animals and guard against the attacks of wild animals and enemies. The herdsmen themselves are only armed with long sticks with which they drive the cattle while whistling. A favourite attitude of these men is to stand on one leg, with the other raised and the sole of the foot placed on the calf or knee of the supporting leg, while they lean on their spear or stick.

As already stated, the bulk of the stock live the greater part of the year on the grazing grounds away from the owners' houses and

---

[1] If the sun shines shortly after a hail storm, work may be done the next day.

Nandi herdsman (Henderson).

Stream near Nandi Fort (Hart).

MODE OF SUBSISTENCE

plantations. The herds are driven forth each morning just before sunrise, when the dew is on the grass, for the Nandi, unlike most East African tribes, believe that the wet grass is fattening. At 10 a.m. the cattle return to the kraal to be milked, and they go off to feed again at 11.30. At 1 and again at 4 p.m. they are watered, and at sun-down they are milked a second time, and the doors of the cattle-fold are closed.

The goats, sheep, and big calves are herded by small boys and girls. They go to the grazing grounds, or they start feeding near the huts at 7.30 a.m., and they return to the kraal two hours later. At 10 o'clock they are again driven forth, at 12.30 they are watered, and at 5 p.m. they are locked up for the night.

Small calves and kids do not go with the herds and flocks. They remain near the huts during the day, and, after being suckled in the evening, go into the huts for the night.

No artificial food is given to the stock, nor are they fed after entering the kraal. They are driven to the salt-licks once a fortnight. The calves are always reared by the mothers, unless the cow dies, when the calf is fed by means of a gourd on to which is fastened a leather mouth-piece. The calves are watered at wooden troughs, a little salt being usually added to the water.

The cows are able to restrain their flow of milk, and do so if their calves are not with them. On this account the calf is allowed to suck first, before any attempt is made to milk. When a calf dies the skin is preserved and produced each time the cow is to be milked.

The milking is usually done by the boys and girls, who at times also milk the animals direct into their mouths. If the cow passes water at the time of milking, the milker rinses his hands in the urine. Cows that are restless when being milked have the hind legs bound together by a leathern thong just above the hocks.

The only vessels that may be used for milk are the gourds or calabashes. If anything else were employed, it is believed that it would be injurious to the cattle. The gourds must be fumigated every time after milk has been put in them, a stick of the *itet* tree being burnt for this purpose. The smoke gives the milk a flavour without which it is not palatable to the taste of the Nandi. When milk is allowed to stand for some while, the gourds are cleansed by cow's urine, after which they are well washed with boiling water. It is the duty of the women to fumigate and cleanse the milk pots.

Butter is made by women, who use it only for oiling their bodies. They churn by striking the gourds, into which milk has been poured, on their thighs.

Each clan has a special mark by which the members know their cattle. Some brand their animals, whilst others clip their ears. There are also smaller marks by which each family and each individual can recognize his beasts. Goats have their ears cut in a special way as distinctive marks, and sheep are branded on the face.

Besides the clan or family marks, cattle are often cauterized when ill, and beautiful patterns are sometimes branded on their backs and sides for ornament. The horns, too, are at times twisted into various shapes.

Donkeys. The Nandi do not keep donkeys like the Masai, as they affirm that these animals spoil the grazing for cattle. Formerly the smiths are said to have owned large herds of donkeys, but they have been obliged to get rid of them, and the only people who may now keep them are the chief medicine man and his relations.

Food. The Nandi eat twice a day, at 9 a.m. and at 7 p.m. On the grazing grounds the morning meal is taken at 5 a.m. The staple food is a kind of stiff porridge, called *kimnyiet*, which is made of eleusine grain or millet mixed with water and cooked. Vegetables are commonly eaten with the porridge as a relish.

Besides vegetable food, cows' and goats' milk is drunk, and the blood of cattle, goats, and sheep is taken hot or mixed with milk. The animals are periodically bled by means of an arrow called *lońgnet*, which is shot into one of the superficial veins of the neck. Every time a cow is milked and every time a beast is bled, a few drops of milk from each teat or a few drops of blood are allowed to fall on the ground as an offering to Asista and to the spirits of the deceased. In former times it was considered wrong to bleed a milch cow, but nowadays it is only necessary to offer an apology to the animal, in much the same way as a man apologizes to his totem when he kills it.[1] *Ko-ii-o sesen* (Dogs have borne),[2] he remarks, and he takes the blood with a clear conscience.

Oxen are butchered by being stabbed in the nape of the neck; sheep and goats are strangled. When cattle are slaughtered, a little

---

[1] *Vide* p. 6.   [2] No explanation of this cryptic saying is known.

Nandi shooting with bow and arrow (Meinertzhagen).

of the meat (liver, kidneys, intestines and fat) is always eaten raw. All meat must be cut at the joints, and the bones may not be stripped before roasting. The tongue and heart must be cut in half lengthways, and divided between two persons. Boys and girls may only eat the meat off the joint of full-grown animals. Warriors, women, and old people may eat any part of the animal. No pregnant woman may eat the flesh of cattle killed by a wild beast, or of a pregnant

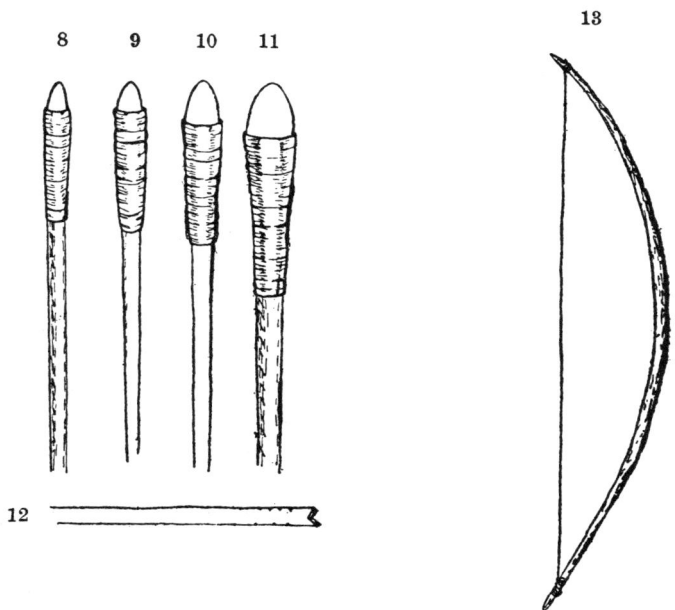

FIGS. 8-12 (scale ¼). Arrows used for bleeding purposes: (8) Goats, (9) Sheep and young calves. (10) Calves and cows. (11) Bulls. (12) Shaft. FIG. 13 (scale ⅛). Bow.

animal. An unborn calf or kid is given to small children if the hide has formed; otherwise it must be thrown away. When cattle, goats, or sheep die or are slaughtered, care must be taken not to step over the carcase or to stand with the carcase between one's legs. If this is done, it is believed that the meat will cause all those who eat it to have pains in their stomachs. All blood-stains must be washed off the hands and knife of the butcher by the undigested food from the animal's intestines.

Milk may be drunk fresh[1] or sour, but it may on no account be boiled, and meat and milk may not be taken together. If milk is drunk, no meat may be eaten for twenty-four hours. Boiled meat in soup must be eaten first, after which roast meat may be taken. When meat has been eaten, no milk may be drunk for twelve hours, and then only after some salt and water has been swallowed. If no salt, which is obtained from the salt-licks, is near at hand, blood may be drunk instead. An exception to this rule is made in the case of small children, boys and girls who have recently been circumcised, women who have a short while before given birth to a child, and very sick people. These may eat meat and drink milk at the same time, and are called *pitorik*. If anybody else breaks the rule he is soundly flogged.

Fish is not known to most Nandi, but is eaten by the western clans, who purchase it from the Kavirondo people.

Game is as a rule much appreciated. It is customary amongst the Nandi to hunt in large numbers, and when a herd has been surrounded, they shoot or spear as many head as they can. They also train dogs to hunt. The clans that live farthest north make wooden traps and also snare game by means of a leather noose, the end of which they fasten to a heavy log of wood, whilst underneath a pit is dug, the whole being carefully hidden.

Certain animals may not be eaten if it is possible to obtain other food. These are waterbuck,[2] zebra, elephant, rhinoceros, Senegal hartebeest, and the common and blue duiker. If a Nandi eats the meat of any of these animals, he may not drink milk for at least four months afterwards, and then only after he has purified himself by taking a strong purge made from the *segetet* tree, mixed with blood.[3] No Nandi will eat the flesh of lion, leopard, hyena, jackal, cat, Colobus monkey, snake, or frog; but baboon meat, rats, moles, locusts, and flying ants are considered delicacies.

There are a few superstitious customs observed by hunters. If a man has started out to hunt he must not be called back, otherwise he will miss his quarry. To step over a snare or trap is to court

[1] People who have been wounded or who are suffering from boils or ulcers may not drink fresh milk.
[2] Waterbuck (*kipsomeret*) is considered an unclean beast. It is often alluded to by the name *chemakimwa*, the animal which must not be talked about.
[3] The members of the Kipasiso clan are exempt from this rule. They may drink milk the day after eating any game.

MODE OF SUBSISTENCE

death and must be avoided at all costs. A man who has recently prepared poison,[1] or one who has shot an animal with a poisoned arrow, or who carries poisoned arrows on his person or in his quiver, may not eat mutton, sleep on a new ox-hide, or associate with women. Before he can do any of these things he must purify himself by bathing in a river and by taking a purge.

Fowls are rarely kept, and are not eaten by women; but wild birds are caught and eaten. The francolin or spur-fowl is looked upon in much the same light as the waterbuck, and although it may be eaten, milk must not be taken for several months afterwards. The crested crane,[2] ox-pecker, woodpecker, African pheasant, sparrow, and all carrion birds are forbidden articles of food, as also are eggs.

Honey is much relished and is an important article of diet. The honey-comb and grubs are likewise eaten. Honey is principally obtained from the hives of wild bees.[3] Hives built in trees are called *pondet*, those made in rocks, *kepenet*. Bees are also kept in a semi-domesticated state, and honey barrels (*moinget*) are placed or

FIG. 14 (scale ¼). *Kesimoret*, knife used for tapping palms.

hung in trees for them to build in.[4] Bees' wax is used for fastening the handles on to knives, spears, bill-hooks, etc.

Intoxicating drinks, which may only be taken by old people in any quantity, are obtained from honey and from the sap of the wild date-palm, whilst beer is made from eleusine and millet grain. Honey wine, which is called *kipketīnik*, is made by mixing honey and a little water in a calabash into which a piece of the fruit of the

[1] The poison is obtained from the wood of the *keliot* tree (*Acocanthera Schimperi*). This is cut up into small chips, which are boiled for some hours until the water has a thick and pitch-like appearance. After straining, the poison is smeared on sheets of bark or put in a half calabash, called *septet*, and kept in trees out of the reach of children.

[2] The Nandi are very fond of the crested crane, owing to its beautiful plumage. Whenever children see these birds they say: *Koñgony! Chepararewa! Chepa-iiti'-moii!* (Crested cranes! The daughters of heifers! The daughters of the calves' ears!)

[3] The Nandi ascertain where the hives are by following the *Cuculus indicator* bird. They prefer honey made from the *tepengwet* flower (*Emilia integrifolia*) to any other.   [4] *Vide* also p. 38.

rotinuet tree [1] is placed. The beverage is allowed to stand for three days, at the end of which time it has fermented and can be drunk. The preparation of the wild date-palm wine (*porokek*) is even simpler. The sap is tapped and allowed to stand for one day in a calabash, when it is ready for drinking. The method of brewing beer (*maiyek*) is more complicated. The grain is first mixed with water and put in an ox-hide. It is then buried in a hole in the ground which is lined with the leaves of the wild banana plant, and the hole is filled in with leaves and sticks. At the end of ten days, when the grain has become malt, it is taken out of the hole and roasted in a pot by a slow fire for twelve hours. The women and children at this stage eat a little of the malt and have a dance, in which they represent the men after they have had a carousal, behaving like drunken creatures and rolling on the ground. The malt is next spread in the sun for two days, after which it is boiled for forty-eight hours. It is then put into pots which are placed in the loft, and for the next two days, until it is ready for drinking, the men and women may not sleep together in the house. When the beer is ready for drinking, the women hold a dance at which they go through the

FIG. 15 (scale ½). Drinking straw.

performance of grinding and crushing the grain, to the accompaniment of the scraping of their iron bracelets.

Tobacco is enjoyed by both sexes. Most warriors take snuff; others, and many old men, chew tobacco, and a few old men and women smoke it. Snuff-boxes (*chepkiraut*) are made of wood, gourds, ox-horn, or, rarely, of ivory; they have a leather cap, and both the box and cap are ornamented with beads. Tobacco pouches are made out of the scrotum of a goat or the horn of an ox (*olpesienyet* or *kipraut*). Both pouches and boxes are slung round the neck by a thin chain. The Lumbwa or Kipsikīs people make a liquid snuff; but although the Nandi employ the Lumbwa word for the snuff-box (*kirongesiet*), they do not take tobacco in this way themselves. Their pipes they purchase from the Kavirondo.

Bhang or hashish (*nyasoret*) grows wild, but is not used by the

[1] *Kigelia aethiopica.*

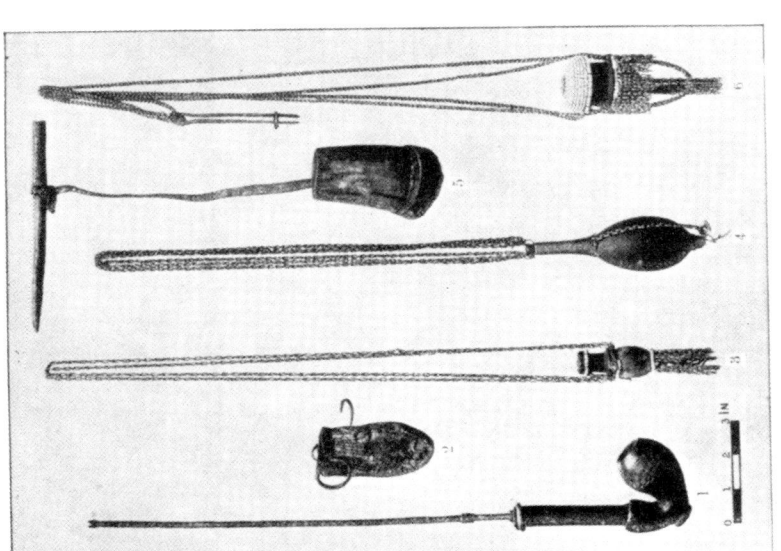

1. Pipe. 2. Olpesienyet. Tobacco pouch.
3 and 4. Kipraut. Snuff-box.
5. Kirongesiet. Liquid tobacco pouch (Lumbwa).
6. Kipraut. Snuff-box, with tweezers.

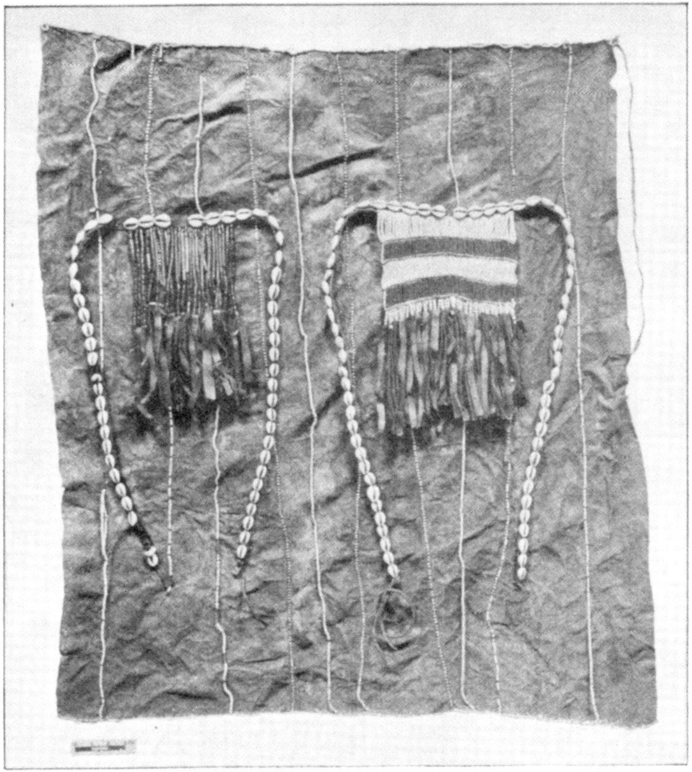

GIRLS' DRESSES.
The dress in the background is an ingoriet-ap-ko. The two in the foreground are osiek aprons.

To face p. 26

MODE OF SUBSISTENCE

Nandi, though it is well known and is smoked by some of the neighbouring tribes, *e. g.* the Kavirondo.

Cannibalism is not practised; but in former times, whenever a Nandi warrior killed an enemy, he used to eat a small portion of the dead man's heart to make himself brave. To the present day, when a person of another tribe has been slain by a Nandi, the blood must be carefully washed off the spear or sword into a cup made of grass, and drunk by the slayer. If this is not done it is thought that the man will become frenzied.

Cooking. Food is cooked in earthen pots inside the houses, and is served up on a piece of smooth hide. The men eat first and the women afterwards. Children have their meals separately. The young girls wait on their parents and brothers.

WEARING APPAREL, WEAPONS, ETC.

Dress and ornaments. Both men and women are scantily dressed. The former show no signs of shame at being seen naked, but women must not appear without their lower garments.

Babies and small children run about naked. Young boys wear a goat's skin garment (*ingoriet*) and a necklace of black beads (*sonaiek*). Young girls wear an apron called *osiek*, the name of the seeds of the *murguyuet* tree with which it is adorned.[1] It is made of strips of leather fastened on to a belt ornamented with cowries. They also at times wear a dressed skin or cloth, called *ingoriet-ap-ko*. Their ornaments consist of iron wire and iron chain necklaces (*asingaiit* and *sirimwagik*), iron wire bracelets (*makirariot*), armlets (*indinyoliet*) and leglets (*tapakwet*), and bead armlets (*sonaiek*) and anklets (*kipkarkarek* or *ingipiliek*). Boys and girls stretch the lobe of the ear by inserting enormous pieces of wood, called *ketit-ap-iit*; the former also wear wooden ear-rings, called *kipalpaliot*, which are polished, ornamented, and cut into various shapes. The Nandi tribal mark, like the Masai, is a small hole bored in the upper part of the ear. Into this boys and girls fix small pegs or reeds called *soliot*.

The dress of the warriors consists of two or three black goats' or calves' hides sewn together and loosely fixed by a strip of leather over one shoulder. The hair is left on the hides, which are ornamented with white or coloured beads. This garment is called *kipoiet*, and the

---

[1] No boy or man may ever wear a girl's apron.

edge, which is worked with beads, is known as *kurmonutiet*. Nowadays a piece of cotton cloth dyed brown often takes the place of the skin garment.[1] Warriors also wear an apron behind called *koroiisit*. Their ornaments consist of a horn arm-clamp (*cheposta*), chain armlets (*sirimwagik*), iron wire, chain, or lead ear-rings (*chepo-lungu, sirimwagik, engosholai* or *kimeiteitiot*), iron or bead bracelets (*asingaiit* or *sonaiek*), and necklaces of beads, berries, or iron wire (*nongoiinik, kaiiñganik, ndaliñgu, asingaiit* or *päk-ap-sosik*). A leather or Colobus monkey-skin leglet (*marikchot* or *munganiet*), an anklet of small bells (*kipkurkuriet*), and a snuff-box (*chepkiraut*) complete the costume. In times of war they wear an ostrich-feather,[2] lion-skin, or ox-hide head-dress (*sombet, kutuet* or *eurto*), a cape of vultures' feathers (*kororik*), a thigh bell (*kipkurkuriet*), sandals (*kweyot*), and a long piece of white or coloured cloth (*anget*), which is fastened to the neck and flows out behind. If a man is noted for his bravery he may wear the skin of a leopard's tail from his right shoulder. At the end of the leopard's tail is generally suspended a Colobus monkey's tail as well.

Married women wear two garments of dressed leather, sometimes ornamented with beads. The lower one, which is fixed by a belt (*legetiet*), is called *chepkawit*; the upper one, *koliket*. Their bracelets and armlets are larger than those worn by girls, but have the same names; they also wear an additional bracelet called *asielda*. Their necklaces are made of glass beads, ostrich egg-shell beads, or of iron wire and chains (*semwet, kelelik, mukuriot, asingaiit* or *sirimwagik*), and their ear-rings are large round disks of brass wire (*taet*).[3] They also wear bead rings (*chepuchechot*) in the upper part of the ear. Old women wear the same garments as married women, but their ornaments are slightly different. They have iron wire, glass bead or ostrich egg-shell bead necklaces, called *ngänemoru, merenget*, and *kelelik*, and small circular ear-rings, called *asuleyot*. Women, both old and young, frequently carry a stick about with them, which is called *sigilgiliot*.

Old men attire themselves in a *kaross*, or fur garment made of hyrax, gazelle, ox, or goat hide (*sambut, sumet, tisiet*, or *ingoriet*), which they sling toga-fashion from the shoulder.[4] They wear iron

[1] Big boys likewise frequently wear cotton cloth in place of the goat's skin.
[2] When an ostrich-feather head-dress is worn, a small box (*olgitongit*) for carrying spare feathers (*songolik*) is worn over one shoulder.
[3] No married woman may, during her husband's life, lay aside her earrings. Should the weight of them hurt her ears, she may wear them as a necklace, and put small bead rings, called *soienik*, in her ears.
[4] Trade blankets have now to a large extent taken the place of the *kaross*.

PLATE IX

Nandi girl wearing the ingoriet-ap-ko garment and the osiek apron

Nandi woman wearing her ear-rings as a necklace (Henderson).

WEARING APPAREL, WEAPONS, ETC. 29

wire bracelets (*samoiyot*) and necklaces (*asingaiit*), and iron wire or chain ear-rings (*sirimwagik* or *kimeiteitiot*). They also frequently wear iron rings on their fingers (*tamokyet*), an ivory arm-ring, and a fur or skin cap (*cheptulet*).

If a person dies, his next younger brother or sister has to wear a certain ornament for the rest of his or her life. This is not a sign of mourning, but is to prevent the evil spirit or disease from attacking the next member of the family. Little girls generally have an arrangement of beads called *songoniet*, which is attached to their hair and hangs over the forehead and nose. Boys and girls wear a necklace made of chips of a gourd (*sepetaiik*), and boys also at times wear a garment made of Colobus monkey-skin instead of goat-skin. Women wear an iron necklace, called *karik-ap-teget*, and men an iron armlet, called *asielda*. Men and women also frequently wear a claw or a piece of the hide of a lion or leopard.

Twins wear an ornament known as *samoiyot*. Boys, girls, and women wear it as a necklace, men as an armlet.

If a man has been wounded in one of his limbs he wears a chain bracelet or leglet; if he suffers from rheumatism or if his ear aches, he wears an ostrich egg-shell armlet, leglet, or ear-ring ; and if his head aches he wears strapped on to his forehead a piece of iron called *sengwetiet*.

Hair. Nandi women and small children have their heads shaved once a month ; old men and boys once a quarter. Some women, however, do not shave the whole head, leaving the crown covered with short hair and shaving only over the temples, ears, and back of the neck. This custom is called *piur*, and may not be followed by girls.

Boys are fond of twisting the seeds of a tree called *murguyuet* into their hair. This gives them a curious appearance, their hair standing up in a number of little knots on their heads. They also frequently wear a single feather of a hawk or vulture hanging down the back of the head.

Warriors let their hair grow long and plait cloth or wool into it to give them a good pigtail behind. They also sometimes wear their hair plaited into three pigtails behind and at other times let it hang loose. In front they either wear their hair in about a dozen tags hanging over their foreheads, or, like the Masai, in one pigtail over each ear and between the eyes, or gathered up in a bunch, or hanging loose and flapping about on their heads as they move.

It is customary amongst the Nandi to shave the head as a sign of grief, and to throw the hair away towards the west in the direction of the setting sun. At other times when the head is shaved the hair is thrown towards the rising sun, or taken towards the east and hidden in the grass. When a prisoner of war is taken his head is shaved by his captor and his hair kept until he is ransomed. The hair is returned with the prisoner. When a person is adopted, his foster father shaves his head and throws the hair away towards the east.

All Nandi shave their eyebrows. The hairs of the beard, arm-pits, pubes, and shins are plucked out, but not shaved.

Teeth. All Nandi have the two middle incisors of the lower jaw extracted as soon as the milk teeth have been replaced by the permanent set.[1] The operation is performed by means of a *loñgnet*, or arrow used for bleeding cattle, and a *katet*, or large needle. The child must throw the teeth away towards the rising sun and say, *Asis, ee kelek che-muruonen, kōn-o che-lelach a-lu-ote che po moi* (God, take the

Fig. 16 (scale ¼). Needle.

brown teeth and give me white ones, so that I may drink calf's milk). As with the Masai, the origin of this custom is said to be in order to enable a person suffering from tetanus to be fed.[2]

The cast milk teeth of children and the extracted teeth of adults must be hidden or buried in goats' dung.

If children cut their upper teeth before the lower ones or the side teeth before the front ones, the old men of the clan make a medicine out of certain trees. Some of this medicine is given to the child to drink, after which the teeth, which are called needles, are said to stop growing until the other ones have come. Children who are born with teeth in their mouths are made away with at birth.

Tattoo. Some Nandi girls tattoo themselves by cutting three horizontal lines in their cheeks below the eyes, or, like the Kavirondo, by drawing one line down the forehead and nose, or, like the Masai, by making a pattern round the eyebrows and eyes. A black dye is rubbed in to make the mark permanent.

[1] Sir H. Johnston (*The Uganda Protectorate*, p. 868) and Mr. Hobley (*Eastern Uganda*, p. 38) are incorrect in stating that a chief or medicine man also has a tooth of the upper jaw removed.

[2] For another possible explanation *vide* p. 82.

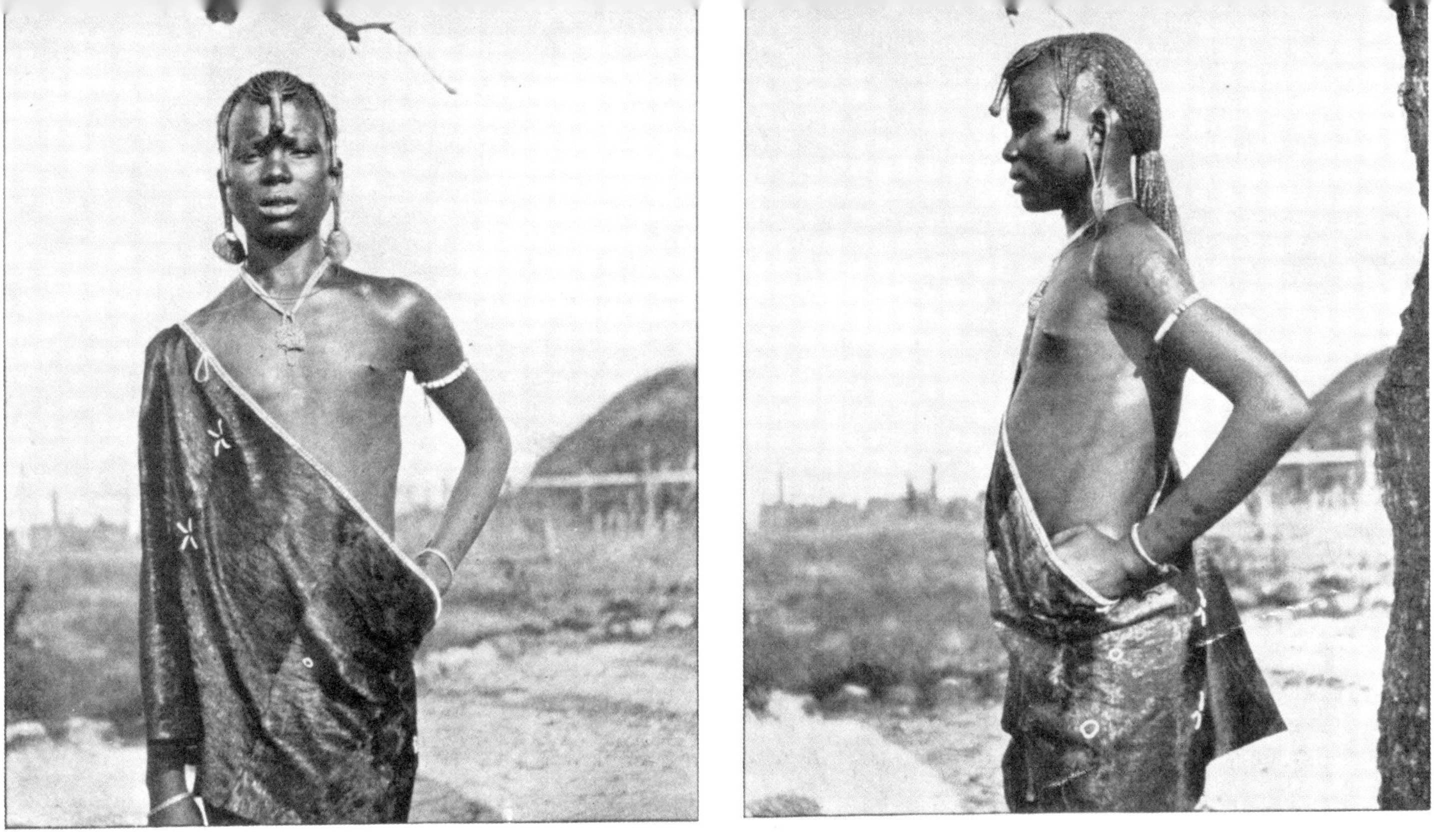

Nandi warrior, showing cicatrices raised on shoulder and scars burnt on wrist (Henderson).

WEARING APPAREL, WEAPONS, ETC. 31

Warriors frequently burn five or six scars on the front of the thighs and on the wrists, and raise a dozen cicatrices on their shoulders. Girls sometimes also make similar marks on their shoulders.

Weapons. The arms of the fighting men usually consist of a spear, shield, sword, and club.[1] There are four kinds of spears in use. The warriors of the western counties have small-bladed, long-shafted spears called *ndɨrit* (Fig. 19); those of the eastern, northern, and southern counties use a weapon which is similar to that of the Masai, *i.e.* long and narrow-bladed, with long iron butt, short socket and short shaft (Fig. 17); and those who live in the central county (the Em-gwen) have short and broad-bladed spears with short iron butts (Fig. 18). These spears are both known by the name of *ñgotit*. The old men use a spear called *ereñgatiat* (Fig. 20), which resembles the Masai spear of thirty or forty yearss ago. It has a short and small leaf-shaped blade with a long socketed shank and a long butt. The spears are used for stabbing, not for throwing.

In order to remind one another of war, warriors sometimes fix a knot of the feathers of the plantain-eater bird on the end of their spears.

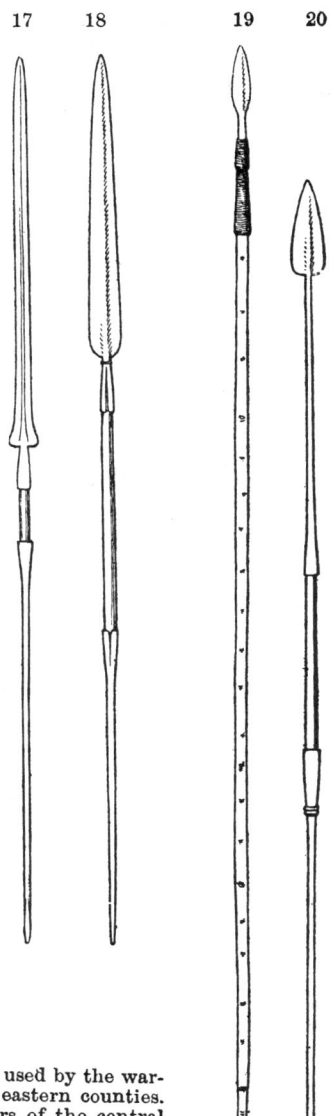

FIGS. 17-20 (scale $\frac{1}{16}$). (17) *Ñgotit*, spear used by the warriors of the northern, southern, and eastern counties. (18) *Ñgotit*, spear used by the warriors of the central county. (19) *Ndɨrit*, spear of the warriors of the western counties. (20) *Ereñgatiat*, old men's spear.

[1] No female may make pretence of using a spear or gird on a sword.

This knot is similar in appearance to the Masai peace-knot of ostrich feathers. When a man has thus decorated his spear, he may not associate with a woman.

The shields (*loñget*) are much like those of the Masai. They are made of the skin of the buffalo, eland, or giant pig, and are nearly

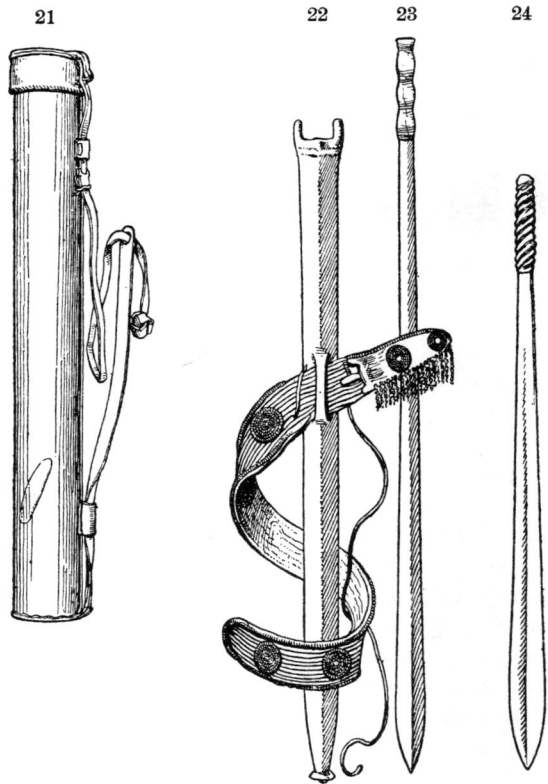

FIGS. 21-24 (scale ⅛). (21) Quiver. Note the patch of leather sewn on to mend a tear. (22) Scabbard. (23) Sword, present (Lumbwa) style. (24) Sword, old (Masai) style.

oval in shape. A narrow piece of wood is sewn tightly round the edge and a broader piece down the centre of the inside. This latter is detached from the shield in the middle and thus forms the handle. Nandi shields are painted, and each geographical division has its own design. The various *siritaiik* (parishes or geographical subdivisions) are also represented by different marks in the main design. The

PLATE XI

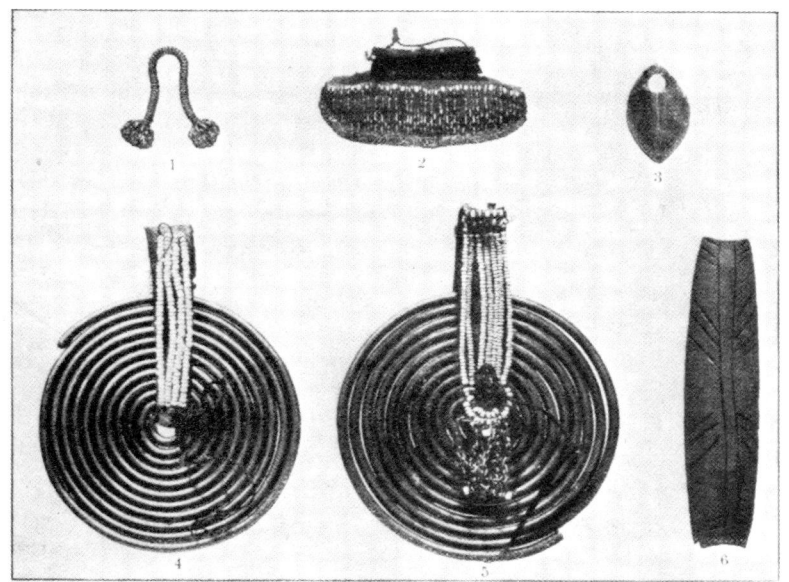

1. Kimeiteitiot. Old men's ear-ring.   2. Chepolungut. Warrior's ear-ring.
3. Engosholaiit. Ear-ring worn by men in the upper part of the ear.
4 and 5. Taōk. Married women's ear-rings.   6. Kipalpaliot. Boy's ear-ring.

1. Ostrich feather head-dress.
2. Olgitongit. Receptacle for keeping ostrich feathers in.

To face p. 32

WEARING APPAREL, WEAPONS, ETC. 33

colours used in painting these shields are white, red, black, and grey or blue.[1]

The swords (*rotuet* or *rotuet-ap-chōk*) are of a peculiar shape, being long, slender, and ill-balanced. They are narrow towards the hilt and broader towards the tip. The swords of the present day are longer than they were formerly, and the fashion seems rather to follow the Lumbwa or Kipsikīs, whose sword blades measure as much as $2\frac{1}{2}$ feet in length. The sheath or scabbard (*chōket*) is attached to a leather belt (*pireyuot*), which is ornamented with cowries and is worn round the abdomen.

The club or knobkerry (*rungut*), which is used for throwing at an advancing or retreating foe, or for giving a fallen enemy the *coup de grâce*, is twisted into the leather fastening (*torokeyuot*) of the sword belt. Old men use a club with a long handle, called *sharit*.

Some warriors, like the old men and boys, carry a bow (*kwanget*) and arrows (*kôtet*). The quiver of arrows (*mootiet*) contains between twenty and thirty, some of which are usually poisoned. Fire sticks (*piōnik*), a needle (*katet*), and spare arrow heads and barbs are also carried in the quiver.

No war party is complete without a greater kudu horn (*ikondit*), which is used as a trumpet, and when sounded can be heard at a great distance.

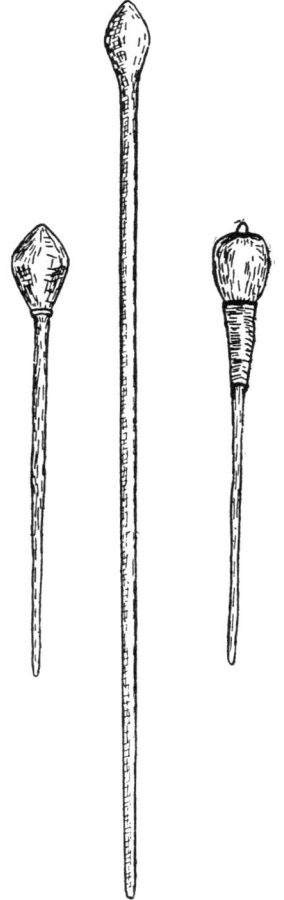

Figs. 25–27 (scale ⅛). (25) Warrior's club. (26) Old man's club. (27) Club with rhinoceros-horn head, used by a man who is unclean.

---

[1] White is obtained by mixing water with white clay; red clay mixed with the juice of a *solanum* and blood produces the red paint; black is procured from charred potsherds and gourds; and grey or blue from cinders mixed with white clay.

NANDI   D

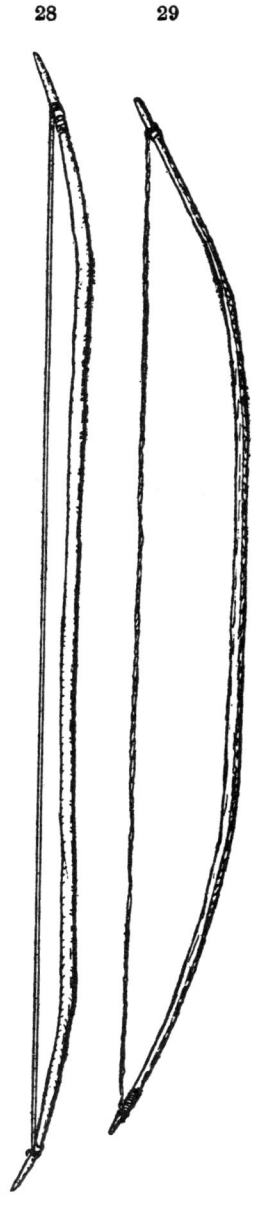
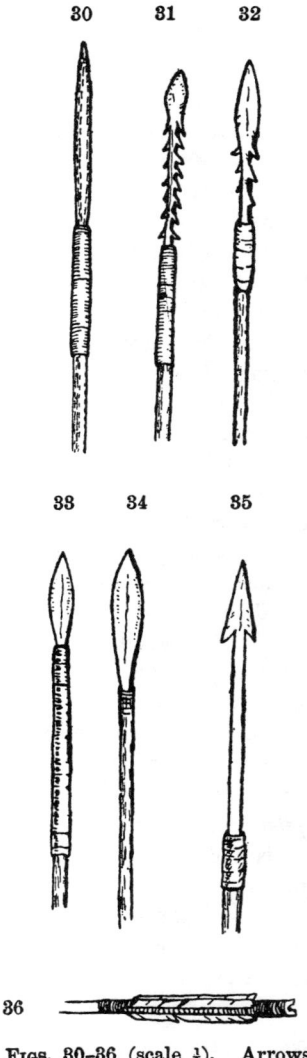

Figs. 28–29 (scale ⅛). (28) Old man's bow. (29) Boy's bow.

Figs. 30–36 (scale ¼). Arrows:
(30) *Supetiet* (wooden head).
(31 and 32) *Tukwariot* (iron head).
(33) *Chepiloñgiot* (iron head).
(34) *Kipchapet* (iron head).
(35) *Kipitinyot* (iron head).
(36) Shaft.

PLATE XII

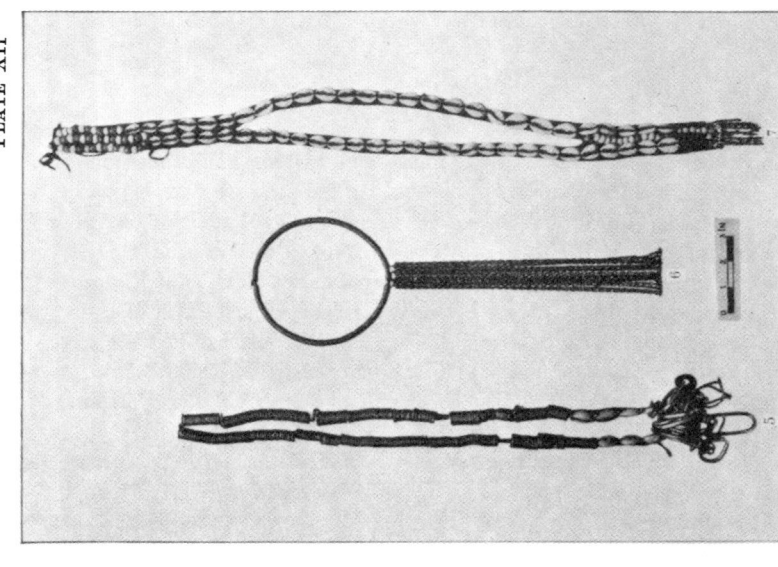
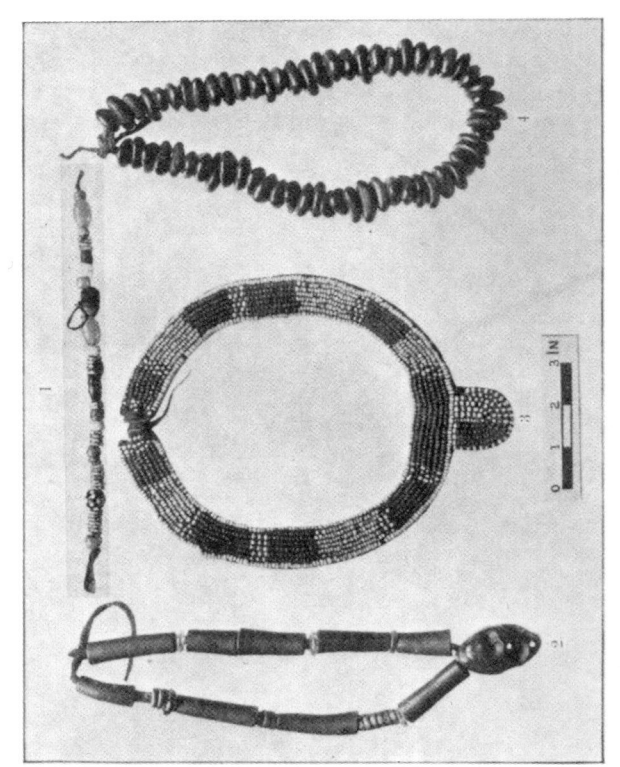

NECKLACES.

1. Kelelik. Worn when the arm is painful. 2. Sepetaiik. Worn by girls and boys of the Talai clan and by children who have lost their next elder brother or sister. 3. Muit'-ap-sonai. Women's necklace. 4. Lapuonik. Worn by children and calves to protect them from the evil eye.

INDUSTRIES.

Earthenware. The Nandi use a number of cooking and other pots which are the handiwork of certain women of the tribe who are known as *chepterēnik.* The work is performed in or near the huts erected for this purpose and called *karik-ap-terēnik.* From the outside these huts closely resemble the ordinary dwelling houses, but inside there is no partition dividing off the goats' compartment from the rest of the house, nor are there any beds or pegs or a loft, for neither goats nor people may sleep in them, nor may grain or utensils be kept in them. No man may go near the *karik-ap-terēnik* or watch the women at work.

A place in which pottery is made is called *Kâmenon*; the two best known spots where the potters' clay (*menet*) is found are Kâpkepen and Kâpimen.

The only implements employed by the potters in making their wares are the handle of a hoe, which is used for pounding and stirring the clay, and the shoulder-blade of an ox, a stone, a seed pod called *cheptaipesiet,* some plaited *taparariet* grass, and three pieces of straw called *saatyet,* with which the pots are smoothed and ornamented. The pottery is unglazed, but is ornamented by patterns, each *cheptereniot* having her own designs. A favourite pattern is the handles, or, as they are called, ears, of the meat cooking-pot.

After the pots have been baked, the potters recite the following prayer :—

Asis! kōn-ech koweit.
God! give-us strength.

Inge-kwañg-e ko-cham piich.
Let-us-cook-in-them that-they-may-like-them men.

In the following list the principal earthen pots, jars, and cups are given :—

Kipanyinyit, cooking-pot for vegetables only.
Kipungut, cooking-pot for vegetables and meat.
Kimwanit, cooking-pot for fat.
Kipiitinit, cooking-pot for meat.
Kipkarotit, cooking-pot for blood.
Loet, pot used for roasting malt.
Kipteregit, pot used for boiling malt (large size).
Riseyuot, pot used for boiling malt (small size).
Tapokut, pot used for standing beer in.

Teret-ap-kimoi, pot used for cooking porridge in.
Teret-ap-pei, water-jar.
Saiget, men's drinking cup.[1]
Tapet, cup used when eating porridge.

Nobody may step over a pot, and were anybody to do this it is believed that he would fall to pieces when the pot is broken. A thief dare not steal from a potter, as he would be cursed the next time she heated her wares. *Ipet-aki ko-uu ter, pirit-it-u-n ko* (Burst like a pot, and may thy house become red), she would say, and the thief would die. If a cooking-pot is broken when food is being prepared in it, no Nandi man may eat the food, but Nandi women may eat food cooked or served up in a broken pot. Warriors may not eat food that has been cooked in new pots; and warriors who have killed an enemy may not stand or sit near the cooking utensils.

Gourds. Gourds or calabashes are obtained from pumpkins, which are planted for this purpose. They are used as cups and jugs for milk and blood, and are of various sizes. Small gourds also at times take the place of the ox-horn or wooden snuff-boxes, this custom having been introduced by the Kamasia.

Each owner of a gourd has his own private mark, which is burnt on the gourd. Warriors' gourds are ornamented with cowries.

No warrior may drink from a new gourd.

The smelting and forging of iron. There live with the Nandi a number of Uasin Gishu Masai who have become smiths (*kitoñgik*). These people speak both Nandi and Masai. The following account is given by the smiths of the arrival of their ancestors in Nandi. After they had lost all their cattle from various causes, the Uasin Gishu Masai quitted their homes and split up in different directions. Some of those who wandered into Nandi were hospitably received by an old man named Ar-ap-Sutek, who was the only smith in the country at the time. Ar-ap-Sutek taught his protégés his trade, and when he died the secret passed into their hands. In those days the Nandi spear-heads were very small, they had no hoes, but used wooden digging sticks; and they bought their axes and other implements from neighbouring tribes. Each clan now has its own smiths, who are for all practical purposes members of the clan, and are treated by the Nandi almost as equals. Very few of the Nandi clans will, however, openly intermarry with the smiths or allow their cattle to

[1] Women's drinking cups, called *mwendet*, are made from gourds.

PLATE XIII

NANDI POTS AND JARS.
1. Kipungut. Cooking-pot for vegetables and meat.   2. Saiget. Men's drinking cup.
3. Kipiitinit, with four handles. Cooking-pot for meat.
4. Teret-ap-pei. Water-jar.   5. Kipiitinit, with three handles. Cooking-pot for meat.

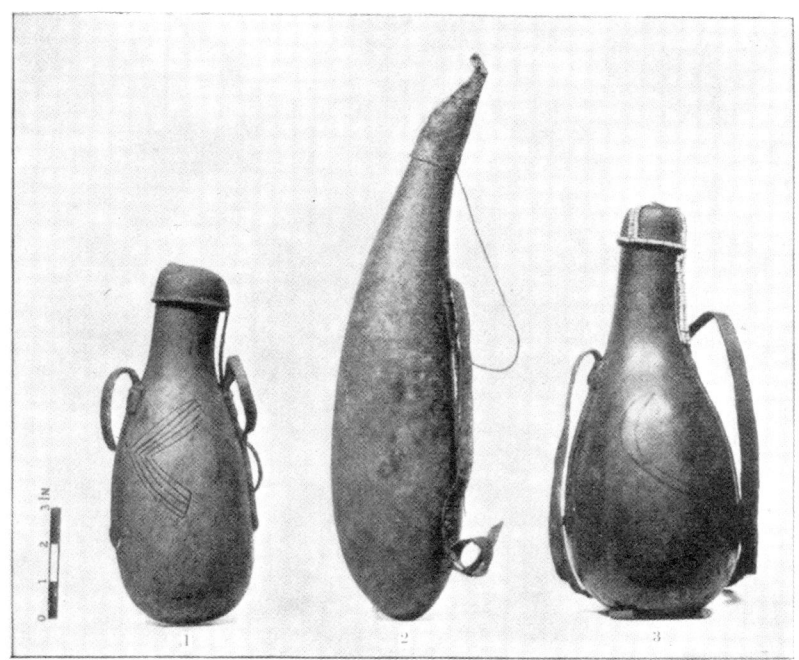

1. Women's milk gourd.   2. Calves' feeding bottle.   3. Warriors' milk gourd.

To face p. 36

INDUSTRIES

herd or breed with the cattle belonging to the smiths; and whenever a Nandi picks up anything new which a smith has made, he first spits into his hand.

The smiths work in small open huts or smithies called *kâp-kitanyit*. They smelt iron by means of a clay furnace, which they heat with charcoal and work with bellows (*kopanda*). The bellows are made of wood and covered at the top with a goat's skin, in the middle of which is a hole known as the mouth (*kutit*). The end of the tube of the bellows is called *rupeitit*, and the small clay pipe in the fire, through which the air is blown, *soiyot*. The *rupeitit* is said to be the male, the *soiyot* the female. Nobody may step over the tube or over the bellows. The pig iron is beaten out on a stone anvil (*topet*) by means of an iron hammer (*kirisuet*).[1] The only other implements used are a knife or cutting iron (*laita*) and pincers or tongs (*konameito*). Spears, swords, arrow-heads, tools, and ornaments are made.

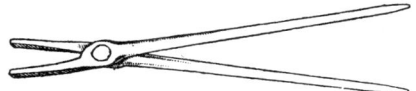 

FIG. 37 (scale ⅛). Smith's pincers or tongs.   FIG. 38 (scale ¼). Cutting iron.

No woman may enter a smithy or watch the smiths at work; and nobody dares to steal anything from a smith, as the owner of the stolen article will heat his furnace, and, while blowing the bellows, will curse the thief, who will surely die.

A number of smiths live at a place called Kâptilol in Em-gwen, as plenty of iron ore is found near there. A place in which iron ore occurs is known as *Ñgoriamuk*. When the smiths search for the ore they recite the following prayer:—

Asis ! kōn-ech sapon,
God ! give-us health,

Asis ! kōn-ech karik.
God ! give-us iron. }
wealth. }

The task of digging for the ore is performed by the men, whilst their women-folk carry it to the smithies. Nowadays, owing to there

---

[1] No Nandi smith will part with his hammer, though he will readily sell his other implements, and even his forge, if a good price is offered.

being so much trade iron in the country, it is scarcely worth the smiths' while to dig for the ore.

Miscellaneous Industries. Besides the industries already mentioned, a number of utensils and articles of furniture, &c., are made by the Nandi. Among these are the *kenut* or mortar for grinding corn, and the *mosit* or pestle. The former is said to be the female and the latter

FIGS. 39 and 40 (scale $\frac{1}{12}$). Pestle and Mortar.

the male. The mortar is beaten by the pestle when a child or a chicken is very ill, and when a woman suffers much at birth. Nobody may sit on or step over either the pestle or the mortar. When a maker

FIG. 41 (scale $\frac{1}{4}$). Nandi stool.

sells a mortar he spits in it, and says: *Ui poiisie* (Go and work for him).

A honey barrel, *moinget*, is made in two halves, the upper part being called the male, and the lower the female. When a man is about to hang a honey barrel in a tree for the first time, he makes marks on it with his knife, taps the tree, and says: *Iro ni kot ne-lalañg,*

PLATE XIV

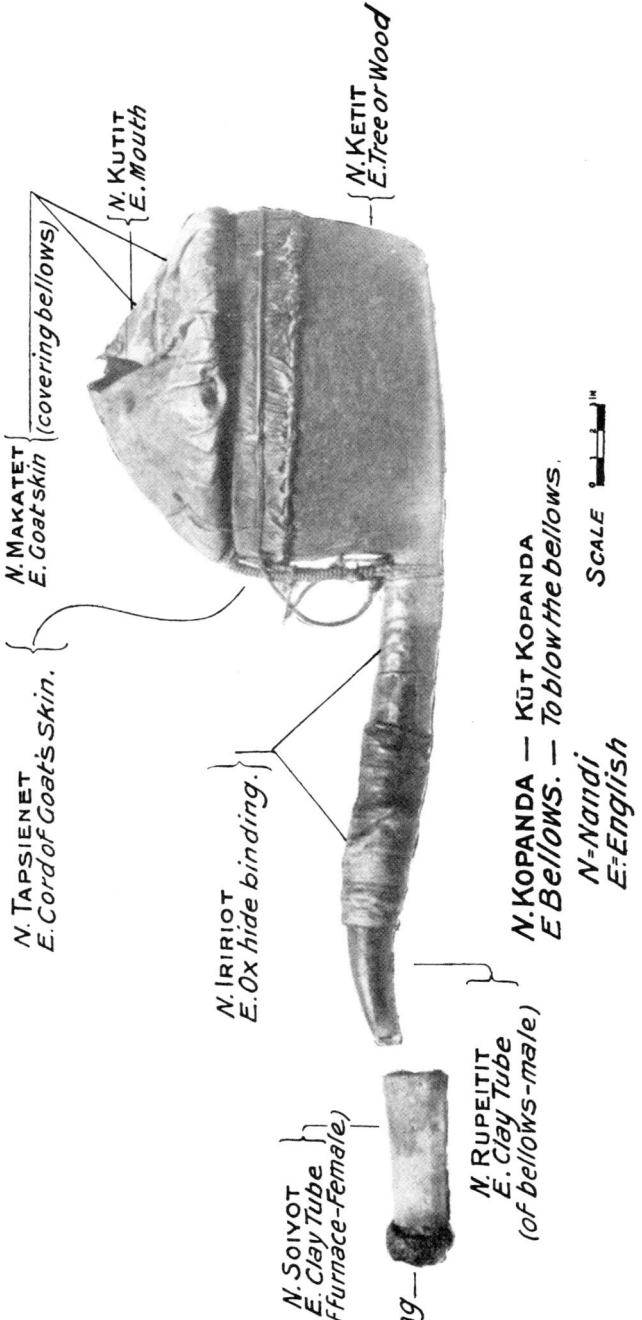

Nandi bellows.

INDUSTRIES 39

chololion che-mi-i Keyu (Look, here is a warm house, pour your honey in here, all ye who are in Elgeyo).

Stools, baskets, doors, clubs, the handles of weapons and implements, &c., are all made by men. There is, however, nothing of

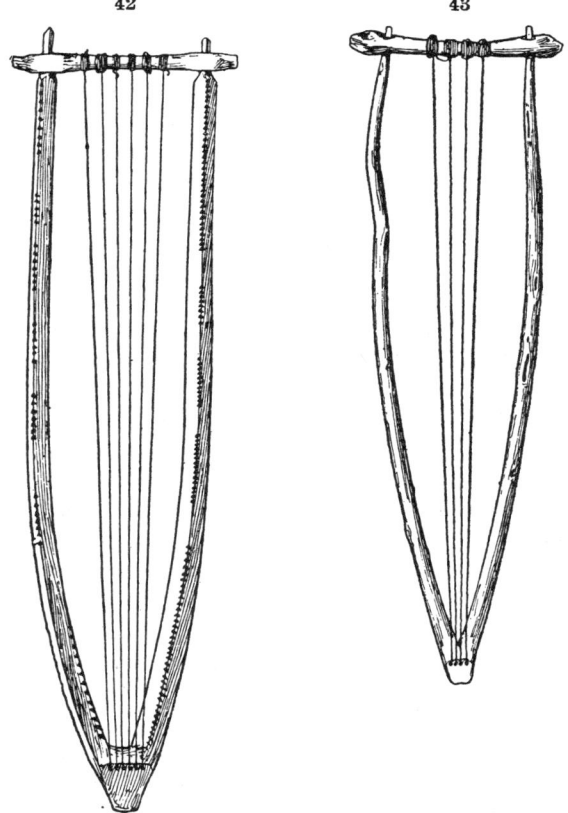

FIGS. 42-43 (scale ⅛). (42) Nandi lyre. When played upon, only five strings are used, the sixth one being unfastened and kept in case one of the others breaks. (43) Lumbwa lyre. Only four strings are used. In both the Nandi and Lumbwa lyres a small piece of wood is sometimes placed under the strings as a supporter, like the bridge of a violin.

interest to be recorded regarding them, and no superstitious customs are observed in connexion with them.

Musical Instruments. The art of music has not reached a very advanced stage in Nandi. With the exception of a five-stringed lyre (*kipokandet*) and a pipe (*indurerut*), they have no musical instruments, though boys use a wooden horn called *serengwet*, and antelope horns are sometimes blown by warriors when taking their cattle to the salt-licks, and by raiding parties. The war-horn which is echoed from parish to parish throughout the land in the event of an attack is a greater Kudu horn.

No ordinary drum is used, though there is a name for the drum of other tribes (*sukutit*). At some feasts old shields are beaten by sticks as a substitute for drums, and at the *rīkset* ceremony, after boys and girls have been circumcised,[1] a friction drum is employed. For boys a *ketet* is used. This is a small wooden barrel, in which the old men keep their fur garments when not wearing them, and a drum is made by covering one end with a goat's skin. For girls a water-jar is treated in a like manner. A deep noise, said to resemble a lion's roar, or a leopard's growl, is produced by drawing both hands, which have been previously wetted, along a stick resting against the centre of the drum head. The boys' friction drum is called *ñgetundo* or lion, the girls', *cheplanget* or leopard. The stick is known as the male and the drum as the female. It is regarded as an unlucky omen if the stick perforates the goat-skin.

There is also a bull-roarer, which is likewise called *ñgetundo* or lion. This is employed by the warriors to frighten boys who have been recently circumcised into staying in their huts after dark.[2] It is made of a small flat piece of wood[3] cut into an oval shape, and it is whirled round the head at the end of a strip of goat's hide. A booming sound is produced, which reminds one of a lion purring and grunting.

No uncircumcised person and no woman may see the bull-roarer or the boys' friction drum, and no uncircumcised person or man may see the girls' friction drum.

At some dances women accompany the dancers by scraping their bracelets one against the other. The sound produced is by no means an unpleasant or unmusical one.

RELIGIOUS BELIEFS.

The religious beliefs of the Nandi are somewhat vague and unformulated. The supreme deity is *Asista*, the sun, who dwells in the

---

[1] *Vide* pp. 57 and 60.   [2] *Vide* p. 56.
[3] The *tumoiyot* tree is used for this purpose.

PLATE XV

Kerepet. Basket.

Barrel used by old men for putting
their garments in.

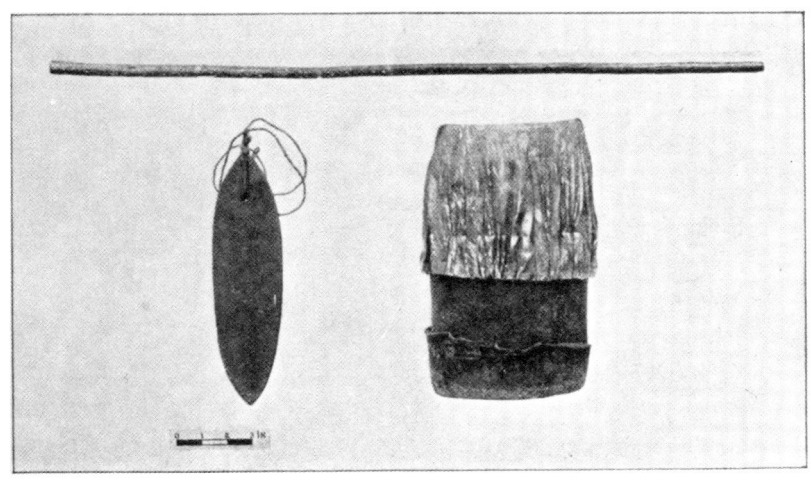

Boys' bull-roarer and friction drum.

sky: he created man and beast, and the world belongs to him; prayers are addressed to him; he is acknowledged to be a benefactor and the giver of all good things; and offerings are at times made to him in return.

Besides Asista, there are two other superhuman beings, the kindly and malevolent thunder-gods called respectively *Īlet ne-mie* and *Īlet ne-ya*. The tradition regarding these two gods and their battles [1] is very similar to the Masai tradition of the Black and Red gods.[2] The thunder-gods are not worshipped, nor are offerings made to them.

The *Oiik*, i.e. the spirits of departed ancestors and adult relations, are held to be responsible for sickness and death, and they are appealed to and propitiated with milk, beer, and food whenever necessary. The human soul is embodied in a person's shadow, and it is firmly believed that after death the shadows of both good and bad people go underground and live there. People who have great possessions on earth are equally blessed when they die, whilst the spirits of poor people have as bad a time after death as they had during life. Years ago a man is said to have gone to the land in which the spirits live. He fell into a river one day and lost consciousness (or died). When he came to himself again he was in a strange country, where there were hills, rivers, plantations, and oxen, just as on earth. The spirits came to him and said: 'Young man, your time has not yet come when you should join us. Go back to the earth.' With that they struck the ground and the man lost consciousness again to wake up near the place where he had fallen into the river.

There is also a devil called *Chemosit*, who is supposed to live on the earth and to prowl round searching to devour people, especially children. He is said to be half man, half bird, to have only one leg but nine buttocks, and his mouth, which is red, is supposed to shine at night like a lamp. He propels himself by means of a stick which resembles a spear and which he uses as a crutch. His method of catching children is to sing a song at night-time near where they are living, and the children seeing the light and hearing the music think that a dance is being held, and are lured on to their destruction.

The prayers of the Nandi, like their religious beliefs, are somewhat vague. The commonest form of prayer, which is supposed to be recited by all adult Nandi twice a day, but which is more particularly used by old men when they rise in the morning, especially if they have had a bad dream, is addressed to both Asista and to the spirits

[1] *Vide* p. 99. [2] *Vide The Masai*, p. 264.

of deceased ancestors. The attitude assumed when saying this prayer is a sitting one, with the arms crossed so that the elbows rest in the palms of the hands. It is as follows :—

Asis,	ka-a-sa-in	tuk-u-a	lakōk	ak
God,	have-I-besought-thee	cover-for-me } guard	the-children	and

tuka.
the cattle.

	Ka-a-mus-in	korirun	ak	lakat.
	Have-I-approached-thee	morning	and	evening.
Asis,	ka-a-som-in	i-ru-e	ak	i-wend-i.
God,	have-I-prayed-thee	thou-sleepest	and	thou-goest.
Asis,	ka-a-som-in	a-mati-ile :		'Ka-a-ñget.'
God,	have-I-prayed-thee	and-do-not-say :		'Have-I-become-tired.'

Oiſk-chok,	amu	ki-o-pek-u,	a-mo-o-'len :	
The-spirits-our,	for	you-died,	and-do-not-(ye)-say :	
'Ki-par-ok	chii ',	o-tuk-w-ech	che-mi-i	parak.[1]
'He-killed-us	man ',	(ye)-cover-for-us } guard	who-are-there	above.

War. When warriors have gone to the wars, the men's mothers tie four knots in their belts, and every morning go outside their huts at about seven o'clock, and, after spitting towards the sun, cry out aloud :—

Asis ! kōn-ech sapon.
God ! give-us health.

The fathers meet together regularly, and before drinking their beer one old man rises and says : *Pwo-ne, o-'le, pwo-ne* (They will return, say, they will return). The rest reply, *Pwo-ne* (They will return). The old man who is standing then says : *Cham-i-ke, o-'le, cham-i-ke*

---
[1] Free translation :—
O God, do Thou Thine ear incline,
Protect my children and my kine,
E'en if Thou 'rt weary, still forbear
And hearken to my constant prayer.
When shrouded 'neath the cloak of night,
Thy splendours sleep beyond our sight,
And when across the sky by day,
Thou movest, still to Thee I pray.
Dread shades of our departed sires,
Ye who can make or mar desires,
Slain by no mortal hand ye dwell,
Beneath the earth, O guard us well.

PLATE XVI

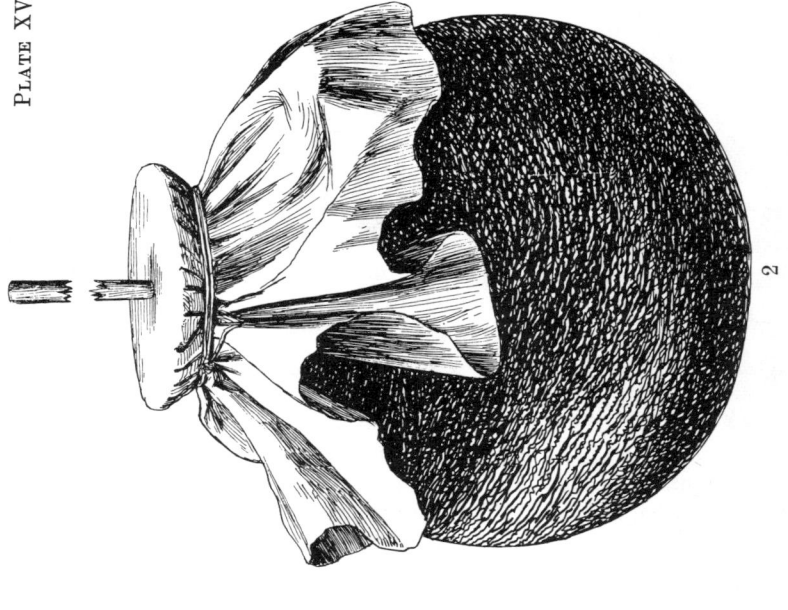

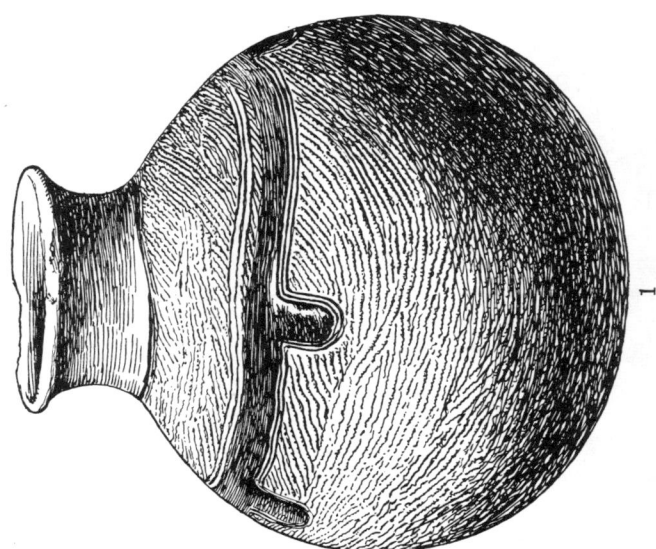

RELIGIOUS BELIEFS

(They are well, say, they are well), and the others say, *Cham-i-ke* (They are well). After this they all sing:—

<table>
<tr><td>Asis!</td><td>uk-w-ech</td><td>lakōk.</td></tr>
<tr><td>God!</td><td>tie-knots-for-us</td><td>the-children.[1]</td></tr>
<tr><td colspan="2">Ki-toroch-i,</td><td>ki-toroch-i.</td></tr>
<tr><td colspan="2">That-we-may-greet-them,</td><td>that-we-may-greet-them.</td></tr>
</table>

When each man has taken his calabash of beer in his hand, he sprinkles some on the ground and on the walls of the hut, and says:—

<table>
<tr><td>Oiík-chok!</td><td>ka-ki-sa-ak.</td></tr>
<tr><td>The-spirits-our!</td><td>have-we-prayed-to-you.</td></tr>
<tr><td>Iro-cho</td><td>maiyo.</td></tr>
<tr><td>Regard-this</td><td>beer.</td></tr>
<tr><td>O-kōn-ech</td><td>sapon.</td></tr>
<tr><td>(Ye)-give-us</td><td>health.</td></tr>
</table>

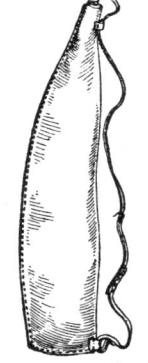

FIG. 44 (scale ⅛). *Superet.* Bag in which warriors carry eleusine flour when proceeding on a raid.

Whilst their sons are absent, the old men frequently pay visits to the chief medicine man, to learn how the expedition is faring. The chief medicine man consults his oracle and gives guarded replies.

During the expedition nobody at home may mention the warriors by name: they must be referred to as birds. Should the children forget themselves and mention the name of one of the absentees, they are rebuked by their mothers, who say: *Mo-o-mwa-i tarīt che-mi-i parak* (Don't talk of the birds who are in the heavens). The warriors themselves, during an expedition, may not sneeze, eat meat alone, or relieve nature on the right side of the road, and, instead of making use of the word *chepkeswet* (knife), they must say *loñgnet* (arrow for bleeding cattle). No man may mention the ordinary greeting for males, but must say, *Takwenya, lukôn-ni* (Takwenya, O war party). The reply is, *Igo*. Every morning when away from home, an elder, who accompanies the party, must spit at the rising sun, and say:

<table>
<tr><td>Asis!</td><td>inak-e-ech</td><td>cheko.</td></tr>
<tr><td>God!</td><td>give-us-to-drink</td><td>milk.</td></tr>
</table>

As soon as cattle are captured during an expedition, the *maotiot*, or chief medicine man's representative, cries out the name of the chief medicine man, *e.g.*, *Kipeles*, and adds, *Ip tuka* (Take the cattle).

---

[1] Guard our children.   [2] *Vide* p. 90.

If this is not done, it is thought that the cattle will vanish from sight.

On the return of a war-party, a thank-offering is made if the expedition has been a success. A *kambakta*, or war-dance, is held, at which the warriors wear their full war dress, and sing and dance. Curiously enough, the song which they sing, and which is repeated over and over again, is in Masai. It is as follows :—

    A-ōmon   eng-Aï   ai,   n-a-ōmon   M-Batyany.
    I-pray   the-God   my,   and-I-pray   Mbatian.[1]
    W̌o-hoo,   W̌o-hoo,   W̌o-hoo.
    Wo-hoo,   Wo-hoo,   Wo-hoo.

The cattle are afterwards distributed, the chief medicine man, the lesser medicine men, and the rain-makers, each receiving a share, as well as the relations of warriors who fell during the fight. When the cattle have been distributed, they are taken by each man to their future homes. The first night they are not allowed inside the cattle kraal, but are tethered outside. On the following day the elders make a bonfire near the entrance to the kraal, and milk and beer are poured on the ground to the accompaniment of the following song, which is taken up and repeated again and again by all present :—

    Koiyo ee !   Koiyo ee !   Koiyo ee !
    The-raided-cattle, oh! The-raided-cattle, oh! The-raided-cattle, oh!
    Asis   ka-kōn-ech   sapon !
    God   he-has-given-us   health !

The cattle are then driven into the cattle-kraal, and are thus welcomed by the owner :—

    Túk'-chōk !   ine-ni   kot   ne-lalañg.
    The-cattle-my !   it-this   the-house   which-is-warm.
    A-ma-to-le :   ' Ki   ñgeriñg.'
    And-do-not-ye-say : ' We-are   few.'
    O-pwa   mitio   ak   o-tep   ko-mie.
    Ye-come   slowly   and   ye-stay   quietly.

If the expedition has not been successful and a number of warriors have been killed, the survivors must all go to a river on their return to their homes and bathe. They then hold a *kambakta* or warriors'

---

[1] Mbatian was a great Masai medicine man, the father of the present Chief of the Masai, Ol-Ōnana, or as he is commonly called, Lenana.

PLATE XVII

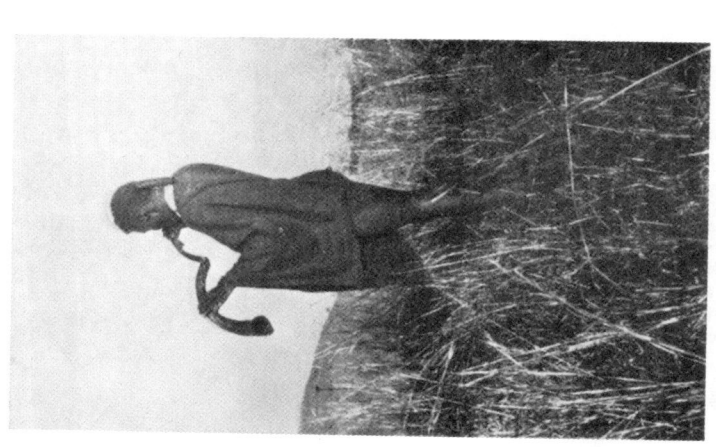

Nandi warrior blowing a war-horn (Meinertzhagen).

Kambakta. Nandi warriors' dance (Meinertzhagen).

RELIGIOUS BELIEFS

dance, at which they wear their full war dress. This dance is called *ki-pir-i pei* (the waters are beaten). After the dance, at which the women wail and cry at intervals, an old man stands amongst the seated warriors, and says:—

Asis!	ka-ki-'le,	'Oiyo'.[1]
God!	have-we-said,	'Oiyo'.
	Ka-ki-sa-in,	'Emuro'.[2]
	Have-we-prayed-thee,	'Emuro'.

Cattle. When cattle have been raided by an enemy or killed by lightning, the *iset-ap-tuka* (sprinkling of cattle) ceremony takes place. A procession is formed and the cattle are driven to the nearest river, where the warriors are drawn up in two lines along the banks, whilst the unmarried girls, who are stripped, stand in front of them in the water. The herd is driven between the girls, and each cow is sprinkled with water as it passes. After this the girls drive the cattle home whilst the men sit down near the river. One old man then rises and recites the following lines, all present repeating them after him:—

Asis!	tuk-w-ech	chu-to,
God!	cover-for-us[3]	these-here,
	Ka-ki-sa-in,	
	Have-we-prayed-thee,	
	Iuit-w-ech	chu-to.
	Guard-for-us	these-here.

When disease breaks out in a herd, a large bonfire is made of *emdit*[4] wood, on the top of which is thrown some brushwood of the *lapotuet*[5] and *kemeliet* shrubs. As soon as there is a good blaze, the sick herd is driven to the fire, where the animals remain standing whilst a pregnant sheep is brought to them. The sheep is anointed with milk by an elder, who says at the same time:—

| Asis! | kōn-ech | moiet | ne-mie, |
| God! | give-us | the-belly | which-is-good, |

after which all present sit down and wait till it passes water. When it has done this, two men belonging to clans that may intermarry seize it and strangle it. The intestines are inspected, and if it is

---

[1] Said when a man stumbles. It is here equivalent to *We admit ourselves beaten.*
[2] Said when a man wants peace, like a schoolboy crying *Pax.*
[3] Guard for us.   [4] *Olea chrysophilla.*   [5] *Solanum campylanthum.*

found that the occasion is propitious, the meat is roasted and eaten, whilst rings are made of the skin and worn by the cattle-owners. If the result of the inspection of the entrails is unsatisfactory, another pregnant sheep has to be slaughtered. After the meat has been eaten, the herd is driven round the fire, and milk is poured on each beast. Before the gathering separates, the following prayer is recited by all present:—

    Asis!   ka-ki-sa-in,
    God!   have-we-prayed-thee,

    Tuk-w-ech   chu-to.
    Cover-for-us [1] these-here.

If cattle are poisoned at a salt-lick, a similar ceremony is performed, but the prayer is slightly different. The elders say:—

    Asis!   ianyiny-w-ech   ñgenda.
    God!   make-good-for-us the-salt-lick.

    'Ngw-am   tany tukul,   ko-cham.
    If-it-eats-(it) ox   any,   may-it-like-(it).

Harvest. During the months of September and October, *i. e.* during the ripening of the eleusine grain, and after the grain has been harvested, the *kipsunde* and *kipsunde oieñg* ceremonies are held. At the former, each owner of a plantation goes with her daughters into the cornfields and makes a bonfire of the branches and leaves of the *lapotuet* [2] and *pêk-ap-tarīt* [3] trees. Some eleusine is then plucked, and whilst one grain is fixed in the necklaces, another one is chewed and rubbed by each woman and girl on her forehead, throat and breast. No joy is shown by the womenfolk on this occasion, and they sorrowfully cut a basketful of the corn which they take home with them and place in the loft to dry. As the ceiling is of wickerwork, a good deal of the grain drops through the cracks, and no attempt is made to prevent it from falling into the fire, as it is supposed when it explodes that the spirits of the deceased are accepting it. A few days later, porridge made from the new grain is served with milk at the evening meal, and all the members of the family take some of the food and dab it on the walls and roofs of the huts. They also put a little in their mouths and spit it out towards the east and on the outside of the huts. The head of the family then holds some of the eleusine grain in his hand, and offers up the following prayer, everybody present repeating the words after him:—

[1] Guard for us.   [2] *Solanum campylanthum.*   [3] *Lantana salvifolia.*

PLATE XVIII

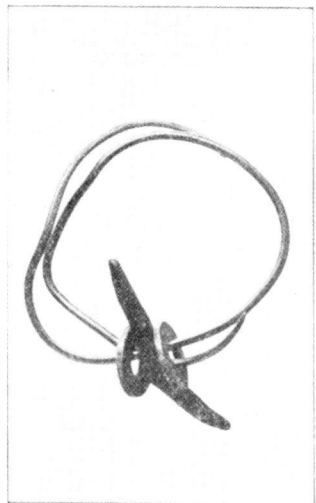

Lokosta. Bracelet used by archers for protecting the wrist.

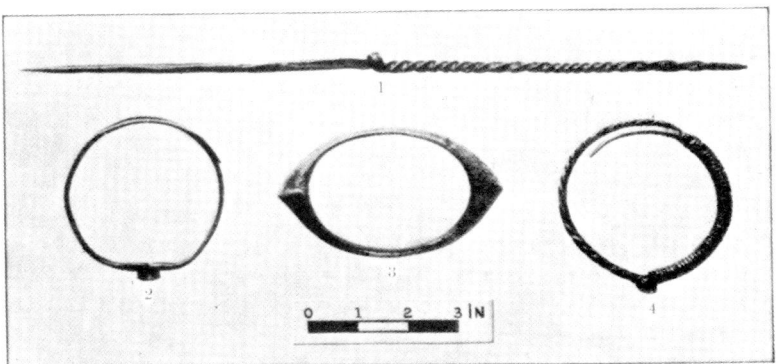

ARMLETS.
1. Samoiyot. Worn by twins (unbent).
2. Asielda. Worn by men who have lost their next elder brother or sister.
3. Old men's ivory arm-ring.   4. Asingaiit.   Worn by old men.

RELIGIOUS BELIEFS 47

Asis! kōn-ech sapon,
God! give-us health,
A-ki-kōn-ech uio,
And-that-it-may-be-given-to-us strength,
A-ki-kōn-ech che.
And-that-it-may-be-given-to-us milk.
'Ngw-am chii tukul, ko-cham.
If-he-eats-(it) man any, may-he-like-(it).
'Ngw-am tomono, ko-cham.
If-she-eats-(it) pregnant-woman, may-she-like-(it).

After the harvest has been gathered in, permission is obtained from the chief medicine man to hold the *kipsunde oieñg* or *kipsunde nepalet* feast. Each *pororiet* or geographical division holds its own feast on the top of a hill or in a large open plain, and all the warriors collect together and take part in a *kambakta*, or war-dance. A large bonfire is made of *emdit*[1] and *tekat*[2] wood, on the top of which *lapotuet*[3] and *kemeliet* shrubs are thrown, and when there is a big blaze *simotuet*[4] wood is cast on the fire. An erection like a door of a cattle-kraal is built near the fire, and as the warriors file past, the old men, who stand by the door-posts, take a little milk and beer in their mouths and spit it on them. The old men then sing as follows:—

Asis! kōn-ech sapon.
God! give-us health.
Asis! kōn-ech koiyo.
God! give-us raided-cattle.
Asis! kōn-ech iiot
God! give-us the-offspring
Nepo piich ak tich.
Of men and cattle.

Before the gathering separates, the old men kill and eat a pregnant goat, and the women, who have oiled their bodies, proceed to the nearest river and take from the water two pebbles, one of which they put in their water-jars, keeping it there till the next *kipsunde oieñg* season, and the other they place in their granaries.

After the *kipsunde oieñg* festival it is customary to hold the girls' circumcision ceremonies, and the warriors were wont formerly to start

---

[1] *Olea chrysophilla.*
[2] *Arundinaria alpina.*
[3] *Solanum campylanthum.*
[4] *Ficus sp.* near *F. elegans.*

their raiding expeditions at this season. It is noticeable that all the Nandi punitive expeditions have commenced in October.

Drought. When there is a drought, it is customary for people to look towards the Tindiret or Chepusio Hill every morning, and say, *Robon, Tindiret* (Rain, Tindiret). If the drought is protracted and a famine is threatened, the old men collect together and take a black sheep with them to a river. Having tied a fur cloak on to the sheep's back, they push it into the water, and take beer and milk into their mouths which they spit out in the direction of the rising sun. When the sheep scrambles out of the water and shakes itself, they sing the following prayer :—

Asis!	ka-ki-sa-in,				
God!	have-we-prayed-to-thee,				
Kōn-ech	rob.				
Give-us	rain.				
Iro-cho	maiyo	ak	che.		
Look-at-these	beer	and	milk.		
Ma-mi-i	chii	ne-ma-ii-o.			
It-is-not-there	man	who-does-not-bear.[1]			
Tuk-w-ech	tomono	nepo	chii	ak	tany.
Cover-for-us[2]	pregnant-woman	of	man	and	ox.

Other occasions on which prayers are offered are given on pages 15, 30, 35, 37 and 65.

GOVERNMENT.

For the purposes of government the Nandi country is divided into fifteen districts (*pororiet*), and subdivided into parishes (*siritiet*).[3] The whole country acknowledges the over-lordship of the *Orkoiyot*, or chief medicine man ;[4] but each district is governed by two men, one called *Maotiot*, who is elected by and represents the *Orkoiyot*, and the other, called *Kiruogindet*,[5] the spokesman or counsellor, who is chosen by the people. The real rulers are the *Kiruogik*, who are responsible to the *Orkoiyot* (through their *Maotik*) for the good

---

[1] We are suffering like women labouring with child.   [2] Guard for us.
[3] *Vide* p 4.   [4] Equivalent to the Masai *Ol-oiboni.*
[5] Equivalent to the Masai *Ol-aigwenani.*

GOVERNMENT

government of their respective districts, and for the enrolment of troops in time of war. Each parish is under a captain called *Olaitoriot*, who is responsible to his *Kiruogindet*. A parish generally contains from twenty to fifty warriors.

The old men of each district meet together from time to time to discuss the affairs of state, the *Maotiot* and *Kiruogindet* being present. The assemblies are held in the shade of a *teldet*[1] tree, and the places of assembly are called *kâp-kiruogutik*.

The Medicine Men. The *Orkoiyot*, or principal medicine man holds precisely the same position as the Masai *Ol-oiboni*, that is to say, he is supreme chief of the whole race. He is a diviner, and foretells the future by such methods as casting stones, inspecting entrails, interpreting dreams, and prophesying under the influence of intoxicants. He is also skilled in the interpretation of omens and in the averting of ill-luck. When foretelling the future by casting stones (*parparek*), he uses a box called *ketet*, or a piece of bamboo stalk called *soiyet*, and he throws the stones on to a fur *kaross*; when making amulets or medicine (*pusaruk* or *kerichek*), he uses an ox-horn and pours the ingredients into the person's hands.

The Nandi believe implicitly in the powers of their *Orkoiyot*. They look to him for instruction when to commence planting their crops; he obtains rain for them, either direct or through the rainmakers, in times of drought; he makes women and cattle fruitful; and no war-party can expect to meet with success unless he has approved of the expedition. On these occasions his official sanction is given when he hands a club, on which has been smeared a concoction called *setanik*, to one of the leading men. Before an attack is made each warrior touches his forehead and breast with the *setanik*, and the club is carried in front of the party.

The position of *Orkoiyot* is a hereditary one. The medicine men are descended from the Segela Masai, and belong to the Talai clan, whose totem is a lion. The following genealogical table will show that the position is not an ancient one, and it seems probable that it has been borrowed from the Masai, just as the Lumbwa seem to have borrowed it from the Nandi in recent years. It will be observed that Ar-ap-Kipsegun and Kopokoii are both termed second Nandi *Orkoiyot*. There was apparently a dual administration until the former was ousted.

[1] *Ficus sp.*

Kipsegun
1st Nandi Orkoiyot
|
Kopokoii   Ar-ap-Kipsegun
2nd Nandi Orkoiyot   2nd Nandi Orkoiyot
|
Turukat
3rd Nandi Orkoiyot
|
Kimnyole
4th Nandi Orkoiyot,
killed by the Nandi in 1890
|
——————————————————————————————————
| | |
Kipchomber   Koitalel   Kipeles
(or Ar-ap-Koileke)   (or Samwei)   (or Tamasun)
1st and present   5th Nandi Orkoiyot,   6th and present
Lumbwa Orkoiyot.   killed by our forces Nandi Orkoiyot.
                     1905.

The person of the *Orkoiyot* is usually regarded as absolutely sacred. Nobody may approach him with weapons in his hand or speak in his presence unless first addressed, and it is most important that nobody should touch his head, otherwise it is feared that his powers of divination, &c., will depart from him.[1] The fourth *Orkoiyot* was, however, clubbed to death by his own people. This was done as he was held to be responsible for several public calamities. First of all came famine; this was followed by sickness; and then a raid, which the *Orkoiyot* had sanctioned against the Kavirondo, was so disastrous that out of 500 warriors who set out but two returned alive. Before he was put to death, Kimnyole is said to have prophesied that white people would come who would wage war with the Nandi, kill their sons, seize their cattle, and drive them out of their homes, and that they would bring with them a strange being like a serpent that would crawl along the ground, shriek, and puff smoke.[2] He advised all those who could do so to go and live in the heavens, as the earth would no longer be a proper place to live in. All the misfortunes which have since befallen the Nandi are attributed to their having murdered their *Orkoiyot*.

[1] It is commonly believed that the *Orkoiyot* can detach his head from his body, and that he is able during a fight to send it to the scene of hostilities to watch his troops.

[2] The engines of the Uganda Railway.

Kipchomber or Ar-ap-Koileke, the Chief Medicine Man of the Kipsikīs or Lumbwa, with his son, Sonaiet or Ar-ap-Kipchomber, his principal advisers, and the headmen of Buret and Sotik. Kipchomber is the second from the spectator's left in the second row; his son is sitting below him. This photograph was taken at Mombasa, hence the garb of the Coast people (Powter).

To face p. 50

The *Orkoiyot* is said never to pray to *Asista*, but only to the spirits of his deceased ancestors. He is also supposed to receive power from certain snakes which he is believed to carry about with him in his bag.

The wives of the principal medicine man may do no work, all their household duties being performed by servants, called *otuagik*. Whenever a wife of the *Orkoiyot* gives birth to a son, the child is surreptitiously taken away from its mother's side, when three or four days old, and not returned until the next night. If the mother does not complain, the child is probably found to have in its hands some hairs of a cow's tail, some grass and a tick, which is a sign that he may one day become paramount chief; if, on the other hand, she has worried about the boy, he will bring back with him the bark and root of a tree and a frog. In this case he can never succeed to the position held by his father.

Besides the *Orkoiyot* there are two classes of lesser medicine men, one of whom is called *Kipsakeiyot*, the other *Kipungut*. The former all belong to the Talai clan, whilst the latter are not Nandi at all, but hail from Marokor, and no blood-money need be paid if one is killed. The duty of these men is to ascertain who is to blame if a person has died mysteriously, or if a corpse has not been taken by the hyenas, to find out the cause of illnesses, and to detect criminals. The *Kipsakeiyot*, like the *Orkoiyot*, divines at his own house; the *Kipungut* proceeds to the spot where the misfortune or crime has occurred and divines there.

Magicians. The people who are believed to practise witchcraft (*ponik*) are much dreaded, and if one of the medicine men divines that a certain person is responsible for the death of anybody, that person is put to death, unless he can escape and leave the country, when he becomes an outlaw.[1] The principal method employed for bewitching or injuring people is said to be to 'catch' their footprints. People can also be bewitched by a portion of their clothing or a bead that they have worn, by their hair, nail parings, teeth, spittle, or anything that has passed from their bodies falling into the hands of a wizard or witch, and care must be exercised to prevent this from happening. When the head is shaved, the hair is thrown away towards the rising or setting sun, or hidden in grass;[2] after the nails have been cut, the parings must be collected and disposed of when nobody is looking;

[1] For further particulars *vide* p. 71.   [2] *Vide* p. 30.

when teeth are cast or extracted they must be hidden in goats' dung;[1] and when anything passes out of a person's body it must be covered with grass.

Rain-makers. There is a class of men called *Uindet* (pl. *uik*) who practise rain-making. They belong to no special clan, and several of them come from Kamasia.

Successful rain-makers are usually very well off. They receive large presents of grain when the crops are harvested, and of oxen after a raid.

The rain-medicine (*kiptakchat*) is a root, and rain is said to be produced by putting this root in water.

When a rain-maker is procuring rain, he may not wash his hands or drink water, he may not have sexual intercourse, and he must not sleep on the hide of an ox which has been recently slaughtered.

CIRCUMCISION FESTIVALS.

Boys' circumcision. A circumcision festival is held every 7½ years,[2] when most youths between the ages of, say, ten and twenty, undergo the operation which transforms them from boys into warriors. Young boys are only circumcised if they are fairly rich orphans or if their fathers are old men. The commonest age is between fifteen and nineteen.

A month before the event the old women start collecting milk, which they put in big jars and set on one side for the boys' consumption after the operation. It is generally taken mixed with blood.

The ceremony is commenced when the moon is in the first quarter. Three days before the operation the boys are handed over by their fathers or guardians to a number of elderly men called *moterēnik* (s. *moteriot*).[3] These men act as nurses or godfathers, and as many as ten boys are placed in charge of two men. The *moterēnik* proceed with their boys to a neighbouring river that has plenty of forest on its banks, and set to work to build a hut, which is called *menjet*. In this hut the two men live with their boys for about six months after the operation.

[1] For an exception to this rule *vide* p. 30.
[2] Since 1905 it has become customary to circumcise boys at frequent intervals, as is done with girls.
[3] The senior man is called *moteriot ne-oo*, the junior, *moteriot ne-mining*. The boys and their *moterēnik* call one another *Pa-mwai*.

PLATE XX

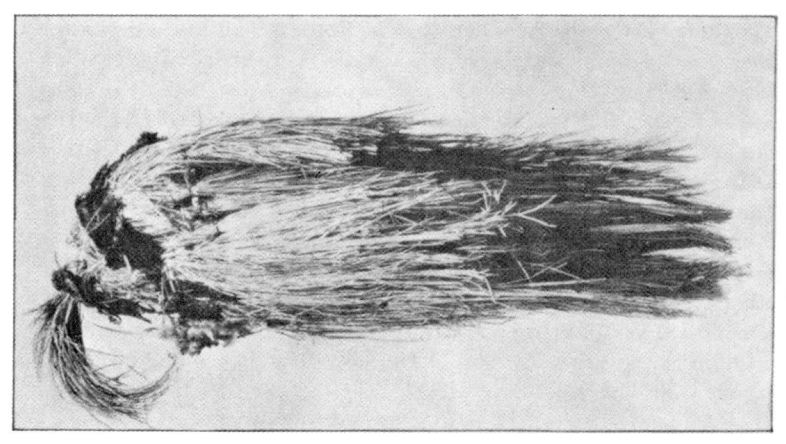
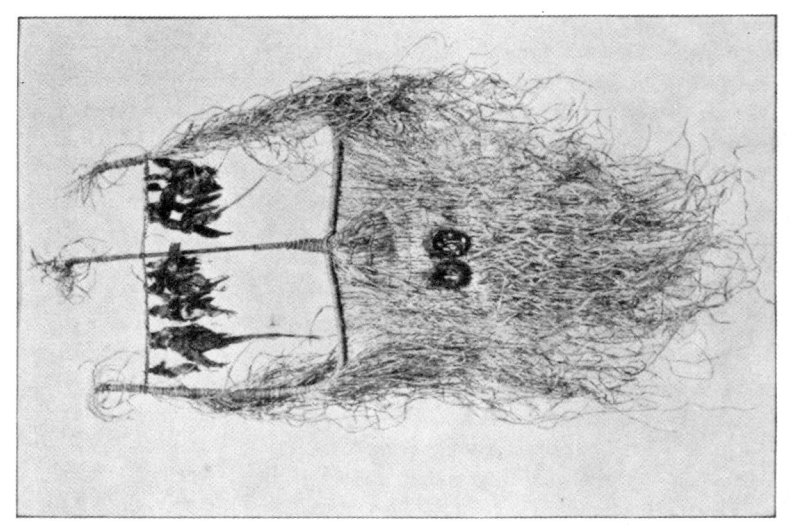

Two specimens of Kimaywanahet head-dress (worn by boys after circumcision).

CIRCUMCISION FESTIVALS 53

On the morning following the erection of the *menjet* huts, the *moterēnik* pour some milk and water mixed with salt on a stool which has a depression in the centre and rub a little on the boys' heads. They then shave the boys, and having collected all the hairs, throw them away towards the rising sun. After being shaved the boys are given a strong purge, which is made from the *segetet, usuet,*[1] or *sukemeriet* trees. During the course of the morning warriors visit the *menjet* huts and seize and take away with them all the boys' clothes and ornaments. Young girls next pay them a visit, and give them some of their own garments (*ingoriet-ap-ko*) and ornaments. Having attired themselves in these, the boys, who now receive the name of *tarusiek* (s. *tarusiot*), start off to inform their maternal uncles and other relations living in the neighbourhood that they are going to be circumcised and invite them to be present. If they have no maternal uncle living, a maternal cousin may take his place. Without the

Fig. 45 (scale ¼). *Kipōs*, boys' circumcision knife.

sanction of a maternal uncle or his representative no operation can be performed.

The next day dances are held which are called *cheptilet* and *aiyuet*. The boys are still dressed as girls and wear a bunch of *sinendet*[2] in their ears. Towards evening they are led away by the warriors, who make them sit down and scrutinize their faces and eyes to see whether they are likely to behave in a cowardly or brave manner when they are operated on. Should the former be anticipated the performance, which is called *kâponyony*, is repeated several times. When the boys have been passed by the warriors, their girl friends give them bead necklaces to wear. Favourites are often smothered with strings of beads.

After sunset the boys are taken by their *moterēnik* to a large empty house and made to sit down outside and gaze at the stars. Presently they hear inside the house the operator's knife being sharpened ready for the next day. This knife is called *kipōs*, which means *bald temples*, as it is double-bladed with the dividing line down the centre. Many warriors are present and make fun at the boys' expense, telling them that *Kipōs* is growling and wants something to eat.

[1] *Ardisia sp.* [2] *Ficus sp.*

Later on everybody strips and a procession is formed, which is led by one *moteriot* and closed by the other. Each boy holds the one in front of him round the waist and stoops down so as to place his head against the other's buttocks. The building is entered by the back door, and inside the goats' compartment is a small cage called *kimusanyit*, through which the procession has to crawl four times. At the entrance and exit of this cage stand warriors armed with stinging nettles and hornets. With the former they beat the boys on the faces and private parts, the latter they drop on the boys' backs. At the end of the other compartment is a kind of throne on which is perched an old man who is enveloped in furs and who wears a lion-skin headdress. In the centre of the room is a fire, round which a number of old men are seated. Each boy has now to appear before the old men and ask for permission to be circumcised. This ordeal is called 'Going to *Kimasop*', *Kimasop* being the name for the old man wrapped in furs. On his entrance the boy is shown a torch and told that if he does not speak the truth the fire will enter his nose. He has then to make a confession of his past life. Should the old men believe that he is not speaking the truth or is hiding something from them, a little eleusine grain is surreptitiously dropped on the fire, and when it explodes he is warned to be careful, as he is displeasing the spirits of the dead. Should he still be reticent about his former misdeeds or refuse to disclose any of his past doings, he is made to sit on a stool covered with stinging nettles. When the old men are satisfied with their examination, the boy describes the cow which he or his father is willing to pay for the permission, and the *Kimasop* nods his head. The boy is then taken outside by his *moterēnik* and hidden under a fur *kaross*. After all the boys have been examined, the *kimusanyit* is broken to pieces and buried in cow-dung. The fur covers are next removed from the boys, who are led back by their *moterēnik* to their hut by the river, where they wait and watch till 5 a.m.

At that hour the warriors and old men collect together round the *menjet* huts, the boys are brought out, and at sunrise the operation commences. All weapons must be removed to a distance, and nobody may speak. The boy to be operated on stands up and is supported by the senior *moteriot* from behind. The other boys with the junior *moteriot* sit in a line close by, looking on. The operator, who is called *poiyot-ap-tum*,[1] kneels in front of the boy, and with a deft cut of the *kipōs* performs the first part of the operation, the foreskin being

[1] The boys and their operators call one another *Pa-tum* ever afterwards.

PLATE XXI

Tarusiot, or boy recently circumcised, wearing the nyorkit garb and the kimaranguchet head-dress (Champion de Crespigny).

CIRCUMCISION FESTIVALS

drawn forward and severed just in front of the tip of the glans penis. The boy's face is carefully watched by the surrounding crowd of warriors and old men to see whether he blinks or makes a sign of pain. Should he in any way betray his feelings, he is dubbed a coward and receives the nickname of *kipite*. This is considered a great disgrace, and no *kipite* may ever attend another circumcision festival or be present at children's dances. Those boys that are brave receive presents of bunches of *sinendet*[1] from the women, who greet them with cries of joy when they hand the bead necklaces they received after the *káponyony* ceremony back to their girl friends. The foreskins are collected by the old men, who pour milk and beer on them and put them away in an ox-horn. This done, all the friends and relations make merry whilst the second part of the operation is performed, at which only barren women and women who have lost several brothers or sisters in quick succession may be present. The skin of the penis is retracted well back, and the inner covering of the glans is slit up, peeled off, and cut away behind the corona. The skin is next pulled tightly over the glans, and a transverse slit is made on its dorsal surface about half an inch long and about the same distance from its bleeding edge. Through this slit the glans is pushed, and the final stage of the operation is the trimming away of the resulting pucker of skin thus formed. During this part of the operation many boys collapse from the pain. Only cold water is administered to the lacerated parts, after which the boys are taken by their *moterēnik* to the *menjet* hut, where they live quietly for the next few weeks. For the first four days they may not touch food with their hands, but must eat out of a half-calabash or with the help of a leaf of the *sokot* tree. They are fed on delicacies, and may eat anything they fancy, including meat and milk mixed. During these four days nobody may go near or regard them except their *moterēnik*. At the expiration of this period the *lapat-ap-ēun* (washing of hands) ceremony is held. Their hands are washed, the girls' clothes are exchanged for women's garments, called *nyorkit*, which, together with a *merenget* necklace, are provided by their mothers, and the old men take the foreskins out of the ox-horn and, after offering them to God, bury them in cow-dung at the foot of a *tepesuet*[2] tree. The boys may now use their hands when eating, but instead of the ordinary pieces of hide which serve as plates, their food is dished up in honey barrels, and they must drink out of gourds instead of cups. They may still

[1] *Ficus sp.*   [2] *Croton sp.*

see nobody except the young children who bring them their food. Any scraps that are left over after they have had their meals are called *tolongik*, and may only be eaten by small children.

During the next three months or so, whilst the boys are recovering, they spend their days shooting small birds, which they attach to a special kind of head-dress, called *kimaranguchet*. They must, however, never be out at night-time, and to frighten them into obeying this order the warriors, armed with bull-roarers (*ñgetunyik* or lions), often visit the *menjet* huts after dark and make the boys think that lions are prowling about outside ready to devour them. One month after the operation the boys and the *moterēnik* sing a song three times every day. This is called *kaandaet*, and records the praises of those who were brave during the operation. On these occasions warriors and old men may be present.

When the boys have recovered, the *kâpkiyai* ceremony is held. A pool is made in the river by means of a dam, and a small hut built in it. All strip, and, preceded by the senior *moteriot*, the boys crawl in procession four times through the hut. They are thus completely submerged by the water. If anybody is affected by the submersion, a goat has to be slaughtered by his father. The boys may now go forth and see people, but they must still wear women's clothes, and they may not appear without the *kimaranguchet* head-gear. They must also carry a bow and half a dozen arrows in their hands. Whenever they talk to anybody, they must stand some distance off; they may call nobody by name, but, if they wish to attract attention, they must clap their hands together or slap their thighs. They must be up and dressed very early in the morning, and every day must leave their huts before the sun rises, and spit towards the east; they may not enter a cattle-kraal or go near the stock, and when referring to a cow and goat must say *soet* (buffalo) and *cheptirgichet* (duiker); they may not mourn if anybody dies; they must spit in their hands and not on the ground; and, most important of all, they must not be out of doors when a hyena howls. To ensure this the warriors still frequently visit the *menjet* huts after dark and sound their bull-roarers.

The period of semi-seclusion lasts about eight weeks, during which the boys and their *moterēnik* hold a dance, called *suiyet*, daily. At the end of this time the *rīkset* feast is held. A large house is set aside for the purpose, and the boys, dressed in the *nyorkit* garb, are shown in one at a time. At the entrance stand one or two warriors, who, as the *moteriot* enters, say, *Moter, ile oi!* (Godfather, ask for permission!)

Plate XXII

Tarusiot, or girl about to be circumcised, wearing warrior's garments (Wilson).

CIRCUMCISION FESTIVALS

The warriors then seize the boy by the left hand, fasten a leather thong to his little finger, and ask him a question, the answer to which is only known to persons who have been circumcised. It is: *Inge-kwir-chi korko njolia kuu 'le ne?* (*Quid simile est sono vaginae in coitu?*) And the reply is, *Kuu 'le chelelel* (*Crepitus pinguis quod super ignem sibilat*). In order that the boy shall not forget the answer the thong is given a sharp jerk, which nearly dislocates his finger. Whilst this is taking place two or three old men are performing on friction drums called *ñgetunyik*[1] in the hut. After all the boys have entered the hut, they are shown both the friction drums and the bull-roarers, and taught how to play them. They are also taught their duties as warriors.

They have now left the *menjet* huts for good, and they spend the next three or four days in the house, in which their *moterēnik* further enlighten them as to their duties. The *ñgetunot* feast is then held by the boys' parents. Each boy returns to his father's home, but finds the doors closed and barred. He calls out, and his favourite sister opens a door for him. For the rest of their lives the brother and sister call one another *Pa-mwai*. The mother now comes forth and proudly presents her son with a complete set of warrior's accoutrements. At the conclusion of the feast the newly-fledged warriors must live by themselves in a *sigiroinet* or warriors' kraal for one month, after which they may live where they like, they may have sweethearts, they may accompany their elders on raiding expeditions, and may generally enjoy the free life of fighting men.

There is, however, yet another feast which has to be held before a warrior is considered fit to have a voice in the government of the country. This is called *kirie korokon*. The warrior selects an ox with a good head, which is slaughtered and eaten by all present except the donor. His friends then proceed to strike him on the face with stinging nettles to make him look fierce, after which he ties a piece of the ox-hide on his milk calabash, and the head and horns he fixes over the back door inside his mother's hut. He is now regarded as an adult; his spirit lives after death; and on his death his name may be given to a member of his family.

Girls' circumcision. When a few girls living in the same neighbourhood have reached a marriageable age, their fathers decide to arrange a circumcision festival.

[1] *Vide* p. 40.

Three days before the date fixed for the operation the *moterēnik*, or godmothers, give the girls a strong purge and shave their heads. The hair is collected and thrown away towards the rising sun, after which their fathers smear their daughters' heads with fat and red clay, and present them with the arm-clamp worn by warriors, which they don, and a tobacco pouch, which they hang round their necks. Each girl's sweetheart gives her his garment, thigh bells, leglets of Colobus monkey skin, and club. These she wears in lieu of her ordinary clothes and ornaments. Other friends give her their thigh bells, so that a popular girl frequently wears as many as ten or twenty of these bells at the same time.

Having attired themselves in men's garments and carrying clubs in their hands, the girls set forth to show themselves to their maternal uncles and other relations, and to invite them to a feast which their fathers provide on the next day. The feast is held in the afternoon, the girls having spent the morning in grinding eleusine grain and preparing for it.

On the day before the operation, the warriors bring their girl friends bunches of *sinendet*,[1] which they may wear in their ears if they behave themselves bravely. The girls kneel down to receive these presents, and each warrior makes a speech to his particular friends and exhorts them not to be cowards. In the evening another feast and dance called *kipsirgoiit* is held. At eleven o'clock the old people leave their houses, where they have been drinking honey-wine and beer, and join the warriors and girls who have been dancing. If one of the girls is a virgin, her father at this stage in the proceedings wears a *nariet* head-dress.[2] At midnight the fathers ask their daughters in the presence of all whether they have any enemies amongst the warriors. If they have, they mention the names, and steps are taken to prevent these men from attending the ceremony the next day, in case their presence might make the girls afraid. After this the old people keep up the feasting till daylight, whilst the warriors and girls retire to rest.

The operation is performed an hour after sunrise. The fathers, maternal uncles, and eldest brothers anoint with milk the girls' faces, breasts, and legs, and pour milk on the heads of the *moterēnik*. Only a few old women are actually present at the operation,[3] which is

---

[1] *Ficus sp.*   [2] *Vide* p. 61, n. 5.
[3] A man who has lost several brothers or sisters in quick succession may witness the operation, as it is supposed to break the spell that has fallen on his family.

PLATE XXIII

Soiyuet head-dress. Worn by girls after circumcision.

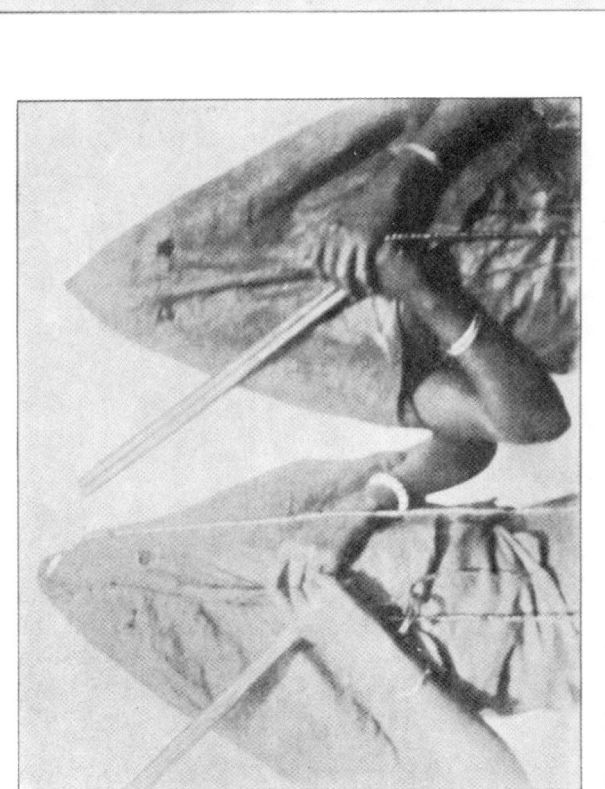

Tarusiek, or girls recently circumcised, wearing the nyorkit garb, the soiyuet head-dress, and carrying the motolik sticks (Stordy).

CIRCUMCISION FESTIVALS

performed in the open, but a large gathering of warriors and others is assembled less than a quarter of a mile away. Whilst the operation is taking place the girls' mothers run round the group weeping and wailing. The girl sits down, the senior *moteriot* sits behind her and supports her, and the operator, who is called *kork'-ap-tum*, sits in front of her. Only the clitoris is excised, and a small curved knife, called *mwatindet*, is used. If the girl shows no sign of pain, she stands up after the operation, puts some *sinendet*[1] into her ears, shakes the warriors' thigh bells above her head, and goes to meet her lover, who runs out to receive back his club, thigh bells, &c. She then retires to her mother's house. If the girl behaves in a cowardly manner, the warrior's things are thrown away.[2]

The *moterēnik* see to the girls' food, which must be the best obtainable. They may not touch food with their hands, but have to eat with the help of a half-calabash. Four days after the operation the *lapat-ap-ēun* (washing of hands) ceremony is held. The patients are clothed

FIG. 46 (scale ¼). *Mwatindet*, girls' circumcision knife.

in long garments, called *nyorkit*, which reach from the neck to the feet; their heads and faces are enveloped in a kind of mask, called *soiyuet*, which has only two holes in front for the eyes; a *malingotiet* necklace is thrown over their necks, and they use wooden spoons called *segetiet* instead of the half calabashes. The girls may now be engaged to be married. For the next month or two they stay in their mothers' huts in complete seclusion. When they are recovering, the *moterēnik* build a small kraal call *kâpteriot*. In this kraal four small huts are erected, two of which are supposed to be for the reception of the future husband and two of his wives, the third for the girl's mother, and the fourth for her warrior friends. The girls appear before this kraal three times every day and sing the *kaandaet* songs extolling the

---

[1] *Ficus sp.*
[2] The test is a severe one. One ball of goat's dung is balanced on the girl's head, another on her knee, and a third on her big toe. If one of them falls to the ground, the girl is said to have flinched, and is considered a coward.

bravery of those who did not behave as cowards during the operation. Married women often join the girls at these songs.

After the girls have all recovered, the *kâpkiyai* ceremony is held. As with the boys, a pool is made in a neighbouring river by means of a dam, and a small hut is built in it. Preceded by their *moterēnik*, the girls, having stripped, form a line and walk in procession completely submerged by the water through the hut. This is done four times.

The girls may now be married. If no husband comes for them, however, they continue to live in a secluded state for the next few weeks, and they must wear their long garments and masks or veils. Whenever they wish to go abroad, they must carry four little sticks of the *kerundut* tree, called *motolik*, and they must be retiring in their behaviour. They may not stand near anybody or call a person by name; they may not enter a cornfield or a cattle-kraal; they may do no work; they may not go near a fire, harvested grain, or cattle; and they may not mourn if anybody dies. They must leave their mothers' huts at daybreak and spit in the direction of the rising sun, and they must be indoors by sundown.

As with the boys, the *rīkset* feast is held some eight or ten weeks after the *kâpkiyai* ceremony. The girls are taken to a large house in which some old women are seated playing on the friction drums,[1] and they are taught their duties as wives. After the feast they are clothed in married women's garments, but instead of the catherine-wheel-shaped ear-rings of married women they wear the *nariet* head-dress [2] and a calf-bell suspended from the back of the neck. The head-dress and bell are worn for one month, after which they are discarded, and the girls assist their mothers in the household work until they are married.

MARRIAGE.

When a Nandi wishes to marry, his father and mother start early one morning at the waxing of the moon [3] and proceed to the house where the parents or guardians of his intended bride live. This journey is called *koito*, and the father carries in his hand a sprig of *nokiruet* [4] and the mother a bunch of leaves of the *senetwet* plant.[5]

On their arrival at the house where the girl's parents live they

[1] *Vide* p. 40. [2] *Vide* p. 61, n. 5.
[3] May or June is the usual season for weddings. [4] *Grewia sp.*
[5] *Cassia didymobotrya*.

PLATE XXIV

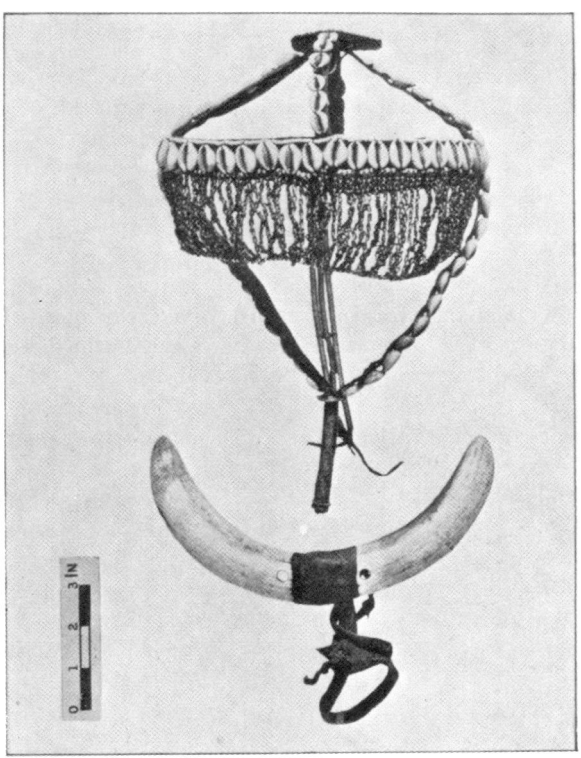

Nariet head-dress. The wart-hog's tushes may be affixed to the head-dress and worn on the forehead if the girl is a virgin.

To face p. 60

MARRIAGE 61

go to the back door, the *kurket-ap-injor*, and enter the goats' compartment, where they remain. The owner of the house looks through the *ñgotie*, or door in the mud partition, and on seeing them joins them and listens to what they have to say. He then tells them to go away in order that he may think over the proposal, and after they have gone he makes inquiries regarding the young man's character and financial prospects.

The old people return the next morning, and the first question which the girl's parents ask is: *Tiony-ñgwañg ko ne ?* (What is your animal ? *i.e.* To what clan do you belong?). This information is required as certain of the clans may not intermarry,[1] the reason being that according to tradition all such marriages are sterile. On learning that the young man does not belong to a forbidden clan or family, which information the young man's parents had of course been careful to ascertain before starting on their journey, and being satisfied with the proposal, the price to be paid for the girl is discussed. At the present time one bull, one cow, and ten goats are the usual amount, though formerly the price was higher. When this matter has been arranged,[2] the old people are given butter or fat which they smear on their faces, bodies, and legs, and then return home. On their arrival they are greeted with shouts of *Ka-ki-'il* (They have been oiled), and everybody knows that the preliminaries have been satisfactorily settled.

Feasts are now prepared by both families, and the next day the bridegroom's relations engage the services of a boy, who is called *mistōat* (herdsman), a girl, who is called *cheplakwet* (nurse), and the bride's two *moterēnik* or godmothers.[3] In the afternoon these four are sent to the house of the girl's parents. They enter by the back door and remain in the goats' compartment, where they are given food. The bride having been freshly oiled, shaved, and dressed in the *kiskisto*[4] and *nariet*[5], or wedding garment and head-dress, and

[1] *Vide* p. 8 *sqq.*
[2] If the parents cannot come to terms, it is a common custom, except among the Tungo clan, for the man to elope with his bride, in which case the price is arranged at a later date.
[3] *Vide* p. 58.
[4] The *kiskisto* is a finely dressed skin lined with black beads.
[5] The *nariet* head-dress is made of leather and iron wire, and is ornamented with chains and cowrie shells. A pair of wart-hog's tushes in the shape of a crescent is bound to the front of the head-dress if the girl is a virgin.

with the *taōk*, or married woman's ear-rings, hanging on her shoulders, then enters the house by the front door. She has, however, to be coaxed into the goats' compartment, and must be promised a cow by her father before she consents to enter. Some time therefore elapses before she can be handed over to the bridegroom's emissaries. When this is done, she has various household articles tied on to her back. These consist of a child's gourd, a *sosiot* or stick used for cleaning gourds, and a *loñgnet* or cupping arrow, whilst a calf's bell is suspended from her left shoulder. All being now ready, the bridal party sets out for the village or cluster of huts of the bridegroom's father. The boy and one old woman precede, and the girl and the other old woman follow, the bride. The journey has to be undertaken with great care; nobody must stumble, as this would be a sign of an unhappy marriage, and were one of the party to look behind, it would mean that the bride would be driven out of, or would fly from, her husband's house back to her parents. The party is timed to reach the house set aside for the purpose at six o'clock in the evening. On arrival the boy and the first old woman enter by the back door, but nothing will induce the bride to follow until her father-in-law and mother-in-law bribe her by promising her a cow and a goat respectively. She then stoops down and enters, and the others follow. In the house is the bridegroom, dressed as an old man in the toga-like robe called *sumet*, and without arms or warrior's ornaments. If it is his first marriage he has also been shaved and his hair cast towards the rising sun.

When the bridal party have entered the house, all seat themselves except the bride, who remains standing and refuses to take off the things which have been tied on to her back. Her father-in-law must promise her another cow before he can prevail upon her to lay aside her impedimenta. The bridegroom and bride then bind a sprig of *sekutiet* grass[1] on to each other's wrists, after which much feasting and dancing are indulged in. This is kept up all night long, and the bridegroom and bride are instructed by the old men and women as to their duties to one another.

At daybreak some of the husband's friends (of the same *mat*[2] as himself), accompanied, whenever possible, by members of the Kipaa clan, go into the woods and fetch a few sticks cut from one of the four following trees, according to the husband's clan: *cheptuiyet, kosisitiet, choruet,* or *tepesuet*.[3] They also make rope from the *sinendet*[4]

[1] *Vernonia sp.*   [2] *Vide* p. 12.   [3] *Croton sp.*   [4] *Ficus sp.*

PLATE XXV

A Nandi bride (Henderson).

MARRIAGE

and *chemnyelilet* trees. The sticks they plant in a circle and bind together near the back entrance of the bridegroom's hut. This erection is called *korosiot*. A bonfire is then made, and the bridal pair with a few relations and friends walk or dance round it four times, after which a goat, called *tet'-ap-tumdo*, is slaughtered near the spot. This goat is specially selected as a strong, healthy animal from the flock, and has been anointed during the course of the morning by the bridegroom's parents with milk and cow's urine, the old people at the same time praying to God that the marriage may be a happy one. Before the goat is strangled, all persons who have been recently shaved and all weapons have to be removed to a distance. After it has been killed, the entrails are examined. If there is no sign of disease, the event is declared auspicious. If, on the other hand, the goat is found to be ailing—a most improbable event, as it has been specially chosen out of a large flock—another one has to be anointed and killed. When the bridegroom's friends have given a favourable report, the parents and the two godmothers sprinkle milk and beer over the pair as well as over the bystanders, which include the girl's *mistōat* and *cheplakwet* of the day before, who may be termed page and bridesmaid. The goat is then skinned, and while the women roast and eat the meat, the skin is rapidly dressed and given to the bride to wear. A ring and bracelet of the skin are also made. The former is put on the middle finger of the bridegroom's right hand, and the latter on the girl's left wrist. The rest of the day is spent in feasting.

Soon after sunset the bridegroom conducts the bride to a friend's house, which has been prepared for them. After she has entered, he performs the duties otherwise performed by the wife, closing the door, making the beds, and attending to the fire. The marriage may not yet be consummated.

The next morning the bride opens the door and cooks some food for her husband, whilst her mother brings milk and assists her. The girl also brings water with which to wash his hands, and a stool for him to sit on; but he refuses to have anything to do with her. At length, after she has promised him the cow her father has given her, he consents to allow her to wait on him, but he will not touch the food until one of his friends (of the same *mat* as himself) has been brought in to taste it. He then eats and drinks, and that night the marriage is consummated.

Four days later the bridal pair move into their own house, and for a whole month are waited on by the bridegroom's mother, as it is unlawful for the bride during this period to work.

Some time after the first marriage the bridegroom has to slaughter a bullock, which is called *eit'-ap-muket*, and give a feast to his friends. This ceremony is similar to the *kirie korokon* feast.[1] An animal with a good pair of horns is chosen, and after the donor, who may not partake of the meat, has been well beaten about the face with stinging nettles, he is permitted to fix the head and horns over his back door. He may then settle down to the humdrum life of a married man.

Polygamy. A man may marry as many wives as he can support, and rich men have had as many as forty wives.[2] Each wife has her own house, and with her children attends to a portion of her husband's property, both live-stock and plantations.

The first wife is always the chief wife, and her eldest son is considered the eldest son of the family, even if one of the other wives bears a son first.

BIRTH.

In the ordinary course of events, a feast, called *rutet-ap-karik* (the boring of iron), is held a few months after marriage, when the wife discovers she is pregnant for the first time. Her relations and friends are invited, and whilst the old people are drinking and the young ones dancing, she borrows an apron from an unmarried girl and takes off the seeds with which it is ornamented. Into these she bores holes with a piece of iron, and then threads them on to a cord and sews them on to her lower garment (*chepkawit*). She wears this charm until her child is born, when it is hung round the babe's neck.

A few days before the birth she retires to her house, where she is attended by an elderly friend, who is called *kork'-ap-sikisis*. When the child is expected, the female relations and neighbours go to the mother's house, and remain outside for some hours discussing the happy event.

As soon as the labour pains begin, the mother sits on the edge of a large stone and seizes a *pambaniat* or rafter of the ceiling. She is supported from behind by an old woman, whilst the *kork'-ap-sikisis* receives the child. Immediately after the birth the mother's belt is tied tightly round her waist. If she suffers much, the women outside

[1] *Vide* p. 57.
[2] The present chief medicine man of Lumbwa has twenty-eight wives.

PLATE XXVI

A wife and daughter of Ar-ap-Koileke, the Chief Medicine Man of the Lumbwa (Hobley).

To face p. 64

BIRTH

beat grain mortars with pestles to drown her cries. The *kork'-ap-sikisis* washes the child and buries the placenta in cow-dung.

After the birth of a child the mother remains in her house for three days. On the fourth day a feast is prepared, which is called *ki-iñgêt Asis* (that God may be awakened). To this feast women only are invited. A short time before the guests arrive the *kork'-ap-sikisis* shaves the mother's head and throws away the hair towards the rising sun. The mother then cuts the rest of the umbilical cord with a *loñgnet*, or arrow used for bleeding cattle. *A-til-i annan a-'tuch-i?* (Shall I cut it off, or shall I leave a piece?) she asks. *Ituch* (Leave a piece), the *kork'-ap-sikisis* replies, whereupon the mother cuts the cord, which the *kork'-ap-sikisis* buries in cow-dung.[1]

For one month after the birth the mother is considered unclean and may not touch food with her hands, using a stick of the *segetiet* tree to feed herself with, whilst her house is washed out daily with water and cow-dung. At the end of this period she proceeds to the nearest river and washes her hands and arms, after which she returns home and resumes her ordinary daily tasks. It is usual for a woman to engage the services of a girl nurse (*cheplakwet*) about this time to assist her with the baby.

When a child is four months old a feast called *tumd'-ap-lakwet* is held. An ox or goat is slaughtered (male animal for a boy and female animal for a girl), and after the mother, child, and animal have been anointed with milk by one of the elders of the clan, the child's face is washed in the undigested food in the animal's stomach. The elder then prays as follows:—

Asis!	kōn-ech	sapon.
God!	give-us	health.
Asis!	iuit-ech.	
God!	protect-us.	
Oiík-chok!	iuit-w-ech	lakwán-ni.
The-spirits-our!	protect-for-us	the-child-this.
Moión-ni!	iuit-w-ech	lakwán-ni.
O-Stomach!	protect-for-us	the-child-this.

After this he turns to the child and says:—

Eku	chii!	lak-te	tuñgwo.
Become	a-man!	throw-away	cough.

A child is not weaned until it is two years of age, and it is a common

---

[1] For further particulars regarding the *ki-iñgêt Asis* feast vide p. 66.

sight to see prolific women suckling two children at the same time. Until the child is weaned the mother must wash her hands and arms daily. In the case of her first two children she must proceed to the river every morning: with other children a *septet* or half-calabash is used in the house.

A man must abstain from cohabiting with his wife as soon as she finds she is pregnant, and after the birth of a child three months must elapse before he may have his meals in his wife's house or have sexual intercourse with her. Until a child is weaned its mother must wash her breasts with water every time before she sleeps with her husband.

If the father is a young man, he may not touch his child until it can speak, and the child may not touch its father or anything belonging to him. If the father wishes to give his child some food he must place it on his foot or on the floor. Children are taught by their mothers to respect and obey their fathers.

No man may touch the threshold of his wife's house or anything in the house except his own bed if his wife has a child that has not been weaned.

Names. As soon as all the guests have assembled at the *ki-iñgêt Asis* feast (see p. 65) a ceremony known as *kurset-ap-lakwet* (the naming of the child) takes place. The child receives the name of a deceased ancestor or relative; this name is called *kainet-ap-oiik* (the spirit's name), and the deceased ancestor or relative, who is henceforth known as *kurenet*, is expected to watch over and keep his namesake from harm. The child is supposed to choose its own name, and the ceremony is performed in the following manner: the paternal grandmother, or other near relation of the father, mentions the names of various ancestors or relatives who have died, and the child's assent to a certain name is signified by it sneezing. In order to make sure that the child will sneeze, a little snuff is blown up its nostrils just before the ceremony. If the child is posthumous, care is taken to make it sneeze when its father's name is mentioned. When the babe has sneezed, the women laugh loudly (three times if a girl, and four times if a boy) to let the men know that the name has been given. The feast which has been prepared is then consumed.

The original name given to a child, that is to say the name of a deceased ancestor or relative, is not used, another one being substituted for it, generally a few days later.[1] The second name is usually

[1] The Toiyoi and Kipasiso clans do not name their children until they are six or seven years old.

BIRTH

given to commemorate the time of the child's birth or some event which has occurred at that period. In the following list a few of the commonest names, and the reasons therefor, are given :—

Kâp-tich, born in the cattle kraal.
Kip-ruto, Chep-ruto, born on a journey.
Kip-or,[1] born by the roadside.
Kim-ñgeny, born when the oxen have gone to the salt-lick.
Kip-ru-kut, born when there is little food in the land.
Ki-muike, born shortly after a relation has been killed.
Ki-pir-ken, born when the mortars had to be beaten to drown the mother's cries.
Kip-yator, born in the early morning when the door is opened.
Ki-pēt, born in the morning.
Kip-kemboi, born in the evening.
Kip-ruiot, born at night-time.
Ki-maiyo, born at the time of drinking beer.

The prefix is not necessarily *kip* if the child is a boy or *chep* if a girl. In the event of a father having recently acquired a cow with a crumpled horn, a boy or girl born at the time might be called *Chepseta,* and if a hornless bull had been purchased or looted the child might receive the name *Kip-karai.*

These names, unlike the first or ancestor's name, which is rarely, if ever, used, are maintained through life, and may be said to be equivalent to our Christian names.

Nicknames are frequently given to children of ten or twelve years of age, or even to warriors, old men and women, if any peculiarity of the child or person is particularly noticeable. Thus, *Kip-katam,* the left-handed, *Kip-'o-iit,* the big-eared, *Sirtoi,* the jumper, *Chep-uny-e,* he who hides his arm, are common names given to big boys or grown-up men, and, at any rate amongst acquaintances, take the place of the second name. Girls' or women's nicknames invariably commence with *Tap,*[2] e. g. *Tap-kiken,* she who waits; *Tap-rap-koi,* the wealthy one; *Tap-arus-ei,* the owner of the blue (black) bullock; *Tam-nyole,* the well-dressed one.

After circumcision the name is changed for the last time, and both men and women are known for the rest of their lives to the outside world by what is equivalent to our surname, *Ar-ap* and *Che'-po* (meaning *son of* and *daughter of* respectively) being prefixed to the

[1] The feminine prefix, *chep* (*chem, che*), is used in all the following names if a girl.
[2] An abbreviation of *Chepto-ap,* the girl of.

father's second name. In the case of younger sons *Ar-ap* is frequently prefixed to an uncle's name or to some other word, e.g. *Ar-ap-koko* (son of the old woman), *Ar-ap-Koileke* (son of the Koileke division).

The following is an example of Nandi names:—

A man of my acquaintance received shortly after his birth the name of one of his ancestors, *Paroret*, his second name was *Chepsiet*, he has no nickname, but after he became a warrior he was called *Ar-ap-Kipletiñg*. His son was originally called *Kimosoñg*, his second name was *Kipēt*, his nickname *Tech-teget* (he who shields his chest), and his surname *Ar-ap-Chepsiet*. *Ar-ap-Chepsiet* now has a son whose ancestor's name was *Kipsum*. This boy's second name is *Kimuike*, and his surname will be *Ar-ap-Kipēt*.

Twins. The birth of twins is looked upon as an inauspicious event, and the mother is considered unclean for the rest of her life. She is given her own cow and may not touch the milk or blood of any other animal. She may enter nobody's house until she has sprinkled a calabash full of water on the ground, and she may never cross the threshold of a cattle kraal again.

One of the twins is always called *Simatua* (*Ficus sp.* near *F. elegans*), whilst the other receives an animal's name such as *Chep-tiony, Chepsepet, Che-maket, Che-makut*, &c.

Infanticide. Children are buried alive in cow-dung if they cry in their mother's womb, or if at birth they present their legs first, or are born with teeth, as these events are considered unlucky. Rich people, however, often pay a medicine man a large sum to avert the misfortune and save their children's lives. Children who are blind or badly deformed, and illegitimate children, *i.e.* the offspring of unmarried girls, are likewise made away with at birth.

Barren women. If a woman has no children, it is usual for her husband to give her some of her step-children to look after and bring up.

Childless women are permitted to attend the boys' circumcision festivities and are present during the second part of the operation, as it is believed that they will afterwards become pregnant. They also go from time to time to the principal medicine man, who gives them an amulet to wear, and who, whilst preparing medicine for them, is often closeted with them alone for some time.

On the death of a childless woman the husband or his heirs expect to have the cattle and goats paid for her refunded.

PLATE XXVII

Nandi hut (Hart).

Granary and hut (Henderson).

To face p. 69

Divorce. A man may divorce a barren woman if she is a bad woman, but he cannot claim back the marriage-portion unless he can find somebody else to marry her. A woman who has had a child cannot be divorced, though the husband and wife may live separated. In a case of this kind it is usual for the eldest child to remain with the father and for the second child to go with the mother to live at her brother's house or elsewhere.

A divorce ceremony takes place in the presence of a number of people, and is performed by the husband cutting or tearing a bag of sand in half, and saying, *Tun 'ngo-to-i-tep-a i-pêt-aki kuu lolón-ni* (The next time thou askest for me thou wilt be torn like this bag).

When men beat their wives it is usual for the women to take shelter with a member of their husband's *mat*,[1] who is expected to act as intermediary and to restore peace. If a man frequently ill-treats his wife, he is cursed by the members of his *mat*.

A woman who has done wrong and who expects to incur her husband's anger generally goes to her father and begs an ox, which she takes to her husband as a peace-offering.

ILLNESS AND DEATH.

If a person falls ill, it is attributed to one of his or her deceased ancestors or relatives, and a brother or other near relation is sent for to propitiate the angry spirit.

A fragment of a broken pot is taken, and after water has been poured into it, it is placed on or near the sick bed. Some castor-oil leaves with long stalks or some millet stalks (four for a man, three for a woman) are then plucked, and the brother endeavours to stand them up in the potsherd. Each one is taken in turn, and at the same time the name of one of the dead relations is called out. This performance is continued until one of the stalks stands upright. The brother then cries out: *Ka-ko-sich-in, orkoiyo!* (I have got thee, O medicine man!); and the sick person solemnly kicks it over with his big toe. One stalk is thrown on the bed, one in the goats' compartment, one between the two rooms of the house,[2] and one outside. Mud or sand is mixed with the water and a little smeared on the forehead and throat of the invalid, whilst the rest, together with some eleusine grain, beer and milk is sprinkled between the bed and the door, and also thrown outside the house, the brother saying to the spirit responsible for the

---

[1] *Vide* p. 12.   [2] This is omitted if the patient is a woman.

illness : *Ui, anum, iro-cho maiyo ak pai ! Ka-ki-'nak-in maiyo ak pai, 'e-at-e !* (Go away, so and so, look at this beer and eleusine grain! Beer and eleusine grain have been poured and sprinkled on thee, enjoy them as thou goest!) The ceremony is concluded by everybody present taking a handful of eleusine grain and throwing it away for the benefit of the angry spirit. If any falls in the fire and crackles, it is looked upon as a good sign.

The Nandi make medicines out of the bark, roots, and leaves of various trees and plants. These medicines are made use of after the spirit of the deceased ancestor or relative has been appeased. Cupping is also frequently resorted to, and wounds are at times cauterized with fire-sticks. Surgery is practised, and limbs are skilfully set and amputated. When a man has been mauled by a wild beast or bitten by a snake, it is customary to scarify his body and to give him tobacco and water to drink.

When a person is nearing death he is carried outside the house. The male relatives say : *Ka-ko-nyarat-it* (The soul has become very small), and the women reply : *Ki-rīp-e konda* (The eye is being watched). Just before death, milk is poured into the dying person's mouth.

After a death has occurred the body is taken away at nightfall a few hundred yards to the west of the hut, towards the setting sun, and placed on the ground. Three adult relations are charged with the duty of conveying the corpse to its last resting-place, and great care must be taken that nobody stumbles, as this would bring misfortune on the whole family. A man is laid on his right side, a woman on her left, with the hand supporting the head, and the legs outstretched. The body, which is left for the hyenas to devour, is not covered with anything except the skin garment which the deceased wore when alive and a few handfuls of grass or leaves of the *tepengwet* plant.[1] When depositing the body the relations say, *Kimaketoi! O-pwa o-am* (Hyenas ! Come and eat).

On their return to the place where the death occurred, the persons who handled the corpse wail and cry aloud the name of the deceased. They then bathe in a river, anoint their bodies with fat, partially shave their heads, and live in the deceased's hut for four days, during which time they must not be seen by a boy or a female. They may also touch no food with their hands, but must eat with the help of a potsherd or chip of a gourd, and they may drink no milk.

[1] *Emilia integrifolia.*

ILLNESS AND DEATH

The body is visited on the second day after death to see if the hyenas have eaten it. If it is found that they have not been near the spot, a goat is killed and the meat is placed on and near the corpse to attract their attention. Except with the Tungo clan, the body is also turned over on the other side. Should the hyenas still not come it is understood that the deceased has been killed by witchcraft, and the relations proceed to a medicine man [1] to ascertain who is responsible for the death. They take iron wire with them as a present, but if this is not accepted, they give the medicine man a goat. He then divines, by casting pebbles from a divining-box, who the guilty person is, and describes him without mentioning his name. The relations of the deceased thereupon seize a brother or other near relation of the accused and take him before the medicine man, who states what he has divined, after which they search for the accused himself, and if they find him, kill him. Even if he escapes he must flee the country.

On the death of anybody but a baby or an old man or woman great sorrow is shown, not only by the near relations, but by the whole family, and, if the person is well known, by the whole clan. The deceased may not again be mentioned by name except at the naming of a child or the curing of a sick person.[2] If a dead person is spoken of, he must be referred to as *kimaitet*, the deceased, or as *puresik*, rubbish.

When a married man dies, his widows and unmarried daughters lay aside all their ornaments, and the eldest son wears his garment inside out. Before the next new moon all the relations of the deceased shave their heads and throw away the hair towards the setting sun. Distant relations shave only over their ears. Widows mourn for a whole year, other persons for from ten days to a month. On the death of a married woman her youngest daughter wears her garment inside out, whilst her other relations put rope on their ornaments and shave their heads. In the case of unmarried people the female relations cover their ornaments with rope and the male relations shave their heads.

When the moon is in the last quarter after the head of a family has died, an ox is slaughtered and the deceased's relations and friends partake thereof. This ceremony is called *kaiilet ap karik*, as all present put oil on their ornaments. One of the brothers, or, if there is no brother or half-brother, a paternal cousin, climbs on to the roof

---

[1] *Kipsakeiyot* or *Kipungut* (*vide* p. 51).
[2] *Vide* pp. 66 and 69.

of the huts and solemnly breaks off the stick called *kimonjōkut* which is bound on to the central pole.¹ After this he enters the huts and breaks the pegs from which the weapons were suspended, the beds, and the mud partition between the rooms; he also cuts pieces out of the stools and baskets, and chips the drinking-cups. The stools and cups are chipped as no warrior may sit on or drink out of a dead man's things. As long as a widow is in mourning, no warrior may enter her house. She is considered unclean, she must speak in a whisper, and she may not go near a warrior or stand up whilst warriors are sitting down. She may also never re-marry or again wear married women's ear-rings.

In the case of very old men or women and very young children (*i. e.* nominally those who have no teeth), the body is buried in the dung-heap near the cattle kraal. No sorrow is shown when old people die, and the relations laugh and talk at the burial, for it is said, *Ka-ko-it ye-ki-iken-i* (He has now arrived where he expected to arrive a long while ago). The corpse is placed in the grave in the same position as with ordinary people, that is to say, males are laid on the right side and females on the left, with the hand supporting the head and the legs outstretched. Old men are sewn up in ox or goats' hides, and milk, beer, and food are put in their graves. After the grave has been filled in, a *lepekwet*² tree is planted in the cow-dung.

When warriors are slain on the field of battle, or when hunters fall victims to the onslaught of wild beasts, the same ceremonies are performed as with people who die at home. Their bodies are placed ready for the hyenas, and their ornaments are taken to their relations to be oiled at the *kaiilet ap karik* ceremony.

INHERITANCE.

On a man's death his sons inherit his herds and flocks. It is customary for the Nandi to distribute their stock amongst their wives during their lifetime, each one being given a certain number to look after, tend, and milk. The sons of each wife inherit the property thus placed in their mother's charge. It is also usual for a man to give his sons from their earliest youth upwards a certain number of cattle—for instance, when a boy's two middle incisor teeth are

[1] *Vide* p. 15. [2] *Dracaena sp.*

INHERITANCE

extracted and when his ears are bored, he is given a cow. These beasts are herded with their mother's cattle until the boys become warriors, when they generally separate their herds from those of their parents.

The eldest son of the principal wife inherits the lion's share of his father's property. He also receives all the cattle which his father lent to his childless wives, unless these wives have taken charge of any of their step-children, when they are inherited by them. It is usual for a father to give or bequeath to each of his sons, if he loves them and they have been dutiful, a stick with which to herd their stock after his death. If, on the other hand, a father dislikes his son he leaves him a knife to enable him to slaughter the cattle he will inherit.

Widows nominally become the property of either their husband's next elder or next younger brother; but they frequently live in their old homes with one of their sons, or they go and live with their father or with one of their own brothers. The eldest son is expected to give a cow to each of his father's widows for her own use.

The eldest son of each wife looks after his sisters and receives the stock which his father would otherwise have received when they marry. The cattle paid to a man when his daughters are married are inherited by the girl's own brothers.

When an unmarried warrior or a man with no sons dies, his brothers inherit his property and make a home for his daughters if he has any. If he has no brothers, his step-brothers are his heirs, and failing them his paternal cousins. A father can only inherit from his sons when they have not yet reached man's estate.

Daughters inherit their mother's ornaments and household utensils. The sons and daughters inherit her plantations and retain an interest in them until they become warriors or are married, when the land is taken up by one of the sons' wives or is handed over by the father to one of his other wives. On a woman's death her plantation, if a new one, is frequently allowed to go out of cultivation.

PUNISHMENT FOR CRIME.

Murder and homicide. If a Nandi kills one of his countrymen, but a member of a different clan from his own, the brothers and cousins of the murdered man try to capture a herd of cattle belonging to the murderer or to one of his relations. To prevent this, the murderer and his relatives drive their cattle to a friendly clan, where the herds are mingled with other cattle. If this is accomplished, the aggrieved persons may not touch the cattle. They then seek for the murderer, whom they club to death should they discover his whereabouts. But after bringing his cattle into safety the murderer will hide until the old men of his clan have arranged to pay the blood-money to the murdered man's relations. The price for a man's life is five cows, five bulls and thirty goats; for a woman's or a child's, five cows, four bulls and fifteen goats. One cow at least has to be paid by the murderer himself: this cow is called *iri-ñgot* (the breaking of the spear). The object of seizing a herd of cattle belonging to the murderer's family is to pick out the finest beasts, as well as to slaughter one or two, after which the herd is returned.

When the blood-money is paid, five or six elders of both clans meet together, each man carrying a handful of grass called *tapariet*. An influential elder of another clan (probably the Tungo clan) is also present and hands to each a little food and water. This is taken on the spot, after which peace is restored.

If a Nandi kills a member of his own clan, he is regarded as unclean for the rest of his life unless he can succeed in killing two other Nandi of a different clan, and can pay the fine (*tuk'-am-met*) himself. He may never again enter a cattle kraal except his own, and whenever he wishes to go into a hut he must strike the earth twice with a rhinoceros-horn club before crossing the threshold.

A Nandi who murders a Nandi is known as *rumindet*; one who kills a person belonging to another tribe is called *parindet*. The former name is one of opprobrium, the latter one of praise. A *parindet* paints one side of his body, spear and sword red, and the other side white. For four days after the murder he is considered unclean and may not go home. He has to build a small shelter by a river and live there, he must not associate with his wife or sweetheart, and he may only eat porridge, beef, and goat's flesh. At the end of the fourth day he must purify himself by drinking a strong purge made from the bark of the *segetet* tree, and by drinking goat's milk mixed with bullock's blood. A Nandi will not slay a foe if he sees that the man has grass in his hand or if the enemy can throw some of his own excrement at him. Trees and rivers are regarded as sanctuaries, and no Nandi may kill a man who has taken refuge in one of these. He exchanges his garment with his enemy, who becomes his prisoner or slave, and remains as such until ransomed. To ensure a prisoner not attempting to escape the captor shaves his head and keeps the hair, thus placing him at the mercy of his magic.

Assault. There is no penalty for assault even if the injured person loses an eye or a limb, but while he is suffering from the effects of the injury, the man who assaulted him has to slaughter oxen and goats fairly frequently to provide him with food. Should the person eventually die from the effects of the wound it is regarded as murder, and the *tuk'-am-met* fine has to be paid in full, notwithstanding the fact that a dozen bullocks may have been slaughtered during the person's illness.

Theft. Theft is looked upon as a mean and contemptible crime, and a thief is severely dealt with.

If a man is caught stealing, or if a theft is brought home to him, he is beaten and fined four times the value of the stolen property. The fine has to be paid by the relations if the man is himself too poor. Should a thief be caught a second time, or even suspected, he is tortured. A thong or bow-string is tied tightly round his head just above his eyebrows and ears, and the ends after being twisted are fixed to stakes in the ground. They are then beaten with sticks which makes the thong cut deeply into the flesh. Twigs are also thrust in underneath the thong, and water is poured over the man's head to make the wound smart. After a couple of hours of this torture, during which time the wretched man has seen his houses and granaries burnt, his crops destroyed, and half his goats and cattle confiscated, he is released; but he bears the mark of the thong and is branded as a thief to his dying day.

On the occasion of a third theft the thief is killed and his goats and cattle slaughtered. The animals are not killed in the ordinary way, but are thrown on their sides and cut or hacked in half. The mode of execution adopted is partial strangulation, after which the person is clubbed to death. Two thongs are tied tightly round the neck and pulled in opposite directions by about twenty people; other people then rush in and use their clubs.

If a woman steals, she is severely beaten the first time, and on the second occasion she is tied up and thrashed with stinging nettles, her face and body being in a terrible state before she is released. The same treatment is meted out to children; and if goats enter the plantations they are also tortured with stinging nettles, which are thrust up their nostrils, into their mouths, and wherever they are most vulnerable.

The equivalent of a spear is a bull-calf or a she-goat; a sword, shield, ostrich-feather or lion-skin head-dress, axe, hoe, honey-barrel, quiver full of arrows, ornament, &c., are each valued at one goat, and for the first theft of any of these articles four times the value must be paid. When grain or stock is stolen, the fine is in kind.

Adultery. There is no recognized punishment for adultery, but, if a man were to find anybody but a member of his own *mat*[1] having intercourse with one of his wives, he might beat him severely.

Should a youth encroach on the warriors' preserves, he would be soundly thrashed; whilst an old man would be so heartily laughed at and so ashamed of himself that he would not dare to put in an appearance at any of the meetings, or, in fact, show himself outside his house for many months to come, during which time his flocks, herds, and crops would all suffer. No warrior would dream of committing adultery with the wife of a member of another *mat* than his own, unless she was an old friend with whom he had formerly lived in a state of free love in a *sigiroinet* or warriors' house, in which case no notice would be taken of the offence.

Incest, intercourse with a step-mother, step-daughter, cousin or other near relation, is punished by what is known as *injoket*. A crowd of people assemble outside the house of the culprit, who is dragged out, and the punishment is inflicted by the women, all of whom, both young and old, strip for the occasion. The man is flogged, his houses and crops destroyed, and some of his stock confiscated.

In the event of a warrior causing a girl to conceive, he has to slaughter an ox when the child is born. He may take the head away himself, but the rest of the animal belongs to the girl's father. Except with the Toiyoi clan, the girl is punished by being put in Coventry, none of her girl friends being allowed to speak to or look at her until after the child is born and buried. She is also regarded with contempt for the rest of her life and may never look inside a granary for fear of spoiling the corn. In the event of a girl dying at child-birth no compensation is payable by the man who caused her to conceive.

Suicide is practically unknown in Nandi, but of late there have been a few cases of Nandi girls living in Lumbwa who, when they found that they were *enceinte*, tried to hang themselves.

Trial by ordeal. If a person is accused of having committed any crime except theft, he may demand a trial by ordeal (*par mumek*).

[1] *Vide* p. 12.

PLATE XXVIII

Nandi elder (Ar-ap-Sirtoi) with two of his daughters (Rayne).

A Nandi family (Meinertzhagen).

PUNISHMENT FOR CRIME

He must search for a human skull, which he takes to the house of the accuser and deposits at his door, saying at the same time: *'Ngo-k-ai kii-i, kw-am-a met-i*; *'ngo-m-â-ai, kw-am-in* (If I have done this thing, may this head eat me; if I have not done it, may it eat thee). If the accused is guilty, it is believed that he will surely die within a few days; but, if he is innocent, his accuser dies.

In the event of a man being falsely accused of theft, he will take a handful of grass, and whilst holding it at one end himself will offer the other end and a knife to his accuser. Should the latter accept the challenge and cut the grass, it is believed that he will die if the accused is innocent. But if he does not die, the accused is considered guilty and punished accordingly.

If a person is accused of stealing food he may, before being punished, ask to be given a quantity of water to drink. He then puts a stick down his throat, and it can be seen when he vomits whether the accusation is correct. Should he be innocent he can demand a good meal from his accuser.

MISCELLANEOUS CUSTOMS.

Hospitality. When a Nandi is travelling or proceeding on a visit to friends, he asks on reaching a place where he wishes to halt for the night whether there is anybody belonging to the same *mat*[1] as himself. On being shown a house he leaves his arms outside and enters. If both men are married, the host charges his wife to attend to the wants of the visitor, and leaves his hut to sleep elsewhere. The wife pours water on the guest's hands, brings him a stool to sit upon, gives him food, takes his arms, and passes the night with him. If the visitor is unmarried, no attention is paid to him beyond giving him food; he sits on the ground and passes the night in the warriors' hut.

In the event of there being nobody of his own *mat* near at hand, the visitor asks to be directed to the dwelling of a member of the next *mat* to his, and when he explains matters to the owner of the hut, he is just as hospitably received as if the two men belonged to the same *mat*. But he cannot expect, and will not receive, hospitality from anybody belonging to another *ipinda*, or age, than his own.

Grass. Grass is held to be sacred, as it is the food of cattle. It

---

[1] *Vide* p. 12.

may not be cut except by women for thatch, and warriors are not permitted to till the ground, as they would have to kill the grass.

When a man or boy is being beaten, he is allowed to go free if he can tear up some grass. A Nandi, too, will not kill a native of another tribe if he has grass in his hand or on his person. A handful of grass held above the head is a sign of peace, and when two people fight, one of them has only to pluck some grass to ensure that his opponent will desist from attacking him.[1] Peacemakers carry grass in their hands after a murder has been committed; and warriors returning from raids and expeditions are greeted by their women-folk who run out to meet them singing, and as a sign of peace bearing bunches of grass.

When a man pays a debt in cattle, or when cattle are paid for a wife, some grass has also to be handed to the receiver, otherwise it is thought that the cattle will die.

Grass is used on many occasions. For instance, it is thrown on the mounds made by the black ant (*songotiet*), as this insect is considered unlucky; it is held in the hand when an ox, calf, goat, or sheep is bled for the first time, or when an unborn calf or kid is removed from its mother's carcase; a bracelet of grass takes the place of the wedding ring of civilized nations; grass is bound round the central pole of the house as a sign of life and strength; and dead bodies are partially covered with grass when laid ready for the hyenas. If a warrior drops a weapon he must throw some grass on it before he picks it up; and when a person urinates or defaecates, he must cover the spot with grass. Grass is also put in the mouth of gourds used for sprinkling warriors with milk when they start on a raid, and for anointing boys and girls during the circumcision festivals. It is likewise employed when the *tet'-ap-tumdo* goat is killed at weddings. Grass must never be used for beating either people or cattle.

Spitting. Spitting is principally used to avert ill luck or to bring good luck. It is also used to express astonishment at anything phenomenal, as a form of blessing, and in making agreements.

If a man tells a lie or says anything that is wrong, he spits. He also spits when he visits a sick person, when he prays, when he smells anything obnoxious, when he has had a bad dream, when he

---

[1] If there are two or three people fighting on each side, a bow stood up on end is the usual sign of peace; if there are several combatants, an ostrich feather is shown (*vide* p. 84).

bleeds his cattle, or takes a beehive, when he sees his totem animal, chameleon, or other strange creature, when he eats game, when he is startled, when he puts on sandals, when he takes anything from a smith's hand, or touches a newly-made cooking-pot, and when he hears the name of a dead person mentioned. Formerly it was customary to spit whenever a person was seen dressed in cloth, and to the present day most Nandi spit when they meet a European. If a warrior sees a baby for the first time, he spits on it and says: 'This child is bad,' at the same time calling it by an animal's name. To himself, however, he says: 'This child is good ; it is like a calf.'

When the new moon is seen, when shooting-stars or a comet are visible, or when there is an eclipse of the sun or moon, the Nandi spit and pray for good luck.

Old people and warriors often spit on children when they greet them, and old men spit in their hands before shaking hands with warriors. A dying father, uncle, or elder will spit in a boy's hand when the latter comes to bid him farewell, and the boy will rub the spittle on his face.

At peace ceremonies, and when marriages are arranged, both parties spit to ensure the agreement being propitious. When cattle, grain, or household utensils are sold, the seller spits after payment has been made to show that the sale has been completed.

Omens. If a person is proceeding on a journey and strikes the sole of his foot or the big or little toe against a stone, it is a good omen. If, on the other hand, he strikes his second, third, or fourth toe, it is a bad omen. To call back a person who has started on a journey portends evil. Should he be wanted, someone must run after him and tell him whilst accompanying him what is required. If a fly enters a traveller's mouth and he spits it out, he may expect a good reception at his journey's end; but if he swallows it, it is a sign that he will go to bed hungry. A rat crossing the path in front of one is propitious, whilst a snake is unlucky.

Like the Masai, the Nandi are great believers in the *kiptiltiliat* bird.[1] A war party starting on an expedition listens intently for the first sound of this bird's note. Should it be on the left side of the road all is well, but if it is on the right side the party will probably return at once. When a man is driving home goats, it is a good sign if he hears the bird calling on the right side of the road, but a bad sign

---

[1] *Mesopicus spodocephalus*, Bp.

if on the left side. With sheep it is the reverse—a good sign on the left side and a bad sign on the right. If a person is starting out to plant eleusine grain, he will return home again if he hears the bird's call on the right side of the path; and the same with millet if the bird calls on the left side, as he may look forward to a bad harvest. Should a traveller hear the *kiptiltiliat's* note in front of him it is unlucky; but if he hears it behind him he may expect a successful journey, provided he does not shake hands with a chance acquaintance that he may happen to meet.

If a francolin or spur-fowl is heard by a war party, it is a sign that one or more of the party will die, and should the cry be repeated the head of the expedition would be foolish to continue on his way.

When a buzzard is seen sitting on a tree or pole, it is a bad sign if he shows his back, but a good sign if his breast is visible.

No Nandi will kill a bush-buck or Colobus monkey, as he may expect to die shortly afterwards if the animal cries. For the same reason trees are rarely felled, as it is believed that if the branches when rubbing against one another make a scraping noise, or, as the Nandi say, cry, the axe-man will die.

If a hyena or snake is killed and a mess made on the ground, the slayer must slaughter a goat, otherwise he will fall ill and die.

It is a most lucky sign if a grasshopper settles on a warrior's spear. Not only does it affect the owner of the spear but all the members of his *mat*.

To have one's garments carried away by the wind is very unlucky and portends great distress. It is also a bad omen to have one's garment caught by a bush.

A man who has no calf to his leg is looked upon as an evil person, and a long-armed man is put down as a thief. A one-eyed man and a one-eyed cow are considered lucky.

A cow that protrudes its tongue to an excessive length, one that grinds its teeth, and one that twists its tail round a tree, are objects of ill omen and must be killed, the head being roasted the same day. Likewise, if a goat or a sheep seats itself like a dog, or if a sheep climbs on to the roof of a hut, it must be slaughtered, and the flesh eaten at once or thrown away. Should a dog climb on to the roof of a house, it is a sign that the head of the family will die. It is said that both of the late *Orkoiik* or chief medicine men (Kimnyole and Koitalel) were warned that their death was near by dogs climbing on to the roofs of their houses a day or two before they were killed. In the case of Koitalel, the dog was shot by Ar-ap-Chemongor, the *maotiot* of Murk'-ap-Tuk' (Kâpwaren).

If a goat goes to the front door of a house it is an omen of good luck, but a sheep that attempts to do the same thing must be driven away, as it is a sign that a death will occur in the family.

When a spider spins its web across an open door, it is a sign that misfortune will befall the household, and unless the house is a new one, it must be pulled down and re-erected by the owner. If it has only recently been built, the elders must be paid to come and pray that the house may be freed from the spell cast upon it.

Shooting stars and comets are a sign of great ill-fortune—especially the latter—and when people see them they must spit and offer up a prayer.

At all ceremonies, such as births, deaths, and marriages, and on all important occasions, as, for instance, when cattle fall sick, when warriors start on an expedition, or when people dream of the dead, a bullock or goat must be slaughtered, and the entrails examined to ascertain whether the omen may be regarded as propitious or otherwise.

Sneezing, Hiccoughs, Yawning, &c. When a person sneezes, those present say, *Ko-'weit-in Asis* (May God be good to thee). The reply is, *Iweit* (He is good).

Should a person ask for something which the owner does not wish to give away, he (the owner) sneezes before replying. It would then be unlucky for the person to receive it. But if the owner were to refuse and then to sneeze, he would have to part with it. A common practice is for a man, who intends to ask for something which he does not expect to get, to take some one with him. The third party then sneezes before the owner has time to reply, and the man gets what he wants.

If a man wishes to buy something and the owner refuses to sell, the intending purchaser will sneeze and throw a piece of wood in the direction of the owner. No one else will then purchase the article, and the man who wants it will probably be able to get it at his own price.

When a person hiccoughs, it is a sign that he will shortly eat meat. A throbbing of the pulse leads a person to expect sexual intercourse. To yawn is bad : it is said to bring illness into the house.

Sleep, Dreams, Madness, Intoxication, &c. During sleep the soul is supposed to leave the body, and a person must not be awakened roughly or boisterously for fear of the soul not finding its way back again.[1] If a person falls into a trance or faints, he is said to die. It is believed by some that the soul leaves and returns to the body through the gap caused by the extraction of the middle incisor teeth of the lower jaw.

The Nandi believe in the reality and truth of what they see in dreams, and, when a person dreams, he is supposed to be holding communication with the spirits of the deceased. The meaning of dreams is interpreted by the medicine men, who themselves are believed to obtain oracles and to be able to foretell future events from what they see in dreams. Adults always pray after they have dreamt a bad dream.

The theory of madness and intoxication are the same. A person is said to lose the power of his head and is rather pitied. The insane are left to themselves unless they become dangerous, when they are kept under restraint. People who make themselves obnoxious when drunk are forbidden by the elders of their clan to drink fermented liquor.

Menstruation. Menstruous girls and women keep themselves in seclusion. They may not cook food or shake anybody by the hand, and they must not be struck. When men allude to them during the time they have their periods, they do not make use of the ordinary word, *sunonik* (menstruous people), but refer to them as having been killed by the Kavirondo (*tāpīk che-ko-par Lemek*).

All women must bathe when their periods are finished, and girls must be careful not to go to the warriors' huts for some days afterwards for fear of becoming pregnant after intercourse with the men.

Games. As elsewhere in Africa and in other parts of the world, Nandi children have toys and play at different games. Small children are fond of building huts in the sand, and collecting snails, pebbles, and solanum berries, which they say are cattle, goats, and sheep; boys make tops out of the *Kimoluet*[2] fruit and

FIGS. 47, 48 (scale $\frac{1}{15}$). Boys' wooden spears.

[1] See also enigma No. 48, p. 144.   [2] *Vangueria edulis.*

PLATE XXIX

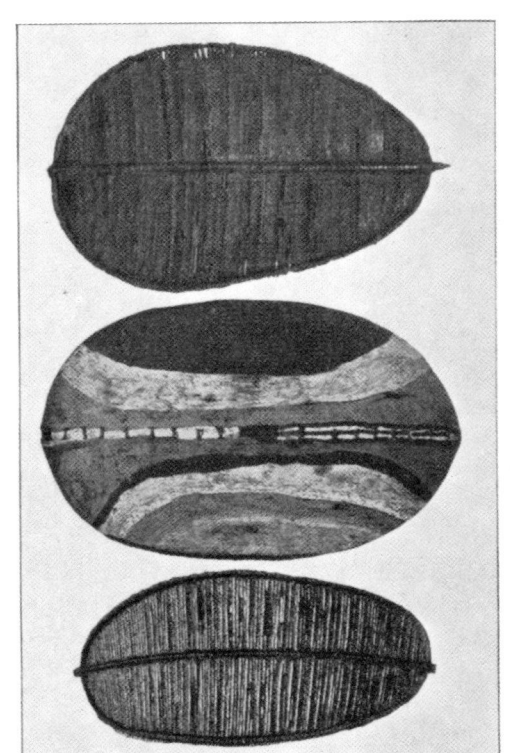

Boys' wooden shields.

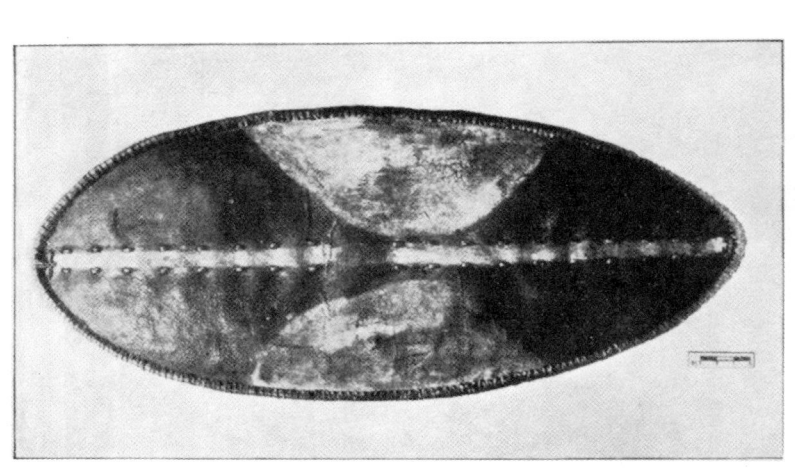

Warrior's shield (painted).

MISCELLANEOUS CUSTOMS 83

clubs out of bulrushes, and they arm themselves with wooden spears and shields; and girls dress dolls, which they make out of the fruit of the sausage tree,[1] in skins, and make necklaces and bracelets of vegetables and seeds.

A game little boys and girls frequently play is called *mororochet* (frog). They jump round in a circle, sitting on their heels and singing: *Kipchokchok koñgoñgoñg supeet*.[2] Another game is to hop on one foot whilst holding the other one, and to sing, *Ka-pel-a koko, kw-eet-a mama* (Grandmother has burnt me, but uncle has stopped her). In the game called *kimnis* from ten to twenty children sit in a circle and take a piece of live charcoal, which they pass from one to another. One child stands outside the circle and guesses who has the charcoal. If he guesses correctly he is told he will have meat for supper, but if he is wrong he will be given donkey's flesh. A game which only the children of the chief medicine man are allowed to play is to form a ring, hold hands, and sing: *Ki-po kip-set-met, ko-mi*

FIGS. 49-51 (scale ¼). Boys' arrows (wooden heads): (49) for killing rats (kipiriot); (50) for killing birds (koiisit); (51) shaft.

porto ka (We belong to the person whose head goes to war whilst his body remains in the kraal).[3]

Big boys and girls sometimes have mock circumcision festivals. As children may not talk of circumcision they call the rite 'branding', and they use in place of the circumcision-knives pieces of wood cut into shape like branding irons. Boys also play at war, when they take girls prisoners, keeping them as such until ransomed or rescued by their friends. Other games which big boys play at are called *talus, chemosiraitet*, and *kañgetet*. The first-mentioned is supposed to represent the bleeding of oxen. A tick is shot with an arrow and the blood caught in a shell. *Chemosiraitet* is a high jump and *kañgetet* is lifting the spear.

The almost universal game of *bau* (a kind of draughts) is known,

---

[1] *Kegelia aethiopica*.
[2] This is untranslatable, but is said to mean, 'Thus jump the frogs.'
[3] *Vide* p. 50, n. 1.

and is sometimes played by grown-up people, but they do not use a board containing compartments, like the Bantu tribes. Instead of this they make holes in the earth in which they circulate seeds. This game the Nandi call *kechuiek*.

Peace ceremonies. Somewhat elaborate ceremonies are performed by the Nandi in the making of peace after war. The placing of an ostrich feather in a prominent position in a high-road is a sign that peace is desired, and after the terms have been settled, one of the following ceremonies is gone through. Perhaps the most binding ceremony of all is when the chiefs and elders go to a soldier ant-heap, and having spat in it, say: *Chiito ne-ñgem-e tilión-ni, ko-ii-chi keringón-ni* (May the children of the man who breaks this peace be born in this hole). Some Nandi cut a dog in half, one man of each of the parties who have met to make peace holding it, whilst a third man says: *Chiito ne-ñgem-e tilión-ni, ki-par sesón-ni* (May the man who breaks this peace be killed like this dog). Others kill with blows of a club a tortoise, or smash a calabash full of water and flies, and say: *Chiito ne-ñgem-e tilión-ni, ki-par tukú-chu* (May the man who breaks this peace be killed like these things). Others again castrate a goat, and after one man of each party has taken one of the testicles in his hand, say: *Chiito ne-ñgem-e tilión-ni, ko-lat Asis* (May God castrate the man who breaks this peace).

When two men wish to make peace, they either cut a bow-string and say: *'Ngo-a-ñgem tilión-ni, kw-am-a inón-ni* (If I break this peace, may this bow-string eat me); or they cut their fore-arms slightly and, touching the other man's blood, say : *'Ngo-a-ñgem tiliónni, kw-am-a koroti-chu* (If I break this peace, may this blood eat me).

When women make peace after a quarrel, they step over a belt which has been placed on the ground, and say: *'Ngo-a-ñgem kii-ñguñg, kw-am-a legetión-ni* (If I spoil thy thing, may this belt eat me).

Blood-brotherhood. A ceremony of blood-brotherhood was formerly unknown to the Nandi, but when the Coast traders obtained access to the country, they induced the Nandi to enter into blood-brotherhood with them. A Swahili and a Nandi would sit opposite to each other, and, after each had cut the back of his hand, the wound was sucked by the other. The Nandi, however, never considered this ceremony binding.

During the last eight or ten years a ceremony common amongst the Masai has been introduced into Nandi. It is called *Patureshin*, or the ceremony of the red bead. When two friends wish to regard one

MISCELLANEOUS CUSTOMS

another as brothers or sisters they exchange a red bead, and ever afterwards call one another *Patureshi*, instead of by their proper names.

Form of oath. If a Nandi is accused of telling a falsehood, he will pluck a few blades of grass or pick up a little earth and say : *Kw-am-a susuondón-ni* or *Kw-am-a ñguñgunyê-chu* (May this grass [or this earth] eat me). One cannot, however, depend on this oath. The form of oath which is binding on all Nandi men is to strike a spear with a club or to step over a spear (preferably one which has killed a man) and to say : *Kw-am-a melei* (May the blade eat me). Nandi women are bound to speak the truth if they step over a woman's belt, as when making peace, and say: *Kw-am-a legetión-ni* (May this belt eat me).

Curses. The worst thing that can be said to a Nandi man is : *Am-in melei* (May a blade eat thee, *i.e.* mayest thou die after perjuring thyself), and nothing can be said which is more hateful to a Nandi woman than *Am-in kâpkwony* (Mayest thou die of impossible labour).

Other curses are given in the following list :—

Am-in Īlat! May the thunder eat thee, *or* Mayest thou be struck by lightning !
Am-in chesirun ! Mayest thou die of small-pox !
Am-in eset ! Mayest thou die of fever !
Am-in chelole ! Mayest thou die of dysentery !
Am-in motony ! Mayest thou be eaten by vultures !
Imelel ! Mayest thou get no oxen on a raid !
Isagit ! Become thin !
Pet-in konyit ! Mayest thou lose all honour !
Ip-in goris ! May the cold seize thee !
Iyei-n koñg ! May thine eye be broken !
Ipanan ! Mayest thou become poor !
Par-in Asis ! May God kill thee !
Ipet ! Be lost !
Perper-itu ! Become a fool !

Fire. Fire is produced by means of fire-sticks (*piōnik*), a hard pointed stick being rapidly drilled into a small hole in a flat piece of soft wood. The hard stick is called *kirkit* (the male), and the soft piece of wood *kôket* (the female). Fire making is the exclusive privilege of the men of the tribe.

Fire may be taken from one house to another once, or at the outside twice, a day, but if there is a very sick person in the house, no fire may leave the premises.

Fires, which might be termed sacred fires, are occasionally kindled at certain ceremonies, as for instance at marriage festivals before the *tet'-ap-tumdo* goat is slaughtered, when cattle are attacked by disease, or when raided cattle are brought to their new home, and at the *kipsunde* festivals at harvest time.[1]

Land Tenure. In Aldai, individual or family ownership of land is recognized. Land is inherited from generation to generation and can be bought or sold, together with the trees on it.

Elsewhere in Nandi no proprietary rights are acknowledged, and when a person wishes to settle on waste land, it is only necessary to obtain permission from the nearest neighbours.

If, however, the great forests, which form natural fastnesses, were to be cut down, the *maotik* or chief medicine man's representatives would probably interfere, and the *kiruogik* or people's representatives would call upon the offenders to desist. Land may not be alienated, but strangers may be given permission to squat, and in course of time they acquire squatters' rights.

Trees. Certain trees are owned by families and private individuals. The *mopet*[2] tree, for instance, the timber of which is much sought after for building purposes, is inherited from generation to generation. Trees which are situated in good positions, and are well shaped for the hanging of honey barrels, may be appropriated and marked as belonging to a family or person. Trees so marked are called *kuketuet.*

Next to the *mopet* tree, the *tepengwet*[3] is mostly used for building huts and cattle-kraals. The timber which is most appreciated for burning is cut from the following trees: *Emdit,*[4] *cheptuiyet, martit, tenduet, masomboriet, osenuit,* and *kimeliet.*

There are a few superstitious customs with regard to various trees. Some trees may not be used either for building huts or as firewood.[5] Such are *kipuimetyet, chepkererlong, chemusariot,*[6] *kakoluet, irokwet,* and *teldet.*[7] The last mentioned, a fine shady tree, is always left standing for the *kápkiruog* or old men's council place. No Nandi may strike anybody with a stick of the *chesagit* tree, and no cattle may be struck with a stick if the bark has been taken off it. A stick of the *legetetuet*[8] tree is generally fixed in the roof of huts as a charm against snakes, a branch of the *chemusariot*[9] tree is planted in the eleusine fields to keep away the locusts, and a few bunches of the *pêk-ap-tarīt*[10] tree are tied on to the hedges to drive off the birds.

[1] *Vide* pp. 63 and 45 sqq.   [2] *Dolichandrone platycalyx.*
[3] *Emilia integrifolia.*   [4] *Olea chrysophilla.*
[5] A tree that has been struck by lightning may also not be cut up for building purposes or for firewood.   [6] *Lippia sp.*
[7] *Ficus sp.*   [8] *Carissa edulis.*   [9] *Lippia sp.*   [10] *Lantana salvifolia.*

PLATE XXX

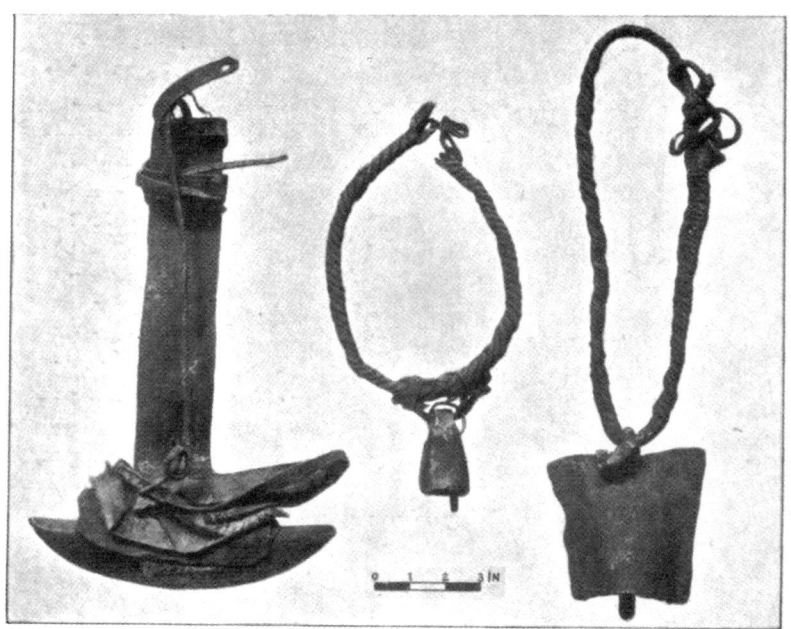

Nandi woman and child. The ornament which the child is wearing on its forehead shows that its next elder brother or sister is dead (Stordy).

Warriors' thigh bell.   Calves' bell.   Cows' bell.

To face p. 87

The bamboo, which is called *tekat*,[1] and a parasite called *simotuet*[2] are regarded almost as sacred. The former may only be used at the *kambakta* or warriors' dances, when a stick is planted in the ground, and for making the old men's divining boxes; from the latter, cord only may be made, with which the warriors bind their pigtails. Wood from both the *tekat* and *simotuet* are at times thrown on sacred fires.

If a tree is lopped, the central branch must always be left standing. Though the Nandi dislike felling trees,[3] they have no objection to cutting off the branches.

Amulets and Charms, Rings, &c. The *orkoiyot*, or chief medicine man, gives amulets called *pusaruk* to barren women to make them fruitful. They are made of wood ash and are wrapped in pieces of skin and worn on the breast. He also gives warriors a concoction, called *setanik*, when they go to the wars, to protect them against the weapons of their enemies.

Rings made of pieces of bullock, sheep, or goat's hide are worn as amulets at certain times, *e. g.* at the *saket-ap-eito* ceremony, at marriages, and when cattle sicken.[4]

A small piece of the *ikomiot* tree is worn by travellers to guard against snake bites, and a strip of lion-skin is attached by warriors to their belts to ward off the attacks of wild beasts. Charms to keep locusts and birds out of the cornfields, and snakes out of houses, are made from the *chemusariot*, *pêk-ap-tarīt*, and *legetetuet* trees respectively[5]; and a porcupine quill is frequently stuck into the roofs of houses to drive away vermin.

When a person's next elder brother or sister dies, it is customary to wear a certain ornament to prevent the disease from attacking the next member of the family; and a necklace of *lapuonik* berries is at times worn by children and calves to protect them from the power of the evil eye.[6]

Bells. The Nandi have four kinds of bells, two of which (one large and one small) are worn by warriors on their legs. They are oblong in shape and made of iron, and the clappers are round like bullets. The other bells are worn by oxen, calves, and goats. They are nearly round in shape and closely resemble those seen in Switzerland. The case is called *kôket* (the female); the clapper, which is attached to the top of the bell, is known as *kirkit* (the male).

[1] *Arundinaria alpina.* [2] *Ficus sp.* near *F. elegans.*
[3] *Vide* also pp. 19 and 80. [4] *Vide* pp. 12, 63, and 46. [5] *Vide* p. 86.
[6] For further particulars see pp. 29 and 90.

The large warriors' bells are worn by girls during the circumcision festivities: calves' bells are worn by young women after the *rīkset* ceremony at circumcisions, and at weddings.

Arithmetic. The Nandi formerly only counted up to fifty, any number above this figure being styled *pokol*. Of late, however, they have introduced numbers for sixty, seventy, &c., which they express by saying six tens, seven tens, and so on, and *pokol* is now generally used for one hundred. Large numbers which cannot be counted are rendered by *pokol-pokol, pokolaiik che-chañg* (many hundreds) or *pokol che-mo-ki-rar-e* (hundred which cannot be counted). Eleven is styled ten and one, twelve is ten and two, and so on up to twenty; twenty-one is twenty and one.

Counting is done on the fingers, beginning with the little finger on the left hand and working up to the thumb, then continuing in the same order on the right hand.[1] There are various signs to denote the numerals, which are similar to those used by the Masai. They are as follows:—

1 (*akenge*). The first finger of the right hand is held up and the rest of the fist closed. The hand must be kept still.

2 (*aeñg* or *oieñg*). The outstretched first and second fingers are rubbed rapidly one against the other.

3 (*somok*). The first finger is rested on the thumb and the first joint of the middle finger is placed against the side of the middle joint of the first finger, the other two fingers remaining closed.

4 (*añgwan*). The fingers are outstretched, the first and middle ones being crossed.

5 (*mut*). The fist is closed, with the thumb placed between the first and second fingers.

6 (*įllo* or *kullo*). The nail of one of the fingers—generally the ring finger—is clicked three or four times by the thumb nail.

7 (*tisap*). The tip of the thumb is rubbed rapidly against the tip of one of the fingers—generally the middle finger—the hand remaining open.

8 (*sisiit*). The hand is opened and the fingers are either all pressed together or all kept apart. A rapid movement with the hand in this position is then performed, first in a downward and then in an upward direction. This movement is made by the hand only, the wrist acting as lever.

9 (*sokol*). The first finger is bent so that the tip touches the tip of the thumb, the other fingers being at the same time opened.

[1] The Lumbwa continue to count on their toes, but this method of counting is unknown in Nandi.

PLATE XXXI

Parparek. Stones used by medicine men for divining purposes.

Soiyet and Ketet. Divining boxes.

MISCELLANEOUS CUSTOMS 89

10 (*taman*). The closed fist is thrown out and opened, the nail of the middle finger being at the same time clicked against the tip of the thumb.

20 (*tiptem*). The open fist is closed and opened two or three times.

30 (*sosom* or *tomonuagik somok*). The fingers are placed in the same position as when representing 1, *i.e.* the first finger is held up while the rest of the hand is closed. When in this position the hand is shaken slightly from the wrist.

40 (*artam* or *tomonuagik añgwan*). The hand is opened, and the first and middle fingers are pressed together, as are also the ring and little fingers, a gap thus existing between the middle and ring fingers. When in this position the hand is shaken.

50 (*konom* or *tomonuagik mut*). The tip of the thumb is placed between the ends of the first and middle fingers. The other fingers can be opened or closed at the same time.

60. For *pokol*, that is to say anything above fifty, the closed fist is jerked out from the body, the fingers being at the same time opened.

People may not be counted as it is supposed that they will die, but there is no harm in counting cattle.

If it is desired to keep a record of days, or of anything else, knots are tied in a piece of cord, or a stick is notched.

The medicine men divine by counting pebbles. Lucky numbers are 2, 3, 5, 8, and 10, 3 and 5 particularly so; unlucky numbers are 1, 4, 6, 7, and 9. 1 is the most unlucky number and 4 the least so. The counting is generally commenced at 20, *i.e.* after four groups of five stones each have been arranged on the ground.

Knots. There are a few superstitions about the making and loosing of knots. When warriors depart on an expedition their mothers tie four knots in their belts, and every day when their fathers meet together to drink beer they pray to God to tie knots for their children (*i.e.* to guard them).

If a person borrows a cow or a goat, he plucks four blades of grass and hands them to the owner, who ties them in a knot in his garment to ensure the loan being returned. On the arrival of the goats from the grazing ground the knot in the garment is untied and the blades of grass placed on the ground so that the goats can tread on them.

Should a relation of a sick person proceed to a medicine man to procure medicine, he plucks four blades of grass and ties them in a knot in his garment. When he loosens the knot, the medicine man is able to divine what sickness he has to treat.

A traveller, when starting on a journey, ties a knot in some grass by the way-side, as he believes that by so doing he will prevent the people he is going to visit from having their meal until he arrives, or at any rate he will ensure there being sufficient food left over for him. When a woman or a cow is about to bear, everybody near at hand ties a half-bow knot in his or her garment and pulls it rapidly undone when the labour pains commence. This is said to facilitate delivery.

The Evil Eye. The Nandi believe that certain persons have the power of causing children and calves to fall ill, and pregnant women and cows to abort, when they regard them. Such persons are called *sakutik*, and whenever a man or woman has the reputation of being possessed of the evil eye, he or she must spit if they see a person or animal approaching them who might be harmed by contact with them. Children and calves who are supposed to be particularly susceptible to the powers of the *sakutik* wear a necklace of seeds called *lapuonik*.

Young people may never look their elders in the face. This has nothing to do with the evil eye, but is considered disrespectful. Old people say that they can always tell when a person has committed a crime by the look in his eyes.

Snakes. Under ordinary circumstances a snake is killed at sight. A snake is also killed if it enters a house, and a hole has to be made in the wall in order to eject the body, as it may not be thrown out of the door. But if a snake goes on to the woman's bed, it may not be killed, as it is believed that it personifies the spirit of a deceased ancestor or relation, and that it has been sent to intimate to the woman that her next child will be born safely. Milk is put on the ground for it to drink, and the man or his wife says: *Ingi-moch-e kurat, i-nyo ki-kur-in* (If thou wantest the call, come, thou art being called). It is then allowed to leave the house.

If a snake enters the houses of old people they give it milk, and say: *Ingi-moch-e kurat, i-we karik-ap-lakōk* (If thou wantest the call, go to the huts of the children), and they drive it away.

Salutations. When two men meet, the elder says, *Sopai*, and the younger replies, *Epa*: when two women meet, the elder says, *Takwenya*, and the other replies, *Igo*.[1] Old men greet warriors by saying, *Sopai, murēn-ju* (Sopai, O warriors), and they greet women by saying, *Takwenya, chepiosó-chu*, or *Takwenya, kwanyí-chu* (Takwenya, O women, *or* Takwenya, O wives). After the usual reply, the old men

[1] These expressions are meaningless in Nandi, but *Takwenia* is equivalent to 'Laugh' (imp.) in Masai, and *Īgó* to 'Go away' (imp.) in Bari.

PLATE XXXII

Nandi boy wearing the kipalpaliot ear-rings, lapuonik necklace, and the seeds of the murguyuet tree in his hair (Henderson).

Nandi women carrying their children (Stordy).

To face p. 90

shake warriors by the hand, and say to women, *Cham-ke sapon, cham-ke lakōk, cham-ke tuka, cham-ke ka* (May your health be good, and may the children, cattle, and all at home be well). When old women meet warriors they say, *Takwenya, murên-ju* (Takwenya, O warriors), and the warriors reply, *Igo*. Women and big girls say *Sopai* to small boys, and warriors and big boys say *Takwenya* to small girls. Brothers and sisters greet one another with *Takwenya*. Old men and warriors say *Sopai* to quite small children, and if they are too young to reply themselves, the mother replies for them. Young children embrace adults by hugging their legs, and old people take children by the hand and kiss them several times on the face.

If a man may have sexual intercourse with a woman, he may not say anything to her when he meets her. Thus a husband does not salute his wife, nor does he even ask after her health or after anything else when he returns from a journey, and warriors take girls by the hand when they meet, but they do not speak.

The parting salutation is, *A-'kot-in* (I salute thee), or *Saiseri* (Goodbye). The reply is, *A-'kot-in ok inye* (I salute also thee), or *Saiseri*. An old man having said *Saiseri* frequently adds, *A-'kot-ok tuka ak piik* (I salute you, cattle and people).

Ceremonial uncleanness or tabu. Ceremonial uncleanness or tabu, which has been frequently alluded to above, may be said to resemble our idea of pollution, though at times it might be defined as being equivalent to sacredness, *e.g.* the prohibition to touch the chief medicine man's head and to fell certain trees.

There are three names for persons who are regarded as ceremonially unclean, *ñgwonik, kerek,* and *simwek*. To the first belong the mothers of twins and the murderers of their own clansmen. These people are *ñgwonin, i.e.* bitter or unclean for the rest of their lives. Others who come temporarily in this category are the *tarusiek*, or boys and girls recently circumcised, when they do anything they should not do, such as talking loudly, falling down, spitting on the ground, &c.,[1] or when an earthquake occurs, or their *menjet* huts catch fire; a child who imitates a hyena's cry; a person who defaecates in a house; a girl whose sweetheart dies; a bride who stumbles when on the way to her future husband's house; and people who fall when carrying a corpse. The mode of lustration employed in these cases is to kill a goat and to rub some of the offal on the person's face and legs.

To the *kerek* belong all *tarusiek* (*i.e.* people circumcised a short

[1] *Vide* pp. 56 and 60.

while before), until the *nyorkit* garb and the *kimaranguchet* or *soiyuot* head-dresses have been discarded, and all women after the birth of a child until the child is weaned. When boys are circumcised they may not eat with their hands until the *lapat-ap-ēun* ceremony has been held, after which they may use their hands provided they wash before eating. Girls must first of all eat with the help of a half-calabash, and, after the *lapat-ap-ēun* ceremony, with a spoon. No *tarusiot* may be shaved, and, as already stated, they must be retiring in their behaviour, they must not talk loudly or approach people, cattle, grain, or fire, and they may not do various other things which are enumerated on pages 56 and 60.

For one month after the birth of a child, a woman may not touch food with her hands, and her house must be washed out daily with water and cow-dung. At the end of this period until her child is weaned she must proceed to a river every morning and wash her hands and arms. During this time, too, she may not touch any part of her body with her hands except at night-time, and even if she wishes to scratch herself she must do so with a stick.

People are said to be dirty (*simwek*) when they have had sexual intercourse, during menstruation, and after involuntary seminal emission; when they have killed an enemy; when they have made poison, or eaten the flesh of an animal killed by a poisoned arrow, or by lightning; when they have eaten an animal that has died of disease; after eating locusts; when they have touched a corpse; and when they have been defeated in war. They must purify themselves by bathing in a river, and in some cases by taking a purge.

RELATIONSHIP.

The principal terms of relationship are given in the following list :—

	When spoken of indirectly.	When addressed directly.
Father	*kwanda* or *kwanit*	(boy) *papa*, (man) *apoiyo*, (girl *or* woman) *pakwa*.
Mother	*kamet* or *kametit*	(boy, girl *or* woman) *eiyo*, (man) *korket*.
Brother	*tupchet* or *ñget-ap-kamet*	(boy *or* man) by name, (girl *or* woman) *tete* or by name.
Sister	*tupchet* or *chep-kamet*	(boy *or* man) *tete* or *lakwán-ni*, (girl *or* woman) by name.
Husband	*manoñgotiot*	*manoñgotiondón-ni*, *murenón-ni* or *poiyondón-ni*.
2nd husband [1]	*kipkondiit*	

[1] *I. e.* husband's brother after husband's decease (*vide* p. 72).

RELATIONSHIP

	When spoken of indirectly.	When addressed directly.
Wife	*kwando* [1]	*kaita.*
Co-wife	*siyet*	*siyén-nyō.*
Son	*lakwet*	*lakwán-ni, weir-i* or *apoiyo.*
Daughter	*lakwet*	*lakwán-ni.*
Father's father	*inguget*	*agwi* or *kuko.*
Father's mother	*ingoget*	*koko.*
Mother's father	*inguget*	*agwi* or *kuko.*
Mother's mother	*ingoget*	*koko.*
Father's brother	*ne-tupche-ap-papa* ⎫	(boy) *papa,* (man) *apoiyo,*
Father's elder brother	*kwanda ne-oo* ⎬	(girl or woman) *pakwa.*
Father's younger brother	*kwanda ne-mining* ⎭	
Father's sister	*senget*	*senge.*
Mother's brother	*imamet*	*mama.*
Mother's sister	*kamet* or *kametit*	(boy, girl or woman) *eiyo,* (man) *korket.*
Father's brother's wife	*kamet* or *kametit*	(boy, girl or woman) *eiyo,* (man) *korket.*
Father's sister's husband	*sandit*	*sandanaa.*
Mother's brother's wife	*imamet*	*mama.*
Mother's sister's husband	*kwanda* or *kwanit*	(boy) *papa,* (man) *apoiyo,* (girl or woman) *pakwa.*
Father's brother's son	*tupchet*	(boy or man) *ar-'t-'apa* or by name, (girl or woman) *tete* or by name.
Father's brother's daughter	*tupchet*	(boy or man) *tete,* (girl or woman) by name.
Father's sister's son	*weirit-ap-chepto*	*mama.*
Father's sister's daughter	*lakwet-ap-chepto* or *lakwet-ap-taptel*	*mama.*
Mother's brother's son	*imamet*	*mama.*
Mother's brother's daughter	*kamet* or *kametit*	(boy, girl or woman) *eiyo,* (man) *korket.*
Mother's sister's son	*tupchet*	(boy or man) by name, (girl or woman) *tete.*
Mother's sister's daughter	*tupchet*	(boy or man) *tete,* (girl or woman) by name.
Grandson ⎫ Granddaughter ⎬	*machokoret*	*machokorón-ni.*
Wife's father	*káp-yukoiit*	*apoiyo.*
Wife's mother	*karukinit*	*karucho.*
Wife's brother	*káp-yukoiit*	*apoiyo.*
Wife's sister	*pamurto*	*pamuru.*
Wife's sister's husband	*lemenyit*	*lemény-i.*
Husband's father	*pamoñget*	*pamoñgo.*
Husband's mother	*pókirto*	*pókir.*
Husband's brother	*pamurto*	*pamuru.*
Husband's sister	*kamatit*	*kamát-i.*
Husband's brother's wife	*pokinit*	*pokin-i.*
Son's wife	*lakwet*	(man) *lakwán-ni,* (woman) *pókir.*
Daughter's husband	*sandit*	*sandanaa.*
Sister's husband	*sandit*	*sandanaa.*
Brother's wife	*pamurto*	*pamuru.*
Sister's son	*lakwet*	*lakwán-ni* or *mama.*
Sister's daughter	*lakwet-ap-taptel*	*lakwán-ni* or *mama.*
Brother's son or daughter	*lakwet*	*lakwán-ni.*

[1] Senior wife is called *kwando ne-oo,* junior wife *kwando ne-mining.*

The eldest child of a family is known to the members of the family as *kiporetit* or *taeta*, the youngest as *toet*, and all the intervening ones as *chep-kwen*.

There are no special terms for step-mother, step-son, half-brother, half-sister, &c., and such persons are called by the same appellation as mother, son, brother, sister, &c. Second-cousins, like cousins, are called brothers; more distant cousins are styled *piik-ap-oret* (people of the family).

The maternal uncle plays an important part in the existence of every Nandi. An understanding exists between a boy and his maternal uncle which is not met with between other relations, and the maternal uncle is appealed to for intervention when a boy is in disgrace. No circumcision ceremony can be performed until a maternal uncle or his representative has given his sanction, and the maternal uncle is consulted before a boy's teeth are extracted or the lobes of his ears are pierced. It is always usual for warriors to give their maternal uncles a cow after a raid in return for the kindness shown them as children. The most terrible thing that can happen to a Nandi is to displease his maternal uncle. If such an event occurs, the uncle formally curses his nephew. He does this by scratching his shin till the blood flows, when he rubs in ashes, and says: *Lakwet-ap-lakwén-nyo ! Am-in koroti-chu, amu ki-ki-sich komit si ko-sich-in* (The child of our child! May this blood eat thee, for we gave life to thy mother that she might bear thee). It is believed that the nephew will surely die in a few days if he has been thus cursed, unless he can persuade his uncle to remove the curse by giving him some cattle.

DIVISIONS OF TIME.

The year (*kenyīt*) is divided into two seasons (*olto*, pl. *oltōsiek*), and twelve months or moons (*arawet*, pl. *arawek*). The seasons are from March to August and from September to February. The former, the wet season, is called *olt'-ap-iwot* or *iwotet*; the latter, the dry season, *olt'-ap-keme* or *keméut*. The names of the months are as follows:—

1st month. *Kiptamo*, meaning 'hot in the fields' (February).
2nd month. *Iwat-kut*, meaning 'rain in showers' (March).
3rd month. *Wake*, meaning unknown (April).

Group of Nandi with goats and sheep (Meinertzhagen).

DIVISIONS OF TIME 95

4th month. *Ñgei*, meaning 'heart pushed on one side by hunger' (May).
5th month. *Rob-tui*, meaning 'black rain or black clouds' (June).
6th month. *Puret*, meaning 'mist' (July).
7th month. *Epeso*, meaning unknown (August).
8th month. *Kipsunde*, meaning 'offering to God in the corn fields' (September).
9th month. *Kipsunde oieñg*, meaning 'second offering to God' (October).
10th month. *Mulkul*, meaning 'strong wind' (November).
11th month. *Mulkulik oieñg*, meaning 'second strong wind' (December).
12th month. *Ñgotioto*, meaning 'the *Brunsvigia Kirkii* or pincushion plant' (January).

There are no special names for the days of the week or for the weeks, but the following days and periods are described by the phases of the moon :—

1st day. *Ke-'ro kutik arawet*, the tanners have seen the moon.
2nd day. *Ko-lēl arawet*, the moon is white or new.
3rd and 4th days. *Ke-'kweny arawet*, the moon has cast a light.
5th and 6th days. *Ka-lalañgit arawet*, the moon has become warm.
7th and 8th days. *Ka-paraït arawet*, the moon has leisure.
9th and 10th days. *Ko-tien-e mistōek arawet*, the herdsmen play in the light of the moon.
11th and 12th days. *Ko-imen-ji parak arawet*, the moon is high in the evening.
13th day. *Ko-wek arawet*, the moon turns.
14th day. *Ke-'omis-chi nêko ka arawet*, the moon has accompanied the goats to the kraal.
15th day. *Ke-'omis-chi tuka ka arawet*, the moon has accompanied the cattle to the kraal.
16th day (full moon). *Ke-'chut-ke arawet*, the moon has passed along (the heavens).
17th day (morning). *Ka-och tarītik arawet*, the birds have driven away the moon.
„ (evening). *Ke-'lingan arawet*, the moon has disappeared for a short while.
18th day. *Ka-koi-ek-chi arawet*, the moon has commenced to rise late.
19th to 21st days. *Koi-ek-chi arawet*, the moon is late.

22nd day. *Ka-tokos arawet*, the moon has climbed up.
23rd to 25th days. *Koi-ek-chi parak arawet*, the moon is late up above.
26th and 27th days. *Ka-wek arawet*, the moon has turned, *i.e.* goes towards the west.
28th day. *Ka-rik-ta myat arawet*, the moon is nearing death.
29th day. *Ok tii-yo arawet*, and they discuss the moon (whether she is dead); *Ka-par Asista arawet*, the sun has murdered the moon.
30th day. *Ka-me arawet*, the moon is dead; *Mesundeit'-ap-arawet*, the moon's darkness.

The day is divided as follows:—
Kaech, from 5 a.m. to 6 a.m.
Korirun, from 6 a.m. to 9 a.m.
Pēt, from 9 a.m. to 2 p.m.
Koskoling, from 2 p.m. to 6 p.m.
Karap or *koimen*, from 6 p.m. to 7 p.m.
Kemboi or *lakat*, night.

The different hours of the day and night also have special terms to describe them.

2 a.m. *Ka-pa pele' pei*, the elephants have gone to the waters.
3 a.m. *Ke-'soi-yo pei*, the waters roar.
4 a.m. *Ke-'rir kiet*, the land (sky) has become light.
5 a.m. *Ka-ki-yat-at korik*, the houses are opened.
5.30 a.m. *Ka-pa tich līmo*, the oxen have gone to the grazing ground.
6 a.m. *Ka-ki-yat kechīr*, the sheep have been unfastened.
6.30 a.m. *Ka-chor asis*, the sun has grown.
7 a.m. *Ka-lalañg-it*, it has become warm.
7.30 a.m. *Ka-pa nêko līmo*, the goats have gone to the grazing ground.
9 a.m. *Ka-rot nêko eñg-līmo*, the goats have returned from the grazing ground.
9.30 a.m. *Ru-itos nêko ka*, the goats sleep in the kraal.
10 a.m. { *Ko-ñgêt-io nêko*, the goats have arisen.
{ *Ka-rot tuka*, the oxen have returned.
10.30 a.m. *Ru-itos tuka*, the oxen sleep.
11 a.m. { *O-'tiok-chi tuka*, untie the cattle, *i.e.* let the calves get their food.
{ *Ake-tos nêko*, the goats feed.

DIVISIONS OF TIME

11.30 a.m. *Ko-ñgêt-io tuka,* the oxen have arisen.

12 a.m. { *Ka-tonun asis* or *ka-telel asis,* the sun has stood upright.
Ka-ru-iot nêko eñg-dim-in, the goats sleep in the (*or* that) wood.

12.30 p.m. *Ka-'e nêko pêk,* the goats have drunk water.

1 p.m. { *Ka-wek asis,* the sun turns, *i. e.* goes towards the west.
Ka-'e tuka pêk, the cattle have drunk water.

1.30 p.m. *Ke-'te-io chepkopiren,* the drones hum.

2 p.m. { *Ka-sen-ge asis,* the sun continues to go towards the west.
Ake-tos tuka, the oxen feed.

3 p.m. *Ka-ision nêko,* the goats have been collected.

4 p.m. { *Ka-nyil tuka pêk,* the oxen drink water for the second time.
Ka-rot nêko, the goats have returned.

4.30 p.m. *Ru-itos nêko,* the goats sleep.

5 p.m. { *Ka-ki-iun-ech päk,* the eleusine grain has been cleaned for us.
O-kwe nêko, take the goats home.
O-ker moiek, shut up the calves.

5.30 p.m. *Ke-'kesi-ke nêko ka,* the goats have entered the kraal.

6 p.m. { *Ka-rarok-te asis,* the sun is finished.
Ka-rot tuka, the cattle have returned.

6.15 p.m. *O-ke cheko,* milk (the cows).

6.45 p.m. { *Ma-ki-'nyit chii ak ket,* neither man nor tree is recognizable.
A-ki-ker ormarichōk, the cattle-fold doors have been closed.

7 p.m. *Ka-rat-arat,* the heavens are fastened.

8 p.m. *A-ki-tar-at kimoi,* the porridge is finished.

9 p.m. *Ru amba-che,* those who have drunk milk are asleep.

10 p.m. *A-ki-ker-at korin,* the houses have been closed.

11 p.m. *A-ki-'o-chi,* those who went to sleep early wake up.

12 p.m. *Kemboi kwen,* the middle of the night.

MYTHS.

Sky and Earth, Sun and Moon. In the Nandi natural philosophy all things are supposed to have been created by the union of the sky and earth. When the sun, who married the moon, proceeded to the earth one day to arrange about the creation, or to prepare the present condition of things, he found there the thunder, a Dorobo,[1] and an elephant, all living together. The thunder became afraid of the Dorobo

[1] *Vide* p. 2.

because he was able to turn over in his sleep without waking or getting up, so he decided to leave the earth and go and live in the sky. The elephant refused to accompany him, and was shot by the Dorobo, who thus became lord of the earth.[1]

The sun is said to enter his scabbard at night-time, and to return to his home in the east by a different route to that which he traverses during the day. The moon is supposed to fall when she disappears and also to return home by a different road. When there is no moon people say that the sun has killed his wife, but the old men know that he has only beaten her, and that she has gone to hide by the river for a couple of days, at the end of which time he will go and fetch her home.

The origin of man. Amongst the Moi clan there is a tradition that the first Dorobo gave birth to a boy and a girl. His leg swelled up one day and became pregnant. At length it burst and a boy issued from the inner side of his calf, whilst a girl issued from the outer side. These two in course of time had children, who were the ancestors of all the people upon earth.

The origin of death. When the first people lived upon the earth a dog came to them one day and said : 'All people will die like the moon, but unlike the moon you will not return to life again unless you give me some milk to drink out of your gourd and beer to drink through your straw. If you do this, I will arrange for you to go to the river when you die and to come to life again on the third day.' The people, however, laughed at the dog, and gave him some milk and beer to drink off a stool.[2] The dog was angry at not being served in the same vessels as a human being, and although he drank the milk and beer he went away saying : 'All people will die, and the moon alone will return to life.' This is how it is that when people die they remain away, whilst when the moon dies she reappears after three days' absence.

The origin of cattle, goats, and sheep. Cattle, goats, and sheep are said to have come out of a great lake. There lived in olden days a person of importance who on one occasion went to the lake and struck the water eight times with a long stick. Cattle, goats, and sheep issued from the water in large numbers, and everybody was able to take away as many as he required and put them in cattle-kraals.

[1] For a fuller account *vide* pp. 111-13.
[2] Milk and water mixed with salt are poured on a stool and used during the boys' circumcision festival (*vide* p. 53).

Nandi elder with his goats and sheep (Meinertzhagen).

The origin of circumcision. The first man who practised circumcision in Nandi is said to have been one Kipkenyo, who came from a country called Do, and who, after staying on the hills called Tuluet-ap-Seike and Tuluet-ap-Rir, passed through the Añgata nanyokie, and settled in the Kakipoch division of Nandi. In those days Nandi was known as *Chemñgal*, a name which is still used by the Elgeyo and other allied tribes when referring to the Nandi country and people.

The story goes that Kipkenyo had a number of brothers and sisters who all died when they reached puberty, so Kipkenyo decided when he had a number of children of his own to 'change' them all at this age. He therefore circumcised them, and as none of his children died, the Nandi followed his example, with the result that circumcision became general.

Thunder and lightning. There is a good and a bad thunder-god (*Ilet ne-mie* and *Ilet ne-ya*). The crashing of thunder near at hand is said to be the bad *Ilet* trying to come to earth to kill people, whilst the distant rumbling is the good *Ilet*, who is protecting them and driving away his namesake. Forked and sheet lightning are said to be the swords of the bad and good *Ilet* respectively. Whenever forked lightning is seen, all Nandi women look on the ground, as it is considered wrong that they should witness the work of devastation which the sun or God (*Asista*) is allowing to take place. During a thunderstorm it is usual to throw some tobacco on the fire, and the youngest child of a family has to put a *sosiot*, or stick used for cleaning gourds, in the ashes of the fire, and then throw it outside the hut. The members of the Toiyoi clan throw out of doors an axe which has been rubbed in the ashes, and exclaim at the same time: *Toiyoi, sis kain-nyo* (Toiyoi, *or* thunder, be silent in our kraal). If cattle have been struck by lightning, some of the Toiyoi clan are called to turn them over on the other side to which they have fallen, after which any grown-up man or woman may go to the place, cut off a piece of meat, and roast and eat it on the spot. They may not converse, and after the meal the bones must be put in a heap so that they can be burnt. They must then proceed to the nearest river and bathe before returning home. The ceremony of burning the bones is performed by people from Kamasia. The spot must afterwards be covered with thorns and stones, so that it cannot be trodden on by man or beast. When a hut has been struck by lightning a person of the Toiyoi clan is called in to burn it down.

Earthquake. When an earthquake is felt, it is said that spirits or devils (*oiik*) are moving from one place to another underground. *Ka-u oi* (Spirits are moving their abode), the Nandi say, and no work may be performed for a whole day afterwards.

Waterfall, steam jets, and hornets' nests. The spray of a waterfall and steam jets (*mat-ap-oiik*) are supposed to be the smoke of the spirits' fires. Hornets' nests when built in the ground are called *konyek-ap-oiik*, and are believed to be the spirits' peep-holes.

The Hill Chepeloi. There is a sacred hill on the borders of western Nandi near Kâpwaren which is called *Che-pel-oi* (The hill which the spirits set fire to). It is believed that the spirits of the deceased set fire to the grass on this hill once every year, and no Nandi will go near the place.

Halo round the sun or moon. A halo round the sun or moon (*ormarichet*) is said to represent a cattle-stockade. A break in the halo is supposed to be a road. If the break is on the east side it is unlucky; if on the west side it is lucky.

Eclipse of the sun or moon. When there is an eclipse of the sun or moon it is said that the sun or moon has died (*Ka-mé Asista* or *Ka-me Arawet*). An eclipse is looked upon as an ill omen.

Comet. A comet (*cheptapisiet* or *kipsaruriet*) is regarded as the precursor of great misfortune. When one is seen, war, drought, famine, disease, and ruin may be expected as a result.

Rainbow. When a rainbow is seen, people know that the rain will soon stop. The outer circle is called *kwapaliet*, the inner circle *chemñgisiriet*. A rainbow is said to be the thunder-god's discarded garments.

Stars. The milky way is called the sea of stars (*Poit'-ap-kechei*). It is supposed to be a great lake in which children are bathing and playing. The Evening Star is known as the Dorobo's star (*Kipokiot*), as the wives of the Dorobo are aware, when it becomes visible, that their husbands will shortly return from the chase. The Morning Star is called *Tapoiyot*; the Midnight Star, *Kokeliet*; and Orion's belt and sword, *Kakipsomok*. The Pleiades are known as *Koremerik*, and it is by the appearance or non-appearance of these stars that the Nandi know whether they may expect a good or a bad harvest.

Dew. Dew is said to be the stars which have fallen on the earth.

PLATE XXXV

Waterfall in Nandi (Meinertzhagen).

FOLK-TALES

THE STORY OF THE HARE AND THE ELEPHANT.

A hare and an elephant were once great friends and always went for walks together. One day they saw a bull and a cow that had wandered away from the rest of the herd, so they took possession of them, the hare taking the bull and the elephant the cow. After a time the cow had a calf. When the hare saw this he said: 'Why should the elephant have two animals, whilst I have only one? I will take the calf.' He did so, and the elephant pretended not to notice what had happened. In the course of time the cow gave birth to twins. 'This is too bad,' said the hare, 'the elephant's animal has had three calves whilst mine has had none. I must take these two calves as well.' Whilst he was driving off the calves, the elephant saw him and said: 'Hi, friend, what are you doing with my calves? You took the first one, and I said nothing, but I cannot let you take these too.' The hare replied: 'It is all right, I am only going to drive them down to the cave, where we can go and discuss the matter. You bring your cow and I will slaughter my bull so that we can have some food, and I will take the first calf with me as well.' The elephant brought his cow which, together with the calves, was driven into the cave. The bull was then slaughtered and the meat passed down, after which the hare entered. When, however, the elephant tried to follow, he found he was too big. The hare laughed at him, and said: 'Go some distance back and run against the stone with your head, so as to break open the entrance. The elephant did as he was bid, but he made no impression on the stone. The hare then called to him to go back further, and so get a good run in order to enable him to strike the stone harder. The elephant again butted the stone, but instead of damaging it, he dashed out his brains. The hare then ate his meat alone, and became possessed of the cow and calves.

THE STORY OF THE HARE WHO ACTED AS NURSE.

A hare once went to a woman who had a small child, and said: 'I want to be engaged as nurse.' The woman had nobody to help her in her household duties, so agreed to engage the hare, and gave it her child to look after, whilst she went about her other work.

The next day the woman's husband slaughtered a goat, and his wife took the meat in order to cook it. Having put the meat in a cooking-pot on the fire, she went out, leaving the hare in charge of the baby. As the baby slept, the hare soon became tired of sitting still, so he went to the cooking-pot and tasted the meat. Finding it very good he took it all and ate it. He then slept for a short while, and when he awoke he said to himself: 'What will the good woman say when she finds her meat gone?' He was uncertain what to do for some time, but at last he decided to put the baby into the pot in the place of the meat. He took a knife and cut the baby into small pieces, as he had seen done with the goat, and dropped the pieces in the cooking pot. He then searched for a beetle, which he put into the mortar for crushing grain, and covered it with the goat's hide

The woman returned home shortly afterwards, and, hearing the beetle buzzing in the mortar, called to the hare to take up the child, as it was crying. The hare took the cover off the mortar and went away. In due course the husband returned home, and was given his meat to eat, after which the wife also ate. The woman then looked for the hare and the baby, but found they were gone, and they have not been seen since.

THE STORY OF THE HARE AND THE OLD WOMAN.

There once lived an old woman all by herself, and one day a hare went to her and said: 'Since you have no child, I want you to adopt me. You are old, and cannot go to the fields to dig. I will do this work for you, and you in return will give me my food.' The old woman was very glad to accept the hare's proposal, as she found digging a very laborious task. She therefore gave the hare a hoe, with which to till the soil, and some seed to sow, whilst she remained at home and prepared the daily meal.

Early each morning the hare left the old woman's hut and went to a place near to which some people were making a plantation, but he did no work and only slept all day. In the evening he rubbed a little wet mud on his hoe and returned to the old woman's hut, where he was given his food.

The old woman went once or twice with the hare to look at her plantation, and the hare showed her the cultivation near to which he went every day. When the crops had ripened, he took her to the field, and she commenced to gather some grain, whereupon the owner appeared and asked her what she was doing. 'I am cutting the crops which my child the hare has cultivated,' said the old woman. At this the owner laughed and told her that the hare had done no work at all, but had slept in the sun all day with his hoe beside him. The old woman then saw that the hare had deceived her, and decided to flog him when he returned home, but he had witnessed the scene between the old woman and the owner of the plantation, and he never went back to the house.

THE STORY OF THE HYENA'S PROPHECY.

Once upon a time a woman was about to bear, but as she suffered a great deal her husband went to seek the advice of a medicine man. While he was gone two hyenas arrived at the door of the hut and looked in. They then went away and on the road met another hyena, whom they informed that they had witnessed a woman giving birth to twins, one a boy and the other a girl. The third hyena said: 'Poor things, one will be killed by a buffalo and the other will die in childbirth.' The husband passed at this moment and heard what the hyenas were saying. He went on his way and when he reached his house he found that his wife was the mother of twins, one a boy and the other a girl. He guessed therefore that the hyenas had talked about his wife and children.

Some years passed and the children grew up and were circumcised, after which the girl was married. Not long afterwards, however, she died in childbirth. The father remembered what the hyenas had said, and took great care of his son.

One day when the two men were herding their cattle on the grazing grounds a buffalo suddenly appeared in their midst. The warrior wished to go and kill it, but his father, remembering the prophecy, forced him to remain behind, whilst he himself with a few friends went and slew the animal. The old man was very pleased when he saw the dead beast at his feet, and cried out: 'What now, O hyenas, I have defeated you.' But when his son went to look at the dead buffalo he tripped over a stone, and fell on the upturned horn, which pierced his body, and he died.

THE ORIGIN OF THE LEOPARD AND HYENA.

A lion once had two cubs, who, when out one day, saw some warriors in their war paint. 'Let us make ourselves beautiful like those men,' said one of the cubs, 'we will get some paint and decorate our bodies.' They procured some paint, and one of the cubs marked the other one by painting a number of black spots on his coat. When he had finished, the spotted cub began to paint his fellow, but at that moment they heard a cry of, 'A goat has been lost,' so the spotted cub threw the paint pot at his friend, and ran off to see if he could find the goat. The spotted cub became a leopard and the other one, whose coat was only partially painted, became a hyena.

THE STORY OF THE HYENAS AND THEIR MEDICINE MAN.

Once upon a time the hyenas all met together and decided to appoint a chief medicine man, who would be able to advise them in all matters concerning the welfare of their country, and who would divine future events and interpret omens and dreams. There was some discussion as to who should be invited to take up these important duties, and the choice eventually fell on the ground-hornbill.[1] A deputation was sent to him, and when he was informed what was required of him, he accepted. He thought it would be well to prophesy something at once, so he told the hyenas that there would be no more day, and that if they required light other than that afforded by the moon they would obtain it from his red gills. The hyenas rejoiced at this good news, and immediately set off to raid their enemy, man, who possessed a number of donkeys not very far off. They attacked the kraal in the middle of the night and killed several donkeys, which they proceeded to eat. Before they had satisfied their hunger, however, they were horrified to find that the sun was rising, just as it used to do before their medicine man told them there would be no more day. They at once saw that there was nothing left for them to do but to abandon their feast and make off as fast as they could. But there was one old hyena with them who had

---

[1] The ground-hornbill (*Bucorax caper*) is a large black bird with red gills and white markings on its wings.

difficulty in walking, so they buried him under a mound of donkeys' dung and then fled to the woods. They had scarcely left before the owner of the donkeys appeared on the scene, and when he saw what had happened he called together his friends, and decided to avenge himself on the raiders. Just as he was leaving he put his spear into the mound of donkeys' dung and stabbed the old hyena. He knew by this that it was the hyenas that had killed his donkeys during the night, so he followed their tracks to their lair in the woods, where he slew a large number of them. Those that escaped met together the same evening and decided to depose their chief medicine man and to elect someone else in his place. The choice this time fell on the francolin, who was duly elected, and who has ruled so wisely ever since that he has remained in power to the present day. If you listen in the fields in the evening you will hear him calling to the hyenas to come out and feed, and again in the morning, long before the other birds are up, he is there warning them that it is time to go home. The ground-hornbill, however, has never been forgiven, and whenever a hyena sees him he gives chase and drives him away.

THE STORY OF THE TAPKŌS BIRD AND THE CHILD.

Once upon a time a girl, who was in the fields weeding, was accosted by a tapkōs bird, who said to her : 'Why do you do so much hard work ? If you want food, I will give you whatever you require. Follow me.' The girl followed the bird, who showed her a granary full of eleusine grain, and told her to take as much as she wanted. The girl did so, and returned the next day, but she found the granary had disappeared. The bird, however, was there, and whistling 'Follow me' he flew away. For many weary miles the girl followed him, until she found herself in a great plain, where she lost him. She looked round to see where she was and found a very handsome young man standing beside her. 'I am the tapkōs bird,' he said, 'I want to marry you.' But the girl disbelieved him, and laughed, whereupon he changed again into the tapkōs bird. 'I cannot marry you now,' he said, 'because you disbelieved me. Follow me.' And he flew away again and led her back to her home, where he left her.

HOW THE MASAI WERE FIRST REPULSED BY THE NANDI.

At the time when the Masai occupied some of the Nandi grazing grounds there lived near the Masai kraals a Nandi woman with her two sons. One day this woman took off her clothes, tied grass round her body, and fastened bells to her arms and legs. She then went to the Masai kraals and danced like a mad woman. Everybody in the kraals laughed at her, and the warriors on the grazing grounds hearing the bells went to see what was the cause of the commotion. As soon as the cattle were left unprotected, the woman's sons dashed out of their hiding place and drove the animals off into the hills, where they were joined by friends and where the Masai warriors dared not pursue them. The woman at the same time slipped off the bells and made good her escape. This was the first check the Masai received at the hands of the Nandi, who eventually succeeded in driving them out of their lands.

THE STORY OF THE WARRIORS AND THE DEVIL.[1]

An old man once had two warrior sons who asked him to give them a bullock, as they wished to go to the woods to slaughter it. The father, however, refused, so the two men stole an animal and went to a neighbouring river where they killed it.

As the younger warrior went to draw water he saw a devil who said to him: 'If you draw water and find it is blood, pour it away; if you find it is water, take it, but do not look behind.' The warrior drew some water and found it was blood, so he poured it away. He then drew some more, and as it was water this time he took it. When he ran back to his brother, however, he forgot the words of the devil and looked behind him.

That night the devil came to where the brothers were sleeping and put out their fire, but as his mouth shone like a fire the warriors noticed no difference. Presently it became cold, and the elder brother

[1] This story, and the story entitled, *The demon who ate people, and the child*, are somewhat similar to the Masai stories given in *The Masai*, pp. 108 and 215. Other stories which are related by both the Nandi and the Masai are *Konyek and his father* and *The Dorobo and the giraffe* (*The Masai*, pp. 133 and 230).

awoke the younger one and told him to make up the fire. The latter took a stick and pushed it into the mouth of the devil, who seized and ate him and then went away. When the elder warrior found his brother had been eaten he followed up the devil and found him asleep. He promptly killed the devil and cut off his big toe, out of which the younger warrior emerged, as well as various kinds of animals.

THE STORY OF THE DEMON WHO ATE PEOPLE, AND THE CHILD.

There was once upon a time a demon who lived on people and cattle, and so rapacious was he that he ate all the inhabitants of one district, except one woman who hid herself in a pit with her baby boy.

The child was brought up in the pit, and when he was old enough to understand, his mother told him the story of the demon, and advised him not to go far from home. The boy made a bow and some arrows and went out daily to shoot birds and animals which he brought back to the pit. On each occasion he asked his mother whether he had shot the demon.

One day the boy lit a large fire and put some stones in the fire which became red hot. When the demon saw the fire he said to himself: 'How is this? I thought I had eaten everybody, yet there must be people living over yonder.' So he went to the spot to investigate. On his arrival, the boy said: 'Ah! you have come to eat us. Wait a little and I will give you the food I am cooking.' He then took the stones out of the fire and told the demon to open his mouth. He thrust the stones down the demon's throat and killed him. As the demon was dying he said: 'Cut off my little finger with grass and your cattle will be given back to you, cut off my thumb and you will get back your people.' The boy did as he was told, and all the people and cattle that had been eaten were restored to life.

The people returned with their cattle to their former homes, and after a consultation appointed the boy their chief.

HOW THE DOROBO DISCOVERED POISON.

There once lived a poor Dorobo woman, who, with her children, lived on the fruits of trees. When out searching for food one day she saw several dead birds under the *keliot* tree,[1] so she took them home, together with some of the fruit of the tree, and gave them to her children to eat. As all the children fell ill after their meal, the woman took a stick of the tree and rubbed some of the juice on an arrow, which she gave to a boy and told him to go and shoot an animal. The boy returned almost immediately with a duiker, which, although only slightly wounded, had died at once. The woman then tried putting some of the juice of the tree by a salt-lick, and had the satisfaction the next day of finding a dead buffalo near at hand. She at once told her friends of her discovery and became rich and greatly honoured amongst her people.

THE PHILOSOPHY OF THE DOROBO.

There was once upon a time a Dorobo who was a great hunter, and this Dorobo lived for many days happily with his wife and children. One day, however, he saw a very beautiful girl, and immediately fell in love with her. 'My wife is now becoming an old woman,' he said, 'I must try and marry this young girl.' But the girl would have nothing to say to the Dorobo, who became so love-sick that he gave up hunting and could only sit at home moping. His wife frequently asked him what ailed him, and prepared such delicacies as she was able to obtain for him, but he would take no notice of her, nor would he eat or drink. At last his wife advised him to go and see a medicine man, so he set forth, but on the way he said to himself: 'I will tell my wife that the medicine man advises me to make love to this beautiful girl, and that unless I do so I shall not recover.' He therefore waited a short while in the wood, and then returned home and told his wife the story he had invented. His wife not suspecting anything at once took all her ornaments and went to the girl and said to her: 'My husband is very sick, and the medicine man has advised him to see you, as you alone are able to cure him. Take these ornaments and go to our house, whilst I go elsewhere.' But the girl only laughed at her. So the woman returned home and brought her household utensils. 'Take these also,' she said, 'only cure my husband.' 'No,' replied the girl, 'I want your skins and your honey-pots and your husband's spear and bows and arrows. If you bring these and leave them with the other things, I will go and

[1] *Acocanthera schimperi.*

spend the night in your house.' The poor woman fetched all her own and her husband's possessions and gave them to the girl, after which she escorted the girl to her own house, showed her in, and went to sleep elsewhere. The husband, notwithstanding the great sacrifice which he and his wife had made, was overjoyed and made love to the girl. But the next morning, when he arose and went outside, he realized what a fool he had been. *Kerke, kerke* (They are all alike, they are all alike), he cried; *kororon alake ko-yaach alake, ta tun ko-kerke* (Some are beautiful and others are ugly, but presently they are all alike). And he became a wiser man and again took to hunting. In course of time, too, he was able to buy new utensils for the house and new ornaments for his wife, with whom he lived happily till the end of his life.

THE SAYINGS OF ANIMALS AND BIRDS.

Many animals and birds and a few insects are supposed to talk like human beings, when they emit sounds or call to one another. Some instances are given below.

When the lion growls he is supposed to be saying: *Sapon chii tin'der ko-oi mukulel* (The owner of a cooking-pot is lucky, he can cook his meat).[1]

The hyena howls: *Rip-u-a ñgô kot a-ker-to oret-i ?* (Who will guard my house for me in order to enable me to take to the road?).

The hare says: *Tak a-lal kiet ki-inyit chii tukul kereñg* (I hope the country will be set on fire so that everybody's footprints will be recognizable).

The wild cat mews: *A-oo, a-oo* (I am big, I am big).

The rat squeaks: *'Nge-pche kesuek* (Let us divide the grain), but when he is caught in a trap he cries: *Ip tukul* (Take it all).

The dog when beaten whines: *Nyil, nyil!* (Do it again, do it again!), and a Nandi consequently always strikes him a second time.

The dove and the green pigeon coo respectively: *Ile-chi Kipkut am-e lakwet teget, ile-chi ko-nyo tun* (Tell Kipkut [2] the child's breast is paining him, tell him to come soon); and *Weirit ak kwan nunanun, chepto ak kamet sakuren* (The boy and his father will rot, the girl and her mother will fly away).

The cock owl hoots: *Tip-chu, o-pwa o-ngephe sukus tukul* (*Venite,*

[1] The translations are not quite literal.
[2] Or, more commonly, *Chepkutkut*, the African pheasant.

puellae, eamus omnes ut mingamus). When the hen bird hears him, she hoots back: *Ke-'lé ne ? Kip-te-pirit tiñgwa* (*Quid aiebas ? Membrum tuum simile funi est*). The cock bird then replies: *Ke-'lé ne ? chep-te-kuset ipero* (*Quid aiebas ? Pudendum tuum simile congeriei foliorum nicotianae*).

There is a small bird that lives near the rivers, called *Kipkamoiyet*. This bird's great delight is to make fun of the herdsmen, and when the cows are driven to water, he starts whistling to them, after which he cries out: *Chaluogin mistōandón-ni. 'Ngo-'kochi tuka pinyiny mwo-chi ñgô chii chepo ?* (This herdsman is a bad man. Who will tell the owner that he has given the cattle some leeches ?). At other times he says: *O-char kechiriet ne-sero ak o-kaikai Cherob, chaluogin Cheserem* (Bleed the many-coloured sheep and give plenty of blood to Cherob,[1] for Cheserem[2] is bad). And then he sings as follows: *Lakwa ake tukul ko-nyoput pitorin Cheserem* (Let each child put his gourd to his mouth, for Cheserem is a person who eats meat and drinks milk at the same time). When a sheep is about to be slaughtered the *Kipkamoiyet* bird laughs and says: *Chati-'p-kechir kó ne ? meti-'p-pirech!* (What is the use of a leg of mutton ? It is not so good as the head of a soldier ant).

There is a small bird, called *Kokopkonyinyit*, that builds its nest on the ground. If you go near its nest, it cries out: *A-me-tiech metit* (Don't tread on my head), and then, when you go away, it laughs at you, and says: *Ka-a-chombil-in* (I have told thee a lie).

Another small bird, called *Chepkoropitiet*, asks when he sees you to be allowed to feed out of your hand: *Rubei, rubei* (Palm of the hand, palm of the hand), he chirps, and if you give him nothing he adds: *Suruch ko-roroch totegin a-ip-eki Chemeitoi. Tuch a-ma-pir-in gōn* (Pick up and let drop a few white ants, that I may take them to Chemeitoi. Cover them up, and thy father will not beat thee).

The guinea-fowl goes into the fields in February, and cries: *O-kol, o-kol, mi-i tokoch* (Plant, plant, there is luck in it). The Nandi know by this that the time has come when their planting operations should commence.[3]

The francolin calls to the hyenas in the evening: *Chur-u kiportot* (Come out, ye who defaecate), and in the morning he says to them: *Timdo sokor* (Hide in the woods).[4]

---

[1] Person's name, meaning *Born during the rains*.
[2] Person's name, meaning *Born in front of the house*.
[3] *Vide* p. 19.   [4] *Vide* also p. 105.

PLATE XXXVI

Group of Nandi warriors (Hart).

Drinking-place for cattle (Meinertzhagen).

FOLK-TALES

A small kind of partridge, known by the name of *Kokoptitiliat*, cries plaintively: *Chor-u koru ak tiomb'-a'-tororot*[1] (All women and birds steal).

When the ground-hornbills are out foraging, the hen bird is continually calling to her mate: *Iit, iit kuu choto* (Peep, peep, into those holes), whereupon the cock bird reassuringly replies: *Ka-a-'it, ka-a-'it, ma-mi-i kii* (I have looked, I have looked, there is nothing there).

A small lark, called *Chepkelembut*, always flies on ahead of his mate when they are looking for food, and if he sees some insects he sings to her: *Iro chu alak, Tapkello !* (Here are some more, Tapkello !).

A kind of sparrow, known as *Chemeremere*, who hops about in front of the houses when the grain is drying in the sun, chirps: *Chang, miach, kororon* (Here is plenty of food. It is good and looks nice).

The honey-bird calls out to the Nandi when they follow him to the bee-hives: *A-wech-e Terik* (I hate Nyangori).

Other small birds are the *Segeriewendet*, the *Chepololet*, and the *Kipwarere*, and their cries are respectively as follows: *O-wei-ke, o-ai etiet* (Return and make a bridge),[2] *A-sop-e koi engumesio* (I shall get well presently when I have had sexual intercourse), and *Tak ki-oi tak ki-rirun-ji* (I hope for something to cook, and I hope to put it forcibly into the cooking-pot).

Locusts chirp: *Te muren geny* (Our warriors are still there); and the tree lizard, who is supposed to attract lightning, sings after the sun has set: *Tak a-rot, ke-ke* (I hope I shall be able to drive the cattle home, so that we can milk them).

Tapand'-ap-emet.
The-beginning-of-the-earth.

Ki-añg-nya-nyo	Asista	kw-ai-ta	emet,
When-he-came	the-Sun ⎱ God ⎰	and-he-prepares	the-earth,
ko-'ro	tukuk	somok,	ko-'ro	īlet	ak
and-he-sees	the-things	three,	and-he-sees	the-thunder	and
pēliot	ak	Okiot.[3]	Ko-tepi	tukul	eñg-olt'
the-elephant	and	the-Dorobo.	And-they-stay	all	in-the-place
akenge.
one.

[1] For *tiond'-ap-tororot*, the animal of the heavens.
[2] If the people of Nyangori hear this bird when on the war-path, they return home.   [3] *Vide* p. 2.

112 THE NANDI

Ko-'le	īlet	petunak :	'Ne	chií-chi ?
And-he-says	the-thunder	one-day :	'What	the-man-this ?
Ingo'ngo-we-chi-ke	ine	ko-ru-e		ko-ma-ñgêt-e
If-he-turns-over-himself	he	and-he-sleeps		and-he-not-arises
ine ;	ingo'ngo-a-moch-e	a-we-i-ke	ane,	a-ñgêt
he ;	if-I-wish	and-I-turn-myself	I,	and-I-arise
korok.'				
first-of-all.'				

Ko-'le	pēliot :	'Akut ane,	ingo'ngo-a-moch-e
And-he-says	the-elephant :	'Even I,	if-I-wish
a-we-i-ke,	a-ñgêt	korok.'	
and-I-turn-myself,	and-I-arise	first-of-all.'	

Ko-'le	īlet :	'M-â-kony-e	ane	chií-chi ;
And-he-says	the-thunder :	'Not-I-venture	I	the-man-this ;
a-mwe	a-we	parak.'		
I-run-away	and-I-go	above.'		

Ko-rori	pēliot,	ko-'le :	'I-mwé
And-he-laughs	the-elephant,	and-he-says :	'Thou-runnest-away
ne ?	Mining	chií-chi.'	
what ?	He-is-small	the-man-this.'	

Ko-'le īlet : 'Ya chií-chi. Añg-nya-ru-e,
And-he-says the-thunder: 'He-is-bad the-man-this. When-he-sleeps,
ko-we-chi-ke.'
and-he-turns-over-himself.'

| Kwa | īlet | parak, | ko-tepi | oñg-ni. |
| And-he-goes | the-thunder | above, | and-he-stays | until-now. |

Ko-'le	chiito :	'Ka-kwa	īlet
And-he-says	the-man :	'He-has-gone-away	the-thunder
ni-ki-a-'yue-i ;	m-â-'yue-i	pēliot.'	
whom-I-was-fearing ;	not-I-fear	the-elephant.'	

Kwa	timdo	ip-kw-ai-ta	ñgwanet,
And-he-goes	the-wood	go-and-he-makes ⎫	the-poison,
		and-he-afterwards-makes ⎭	
ko-'nyul	kôtet,	kw-ai-ta	kwanget,
and-he-rubs-it-on	the-arrow,	and-he-makes	the-bow,
ko-riich,	ko-wek ka,	ko-mwog	pēliot.
and-he-bends-it,	and-he-returns kraal,	and-he-shoots	the-elephant.
Ko-rir	pēliot,	ko-ip-e	ēut
And-he-cries	the-elephant,	and-he-causes-to-carry	the-arm ⎫ trunk ⎭
parak,	ko-'le-chi	īlet :	'Nam-a.'
above,	and-he-says-to	the-thunder :	'Take-me.'

FOLK-TALES

Ko-'le-chi	īlet:	'M-â-nom-in	amu
And-he-says-to-him	the-thunder:	'Not-I-take-thee	for
ki-ka-mwa-un	ole:	"Ya	chií-chi,"
I-already-told-thee	thus:	"He-is-bad	the-man-this,"
i-rori,	ile:	"Mining."'	
and-thou-laughest,	and-thou-sayest:	"He-is-small."'	
Ko-'le	pēliot:	'Nam-a amu	ka-a-me.'
And-he-says	the-elephant:	'Take-me for	I-have-died.'
Ko-'le-chi	īlet:	'Me	i-te-ke.'
And-he-says-to-him	the-thunder:	'Die	alone.'
Ko-me.			
And-he-dies.			
Koi-ek	chiito	ne-oo	eñg-emotinuek tukul.
And-he-becomes	the-man	who-is-great	in-the-countries all.

THE STORY OF THE CREATION.

When God came to the earth to prepare the present order of things, he found three beings there, the thunder, an elephant, and a Dorobo, all living together.

One day the thunder remarked: 'What sort of a creature is this man? If he wishes to turn over from one side to the other when he is asleep, he is able to do so. If I wish to turn over, I have first of all to get up.'

The elephant said: 'It is the same with me; before I can turn over from one side to the other, I have to stand up.'

The thunder declared that he was afraid of the man and said he would run away and go to the heavens. At this the elephant laughed and inquired why he was running away, for the man after all was only a small creature. 'But he is bad,' the thunder replied, 'he can turn over when asleep'; and with that he fled and went to the heavens, where he has remained ever since.

The man seeing the thunder go away was pleased, and said: 'The person I was afraid of has fled. I do not mind the elephant.' He then went to the woods and made some poison into which he dipped an arrow, and having cut a bow, he returned to the kraal, and shot the elephant.

The elephant wept and lifted his trunk to the heavens, crying out to the thunder to take him up.

The thunder refused, however, and said: 'I shall not take you, for when I warned you that the man was bad, you laughed and said he was small.' The elephant cried out again and begged to be taken to heaven, as he was on the point of death. But the thunder only replied : ' Die by yourself.' And the elephant died, and the man became great in all the countries.

Ñgalek-ap-sesēnik.
The-news-of-the-dogs.

Ki-mi	ole-kinye	sesēnik,	ko-'tun-i
They-were-there	formerly	the-dogs,	and-they-used-to-marry
korusiek	piik,[1]	ko-tepi	kain-nywa,
the-women	the-men,	and-they-stayed	the-town-their,
ko-tinye	tuka,	ko-uu	piik.
and-they-had	the-cattle,	and-they-were-like	the-people.
Añg	dun	petunak	ko-mi	lukōsiek
Now	afterwards	one-day	and-they-are-there	the-wars
chepo	punik,	ko-nam		punik
of	the-enemies,	and-they-take		the-enemies

tuka-ap-sesēnik.
the-cattle-of-the-dogs.

Kw-awen-ji	sesēnik	tuka,	ko-'sup
And-they-run-after	the-dogs	the-cattle,	and-they-follow

punik.
the-enemies.

Añg-nya-kas-an [2]	punik	sesēnik,	ko-mukut
When-they-hear-hither	the-enemies	the-dogs,	and-they-take-up
ñguñgunyek,	ko-lany	ketik	parak.
the-sands,	and-they-climb	the-trees	above.
Añg-nya-pwa	sesēnik,	ko-'nyal	ketik	parak,
When-they-come	the-dogs,	and-they-look-up	the-trees	above,
ki-ser-chi	ñguñgunyek	konyek.		
and-it-is-thrown-to-them	the-sands	the-eyes.		
Ko-chilil	sesēnik,	ko-pa	ka.	
And-they-escape	the-dogs,	and-they-go	town.	

[1] For *korusiek-ap-piik*.   [2] *Vide* p. 222.

FOLK-TALES 115

Ip-ko-wek	sesēnik,	ko-'sup
Go-and-they-return	the-dogs,	and-they-follow
And-they-afterwards-return		
tuka.		
the-cattle.		

Añg-nya-kas-an	punik	sesēnik,		ko-mukut
When-they-hear-hither	the-enemies	the-dogs,		and-they-pick-up
ñguñgunyek	kokeny,	ko-lany	ketik	parak,
the-sands	again,	and-they-climb	the-trees	above,

ko-roñg-ji	ñguñgunyek	konyek.
and-they-pour-into	the-sands	the-eyes.
Ko-rua	sesēnik,	ko-pet-i-ot.
And-they-run-away	the-dogs,	and-they-become-lost.
Ip-koi-ek		otuagik-ap-piik.
Go-and-they-become		the-slaves-of-the-men.
And-they-afterwards-become		

THE STORY OF THE DOGS.

In olden times dogs were just like men; they lived in kraals, they kept cattle, and they married like men and women.

On one occasion they engaged in war with their enemy man, and were beaten. Their cattle were taken from them and driven to a far-off country. They at once made an attempt to re-capture their cattle and pursued their enemies, but when the latter heard the dogs approaching they took some sand and climbed up into some high trees. The dogs being unable to follow them stood at the bottom of the trees looking up, and their enemies threw the sand down into their eyes. They were thus defeated and retired to their kraals; but as soon as they had collected their forces together again, they returned to the attack. The men pursued the same tactics as before and took a lot of sand with them into some high trees. When the dogs approached them, they poured the sand down into their eyes, and so effectually prevented them from seeing that the dogs lost themselves and have never since been able to find their kraals. Thus the dog became the slave of man.

Ñgalek-ap-tuka.
The-news-of-the-cattle.

Ki-uu	tuka	ole-kinye	piik,	ki-mo-ko-tinye
They-were-like	the-cattle	formerly	the-men,	not-they-had
siōk-ap-tuka		ko-uu	rani,	ki-uu
the-hoofs-of-the-cattle		and-it-is-like	now,	they-were-like
chepo piik,		ko-nai		ñgalek-ap-piik,
of the-men,		and-they-know		the-language-of-the-men,
ko-tepi	tukul	ak		piik.
and-they-stay	all	and together-with }		the-men.
Tun	ko-ñgêt		ko-mi-te	chiito,
Afterwards	and-he-arises		and-he-is-there	the-man,
koi-ya,	ko-tepi	ak	lakwet ak	teta.
and-he-is-bad,	and-he-stays	and with }	the-child and	the-cow.
Ko-mach	chií-chi		koi-eny	tány-i,
And-he-wants	the-man-this		and-he-slaughters	the-cow-this,
ko-'yue,	ko-'le :	'O-lio-chí	ni	'nga-a-eny ?'
and-he-fears,	and-he-says :	'I-do	how	if-I-slaughter-it ?'
Ko-'le-chi	lakwén-nyi :	'Mian.'		
And-he-says-to	the-child-his :	'Sicken.'		
Ko-mian	lakwet.			
And-he-sickens	the-child.			
Ko-'le-chi	chiito	teta :	'Mion-i	lakwén-nyō.'
And-he-says-to	the-man	the-cow :	'He-is-sick	the-child-my.'
Ko-'le	teta :	'Ara,	moch-é	ne ?'
And-she-says	the-cow :	'Well,	he-wants	what ?'
Ko-'le	chiito :	'Moch-e	mwaita.'	
And-he-says	the-man :	'He-wants	the-fat.'	
Ko-'le	teta :	'Nyo,	ke-a,	s'
And-she-says	the-cow :	'Come,	milk-me,	so-that
ip-ipir-chi		asis	cheko,	si
go-and-it-causes-to-strike-on		sun	the-milks,	so-that
i-nyo		isach,		si
and-thou-comest		and-thou-shakest-them,		so-that
koi-ek	mwaita,	si	ikochi	lakwet,
they-may-become	the-fat,	so-that	and-thou-givest-it	the-child,
ko-sop.'				
and-he-recovers.'				

FOLK-TALES

Ko-ke,	ko-'pir-chi	asis	cheko,
And-he-milks-her,	and-it-causes-to-strike-on	sun	the-milks,

ko-'sach,	ko-'ro	ko-ka-ko-nyo	mwaita,
and-he-shakes-them,	and-he-sees	finished-it-comes	the-fat, } butter, }

ko-'koch	lakwet.
and-he-gives-it	the-child.

Ko-'le-chi	chiito	lakwén-nyi	pesiet	ake:
And-he-says-to	the-man	the-child-his	day	other:

'Mian kokeny.'
'Sicken again.'

Ko-mian	lakwet	kokeny.
And-he-sickens	the-child	again.

Ko-'le-chi	chiito	teta:	'Mion-i	lakwén-nyō.'
And-he-says-to	the-man	the-cow:	'He-is-sick	the-child-my.'

Ko-'le	teta:	'Ara,	moch-é	ne?'
And-he-says	the-cow:	'Well,	he-wants	what?'

Ko-'le	chiito:	'Moch-e	korotik.'
And-he-says	the-man:	'He-wants	the-bloods.'

Ko-'le	teta:	'Nyo,	iket-a,	si
And-she-says	the-cow:	'Come,	strangle } -me, bind }	so-that

i-char	kepet,	si	ingi-sich
and-thou-shootest	the-jugular-vein,	so-that	mayest-thou-get

korotik,	ikochi	lakwet.'
the-bloods,	and-thou-givest-them	the-child.'

Ko-'ket,	ko-char	kepet,
And-he-strangles } -her, binds }	and-he-shoots	the-jugular-vein,

ko-sich	korotik,	ko-'koch	lakwén-nyi,
and-he-gets	the-bloods,	and-he-gives-them	the-child-his,

ko-sop.
and-he-recovers.

Ko-'le-chi	chiito	lakwet	pesiet	ake:	'Mian
And-he-says-to	the-man	the-boy	day	other:	'Sicken

kokeny.'
again.'

Ko-mian	lakwet.
And-he-sickens	the-boy.

```
Ko-'le-chi        chiito       teta:       'Mian-i       lakwén-nyō
And-he-says-to    the-man      the-cow:    'He-is-ill    the-child-my
kokeny.'
again.'
    Ko-'le        teta:        'Ara,       moch-é      ne?'
    And-she-says  the-cow:     'Well,      he-wants    what?'
    Ko-'le        chiito:      'Moch-e     mwaita.'
    And-he-says   the-man:     'He-wants   the-fat.'
    Ko-tep        teta:        'Añg?                   Ne-kínye?'
    And-she-asks  the-cow:     'What-sort-of?          Which-is-formerly?'
    Ko-'le        chiito:      'Ma-moch-e              ne-kínye,
    And-he-says   the-man:     'Not-he-wants           which-is-formerly,
moch-e        amset.'
he-wants      the-marrow.'
    Ko-'le            teta:                     'Ka-a-ko-rok,
    And-she-says      the-cow:                  'Have-I-become-finished,
    ka-o-eny-a,               ip-u          rotuet,      nyo,      tor-a
    have-you-slaughtered-me,  bring-hither  the-knife,   come,     stab-me
    kimutit.'
the-nape-of-the-neck.'
    Ko-ip          chiito        rotuet,           ko-tor
    And-he-takes   the-man       the-knife,        and-he-stabs-her
    kimutit,                ko-me.
the-nape-of-the-neck,     and-she-dies.
    Otkote     atkinye       ip-ko-wek                          tuka
    Since      then          go-and-they-change       }         the-cattle
                             and-they-afterwards-change}
tukul,      ko-wek            keliek,         ko-sich            siōk,
all,        and-they-change   the-legs,       and-they-get       the-hoofs,
    ko-ma-ta-ko-much                    ko-mwa          ak       piik.
and-not-again-they-have-been-able       and-they-talk   with     the-men.
    Inyo                ip-ko-nai                                piik
    And-it-comes        go-and-they-know         }               the-men
                        and-they-afterwards-know }
    kw-ai-ta                 mwait'-ap-cheko,                    inyo
    and-they-prepare         the-fat } -of-the-milks,            and-it-comes
                             butter  }
    ip-ko-char                     a-koi-eny            túk'-chwak.
    go-and-they-bleed          }   and-they-slaughter   the-cattle-their.
    and-they-afterwards-bleed  }
```

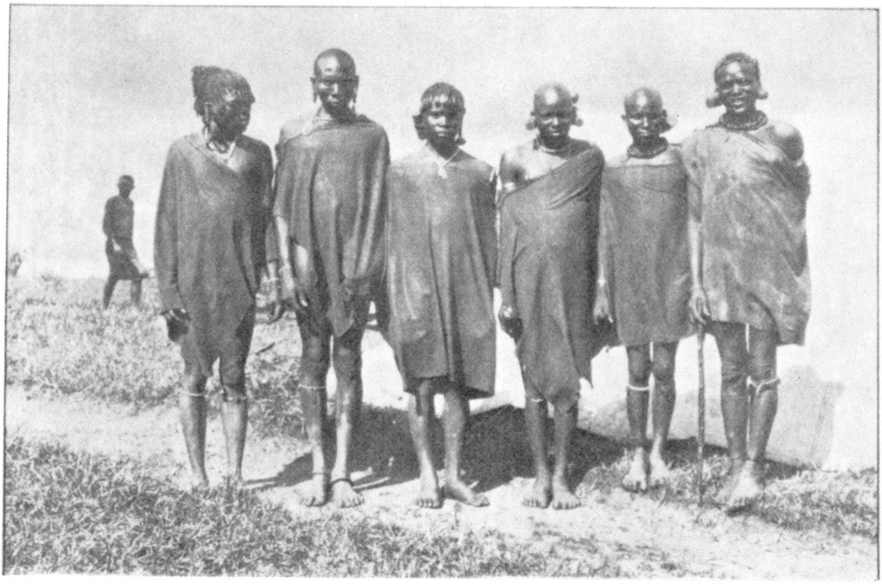

PLATE XXXVII

Group of Nandi boys and warriors. Reading from left to right—Nos. 1, 2 and 3 are warriors, and Nos. 4, 5 and 6, boys (Meinertzhagen).

Group of Nandi women and children (Meinertzhagen).

Inyo	ip-ko-'le	piik:	'Tuka
And-it-comes	go-and-they-say and-they-afterwards-say	the-men:	'The-cattle
ko	kametuagik-chok.'		
and-they-are	the-mothers-our.'		

THE STORY OF THE CATTLE.

In olden days cattle were like human beings; they had men's feet —not hoofs as they have at present—they lived together with men, and they could talk their language.

In course of time a man who lived with his son and a cow made up his mind to kill the cow, but he was afraid to do so openly. He therefore told his son to pretend to be ill, and he went to the cow and said, ' My child is ill, he wants some fat to cure him.'

The cow told him to milk her, and after putting the milk in the sun, to shake it, and he would get what he required. The man did as he was bid, and his boy recovered.

He then told the child to pretend to be ill again, and he went to the cow, and said he wanted some blood to cure him. The cow told him to tie a ligature round her neck, and to shoot an arrow into her jugular vein. This the man did, and obtained some blood which he gave to the child who, as on the former occasion, recovered.

Later on, the man told his son to feign sickness again, and he went to the cow and said he wanted some more fat. The cow asked him if the same kind of fat as he had had on the former occasion would do, but the man replied that he wanted marrow-fat. The cow then knew that she must be slaughtered, and she told the man to bring a knife, and to pierce her in the nape of the neck. This was done, and the cow died.

The legs of the cattle then changed, they developed hoofs, and they were unable any more to converse with men. This is how men learnt to obtain milk and make butter, to draw blood from the living animals, and to butcher their cattle; and it is for this reason that men say that the cattle are their mothers.

Kâpchemosīnik-ap-päk.
The-stories-of-the-eleusine-grains.

Ki-ki-kas	ole-kinye,	ko-'len	poiisiek,	ki-mwog-se
We-heard	formerly,	and-they-say	the-old-men,	they-hunted

Nandi, ki-mwog-e tioñgik, ki-ma-nai
Nandi, they-hunt-used-to the-wild-animals, they-not-knew
ko-'pat.
and-they-cultivate.

Tun ko-set murenik petunak luket,
Presently and-they-go the-warriors one-day the-war,
ko-nyor piek-ap-pēliot, ko-'ro
and-they-get } the-excrements-of-the-elephant, and-they-see
see

päk che-ko-rur em-parak,
the-eleusine-grains which-have-ripened at-above,
ko-kes, ko-ip ka.
and-they-gather-them, and-they-take-them kraal.

Ip-ko-'pat imbaret,
Go-and-they-cultivate } the-plantation,
And-they-afterwards-cultivate

ko-kol, ko-rur päk.
and-they-plant-them, and-they-ripen the-eleusine-grains.
Ko-mwo-chi-ke kule : 'Am totegin.'
And-they-say-to-themselves thus : 'Eat a-little.'
Ko-esi-o chii tukul.
And-they-refuse man all.

Ko-mi korko ka ne-mo-tinye murenet,
And-there-is-there woman kraal who-not-has the-warrior, }
husband,
ako tinye lakwet ne-kararan.
but she-has the-child who-is-beautiful.

Ko-mwo-chi-ke piik-ap-ka kule :
And-they-say-to-themselves the-people-of-kraal thus :

'Ingen ñgô ingo-pokoch-i piich ingi-am ?
'He-knows who if-they-kill people if-we-eat-them ?
Onge-'kochi korket si ingo-pokoch-i piich,
Let-us-give-them the-woman so-that if-they-kill people,
ko-me, ki-nam lakwet.'
and-she-dies, and-we-take the-child.'

Ko-'koch,		ko-ñga
And-they-give-them-her,		and-she-grinds-them
eñg-goiit'-ap-pai,		ko-korkoren-ji-ne
with-the-stone-of-eleusine,		and-she-causes-them-to-stir-in
pêk, kw-am.		
the-waters, and-she-eats-them.		

Mutai ko-'le:	'O-kōn-o	alak.'	
Morrow and-she-says:	'Ye-give-me	others.'	
Ko-'le	piik:		'Ingo-ma-me,
And-they-say	the-people:		'If-she-not-dies,
onge-kwany-ji-ne		mat	si
let-us-cause-them-to-approach-to		the-fire	so-that
ko-pel,	kw-am,		ko-me.'
and-she-roasts-them,	and-she-eats-them,		and-she-dies.'
Ko-'koch	piik	alak,	ko-pel,
And-they-give-her	the-people	others,	and-she-roasts-them,
kw-am.			
and-she-eats-them.			
Mutai ko-'le:	'O-kōn-o	alak.'	
Morrow and-she-says:	'Ye-give-me	others.'	
Ko-'koch	piik	alak,	kw-am,
And-they-give-her	the-people	others,	and-she-eats-them,
ko-ner.			
and-she-fattens.			
Añg-nya-iro	piik		ko-ner-e,
When-they-see	the-people		and-they-cause-her-to-fatten,
kw-am tukul.			
and-they-eat all.			
Kw-am otkote kuni.			
And-they-eat until now.			

THE STORY OF THE ELEUSINE GRAIN.

Our fathers have told us that in olden days the Nandi lived by hunting, and did not know how to cultivate the soil.

One day some warriors went on a raiding expedition, and on the path saw some elephant excrement, out of which some eleusine plants were growing. They gathered the ripe grain, which they took home with them and planted. In course of time it grew and ripened.

Nobody would eat it, however, for fear of it being poisonous, and each man attempted to persuade his neighbour to try a little, but without success.

There lived a woman in the kraal who had no husband, but she had a beautiful child. The inhabitants of the kraal decided to give some of the grain to this woman, to see whether it was good to eat or poisonous. 'If it kills her,' they said, 'it will not matter, for we can then take the child.'

The woman took the grain, and ground it with a stone, after which she stirred it in water, and ate it.

The next day she asked for more, and the people, seeing that nothing happened to her, suggested putting the grain near the fire to see if it was good when roasted. The woman ate the roasted grain, and again asked for more. When she had eaten a third time, the people noticed that she was getting fat, and they all partook of the grain. And they have eaten it ever since.

Arawet ne-ko-lel.
The-moon which-is-new.

Ingo-'ro lakōk-ap-Nandi arawet ko-ko-lel,
If-they-see the-children-of-Nandi the-moon and-it-is-new,

ko-ñgut-yi, ko-'le-chi :
and-they-spit-at-it, and-they-say-to-it :

'Pelepele, arawa!
'Welcome, moon!

Ingi-am kii, ko-'ket-in;
If-thou-eatest anything, may-it-choke-thee;

Ingâ-am kii, ko-'is-a.'
If-I-eat anything, may-it-do-me-good.'

Ingo-'ro poiisiek arawet, ko-'le-chi :
If-they-see the-old-men the-moon, and-they-say-to-it :

'Ptu, tuk-u-a lakōk ak
'(noise resembling spitting), cover-for-me the-children and

tuka.
the-cattle.

Nyo, arawán-ni ne-mie,
Come, O-moon who-art-good,

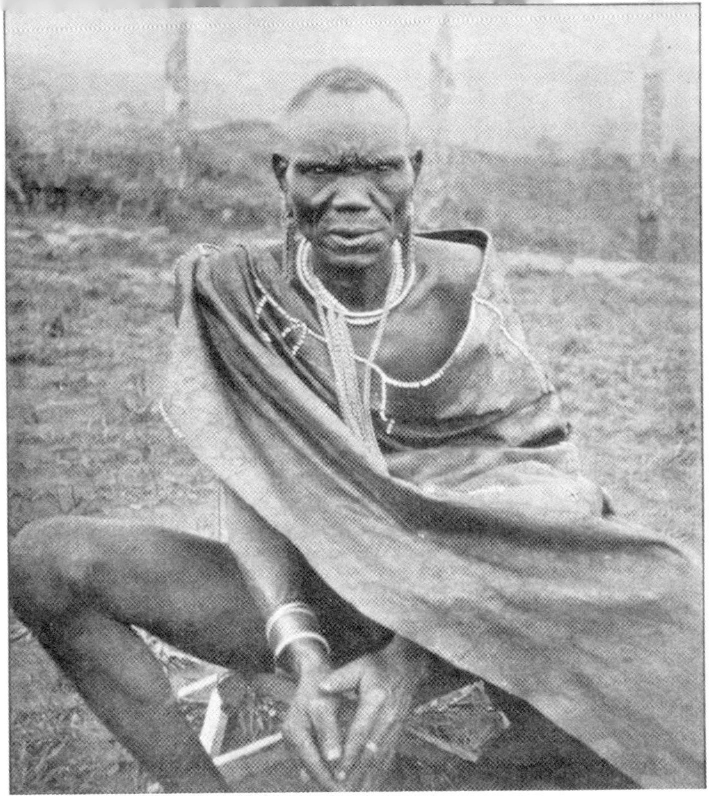

Nandi elder—full face (Hobley).

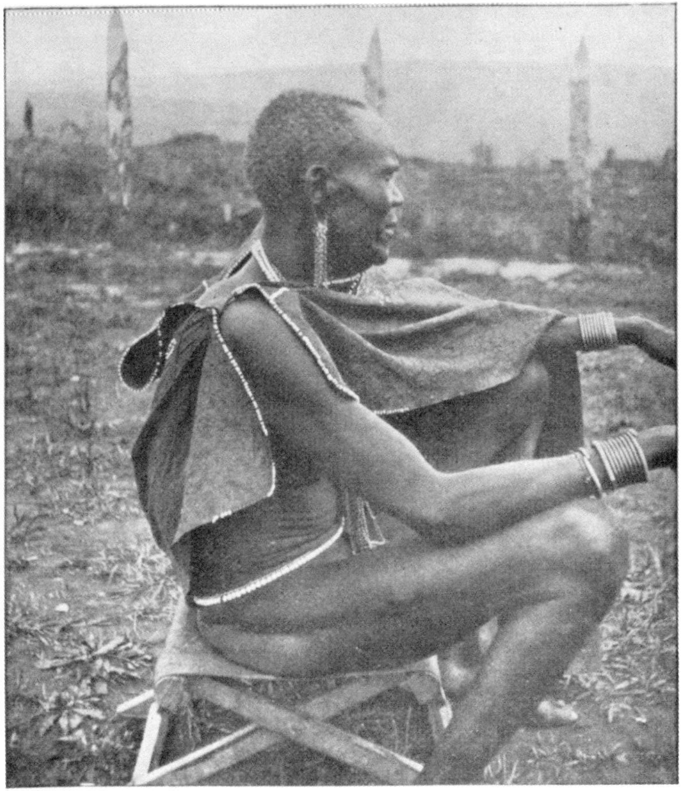

Nandi elder—profile (Hobley).

To face p. 122

Tuk-u-a	lakōk	ak	tuka,		
Cover-for-me	the-children	and	the-cattle,		
Tuk-u-a		koi	tun		ingi-me.'
Cover(them)-for-me		afterwards	presently until	}	thou-mayest-die.'

THE NEW MOON.

When Nandi children see the new moon, they spit at it, and say:—
  'Welcome, moon!
  May anything that thou eatest choke thee,
  Whilst anything that I eat, may it do me good.'

Old men also spit at the new moon, and sing:—
  'O kindly moon, thine influence benign
  Withhold not from our children and our kine,
  And through thy life's short span of thirty days,
  May nought but blessings issue from thy rays.'

THE NANDI HOUSE THAT JACK BUILT OR THE OLD WOMAN AND HER PIG.

Wirua ñgô soroiyo?	Who will cast goats' dung at me?
Iliochi soroiyo?	What will you do with goats' dung?
Awirchi tororot.	I will throw it at the heavens.
Iliochi tororot?	What do you want with the heavens?
Kosoiua tupa pei.	That they drop a little water on me.
Iliochi tupa pei?	Why do you want a little water?
Kopīte iwasto.	That the burnt grass may grow.
Iliochi iwasto?	Why do you want young grass?
Kwamua osén-nyō.	That my old cow may eat.
Iliochi osén-ñguñg?	What will you do with your old cow?
Oienyji orokí-chun.	I will slaughter it for those eagles.
Iliochi orokí-chun?	What do you want with those eagles?
Kometua tareyuo.	That they drop their feathers for me.
Iliochi tareyuo?	Why do you want feathers?
Atare kótén-nyō.	That I may fasten them on my arrow.
Iliochi kótén-ñguñg?	Why do you want your arrow?
Amwoge tuk'-ap-pun.	That I may hunt the enemies' oxen.
Iliochi tuk'-ap-pun?	Why do you want the enemies' oxen?
A'tune kaitán-nyō.	That I may obtain my wife.
Iliochi kaitán-ñguñg?	Why do you want your wife?
Kosichua lakwén-nyō.	That she may bear me a child.
Iliochi lakwén-ñguñg?	Why do you want your child?
Kocheñgwa iseria.	That he may look for my lice.
Iliochi iseria?	Why do you want lice?
Awe ko'lilot.	That I may go and die (with them) as an old man.

ATINDONIK-AP-NANDI
NANDI PROVERBS

No. 1. Chii   ne-ki-kw-am-e   soet   ko-'ngo-'ro   tany
        Man   who-is-eaten-by   the-buffalo   and-if-he-sees   ox
dui   ko-'le   ka-it.
black   and-he-says   it-has-arrived.

If a man has been once tossed by a buffalo he thinks when he sees a black ox coming towards him that it is another buffalo.
['Once bit, twice shy.']

No. 2.   Ii-e   ñgetūny   lel.
          He-bears   lion   hyena.

The lion bears a hyena.
[Said when a son is unworthy of his father.]

No. 3.   I-much-i-ke   cheposta;   'ngo-iam-in
          Try-thyself   the-arm-clamp;   if-it-suits-thee
in-de-ke,   'ngo-ma-iam-in   i-met-te.
and-thou-wearest-it,   if-it-not-suits-thee   and-thou-throwest-it-away.

Try this arm clamp; if it fits you, wear it, if it does not fit you, throw it away.
[Don't wear an ornament if it inconveniences you, and don't do anything for show unless you derive some benefit from your action.]

No. 4.   Inga-i   ñgom,   i-ker-i-ke   kimut-i?
          (Even)-if-thou-art   clever,   dost-thou-see-thyself   nape-of-the-neck?

However clever you may be, can you see the back of your neck?
[Said to a boaster.]

No. 5.   Inge-ñgor-a   ke-ñgor   Kipkeny.
          If-I-am-divined   and-he-is-divined   Kipkeny.

[Kipkeny is the name of a well-known wizard who was never found out. This saying is much used by a person who boasts of having done wrong and is equivalent to: 'They might as well expect to catch Kipkeny as me.']

No. 6.   Iñgêt-i   kimereñg   minde.
          It-causes-to-arise   blue-duiker   red-duiker.

The small gazelle (blue duiker) causes the big gazelle (red duiker) to get up.

NANDI PROVERBS

[The blue duiker and the red duiker feed together. If danger approaches, the former warns the latter and sets him running off. Similarly, if a rumour of small importance gets abroad, it is soon magnified and exaggerated.]

No. 7.   Iok-toi   kiplengoi   pēlio.
          They-send   hares   elephant.

Send hares to the elephant, not elephants to the hare.

[It is the duty of children to wait on elders, not elders on children. 'Seniores priores.']

No. 8.   Iput-i   tany   aku   pa-kelek   añgwan.
          It-falls ox   but   of-the-legs   four.

The ox falls in spite of its four legs.

[A man often makes a mistake, notwithstanding the fact that he is an intelligent being. 'Accidents happen even in the best-regulated families.']

No. 9.   Ka-al-ke   makata   ak   sot.
          They-have-bought-themselves   goat's-hide   and   gourd.

A goat's hide buys a goat's hide and a gourd a gourd.

['An eye for an eye and a tooth for a tooth.']

No. 10. Ke-girgir te pirtit ap toot 'nge-kir-chin pêk ko-ñgêt-e.

Festinavit veluti mentula viatoris quae superba fit cum coniux amici in cuius domum intravit manus eius aqua lavat.

['Haste, haste, has no blessing.']

No. 11.   Ke-'pwat-e   che   logot.
          He-has-been-remembering   milks   hunt.

He thought of milk during the hunt.

[When driven by adversity to obtain his living by hunting, a man during an arduous stalk is apt to think of the days of plenty when he could quench his thirst by copious draughts of milk. 'O fortunatos nimium, sua si bona norint.']

No. 12. Kerichek-ap-erenet   ak   chepo-lakwet   kw-akenge.
         The-medicines-of-the-snake and of-the-child   and-they-are-one.

It is all one whether one is bitten by an old snake or by its offspring: both are poisonous.

[A crime is none the less a crime because the person who commits it is a minor.]

No. 13. Kerke ki-mutio ak ki-mīsing.
They-are-alike slow-person and very-person.
fast

[There is no difference between the slow speaker (or the person who speaks little) and the fast speaker (or the person who talks a great deal). It is quality not quantity that tells.]

No. 14. Kerke kipset ak kiptep.
They-are-alike raider and home-stayer.

[There is no difference in the long run between a man who raids and one who stays at home. Both run somewhat similar risks. The one may be killed in the enemy's country, the other may be killed by the enemy in his own home; and cattle diseases, drought, &c., affect both in much the same way.]

No. 15. Ki-am-doi Asis a-mo-ki-am-doi
He-is-owned-in-partnership Sun and-it-is-not-owned-in-partnership
atep.
seat.

The Sun is owned by everybody, but a man's body is owned by himself alone.

['Each for himself and God for us all.']

No. 16. Ki-'ēn-i tany koñg si ki-char-e.
It-is-closed ox eye in-order-that it-may-be-bled.

Cover the eyes of the ox you wish to bleed, or he will see the preparations you are making and fidget or run away.

['Surely in vain the net is spread in the sight of any bird.' Proverbs i. 17.]

No. 17. Ki-mwa Asista: 'Ki-a-we inyalil-o
It-said the-Sun: 'I-went they-bully-me
mee.'
agricultural-people.'

The Sun said, 'Whatever I do, the farmers curse me. If there is no rain, they say I burn their crops; if there is much rain, they complain that I do not shine.'

[Said of discontented people.]

No. 18. Ma-am-e īlat ket oieñg.
It-does-not-eat thunder tree twice.

A tree is not twice struck by lightning.

[If you have to punish a person or a tribe, do it so thoroughly that it will not require to be done a second time.]

No. 19. Ma-chut-e   ñgwanet   ye-ma-mi-i
         It-enters-not the-poison   where-they-are-not-there
korotik.
the-bloods.

The poison (of a poisoned arrow) does no harm if it does not enter the blood.

['Hard words break no bones.']

No. 20. Ma-ki-eny-jin   kamet   moita   met.
         It-is-not-slaughtered-to   the-mother   the-calf   head.

One does not slaughter a calf before its mother's eyes.

['Thou shalt not seethe a kid in his mother's milk.' Deut. xiv. 21.]

No. 21. Ma-ki-'ep-chin-iit   chii   rir-e.
         It-is-not-cut-to-ear } man   he-cries.
         listened-to   }

A man who is always crying is not listened to.

[Credence is not given to a man who is always crying 'wolf'.]

No. 22. Ma-ki-'lok-toi   'ngor   cheput.
         It-is-not-worn-thither garment   caterpillar.

A person does not put on a garment if there is a caterpillar in it, as its spikes will irritate him.

['Cut off your nose to spite your face.']

No. 23. Ma-ki-lol-e   ma   pei.
         It-is-not-lit   fire   waters.

You cannot light a fire in water.

[Said to a liar.]

No. 24. Ma-ki-met-toi   mokoiyo
         It-is-not-thrown-away   the-fruit-of-the-wild-fig-tree

ne-mi-i   'ngoiny   a-ki-sor   ne-mi-i
which-are-there below   and-they-may-be-run-after which-are-there
parak.
above.

Don't throw away the figs which grow at the bottom of the tree and hasten to pick those which grow at the top.

['A bird in the hand is worth two in the bush.']

No. 25. Ma-ki-mon-doi   karna   ma.
         It-is-not-despised iron   fire.

Do not despise a piece of iron in the fire, for it will not be burnt, but when red hot it will be beaten into shape and may possibly become a formidable weapon.

[Despise not your enemies when they are in straitened circumstances.]

No. 26.　　Ma-ki-mus-chin　　　　　　gai-pa-muren.[1]
　　　　　It-is-not-gone-in-the-morning-to　house -of-warriors.
　　　　　　　　　　　　　　　　　　　kraal

It is not usual to pay a visit to the warriors' hut in the early morning, as the visitor may be mistaken for a thief and killed.

['Look before you leap.']

No. 27.　　Ma-ki-mwo-e　　kii　　　kut.
　　　　　It-is-not-said　　thing　　mouth.

Do not say the first thing that comes into your head.

['Think twice before you speak.']

No. 28.　　Ma-ki-'por-chin　　kimaket　　susut.
　　　　　It-is-not-shown-to　hyena　　　bite.

Don't show a hyena how well you can bite, for his jaws are more powerful than yours.

['Pride comes before a fall.']

No. 29.　　　Ma-ki-rīp-e　　　　　pai　　　　　puch
　　　　　They-are-not-guarded　eleusine-grains　for-nothing
　a-ma-am　　　toroi.
and-they-eat-not　pigs.

Don't guard your plantations until the pigs begin to enter.

[Don't wear yourself out by needless work, for the time will come when you will require all your strength.]

No. 30.　　　Ma-ki-sar-u-ne　　chii　　ma.
　　　　　It-is-not-caused-to-rescue　man　　fire.

A man cannot be saved if he wishes to throw himself in the fire, and a quarrelsome person is sure to come to harm in course of time.

No. 31.　　　　　Ma-ki-sos-e　　　　　　　　　kâp
　　　　　　　It-is-not-disliked　　　　　　the-house-of
　　　kip-kas-an　　　　　　　　a-ma-ki-ru　　　kaita.
the-person-one-hears-is-coming-hither　and-it-is-not-slept　the-house.

One cannot say that one dislikes the house of somebody one has heard about if one has not had an opportunity of sleeping in his house.

[Do not condemn a person on hearsay.]

No. 32.　　　Ma-ki-tar-e　　　ndara.
　　　　　It-is-not-finished　remorse.

After a foolish action comes the remorse.

No. 33.　　　Ma-ki-'un-jin　　　e　　　korko.
　　　　　It-is-not-washed-to　hand　woman.

A man does not wash a woman's hand.

---

[1] For *kait'-am-murenik*.

PLATE XXXIX

Nandi outpost (Meinertzhagen).

Nandi outpost (Author).

NANDI PROVERBS

Also: Ma-ki-ōt-e korko.
It-is-not-worked-for woman.
A man does not slave for a woman.
[It is a woman's duty to wait on her husband and on her husband's guests.]

No. 34. Ma-me-i chii nepo chii.
He-does-not-die man of man.
A man may strike a man, but death is sent to him by God.

No. 35. Ma-mi-i konyit kimosak kuu rotua.
It-is-not-there shame one-sided ⎱ like knife.
one-edged ⎰
Shame is not one-edged like a knife; it cuts in every direction and goes deep into one's heart; or it affects the relations as well as the guilty person.

No. 36. Ma-mi-i myat ake ne-rom-chin
It-is-not-there death the-one who-draws-for
ake pei.
the-other waters.
One death does not draw water for another death.
[Death fights his own battles unassisted, and always wins in the end.]

No. 37. Ma-mi-i ñgolio ne-ma-tinye aino.
It-is-not-there saying which-has-not river. ⎱
proverb. ⎰
There is no saying without a double meaning.
[Look for a hidden meaning in every word that is spoken.]

No. 38. Ma-nom-e riria kâp-ingui.
It-takes-not ox-pecker-bird ⎱ land-of-vegetables. ⎱
beefeater-bird ⎰ plantations. ⎰
The ox-pecker bird does not steal grain.
[The ox-pecker birds[1] live on the ticks and insects which are to be found on every ox, donkey, or other animal, and as many as ten or even twenty are sometimes to be seen on a single cow's back. If a man wanted to protect his crops from the birds, the ox-pecker bird would be amongst the last he would attempt to destroy. In like manner, if a man quarrelled with a neighbour he would not wage war on a third party.]

No. 39. Ma-oi-tos ma pei.
It-crosses-not fire waters.
A grass fire is stopped by a river, and an enemy or beast of prey is in a like manner hindered by a good zariba or hedge.

[1] *Buphaga erythrorhyncha*, Stanl.

No. 40.　　Ma-tinye　　chorin　　doondon.¹
　　　　　　He-has-not　　thief　　the-stranger.

A born thief will respect nothing, not even hospitality, and will as soon steal from his host as from anybody else.

No. 41.　　Ma-tinye　　oliot　　chep-kam.
　　　　　　It-has-not　　the-trade　　sister.

If a man wishes to make a bargain, he will cheat his own sister.

No. 42.　　Mai-'os-e　　kimaket　　puch　　pamb-a'-pēt.²
　　　　　　It-refuses-not　　hyena　　for-nothing　　the-journey-of-morning.

A hyena does not remain out during the hot hours of the day unless there is some reason for it.

[If one notices a change in the habits of a man or in the tactics of a foe, there is always some cause for it, and it is as well to be on one's guard.]

No. 43.　　Me-men-e　　che-ki-men-e　　Cheptol.
　　　　　　Do-not-be-puffed-up　　who-are-puffed-up　　Cheptol.

Do not be puffed up like the people of Cheptol.

[On one occasion when a great raid was projected the people of Cheptol, one of the geographical divisions, are said to have slaughtered and eaten all their oxen, so certain were they that they would capture large herds of cattle. They were, however, beaten, and had to return empty-handed to empty kraals. ' Pride comes before a fall.']

No. 44.　　Me-pun　　kamasanet,　　pun　　kiboñgboñgit.
　　　　　　Do-not-take　　the-by-path,　　take　　the-broad-road.

[A favourite saying when bidding a person farewell. Thieves and wild animals are supposed to frequent the by-paths ; honest people and cattle use the broad roads.]

Another proverb of a like nature is the following :—

　　　　Me-torok-te,　　　　têk-u.
　　　　Do-not-go-to-meet-it,　　take-shelter.

If you see danger ahead, do not take any risk and go to meet it ; hide by the roadside till the danger has passed.

No. 45.　　Me-'ut-e　　kiruk　　korōsiek ³　　oieñg.
　　　　　　He-bellows-not　　bull　　the-countries　　two.

A bull cannot bellow in two places at once.

No. 46.　　Mur　　kimaket　　a-ki-sīl-e.
　　　　　　It-is-brown　　hyena　　but-it-is-clawed.

¹ For *toondet.*　　² For *pand'-ap-pēt.*　　³ For *korotinuek.*

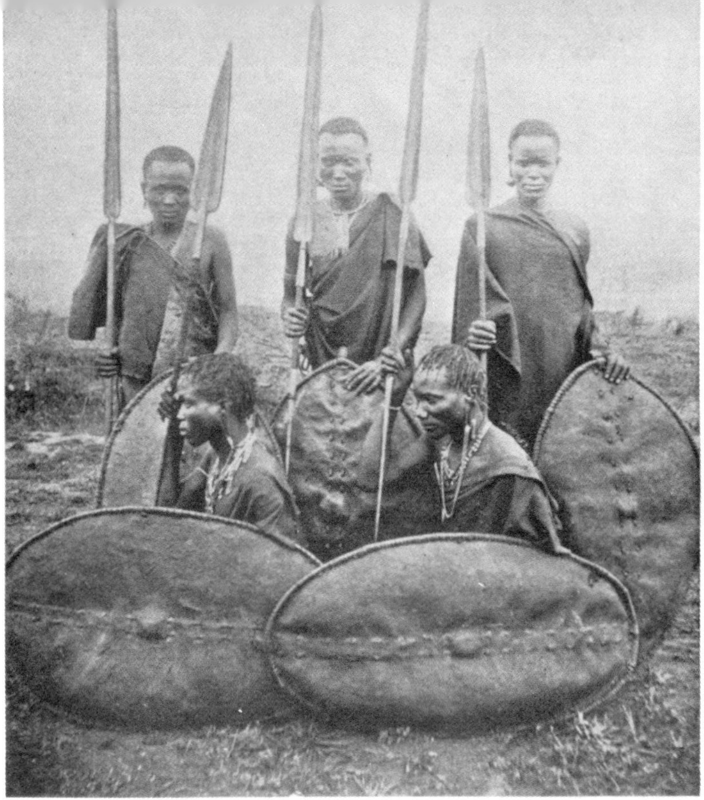

Nandi warriors (Hobley).

Nandi girls (Stordy).

To face p. 130

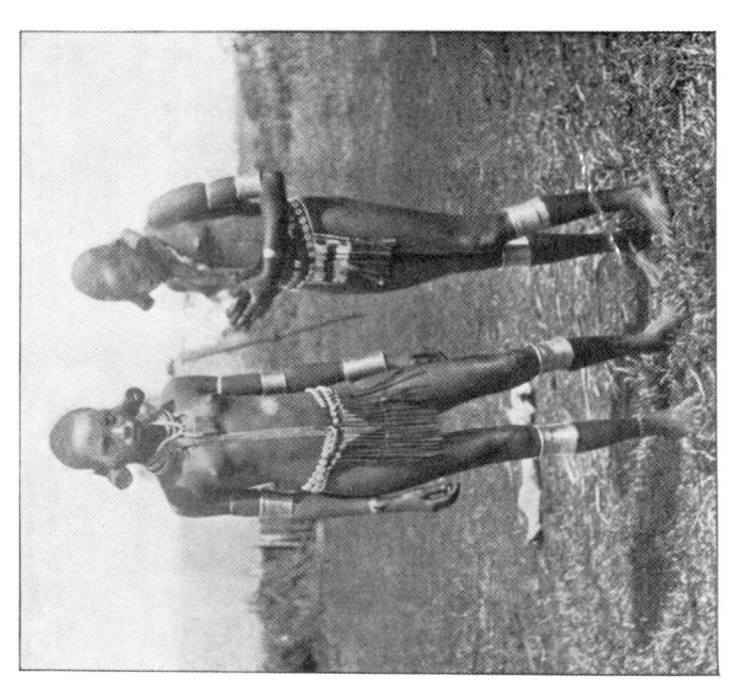

Although the hyena is brown in colour it has the marks of people's nails on its body (stripes).

[Whenever a striped hyena is seen in the neighbourhood of a house, people point at it, and everybody claims to have made a mark on it at some former time in order to recognize again the thief. 'Give a dog a bad name and hang him.']

No. 47.   'Nga-ñgom   chorin,   ko-tamne
    (Even)-if-he-is-clever   thief,   and-he-is-more-so
kinindet.
the-person-who-finds-him-out.

However clever a rogue may be, when he is found out he must admit that there is somebody cleverer than he.

No. 48.   'Nga-oo   pēlio   ko-ma-ii-e
    (Even)-if-it-is-big   elephant   and-it-does-not-bear
moiek   oieñg.
the-calves   two.

Notwithstanding the fact that the elephant is a big animal, it does not give birth to more than one at a time.

[However generous a rich man may be, there is a limit to everybody's generosity.]

No. 49.   'Ngi-'om-e-chi   pôton   kel-ok.
    Let-us-put-together-in   tremble   leg-one.

Let us put our trembling legs together in one place, and we shall obtain support one from the other.

[The necessity of joint action *or* 'Union is strength'.]

No. 50.   'Ngi-rep-e   lakwa   rotua   ke-ken-ji   ket.
    If-thou-seizest   child   knife   and-thou-coaxest-him   tree.

If you take a knife away from a child, give him a piece of wood instead.

[If you have to perform an unpleasant duty and hurt a person's feelings, do it as gently as possible.]

No. 51.   'Ngo-lul   ket   ne-yâmat   ko-ti-to
    If-it-falls   tree   which-is-dry   and-it-takes-with-it
ne-tuon.
which-is-green.

If a dead tree falls, it carries with it a live one.

[If a criminal is punished, his innocent relations suffer as well.]

No. 52. 'Ngo-pan   jii   kwe,   ko-me-pan-e kiruk.
         If-he-bewitches man   he-goat,   and-thou-bewitchest-not bull.

Because a man has injured your goat, do not injure his bull.
[Do not seek revenge.]

No. 53. 'Ngo-'put-yi   kororia   ma   a-ko-loñg   tukul-i ?
         If-it-falls-into feather fire and-it-crosses all ?

If a feather falls into the fire, can it be wholly saved ?

Also: 'Ngo-'put-yi   tany   kering   ko-mo-loñg-u kororik.
         If-it-falls-into ox   pit   and-it-does-not-cross-hither the-feathers.

If an ox falls into a pit, it will at least leave some of its hairs at the bottom.
[If a foe attacks you, you will suffer some damage, even if you are in a position to beat him off.]

No. 54. 'Ngo-samis-it   muria   kwa   ko.
         If-it-stinks   rat   and-it-goes home.

If a rat stinks, it goes home; and if a man is ill, he goes to his relations to be attended to and cared for.
['Blood is thicker than water.']

No. 55.   Somnyo   mesundei.
                  Uncircumcised-girl darkness.⎫
                                      no-moon. ⎭

Darkness is like an uncircumcised girl.

[Just as an uncircumcised girl, who only wears a small apron of strips of leather, feels no shame, so a woman does not mind being naked in the dark.]

No. 56. Tandus   ko   po-tiony   ñgwan   ko   po-chii.
         Pleasant   it-may-be of-animal   bitter   it-may-be   of-man.

What is pleasant to an animal may be bitter to a man.
['One man's meat is another man's poison.']

No. 57. Tapen !   korán-ni   ki-'pat   ilat.
         Look !   land-this   it-cultivated thunder.

Look ! This land has been struck by lightning.

[Said of a plot made ready for planting where the soil has been well turned over. It is supposed that the earth has been torn to pieces like a tree struck by lightning.]

TONGŌCHIK-AP-NANDI
NANDI ENIGMAS

Riddles or enigmas are the sport of children and young people. They are only asked after dark. The propounder says: Tongoch. The others reply: Cho.

No. 1.   A-koi   ak   a   po-minan.
Enigma.   I-am-tall   and   I-am   of-red-earth-in-my-hair.
Reply.   Mosongiot.
     The-millet-plant.

I am tall and my hair has red earth in it. What am I? The millet plant.

[The millet plant is tall, and the flower at the top is coloured much like hair dyed red.]

No. 2.   Alak-u   yu   a-alok   yu
Enigma.   Go-round   here   and-I-go-round   here
     te-'p-ki-tui-ye   ko-pirir-ech   ēun.
     again-afterwards-we-meet }   and-they-are-red-to-us   hands.
     when-we-meet-again

Reply.   Kopchopinek.
     The-kopchopinek-fruit.

If you go round there and I go round here, why will our hands be red when we meet again? Because we shall have eaten kopchopinek fruit.

[Cf. the Masai riddle, 'What will your hands be like if we meet after you have gone round that part of the mountain? The fruit of the *Ximenia americana*, which stains everything blood-red.']

No. 3.   Anyiny   ingua   tere'-'p-oiin.
Enigma.   It-is-sweet   vegetable   cooking-pot-of-spirits.
Reply.   Kongaiyat.
     The-white-ant-in-flying-stage.

What is the sweet vegetable that comes out of the cooking-pot of the spirits of the deceased? The white ant.

[The white ant is considered a great delicacy, especially during the flying stage. As it lives in the ground, it is supposed to come from the cooking-pot of the spirits of the deceased.]

134 THE NANDI

No. 4.   Apuk   ma-pa.
Enigma.   It-pours-out   it-does-not-go.
Reply.   Kīna-ap-teta.
   The-teat-of-the-cow.

What is it that produces liquid and yet cannot let the liquid flow when it wishes? A cow's udder.

No. 5.   A-tenden   ak   a   po-Tuken.
Enigma.   I-am-thin   and   I-am   of-Kamasia.
Reply.   Etiet.
   The bridge.

I am thin and I come from Kamasia. What am I? A bridge.
[The Nandi are said to have learnt the art of making bridges from the Kamasia.]

No. 6.   A-tinye   cheptán-nyō   ne-'ngo-wendi   kâp-tich
Enigma.   I-have   the-girl-my   who-if-she-goes   the-cattle-kraal
   ko-'sīk-ot   ta-nyo-ne   ka
   and-she-sings-as-she-goes   again-she-comes   hut
   ko-sis-anu.
   and-she-is-silent-as-she-comes.
Reply.   Sotonik.
   The-milk-calabashes.

What are the things which as they go to the cattle-kraal sing, whilst as they return home are silent? The milk calabashes.
[When empty the milk calabashes knock against one another and make a noise; but when full they make no sound.]

No. 7.   A-tinye   cheptán-nyō   ne-piiy-onyi
Enigma.   I-have   the-girl-my   who-has-enough-to-eat
   mutai   ko-rukut   lakat.
   every-morning   and-she-sleeps-hungry   night.
Reply.   Kweyot.
   The-broom.

I have a daughter who gets a good meal every morning, but she goes to bed hungry at night. What is she? A broom.
[The huts and compounds are swept out every morning, and a broom has a good meal of dust and dirt; but it goes hungry till the next morning.]

No. 8.   A-tinye   choruén-nyō   n-ingo-'ok-te   ko-lapat.
Enigma.   I-have   the-friend-my   whom-if-I-send   and-he-runs.
Reply.   Moiet.
   The belly.

PLATE XLI

Nandi honey barrel (Hart).

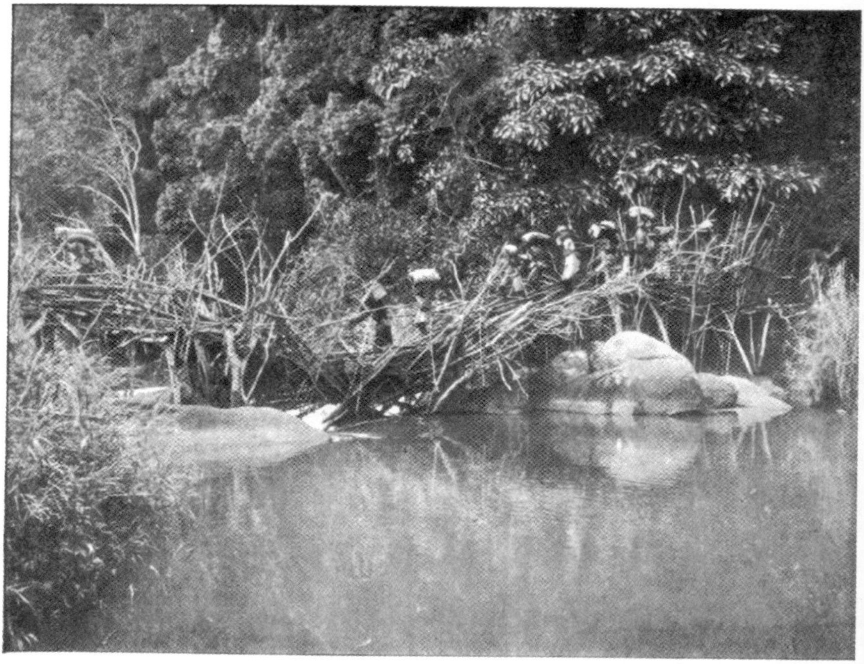

A Nandi bridge (Meinertzhagen).

NANDI ENIGMAS

I have a friend, and if I send him anywhere he runs with me. What am I ? The belly.

[If a person feels the pangs of hunger, his legs will move quickly in order to bring him to a place where food can be obtained.]

No. 9. *Enigma.*	A-tinye I-have	choruén-nyō the-friend-my	ne-ki-mo-koto-me who-did-not-yet-die
	ko-re and-it-brings-him	mo kut belly until	ko-me. he-may-die.
Reply.	Motonda. The vulture.		

I have a friend who would not die were it not for his belly's sake. What is my friend ? A vulture.

[A hungry vulture will run any risk to obtain food, and can be easily killed when settled on the ground feeding. Were it not for this he might remain flying about in the heavens and never be touched.]

No. 10. *Enigma.*	A-tinye I-have	lakwén-nyō the-child-my	ne-ki-ko-nai who-is-known	ko-chor-e. and-it-steals.
Reply.	Muriat. The rat.			

I have a child who is known to steal. What is my child ? A rat.

No. 11. *Enigma.*	A-tinye I-have	lakwet the-child	ne-mīban. who-runs-fast.
Reply.	Segemyat. The-bee.		

What is it which I possess that moves very rapidly ? A bee.

No. 12. *Enigma.*	A-tinye I-have	lakwet the-child	ne-sil-u-o who-draws-hither-me
	pêk-ap-Kepen. waters-of-Kepen.		
Reply.	Segemyat. The-bee.		

I have a child that draws water for me from the rocks. What is my child ? A bee.

[A beehive made in the rocks is called Kepen, or cave.]

No. 13. *Enigma.*	A-tinye I-have	lakōk the-children	pokol hundred	añg and	tukul all
	ko-chuchun-o. and-they-suck-me.				

Reply.   Toloita   ak   kureyuek.
           The-central-pole-of-the-house   and   the-poles-of-the-roof.

I have a hundred children and I support them all. What am I and what are they?
The central pole of the house and the poles of the roof.

No. 14.   A-tinye   mukulen   aku   pa-papa.
Enigma.   I-have   circular-things   but   of-Father.
Reply.   Chepwilpwilōk.
             The-biceps.

I have something which is round, but which really belongs to my father. What is it?   My biceps.
[A child's strength is always at his father's disposal.]

No. 15.   Chapoi-i   litei.
Enigma.   It-slips   whetstone.
Reply.   Koito.
             The-liver.

What slips in the hand like a knife on the whetstone?   Liver.

No. 16.   Char-chi-n   asis   kulua.
Enigma.   It-rises-out-of   sun   valley.
Reply.   Taet.
             The-brass-wire.

What is the sun rising out of the valley like?   Brass wire.
[If the sun comes out when one is in the valley, the glare is like polished brass wire.]

No. 17.   I-ie   tururik   annan   i-ie
Enigma.   Thou-drinkest   the-dirty-waters   or   thou-drinkest
   che-tililin.
   which-are-clean.

Reply.   Oi-'e   tururik.
             I-drink   the-dirty-waters.

Which would you prefer, water made dirty by the feet of oxen or clean water?
I would rather have the dirty water, as I should then own cattle.

No. 18.   I-let-u   annan   i-'ndoï-i.
Enigma.   Thou-comest-after   or   thou-precedest.
Reply.   A-let-u.
             I-come-after.

[This is equivalent to: 'Will you die after or before me?' The reply is obvious.]

NANDI ENIGMAS

No. 19. I-lu-e   sotet   ne-marīch-kut
Enigma. Thou-drinkest-milk the-calabash which-is-wide-mouth
   annan   ne-para-kut.
   or   which-is-narrow-mouth.

Reply. M-a-lu-e.
   I-drink-not-milk.

Which would you prefer, to drink milk from a calabash which has a wide mouth or from one which has a narrow mouth ?
I will drink from neither.
[Calabashes with narrow mouths are said to be males; those with wide mouths, females.]

No. 20.   Inga-'añg-anu   chepo-mee
Enigma. If-I-see-coming-towards-me of-agricultural-people
   a-rori   kut   a-siep patai.
   and-I-laugh very-much I-lie-on back.

Reply. Iseriat.
   The-louse.

If I see a person coming towards me I only laugh and turn over on my back. What am I ?   A louse.
[Cf. the Masai proverb, 'One finger will not kill a louse.']

Also: Inga-'añg-anu   ane   a-tior-chi
   If-I-see-him-coming-towards-me I I-kick-at
   pures   konyan.
   thing-of-no-value eyes.

Reply. Kimitia.
   Flea.

If I see a person coming towards me I kick dust into his eyes, *i. e.* I escape. What am I ?   A flea.
[A flea jumps and escapes if it sees a finger coming towards it.]

No. 21. Inga-i koiītin iīt marinwek-ap-Kony.
Enigma. If-thou-art counter count the-nullahs-of-Mt.-Elgon.
Reply. Pôk.
   The-honey-comb.

What is counting the nullahs on Mt. Elgon like ?
Counting the cells in honey-comb.

No. 22. Ingephe ainón-ni inge-cheñg gorko
Enigma. Let-us-go the-river-this let-us-search woman
   ne-chañg-ingorai.
   who-many-garments.

Reply. Sasurik.
The-wild-bananas.

There lives by the river a woman who has many garments. What is she? The wild banana plant.

[The wild banana plant grows in great luxuriance in Western Nandi.]

No. 23. Ingephe ainón-ni inge-cheñg gorko
Enigma. Let-us-go the-river-this let-us-search woman
 ne-tui.
 who-is-black.

Reply. Sengwet.
The-obsidian.

There lives by the river a black woman. What is she? Obsidian.

[Obsidian, which is generally black in colour, is a glass produced by volcanoes. It is found in large quantities in various parts of East Africa.]

No. 24. Ip-u tapet ki-am-e ilet.
Enigma. Bring the-cup and-we-eat-with the-thunder.

Reply. Kumiat.
The-honey.

What is in the cup from which both the thunder-god and ourselves obtain food? Honey.

[The thunder-god is supposed to visit the honey-barrels from time to time and take his supply of honey from them.]

No. 25. I-'u-i-e-ke cheptam annan
Enigma. Thou-bindest-thyself-the-waist-with dry-thing or
 ingiriren.
 soft-piece-of-hide.

Reply. Legetio ak eren.
 Belt and snake.

Which would you rather bind round your waist, a dry stick or a soft cord? A dry stick, because a soft cord is a snake.

[There is some play on the words 'ingiriren' and 'eren'. 'Ingiriren' means a piece of dressed hide, 'ingi-iur eren,' May he prod (the) snake.]

No. 26. Iro! Kechiré-chun ko-mo tuiyot.
Enigma. Look! The-sheep-those and-they-are-not the-crowd.

Reply. Tindinyek.
The-turfs.

PLATE XLII

Nandi women crushing grain (Rayne).

Nandi women going to market (Henderson).

There is a flock of sheep grazing, and the animals are not crowded together. What do they remind you of?
Turf cut ready for burning.
[Manure is made from the ashes of turf which is cut into sods, turned over, and dried. Only portions of the turf are visible when it is being dried, and the patches of green amongst the black or red earth are said to resemble a flock of sheep scattered over a large field.]

No. 27.   I-ru-e   kot-ap-tesiimik   annan
Enigma.   Wilt-thou-sleep   the-hut-of-the-castrated-goats   or
     nepo-mengīchek.
     of-the-rams.
Reply.   Leluek   ak   kimaketōk.
     The-jackals   and   the-hyenas.

Would you rather sleep in the goats' shed or in the sheep pen?
I will sleep in neither, for the goats are the jackals and the sheep the hyenas.
[Goats and sheep are sometimes styled jackals and hyenas, for when they enter a plantation they eat up everything.]

No. 28.   Iut-yin-dos   a-ma-par-i-ke.
Enigma. They-bellow-at-one-another and-they-do-not-kill-one-another.
Reply.   Aiyuet.
     The-axe.

What are the things which make a noise at one another, like bulls bellowing before a fight, but which do not hurt one another? Axes.
[It is usual in Nandi, when women cut firewood, for two to chop at the same tree, like blacksmiths in England hammering on an anvil. Each axe in turn is said to challenge the other to fight, but no harm is done.]

No. 29.   Ka-a-'chut   rīke   kwe   Lem.
Enigma.   I-have-pulled   thong   and-it-goes   Kavirondo.
Reply.   Luket.
     The-war-party.

What is like a thong which when stretched reaches from Nandi to Kavirondo? A war-party.
[When on the war-path the Nandi always march in single file.]

No. 30.   Ka-a-nyor-u   koko
Enigma.   I-have-met-with   grandmother
     ko-kesen-isye.
     she-was-carrying (something)-on-her-back.

Reply. Iseriat.
The-louse.

What does an old woman carry on her back? Lice.
[An old woman is unable to carry a load of any description.]

No. 31. Ka-a-nyor-u komit ko-pun-u pukaa kut.
Enigma. I-have-met-with thy-mother and-it-issues froth mouth.
Reply. Teret-ap-kimoi.
The-pot-of-porridge.

I saw your mother, and there was froth coming from her mouth. What is she? The pot of porridge bubbling over at the fire.
[After a child has been weaned the porridge-pot is said to be his mother.]

No. 32. Ka-a-tui-ye kamet ko-ip-e
Enigma. I-have-met-together-with the-mother she-was-carrying
meti'-'p-chii.
the-head-of-man.
Reply. Chepololet.
The-pumpkin.

I met a woman carrying something which resembled a man's head. What was it? A pumpkin.

No. 33. Ka-a-tui-ye kōnut
Enigma. I-have-met-together-with thy-father
ko-'lak-anu sambu.
and-he-wore-and-came-hither fur-cloak.
Reply. Cheputiet.
The-caterpillar.

I have met your father wearing his fur cloak. What does he resemble? A caterpillar.
[An old man wrapped up in a fur cloak and walking slowly is said to look like a caterpillar.]

No. 34. Karap i-nyo koín-nyō i-iro
Enigma. Evening and-thou-comest the-house-my and-thou-seest
lakók-chōk inga-a-'uriet.
the-children-my if-I-drive-them-away.
Reply. Cherengis.
House-lizard.

If you come to my house in the evening you will see me drive away my children. What am I? The house lizard.
[When the house lizard falls from the roof or ceiling of a hut on to

---

[1] For *metit-ap-chii*.

NANDI ENIGMAS

the floor—a frequent occurrence when there is a big fire in the house—everybody present gets up and goes outside.]

No. 35. Ki-a-ai imbaret nette yu ok yun
Enigma. I-made the-field from here and } there
                                                                                                                               to }
        ko-ur   kwen-u.
and-it-is-out-of-cultivation   in-between-(hither).

Reply.   Kutund'-ap-artet.
          The-knee-of-the-goat.

I had a large plantation, but it went out of cultivation in the middle. What did it remind one of?
A goat's leg, the knee of which had worn bare.

No. 36. Ki-a-eny giplelyo ak kipsitye
Enigma. I-slaughtered white-ox and red-ox
     kw-'oiechin   muiuek.
and-they-resembled-each-other   the-hides.

Reply.   Parak   ak   ingoiny.
         Above and beneath.

I slaughtered two oxen, one red and the other white, and their hides were alike. What were they?   The earth and the sky.
[Cf. the Masai riddle, ' I have two skins, one to lie on and the other to cover myself with. What are they? The bare ground and the sky.']

No. 37. Ki-a-ep-e korok pitón-i ak a-ep-e
Enigma. I-was-chopping stick the-bank-this and I-chop
   pitón-in   te-'p-a-tui-ye
the-bank-that   again-afterwards-I-place-them-together
   kw-'oiechin.
and-they-are-alike.

Reply.   Osotik.
         The-married-women.

I cut one stick on this side of the river and another one on the far side, and when I placed them together, I found they were alike. What were my sticks?   Two women.
[It makes no difference which clan or family one selects one's wife from, they are all women.]

No. 38. Ki-a-mwok-te kótén-nyō ko-ma-tar-at,
Enigma. I-shot-thither the-arrow-my and-it-is-not-feathered,
  tun   te-'p-a-ip-u   ko-tar-at.
presently again-afterwards-I-bring-it and-it-is-feathered.

142   THE NANDI

Reply.   Paiyuat.
               The-eleusine-plant.

I shot off my arrow and it was not feathered, but when I went to fetch it, it was feathered. What was my arrow ?   The eleusine plant.

[The head of the eleusine plant resembles somewhat the feathered end of an arrow. When sown, the grain has no feathers, but when reaped the head has formed.]

No. 39.	Ki-a-'ok-te	kiruog	ko-pa	ingoiny.
Enigma.	I-sent	advisers	and-they-went	below.
Reply.	Lumeyuek.			
	The-poles.			

I dispatched the advisers, and they entered the earth. What were they ?   The poles of a house.

[Here the word adviser, counsellor, or spokesman—the prop or mainstay of the Nandi system of government—is used as synonymous with the outside poles (*i. e.* the principal support) of a house.]

No. 40.	Ki-a-'pat	imbarén-nyō	nette	yu	ok
Enigma.	I-cultivated	the-plantation-my	from	here	and to
	yun	ko-tar	siiya.		
	there	and-it-has-finished-it	nail.		
Reply.	Chepkeswet.				
	The-knife.				

Fig. 52 (scale ¼).   *Chepkeswet*, small knife.

I have a large plantation, and I finished the work on it with my nail. What is my nail ?   A small knife.

[The last part of the work on a millet plantation, *viz.* the harvest, is performed with the help of a small knife, scarcely bigger or sharper than one's nail.]

No. 41.	Ki-a-wir	chepkemis	ko-put-ye
Enigma.	I-threw	chepkemis-bird	and-it-fell-thither
	mesua.		
	mesuot-tree.		
Reply.	Ñgariet.		
	The-red-clay.		

PLATE XLIII

A salt-lick (Meinertzhagen).

River in Nandi (Meinertzhagen).

NANDI ENIGMAS 143

I threw a club at the chepkemis bird, and it fell by a mesuot tree. What was the bird? Red clay.

[The chepkemis bird—a small bird with a red breast—is said to live where the red clay is found with which the warriors paint their faces and bodies. If one of these birds were seen, it would be almost certain that some of the red clay would not be far away.]

No. 42.	Ki-a-tarñgañg-e	a-tar	are.
Enigma.	I-lay-on-my-back	I-may-finish	kids.
Reply.	Koiit'-ap-pai.		
	The-grindstone.		

I lay on by my back in order that I might finish (eating) the kids. What am I? A grindstone.

[A grindstone when not in use is placed on its side against the wall of the hut. When laid on its back, it is for the purpose of crushing grain. *Are*, though originally the equivalent of kids, is also used for the young of any animal, and is here employed for the young or seed of corn.]

No. 43.	Ki-a-u,	'ngo-a-u-e	ko	somok
Enigma.	I-moved,	when-I-moved	and-they-are	three
	nêko,	te-'p-a-ket-u-ke		ko
	the-goats,	again-afterwards-I-return-hither-myself		and-they-are
	somok	ko-keny.		
	three	still.		
Reply.	Koiik-am-ma.			
	The-stones-of-the-fire.			

I moved my abode and left three goats behind; when I returned there were still three goats. What were the goats? The fire stones.

[Cooking-pots are always rested on three stones, which are left behind when a person moves.]

No. 44.	Ki-a-u	kut	a-meny	or-tapan.
Enigma.	I-moved	until	I-may-stay	road-side.
Reply.		Kosomek.		
	The-small-flies-which-follow-bees.			

What is the thing that continually changes its abode until it finally settles by the way-side? The small fly which follows the bee into its hive, where it dies.

No. 45.	Ki-a-u	kut	ko-put	terget-ap-lakwet.
Enigma.	I-moved	until	it-may-drop	the-calabash-of-the-child.
Reply.	Talusiet.			
	The-tick.			

What does it remind one of if a journey is so long that a child at length drops the gourd it is carrying from sheer weariness?

A tick which, having gorged itself on an ox, is unable to keep its hold any more and falls off.

No. 46.   Ki-a-u,   tun   'nga-it-u
Enigma.   I-moved,   afterwards   if-I-arrive-hither

     ki-tien-e   kot   sondoiyo.
     it-is-being-danced   the-house   old-men's-dance.

Reply.   Kimitek.
     The-fleas.

What should I find dancing the *sondoiyot* dance in my house were I to leave it for a time and then return?   Fleas.

[Vermin of all kinds are common in Nandi, especially in deserted huts or kraals.]

No. 47.   Ki-a-u,   tun   'nga-it-u   kwa
Enigma.   I-moved,   afterwards   if-I-arrive-hither   and

     ki-'tur-e   kot   sigilgil.
     they-lean-against   the-house   women's-walking-sticks.

Reply.   Susuek.
     The-grasses.

Fig. 53 (scale $\frac{1}{10}$). Woman's walking-stick.

If I were to move and then to return to my house I should find women's walking-sticks standing up against the walls. What are the walking-sticks?   Blades of grass.

[Women use thin walking-sticks like reeds. When weeds have sprung up around and in a deserted hut, they are said to be leaning up against the walls like walking-sticks.]

No. 48.   Ki-a-we   koi-in   añg-nya-it-ite
Enigma.   I-went   the-house-that   when-I-arrived-thither

     ke-me,   a-me   akine.
     they-have-died,   and-I-die   myself.

Reply.   Ruondo.
     The-sleep.

When I arrived at a certain house and found the occupants dead, I died myself. What was the death?   Sleep.

Two young Nandi warriors—full face (Henderson).

Two young Nandi warriors—profile (Henderson).

To face p. 144

NANDI ENIGMAS 145

No. 49.   Ki-a-wir-te   mukurio
Enigma.   I-threw-thither   women's-iron-wire-bracelet
     kwa   Soiin.
   and-it-goes   Soiin.
Reply.   Mukunget-ap-pēliot.
     The-spoor-of-the-elephant.

If I throw down a woman's iron-wire bracelet, what does the mark made in the ground remind one of?
The spoor of an elephant.

[Nandi women wear a bracelet made of iron wire wound round the arm from the wrist to the elbow. Soiin is the southern county of Nandi. It is a barren country, but herds of elephants occasionally visit it.]

No. 50.   Ki-ip   rokchet   a-mo-ip-u.
Enigma.   He-took   the-potsherd   and-he-did-not-bring-it-(back).
Reply.   Sakot.
     The-grass-basket.

A man took away a potsherd, but did not return it. What was the potsherd?   A grass basket.

[A piece of broken pot and a basket made of a few wisps of straw plaited together are equally valueless, and would be thrown away as soon as they had done what was required of them.]

No. 51.   Ki-ki-ñgot   kaita,   kut   ki-ñgot-e
Enigma.   It-was-made   the-house }   even   and-it-was-being-made
                             kraal }
   tilatit.
   the-thorn-enclosure.
Reply.   Konda.
     The-eye.

A hut has been made and the thorn enclosure is in course of construction. What are they?   The eye and the eyebrow.

No. 52.   Ki-lul   ket   eñg-Gipsikīs,   ko-it
Enigma.   It-fell   tree   in-Lumbwa,   and-it-arrived
   oli   simamik.
   here   the-twigs.
Reply.   Wakat.
     The-shout.

A tree fell in Lumbwa and its branches reached Nandi. What was the tree?   A great noise.

No. 53.	Kipkeleny	tulua.
Enigma.	The-lifter	mountain.
Reply.	Popat.	
	The-mushroom.	

What lifts up a mountain? A mushroom.

[A mushroom in sprouting frequently pushes aside a clod of earth which, owing to its size, might well have prevented it from growing at all.]

No. 54.	Kipkurkur	ki-wo	to.
Enigma.	Warrior's-bell	it-went	hiding-place.
Reply.	Puñguñgwet.		
	The-mole.		

What does a warrior's bell which is hidden away (*i.e.* muffled) remind you of? A mole.

[A mole in its hole makes much the same noise as a muffled bell.]

No. 55.		Kororon	tarīt
Enigma.		They-are-beautiful	birds
	a-m-oon-e	takipos.	
	and-they-do-not-chase-away }	wagtail.	
	surpass		
Reply.	Koroiityet.		
	The-Colobus-monkey.		

There are many beautiful birds, but they do not surpass the wagtail. What does this bird remind you of? The Colobus monkey.

[The colour of both the wagtail of Nandi and the Colobus monkey is black and white, and although there are other handsome birds and monkeys it would be difficult to find anything to surpass either in beauty. The wagtail is one of the few songsters in East Africa, its song often reminding one of a canary bird.]

No. 56.	Mwaib'-a'-pēlio [1]	ki-'le	kor.
Enigma.	The-fat-of-elephant	it-said	it-is-dry.
Reply.	Ñgenda.		
	The-salt-lick.		

The fat of the elephant said: 'What is the use of me? I am dry.' What is the fat? The salt-lick.

[The Nandi prize the fat of elephants, which they use to anoint their bodies with, and even when it becomes dry and hard, it is as good as when liquid and moist, just as the salt of the salt-licks, which though mixed with mud and sand, is as good as pure salt.]

---

[1] For *mwait'-ap-pēliot*.

NANDI ENIGMAS

No. 57.   Kot-ap-koko   ikongen   tukul.
Enigma.   The-hut-of-grandmother   small-baskets   all.

Reply.   Keringonik.
         The-pits.

Why is the floor of grandmother's hut like small baskets ?
Because the goats and sheep have stamped or made holes in it.
[After a house has been erected for some time the floor of the goats' compartment becomes full of holes.]

No. 58.   Lamaiyua   ka-'ñgat-an.
Enigma.   *Ximenia-Americana*   it-has-grown-hither.

Reply.   Saruriet-am-mengit.
         The-tail-of-the-ram.

What grows rapidly like a *lamaiyuet* tree ?
The tail of a (fat-tailed) sheep.

No. 59.   Mi-i-te   ket   Soiin   ne-mo-tinye   soko.
Enigma.   It-is-there   tree   Soiin   which-not-has   leaves.

Reply.   Koiita.
         The-stone.

There are trees in Soiin which have no leaves. What are they ?
Stones.

Also :   Mi-i   ket   Soiin   ne-mo-tinye   tīkītio.
        There-is   tree   Soiin   which-not-has   root.

Koiita.
The-stone.

There are trees in Soiin which have no roots. What are they ?
Stones.
[Soiin, the southern county of Nandi, is a mountainous and barren land, in which there are but few trees.]

No. 60.   Nĕget   ko-'p-chep-komit   a-me-i-it-e.
Enigma.   It-is-near   house-of-thy-sister   and-thou-dost-not-arrive.

Reply.   Oret-ap-patai.
         The-road-of-back. }
         The-back-bone. }

Thy sister's house is near, yet thou canst not reach it. What is thy sister's house ?   The back-bone.

No. 61.   'Nga-a-we   koi-in   a-pan,
Enigma.   If-I-go   the-house-that   and-I-leave-magic,

    ta-a-we   koi-in   a-pan.
    again-I-go   the-house-that   and-I-leave-magic.

Reply.   Ñgulek.
             The-spittle.

No matter where I go I am sure to leave something behind by which a wizard or a witch can make me ill. What do I leave behind? Spittle.

[The Nandi spit freely, not only to avert ill-luck but to relieve the excessive amount of saliva that collects in their mouths. If a wizard or a witch were to collect any of this saliva, it is believed, the person from whom it emanated could be bewitched.]

No. 62.   Ngiri,   ngiri.
Enigma.   That-yonder,   that-yonder.
Reply.   Tomirimir.
                 A-man's-shadow.

[All Nandi, but more particularly children, are very afraid of a shadow, as it is believed that a man's shadow lives after his death. Riddles, as already stated, are only asked after dark, and this one might be turned as follows: 'What can I see in the dark? Ghosts.']

No. 63.   Ñgurur-in   a-ma-am-in.
Enigma.   It-looks-down-at-thee but-it-does-not-eat-thee.
Reply.   Serut.
                 The-nose.

What is the thing which looks down at you but which does not eat you? The nose.

No. 64.   Nīr[1]   ma-ñget.
Enigma.   It-is-drawn-out not-it-breaks.
Reply.   Ainet   annan   oret.
                 The-river or   the-road.

What is it that does not break though you may draw it out as far as you like? A river or a road.

No. 65.   Oon-w-a   piich   che-koiin
Enigma.   They-chase-me-hither   people   which-are-long
                 kelien.
                 legs.
Reply.   Robta.
                 The-rain.

What are the long-legged people who have made me fly back home? The drops of rain.

---

[1] This word is generally used for drawing the entrails out of a slaughtered animal.

NANDI ENIGMAS 149

No. 66. Oswa-ap-Ilat ko-kwer ingoiny.
Enigma. The-old-things-of-Thunder and-they-arrive ground.
Reply. Chemñgisir ak kwapal.
Inner-rainbow and outer-rainbow.

What are the thunder-god's discarded garments which fall on the earth ? The inner and outer rings of the rainbow.[1]

No. 67. Samo koko samo
Enigma. Many-coloured grandmother many-coloured
chepo-kikat.
the-daughter-of-the-person-who-salutes-(her).
Reply. Kimnyet ak kirokoret.
The-porridge and the-basket.

If you see a child resembling in appearance its grandmother, what does it remind you of?

Porridge which has been put in a basket, and which on being taken out again has assumed the shape and taken the markings of the basket.

[' Like master, like man.']

No. 68. Siisi!
Enigma. An exclamation of despair.
Reply. Toiek.
The-strangers.

When does one say : ' What *shall* I do ? '

When strangers arrive and there is no food in the house.

[The Nandi are most hospitable to people of their own *mat*,[2] but, if some strangers were to arrive after the evening meal, the host might be at his wits' end to know how to procure food for them, and might unwittingly have to run the risk of being considered stingy.]

No. 69. Sot'-ap-kok
Enigma. Gourd-of-warriors'-assembly-place

ma-nye che.
it-has-not-become-full milks.
Reply. Ñgototek.
The-cow-dung.

The milk calabashes taken to the warriors' assembly place are never full. What does the milk resemble in this respect ? Cow-dung.

[The warriors' assembly places are generally in or near the cattle kraals, and just as these places are never allowed to fill with cattle dung, so the warriors never leave their milk calabashes full of milk.]

[1] *Vide* p. 100.   [2] *Vide* p. 77.

No. 70.   Tapalia-kuk.
Enigma.   Thing-against-which-one-has-struck-one's-foot.
Reply.   Kanōkut.
             Omen.

If I strike my foot against something, what does it signify? It is an omen for good or evil.[1]

No. 71.   Tapen!   Tōtón-nin   ki-tet
Enigma.   Look!   The-wall-that-(inside-the-house) it-arranged-(it)
  oi.
  spirits.
Reply.   Kelek.
           The-teeth.

What is the wall inside a man's house (body) which was made by the spirits (of his ancestors)?   His teeth.

No. 72.   Tapen   tu-chun!   Iok-i
Enigma.   Look-at   the-oxen-those!   It-is-herding-them
  kimnyelnyel.
  thing-which-is-blown-about-by-the-wind.
Reply.   Sombet.
           The-ostrich-feather-head-dress.

What is the thing which, though so weak that it is blown about by the wind, is able to herd oxen?
The ostrich-feather head-dress.

[In Nandi the grass is frequently so high that only a warrior's head-dress can be seen above it, and at first sight it often appears as if a herd of oxen were being guarded by the ostrich feathers, which are the plaything of every gust of wind.]

No. 73.   Tapen   tu-chun!   Iok-i
Enigma.   Look-at   the-oxen-those!   It-is-herding-them
  kipsitye.
  red-brown-thing.
Reply.   Kwanget.
           The-bow.

What is the red-brown thing that is herding the cattle?
The bow.

[As in the last riddle, when the grass is long a person herding cattle is often quite concealed from view, and it appears as if his bow, which is red-brown in colour, is doing the work of herdsman.]

---

[1] *Vide* p. 79.

NANDI ENIGMAS

No. 74. Telel koiech.
Enigma. Stand all-night.
Reply. Arawet ak kuinet-ap-teta.
The-moon and the-horn-of-the-ox.

What remains erect all night ?
The moon and the horn of an ox.

No. 75. Tos! I-lany kōn met-i ?
Enigma. I-don't-know! Thou-climbest thy-father head ?
Reply. Ñgotit.
The-spear.

What would climbing on to your father's head be like ?
Climbing a spear.

[A Nandi *paterfamilias* would resent his son climbing on to his head, and the son's appearance, were he bold enough to attempt this, would be much the same as if he were to try and climb a spear.]

No. 76. Tui a-ma-po ke-rar
Enigma. Black and-they-do-not-make-it it-is-cut
kipoia.
warrior's-garment.
Reply. Chepkwogit.
The-crow.

What is it that is not made by hand, that is black, and is fashioned like a warrior's garment (*i. e.* with hairs on it) ? A crow.

PART II

ÑGALEK-AP-NANDI
NANDI GRAMMAR

ALPHABET AND PRONUNCIATION.

Vowels.

A represents the English *a* in father.
Ē   ,,   ,,   *a* in fate.
E   ,,   ,,   *e* in benefit.
Ä   ,,   ,,   *a* in dare.
I   ,,   ,,   *i* in hit.
Ī   ,,   ,,   *i* in ravine.
O   ,,   ,,   *o* in not.
Ō   ,,   ,,   *o* in mote.
U   ,,   ,,   *u* in bull.
Ū   ,,   ,,   *u* in flute.
Ai ,,   ,,   *ai* in aisle.

Ae is a diphthong similar to *ai*, but formed by a unison of the vowels *a* and *e*.

Au represents the English *ow* in how.

Oi   ,,   ,,   *oi* in oil.

Ei. These two letters are usually pronounced separately, but they are sometimes slurred over and are scarcely distinguishable from *ei* in eight or *ey* in they.

Whenever *ai* or *oi* are not pronounced as diphthongs, the *i* is marked by a diaeresis, thus *aï*.

Vowels are only doubled when there is a distinct repetition of a single sound.

Â is used to express a prolonged short *a* not amounting to *aa*, or a contracted *aa*.

Ế is used to express a prolonged short *e* not amounting to *ee*.

Ô represents the English *aw* in paw.

There is a dull vowel sound (*i̯*) at the commencement of a few words

ALPHABET AND PRONUNCIATION 153

like the Russian ы, or the unaccentuated *i* in some English words, e.g. *Charity*. This sound reminds one of the dull vowel sound which precedes substantives commencing with *m* in Swahili. Examples: *ïllo*, six; *ïpche*, to divide; *ïmrok*, to cross a road.

CONSONANTS.

B, d, k as in English.
G is hard as in the English word go.
H is not used as a separate letter.
J nearly resembles the English *j*.
Ch as in church.
Sh, l, m, n as in English.
Ng has two separate sounds, the one hard as in the English word finger, the other as in singer. The latter sound is written *ñg*.
Ny. This sound is similar to *ni* in the English word minion, or *ñ* in Spanish.
P as in English. This letter is often exchangeable with *v*.
Ph is a *p* followed by an *h*.
R is always well pronounced or rolled on the tongue.
S, t, w as in English.
Y is a consonant, as in yard.
Z as in English.
Consonants are only doubled when there is a distinct repetition of a single sound.

CHANGES OF LETTERS.

A and *o* are frequently interchangeable; e.g. añg? or oñg?, what sort of ?; ak *or* ok, and.

A usually changes to *o* in the formation of the plural:

    Kararan, pl. kororon, beautiful.
    Pananet, pl. pononik, the poor person.

When *a* is the vowel of the verbal root, it generally becomes *o* in the present tense. Thus:

    Itany, to forge;   a-'tony-i, I forge.
    Wal, to alter;   a-wol-e, I alter.

O is also sometimes used for *a* as the personal prefix in the first person singular:

    Ai, to do;   o-oi-e, I do.
    Iiny, to squeeze;   o-'iny-i, I squeeze.

E sometimes changes to *i* in the formation of the plural of adjectives:

> Wesis, pl. wisisin, gentle.
> Sames, pl. somis, rotten.

When a substantive commences with *i*, that letter is at times not pronounced in conversation; *e. g.*

> 'Ngotiot *for* Ingotiot, the giraffe.

Verbs commencing with *i* frequently drop that letter. For particulars see pp. 189–90; it will be sufficient to give here one or two examples:

> iput, to drop;   a-'put-i, I drop (it);
> o-'put-i, you drop (it);   ke-'put, he *or* she has dropped (it).

K, *t*, and *ch* change to *g*, *d*, and *j* respectively after *n*, *ñg*, or *ny*. Examples:

> Ka-a-'un-ge (*for* ka-a-'un-ke), I have bathed.
> A-un-doi-i (*for* a-un-toi-i), I am letting (him) go.
> Sesén-ju (*for* sesén-chu), these dogs.
> Añg gitonga (*for* añg kitonga)? What sort of a basket?
> Añg duluo (*for* añg tuluo)? What sort of a mountain?
> Añg jorua (*for* añg chorua)? What sort of a friend?
> Ka-a-uny-ge (*for* ka-a-uny-ke), I have hidden myself.
> Tany dui (*for* tany tui), black ox.
> Kwany-ji (*for* kwany-chi), they approach it.

T becomes *d* after *m* and *l*,[1] and *s* becomes *z* after *n*:

> Sirimdo (*for* sirimto), the chain.
> A-'ul-dos-i (*for* a-'ul-tos-i), I cause (him) to squabble with someone.
> Iun-ze (*for* iun-se), to wash.

T becomes *n* and other changes of spelling occur when a singular substantive joined to the article is followed by a demonstrative or possessive pronoun. For particulars see pp. 160–3.

In conversation, the *t* of the singular article is often slurred over or changed to *n* if the word which follows commences with *n*. If, however, the speaker is not understood, and the sentence has to be repeated, care is taken to pronounce the *t*; *e. g.*

> Sesen ne-oo *for* seset ne-oo, the big dog.

When *ch* is the terminal letter of simple verbs, it changes to *k* in the formation of derivatives:

---

[1] The only exception to this rule appears to be the word *olto*, the place.

CHANGES OF LETTERS

Tuch, to cover ;   tuk-u, to cover hither.
Iwech, to return (act.);   wek-e, to return (neut.).
Iroch, to dip ;   irok-te, to dip thither.

Ch changes to *y* after *t* :

Met-yi (*for* met-chi), to throw at.

Io or *yo* change to *cho* after *p* :

Mopcho (*for* mopio *or* mopyo), sugar cane.

The *p* of the masculine and feminine prefixes, *kip* and *chep* (see p. 158), becomes *m* before *n*, *ñg*, or *ny* :

Kim-naria, a bull with white marks round its eyes.
Chem-naria, a cow with white marks round its eyes.
Kim-ñgosos, a shy bull.
Chem-ñgosos, a shy cow.
Kim-nyokorio, a cowardly man.
Chem-nyokorio, a cowardly woman.

P usually changes to *m* when followed by *m* :

Kond'-am-moita (*for* kond'-ap-moita), the calf's eye.

But when the masculine and feminine prefixes are followed by *m* the *p* is omitted :

Ki-makoñg, a one-eyed bull.
Che-makoñg, a one-eyed cow.

The *p* of the masculine and feminine prefixes is also omitted when followed by another *p* :

Ki-porus, a grey bull.
Che-porus, a grey cow.

The *p* of the feminine prefix is omitted when followed by a word beginning with *sa* or *so*. When followed by a word commencing with *er*, the *ep* of the feminine prefix falls out :

Che-samo, a dapple grey cow.
Che-soleyua, colour.
(*But* Chep-seta, a cow with a crumpled horn.
Kip-samo, a dapple grey bull.)
Ch-eringis, lizard.
Ch-ereñgen, locust.
(*But* Kip-ereñgen, a cloud of locusts.)

K sometimes changes to *ñg* when followed by *m* or *n* :

Chept' añg murenet (*for* chept' ak murenet), the girl and the warrior.
Kipsikīsiek añg Nandiek (*for* Kipsikīsiek ak Nandiek), the Lumbwa and the Nandi.

Ñg changes to m before p and k. The k at the same time changes to g:

Em-pēliot (*for* eñg-pēliot), on the elephant.
Em-gwen (*for* eñg-kwen), the central county of Nandi.

Nd frequently changes to mb when followed by a genitive:
Pamb'-a'-pēt (*for* pand'-ap-pēt), the morning's journey.
Kwamba-anum (*for* kwand'-ap-anum), so-and-so's father.

T likewise sometimes changes to b when followed by a genitive:
Mwaib'-a'-pēliot (*for* mwait'-ap-pēliot), the elephant's fat.

I and y are often interchangeable, as are also u and w when followed by a, e, or o:

Poiisio *or* poiisyo, work.
Poiisiet *or* poiisyet, the work.
Tilia *or* tilya, peace.
Kesua *or* keswa, seed.
Kesuot *or* keswot, the seed.
Kesuek *or* keswek, the seeds.

THE ACCENT.

The general rule is that all syllables are accentuated alike, a slight stress being perhaps laid on the penultimate.

There are, however, exceptions to this rule:

1. If the penultimate syllable of a substantive (not joined to the singular article or other part of speech) is i or u followed by a, e, or o, the accent generally rests on the antepenultimate syllable:

Poiísio, work.
Késua, seed.
Kepenósiek, the caves.
Lolotínuek, the bags.

2. When the singular substantive joined to the article ends in t, the two words are spoken as one, and the article is usually lightly accentuated. All syllables are, however, frequently accentuated alike:

Sése, dog;	sesét, the dog.
Niánja, lake;	nianjét, the lake.
Poiísio, work;	poiisiét, the work.
Múren, warrior;	murenét, the warrior.
Mistóa, herdsman;	mistōát, the herdsman.
Segémya, bee;	segemyát, the bee.
Koñgónyo, crested crane;	koñgonyót, the crested crane.
Nandíin, Nandi;	Nandiindét, the Nandi (man).
Cheptíbi, ground-hornbill;	cheptībít, the ground-hornbill.
Tárit, bird;	tarityét, the bird.
Rúngu, club;	rungút, the club.

THE ACCENT

But when the substantive joined to the article ends in *ta, to, da,* or *do,* the accent rests on the penultimate :

Ñgélyep, tongue ; ñgelyépta, the tongue.
Kóris, air ; korísto, the air.
Koñg, eye ; kónda, the eye.
Sírim, chain ; sirímdo, the chain.

3. When the plural substantive (without the article) is the same as the singular substantive, or when a difference is made by only lengthening the last vowel, the accent rests on the last syllable :

Múren, warrior ; murén, warriors.
Tárit, bird ; tarít, birds.

4. When the plural substantive joined to the article is an abbreviated form of the true word, the article is lightly accentuated :

Mureník (*for* murenáiik), the warriors.
Kiptiltilók (*for* kiptiltiláiik), the woodpeckers.
Rotók (*for* rotonáiik), the swords.
Nianjók (*for* nianjásiek), the lakes.
Sirimwék (*for* sirimwágik), the chains.

5. In interrogative sentences, an accentuated *i* is generally affixed to the last word if that word is a noun or verb ending in a consonant. The voice is at the same time raised to a higher pitch than in European languages :

Ka-ko-rok, it is ready. Ka-ko-rok-í ? Is it ready ?
Ka-ko-rok pêk-í ? Is the water ready ?
Ka-ko-pa korúsiek, the women have gone.
Ka-ko-pa korusiek-í ? Have the women gone ?
Ka-a-'sup, I have followed (him).
Ka-a-'sup-í ? Have I followed (him) ? [1]

6. Whenever a word of two or more syllables is followed by a monosyllabic word the two words are spoken as one, and the last syllable of the longer word is distinctly accentuated : [2]

---

[1] No change takes place in the spelling of words ending in a vowel. In such cases the voice only is raised ; *e. g.*
A-'sup-i, I follow (him), *or* Am I following (him) ?
Ka-ko-rok cheko, the milk is ready, *or* Is the milk ready ?

[2] This is also the case in Masai, though not quite so marked. Examples :
Ol-chóre, the friend ; ol-choré lai (*pronounced* ol-chorélai), my friend.
Añgáta (*or* oñgóta), the plain ; añgatá pus (*pronounced* añgatápus *or* oñgotápus), the blue plain.
Metíu, it is not like ; metiú ae (*pronounced* metiúae), it is not like anything, *or* it does not matter.

A-wénd-i, I go.
A-wend-í ko (*pronounced* awendíko), I go to the house.
I-móch-e, thou wantest.
I-moch-é ne (*pronounced* imochéne)? What dost thou want?
Imbarán-ni (*pronounced* imbaránni), this plantation.
Kerichondón-ni (*pronounced* kerichondónni), this medicine.
Kutundán-nyō (*pronounced* kutundánnyō), my knee.
Oriandén-nyō ⎫　　　　　　　　oriandénnyō ⎫
　　or　　　 ⎬ (*pronounced*) 　or　　　　⎬ my ash.
Orián-nyō　 ⎭　　　　　　　　oriánnyō)　 ⎭

7. Whenever a word of two or more syllables is preceded by a monosyllabic word, the two words are spoken as one. If the second word is of two syllables, the accent rests on the first syllable. Examples:

Am ómdit (*pronounced* amómdit), eat the food.
(*But* Am omituágik (*pronounced* amomituágik), eat the foods.)
Pir séset (*pronounced* pirséset), beat the dog.
Kur áke (*pronounced* kuráke), call the other one.

8. If two or three monosyllabic words follow one another they are spoken as one, and the accent rests on the penultimate syllable. Example:

Pêk-ám-ma (*pronounced* pêkámma), hot water (*lit.* the waters of fire).

GENDER AND NUMBER.

The Nandi language distinguishes by the particles *kip* and *chep*[1] two genders or classes answering approximately to masculine and feminine. The former signifies big, strong, or masculine; the latter something of a small, weak, or feminine nature.

These particles are prefixed to certain substantives and often form a part of the word, which would be unintelligible without them; *e.g.*

Kipsikīsiek, the Lumbwa people.
Kipsirīchet, the rhinoceros.
Kipsoiyuet, the cock.
Cheptirgichet, the gazelle.
Chepkeswet, the small knife.
Chepkildet, the little finger.

At other times the particles are used to draw a distinction between the sexes, or between something great or small, and can be omitted; thus:

Sirue, a white ox, bull, bullock, or cow.
Kip-sirue, a white bull; chep-sirue, a white cow.

[1] Certain changes take place in the spelling of the particles *kip* and *chep* when the word which follows commences with *m, n, ñg, ny,* and *p,* &c. For particulars *vide* p. 155.

Koñgak, one-eyed.
Kip-koñgak, one-eyed (man); chep-koñgak, one-eyed (woman).
Ch-ereñgen, locust.
Kip-ereñgen, cloud of locusts.
Morin, fingers.
Ki-morin, centipede.

The particles *kip* and *chep* are occasionally also used in compound words without any substantive, in much the same way as the article is used in Masai.[1] Examples:

Kip-uny-i-ke, the (person) who hides himself.
Chep-eiyo (the-of-mother), my sister.
Kip-set-met, the (person) whose head goes to the wars (a name given to the chief medicine man : *vide* p. 50, n. 1, and p. 83).
Kip-kas-an, the (person) one hears is coming hither (Proverb No. 31).
Kerke ki-mutio ak ki-mīsing, the slow (speaker) and the fast (speaker) are alike (Proverb No. 13).
Kerke kip-set ak kip-tep, the raider and the home-stayer are alike (Proverb No. 14).

The particles *akut* and *angut*, which are prefixed to a few substantives and to one or two classes of pronouns to form the plural, appear to have in former times also marked the gender, *akut* being used for the masculine and *angut* for the feminine; but the distinction has now been nearly lost sight of, and *akut* or *angut* are used somewhat indiscriminately by the present generation. Old people, however, still generally use 'akut-kwanda' for *the fathers*, 'angut-kamet' for *the mothers*; 'akut-ñgô' (m.) and 'angut-ñgô' (f.) for *Who?* The Kipsikīsiek or Lumbwa are said to use *ingut* for both genders : they, however, also at times use *akut* for the masculine.

One word, *olto* (the place), might perhaps be classed by itself, as the demonstrative pronoun and some other parts of speech assume special forms when agreeing with it.

There are two numbers, singular and plural, which are marked by variations in the termination of nouns. Except for the interrogative pronoun *Who?*[2] there are no indications of reduplication being used to mark the plural of any part of speech. Nouns are not susceptible to any inflexions to mark the cases or the gender.

[1] *The Masai*, pp. 13-14.   [2] *Vide* pp. 188-9.

THE ARTICLE.

The article, which is affixed to the noun, is generally *t* in the singular and *k* in the plural. The singular article is also at times *ta, to, da,* or *do*,[1] and in a few instances the plural article is *ka* or *ko* (*e.g.* tuka, the oxen; cheko, the milk). The article is, as a rule, joined to the noun by one or more letters, and the last one or two letters of the noun are frequently changed when the article is employed. Examples:

Singular without article.	Singular with article.	Plural without article.	Plural with article.	English.
Sese	Seset	Sesen	Sesēnik	Dog.
Lol	Lolet	Lolotinua	Lolotinuek	Bag.
Punyo	Punyot	Pun	Punik	Enemy.
Legetio	Legetiet	Legetai	Legetaiik	Belt.
Morna	Mornet	Morin	Morīk	Finger.
Sirim	Sirimdo	Sirimwag	Sirimwagik	Chain.
Koñg	Konda	Konyan	Konyek	Eye.

The article is separable from the substantive, and in certain cases is not employed; but whenever it is joined to its noun the two words are spoken as one, and were it to be omitted, the speaker would not be understood. The place of the article can be taken by the indefinite pronoun, *tukul*, each, &c.,[2] by the interrogative pronouns, *ñgô*, &c., which?, and *añg?* what sort of?, and by the numeral *akenge*, one. Examples:

    Sese tukul, each dog.
    Sesé ñgô? Which dog?
    Añg sése? What sort of a dog?
    Sese akenge,[3] one dog.

The article and the termination of substantives undergo certain changes when the noun is accompanied by a demonstrative pronoun. When the singular substantive joined to the article ends in *ut*, the *t* is changed to *n*; when it ends in *et*, the *t* is changed to *n*, and the *e* to *a* or *o*; when it ends in *at* or *ot*, the *t* is changed to *ndan* or *ndon*; and when it ends in *it*, that termination is usually dropped as well as the

---

[1] When this form of the article is employed, the vowel is usually dropped when followed by a word commencing with *a* or *o*.
[2] When *tukul* is used to translate *all*, the article is retained, e.g. *sesēnik tukul*, all dogs, *or* all the dogs.
[3] *Seset akenge* may also be used.

THE ARTICLE

n of the demonstrative. Sometimes, however, words ending in *it* change the *t* to *n*, or the *it* to *on*, and omit the consonant of the demonstrative. When the singular substantive joined to the article ends in *ta* or *to*, these terminations are dropped if the demonstrative is used, as well as the *n* of the demonstrative. Similar changes take place in words ending in *da* or *do*, unless the letter which precedes the *d* is *n*, in which case the *d* is generally changed to *g* or *y*. Examples :

Ēut, the arm;	ēún-ni, this arm.
Itōkut, the bedstead;	itōkún-ni, this bedstead.
Seset, the dog;	sesón-ni, this dog.
Teret, the cooking-pot;	terón-ni, this cooking-pot.
Imbaret, the plantation;	imbarán-ni, this plantation.
Kaliañget, the fly;	kaliañgán-ni, this fly.
Oriat, the ash;	oriandán-ni, this ash.
Segemyat, the bee;	segemyandán-ni, this bee.
Kerichot, the medicine;	kerichondón-ni, this medicine.
Ingotiot, the giraffe;	ingotiondón-ni, this giraffe.
Iitīt, the ear;	iít-i, this ear.
Metit, the head;	mét-i, this head.
(*But* Kutit, the mouth;	kutín-i, this mouth.
Pītit, the bank of a river;	pītón-i, this bank of a river.)
Mwaita, the oil;	mwāi-i, this oil.
Rorta, the heifer;	rór-i, this heifer.
Porto, the body;	pór-i, this body.
Eito, the bullock;	eí-i, this bullock.
Sirimdo, the chain;	sirím-i, this chain.
Keldo, the leg;	kél-i, this leg.
Kutunda, the elbow, knee;	kutúñg-i, this elbow, knee.
Konda, the eye;	kóñg-i, this eye.
Tiondo, the animal;	tióny-i, this animal.
Ñgetundo, the lion;	ñgetúny-i, this lion.
(*But* Tiendo, the dance;	tién-i, this dance.
Miondo, the disease;	mión-i, this disease.)

When the plural substantive joined to the article is accompanied by a demonstrative pronoun, the *k* of the article is dropped. If the termination is *enik* or *onik* the *i* is likewise omitted, and the *ch* of the demonstrative pronoun becomes *j*. Examples:

Ēunek, the arms;	ēuné-chu, these arms.
Iitīk, the ears;	iití-chu, these ears.
Kerichek, the medicines;	keriché-chu, these medicines.
Mwanik, the oils;	mwaní-chu, these oils.
Tioñgik, the animals;	tioñgí-chu, these animals.
Tienwagik, the dances;	tienwagí-chu, these dances.

Lakōk, the children;	lakó-chu, these children.
Sotonik, the gourds;	sotón-ju, these gourds.
Sesēnik, the dogs;	sesén-ju, these dogs.

If the demonstrative is used predicatively, the article and the termination of substantives undergo changes somewhat similar to those enumerated above. When the singular substantive joined to the article ends in *ut*, no change is made; when it ends in *et*, *at*, or *ot*, the *t* is changed to *n*; and when it ends in *it*, the *t* is usually omitted, though it is in some words changed to *n*. When the singular substantive joined to the article ends in *ta*, *to*, *da*, or *do*, *n* is added.

Examples:

Ēut, the arm;	ēút-ni, this is the arm.
Seset, the dog;	sesén-ni, this is the dog.
Imbaret, the plantation;	imbarén-ni, this is the plantation.
Oriat, the ash;	orián-ni, this is the ash.
Kerichot, the medicine;	kerichón-ni, this is the medicine.
Iitīt, the ear;	iití-ni, this is the ear.
(*But* Kutit, the mouth;	kutín-ni, this is the mouth).
Mwaita, the oil;	mwaitán-ni, this is the oil.
Porto, the body;	portón-ni, this is the body.
Sirimdo, the chain;	sirimdón-ni, this is the chain.
Kutuṇda, the elbow, knee;	kutundán-ni, this is the elbow.
Ñgetundo, the lion;	ñgetundón-ni, this is the lion.
Tiendo, the dance;	tiendón-ni, this is the dance.

In the plural no changes take place when the demonstrative is used predicatively:

Ēunek, the arms;	ēunék-chu, these are the arms.
Iitīk, the ears;	iitík-chu, these are the ears.
Mwanik, the oils;	mwaník-chu, these are the oils.
Lakōk, the children;	lakók-chu, these are the children.
Sesēnik, the dogs;	sesēník-chu, these are the dogs.

When the singular substantive joined to the article is accompanied by a possessive pronoun, certain changes also take place. No alteration, however, occurs in the plural. If the article ends in *t*, that letter changes to *n* unless it is preceded by *a* or *o*, in which case it usually changes to *nden*. If the article ends in *ta* or *da*, *n* is added; if in *to* or *do*, these terminations change to *tan* or *dan*. Examples:

Seset, the dog;	sesén-nyō, my dog.
Sesēnik, the dogs;	sesēník-chōk, my dogs.
Ēut, the arm;	ēún-nyō, my arm.
Ēunek, the arms;	ēunék-chōk, my arms.
Punyot, the enemy;	punyondén-nyō *or* punyón-nyō, my enemy.

Oriat, the ash; { oriandén-nyō *or* orián-nyō } my ash.
Rorta, the heifer ; rortán-nyō, my heifer.
Kutunda, the knee ; kutundán-nyō, my knee.
Tiondo, the animal ; tiondán-nyō, my animal.
Muito, the ox-hide ; muitán-nyō, my ox-hide.

The article is omitted in the following cases:

(1) When the substantive is used in a general sense or as an adverb.
Examples :

A-'onyi kii (*not* kiito), I see something.
A-wend-i oii (*not* olto), I am going somewhere.
Mi-i chii (*not* chiito), there is somebody there.
A-nom-e tuka kwa muren (*not* murenet), when I am a warrior I shall seize cattle.
Ole-kinye ko-ki ñgeta (*not* ñgetet), formerly he was a boy.

(2) When the meaning is *motion to* or *from*, or *resting at*, a kraal or hut (similar to our phrases *to* or *from town* or *at home*), no possessive case being used. Examples :

A-wend-í ko (woman speaking), I go *or* am going to the hut or kraal.
A-pun-ú ka (man speaking), I come *or* am coming from the hut or kraal.
A-mi-í ko }
A-mi-í ka } I am in the hut or kraal.

But A-wénd-i kóin-nyō (woman speaking), I go *or* am going to my hut or kraal.
A-pún-u kaín-nyō (man speaking), I come *or* am coming from my hut or kraal.
A-mí-i kot-ap-pápa }
A-mí-i kâp-papa } I am in father's hut.

(3) When the time of day is expressed in such sentences as :

When it becomes evening, Añg-nyep-koi-ek koskoling (*not* koskolingut), and
He is going away in the morning, Wend-i korirun (*not* korirunet).

(4) In a few compound words, *e. g.*

Pêk-áp-koñg (*not* konda *or* konyek), the tears.
Chek'-ám-ma (*not* mat), hot milk (*i. e.* fresh from the cow).
Sigiriet-áp-tim[1] (*not* timdo), the zebra.
Nepo-tapan (*not* tapanda), the last (*lit.* of end).

[1] Sigiriet-ap-tím-in (the donkey of that wood) is perhaps more commonly used than Sigiriet-áp-tim.

A few substantives never take the article. Such are:

>Anum, so-and-so, such a one.
>Myat, death, *and* the death.
>Teget, breast, *and* the breast.
>Konyit, honour *or* shame, *and* the honour *or* the shame.
>Kapatut, field without crops, *and* the field without crops.

Most names for cattle (see p. 280).

The article is also frequently omitted with proper names, and one more often hears, for instance:

>Asis, *than* Asista (God, *or* the God).
>Nandi, *than* Nandiek (Nandi, *or* the Nandi).

CASES.

Nouns in Nandi are not susceptible of any inflexions to mark the cases; but the article has special forms to denote the nominative and vocative. The accusative case is the same as the nominative. Special particles prefixed to the governed noun are used to denote the genitive.

THE VOCATIVE CASE.

The form used for the vocative case is the same as when the substantive is joined to the demonstrative pronoun *ni* or *i* (pl. *chu*):

>Korkón-ni! O woman! *or* this woman.
>Korusié-chu! O women! *or* these women.
>Lakwán-ni! O child! *or* this child.
>Lakó-chu! O children! *or* these children.
>Orkoiyondón-ni! O medicine man! *or* this medicine man.
>Orkoií-chu! O medicine men! *or* these medicine men.
>Asís-i! O God! *or* this God.

The commonest way of addressing a young man or woman is by the use of the word *weír-i!* in the masculine and *chép-i!* in the feminine. *Weirí-chu!* and *típ-chu!* are used in the plural.

A superior is addressed by the words *Poiyondón-ni!* (O elder!) or *Murenón-ni!* (O warrior!) if a man; and by *Chepiosón-ni!* (O old woman!) or *Korkón-ni!* (O woman!) if a woman.

The vocative case is frequently expressed by the substantive used in a general sense, *i.e.* without the article. Examples:

>Orkoiyo! O medicine man!
>Asis! O God!

CASES

THE GENITIVE.

There are three methods of forming the genitive case in Nandi. In the most common form the governed word follows the governing substantive, being joined to it by the particle *ap*[1]. This particle does not as a rule vary in number. Examples:

Rotuet-ap-papa, the sword of (my) father.
Kot-ap-eiyo, the hut of (my) mother.
Rotōk-ap-orkoiik, the swords of the medicine men.
Korik-ap-korusiek, the huts of the women.
Ñgalek-ap-keny, the news of formerly (*i.e.* of former times).
Ñgalek-ap-tun, the news of presently (*i.e.* of the future).

In a few instances *ap* becomes *ip* in the plural. Example:

Ñget'-ap-eiyo (the boy of mother), my brother.
Akut-ñget'-ip-eiyo, my brothers.

When *ap* is used in conjunction with *ka* (*kaita*), the house, kraal, or country, *kâp* is used:

Kâp-anum, the house of so-and-so.
Kâp-Tumo, Tumo's country.

When *ap* is used in conjunction with *kwanda*, the father, and *kamet*, the mother, *kwamba* and *kopot* are used:

Kwamba-anum, the father of so-and-so.
Kopot-anum, the mother of so-and-so.

After a man has been circumcised he takes his father's name, *Ar-ap*,[2] meaning *the son of*, being prefixed to it,[3] *e. g.*

Ar-ap-anum, the son of so-and-so.
Ar-ap-Sirtoi, the son of Sirtoi.

The second way of forming the genitive is in conjunction with the relative (which see, pp. 187-8), *nepo* being used for the singular, *chepo* for the plural.[4] These particles, like *ap*, join the governing substantive to the governed word. The particle agrees with the governing noun in number. Examples:

Rotuet nepo metit (the knife of the head), the razor.
Rotōk chepo metit (the knives of the head), the razors.

---

[1] *Ap* becomes *am* before a word commencing with *m*; e. g. kiit'-am-murenet, the thing of the man : ñgalek-am-Mâsaeek, the language of the Masai.

Ap is occasionally changed to *pa*, *e. g.* chii-pa-ka (*for* chii-ap-ka), freeman (*lit.* man of house, *i. e.* independent person).

[2] *Ar-ap* is commonly written *Arab* by Europeans, *e. g.* Arab-Sirtoi *for* Ar-ap-Sirtoi.   [3] *Vide* pp. 67-8.

[4] *Nepo* and *chepo* become *kopa* and *chukopa* when used with *amt* (yesterday).
Examples : Kōn-a ñgoliot kopa amt } Give me yesterday's news.
Kōn-a ñgalek chukopa amt

The third way of forming the possessive case is to place the particle *pa* or *po* before the governing substantive, the governed word following immediately after the latter. This form is used when it is wished to put special stress on the genitive, and is unchangeable:

Po chii rotuet, this is somebody's knife.
Pa anum rotōk, these are such and such a person's knives.
Mo po lakōk Nandi, po lakōk Kipsikīs (not of the children Nandi, of the children Lumbwa), they are not Nandi children, they are Lumbwa children.

SUBSTANTIVES.
THE PLURAL OF SUBSTANTIVES.

By far the most complicated part of the Nandi language is the formation of the plural of substantives, either with or without the article. Many substantives have two or even three forms for the plural, the longest form, which is probably the most correct, being often abbreviated in ordinary conversation and only used when the speaker has difficulty in making himself understood. Thus, a person might remark: A-'onyi rotōk, *or* A-'onyi sirimwek, *or* A-'onyi tabuburik, I see some swords, *or* I see some chains, *or* I see some butterflies. If the person to whom the remark is addressed were to reply, I-ionyí ne ? (What do you see ?), the answer would probably not be Rotōk, *or* sirimwek, *or* tabuburik, but Rotonaiik, *or* sirimwagik, *or* tabuburaiik. In the following lists the most common form of the plural has been given.

The plural of words denoting relationship is made by the prefixes *akut* and *angut*.[1] Examples:

Akut-papa, my fathers.
Akut-kwanda, the fathers.
Akut-ñget-ip-eiyo, my brothers.
Akut-ñget-ip-komituak, thy *or* your brothers.
Akut-ñget-ip-kametuak, his *or* their brothers.
Akut-agwi, my grandfathers.

Angut-eiyo, my mothers.
Angut-kamet, the mothers.
Angut-chep-eiyo, my sisters.
Angut-chep-komituak, thy *or* your sisters.
Angut-chep-kametuak, his *or* their sisters.
Angut-koko, my grandmothers.

CLASS I.
A.

Perhaps the commonest way of forming the plural of nouns is by adding *oi*, or, less frequently, *ai*, to the singular. When employed

---
[1] *Akut* and *angut* are often interchangeable.

SUBSTANTIVES

with the article, the noun takes the affix, *et, iet,* or *yet* in the singular, and *ōk* or *aiik* in the plural. Examples:

Singular without article.	Singular with article.	Plural without article.	Plural with article.	English.
Ñgecher	Ñgecheret	Ñgecheroi / Ñgecherai	Ñgecherōk / Ñgecheraiik	Stool.
Tomirimir	Tomirimiriet	Tomirimiroi / Tomirimirai	Tomirimirōk / Tomirimiraiik	Person's shadow.
Kimaket	Kimaketyet	Kimaketoi / Kimaketai	Kimaketōk / Kimaketaiik	Hyena.
Ormarīch	Ormarīchet	Ormarīchoi	Ormarīchōk	Door of cattlefold.
Cheringis	Cheringisiet	Cheringisoi	Cheringisōk	Lizard.
Kwang	Kwanget	Kwangoi	Kwangōk	Bow.
Temen	Temenyet	Temenoi	Temenōk	Wax.

B.

Nouns belonging to this class which end in *a* form the plural by adding *i* to the singular, or by changing *a* into *oi*. When the noun is employed with the article, the terminal *a* is changed to *et* in the singular and to *ōk* or *aiik* in the plural. Examples:

Makata	Makatet	Makatoi / Makatai	Makatōk / Makataiik	Leather, goat's skin.
Kaina	Kainet	Kainoi / Kainai	Kainōk / Kainaiik	Name.
Kuina	Kuinet	Kuinai	Kuinaiik	Horn.
Kīna	Kīnet	Kīnai	Kīnaiik	Nipple.
Cheplanga	Cheplanget	Cheplangoi	Cheplangōk	Leopard.
Indara	Indaret	Indaroi	Indarōk	Python.

C.

Those nouns which end in *wai, ia, io, o, e, ya, iya, iyua, ua,* &c., and belong to this class, change the terminal letters of the singular into *ai* or *oi* to form the plural. Examples:

Chepkeswai	Chepkeswet	Chepkesoi / Chepkesai	Chepkesōk / Chepkesaiik	Small knife.
Tisia	Tisiet	Tisoi	Tisōk	Monkey.
Sigirio	Sigiriet	Sigiroi	Sigirōk	Donkey.
Īno	Īnet	Īnai	Īnaiik	Bow-string.
Soromya	Soromyet	Soromoi	Soromōk	Kidney.
Siiya	Siiyet	Sioi	Siōk	Nail, claw.
Taiyua	Taiyuet	Taoi	Taōk	Spur-fowl.
Tae	Taet	Taoi	Taōk	Brass-wire.
Kutere	Kuteret	Kuterai	Kuteraiik	Spoon.
Kipisua	Kipisuet	Kipisoi	Kipisōk	Swallow.

D.

A certain number of words—generally those ending in *ua, uo,* or *wa*—which may be included in this class, change the final letters into *oi, onai,* or *ondoi,* to form the plural. The singular article is formed by changing *a* or *o* into *et,* and the plural article by changing *oi, onai,* or *ondoi* into *ōk, onōk, onaiik* or *ondōk.* Such are:

Singular without article.	Singular with article.	Plural without article.	Plural with article.	English.
Rotua	Rotuet	{ Rotoi { Rotonai	Rotōk } Rotonaiik }	Sword or knife.
Kiplengwa	Kiplengwet	{ Kiplengoi { Kiplengonoi	Kiplengōk } Kiplengonōk }	Hare.
Lakwa	Lakwet	Lakoi	Lakōk	Child.
Situa	Situet	Sitonoi	Sitonōk	Impalla gazelle.
Chorua	Choruet	Choronoi	Choronōk	Friend.
Mulua	Muluet	Mulondoi	Mulondōk	Lump.
Urua	Uruet	Uruondoi	Uruondōk	Shadow.
Tuluo	Tuluet	Tuluondoi	Tuluondōk	Mountain.
Turio	Turiet	Turionoi	Turionōk	Unlucky omen.
Rokcho	Rokchet	Rokchonoi	Rokchonōk	Potsherd.

Class II.

A.

There are a large number of words which, as a rule, do not vary in the plural except for the change of the accent from the penultimate to the last syllable, or the changing or lengthening of a vowel. As many of these words, however, can form their plural by adding *ai* to the singular, they might perhaps have been properly considered as belonging to Class I; but they are an important group, and it is more convenient to classify them separately.

The article is formed by adding *et, iet, yet,* or rarely, *det* or *it* in the singular, and *ik* or *aiik* in the plural.

Examples of words which usually do not change except for the accent:

Moróroch	Mororochét	{ Mororóch { Mororóchai	Mororochík } Mororocháiik }	Frog.
Káliañg	Kaliañgét	{ Kaliáñg { Kaliáñgai	Kaliañgík } Kaliañgaíik }	Fly.
Múren	Murenét	Murén	Murenĭk	Warrior, man.

SUBSTANTIVES

Singular without article.	Singular with article.	Plural without article.	Plural with article.	English.
Tapúpur	Tapupuriét	Tapupúr	Tapupurík	Butterfly.
Koroíit	Koroiityét	Koroiít	Koroiitík	Colobus monkey.
Púon	Puondét	Puón	Puoník	Lung.
Két	Ketít	Két	Ketík	Tree.

Examples of words which change or lengthen a vowel :

Panan	Pananet	Ponon	Pononik	Poor person.
Tarit	Tarityet	Tarīt	Tarītik	Bird.
Tangoch	Tangochet	Tongōch	Tongōchik	Enigma.
Torkoch	Torkochet	Torkōch	Torkōchik	Kavirondo shield.

B.

In a few instances the plural article is formed by adding *ek* instead of *ik*. Examples:

Lembech	Lembechet	Lembech	Lembechek	Lie.
Ñgoror	Ñgororiet	Ñgoror	Ñgororek	Goat.
Kechir	Kechiriet	Kechīr	Kechīrek	Sheep.

C.

The following words may be included in this class, but are slightly irregular :

Teget	Teget	Tegēt	Tegētik	Breast.
Kapatut	Kapatut	Kapatut	Kapatutik	Field cleared ready for sowing.
Kurkat	Kurket	Kurkot	Kurkotik	Door.
Sumat	Sumet	Sumot	Sumotik	Old men's garment.
Patai	Patet	Patoi	Patoiik	Back.
Mengich	Mengit	Mengīch	Mengīchik	Ram.
Tokoch	Toket	Tokōch	Tokōchik	Face.
Kunyut	Kundit	Kunyut	Kunyutik	Brain.
Kunyuk	Kungit	Kunyuk	Kunyukik	Handle.

CLASS III.

A.

Class III consists of nouns which usually form their plural by adding *s, is, ōs,* or *us* to the singular, or by changing *a* or *o* into *s, ōs,* or *es*.[1] The singular article is made by adding *t, et, it,* or *ut* to the

---

[1] The full form of the plural is *sio, isio, ōsio,* and *usio,* but this form is not often used. In the word *poiyo,* ancestor or old man, however, the only form for the plural is *poiisio* (*poiisiek*).

singular, or by changing *a* or *o* into *et*; the plural article by adding *iek* to the plural (or by changing *io* into *iek*). Some of the words belonging to this class can also form the plural like nouns of Class I, *i. e.* by adding *oi* to the singular, or by changing *a*, &c., into *oi*. The plural article then becomes *ōk*; *e. g.* nianjoi, nianjōk, *for* nianjas, nianjasiek (lakes). Examples:

Singular without article.	Singular with article.	Plural without article.	Plural with article.	English.
Nianja	Nianjet	Nianjas / Nianjasio	Nianjasiek	Lake.
Rungu	Rungut	Rungus	Rungusiek	Club.
Keny	Kenyīt	Kenyīs	Kenyīsiek	Year.
Kepen	Kepenet	Kepenōs	Kepenōsiek	Cave.
Itōk	Itōkut	Itōkus	Itōkusiek	Bed.
Aina	Ainet	Ainōs	Ainōsiek	River.
Kuto	Kutet	Kutes	Kutesiek	Ant-bear.
Salua	Saluet	Salus	Salusiek	Deformed person.

B.

In a few instances *ua* and *uo* are changed into *ōs* to form the plural:

Chambolua	Chamboluet	Chambolōs	Chambolōsiek	Knife for butchering cattle.
Pireyuo	Pireyuot	Pireyuōs	Pireyuōsiek	Man's belt.

CLASS IV.

A.

A large number of nouns make the plural by adding *n, an, en, yen, in, on,* or *un* to the singular. The singular article is formed by adding *t, et,* or *det* to the singular, or by changing *o* into *et*; the plural article by adding *ik* to the plural. Examples:

Sese	Seset	Sesen	Sesēnik	Dog.
Moso	Moset	Moson	Mosonik	Baboon.
Mukang	Mukanget	Mukangan	Mukanganik	Spoon.
Imbar	Imbaret	Imbaren	Imbarēnik	Plantation.
Chereñgen	Chereñgendet	Chereñgenyen	Chereñgenyēnik	Locust.
Kipokan	Kipokandet	Kipokandin	Kipokandīnik	Lyre.
Sot	Sotet	Sotōn	Sotōnik	Calabash.
Kipkēu	Kipkēut	Kipkēun	Kipkēunik	Kind of rat.

SUBSTANTIVES

B.

When *un* is added to the singular to form the plural, the plural article is sometimes made by adding *ek*. Examples:

Singular without article.	Singular with article.	Plural without article.	Plural with article.	English.
E	Ēut	Ēun	Ēunek	Arm.
Ser	Serut	Serun	Serunek	Nose.

C.

Nouns which belong to this class and end in *ia, ya, io, iyo,* or *yo* change these letters into *en, in,* or *ōn* to form the plural. The article is generally formed regularly by adding *t* in the singular and *ik* in the plural. Examples:—

Sabitia	Sabitiat	Sabiten	Sabitēnik	Porcupine quill.
Tiañgia	Tiañgiat	Tiañgin	Tiañgīnik	Stalk of millet.
Terkekya	Terkekyat	Terkeken	Terkekēnik	Guinea-fowl.
Iririo	Iririot	Iriren	Irirēnik	Piece of hide.
Maïyo	Maïyat	Maen	Maēnik	Digging-stick.
Ingotio	Ingotiot	Ingotin	Ingotīnik	Giraffe.
Samoiyo	Samoiyot	Samoiin	Samoiīnik	Old man's bracelet.
Kweyo	Kweyot	Kweōn	Kweōnik	Sandal, broom.

Sometimes the plural article is formed by changing *in* into *īk*. This is, however, generally the case with words ending in other letters than *ia, ya, io,* or *yo*. Examples:

Kumia	Kumiat	Kumin	Kumīk	Honey.
Twalio	Twaliot	Twalin	Twalīk	Cow-bell.
Tyolio	Tyoliot	Tyolin	Tyolīk	Cooked locust.
Karna	Karnet	Karin	Karīk	Iron.
Morna	Mornet	Morin	Morīk	Finger.
Loñgno	Loñgnet	Loñgin	Loñgīk	Arrow used for bleeding cattle.
Iit	Iitīt	Iitin	Iitīk	Ear.

D.

Nouns belonging to this class which end in *ua, wa, iyua,* or *iyuo* form the plural by changing these letters into *on*. Examples:

Sororua	Sororuet	Sororon	Sororonik	Flower of the banana.
Serengwa	Serengwet	Serengon	Serengonik	Wooden horn.
Kipsoiyua	Kipsoiyuet	Kipsoon	Kipsoonik	Cock.
Lamaiyuo	Lamaiyuet	Lamaon	Lamaonik	*Ximenia americana* (tree).

CLASS V.

A.

Some nouns add *ua* to the singular to form the plural, or change *ia*, *io*, or *yo* into *ua*. The singular article is made by adding *t* or *it* to the singular; the plural article by changing *ua* into *uek*. Examples:

Singular without article.	Singular with article.	Plural without article.	Plural with article.	English.
Ñgot	Ñgotit	Ñgotua	Ñgotuek	Spear.
Os	Osit	Osua	Osuek	Old cow.
Kipeperia	Kipeperiat	Kipeperua	kipeperuek	Portion.
Musio	Musiot	Musua	Musuek	Carcase.
Kwetio	Kwetiot	Kwetua	Kwetuek	Buttock.
Lokoiyo	Lokoiyot	Lokoiyua	Lokoiyuek	Answer.

B.

Nouns ending in *uo* or *wo* change the final *o* into *a*. Examples:

Susuo	Susuot	Susua	Susuek	Grass.
Sokwo	Sokwot	Sokwa	Sokwek	Notch in the butt of arrow.
Tuñgwo	Tuñgwot	Tuñgwa	Tuñgwek	Cough.
Siwo	Siwot	Siwa	Siwek	Stinging-nettle.

C.

Some monosyllabic words which may be included in this class form the plural by adding *tinua* or *otinua* to the singular. The singular article is formed by adding *et* or *iet*; the plural article by changing *tinua* into *tinuek*. Examples:

Lol	Lolet	Lolotinua	Lolotinuek	Bag.
Kor	Koret	Korotinua	Korotinuek	Country.
Em	Emet	Emotinua	Emotinuek	Earth.
Mo	Moiet	Mootinua	Mootinuek	Belly.
Or	Oret	Ortinua	Ortinuek	Path, clan.
Loñg	Loñget	Loñgotinua	Loñgotinuek	Shield.
Ror	Roret	Rorotinua	Rorotinuek	Stubble.

D.

In the following instances the plural of monosyllabic words is made by adding *usua* to the singular:

Kut	Kutit	Kutusua	Kutusuek	Mouth.
Kat	Katit	Katusua	Katusuek	Neck.

SUBSTANTIVES

E.

In one instance *o* is changed to *eyua* to form the plural, and in another *ōa* is added:

Singular without article.	Singular with article.	Plural without article.	Plural with article.	English.
Siro	Siret	Sireyua	Sireyuek	Band, stripe.
Met	Metit	Metōa	Metōek	Head.

CLASS VI.

A few words form the plural by adding *nut* to the singular, or by changing *a* into *onut*. The singular article is made by adding *t* to the singular; the plural article by adding *ik* to the plural. Examples:

Suwe	Suwet	Suwenut	Suwenutik	Loin.
Sombe	Sombet	Sombenut	Sombenutik	Ostrich-feather head-dress.
Tilia	Tiliet	Tilionut	Tilionutik	Peace, relation.

In one instance *ut* only is added:

Kiruog	Kiruoget	Kiruogut	Kiruogutik	Advice, assembly.
Kâp-kiruog	Kâp-kiruoget	Kâp-kiruogut	Kâp-kiruogutik	Place of assembly.

CLASS VII.

A.

Some words ending in *a* or *o* form the plural by changing the terminal letter into *e* or *i*. The singular article is formed by adding *t* or by changing *a* into *ot*; the plural article by adding *k* or *ek*, or by changing *i* into *ek*. Examples:

Kesua	Kesuot	Kesui	Kesuek	Seed.
Ingua	Inguot	Ingui	Inguek	Herb, vegetable.
Lelua	Leluot	Lelue	Leluek	Jackal.
Mistōa	Mistōat	Mistōe	Mistōek	Herdsman.
Kôto	Kôtet	Kôti	Kôtiek	Arrow.

B.

In this class may be included words ending in *o* which add *i*, or change *o* into *ai*, to form the plural. The plural article, instead of being *ōk* or *aiik*, as in Class I, is *ek* or *ik*. Examples:

Kôwo	Kôwet	Kôwoi	Kôwek	Bone.
Ruto	Rutōet	Rutoi	Rutoïk	Visitor.
Akwo	Akwot	Akwai	Akwek	Rag.

Class VIII.

A.

Most words which, when used with the article, take the affix *ta* or *to*, or *da* or *do*, if the last letter is *l*, *m* or *n*,[1] form the plural by adding to the singular *ua*, *uo*, or *wa* (or, to give the full form, *uag*, *uog*, or *wag*). The plural article is made by changing *ua*, *uo*, or *wa* into *uek* or *wek*, or into *uagik*, *uogik*, or *wagik*.

The plural is also at times formed like nouns of the first class by adding *ai*. The plural article then becomes *aiik*. Examples:

Singular without article.	Singular with article.	Plural without article.	Plural with article.	English.
Sirim	Sirimdo	⎧Sirimwag ⎨Sirimwa ⎩Sirimai	⎫Sirimwagik ⎬Sirimwek ⎭Sirimaiik	Chain.
Pesen	Pesendo	Pesenua	Pesenuek	Debt.
Ror	Rorta	Rorua	Roruek	Heifer.
Uk	Ukta	Ukwa	Ukwek	Hump.
Melmel	Melmeldo	Melmelua	Melmeluek	Scorpion.
Litei	Liteito	Liteiua	Liteiuek	Whetstone.

B.

Nouns belonging to this class which end in *ñg* or *ny* drop the *g* or the *y* when joined to the singular article:

Ñgeñg	Ñgenda	Ñgeñgwa	Ñgeñgwek	Salt-lick.
Kutuñg	Kutunda	Kutuñgwa	Kutuñgwek	Elbow, knee.
Matañg	Matanda	Matoñgwa	Matoñgwek	Cheek.
Motony	Motonda	Motoñgwa	Motoñgwek	Vulture.

Class IX.

A few nouns, which when used with the article take *ta*, *to*, *da*, or *do*, form the plural by affixing *i*, *n*, *in*, or *ien* to the singular, or by changing *i* into *n*. The plural article is formed by adding *ik* or by changing *i* into *ek*, or *n* into *k*. Such are:

Moi	Moita	Moii	Moiek	Calf.
Koii	Koiita	Koiin	Koiik	Stone, egg.
Ei	Eito	Ein	Einik	Bullock.
Kel	Keldo	Kelien	Keliek	Leg.
Mwai	Mwaita	Mwan	Mwanik	Oil.

The following belong to the same class, but are slightly irregular:

Koñg	Konda	Koñgin	Koñgik	Hole.
Koñg	Konda	Konyan	Konyek	Eye.
Tiony	Tiondo	Tioñgin	Tioñgik	Animal.
Ñgetūny	Ñgetundo	Ñgetuny	Ñgetunyik	Lion.

[1] The only exception to this rule appears to be the word *olto*, the place.

SUBSTANTIVES

Class X.

A.

A large number of substantives, which were probably first known as collective nouns, form the singular from the plural by affixing *a, o, ia, io, ya,* or *yo*. The singular article is made by adding *t* to the singular, or by changing *a*, &c., into *et*; the plural article by adding *k, ek,* or *ik* to the plural. Examples:

Singular without article.	Singular with article.	Plural without article.	Plural with article.	English.
Kecheia	Kecheiat	Kechei	Kecheik	Star.
Koñgonyo	Koñgonyot	Koñgony	Koñgonyik	Crested crane.
Muria	Muriat	Mur	Murek	Rat.
Kororia	Kororiat	Koror	Kororik	Feather.
Pēlio	Pēliot	Pēl	Pēlek	Elephant.
Robòonio	Robòoniot	Roboon	Roboonik	Potato.
Segemya	Segemyat	Segem	Segemik	Bee.
Imanya	Imanyat	Iman	Imanek	Castor oil plant.
Sumeyo	Sumeyot	Sume	Sumek	Hair.

After *p* and *k*, *ia*, *ya*, *io*, or *yo* become *cha* or *cho*.

Solopcho	Solopchot	Solop	Solopik	Cockroach.
Mopcho	Mopchot	Mop	Mopik	Sugar-cane.
Orokcha	Orokchat	Orok	Orokik	Eagle.

B.

Nouns ending in *a* or *e* generally change that letter into *ia* or *io* to form the singular. Examples:

Makandia	Makandiat	Makanda	Makandek	Bean.
Mumia	Mumiat	Muma	Mumek	Oath.
Ipandia	Ipandiat	Ipande	Ipandek	Indian corn.
Ndorio	Ndoriot	Ndore	Ndorek	Red bead.
Makorio	Makoriot	Mokore	Mokorek	Merchant.

C.

Nouns ending in *o* form the singular by changing that letter into *a*. Examples:

Pusia	Pusiat	Pusio	Pusiek	Flour.
Maiya	Maiyat	Maiyo	Maiyek	Beer.

D.

In some words *yua* or *yuo* is added to the plural to form the singular. When the singular article is used, *t* is added to the singular or *a* is changed into *ot*; when the plural article is employed, *yuek* is added to the plural. Examples:

Singular without article.	Singular with article.	Plural without article.	Plural with article.	English.
Roteyua	Roteyuot	Rote	Roteyuek	Slender pole.
Lumeyua	Lumeyuot	Lume	Lumeyuek	Stout pole.
Tareyuo	Tareyuot	Tare	Tareyuek	Feathers of an arrow.
Kanameyuo	Kanameyuot	Kaname	Kanameyuek	Tongs.

E.

There are a few instances of words belonging to this class being formed in an irregular manner. Examples:—

Poldo	Poldet	Pol	Polik	Cloud.
Perto	Pertet	Per	Perik	Bark of a tree.
Kwendo	Kwendet	Kwen	Kwenik	Fire-wood.
Saanya	Saandet	Saan	Saanik	Lover.
Aruwa	Aruwet	Are	Arek	Kid.
Arawa	Arawet	Araa	Arawek	Moon, month.

Class XI.

A.

The names of tribes of people, and of trades or callings, form the singular from the plural by adding *in*. The singular article is made by the affix *det*; the plural article by the affix *ik, ek,* or *iek*.

Nandiin	Nandiindet	Nandi	Nandiek	Nandi.
Kipsikīsin	Kipsikīsindet	Kipsikīs	Kipsikīsiek	Lumbwa.
Lemin	Lemindet	Lem	Lemek	Kavirondo.
Mâsaein	Mâsaeindet	Mâsae	Mâsaeek	Masai.
Segein	Segeindet	Sege	Segeik	Soldier.
Kitoñgin	Kitoñgindet	Kitoñg	Kitoñgik	Smith.
Ponin	Ponindet	Pon	Ponīk	Wizard.
Chorin	Chorindet	Chor	Chorīk	Thief.

SUBSTANTIVES

B.

The names of a few tribes of people are formed irregularly. This is doubtless due to the Masai form of the words having been adopted, *e. g.* il-Chumba, il-Kōkōyo.

Singular without article.	Singular with article.	Plural without article.	Plural with article.	English.
Chumbin	Chumbindet	Chumba	Chumbek	Swahili.
Kōkōyin	Kōkōyindet	Kōkōyo	Kōkōyek	Kikuyu.
Keyo	{ Keyot / Keyondet }	Keyu	Keyek	Elgeyo.
Asungio	Asungiot	Asungu	Asunguk	European.

Some nouns are only used in the singular. Such are:

Without article.	With article.	English.
Kipurienge	Kipurienget	Fog, mist.
Melel	Melelda	Thirst.
Kâp-walio	Kâp-waliot	Market.
Olisio	Olisiet	Merchandise.
Lapcha	Lapchat	Mud.
Polot	Polotet	Uproar.
Oïn	Oïndo	Old age.
Mieno	Mienot	Goodness.
Yaitio	Yaitiot	Badness.
Kararin	Kararindo	Beauty.

Others are only used in the plural. Examples:

Pusio	Pusiek	Powder.
Pusaru	Pusaruk	Gunpowder.
Kaot	Kaotik	Perspiration.
Purut	Purutek	Pus.
Ñgul	Ñgulek	Saliva.
Kipketin	Kipketīnik	Honey-wine.
Porok	Porokek	Palm-wine.
Mursi	Mursiik	Curdled milk.
Sukut	Sukutek	Cattle pond.
Musar	Musarek	Gruel.

The words for water, *pei* (*pêk*), and milk, *che* (*cheko*), are also generally only used in the plural; but *peiyo* (*peiyot*) can be employed for a pond, and *cheiyo* (*cheiyot*) is used in such expressions as *a little milk* (cheiyot totegin).

178 NANDI GRAMMAR

IRREGULAR PLURALS.

A number of words form their plurals irregularly, and some, when used with the demonstrative pronoun, do not follow the rules given on pp. 160–2. The most important are given in the following list:

Singular without article.	Singular with article.	Singular with demonstrative.	Plural without article.	Plural with article.	Plural with demonstrative.	English.
Tie	Chepto	Chép-i	Tipin	Tipik	Tip-chu	Girl.
Ara	Artet	Artán-ni	No	Néko	Né-chu	Goat.
Kwe	Kwesta	Kwé-i	Kwes	Kwesik	Kwesí-chu	He-goat.
Ko	Kot	Kō-i [1]				
Ko	Kaita	Kaí-i [2]	Korin	Korik	Kór-chu	House.
Chii	Chiito	Chii-chi	Piich	Piik	Pií-chu	Man.
Kii	Kiito	Kii-i	Tukun	Tukuk	Tukí-chu	Thing.
Peny	Pendo	Pény-i	Pany	Panyek	Panyé-chu	Meat.
Tany	Teta	Tány-i	Tich	Tuka	Tú-chu	Ox.
Kiruk	Kirkit	Kírk-i	Kiruk	Kirukik	Kirukí-chu	Bull, male.
Aiyuo	Aiyuet	Aiyuón-ni	Aunoi	Aunōk	Aún-ju	Axe.
Ma	Mat	Má-i	Mostinua	Mostinuek	Mostinué-chu	Fire, gun.
Paiyua	Paiyuat	Paiyuandán-ni	Pai	Pāk	Pā-chu	Elusine grain.
Korko	Korket	Korkón-ni	Korusio	Korusiek	Korusié-chu	Woman.
Oii	Olto	Oltó-yu	Oltōs	Oltōsiek	Oltōsió-uli	Place.
Tae	Tæta	Taé-i	Toiua	Toiuek	Toiué-chu	Front.
Meyuo	Meyuot	Meyuondón-ni	Mee	Meek	Meé-chu	Agricultural people.

[1] Woman speaking. [2] Man speaking.

SUBSTANTIVES

Singular without article.	Singular with article.	Singular with demonstrative.	Plural without article.	Plural with article.	Plural with demonstrative.	English.
Kemboi	Kembaut	Kembaún-ni	Kembaus	Kembausiek	Kembausié-chu	Night.
Kimnyio	Kimnyiet	Kimnyión-ni	Kimoi	Kimoiik	Kimoií-chu	Porridge.
Kelda	Keldet	Keldón-ni	Kelat	Kelek	Kelé-chu	Tooth, ivory.
Ékon	Ékonet	Ékonón-ni	Êkōs [1]	Êkōsiek	Êkōsié-chu	Day.
Karatia	Karaita	Karaí-i	Karatua	Karatuek	Karatué-chu	Site of kraal.
Kâp-tich	Kâp-tugut	Kâp-tugún-ni	Kâp-tugun	Kâp-tugunik	Kâp-tuguní-chu	Cattle-kraal.
Ai	Aita	Ai-i	Aisai	Aisaiik	Aisaií-chu	Calf of leg.

SINGULAR ARTICLE FORMED IRREGULARLY.

Some words ending in *it* and one in *et* form the singular article irregularly. Examples:

Singular without article.	Singular with article.	Singular with demonstrative.	Plural without article.	Plural with article.	Plural with demonstrative.	English.
Omit	Omdit	Ómd-i	Omituag	Omituagik	Omituagí-chu	Food.
Emit	Emdit	Émd-i	Emit	Emitik	Emití-chu	Wild olive.
Pirit	Pirtit	Pirt-i	Pirit	Piritik	Pirití-chu	Penis.
Terit	Tertit	Tért-i		wanting		Dust.
Ponit	Pondit	Pónd-i		wanting		Wizard's medicine.
Sepet	Septet	Septón-ni	Sepetai	Sepetaiik	Sepetaií-chu	Half calabash.

[1] Also *Êkones (ékonesiek)*.

It occasionally happens that there are two forms for the singular when used with the article. Examples:

Singular without article.	Singular with article.	Plural without article.	Plural with article.	English.
Soko	{Sokot / Sokondet}	Sok	Sokek	Leaf.
Too	{Toot / Toondet}	Toi	Toiek	Stranger.
Okion	{Okiot / Okiondet}	Oki	Okiek	Dorobo.
Keyo	{Keyot / Keyondet}	Keyu	Keyek	Elgeyo.

ADJECTIVES.

There appear to be no true adjectives in Nandi, and all words used in an adjectival sense are in reality verbs, which can be either joined to the relative or used by themselves. They are generally joined to the relative.

When used as an attribute, the adjective follows the substantive.[1]

The plural of adjectives is formed in two ways, firstly by adding *en* or *in*, or by changing *i* into *en*, or *en* into *in*; and secondly by adding *ach*, or by changing *e* into *ach*. A few adjectives have the same form for both singular and plural, and two or three form the plural irregularly. The letters *a* and *e* are frequently changed in the plural to *o* and *i* respectively, when they occur in the body of the word.

1. Examples of adjectives which form the plural by adding *en* or *in*, or by changing *i* into *en*, or *en* into *in*:

    Chiito korom *or* chiito ne-korom, the fierce man.
    Piik koromen *or* piik che-koromen, the fierce men.
    Itōkut tepes *or* itōkut ne-tepes, the broad bed.
    Itōkusiek tepesen *or* itōkusiek che-tepesen, the broad beds.
    Ketit koi *or* ketit ne-koi, the high tree.
    Ketik koiin *or* ketik che-koiin, the high trees.
    Korket tui *or* korket ne-tui, the black woman.
    Korusiek tuen *or* korusiek che-tuen, the black women.
    Kwendet ui *or* kwendet ne-ui, the hard firewood (sing.).
    Kwenik uen *or* kwenik che-uen, the hard firewood (pl.).
    Oret tenden *or* oret ne-tenden, the narrow road.
    Ortinuek tendin *or* ortinuek che-tendin, the narrow roads.

[1] In a few rare instances the adjective precedes the substantive. Example: I-lu-e sotet ne-marīch-kut annan ne-para-kut-i? Wilt thou drink milk from a wide-mouthed or from a narrow-mouthed calabash? Here *ne-marīch-kut* and *ne-para-kut* are used for *kutit ne-marīch* and *kutit ne-para*. (Enigma No. 19, p. 137.)

ADJECTIVES

2. Examples of adjectives which form the plural by adding *ach* or by changing *e* into *ach*:
    Ñgetet ya *or* ñgetet ne-ya, the bad boy.
    Ñgetik yaach *or* ñgetik che-yaach, the bad boys.
    Ingoriet lēl *or* ingoriet ne-lēl, the new (*or* white) garment.
    Ingoraiik lelach *or* ingoraiik che-lelach, the new (*or* white) garments.
    Murenet mie *or* murenet ne-mie, the good warrior.
    Murenik miach *or* murenik che-miach, the good warriors.
3. Examples of adjectives which have the same form for the singular and plural:
    Lakwet puch *or* lakwet ne-puch, the naked child.
    Lakōk puch *or* lakōk che-puch, the naked children.
4. Examples of adjectives which form the plural irregularly:
    Lakwet mining *or* lakwet ne-mining, the small child.
    Lakōk mingech *or* lakōk che-mingech, the small children.
    Seset oo *or* seset ne-oo, the big dog.
    Sesēnik echen *or* sesēnik che-echen, the big dogs.
    Chiito mioni *or* chiito ne-mioni, the sick man.
    Piik miondōs *or* piik che-miondōs, the sick men.
5. Examples of adjectives which form the plural by changing *a* into *o* and *e* into *i*, when these letters occur in the body of the word:
    Chepto kararan *or* chepto ne-kararan, the beautiful girl.
    Tīpīk kororon *or* tīpīk che-kororon, the beautiful girls.
    Poiyot wesis *or* poiyot ne-wesis, the gentle old man.
    Poiisiek wisisin *or* poiisiek che-wisisin, the gentle old men.

Many is translated by *che-chañg, few* by *che-ñgeriñg*:
    Piik che-chañg, many men.   Piik che-ñgeriñg, few men.

Male and *female* are rendered by *kirkit* and *kôket* respectively:
    Ñgetundo kirkit, the lion.   Ñgetundo kôket, the lioness.

When the adjective is used predicatively, it precedes the substantive:
    Korom chiito, the man is fierce.   Koromen piik, the men are fierce.
    Chañg piik, the men are many.

A few words, which are merely genitives, are used as attributes (similar to such expressions as *days of old, homme de bien,* &c.). They follow the substantive they qualify:
    Ēut-áp-tai, the right hand.   Oret-ap-kátam, the left hand.
    Tioñgik-ap-tímdo, the wild animals (*lit.* of the wood).

Two or more adjectives can follow a substantive:
    Eito ne-oo ne-tui nepo-ole-kinye, the former big black bullock.

When a noun is qualified by an adjective, and followed by a genitive, the genitive precedes the adjective. It is therefore sometimes difficult to tell whether the adjective qualifies the nominative or genitive; thus

> Chep-kametit am-murenet ne-mining, might mean, The sister of the small warrior, *or* The warrior's small sister.

The Comparison of Adjectives.

There are not, properly speaking, any degrees of comparison in Nandi.

The comparative may be represented in four ways:

1. By the use of *ko-sir*, 'that it may pass':
   > Ane ne-oo ko-sir (I who am greater that it may pass him), I am greater than he.
   > Inendet ne-oo ko-sir-o (he who is greater that it may pass me), he is greater than I.
   > Kararan kii-i ko-sir nin (beautiful this thing that it may pass that), this thing is more beautiful than that.

2. By the use of *lâtit*, the rest:
   > Ka-a-'kochi rupiesiek pokol ak lâtit (I have given him Rs. 100 and the rest), I have given him more than Rs. 100.
   > Tinye tuka taman ak lâtit, he has more than ten oxen.

3. By the use of *kitegin*, a little more:
   > Ip-u kiito ne-oo kitegin, bring something a little bigger.

4. By the use of *tamne* or *mirit*, which may be translated by 'to be more so':
   > A-korom, i-tamne (*or* i-mirit-e), I am fierce, (but) thou art more so (*i.e.* thou art fiercer).

More can be translated by *ake*, &c., other (which see p. 188), or by *tes*, to increase:

> Tes cheko, ip-u chek' alak, increase the milk, bring some more milk.

The superlative is generally rendered by the use of the adjective in its simple form:

> Ñgô ne-mie? Who is the best?

It can also be translated by an adjective (verbal form joined to the relative) followed by the local case:

> Inendet ne-mining eñg-murenik tukul (he who is small from the warriors all), he is the smallest of all the warriors.

Like the comparative, the superlative can be expressed by *ko-sir*, 'that it may pass':

> Mie chií-chi ko-sir tukul (good this man that it may pass all), this man is the best of all.

ADJECTIVES

The superlative may also be represented by other parts of the verb *sir*, to pass, followed by the local case:

Mié nin, ako ni ne-sir-e eñg-miēnot (good that one, but this one who surpasses in goodness), that one is good, but this one is the best.

THE NUMERALS.

Akenge	One.
Aeñg *or* oieñg	Two.
Somok	Three.
Añgwan	Four.
Mut	Five.
Illo *or* kullo	Six.
Tisap	Seven.
Sisiit	Eight.
Sokol	Nine.
Taman	Ten.
Taman ak akenge	Eleven.
Taman ok oieñg	Twelve.
Taman ok somok	Thirteen.
Taman ak añgwan	Fourteen.
Taman ak mut [1]	Fifteen.
Taman ak illo	Sixteen.
Taman ak tisap	Seventeen.
Taman ok sisiit	Eighteen.
Taman ok sokol	Nineteen.
Tiptem	Twenty.
Tiptem ak akenge	Twenty-one.
Sosom *or* tomonuagik somok	Thirty.
Artam *or* tomonuagik añgwan	Forty.
Konom *or* tomonuagik mut	Fifty.
Tomonuagik illo	Sixty.[2]
Tomonuagik tisap	Seventy.
Tomonuagik sisiit	Eighty.
Tomonuagik sokol	Ninety.
Pokol	Hundred.
Pokol ak akenge	Hundred and one.

The numeral always follows the substantive, which, except when *one* is used, must be accompanied by the article. *One* can take the article or not, as the speaker wishes:

Piik oieñg, two men.
Chii akenge *or* chiit' akenge, one man.

[1] *Or* taman añg mut.
[2] Often everything above fifty is simply styled pokol. If it is desired to express a very large number, pokol-pokol, pokolaiik che-chañg, *or* pokol che-mo-ki-rar-e is used.

The ordinal numbers are expressed by the use of the genitive particle:
Chiit'-ap-añgwan, the fourth man.
Lak-te piik oieñg, imut-u nepo somok (leave two men alone, bring the third), bring the third man.

First and *last* are translated by Nepo (*or* chepo) met, and Nepo (*or* chepo) let, respectively. *First* can also be translated by Nepo tae *or* Ne-indoï, and both *first* and *last* by Ole-poch.

Once is translated by Kip-akenge, *twice* and the *second time* by Kip-oieñg *or* Isakte oieñg, *How many times ?* by Ke-'sakte ata ?, and *often* by Isakte che-chañg.

First of all is translated by Isi, which is generally followed by Ta-u, (to begin):
Isi a-ta-u poiisiet, si a-wa, I must first of all do the work, then I may go.

PRONOUNS.

The personal pronouns are:

Singular.		Plural.	
I	Ane	We	Achek.
Thou	Inye	You	Okwek.
He, she, or it	Inendet *or* Ine	They	Icheket *or* Ichek.

The objective cases *me*, *thee*, *him*, &c., can be expressed by the same forms as those given for the nominative.

The possessive case *of me*, &c., is expressed by the possessive pronoun.[1]

The position of the personal pronoun with regard to the verb is given on p. 191.

The personal pronouns, when combined with a verb as subject or object, are indicated by special prefixes and affixes. See pp. 190-1.

Possessive Pronouns.

The possessive pronouns are always placed after the substantive denoting the thing possessed and vary according to number. The singular article and the termination of the noun frequently undergo changes when a possessive pronoun is used. For particulars see pp. 162-3.

---

[1] *Some of us*, &c., is translated by *akut-achek*, *angut-achek*, &c. Example: Ki-mi piik-i? Were any of the men there? Wei, ki-mi akut-ichek. Yes, some of them were there.

PRONOUNS 185

The possessive pronouns are :

	Singular.	Plural.
My	Nyō	Chōk.
Thy	Ñguñg	Kuk.
His, her, or its	Nyi	Chik.
Our	Nyo	Chok.
Your	Ñgwañg	Kwok.
Their	Nywa	Chwak.

Sesén-nyō, my dog; sesēnik-chōk, my dogs.
Rōtuén-ñguñg, thy sword; rōtók-kuk, thy swords.
Chepkeswén-nyi, his knife ; chepkesók-chik, his knives.

The words *mine, thine,* &c., used predicatively or absolutely, take the prefix *na* or *ne* in the singular, and *cha* or *che* in the plural. The forms for *mine, thine,* and *his* also undergo slight changes in the plural :

Mine	Nanyō	Chachōget.
Thine	Neñguñg	Chekuget.
His, hers, or its	Nenyi	Chechiget.
Ours	Nenyo	Chechok.
Yours	Neñgwañg	Chekwok.
Theirs	Nenywa	Chechwak.

Rotōk chwak chu, ngocho chekuget, these are their swords, where are thine?

Kararan kií-nyi ko-sir nanyō, his thing is more beautiful than mine.

Ko-'le orkoiyot : ' Mo-o-par sigirōk, chechok ', the medicine man said : ' Do not strike the donkeys, they are ours.'

There is a short enclitic form of the possessive pronouns of the second and third persons which is used with the words *father* and *mother* :

Kōn, thy or your father ; Akut-kōn (*or* Akut-kōnuak),[1] thy or your fathers.

Kwan, his, her, or their father; Akut-kwan (*or* Akut-kwanuak), his, her, or their fathers.

Komit, thy or your mother; Angut-komit(*or*Angut-komituak), thy or your mothers.

Kamet, his, her, or their mother; Angut-kamet (*or* Angut-kametuak), his, her, or their mothers.

The personal pronouns may be added to the possessive pronoun to give emphasis. The word *porto*, the body, is also sometimes used in this sense :

Rotuén-nyō ane
Rotuén-nyō nepo portán-nyō } My own knife.
Rotuet-ap-portán-nyō

[1] *Akut* and *angut* are often interchangeable.

DEMONSTRATIVE PRONOUNS.

The demonstrative pronoun assumes four forms. The first denotes objects near at hand; the second, objects at a distance; and the third and fourth, objects previously mentioned. The word *olto*, the place, requires a special form to be used with it.

Class I.

This *or* these, of objects at no great distance:

Usual form.	Used with the word olto.	English.
Ni *or* I	Yu	This.
Chu [1]	Uli	These.

Class II.

That *or* those *or* yonder, referring to things at a distance:

Nin *or* In	Yun	That.
Chun	Ulin	Those.

Class III.

This *or* these, mentioned before:

No *or* O	Yo	This.
Cho	Ulo	These.

Class IV.

That *or* those *or* yonder, mentioned before:

Non *or* On	Yon	That.
Chon	Ulon	Those.

The demonstrative pronoun always follows the substantive. When the substantive joined to the article is accompanied by the demonstrative pronoun, certain changes of spelling take place in all three parts of speech. For particulars and examples see pp. 160–2.

If it is desired to lay stress on the demonstrative pronoun, *to* (*d* after *n*) is affixed to it. Examples:

Seson-nito, this dog here, this very dog.
Sirim-ito, this chain here.
Sesen-juto, these dogs here.
Korkon-nindo, that woman there.
Korusie-chundo, those women there.
Yuto, just this place, just here.

Iro, look, can also be prefixed to the pronoun to express emphasis:
Iro-cho, maiyo ok che, look at these (things mentioned before), beer and milk (see p. 48).

---

[1] *Ch* changes to *j* after *n*.

PRONOUNS

REFLEXIVE PRONOUNS.

Most verbs have a special reflexive form which is made by the affix *ke*:

    A-til-i-ke, I am cutting myself.
    Ka-ki-til-ke, we have cut ourselves.

Self is also occasionally translated by *mukuleldo*, the heart:

    Chom-e mukuleldán-nyi, (he loves his heart) he loves himself.

When *self* is added to a pronoun to express emphasis, it is rendered by the affix *-ke* or *-e*, or by the prefix *ak*.

    Chiito ineke, *or* chiito akine, the man himself.
    Piik icheke, *or* piik akichek, the men themselves.
    Aneke *or* akane, I myself; acheke *or* akachek, we ourselves.
    Inyeke *or* akinye, thou thyself; okweke *or* akokwek, you yourselves.

By myself, by ourselves, &c., are rendered in the same way:

    Aneke *or* akane, by myself; acheke *or* akachek, by ourselves.

In place of *aneke*, &c., *i-toi-i-ke* (third person *i-toi-ke*) is often affixed to the present tense and *i-te-ke* to the past tense:

    A-me-i i-toi-i-ke, I will die by myself, *or* alone.
    Ka-me i-te-ke, he has died by himself, *or* alone.

The word *owner* is rendered by *chiito*, the man, *korket*, the woman, &c., not by *-ke*,[1] &c.; *e. g.*

    Chiit'-ap-kot   } the owner of the house.
    Korket-ap-kot
    Piik-ap-korik   } the owners of the house.
    Korusiek-ap-korik
    Chiit'-ap-kepenet, the owner of the (lion's) den.

Kopo may also be prefixed to the governed word to express *owner*:

    Chiit'-ap-kopo-kot, the owner of the house.
    Piik-ap-kopo-korik, the owners of the house.
    Chiit'-ap-kopo-kepenet, the owner of the (lion's) den.

RELATIVE PRONOUNS.

The form for the relative pronoun is *ne* in the singular and *che* in the plural. There is a special form for the word *olto*, the place, which is *ye* in both numbers:

    Chiito ne-kararan, the man who is beautiful.
    Piik che-kororon, the men who are beautiful.
    Olto ye-kararan, the place which is beautiful.
    Oltōsiek ye-kororon, the places which are beautiful.

---

[1] In Masai the word *owner* is rendered by open, *self*.

When the negative is combined with the relative, *ne-ma* is used in the singular, and *che-ma* in the plural. *Ye-ma* is employed with the word *olto*, the place:

>Chiito ne-ma-kararan, the man who is not beautiful.
>Piik che-ma-kororon, the men who are not beautiful.
>Olto ye-ma-kararan, the place which is not beautiful.

Particulars with regard to certain changes which take place in the spelling of the relative are given on pp. 191–3.

INDEFINITE PRONOUNS.

There are two indefinite pronouns. The first, *ake* (pl. *alake* or *alak*), is equivalent to *other, another, the one . . . the other,* and *else*; the second, *tukul,* to *each, every, all, whosoever* and *whatsoever,* and in compound words to *all three,* &c. :

>Chiit' ake, another man.
>Korket ake, another woman.
>Piik alak, other men.
>Korusiek alak, other women.
>Ki-nyo chiit' ake, somebody else came.
>Ki-a-we olt' ake, I went somewhere else.
>Kâ-ai-te kiit' ake, I have done something else.
>Kororon alake ko-yaach alake, some are good and others bad.

When *tukul* is used to translate *each, every, whosoever,* &c., the article is omitted:

>Ki-nyo chii-tukul, each man came.
>Ki-pwa piich-tukul, every man came.
>Ki-pun-u eṅg-oii-tukul, they came from every place.
>Ingo-nyo chii-tukul, ile-chi kwa, whosoever comes, tell him to go away.

When *tukul* is used to translate *all,* the article is retained:

>Ka-pwa piik-tukul, all the men have come.

Both, all three, &c., are translated as follows :

>Towae, both.
>Tukul ko-somok, all three.
>Tukul kw-añgwan, all four.
>Tukul ko-mut, all five.

INTERROGATIVE PRONOUNS.

There is one interrogative pronoun that is declinable, *ñgô,* Who? and three that are indeclinable, *ñgô,* Which ?, *ne,* What ?, **and** *añg,* What sort of ?

PRONOUNS

Who? is declined as follows :

Singular.	Plural.		English.
Masculine & Feminine.	Masculine.	Feminine.	
Ñgô	Ñgô-ñgô		Who? Whom?
	Akut-ñgô	Angut-ñgô	
Po-ñgô	Pakut-ñgô	Pangut-ñgô	Whose?

Ñgô is also used in both numbers to express *Which?* or *What?*; *ne* is equivalent to *What?*; and *añg* to *What sort of?*.

If the interrogative pronoun is the subject, the verb requires a relative with it. When *Which?*, *What sort of?*, &c., are joined to a substantive, the article is omitted. *Who?* precedes the verb, *Whom?* and *What?* follow; *Whose?* and *What sort of?* precede the substantive, *Which?* follows.

When following *añg*, *t* becomes *d*, *ch* becomes *j*, and *k* becomes *g*. Before *p* and *k*, *añg* becomes *am*.

Ñgô ne-mi-í ko? Who is at the house?
Ñgô-ñgô che-mi-í ko? ⎫
Akut-ñgô che-mi-í ko? ⎬ Who are at the house?
Angut-ñgô che-mi-í ko? ⎭
I-moch-é ñgô? Whom do you want?
Po-ñgô rotuán-ni? Whose sword is this?
Pakut-ñgô rotó-chu? Whose swords are these?
Pangut-ñgô ingoraií-chu? Whose garments are these?
Chii-ñgô ne-mi-i? Which man is there?
Korko-ñgô ne-mi-i? Which woman is there?
Piich-ñgô che-mi-i? Which men are there?
Mi-í ne? What is there?
Tinye né chu? What have these? (*i.e.* what is the matter with them?)
I-moch-é ne? What do you want?
Añg-sigiroi che-mi-i? What sort of donkeys are there?
Añg-joruán-ni? What sort of a friend is this?
Añg-dim ne-ke-i-'ro? What sort of a wood hast thou seen?
Am-gorko ne-mi-i? What sort of a woman is there?
Am-perut ne-mi-i? What sort of a mark is there?

VERBS.

Verbs in Nandi fall into two classes: (1) roots beginning with *i*, (2) all other roots. There are also numerous derivative forms which may be assumed by most Nandi verbs where in English either another verb or some compound expression must be used.

The principal difference between verbs commencing with *i* and those commencing with any other letter is the omission of the *i* in certain cases. This omission is to be found in the first person singular and second person plural of all tenses of the active voice,[1] in the third persons singular and plural whenever the personal prefix is *ko*, and in the second person singular and third persons singular and plural of the active voice when the tense prefix ends in *e* or *i*. Examples:

A-'sup-i,[2] I follow (him). Ki-isup-i, we follow (him).
A-pir-i,[3] I strike (him). Ki-pir-i, we strike (him).
Isup, follow (him). O-'sup, follow ye (him).
Pir, strike (him). O-pir, strike ye (him).
Ke-i-'sup, thou hast followed (him). Ko-'sup, that he, she, *or* they may follow (him).
Ki-ki-isup, we followed (him). Ki-'sup, he, she, *or* they followed (him).

When conjugating the verb, special prefixes are used to mark the subject if of the first and second persons. There is also in some tenses a special prefix to mark the subject in the third persons. The following are the subjective or nominative forms.

I, *a*, rarely *o*, *ai*, or *oi*. We, *ki*, rarely *ke*.
Thou, *i*, rarely *e*. You, *o*, rarely *oi*.
He, she, or it, sometimes *ko*.[4] They, sometimes *ko*.

A special affix is also employed when the object is the first or second person singular or plural.[5] When the subject is:

I	and the object	thee,	the affix is	*n* or *in*.
I	,,	,,	you	,,	,,	*ak* or *ok*.
Thou	,,	,,	me	,,	,,	*a* or *o*.
Thou	,,	,,	us	,,	,,	*ech*.
He, she, or it	,,	,,	me	,,	,,	*a* or *o*.
He, she, or it	,,	,,	thee	,,	,,	*n* or *in*.
He, she, or it	,,	,,	us	,,	,,	*ech*.
He, she, or it	,,	,,	you	,,	,,	*ak* or *ok*.
We	,,	,,	thee	,,	,,	*n* or *in*.
We	,,	,,	you	,,	,,	*ak* or *ok*.
You	,,	,,	me	,,	,,	*a* or *o*.
You	,,	,,	us	,,	,,	*ech*.
They	,,	,,	me	,,	,,	*a* or *o*.
They	,,	,,	thee	,,	,,	*n* or *in*.
They	,,	,,	us	,,	,,	*ech*.
They	,,	,,	you	,,	,,	*ak* or *ok*.

[1] There are a few exceptions to this rule, *e.g.* a-it-e, I arrive; a-ipe-i, I seize (it).   [2] From *Isup*, to follow, a verb beginning with *i*.
[3] From *Pir*, to strike, a verb beginning with another letter than *i*.
[4] *Ko* becomes *go* after *n* and *kw* before *a*.
[5] When the verb takes a derivative form, the verbal affix is sometimes changed when the object is the first or second person singular or plural. *Vide* pp. 210, 212.

VERBS

The following examples from the verb *isup*, to follow, will illustrate the use of the affixes:

Singular.
- Ka-a-'sup, I have followed him, &c.
- Ka-a-'sup-in, I have followed thee.
- Ka-a-'sup-ok, I have followed you.
- Ke-i-'sup, thou hast followed him, &c.
- Ke-i-'sup-o, thou hast followed me.
- Ke-i-'sup-ech, thou hast followed us.
- Ke-'sup, he or she has followed him, &c.
- Ke-'sup-o, he or she has followed me.
- Ke-'sup-in, he or she has followed thee.
- Ke-'sup-ech, he or she has followed us.
- Ke-'sup-ok, he or she has followed you.

Plural.
- Ka-ki-isup, we have followed him, &c.
- Ka-ki-isup-in, we have followed thee.
- Ka-ki-isup-ok, we have followed you.
- Ko-o-'sup, you have followed him, &c.
- Ko-o-'sup-o, you have followed me.
- Ko-o-'sup-ech, you have followed us.
- Ke-'sup, they have followed him, &c.
- Ke-'sup-o, they have followed me.
- Ke-'sup-in, they have followed thee.
- Ke-'sup-ech, they have followed us.
- Ke-'sup-ok, they have followed you.

The personal pronoun is only rarely added, and then to prevent ambiguity or for emphasis. It always follows the verb, and is more frequently used in the subjective than in the objective case. If both are used, the former precedes the latter:

A-pir-ok ane okwek, I (shall) strike you.
Ki-pir-o ane, I am struck.

If the personal pronoun is used as the indirect object, it precedes the direct object. Example:

Ka-a-kōn-ok okwek rotōk, I have given you the swords.

The objective prefix is used when anything about the person or thing is about to be stated:

Ka-til-a mornet, he has cut my finger.
Ki-ki-rat-ak ēunek, we bound your arms.

THE RELATIVE.

The relative is inseparable from the verb, and in the present tense is generally used instead of the personal prefixes. Example: Inye ne-isup-i chiito, it is thou who followest the man. It may, however, be placed in front of these prefixes, *e.g.* Inye ne-i-isup-i chiito.

The relative may be used with the present, past, and future, both active and passive. When followed by *a* or *o*, the vowel of the relative changes to *a* or *o*.

If the subject and object are expressed, the former precedes, and the latter follows, the relative and verb. Examples:

Ane ne-isup-i chiito } (it is) I who follow the man.
Ane na-a-'sup-i chiito

Ane na-a-'sup-in, (it is) I who follow thee.
Ane ne-ki-a-'sup chiito, (it is) I who followed the man.
Ane ne-kwo-a-'sup chiito, (it is) I who followed the man yesterday.
Ane ne-ka-a-'sup chiito, (it is) I who have followed the man.
Ane ne-ip-a-'sup-i chiito, (it is) I who will follow the man.
Inendet ne-isup-i chiito, (it is) he or she who follows the man.
Achek che-isup-i chiito } (it is) we who follow the man.
Achek che-ki-isup-i chiito
Okwek che-isup-i chiito } (it is) you who follow the man.
Okwek cho-o-'sup-i chiito
Icheket che-isup-i chiito, (it is) they who follow the man.
Chiito ne-ki-isup-i, the man who is followed.
Chiito ne-ki-ki-isup, the man who was followed.
Chiito ne-ip-ki-isup-i, the man who will be followed.
Piik che-ki-isup-i, the men who are followed.

When the relative is the object of the verb, *n* or *ch* (*ne* or *che* before *k*) precede the personal or the tense prefixes. Examples:

Chiito n-a-'sup-i, the man whom I follow.
Chiito ne-ki-a-'sup, the man whom I followed.
Chiito ne-ka-a-'sup, the man whom I have followed.
Chiito ne-kwo-a-'sup, the man whom I followed yesterday.
Piik ch-a-'sup-i, the men whom I follow.

Adverbs of place and time are often treated as relative particles, *ole, ola,* or *olo* being placed before the personal prefixes:[1]

A-wend-i ole-i-wend-i, I go whither (or when) thou goest.
A-wend-i olto ole-i-pun-u, I am going to the place whence thou comest.
I-wend-i olto ola-a-pun-u, thou art going to the place from whence I come.
A-wend-i olto olo-o-pun-u, I am going to the place from whence you come.

The relative is often employed in Nandi where it is not required in English. Examples:

Ñgô ne-wend-i? Who is going?
Añg gorusio che-ka-pa? Which women have gone?

[1] If an adverb of time is used the relative is frequently omitted. Thus: A-wend-i koi i-wend-i, I go (and) afterwards thou goest, is as intelligible as a-wend-i ole-koi-i-wend-i, *or* a-wend-i ole-i-wend-i, I go when thou goest.

VERBS 193

Piik ata che-ka-pa? How many men have gone?
Chii-tukul ne-nyo-ne, whoever may come.
Tuluet ne-oo, the big mountain.
A-tinye pêk che-oi-'e, I have some drinking water.
Ip-u ñgecheret na-a-tep-e, bring me a chair to sit on.

Somewhat similar changes to those enumerated above occur when the relative is used with the negative (*ne-ma* and *che-ma*). The particle *ma*, which is unchangeable, can however precede a pronoun:

Ma ane ne-isup-i chiito } it is not I who follow the man.
Ane ne-ma-a-'sup-i chiito }

Ma inye ne-isup-i chiito } it is not thou who followest the man.
Inye ne-ma-i-isup-i chiito }

Ma achek che-isup-i chiito } it is not we who follow the man.
Achek che-ma-ki-isup-i chiito }

Ma ane ne-kwo-a-'sup chiito } it was not I who followed the man
Ane ne-kwo-ma-a-'sup chiito } yesterday.

Olto ole-ma-mi-i, a place where there is nobody (a desert place).

FORMATION OF TENSES.
SIMPLE VERBS.
ACTIVE VOICE.
INDICATIVE TENSES.
Present.

There is only one present tense,[1] which is formed by affixing *i* or *e*[2] to the root:

A-'sup-i (ane inendet), I follow *or* am following (him).
I-isup-i (inye inendet), thou followest *or* art following (him).
Isup-i (inendet inendet), he or she follows *or* is following (him).

Ki-isup-i (achek inendet), we follow *or* are following (him).
O-'sup-i (okwek inendet), you follow *or* are following (him).
Isup-i (ichek inendet), they follow *or* are following (him).

When the vowel of the verbal root is *a*, it is generally changed to *o* in the present tense:

A-chom-e,[3] I love *or* am loving (him).
I-chom-e, thou lovest (him).
Chom-e, he or she loves (him).

Ki-chom-e, we love (him).
O-chom-e, you love (him).
Chom-e, they love (him).

[1] See also p. 194.
[2] This affix, it must be remembered, changes when the object of the verb is the first or second person singular or plural. See pp. 190-1.
[3] Verbal root *cham*.

NANDI O

In a few verbs the present tense is formed without the affix *i* or *e* :

 A-mwe,[1] I run away.   Ki-mwe, we run away.
 I-mwe, thou runnest away.   O-mwe, you run away.
 Mwe, he or she runs away.   Mwe, they run away.

When the verbal root ends in *i* or *e*, the present tense is sometimes formed by changing the *i* into *e*, or the *e* into *i* :

 A-tu-e,[2] I pound.   Ki-tu-e, we pound.
 I-tu-e, thou poundest.   O-tu-e, you pound.
 Tu-e, he or she pounds.   Tu-e, they pound.
 A-pwan-i,[3] I swell.   Ki-pwan-i, we swell.
 I-pwan-i, thou swellest.   O-pwan-i, you swell.
 Pwan-i, he or she swells.   Pwan-i, they swell.

Still, yet, or *again* is indicated by *ta* placed before the personal prefixes. In the third persons the prefix changes to *ko* :

 Ta-a-'sup-i, I still follow *or* am still following (him), *or* I am following (him) again.   Ta-ki-isup-i, we still follow (him).
 Ta-i-isup-i, thou still followest (him).   Ta-o-'sup-i, you still follow (him).
 Ta-ko-'sup-i, he or she still follows (him).   Ta-ko-'sup-i, they still follow (him).

Present Perfect.

The present perfect is made by placing *k* and a vowel before the personal prefix. *Ka* is used in the first persons,[4] *ke* in the second person singular and in the third persons if the verbal root commences with *i*. If the verb commences with any other letter, *ka* or *ko* is used in the third persons. *Ko* is used in the second person plural. This tense as a rule denotes an action complete at the time of speaking, and is equivalent to the English tense with *have*. It is, however, at times also used in place of the present imperfect and progressive (I am following) :

 Ka-a-'sup, I have followed (him).   Ka-ki-isup, we have followed (him).
 Ke-i-'sup, thou hast followed (him).   Ko-o-'sup, you have followed (him).
 Ke-'sup, he or she has followed (him).   Ke-'sup, they have followed (him).
 Ka-cham, he, she, or they have loved (him).

---

[1] Verbal root *mwe*, to run away.   [2] Verbal root *tu-i*, to pound.
[3] Verbal root *pwan-e*, to swell.
[4] When the verbal root commences with *a*, *ka-a* is contracted into *kâ*; *e.g.* Kâ-aruny, I have folded, for ka-a-aruny.

A form of the present perfect which denotes a more complete action than the preceding is made by doubling the syllable *ka* or by using *ka* instead of *ke*, &c. In the third persons the personal prefix becomes *ko*:

Kaka-a-'sup *or* ka-a-'sup, I have finished following (him).
Kaka-i-isup *or* ka-i-'sup, thou hast finished following (him).
Kaka-ko-'sup *or* ka-ko-'sup, he has finished following (him).
Kaka-ki-isup *or* ka-ki-isup, we have finished following (him).
Kaka-o-'sup *or* ka-o-'sup, you have finished following (him).
Kaka-ko-'sup *or* ka-ko-'sup, they have finished following (him).

Past Perfect.

A past perfect tense is made by the prefix *ki*. It denotes an action complete in past time, and represents the indefinite past tense in English:

Ki-a-'sup, I followed (him).
Ki-i-'sup, thou followedst (him).
Ki-'sup *or* Ki-ko-'sup, he or she followed (him).
Ki-ki-isup, we followed (him)
Ki-o-'sup, you followed (him).
Ki-'sup *or* ki-ko-'sup, they followed (him).

When it is desired to express a still more complete action in the past, *kika* is used for *ki*:

Kika-a-'sup, I finished following (him).
Kika-i-isup, thou finishedst following (him).
Kika-ko-'sup, he finished following (him).
Kika-ki-isup, we finished following (him).
Kika-o-'sup, you finished following (him).
Kika-ko-'sup, they finished following (him).

If the time of action is qualified by the adverb *amt*, yesterday, slightly different forms are used, *kwo* and *kwoka* taking the place of *ki* and *kika*:

Kwo-a-'sup amt, I followed (him) yesterday.
Kwoka-a-'sup amt, I finished following (him) yesterday.
Kwo-ki-isup amt, we followed (him) yesterday.
Kwoka-ki-isup amt, we finished following (him) yesterday.

Imperfect.

An imperfect tense denoting that the action is not yet complete, and answering to the English *was* followed by the present participle, is formed by prefixing the same letters as are used in the present and past perfect to the present tense:

Ka-a-'sup-i, I have been following (him).
Ki-a-'sup-i, I was following (him).
Ka-ki-isup-i, we have been following (him).
Ki-ki-isup-i, we were following (him).

When the verb is qualified by the adverb *amt*, yesterday, the prefix is changed to *kwo*:

Kwo-a-'sup-i amt, I was following (him) yesterday.
Kwo-ki-isup-i amt, we were following (him) yesterday.

Again is expressed by inserting *ta* between the prefix of the past tense and the personal prefix:

Ka-ta-a-'sup, I have again followed (him).
Ki-ta-a-'sup, I again followed (him).

Future.

A future tense is formed by prefixing *ip* or *inyo* to the present. The former signifies *going*, the latter *coming*. In the third persons *ko* is used for the personal prefix:

Ip (*or* inyo)-a-'sup-i, I go (*or* come) to follow (him), *or* I shall follow (him).

Ip (*or* inyo)-ki-isup-i, we go (*or* come) to follow (him), *or* we shall (follow) him.

Ip (*or* inyo)-i-isup-i, thou goest (*or* comest) to follow (him), *or* thou wilt follow (him).

Ip (*or* inyo)-o-'sup-i, you go (*or* come) to follow (him), *or* you will follow (him).

Ip (*or* inyo)-ko-'sup-i, he or she goes (*or* comes) to follow (him), *or* he or she will follow (him).

Ip (*or* inyo)-ko-'sup-i, they go (*or* come) to follow (him), *or* they will follow (him).

The present tense with or without such words as *koi*, afterwards, *tun*, presently, *mutai*, to-morrow, is often used instead of the future.

CONDITIONAL TENSES.

Present.

There are two present conditional tenses, one of which is formed by the prefix *ingo-nga*, &c.,[1] and the other by *ang-nya*, &c. The former is equivalent to *if*, the latter to *when*. When *ingo-nga*, &c., is used, various changes take place in the personal prefixes:

Ingo-nga-a-'sup, if I follow *or* am following (him).
Ingo-ngi-isup, if we follow (him).

Ingo-ngi-isup, if thou followest (him).
Ingo-ngo-o-'sup, if you follow (him).

Ingo-ngo-'sup, if he *or* she follows (him).
Ingo-ngo-'sup, if they follow (him).

[1] *Ingo* or *inga* is frequently used for *ingo-ngo* or *ingo-nga*, *ingi* for *ingo-ngi*, and *inge* for *ingo-nge*.

VERBS

Ingo-nga-a-par, if I kill (him).
Ingo-ngi-par, if thou killest (him).
Ingo-ngo-par, if he or she kills (him).

Ingo-nge-par, if we kill (him).
Ingo-ngo-o-par, if you kill (him).
Ingo-ngo-par, if they kill (him).

Añg-nya-a-'sup, when I follow or am following (him).
Añg-nye-i-'sup, when thou followest (him).
Añg-nye-'sup, when he or she follows (him).

Añg-nye-ki-isup, when we follow (him).
Añg-nyo-o-'sup, when you follow (him).
Añg-nye-'sup, when they follow (him).

Past.

As in the indicative tenses, there are several ways of forming the past contingent tenses. The most usual way is by prefixing *ki* to the present contingent. *Ingo-nga* and *ingo-ngi* are contracted into *ingo* and *ingi*:

Ki-ingo-a-'sup, if I followed (him).
Ki-ingi-isup, if thou followedst (him).
Ki-ingo-'sup, if he or she followed (him).

Ki-ingi-isup, if we followed (him).
Ki-ingo-o-'sup, if you followed (him).
Ki-ingo-'sup, if they followed (him).

Ki-añg-nya-a-'sup, when I followed (him).
Ki-añg-nye-ki-isup, when we followed (him).

When I was about to, &c., is translated by *kiolen*, &c., placed before the personal prefix. When the verb assumes this form, the prefix of the third persons is changed to *go*, and of the first person plural to *gi*:

Kiolen-a-'sup, when I was about to follow (him).
Kiilen-i-isup, when thou wast about to follow (him).
Kilen-go-'sup, when he or she was about to follow (him).

Kikilen-gi-isup, when we were about to follow (him).
Kiolen-o-'sup, when you were about to follow (him).
Kilen-go-'sup, when they were about to follow (him).

Slight changes in the above forms are made when the verb is qualified by the adverb *amt*, yesterday:

Kwo-nga-a-'sup amt, if I followed (him) yesterday.
Kwo-añg-nya-a-'sup amt, when I followed (him) yesterday.
Kwolen-a-'sup amt, when I was about to follow (him) yesterday.

Kwo-ngi-isup amt, if we followed (him) yesterday.
Kwo-añg-nye-ki-isup amt, when we followed (him) yesterday.
Kwokilen-gi-isup amt, when we were about to follow (him) yesterday.

Again is expressed by inserting *ko-ta* between the verbal and personal prefixes, unless *ko* forms a part of the former, when *ta* only is used:

Ingo-ta-a-'sup, if I follow (him) again.
Ki-añg-nya-ko-ta-a-'sup, when I follow (him) again.

Future.

The future conditional tenses are formed by the prefixes *ingo-ngep* and *añg-nyep*:

Ingo-ngep-a-'sup, if I shall follow (him).
Añg-nyep-a-'sup, when I shall follow (him).

Ingo-ngep-ki-isup, if we shall follow (him).
Añg-nyep-ki-isup, when we shall follow (him).

The Contingent Tenses.

The present and past contingent tenses are formed by prefixing *takoraki* and *ta* to the present and past perfect indicative. *Ko* is used for the personal prefix in the third persons:

Present.

Takoraki-a-'sup-i, I should or if I did follow (him).
Takoraki-i-'sup-i, thou wouldst or if thou didst follow (him).
Takoraki-ko-'sup-i, he or she would or if he or she did follow (him).

Takoraki-ki-isup-i, we should or if we did follow (him).
Takoraki-o-'sup-i, you would or if you did follow (him).
Takoraki-ko-'sup-i, they would or if they did follow (him).

Past.

Ta-ki-a-'sup, I should have or had I followed (him).
Ta-ki-i-'sup, thou wouldst have or hadst thou followed (him).
Ta-ki-ko-'sup, he or she would have or had he or she followed (him).

Ta-kika-a-'sup, I should have or had I finished following (him).
Ta-kwo-a-'sup amt, I should have or had I followed (him) yesterday.
Ta-kwoka-a-'sup amt, I should have or had I finished following (him) yesterday.

Ta-ki-ki-isup, we should have or had we followed (him).
Ta-ki-o-'sup, you would have or had you followed (him).
Ta-ki-ko-'sup, they would have or had they followed (him).

Ta-kika-ki-isup, we should have or had we finished following (him).
Ta-kwo-ki-isup amt, we should have or had we followed (him) yesterday.
Ta-kwoka-ki-isup-amt, we should have or had we finished following (him) yesterday.

VERBS 199

When *again* is used with the present contingent tense, *ko-ta* is inserted between *takoraki* and the personal prefixes. In the other tenses *ta* is used:

Takoraki-ko-ta-a-'sup-i, I should *or* if I did follow (him) again.
Ta-ki-ta-a-'sup, I should have *or* had I followed (him) again.

IMPERATIVE.

The imperative is the simple verbal root. The plural is formed by the prefix *o*:

Isup, follow (him).   O-'sup, follow ye (him).
Cham, love (him).   O-cham, love ye (him).

When the object is the first person, *a* or *o* is affixed in the singular, and *ech* in the plural:

Isup-a, follow me.   O-'sup-a, follow ye me.
Isup-ech, follow us.   O-'sup-ech, follow ye us.

One form of the subjunctive (which see below) may also be used as an imperative or jussive:

Ingo-a-'sup, let me follow (him).   Ingi-isup, let us follow (him).

Another form of the imperative is made by the imperative of the verb *to give*, followed by the subjunctive:

Ikochi ko-'sup, give him that he follows (him), *or* let him follow (him).
Kōn-o a-'sup-in, give me that I follow (thee), *or* let me follow (thee).

Again is expressed by prefixing *ta* in the singular, *to* in the plural:

Ta-isup, follow (him) again.   To-o-'sup, follow ye (him) again.
Ta-cham, love (him) again.   To-o-cham, love ye (him) again.

SUBJUNCTIVE.

There are three ways of forming the subjunctive. In the first, the simple verbal root is preceded by the personal prefixes in the first persons, the imperative is employed in the second persons, and the root, preceded by *ko*, is used in the third persons; in the second method, the simple verbal root is preceded by the personal prefixes; and in the third, *ingo* or *ingi* is placed before the personal prefixes much as in the present conditional tense:

A-'sup, that I may follow (him).   Ki-isup, that we may follow (him).
Isup, that thou mayest follow (him).   O-'sup, that you may follow (him).
Ko-'sup, that he or she may follow (him).   Ko-'sup, that they may follow (him).

A-cham, that I may love (him).
Cham, that thou mayest love (him).
Ko-cham, that he or she may love (him).
A-'sup, may I follow (him).
I-isup, mayest thou follow (him).
Isup, may he or she follow (him).
A-cham, may I love (him).
I-cham, mayest thou love (him).
Cham, may he or she love (him).
Ingo-a-'sup, let me follow (him).
Ingi-isup, let thee follow (him).
Ingo-'sup, let him or her follow (him).

Ki-cham, that we may love (him).
O-cham, that you may love (him).
Ko-cham, that they may love (him).
Ki-isup, may we follow (him).
O-'sup, may you follow (him).
Isup, may they follow (him).
Ki-cham, may we love (him).
O-cham, may you love (him).
Cham, may they love (him).
Ingi-isup, let us follow (him).
Ingo-o-'sup, let you follow (him).
Ingo-'sup, let them follow (him).

The first of these forms is also used both as a narrative tense and where an infinitive is employed in English. In telling a story it is usual to commence with a verb in a past tense, and to put all the verbs that follow in the subjunctive. In some derivative and irregular verbs there is a special form for the narrative tense.

A few instances of the use of the subjunctive are given in the following examples:

Mwa-chi ko-ip omdin-nyō, tell him to bring my food.
Kur ko-nyo ka, call him (to come) to the house.
Kōn-o a-wa, give me permission to go.
Par-in Asis, may God kill thee.
Met-te ko-ru, leave him alone that he may sleep.
Ka-a-'le-ch-in tes omdit, I have told thee to increase the food.
Ko-'le-chi chiito: 'Inge-par,' he said to the man: 'Let us kill him.'
Ki-a-tinye ole-kinye tany-nyō, a-mach a-eny, ko-nai, ko-chilil, I formerly had my ox, I wished to slaughter it, it knew, and it ran away.

PARTICIPLES.

There are no participles in Nandi. The English present participle in -*ing* may sometimes be represented by the present tense. When used in this sense the personal prefix in the third persons becomes *ko*. Example:

Ki-pir ko-'sup-i, he struck him following him.

When the past participle in English is used as a verbal adjective, it is rendered in Nandi by the verbal forms combined with the relative. Example:

Iyue-i lakwet ne-ka-ki-pél mat, a burnt child fears the fire.

INFINITIVE.

There is no form for the infinitive, and the subjunctive is generally used instead. The present indicative at times takes the place of the subjunctive. Examples:

A-'much-i a-'sup, I am able to follow (him).
I-moch-e isup, thou wishest to follow (him).
Sich-e chiito poiisiet kw-ai, the man (will) succeed in doing the work.
Ki-ingen ki-isup, we know how to follow (him).
Mo-o-'much-i oi-eny eito, you were unable to slaughter the bullock.
Ko-sich piik ko-'sup nin, the men succeeded in following that (person).
Isi a-ta-u a-'sup-i, I will first of all follow (him).

THE NEGATIVE CONJUGATION.—ACTIVE VOICE.

INDICATIVE TENSES.

Present.

The negative present is formed by prefixing *m* to the affirmative, with or without a vowel. When the verbal root commences with *i*, the prefix in the third persons is *me*; when it commences with any other letter, the prefix is *ma*:

M-â-'sup-i, I follow (him) not.   Ma-ki-isup-i, we follow (him) not.
Me-i-'sup-i, thou followest (him) not.   Mo-o-'sup-i, you follow (him) not.
Me-'sup-i, he or she follows (him) not.   Me-'sup-i, they follow (him) not.

M-â-chom-e, I love (him) not.   Ma-ki-chom-e, we love (him) not.
Me-i-chom-e, thou lovest (him) not.   Mo-o-chom-e, you love (him) not.
Ma-chom-e, he or she loves (him) not.   Ma-chom-e, they love (him) not.

Again is expressed by the prefix *ma* (*mâ* in the first person plural); *still*, by *tom*. When these forms are used, the personal prefix of the third persons is *ko*:

Ma-a-'sup-i, I follow (him) not again.
Ma-i-isup-i, thou followest (him) not again.
Ma-ko-'sup-i, he or she follows (him) not again.

Mâ-ki-isup-i, we follow (him) not again.
Ma-o-'sup-i, you follow (him) not again.
Ma-ko-'sup-i, they follow (him) not again.

Tom-a-'sup-i, I still follow (him) not.
Tom-ki-isup-i, we still follow (him) not.

Present Perfect.

The present perfect negative is formed by placing *ma* before the personal prefix:

Ma-a-'sup, I have not followed (him).
Ma-i-isup, thou hast not followed (him).
Ma-isup, he or she has not followed (him).

Ma-ki-isup, we have not followed (him).
Ma-o-'sup, you have not followed (him).
Ma-isup, they have not followed (him).

Past Perfect.

The negative past perfect tenses and the imperfect are made by inserting *ma* between the prefix of the affirmative and the personal prefixes:

Ki-ma-a-'sup, I followed (him) not.
Ki-ma-i-isup, thou followedst (him) not.
Ki-ma-isup, he or she followed (him) not.
Kika-ma-a-'sup, I did not finish following (him).
Kwo-ma-a-'sup amt, I did not follow (him) yesterday.
Kwoka-ma-a-'sup amt, I did not finish following (him) yesterday.

Ki-ma-ki-isup, we followed (him) not.
Ki-ma-o-'sup, you followed (him) not.
Ki-ma-isup, they followed (him) not.
Kika-ma-ki-isup, we did not finish following (him).
Kwo-ma-ki-isup amt, we did not follow (him) yesterday.
Kwoka-ma-ki-isup amt, we did not finish following (him) yesterday.

Imperfect.

Ki-ma-a-'sup-i, I was not following (him).
Kwo-ma-a-'sup-i amt, I was not following (him) yesterday.

Ki-ma-ki-isup-i, we were not following (him).
Kwo-ma-ki-isup-i amt, we were not following (him) yesterday.

Again is expressed by the prefix *ma-ta*; *not yet*, by *tom*:

Ma-ta-a-'sup, I have not followed (him) again.
Ma-ta-ki-isup, we have not followed (him) again.
Tom-a-'sup, I have not yet followed (him).
Tom-ki-isup, we have not yet followed (him).
Kaka-ma-ta-a-'sup, I have not finished following (him) again.
Kaka-ma-ta-ki-isup, we have not finished following (him) again.
Kaka-tom-a-'sup, I have not yet finished following (him).
Kaka-tom-ki-isup, we have not yet finished following (him).

Future.

The future negative is formed by the prefix *me'p* or *me'nyo*:

Me'p (*or* me'nyo)-a-'sup-i, I go (*or* come) not to follow (him), *or* I shall not follow him.
Me'p (*or* me'nyo)-ki-isup-i, we go (*or* come) not to follow (him), *or* we shall not follow (him).

CONDITIONAL TENSES.

In the negative conditional tenses *m* and a vowel are inserted between the prefix of the affirmative and the personal prefixes. *Ingo* takes the place of *ingo-nga* or *ingo-ngi*, &c., and *añg-nya* that of *añg-nye*, &c.:

Ingo (*or* añg-nya)-ma-a-'sup, if (*or* when) I follow (him) not.
Ingo (*or* añg-nya)-ma-ki-isup, if (*or* when) we follow (him) not.
Ki-ingo (*or* ki-añg-nya)-ma-a-'sup, if (*or* when) I followed (him) not.
Ki-ingo (*or* ki-añg-nya)-ma-ki-isup, if (*or* when) we followed (him) not.

Again is expressed by *ma-ta* or *ko-ma-ta*:

Ingo-ma-ta-a-'sup, if I follow (him) not again.
Ki-añg-nya-ko-ma-ta-a-'sup, when I followed (him) not again.

CONTINGENT TENSES.

Present.

To form the negative present contingent tense, *koma* is inserted between the prefix *takoraki* and the personal prefix of the verb.

Takoraki-koma-a-'sup-i, I should not *or* if I did not follow (him).
Takoraki-koma-ki-isup-i, we should not *or* if we did not follow (him).

Past.

The past contingent tenses are formed by inserting *ma* between the prefix of the affirmative and the personal prefixes.

Ta-ki-ma-a-'sup, I should not have *or* had I not followed (him).
Ta-ki-ma-ki-isup, we should not have *or* had we not followed (him).

Ta-kika-ma-a-'sup, I should not have *or* had I not finished following (him).
Ta-kwo-ma-a-'sup amt, I should not have *or* had I not followed (him) yesterday.
Ta-kwoka-ma-a-'sup amt, I should not have *or* had I not finished following (him) yesterday.

Ta-kika-ma-ki-isup, we should not have *or* had we not finished following (him).
Ta-kwo-ma-ki-isup amt, we should not have *or* had we not followed (him) yesterday.
Ta-kwoka-ma-ki-isup amt, we should not have *or* had we not finished following (him) yesterday.

IMPERATIVE.

There are two ways of expressing the negative imperative. The first is formed by prefixing to the root *me* in the singular and *mo* in the plural. When the verbal root commences with *i*, that letter is omitted. The second is formed by prefixing *ma-t* in the singular and *ma-to* in the plural.

Me-'sup } follow (him) not.
Ma-t-isup }
Me-'sup-o } follow me not.
Ma-t-isup-o }

Mo-o-'sup } follow ye (him) not.
Ma-to-'sup }
Mo-o-'sup-o } follow ye me not.
Ma-to-'sup-o }

The negative imperative of the verb *to give* followed by the subjunctive is also frequently used for the simple imperative.

Me-kōn-o a-'sup, do not give me that I follow (him), *or* do not let me follow (him).

Me-'kochi ko-'sup, do not give them that they follow (him), *or* do not let them follow (him).

Again is expressed by prefixing *ma-ta-ta* or *ma-t-ko-ta* to the affirmative.

Ma-ta-ta-isup } follow (him) not again.
Ma-t-ko-ta-isup }

Ma-ta-ta-o-'sup } follow ye (him) not again.
Ma-t-ko-ta-o-'sup }

SUBJUNCTIVE.

The negative subjunctive is formed by prefixing *ma-t* to the affirmative.

Ma-t-a-'sup, that I may not follow (him).
Ma-t-i-isup, that thou mayest not follow (him).
Ma-t-ko-'sup, that he or she may not follow (him).
Ingo-ma-a-'sup, let me not follow (him).

Ma-t-ki-isup, that we may not follow (him).
Ma-t-o-'sup, that you may not follow (him).
Ma-t-ko-'sup, that they may not follow (him).
Ingo-ma-ki-isup, let us not follow (him).

VERBS

Again is expressed by *ma-ta-ta* which is sometimes abbreviated into *ma-ta*.

Ma-ta-ta-a-'sup or Ma-ta-a-'sup, that I may not follow (him) again.

Ma-ta-ta-ki-isup or Ma-ta-ki-isup, that we may not follow (him) again.

The Impersonal Form or Passive Voice.

There is an impersonal form which corresponds to the passive in English. The prefix *ki* or *ke* (*gi* and *ge* after *n*) takes the place of the personal prefixes of the verb, and the objective affix is used for the first and second persons.

Indicative Tenses.

Present.

Ki-isup-o, there is following with respect to me, *or* I am followed.

Ki-isup ech, we are followed.

Ki-isup-in, thou art followed.

Ki-isup-i, he or she is followed.

Ki-isup-ok, you are followed.

Ki-isup-i, they are followed.

Ke-cham-a, I am loved.

Ke-cham-ech, we are loved.

Ta-ki-isup-o, I am still being followed, *or* I am being followed again.

Ta-ki-isup-ech, we are still being followed.

Past.

Ka-ki-isup-o, I have been followed.

Ka-ki-isup-ech, we have been followed.

Ka-ki-isup-in, thou hast been followed.

Ka-ki-isup-ok, you have been followed.

Ka-ki-isup, he or she has been followed.

Ka-ki-isup, they have been followed.

Ka-ke-cham-a, I have been loved.

Ka-ke-cham-ech, we have been loved.

Ka-ta-ki-isup-o, I have again been followed.

Ka-ta-ki-isup-ech, we have again been followed.

Kaki-isup-o, I have finished being followed.

Kaki-isup-ech, we have finished being followed.

Ki-ki-isup-o, I was followed, *or* I was being followed.

Ki-ki-isup-ech, we were followed, *or* we were being followed.

Kika-ki-isup-o, I was finished being followed.

Kika-ki-isup-ech, we were finished being followed.

Kwo-ki-isup-o amt, I was followed, *or* I was being followed yesterday.

Kwo-ki-isup-ech amt, we were followed, *or* we were being followed yesterday.

Kwoka-ki-isup-o amt, I was finished being followed yesterday.

Kwoka-ki-isup-ech amt, we were finished being followed yesterday.

Future.

Ip (*or* inyo)-ki-isup-o, I shall be followed.
Ip (*or* inyo)-ki-isup-ech, we shall be followed.
Ip (*or* inyo)-ke-cham-a, I shall be loved.
Ip (*or* inyo)-ke-cham-ech, we shall be loved.

Conditional Tenses.
Present.

Ingo-ngi-isup-o, if I am followed.
Ingo-ngi-isup-ech, if we are followed.
Añg-nya-ki-isup-o, when I am followed.
Añg-nye-ki-isup-ech, when we were followed.
Ki-ingi-isup-o, if I was followed.
Ki-ingi-isup-ech, if we were followed.
Kiolen-gi-isup-o, when I was about to be followed.
Kikilen-gi-isup-ech, when we were about to be followed.
Kwo-añg-nya-ki-isup-o amt, when I was followed yesterday.
Kwo-añg-nye-ki-isup-ech amt, when we were followed yesterday.

Ingo-ngo-ta-ki-isup-o, if I am again followed.

Contingent Tenses.

Takoraki-ki-isup-o, I should be followed.
Takoraki-ki-isup-ech, we should be followed.
Ta-ki-ki-isup-o, I should have been followed.
Ta-ki-ki-isup-ech, we should have been followed.
Ta-kika-ki-isup-o, I should have finished being followed.
Ta-kika-ki-isup-ech, we should have finished being followed.
Ta-kwo-ki-isup-o amt, I should have been followed yesterday.
Ta-kwo-ki-isup-ech amt, we should have been followed yesterday.

Takoraki-ko-ta-ki-isup-o, I should be again followed.

Imperative.

Ki-isup-in, be followed.
Ki-isup-ok, be ye followed.
Ke-cham-in, be loved.
Ke-cham-ak, be ye loved.

Another form of the imperative passive is made by prefixing *ingi* instead of *ki*:

Ingi-isup-in, be followed.
Ingi-isup-ok, be ye followed.
Inge-cham-in, be loved.
Inge-cham-ak, be ye loved.

The imperative affirmative of the verb *to give* followed by the imperative is also much used:

Ikochi ki-isup-in, give that it is followed to thee, *or* be followed.
Ta-ki-isup-in, be followed again.

VERBS

SUBJUNCTIVE.

Ki-isup-o, that I may be followed.
Ki-isup-in, that thou mayest be followed.
Ki-isup, that he or she may be followed.
Ki-isup-ech, that we may be followed.
Ki-isup-ok, that you may be followed.
Ki-isup, that they may be followed.

Ko-ta-ki-isup-o, that I may be followed again.

THE NEGATIVE PASSIVE.

The negative passive is formed in the same way as the negative active:

INDICATIVE TENSES.

Present.

Ma-ki-isup-o, I am not followed.
Ma-ta-ki-isup-o, I am not again being followed.
Ma-ki-isup-ech, we are not followed.
Ma-ta-ki-isup-ech, we are not again being followed.

Past.

Ka-ma-ki-isup-o, I have not been followed.
Ki-ma-ki-isup-o, I was not followed.
Tom-ki-isup-o, I have not yet been followed.
Ka-ma-ta-ki-isup-o, I have not again been followed.
Ka-ma-ki-isup-ech, we have not been followed.
Ki-ma-ki-isup-ech, we were not followed.
Tom-ki-isup-ech, we have not yet been followed.
Ka-ma-ta-ki-isup-ech, we have not again been followed.

Future.

Me-'p-ki-isup-o, I shall not be followed.
Me-'p-ki-isup-ech, we shall not be followed.

CONDITIONAL TENSES.

Ingo (*or* añg-nya-ko)-ma-ki-isup-o, if (*or* when) I am not followed.
Ki-ingo (*or* ki-añg-nya-ko)-ma-ki-isup-o, if (*or* when) I was not followed.
Ingo (*or* añg-nya-ko)-ma-ki-isup-ech, if (*or* when) we were not followed.
Ki-ingo (*or* ki-añg-nya-ko)-ma-ki-isup-ech, if (*or* when) we were not followed.

CONTINGENT TENSES.

Takoraki-koma-ki-isup-o, I should not be followed.
Ta-ki-ma-ki-isup-o, I should not have been followed.
Takoraki-koma-ki-isup-ech, we should not be followed.
Ta-ki-ma-ki-isup-ech, we should not have been followed.

IMPERATIVE.

Ma-ki-isup-in, be not followed. Ma-ki-isup-ok, be ye not followed.
Ma-ta-ki-isup-in, be not again followed. Ma-ta-ki-isup-ok, be ye not again followed.

SUBJUNCTIVE.

Ma-ki-isup-o, that I may not be followed. Ma-ki-isup-ech, that we may not be followed.
Ma-ta-ki-isup-o, that I may not again be followed. Ma-ta-ki-isup-ech, that we may not again be followed.

DERIVATIVE VERBS.

VERBS DENOTING MOTION TOWARDS THE SPEAKER.

Verbs denoting motion towards the speaker take the affix *u*:

ACTIVE VOICE.

Present.

A-'sup-u, I follow (him) hither. Ki-isup-u, we follow (him) hither.

Past.

Ka-a-'sup-u, I have followed (him) hither. Ka-ki-isup-u, we have followed (him) hither.
Ki-a-'sup-u, I followed (him) hither. Ki-ki-isup-u, we followed (him) hither.

Future.

Ip (*or* inyo)-a-'sup-u, I shall follow (him) hither. Ip (*or* inyo)-ki-isup-u, we shall follow him (hither).

IMPERATIVE.

Isup-u, follow (him) hither. O-'sup-u, follow ye (him) hither.

SUBJUNCTIVE.

A-'sup-u, that I may follow (him) hither. Ki-isup-u, that we may follow (him) hither.

PASSIVE VOICE.

Present.

Ki-isup-u-a, I am followed hither. Ki-isup-u-ech, we are followed hither.
Ki-isup-u-n, thou art followed hither. Ki-isup-u-ok, you are followed hither.
Ki-isup-u, he or she is followed hither. Ki-isup-u, they are followed hither.

VERBS

Past.

Ka-ki-isup-u-a, I have been followed hither.
Ka-ki-isup-u-ech, we have been followed hither.
Ki-ki-isup-u-a, I was followed hither.
Ki-ki-isup-u-ech, we were followed hither.

Examples:

Isup-u-a ko-pir-o, he is following me hither to strike me.
Isup-u-n ko-pir-in, he is following thee hither to strike thee.
Kwo-a-'sup-u-ok okwek yu amt; kwo-añg-nya-a-it-u yu, o-rua, I followed you here yesterday; when I arrived here, you ran away.
Ingo-ngo-a-chor-u cheko, ko-lu-e lakōk-i? if I steal milk (and bring it hither), will the children drink it?
Kwo-ki-isup-u-a amt, I was followed hither yesterday.

VERBS DENOTING MOTION FROM THE SPEAKER.

Present.

The present tense is formed by affixing *toi-i* in the first and second persons, and *toi* in the third persons:

A-'sup-toi-i, I follow (him) thither.
Ki-isup-toi-i, we follow (him) thither.
I-isup-toi-i, thou followest (him) thither.
O-'sup-toi-i, you follow (him) thither.
Isup-toi, he or she follows (him) thither.
Isup-toi, they follow (him) thither.

Past.

The past tenses are formed by affixing *te* in the first and second persons, and *to* in the third persons:

Ka-a-'sup-te, I have followed (him) thither.
Ka-ki-isup-te, we have followed (him) thither.
Ke-i-'sup-te, thou hast followed (him) thither.
Ko-o-'sup-te, you have followed (him) thither.
Ke-'sup-to, he or she has followed (him) thither.
Ke-'sup-to, they have followed (him) thither.
Ki-a-'sup-te, I followed (him) thither.
Ki-ki-isup-te, we followed (him) thither.

IMPERATIVE.

The affix of the imperative is *te*:

Isup-te, follow (him) thither.   O-'sup-te, follow ye (him) thither.

SUBJUNCTIVE.

In the subjunctive the affix used in the first person singular and in the third persons is *to*; in the other persons *te*:

A-'sup-to, that I may follow (him) thither.
Isup-te, that thou mayest follow (him) thither.
Ko-'sup-to, that he or she may follow (him) thither.
Ki-isup-te, that we may follow (him) thither.
O-'sup-te, that you may follow (him) thither.
Ko-'sup-to, that they may follow (him) thither.

NARRATIVE TENSE.

In verbs denoting motion from the speaker the narrative tense is formed by the affix *te*:

A-'sup-te, and I follow (him) thither.
Ki-isup-te, and we follow (him) thither.

When the object of the verb is the personal pronoun (first and second persons), slight changes take place in the verbal affixes. Examples:

Present.

A-'sup-toi-i, I follow him thither.
A-'sup-toi-in, I follow thee thither.
A-'sup-to-ok, I follow you thither.
I-isup-toi-i, thou followest him thither.
I-isup-to-o, thou followest me thither.
I-isup-toi-ech, thou followest us thither.
Isup-toi, he or she follows him thither.
Isup-to-o, he or she follows me thither.
Isup-toi-in, he or she follows thee thither.
Isup-toi-ech, he or she follows us thither.
Isup-to-ok, he or she follows you thither.

Past.

Ka-a-'sup-te, I have followed him thither.
Ka-a-'sup-te-n, I have followed thee thither.
Ka-a-'sup-t-ok, I have followed you thither.
Ke-i-'sup-te, thou hast followed him thither.
Ke-i-'sup-t-o, thou hast followed me thither.
Ke-i-'sup-t-ech, thou hast followed us thither.
Ke-'sup-to, he or she has followed him thither.
Ke-'sup-t-o, he or she has followed me thither.
Ke-'sup-te-n, he or she has followed thee thither.
Ke-'sup-t-ech, he or she has followed us thither.
Ke-'sup-t-ok, he or she has followed you thither.

When the verbal root ends in *t*, the affix denoting motion from the speaker is sometimes joined to the root by *i*. Example:

It-it-e, to arrive thither (pr. a-it-itoi-i, I arrive thither, p.p. ka-a-it-it-e, I have arrived thither).

In a few instances the verb denoting motion from the speaker is

VERBS

formed by adding the affix to the verb denoting motion towards the speaker. Example:

Ñgut-u, to spit *or* to spit hither. Ñgut-u-te, to spit thither.

PASSIVE.

Present.

Ki-isup-to-o, I am followed thither.
Ki-isup-toi-in, thou art followed thither.
Ki-isup-toi, he or she is followed thither.

Ki-isup-toi-ech, we are followed thither.
Ki-isup-to-ok, you are followed thither.
Ki-isup-toi, they are followed thither.

Past.

Ka-ki-isup-to-o, I have been followed thither.
Ka-ki-isup-te-n, thou hast been followed thither.
Ka-ki-isup-t-o, he or she has been followed thither.

Ka-ki-isup-t-ech, we have been followed thither.
Ka-ki-isup-to-ok, you have been followed thither.
Ka-ki-isup-t-o, they have been followed thither.

Examples:

A-'sup-toi-i si a-pir, I am following him thither to beat him.
Kwo-isup-te-n amt ka, he followed thee yesterday to the hut.
Kwo-isup-to amt ka, he followed him yesterday to the hut.
Ki-añg-nya-a-it-ite, ko-lapat, when I arrived thither, he ran away.

THE DATIVE FORM.

The dative form is used where in English a preposition is required to connect the verb with its object, and indicates that the action of the verb is performed for or against a person or thing. When this form is assumed, *chi* is affixed to the verb.[1] In the present tense the affix is *chi-ni* in the first and second persons, and *chi-n* in the third persons:

Present.

A-'sup-chi-ni, I follow for (him) *or* I follow (him) to.
I-isup-chi-ni, thou followest for (him).
Isup-chi-n, he or she follows for (him).

Ki-isup-chi-ni, we follow for (him).
O-'sup-chi-ni, you follow for (him).
Isup-chi-n, they follow for (him).

[1] When the object of the verb is the personal pronoun of the first or second persons *chi* changes to *u* (*vide* p. 212).

Past.

Ka-a-'sup-chi, I have followed for (him).
Ka-ki-isup-chi, we have followed for (him).
Ke-i-'sup-chi, thou hast followed for (him).
Ko-o-'sup-chi, you have followed for (him).
Ke-'sup-chi, he or she has followed for (him).
Ke-'sup-chi, they have followed for (him).

Whenever the sound permits, the affix in the third persons of the past tenses is *ch*; *e. g.*

Ka-mwe-ch, he has run away to (him).

IMPERATIVE.

Isup-chi, follow for (him).   O-'sup-chi, follow ye for (him).

SUBJUNCTIVE.

A-'sup-chi, that I may follow for (him).
Ki-isup-chi, that we may follow for (him).
Isup-chi, that thou mayest follow for (him).
O-'sup-chi, that you may follow for (him).
Ko-'sup-chi, that he or she may follow for (him).
Ko-'sup-chi, that they may follow for (him).

As with verbs denoting motion from the speaker, slight changes take place in the verbal affixes when the object of the verb is the personal pronoun of the first or second persons:

Present.

A-'sup-chi-ni, I follow for him.
A-'sup-u-n, I follow for thee.
A-'sup-u-ok, I follow for you.
I-isup-chi-ni, thou followest for him.
I-isup-u-a, thou followest for me.
I-isup-u-ech, thou followest for us.
Isup-chi-n, he or she follows for him.
Isup-u-a, he or she follows for me.
Isup-u-n, he or she follows for thee.
Isup-u-ech, he or she follows for us.
Isup-u-ok, he or she follows for you.

Past.

Ka-a-'sup-chi, I have followed for him.
Ka-a-'sup-u-n, I have followed for thee.
Ka-a-'sup-u-ok, I have followed for you.
Ke-i-'sup-chi, thou hast followed for him.
Ke-i-'sup-u-a, thou hast followed for me.

Ke-i-'sup-u-ech, thou hast followed for us.
Ke-'sup-chi, he or she has followed for him.
Ke-'sup-u-a, he or she has followed for me.
Ke-'sup-u-n, he or she has followed for thee.
Ke-'sup-u-ech, he or she has followed for us.
Ke-'sup-u-ok, he or she has followed for you.

PASSIVE.

Present.

Ki-isup-chi-n-o, I am followed for.
Ki-isup-chi-n-in, thou art followed for.
Ki-isup-chi-n, he or she is followed for.
Ki-isup-chi-n-ech, we are followed for.
Ki-isup-chi-n-ok, you are followed for.
Ki-isup-chi-n, they are followed for.

Past.

Ka-ki-isup-ch-o, I have been followed for.
Ka-ki-isup-ch-in, thou hast been followed for.
Ka-ki-isup-ch-i, he or she has been followed for.
Ka-ki-isup-ch-ech, we have been followed for.
Ka-ki-isup-ch-ok, you have been followed for.
Ka-ki-isup-ch-i, they have been followed for.

Examples:
A-'sup-chi-ni pendo ka, I am following the animal for him to the kraal.
Ki-nyinyir-chi-no ingoiny, I am being crushed to the earth.
It-yi-n ka, he will reach the town.

THE APPLIED FORM.

Where in English a preposition connected with a verb can stand by itself at the end of a sentence, or where a preposition, which is required to connect the verb with its object, does not indicate that the action of the verb is performed for or against a person or thing, a special form is used in Nandi, *e* or *i* being affixed to the verbal root in all tenses. Examples:

Ip-u ñgecheret na-a-tep-e, bring me a chair to sit upon.
Mo-o-mwa-i tarīt, do not talk of the birds.
Ka-tien-e mistōek arawet, the herdsmen have danced in the (light of the) moon.

THE REFLEXIVE FORM.

Many verbs have a reflexive form, which is made by affixing *ke* (*ge* after *ñg* and *ny*) to the simple verb:

Present.

A-'un-i-ke, I bathe. Ki-iun-i-ke, we bathe.
I-iun-i-ke, thou bathest. O-'un-i-ke, you bathe.
Iun-i-ke, he or she bathes. Iun-i-ke, they bathe.
A-til-i-ke, I cut myself. Ki-til-i-ke, we cut ourselves.

Past.

Ka-a-'un-ge, I have bathed. Ka-ki-iun-ge, we have bathed.
Ka-a-til-ke, I have cut myself. Ka-ki-til-ke, we have cut ourselves.

IMPERATIVE.

Iun-ge, bathe. O-'un-ge, bathe yourselves.
Til-ke, cut thyself. O-til-ke, cut yourselves.

SUBJUNCTIVE.

A-'un-ge, that I may bathe. Ki-iun-ge, that we may bathe.
A-til-ke, that I may cut myself. Ki-til-ke, that we may cut ourselves.

THE RECIPROCAL FORM.

The reciprocal form denotes doing something with someone else:

Present.

The present tense is formed by affixing *tos-i* in the first and second persons, and *tos* in the third persons:

A-'rot-tos-i, I bet with (him). Ki-irot-tos-i, we bet with (him).
I-irot-tos-i, thou bettest with (him). O-'rot-tos-i, you bet with (him).
Irot-tos, he or she bets with (him). Irot-tos, they bet with (him).
A-tii-tos-i, I argue with (him). Ki-tii-tos-i, we argue with (him).

Past.

The past tenses are formed by affixing *ie, ye,* or *e* in the first and second persons, and *io, yo,* or *o* in the third persons.

Ka-a-'rot-ie, I have betted with (him). Ka-ki-irot-ie, we have betted with (him).
Ke-i-'rot-ie, thou hast betted with (him). Ko-o-'rot-ie, you have betted with (him).
Ke-'rot-io, he or she has betted with (him). Ke-'rot-io, they have betted with (him).
Ka-a-tii-ye, I have argued with (him). Ka-ki-tii-ye, we have argued with (him).
Ka-a-'tui-e, I have joined with (him). Ka-ki-itui-e, we have joined with (him).

VERBS

IMPERATIVE.

Irot-ie, bet with (him).   O-'rot-ie, bet ye with (him).

SUBJUNCTIVE.

In the subjunctive the affix is *io, yo,* or *o* in the first person singular and in the third persons, and *ie, ye,* or *e* in the other persons:

A-'rot-io, that I may bet with (him).
Ki-irot-ie, that we may bet with (him).
Irot-ie, that thou mayest bet with (him).
O-'rot-ie, that you may bet with (him).
Ko-'rot-io, that he or she may bet with (him).
Ko-'rot-io, that they may bet with (him).

When the meaning is doing something with each other, either the reflexive form is used or the reciprocal affix is joined to the dative form:

Ki-irot-i-ke, we bet with each other.
Ka-ki-irot-ke, we have betted with each other.
Iut-yi-n-dos, they are bellowing at each other.
Ke-'ut-y-io, they have bellowed at each other.

INTRANSITIVE VERBS.

By affixing *se* (*ze* after *n*), *isie,* or *isye* most transitive verbs can be used intransitively.

In the present tense *i* is also affixed in the first and second persons:

Present.

A-mwog-se-i, I shoot.
Ki-mwog-se-i, we shoot.
I-mwog-se-i, thou shootest.
O-mwog-se-i, you shoot.
Mwog-se, he or she shoots.
Mwog-se, they shoot.

A-'un-ze-i } I wash.
A-mwet-isie-i }
Ki-iun-ze-i } we wash.
Ki-mwet-isie-i }

A-kesen-isye-i, I carry on the back.
Ki-kesen-isye-i, we carry on the back.

Past.

In the third persons the affix is *so, isio,* or *isyo*:

Ka-a-mwog-se, I have shot.
Ka-ki-mwog-se, we have shot.
Ke-i-mwog-se, thou hast shot.
Ko-o-mwog-se, you have shot.
Ka-mwog-so, he or she has shot.
Ka-mwog-so, they have shot.

Ka-mwet-isio, he or she has washed.

IMPERATIVE.

Mwog-se, shoot.
O-mwog-se, shoot ye.
Mwet-isie, wash.
O-mwet-isie, wash ye.

SUBJUNCTIVE.

A-mwog-so, that I may shoot.
Mwog-se, that thou mayest shoot.
Ko-mwog-so, that he or she may shoot.
Ki-mwog-se, that we may shoot.
O-mwog-se, that you may shoot.
Ko-mwog-so, that they may shoot.

CAUSATIVE VERBS.

The rule for the formation of causatives is that all verbs which commence with any letter except *i* take the prefix *i*. Verbs commencing with *i* take the affix *e* or *i*, except in the past tense, where there is no change. If the present tense of the simple verb takes the affix *i*, the causative affix is *e*, and vice versa:

Cham, to love.
Lapat, to run.
Isup, to follow.
Ki-chom-e, we love (him).
Ki-lopot-i, we run.
Ki-isup-i, we follow (him).
Ka-ki-cham, we have loved (him).
Ka-ki-lapat, we have run.

Ka-ki-isup, we have followed (him).

Icham, to cause to love.
Ilapat, to cause to run.
Isup-e, to cause to follow.
Ki-ichom-i, we cause (him) to love.
Ki-ilopot-e, we cause (him) to run.
Ki-isup-e, we cause (him) to follow.
Ka-ki-icham, we have caused (him) to love.
Ka-ki-ilapat, we have caused (him) to run.
Ka-ki-isup, we have caused (him) to follow.

In the causative form of derivative verbs, *e* or *i*, which is sometimes preceded by *n*, is affixed to the simple verb. Verbs not commencing with *i* also take the prefix *i*:

A-'lapat-u-ne, I cause (him) to run hither.
Ka-a-'lapat-u-ne, I have caused (him) to run hither.
A-'sup-u-ne, I cause (him) to follow hither.
Ka-a-'sup-u-ne, I have caused (him) to follow hither.
A-'lapat-itoi-e, I cause (him) to run thither.
Ka-a-'lapat-itoi-e, I have caused (him) to run thither.
A-'sup-toi-e, I cause (him) to follow thither.
Ka-a-'sup-toi-e, I have caused (him) to follow thither.
A-'lapat-yi-ne, I cause (him) to run to.
Ka-a-'lapat-yi-ne, I have caused (him) to run to.
A-'sup-chi-ne, I cause (him) to follow for.
Ka-a-'sup-chi-ne, I have caused (him) to follow for.

NEUTER OR QUASI-PASSIVE FORM.

There is a neuter or quasi-passive form which is frequently employed. The following example will show its use:

A-'sup-í ni, ako me-'sup-oksé nin, I am following this one, but that one will not be (*or* become) followed.

VERBS

INDICATIVE TENSES.
Present.

The present tense is formed by the affix *at* or *ot*:

A-'sup-ot, I become followed.
I-isup-ot, thou becomest followed.
Isup-ot, he or she becomes followed.
Ki-isup-ot, we become followed.
O-'sup-ot, you become followed.
Isup-ot, they become followed.

A-rat-at, I become bound.

Past.

In the past tenses the affix in the first and second persons is *ak-e* or *ok-e*, and in the third persons *ak* or *ok*:

Ka-a-'sup-ok-e, I have become followed.
Ke-i-'sup-ok-e, thou hast become followed.
Ke-'sup-ok, he or she has become followed.
Ka-ki-isup-ok-e, we have become followed.
Ko-o-'sup-ok-e, you have become followed.
Ke-'sup-ok, they have become followed.

Future.

There is a special form for the future, which is made by affixing *akse-i* or *okse-i* in the first and second persons, and *akse* or *okse* in the third persons:

A-'sup-okse-i, I shall become followed.
I-isup-okse-i, thou wilt become followed.
Isup-okse, he or she will become followed.
Ki-isup-okse-i, we shall become followed.
O-'sup-okse-i, you will become followed.
Isup-okse, they will become followed.

CONTINGENT TENSES.

The contingent tenses are formed like the past:

Ingo-a-'sup-ok-e, if I become followed.
Ki-ingo-a-'sup-ok-e, if I became followed.

CONDITIONAL TENSES.

The present conditional tenses take the same affix as the future, the past the same as the past indicative:

Takoraki-a-'sup-okse-i, I should become followed.
Ta-ki-a-'sup-ok-e, I should have become followed.

IMPERATIVE.

The affix of the imperative is the same as in the past tenses:

Isup-ok-e, become followed.
Rat-ak-e, become bound.
O-'sup-ok-e, become ye followed.
O-rat-ak-e, become ye bound.

SUBJUNCTIVE.

In the subjunctive the first person singular and the third persons take the affix *ak* or *ok*, the other persons *ak-e* or *ok-e*:

A-'sup-ok, that I may become followed.
Isup-ok-e, that thou mayest become followed.
Ko-'sup-ok, that he or she may become followed.
Ki-isup-ok-e, that we may become followed.
O-'sup-ok-e, that you may become followed.
Ko-'sup-ok, that they may become followed.

NEUTER VERBS.

Most neuter verbs, and particularly those which in English must be translated by an adjective and the verb *to be* or *to become*, form a class to themselves. All these verbs possess a future tense, and in some cases the verbal part takes plural inflexions. With the exception of the present indicative and the subjunctive, all tenses take the affix *-itu*.

INDICATIVE TENSES.
Present.

The present tense is formed by simply adding the personal prefixes to the root:

A-lalañg, I am hot.
A-kararan, I am beautiful.
Ki-laloñg, we are hot.
Ki-kororon, we are beautiful.

Past.

Ki-a-lalañg-itu, I was hot.
Ki-a-kararan-itu, I was beautiful.
Ki-ki-laloñg-itu, we were hot.
Ki-ki-kororon-itu, we were beautiful.

Future.

A-lalañg-itu, I shall be hot.
A-kararan-itu, I shall be beautiful.
Ki-laloñg-itu, we shall be hot.
Ki-kororon-itu, we shall be beautiful.

CONDITIONAL AND CONTINGENT TENSES.

Añg-nya-a-lalañg-itu, when I am hot.
Ki-añg-nya-a-lalañg-itu, when I was hot.
Takoraki-a-lalañg-itu, I should be hot.
Ta-ki-a-lalañg-itu, I should have been hot.

IMPERATIVE.

Lalañg-itu, be hot.
Kararan-itu, be beautiful.
O-lalañg-itu, be ye hot.
O-kororon-itu, be ye beautiful.

SUBJUNCTIVE.

The affix of the subjunctive in the first person singular and the third persons is *it*; in the other persons *itu*:

A-lalañg-it, that I may be hot.
Lalañg-itu, that thou mayest be hot.
Ko-lalañg-it, that he or she may be hot.
Ki-lalañg-itu, that we may be hot.
O-lalañg-itu, that you may be hot.
Ko-lalañg-it, that they may be hot.

The causative form of neuter verbs is made by affixing *ne* to the future:

   A-lalañg-itu-ne, I cause (him) to be hot.
   Ka-a-lalañg-itu-ne, I have caused (him) to be hot.

IRREGULAR VERBS.

I, To be.

Present.

A, I am.
I, thou art.
(wanting), he or she is.

Ki, we are.
O, you are.
(wanting), they are.

Past.

Kw-a, I have been.
Ko-ï, thou hast been.
Ko, he or she has been.

Ko-ki, we have been.
Ko-o, you have been.
Ko, they have been.

Ki-a, I was.
Ki-i, thou wast.
Ki *or* ko-ki, he or she was.

Ki-ki, we were.
Ki-o, you were.
Ki *or* ko-ki, they were.

IMPERATIVE.

I, be.   O, be ye.

The subjunctive is the same as the present perfect.
The verb *to be* must be followed by a substantive. Examples:

  A orkoiyot, I am the chief.
  Ole-kinye ko-ki ñgeta, formerly he was a boy.
  Nyo-ne kw-a orkoiyo, he will come when I am (*or* have been) chief.
  Ko chorīk, they have been thieves.
  O muren! be warriors!

When the verb *to be* is used in English as the copula it is sometimes omitted in Nandi:

  Ñgô orkoiyot? Who is the chief?
  Ane orkoiyot,[1] I am the chief.
  Ane ne-ki-a-ai-te kôtón-ni, it is I who made this arrow.
  Kararan chií-chi, this man is handsome.

---

[1] *A orkoiyot* is also correct. *He is the chief* would be simply *Orkoiyot,* or *Inendet orkoiyot.*

When the verb *to be* is used in English to denote existence in place or time, the verb Mi, or Mi-te, *to be there*, is used in Nandi:

Mi-í yu *or* mi-i-té yu, he is here.
Ki-mi ole-kinye chii, there was once a man.
A̱-mi-i ono? Where am I?
Ñgô ne-mi-í ko? Who is in the hut?
Ma-mi-i chii, there is nobody there.

The present tense is often used to translate the past tense in English:

Ki-nyó ki muren, he came when we were warriors.
A-mi-í yu arawet akenge, I have been here one month.

Eku, To Become.

Present.

Oi-eku, I become. Ki-eku, we become.
I-eku, thou becomest. Oi-eku, you become.
Eku, he or she becomes. Eku, they become.

Past.

K-oi-eku, I have become. Ko-ki-eku, we have become.
Ke-eku, thou hast become. Ko-o-eku, you have become.
Koi-ek, he or she has become. Koi-ek, they have become.

Ki-oi-eku, I became. Ki-ki-eku, we became.

IMPERATIVE.

Eku, become. Oi-eku, become ye.

SUBJUNCTIVE.

Oi-ek, that I may become. Ki-eku, that we may become.
Eku, that thou mayest become. Oi-eku, that you may become.
Koi-ek, that he or she may become. Koi-ek, that they may become.

Examples:

Oi-eku murenet, I shall become a warrior.
Ile-chi koi-ek murenet, tell him to become a warrior.

Ui / O-pa } To Go.

Present.

A-wend-i, I go, am going, *or* shall go. Ki-pend-i, We go.
I-wend-i, thou goest. O-pend-i, you go.
Wend-i, he or she goes. Pend-i, they go.

VERBS

Past.

Ka-a-we, I have gone.
Ke-i-we, thou hast gone.
Ko-wa, he or she has gone.
Ki-a-we, I went.
Ki-i-we, thou wentest.
Ki-kwa } he or she went.
Ki-wo

Ka-ke-phe, we have gone.
Ko-o-phe, you have gone.
Ka-pa, they have gone.
Ki-ke-phe, we went.
Ki-o-phe, you went.
Ki-pa } they went.
Ki-ko-pa

IMPERATIVE.

A-wa, let me go.

Ui, go.

Ingephe, let us go (if of a few only).
O-ngephe, let us go (if of many).
O-pa, go ye.

SUBJUNCTIVE.

A-wa, that I may go.
Ui, that thou mayest go.
Kwa, that he or she may go.

Ke-phe, that we may go.
O-pa, that you may go.
Ko-pa, that they may go.

NARRATIVE.

A-we, and I go.
I-we, and thou goest.
Kwa, and he or she goes.

Ke-phe, and we go.
O-phe, and you go.
Ko-pa, and they go.

Wend-ote } **To go for a walk.**
O-pend-ate

Present.

A-wend-oti, I go for a walk.   Ki-pend-oti, we go for a walk.

Past.

Ka-a-wend-ote, I have gone for a walk.
Ke-i-wend-ote, thou hast gone for a walk.
Ko-wend-ot, he or she has gone for a walk.

Ka-ki-pend-ate, we have gone for a walk.
Ko-o-pend-ate, you have gone for a walk.
Ko-o-pend-at, they have gone for a walk.

IMPERATIVE.

Wend-ote, go for a walk.   O-pend-ate, go ye for a walk.

SUBJUNCTIVE.

A-wend-ot, that I may go for a walk.
Wend-ote, that thou mayest go for a walk.
Ko-wend-ot, that he or she may go for a walk.

Ke-pend-ate, that we may go for a walk.
O-pend-ate, that you may go for a walk.
Ko-pend-at, that they may go for a walk.

Most verbs used in conjunction with the verb *to go* are formed in a similar manner, *e. g.*:

Iñgwal-ate, to go lame (pr. a-'ñgwal-oti).
Sis-ate, to go silently (pr. a-sis-oti).

Nyo } To Come.
O-pwa

Present.

A-nyo-ne, I come, am coming, or shall come.
Ki-pwo-ne, we come.
I-nyo-ne, thou comest.
O-pwo-ne, you come.
Nyo-ne, he or she comes.
Pwo-ne, they come.

Past.

Ka-a-nyo, I have come.
Ka-ke-pwa, we have come.
Ke-i-nyo, thou hast come.
Ko-o-pwa, you have come.
Ko-nyo, he or she has come.
Ka-pwa, they have come.

IMPERATIVE.

A-nyo, let me come.
Ke-pwa, let us come.
Nyo, come.
O-pwa, come ye.

SUBJUNCTIVE.

A-nyo, that I may come.
Ke-pwa, that we may come.
Nyo, that thou mayest come.
O-pwa, that you may come.
Ko-nyo, that he or she may come.
Ko-pwa, that they may come.

NARRATIVE.

A-nyo, and I come.
Ke-pwa, and we come.
I-nyo, and thou comest.
O-pwa, and you come.
Ko-nyo *or* inyo, and he or she comes.
Ko-pwa, and they come.

Verbs used in conjunction with the verb *to come* take the affix *anu*:

Iñgwal-anu, to come lame (pr. a-'ñgwal-anu).
Sis-anu, to come silently (pr. a-sis-anu).

Ikochi (kōn), To Give.

The root of this verb changes from *ikochi* to *kōn* whenever the object is the first or second person singular or plural:

Present.

A-'kochi-ni, I give him, &c.
Ki-ikochi-ni, we give him, &c.
A-kōn-in, I give thee.
Ki-kōn-in, we give thee.
A-kōn-ok, I give you.
Ki-kōn-ok, we give you.

VERBS

I-ikochi-ni, thou givest him, &c.
I-kōn-o, thou givest me.
I-kōn-ech, thou givest us.
Ikochi-n, he or she gives him, &c.
Kōn-o, he or she gives me.
Kōn-in, he or she gives thee.
Kōn-ech, he or she gives us.
Kōn-ok, he or she gives you.

O-'kochi-ni, you give him, &c.
O-kōn-o, you give me.
O-kōn-ech, you give us.
Ikochi-n, they give him, &c.
Kōn-o, they give me.
Kōn-in, they give thee.
Kōn-ech, they give us.
Kōn-ok, they give you.

Past.

Ka-a-'kochi, I have given him, &c.
Ka-a-kōn-in, I have given thee.

IMPERATIVE.

Ikochi, give him.
Kōn-o, give me.

O-'kochi, give ye him.
O-kōn-o, give ye me.

SUBJUNCTIVE.

A-'kochi, that I may give him, &c.
A-kōn-in, that I may give thee.

NARRATIVE.

A-'koch, and I give him, &c.
Ikochi, and thou givest him, &c.
Ko-'koch, and he or she gives him, &c.

Ki-'kochi, and we give him, &c.
O-'kochi, and you give him, &c.
Ko-'koch, and they give him, &c.

PASSIVE.

Ki-kōn-o, I am given.
Ka-ki-kōn-o, I have been given.

Nai, To Know.

Present.

A-'nget } I know.
A-'ngen }
I-inget } thou knowest.
I-ingen }
Inget } he or she knows.
Ingen }

Ki-inget } we know.
Ki-ingen }
O-'nget } you know.
O-'ngen }
Inget } they know.
Ingen }

Past.

Ka-a-nai, I have known.
Ke-i-nai, thou hast known.
Ka-nai, he or she has known.

Ka-ki-nai, we have known.
Ko-o-nai, you have known.
Ka-nai, they have known.

IMPERATIVE.

Nai, know.
O-nai, know ye.

Subjunctive.

A-nai, that I may know.
Nai, that thou mayest know.
Ko-nai, that he or she may know.

Ki-nai, that we may know.
O-nai, that you may know.
Ko-nai, that they may know.

Passive.

Ki-nai-a, I am known.
Ki-ki-nai-a, I was known.

Iro, To See.

Present.

A-'onyi } I see.
O-kere }

I-ionyi } thou seest.
I-kere }

Ionyi } he or she sees.
Kere }

Ki-ionyi } we see.
Ki-kere }

O-'onyi } you see.
O-kere }

Ionyi } they see.
Kere }

Past.

Ka-a-'ro, I have seen.
Ke-i-'ro, thou hast seen.
Ke-'ro, he or she has seen.

Ka-ki-iro, we have seen.
Ko-o-'ro, you have seen.
Ke-'ro, they have seen.

Imperative.

Iro, see.

O-'ro, see ye.

Subjunctive.

A-'ro, that I may see.
Iro, that thou mayest see.
Ko-'ro, that he or she may see.

Ki-iro, that we may see.
O-'ro, that you may see.
Ko-'ro, that they may see.

Me / O-pek-u } To Die.

Present.

A-me-e, I die.
I-me-e, thou diest.
Me-e, he or she dies.

Ke-pek-u, we die.
O-pek-u, you die.
Pek-u, they die.

Past.

Ka-a-me, I have died.
Ke-i-me, thou hast died.
Ka-me, he or she has died.

Ka-ke-pek-u, we have died.
Ko-o-pek-u, you have died.
Ka-pek, they have died.

Imperative.

Me, die.

O-pek-u, die ye.

VERBS

Subjunctive.

A-me, that I may die.
Me, that thou mayest die.
Ko-me, that he or she may die.

Ke-pek-u, that we may die.
O-pek-u, that you may die.
Ko-pek, that they may die.

Ile, To Say, to say thus, to imitate.

Present.

A-len, I say.
I-len, thou sayest.
Len, he or she says.

Ki-len, we say.
O-len, you say.
Len, they say.

Past.

Ka-a-'le, I have said.
Ke-i-'le, thou hast said.
Ka-'le, he or she has said.

Ka-ki-ile, we have said.
Ko-o-'le, you have said.
Ka-'le, they have said.

Imperative.

Ile, say.

O-'le, say ye.

Subjunctive.

A-'le, that I may say.
Ile, that thou mayest say.
Ko-'le, that he or she may say.

Ki-ile, that we may say.
O-'le, that you may say.
Ko-'le, that they may say.

When this verb takes the dative form (*ile-chi*, to say to) it is regular.

Piiy-e, To Be Satisfied with.

Present.

A-piiy-onyi, I am satisfied with food.
I-piiy-onyi, thou art satisfied with food.
Piiy-onyi, he or she is satisfied with food.

Ki-piiy-onyi, we are satisfied with food.
O-piiy-onyi, you are satisfied with food.
Piiy-onyi, they are satisfied with food.

Past.

Ka a-piiy-e, I was satisfied with food.

Ka-ki-piiy-e, we were satisfied with food.

Imperative.

Piiy-e, be satisfied with food.

O-piiy-e, be ye satisfied with food.

Subjunctive.

A-piiy-o, that I may be satisfied with food.
Piiy-e, that thou mayest be satisfied with food.
Ko-piiy-o, that he or she may be satisfied with food.

Ki-piiy-e, that we may be satisfied with food.
O-piiy-e, that you may be satisfied with food.
Ko-piiy-o, that they may be satisfied with food.

Causative Form.
Present.

A-'piiy-onye, I satisfy (him) with food.
Ki-ipiiy-onye, we satisfy (him) with food.

Past.

Ka-a-'piiy-e, I have satisfied (him) with food.
Ka-ki-ipiiy-e, we have satisfied (him) with food.

Ietu / O-'ekitu } To Grow.

Present.

Oi-'etu, I grow.
I-ietu, thou growest.
Ietu, he or she grows.

Ki-iekitu, we grow.
O-'ekitu, you grow.
Iekitu, they grow.

Past.

Ka-a-'etu, I have grown.
Ka-ki-iekitu, we have grown.

Imperative.

Ietu, grow.
O-'ekitu, grow ye.

AUXILIARY VERBS.

Can, may, and *might* are represented by the appropriate tenses of *imuch,* to be able. *Must* is expressed by *tai* followed by the subjunctive:

Tai mutai a-'sup, I must follow him to-morrow.

Ought and *should* are translated by the third persons singular of the present or past tenses of *cham,* to love, followed by *si* and the subjunctive:

Chom-e si a-wa, I ought to go.
Ka-cham si a-wa, I ought to have gone.

Eku, To Become.

The verb *eku,* to become, is used to strengthen the conditional tenses and to assist in the formation of several other tenses:

Ing-oi-ek ka-a-'sup, if it comes to pass that I follow him, *or* if I follow him.
Añg-nya-koi-ek ka-a-'sup, while I was following him.
Eku ka-a-'sup, I shall have followed him.
Eku a-'sup-i, I shall be in the act of following him.

The third person singular of the past tense of *eku*, to become, followed by the relative, is often used to translate such phrases as *about to, on the point of,* &c. :

Ka-koi-ek ne-rarok-toi asista (it has become which descends thither the sun), the sun is *or* was on the point of setting.

Ka-koi-ek ne-ñget-e chiito mukuleldo (it has become which he breaks the man the heart), the man is *or* was on the point of death.

REDUPLICATION.

Doubling a verb often gives an idea of thoroughness :

A-til-e, I cut.
A-cheñg-e, I search.
A-ñget-e, I break.
A-tiech-e, I trample.

A-tilatil-i, I cut up.
A-cheñgcheñg-i, I search everywhere.
A-ñgetñget-i, I break completely.
A-tiechatiech-i, I trample under foot.

At other times the meaning is changed :

A-chom-e, I love.
A-'tum-i, I churn milk.
A-por-e, I kill.
A-sop-e, I am alive.

A-chomchom-i, I taste.
A-'tumtum-i, I shake trees.
A-porpor-i, I rub.
A-sopsopi, I touch gently.

ADVERBS.

All adverbs in Nandi follow the verbs they qualify. Examples :

Ñgalal mútio, speak slowly.
A-kony-e kitegin, I shall wait for him a short time.
Wend-i nguno, he is going now.
Ka-ki-pir-o puch, I have been beaten for nothing.

Substantives without the article may be used as adverbs, and verbs with or without the relative are commonly used in an adverbial sense :

Met, before.
Let, behind.
Mí-i yu-túrur, he is above.
Mí-i ya-póri, he is below.
Mí-i ye-négit, he is near.
Ole-loo, (where it is far) far.
Chok-chi, chok-u, chok-toi, chok-chok-toi, (to do) quickly.

Korirun, morning.
Koskoling, evening.

Adjectives can also be used as adverbs. They are generally prefixed by *ko*, it may be :

>Ko-ñgeriñg, ko-mining, little.
>Ko-chañg, much.
>Ko-ya, ill.
>Ko-kararan, ko-mie, well.

Example :—A-onyi ko-mie, I see well.

Many English adverbs may be translated by *mīsing*, very :

Lapat mīsing, run fast.
Nam mīsing, hold tight.
Kas mīsing, listen well.
Pir mīsing, strike hard.

Mīsing is also used for the comparison of adverbs :

>Ñgalàl mútio mīsing, speak very slowly.
>Ki-ai-te kararan mīsing, he did it very well.

ADVERBS OF TIME.

Rani, to-day.
Nguno, now.
Nguni, instantly.
Atkai, lately, now, a short time ago.
Tun, presently.
Ole-kinye, formerly.
Ole-kinye keny, long since.
Koi, afterwards.
Kitegin, soon.
Mutai, to-morrow.
Tun-gwoiin, the day after to-morrow.
Amut *or* amt, yesterday.
Oiin, the day before yesterday.
Ko-keny, again.
Katukul, always.

Compound words are frequently used as adverbs of time :

>Êkōsié-chu, (these days) nowadays.
>Kosakt' oieñg, twice.
>Kosakta che-chañg, often.

ADVERBS OF PLACE.

There are no true adverbs of place. Sentences beginning in English with *whither*, *where*, and *whence*, are expressed by verbal forms combined with the relative ; substantives without the article take the place of such words as *before*, *behind*, *somewhere*, &c. ; and *here* and *there* are expressed by the demonstratives *yu* or *yun*, &c., or if joined to the verb *to be*, by *mi* :

>A-'ngen ole-i-wendi } I know where you are going.
>A-'ngen olto ole-i-wendi }
>A-wend-i oii, I am going somewhere.
>Ka-a-'ro ko-mí yu, I saw him here.
>Ko-rorok-chí yun, he fell there.

ADVERBS

ADVERBS OF MANNER.

The principal adverbs of manner are:

Noto, thus.
Kitio, only.
Mīsing, very.
Achecha, no.
Toma, not yet.
Wei, weis, yes.
Kwekeny, altogether.
Po-many, indeed.

ADVERBS OF INTERROGATION.

The principal adverbs of interrogation are:

Ni? ne? how?
Ngoro (pl. Ngocho)? where?
Ono? kwano? where? whence? whither?
Au? when?
Kotia au? how long ago?
Kalia si? why?
Ata? how much? how many?

Examples:

O-lio-chi-ní ni? how shall I do this?
O-le-chi-n-ók ne? how shall I tell you?
Ngoro chiito? where (is) the man?
Ngocho piik? where (are) the men?
Ngoro ine? (where he?)
Mi-i ono? (where he is there?) } where is he?
I-wend-i ono? where art thou going?
I-pun-u ono? whence comest thou?
Emen-ñgwañg gwano? (where is your country?) what is your tribe?
Ip-i-wend-oti ono? where wilt thou go for a walk?
I-wend-i au? when art thou going?
Ki-mi-i kotia au? how long has he been there?
Kalia si i-ai-toi-i ni? why dost thou do this?
Kalia si mo-o-yat kurket? why have you not opened the door?
Piik ata cho-om-e omdit? how many men will eat the food?

CONJUNCTIONS.

Conjunctions are often dispensed with by the use of the subjunctive or conditional tenses. *And, but,* or other connective is translated by the subjunctive; *if, when,* and other conjunctions introducing a state, by one of the conditional tenses. The principal conjunctions are:

Ak *or* ok, and, with.
Si, and, then, in order that.
Annan, or.
Amu, amu-ne, for.
Ako, but.
Ko-keny, again.
Toma, before, ere.
Kuu, like.
Kele, because.

PREPOSITIONS.

There appears to be only one simple preposition in Nandi, *eñg*, which is equivalent to *at, by, for, from, in, off, on, out, to,* and *with*. Certain changes of letters take place at the commencement of words following this preposition; *ch* becomes *j*, and *t* becomes *d*. Before *k* and *p*, *eñg* becomes *em*, and the *k* changes to *g*. Examples:

    Ki-a-kas eñg-oriit, I felt in myself.
    Ko-mwa-chi akenge eñg-joto, he told one of (*or* out of) them.
    Ka-ki-iro eñg-dimdo, we found it in the wood.
    Ke-'put-ite em-goiik, he fell on the stones.
    Rur-e em-parak, they will ripen (at) above.

Prepositions can also be expressed by verbs in their simple or applied forms, or by a noun with or without the article. Examples:

    Och-e, he pushes him away.
    It-yi-n ka, he will arrive at the town.
    Ke-'rot-io chiito, he has betted with the man.
    Eñg-met } ahead.
    Eñg-dae }
    Eñg-let, behind.
    Eñg-nyun, beyond.
    Eñg-ono, beside, in the direction of.
    (Kot)-saang *or* saangut (ap kot), outside (the house).
    (Kot)-oriit *or* oriitut (ap kot), inside (the house).

INTERJECTIONS.

The most usual interjections are given in the following list:

	Singular.		Plural.	
	Masculine.	*Feminine.*	*Masculine.*	*Feminine.*
Of address:	Iñgwe	{ Inye { Tete	Leiye.	
Children	Weír-i	Chép-i	Weirí-chu	Típ-chu.
Grown up people	Murenón-ni	Korkón-ni	Murén-ju	Korusié-chu.
Old people	Poiyondón-ni	Chepiosón-ni	Poiisié-chu	Chepiosó-chu.
Very old people	Agwi	Koko	Akut-agwi	Angut-koko.

A man replies, Oo; A woman, Oe.

	Singular and Plural.	Singular and Plural.
	Masculine.	*Feminine.*
Of greeting:	Sopai	Takwenya.
The reply is:	Epa	Igo.

INTERJECTIONS

Of astonishment: Oi! or He! oh!
Of assent: Aiya or Wei! all right! Iman! truly.
Of contempt: Ih! O!
Of defiance: Orid!
Of grief: Eiyo-nyō! O my mother!
Of joy: Oi!
Of surprise: He!
Of taking leave: Saisere! farewell!

Imperatives are frequently used as interjections:

Ee![1] catch hold!   Chok-chi! be quick!
Sis! silence!   Isteke! make way!
Ker!
Iro! } behold!   Nate! move on one side!
Topen! look!   Mite! don't touch! leave it alone!
Kas! listen!   Tos! I don't know!

---

[1] *Ee* is also often used as an equivalent to, *I say! You there*

ENGLISH - NANDI VOCABULARY

ABBREVIATIONS

L. = Lumbwa ; K. = Kamasia ; n. = noun ; v. = verb ; neut. = neuter verb ; act. = active verb ; intr. = intransitive verb ; v. imp. = impersonal verb ; rel. pron. = relative pronoun ; int. pron. = interrogative pronoun ; adj. = adjective ; adv. = adverb ; conj. = conjunction ; prep. = preposition ; poss. = possessive pronoun ; pl. = plural ; pr. = present indicative tense ; p.p. = present perfect tense ; m. = masculine ; f. = feminine.

NOTE.—Nouns are first shown without the article : when joined to the article they are put in brackets. With verbs the root is first given, and the first person singular of the present and present perfect tenses follow in brackets. When a verb has no singular form the corresponding forms of the plural are given.

A what-is-it, kii.
Such-a-one, so-and-so, anum.
Abdomen, ketōe (ketōet), pl. ketōes (ketōesiek).
Abhor, wech (pr. a-wech-e, p.p. ka-a-wech).
be Able, imuch (pr. a-'much-i, p.p. ka-a-'much).
Abort, ōs-u (pr. a-ōs-u, p.p. ka-a-ōs-u).
Abound with, nyītat (pr. a-nyītat, p.p. ka-a-nyītat).
(*become full*), nyi (pr. a-nyi-e, p.p. ka-a-nyi).
About (*near*), nēgit.
Above, parak ; toror.
Abscess, mô (môet), pl. môoi (môōk).
Absorb, tiptipan (pr. a-tiptipon-i, p.p. ka-a-tiptipan).
Abundantly, nyītat ; mīsing.
Abuse, chup (pr. a-chup-e, p.p. ka-a-chup).
Accept, cham (pr. a-chom-e, p.p. ka-a-cham).
(*receive*), tâch (pr. a-toch-e, p.p. ka-a-tâch).

Accompany, iomis (pr. a-'omis-i, p.p. kâ-'omis).
become Accustomed to, nai-te (pr. a-noi-toi-i, p.p. ka-a-nai-te).
Ache, ñgwan (ñgwanet).
(v. imp.), am ; ñgwan.
My head aches, am-a metit (the head eats me).
Add to, tes (pr. a-tes-i, p.p. ka-a-tes).
Adjoin, itui-e (pr. a-'tui-tos-i, p.p. ka-a-'tui-e).
Admire, cham (pr. a-chom-e, p.p. ka-a-cham).
Adorn, lelesan (pr. a-leleson-i, p.p. ka-a-lelesan).
commit Adultery, chor. (See Steal.)
Advance, indoï (pr. a-'ndoï-i, p.p. ka-a-'ndoï).
(*go before*), ui tae.
Advance money, pesen (pr. a-pesen-i, p.p. ka-a-pesen).
Advice, kiruog (kiruoget), pl. kiruogut (kiruogutik).
Advise, iruog-chi (pr. a-'ruog-chi-ni, p.p. ka-a-'ruog-chi).

ENGLISH-NANDI VOCABULARY

Adviser, kiruogin (kiruogindet), pl. kiruog (kiruogik).
be Afraid, iyue (pr. a-'yue-i, p.p. ka-a-'yue).
After, let.
The after part, let (letut), pl. letus (letusiek).
Afterbirth, parpa (parpet), pl. parpas (parpasiek).
Afternoon, koskoling (koskolinget).
Afterwards, kitigin ; tun ; koi ; ip- (prefixed to the verb).
He afterwards digs, or *he will afterwards dig,* ip-ko-pal.
Again, ko-keny, isakte oieñg.
To do a thing again, nyil (pr. a-nyil-i, p.p. ka-a-nyil). sak-te (pr. a-sak-toi-i, p.p. ka-a-sak-te).
Not to do a thing again, ias (pr. ai-'os-i, p.p. kâ-'as).
Age (*periods of about* 7½ *years*), ipin (ipinda), pl. ipinuag (ipinuagik).
Agitate, isach. (See **Shake.**)
Ago, ole-kinye.
Long ago, ole-kīnye ; ole-kīnye keny.
How long ago ? ko-ti-a olto ? kotkoit au ?
Ten days ago, êkonet-ap-taman rani.
Agricultural people, meyuo (meyuot), pl. mee (meek).
Aim, imu-chi. (See **Try.**)
Place an arrow ready preparatory to aiming, ñgat (pr. a-ñgot-e, p.p. ka-a-ñgat).
Shoot after aiming, itar-chi (pr. a-'tar-chi-ni, p.p. ka-a-'tar-chi).
Air, koris (koristo).
Alike, kerke.
This is like that, kerke ni ak nin.
be Alive, sap (pr. a-sop-e, p.p. ka-a-sap).
All, tukul.

All at once, all together, kipakenge ; tukul kip-akenge.
All three, tukul ko-somok.
Allow, ikochi. (See irregular verbs, pp. 222–3.)
I will allow thee to go, a-kōn-in panda i-ue.
Alone, ineke, &c. (see pp. 186–7); kitio.
Along, tapan.
Along with, olt' akenge ak.
I will go along with you (*We will go together*), ki-pendi towae.
Aloud, eñg-ñgoliot ; eñg-ñgoliot ne-oo ; em-polet.
Already, nguno.
I have already followed him, kaka-a-'sup.
Also, ak ; ko-keny.
Alter (act.), wal (pr. a-wol-e, p.p. ka-a-wal).
Although, ako.
Altogether, kwekeny ; mīsing ; katukul.
Always, katukul.
Amalgamation, tuio (tuiet), pl. tuiōs (tuiōsiek).
Amaze, tañgany (pr. a-toñgony-i, p.p. ka-a-tañgany).
Amend, ai-te (pr. o-oi-toi-i, p.p. kâ-ai-te).
Amidst, kwen.
The midst of, kwen (kwenut), pl. kwenus (kwenusiek).
Among, oriit ; kwen.
Amulet (*women's*), pusaru (pusaruk).
(*warriors'*), setan (setanik).
Amuse, ipôten (pr. a-ipôten-i, p.p. ka-a-ipôten).
Amusement, ipôton (ipôtonik).
Ancestor, poiyo (poiyot), pl. poiisio (poiisiek).
(*male*), inguget, pl. akutingugaiik.
(*female*), ingoget, pl. angutingogaiik.

Ancient, ap-kuko.
(*formerly*), ap-keny.
Anciently, ko-rok; ole-kinye.
And, ak *or* ok.
be Angry, nerech (pr. a-nerech-i, p.p. ka-a-nerech).
Animal, tiony (tiondo), pl. tioñgin (tioñgik).
Ankle, kôwet-ap-ñgwanyo.
Anklet (*warriors'*), kipkurkur. (See **Bell.**)
(*girls'*), ingipilio (ingipiliot), pl. ingipiliōs (ingipiliōsiek); kipkarkar (kipkarkarek).
Annoy, iim (pr. a-'im-i, p.p. ka-a-'im).
Another, ake.
Answer, lokoiyo (lokoiyot), pl. lokoiyua (lokoiyuek).
(v.) twek-u (pr. a-twek-u, p.p. ka-a-twek-u); am lokoi.
Answer to, twek-chi (pr. a-twek-chi-ni, p.p. ka-a-twek-chi).
Answer when called, iyan (pr. a-'yon-i, p.p. ka-a-'yan).
iten (pr. a-iten-i, p.p. kâ-iten).
Ant:
Black ant, songōk (songōkiet), pl. songōk (songōkik).
Brown (*soldier*) *ant,* pirech (pirechet), pl. pirech (pirechik).
White ant, termite, toiya (toiyat), pl. toi (toiik).
Ants in their flying stage, kongaiya (kongaiyat), pl. kongai (kongaiek).
Other kinds, ririmio (ririmiot), pl. ririm (ririmek).
cheplilia (chepliliat), pl. cheplil (cheplilik).
Ant-hill, tuluet-ap-toiik, (pl. tuluondōk-ap-toiik).
Ant bear or *Ardvark,* kimakut (kimakutit), pl. kimakutin (kimakutīnik).
L., kuto (kutet), pl. kutes (kutesiek).

Antelope:
Bush buck, poina (poinet), pl. poinoi (poinōk).
Cobus cob, teperetio (teperetiot), pl. teperetin (teperetīnik).
Blue duiker (*C. aequatorialis*), kimereng (kimerengit), pl. kimerengin (kimerengīnik).
Common duiker (*C. grimmi*), cheptirgich (cheptirgichet), pl. cheptirgich (cheptirgichek).
Red duiker (*C. igna issaci*), minde (mindet), pl. mindōs (mindōsiek).
Eland, singoi (singoito), pl. singoiua (singoiuek).
Hartebeest, chemnyōkōso (chemnyōkōset), pl. chemnyōkōson (chemnyōkōsonik).
Impalla, situa (situet), pl. sitonoi (sitonōk).
Kudu, solgoi (solgoita), pl. solgoiuag (solgoiuagik).
Oribi, kenyele (kenyelet), pl. kenyeloi (kenyelōk).
Reed buck, irukut (irukutiet), pl. irukutin (irukutīnik).
Roan, kiplelgut (kiplelgutiet), pl. kiplelgutis (kiplelgutisiek).
Senegal hartebeest (*tope*), mukeiyo (mukeiyot), pl. mukei (mukeiik).
Waterbuck, kipsomere (kipsomeret), pl. kipsomeroi (kipsomerōk).
Anus (*human beings*), kwetio (kwetiot).
(*animals*), kimesto (kimestōet).
Anvil, top (topet), pl. topōs (topōsiek).
Any:
'Any' is expressed by using the substantive it qualifies absolutely (*i.e.* without the article), by the relative, or by *all.*
Anybody, chii; chii tukul.
Anybody's, pa-chii tukul.
Anywhere, oii; oii tukul.

ENGLISH-NANDI VOCABULARY

Any :
I don't see anything, m-â-onyi kii.
Anything whatever, kii tukul.
Take any you like, nam ne-i-moch-e.
Apart, loo.
Appear, tok-u (pr. a-tok-u, p.p. ka-a-tok-u).
(come out), mañg-u (pr. a-mañg-u, p.p. ka-a-mañg-u).
Appoint, letye. (See **Choose.**)
Approach, nēgit-yi (pr. a-nēgit-yi-ni, p.p. ka-a-nēgit-yi).
  rik-chi (pr. a-rik-chi-ni, p.p. ka-a-rik-chi).
  kwany-ji (pr. a-kwany-ji-ni, p.p. ka-a-kwany-ji).
Approach hither, inak-u (pr. a-'nok-u, p.p. ka-a-'nak-u).
  rik-u (pr. a-rik-u, p.p. ka-a-rik-u).
Approach thither, inak-te (pr. a-'nok-toi-i, p.p. ka-a-'nak-te).
  rik-te (pr. a-rik-toi-i, p.p. ka-a-rik-te).
Approve, cham (pr. a-chom-e, p.p. ka-a-cham).
Argue, tii-ye (pr. a-tii-tos-i, p.p. ka-a-tii-ye).
Arise, ñgêt (pr. a-ñgêt-e, p.p. ka-a-ñgêt).
Arm, ē (ēut), pl. ēun (ēunek).
Forearm, chepwalel (chepwalelit), pl. chepwalelis (chepwalelisiek).
  walel (waleldo), pl. waleluag (waleluagik).
Upper arm, rotion (rotionet), pl. rotionai (rotionaiik).
  L., ponoch (ponochet), pl. ponochai (ponochaiik).
Arm oneself, nam karīk ; itiach karīk.
Arms (iron), karin (karīk).
Arm-clamp (men's ornament), chepos (cheposto), pl. cheposua (cheposuek).

Armlet (women's), indinyol (indinyoliet), pl. indinyolai (indinyolaiik).
(men's or girls'), sirimwek (chains); sonaiek (beads).
(worn if the arm is painful), kelel (kelelik).
(worn by a man who has lost his next elder brother or sister), asiel (asielda), pl. asielwag (asielwagik).
(worn by a man who has a twin brother or sister), samoiyo (samoiyot), pl. samoiin (samoiīnik).
Armpit, kulkul (kulkulda), pl. kulkuluo (kulkuluek).
Arrange, ai-te (pr. o-oi-toi-i, p.p. kâ-ai-te).
Arrive, it (pr. a-it-e, p.p. ka-a-it).
  kwer (pr. a-kwer-e, p.p. ka-a-kwer).
Arrive hither, it-u (pr. a-it-u, p.p. ka-a-it-u).
Arrive thither, it-ite (pr. a-it-itoi-i, p.p. ka-a-it-ite).
Make to arrive, iit (pr. a-'it-i, p.p. ka-a-'it).
Reach a person, it-yi (pr. a-it-yi-ni, p.p. ka-a-it-yi).
Arrow, kôto (kôtet), pl. kôti (kôtiek).
Feathers of arrow, tareyuo (tareyuot), pl. tare (tareyuek).
Shaft of arrow, ñgopta (ñgoptet), pl. ñgoptoi (ñgoptōk).
Notch at end of arrow, sokwo (sokwot), pl. sokwa (sokwek).
Binding used for fastening head on to shaft, simol (simoliet), pl. simolai (simolaiik).
Leaf-shaped barb (large), kipchapo (kipchapet), pl. kipchapon (kipchaponik).
Leaf-shaped barb (small), chepiloñgio (chepiloñgiot), pl. chepiloñgen (chepiloñgēnik).

Arrow:
Harpoon-shaped barb, tukwario (tukwariot), pl. tukwarin (tukwarīnik).
   kipitinyo (kipitinyot), pl. kipitinin (kipitinīnik).
Head made of a spike of wood, supet (supetiet), pl. supet (supetik).
Boys' (for shooting rats), kipirio (kipiriot), pl. kipiren (kipirēnik).
Boys' (for shooting birds), koiisi (koiisit), pl. koiisin (koiisīnik).
Arrow used for bleeding cattle, sheep, and goats, loñgno (loñgnet), pl. loñgin (loñgīk).
Artery, tīkītio (tīkītiot), pl. tīkīt (tīkītik).
As, as if, like, kuu; ile; nette; te. *Do as you please,* ai-te kuu ne-i-moch-e.
Ascend, lany (pr. a-lony-e, p.p. ka-a-lany).
Ascend higher, itoch (pr. a-'toch-i, p.p. ka-a-'toch).
Ash, oria (oriat), pl. or (orek).
be Ashamed, têch (pr. a-têch-e, p.p. ka-a-têch).
   tinye konyit.
Aside, tapan ; nepo-tapan ; komasto.
go Aside, mas-te (pr. a-mas-toi-i, p.p. ka-a-mas-te).
Ask, tep (pr. a-tep-e, p.p. ka-a-tep).
Ask after, tepe (pr. a-tepe, p.p. ka-a-tepe).
Ask for (want), mach (pr. a-moch-e, p.p. ka-a-mach).
Make inquiries on behalf of any one, tep-chi (pr. a-tep-chi-ni, p.p. ka-a-tep-chi).
Ass, sigirio (sigiriet), pl. sigiroi (sigirōk).
Assemble, ium (pr. a-'um-i, p.p. ka-a-'um).
Assembly, tuiyo (tuiyot).

Place of Assembly (large), kâp-kiruog (kâp-kiruoget), pl. kâp-kiruogut (kâp-kiruogutik).
Place of Assembly (small), kokwa (kokwet), pl. kokwan (kokwanik).
Place of Assembly (for warriors), kâp-tui (kâp-tuiet), pl. kâp-tuion (kâp-tuionek).
Assent, cham (pr. a-chom-e, p.p. ka-a-cham).
Assert, mwa (pr. a-mwo-i, p.p. ka-a-mwa).
Assist, toret (pr. a-toret-i, p.p. ka-a-toret).
Astonish, tañgany (pr. a-toñg-ony-i, p.p. ka-a-tañgany).
At, eñg.
At first, ko-rok.
At home, kain-nyō, kain-ñguñg, kain-nyi, &c. (*my house, thy house, his* or *her house, &c.*).
   olin-nyō, olin-ñguñg, olin-nyi, &c. (*my place, &c.*).
At last, taiitio.
At night, kemboi.
At once, nguni ; nguní-to.
At the top, parak.
At the bottom, ingoiny.
Attempt, tiem (pr. a-tiem-e, p.p. ka-a-tiem).
Attend, kany. (See **Wait.**)
Aunt :
   (*paternal*), senge (senget) ;
   (*maternal*), kamet *or* kametit, pl. angut-kamet.
Avoid (*escape*), mwe (pr. a-mwe, p.p. ka-a-mwe).
Get out of the way of, is-te-ke (pr. a-is-toi-i-ke, p.p. kâ-is-te-ke).
Await, iken. (See **Expect.**)
Awake (neut.), ñgêt (pr. a-ñgêt-e, p.p. ka-a-ñgêt).
Waken (act.), iñgêt (pr. a-'ñgêt-i, p.p. ka-a-'ñgêt).
be Awake, kas-u (pr. a-kas-u, p.p. ka-a-kas-u).

Away:
I am going away, a-wend-i ; a-we-chi-ni-ke (*I will go myself*).
Come away, nyo.
He is away, ma-mi-i.
Axe, aiyuo (aiyuet), pl. aunoi (aunōk).

Baboon, moso (moset), pl. moson (mosonik).
Baby, cherere (chereret), pl. chereren (chererēnik).
kiplekwa (kiplekwet), pl. kiplekon (kiplekonik).
Back (*human beings*), patai (patet,) pl. patoi (patoiik).
(*cattle*), let (letut), pl. letus (letusiek).
Back-bone (*human beings*), oretap-patai.
(*animals*), rot (rotet), pl. rotōs (rotōsiek).
(*near neck*), kâpiog (kâpioget), pl. kâpiogōs (kâpiogōsiek).
(*near rump*), sukulum (sukulumdo), pl. sukulumwag (sukulumwagik).
Bad, ya, pl. yaach ; samis, pl. somis.
To be bad, ya-itu (pr. a-ya, p.p. kâ-ya-itu).
Bad-tempered, ya-atep, pl. yaach-atep.
Badness, yaitio (yaitiot).
Bag (*small*), lol (lolet), pl. lolotinua (lolotinuek).
(*very small*), supere (superet), pl. superoi (superōk).
(*large*), milo (milet), pl. milōs (milōsiek).
sack, gunia (guniet), pl. gunias (guniasiek).
Bake, pel (pr. a-pel-e, p.p. ka-a-pel).
Baldness, pos (posto), pl. posuo (posuek).
Bamboo, teka (tekat), pl. tek (tekik).

Banana, makomya (makomyat), pl. makom (makomik).
mototia (mototiat), pl. motot (mototik).
Flower of banana, sororua (sororuet), pl. sororon (sororonik).
Wild banana, sasur (sasuriet), pl. sasur (sasurik).
Band (*stripe*), siro (siret), pl. sireyua (sireyuek).
Banded (*striped*), sirat, pl. sirotin.
Banish, oon (pr. a-oon-e, p.p. ka-a-oon).
Bank (*of a river*), ingekut (ingekutiet), pl. ingekutoi (ingekutōk).
(*side of a river*), tapan (tapanda), pl. tapanuag (tapanuagik).
The opposite bank, pīt (pītit) ; pītón-in.
Barber, konimunin (konimunindet), pl. konimun (konimunik).
Bare, puch, pl. puch.
Bargain, kīm (pr. a-kīm-e, p.p. ka-a-kīm).
Bark (*of a tree*), perto (pertet), pl. per (perik).
Barrel (*honey*), moing (moinget), pl. moingon (moingonik).
(*clothes*), keto (ketet), pl. ketōs (ketōsiek).
Barren (*person* or *animal*), son (sonet), pl. sonōs (sonōsiek).
Basin, tapo (tapet), pl. tapoi (tapōk).
Basket, kitonga (kitonget), pl. kitongoi (kitongōk).
mesendo (mesendet), pl. mesendai (mesendaiik).
(*large*), kipserion (kipserionit), pl. kipserionin (kipserionīnik).
(*small*), kerep (kerepet), pl. kerepon (kereponik).

ENGLISH-NANDI VOCABULARY

Basket:
(*small*), kirokoro (kirokoret), pl. kirokoroi (kirokorōk).
(*very small*), ikongo (ikonget), pl. ikongen (ikongēnik).
(*children's grass basket*), soko (sokot), pl. sok (sokek).
Bat, reres (reresiet), pl. reres (reresik).
Bathe, iun-ge (pr. a-'un-i-ke, p.p. ka-a-'un-ge).
Battle, porio (poriet), pl. poriōs (poriōsiek).
Battle-field, kâporio (kâporiot).
Be, i ; mi ; mi-te. (See irregular verbs, p. 219.)
(*stay*), tepi (pr. a-tepi-e, p.p. ka-a-tepi).
Bead, sonaiya (sonaiyat), pl. sonoi (sonoiek).
Bead made of ostrich egg-shell, kelelio (keleliot), pl. kelel (kelelik).
Each kind of bead has a special name. The following are some of the principal kinds :—
    anongoiyo (anongoiyot), pl. anongoiin (anongoiīnik).
    ingopotio (ingopotiot), pl. ingopot (ingopotek).
    ndorio (ndoriot), pl. ndore (ndorek).
    ingupusio (ingupusiot), pl. ingupusin (ingupusīnik).
    sombaiyo (sombaiyot), pl. sombai (sombaiek).
    nongoiyo (nongoiyot), pl. nongoiin (nongoiīnik).
Beak (*bird's*), kutit-ap-tarityet.
Bean, makandia (makandiat), pl. makanda (makandek).
Bear (*fruit* or *children,* &c.), ii (pr. a-ii-e, p.p. kâ-ii).
Person who has recently borne or who is about to bear, tomono (tomonet), pl. tomonōs (tomonōsiek).

(*carry*), ip (pr. a-ip-e, p.p. kâ-ip).
Carry on the back, la (pr. a-lo-i, p.p. ka-a-la).
Beard, kororek-ap-tamnet.
Beast, tiony (tiondo), pl. tioñgin (tioñgik).
Beat, pir (pr. a-pir-e, p.p. ka-a-pir).
(*conquer*), ipēl (pr. a-'pēl-i, p.p. ka-a-'pēl).
Beat a child slightly with a stick, itiol (pr. a-'tiol-e, p.p. ka-a-'tiol).
Be too great a task, temene (pr. a-temene, p.p. ka-a-temene).
Beautiful, kararan, pl. kororon.
To be beautiful, kararan-itu (pr. a-kararan, p.p. ka-a-kararan-itu).
Beauty, kararin (kararindo).
Because, amu ; amu ne ; kele.
Beckon to, ñgwech (pr. a-ñgwech-i, p.p. ka-a-ñgwech).
Become, ek-u. (See irregular verbs, p. 220.)
Bed, itōk (itōkut), pl. itōkus (itōkusiek).
(*warriors*), kitar (kitarut), pl. kitarus (kitarusiek).
The head of a bed, meto (metōut).
The foot of a bed, kâp-kelien (kâp-kelienut).
Bee, segemya (segemyat pl. segem (segemik).
Names of various kinds of bees :
    chepoñgonyo (chepoñgonyot), pl. chepoñgonyin (chepoñgonyīnik).
    kosomyo (kosomyot), pl. kosom (kosomek).
    kiptulonio (kiptuloniot), pl. kiptulon (kiptulonik).
    kulumbio (kulumbiot), pl. kulumben (kulumbēnik).
    imeio (imeiot), pl. imei (imeik).
    chepruecho (chepruechot), pl. chepruechoi (chepruechōk).

ENGLISH-NANDI VOCABULARY

Bee :
Drone, chepkopirio (chepkopiriot), pl. chepkopiren (chepkopirēnik).
Beehive (*natural*), pondo (pondet), pl. pondōs (pondōsiek).
(*artificial*), moing (moinget), pl. moingon (moingonik).
Take a beehive, iñget-te (pr. a-'ñget-toi-i, pp. ka-a-'ñget-te).
Beer, maiya (maiyat), pl. maiyo (maiyek).
Beeswax, temen (temenyet), pl. temenai (temenaiik).
Beetle, cheptoruruog (cheptoruruoget), pl. cheptoruruog (cheptoruruogik).
Before, tae (*place*); toma (*time*).
The front of, tae (taeta), pl. toiua (toiuek).
To go before, indoï (pr. a-'ndoï-i, p.p. ka-a-'ndoï).
Before he goes to sleep, tom-ko-ru.
Beg, som (pr. a-som-e, p.p. ka-a-som).
Beget, ii (pr. a-ii-e, p.p. kâ-ii).
Beggar, somin (somindet), pl. som (somik).
chemñgesusuo (chemñgesusuot), pl. chemñgesusua (chemñgesusuek).
chepsoiso (chepsoiset).
Begin (*hither*), ta-u (pr. a-ta-u, p.p. ka-a-ta-u).
(*thither*), ta-te (pr. a-ta-toi-i, p.p. ka-a-ta-te).
Beginning, olekopoch (olekopochet); tapan (tapanda).
Behind (adv.), let.
(prep.), letut-ap; letun-nyi, &c.
Belch, sie (pr. a-sie-i, p.p. ka-a-sie).
Bell (*warriors'*), kipkurkur (kipkurkuriet), pl. kipkurkurai (kipkurkuraiik).

(*small*),chepkurkur(chepkurkuriet), pl. chepkurkurai (chepkurkuraiik).
(*cows'*), twalio (twaliot), pl. twalin (twalīk).
Bellow (*oxen*), parar (pr. a-poror-i, p.p. ka-a-parar).
(*cows calling their calves*), iut (pr. a-'ut-i, p.p. ka-a-'ut).
Bellows, kopan (kopanda), pl. kopanua (kopanuek).
Belly, mo (moiet), pl. mootinua (mcotinuek).
Below (adv.), ingoiny; ya-pori.
(prep.), ingoinyut-ap; ingoinyun-nyi, &c.
Belt (*women's*), legetio (legetiet), pl. legetai (legetaiik).
(*men's*), pireyuo (pireyuot), pl. pireyuōs (pireyuōsiek).
Bend, ñgwal (pr. a-ñgwol-e, p.p. ka-a-ñgwal).
(*fold*), aruny (pr. a-aruny-i, p.p. kâ-aruny).
Bend wood, &c., kwen (pr. a-kwen-e, p.p. ka-a-kwen); yem (pr. a-yem-e, p.p. ka-a-yem).
Bend a bow, riich (pr. a-riich-e, p.p. ka-a-riich).
Bend down (act.), iñguruch (pr. a-'ñguruch-i, p.p. ka-a-'ñguruch).
(neut.), iñguruk-e (pr. a-'ñguruk-at, p.p. ka-a-'ñguruk-e).
Bequeath, pokok-chi (pr. a-pokok-chi-ni, p.p. ka-a-pokok-chi).
Beseech, sa (pr. a-so-e, p.p. ka-a-sa).
Beside, tapan.
Besides, ko-keny.
Best, better, kaikai, pl. koikoi.
Thou hadst better go, kaikai i-ue.
Bet with some one, irot-ie (pr. a-'rot-tos-i, p.p. ka-a-'rot-ie).
Between, kwen; takoi.
The space between, takoi (takoita), pl. takoiua (takoiuek).

Beware, iro. (See irregular verbs, p. 224.)
Bhang, nyasore (nyasoret), pl. nyasoroi (nyasorōk).
Biceps, chepwilpwil (chepwilpwiliet), pl. chepwilpwiloi (chepwilpwilōk).
Big, oo, pl. echen.
To be big, oo-itu (pr. a-oo, p.p. kâ-oo-itu).
Bile, es (eset); cheptigon (cheptigonit).
Bill-hook, mor (morut), pl. morus (morusiek).
Bind, rat (pr. a-rot-e, p.p. ka-a-rat).
Bind round, ta (pr. a-to-e, p.p. ka-a-ta).
Bird, tarit (tarityet), pl. tarīt (tarītik).
Buzzard, chepkōkōsio (chepkōkōsiot), pl. chepkōkōsin (chepkōkōsīnik).
Crested crane, koñgonyo (koñgonyot), pl. koñgony (koñgonyik).
Crow, chepkwog (chepkwogit), pl. chepkwogin (chepkwogīnik).
Dove, cheptuge (cheptuget), pl. cheptugen (cheptugēnik).
Duck, kokopeno (kokopenet), pl. kokopen (kokopēnik).
taiyuet-ap-pêk.
Eagle, kipsich (kipsichit), pl. kipsichin (kipsichīnik).
orokcha (orokchat), pl. orok (orokik).
Green Pigeon, nengo (nenget), pl. nengai (nengaiik).
Ground Hornbill, cheptībi (cheptībīt), pl. cheptībin (cheptībīnik).
Guinea-fowl, terkekya (terkekyat), pl. terkeken (terkekēnik).
Hawk, chepsirire (chepsiriret), pl. chepsiriren (chepsirirēnik).
Honey-bird, chepkeche (chepkecheit), pl. chepkecheis (chepkecheisiek).
Kite, chepsengwa (chepsengwet), pl. chepsengwen (chepsengwenik).
Lesser bustard, chelokom (chelokomiet), pl. chelokomai (chelokomaiik).
Owl, sukuru (sukurut), pl. sukurus (sukurusiek).
Ox-pecker, ririo (ririet), pl. rir (ririk).
Plantain-eater, merewa (merewet), pl. mereon (mereonik).
Quail, chepiakwai (chepiakwaiet), pl. chepiakwaien (chepiakwaiēnik).
Shrike, kipkekend (kipkekendet), pl. kipkekendai (kipkekendaiik).
Spurfowl, partridge, francolin, taiyua (taiyuet), pl. taoi (taōk).
Stork, kâpcheptalamia (kâpcheptalamiat), pl. kâpcheptalamin (kâpcheptalamīnik).
Sunbird (Calchometra acik), chesilio (chesiliot), pl. chesilen (chesilēnik).
Sunbird (Nectarinia kilimensis), chepkemis (chepkemisiet), pl. chepkemisai (chepkemisaiik).
Swallow, kipisua (kipisuet), pl. kipisoi (kipisōk).
Vulture, motony (motonda), pl. motoñgwa (motoñgwek).
Wagtail, takipos (takiposit), pl. takiposin (takiposīnik).
Woodpecker, kiptiltil (kiptiltiliat), pl. kiptiltiloi (kiptiltilōk).
Bird-lime, pemba (pembet), pl. pembon (pembonik).
Birth-mark, tisio (tisiet), pl. tisioi (tisiōk).
Bite, sus (susut).
(v.), sus (pr. a-sus-e, p.p. ka-a-sus).

ENGLISH-NANDI VOCABULARY

Bitter, ñgwan, pl. ñgwoniu.
To be bitter, ñgwañg-itu (pr. a-ñgwañg, p.p. ka-a-ñgwañg-itu).
Black, tui, pl. tuen.
To be black, tui-itu (pr. a-tui, p.p. ka-a-tui-itu).
Blacksmith, kitoñgin (kitoñg-indet), pl. kitoñg (kitoñgik).
Bladder, chepkule (chepkulet), pl. chepkules (chepkulesiek).
Blade of spear, melei (meleito), pl. meleiua (meleiuek).
Blanket, marangeti (marangetit), pl. marangetis (marangetisiek). sumat (sumet), pl. sumot (sumotik).
Bleed (*oxen*), char (pr. a-chor-e, p.p. ka-a-char).
 (*people*), kwer (pr. a-kwer-e, p.p. ka-a-kwer).
Blind, korat, pl. korotin.
To be blind, kor (pr. a-kor-e, p.p. ka-a-kor).
One-eyed person (m.), kipkoñgak, (f.), chepkoñgak.
Blink, mismis (pr. a-mismis-i, p.p. ka-a-mismis).
Blister, termemut (termemutiet), pl. termemut (termemutik).
Blood, koroti (korotik).
Blood used as food, reges (regesto), pl. regesua (regesuek).
Blood-brotherhood, kalia (kaliet); muma (mumek); patureshin (patureshīnik).
Enter into blood-brotherhood or be on friendly terms with, kaliau; par mumek; nam patureshin.
Blood-vessel, tīkītio (tīkītiot), pl. tīkīt (tīkītik).
Blow (act.), kūt (pr. a-kūt-e, p.p. ka-a-kūt).
 (*of the wind*), imut (pr. a-'mut-i, p.p. ka-a-'mut).
Blow a horn, kūt kuinet.
Blow the nose, ñgu seperik.
Blow bellows, kūt kopanda.

Blunder, ichilil (pr. a-'chilil-e, p.p. ka-a-'chilil).
Blunt, ñgutum, pl. ñgutumen.
Boast, las-ke (pr. a-los-i-ke, p.p. ka-a-las-ke).
 (*be puffed up*), men (pr. a-men-e, p.p. ka-a-men).
Boaster, menotio (menotiot), pl. menot (menotik).
Body, por (porto), pl. porua (poruek).
A dead body, musio (musiot), pl. musua (musuek).
Boil (*blain*), undir (undiriet), pl. undir (undirik).
Boil (*bubble up*), kut-u (pr. a-kut-u, p.p. ka-a-kut-u).
 (act.), ikut-u (pr. a-'kut-u, p.p. ka-a-'kut-u).
Bone, kôwo (kôwet), pl. kôwoi (kôwek).
be Born (v. imp.), sich.
I was born in Nandi, ki-ki-sich-in-o Nandi.
Both, towae; kwoieñg.
Both ... and, ak ... ak.
Bother, iim (pr. a-'im-i, p.p. ka-a-'im).
 iluiluch (pr. a-'luiluch-i, p.p. ka-a-'luiluch).
Bottom, ingoiny (ingoinyut), pl. ingoinyus (ingoinyusiek).
Bough, mornet-ap-ketit.
Boundary, kiwoto (kiwotet), pl. kiwotōs (kiwotōsiek).
People living on the boundary of a country, toroch (toroita); kiptorochin (kiptorochīnik).
Bow, kwang (kwanget), pl. kwangoi (kwangōk).
Bow for bleeding cattle, kirer (kirerto), pl. kirerua (kireruek).
Bow (act.), iñguruch (pr. a-'ñguruch-i, p.p. ka-a-'ñguruch).
 (neut.), iñguruk-e (pr. a-'ñguruk-at, p.p. ka-a-'ñguruk-e).
Bow-string, īno (īnet), pl. īnai (īnaiik).

ENGLISH-NANDI VOCABULARY

Bow-string:
Leather band to keep bow-string in place, tikiseyuo (tikiseyuot), pl. tikise (tikiseyuek).
Piece of leather attached to a bracelet to prevent the bow-string from hurting the wrist, lokos (lokosta), pl. lokosua (lokosuek).

Box the ears, irapach (pr. a-'ropoch-e, p.p. ka-a-'rapach).

Boy, ñgeta (ñgetet), pl. ñget (ñgetik).
  lemin (lemindet), pl. lem (lemek).

Bracelet (*women's*), makiraria (makirariat), pl. makirarin (makirarīnik).
  mukurio (mukuriot), pl. mukure (mukurek).
  (*old men's*), samoiyo (samoiyot), pl. samoiin (samoiīnik).
  (*of iron, bound with small iron rings, worn by boys and warriors*), asingai (asingaiit), pl. asingaiin (asingaiīnik).
  (*worn by men if wounded in the arm*), sirimdo-ap-ēut.

Brain, kunyut (kundit), pl. kunyut (kunyutik).

Branch, mornet-ap-ketit.

Brand, pel (pr. a-pel-e, p.p. ka-a-pel).

Branding-iron (*cattle*), mechei (mecheito), pl. mecheiua (mecheiuek).
  (*sheep*), samoiyo (samoiyot), pl. samoiin (samoiīnik).

Brass wire, tae (taet), pl. taoi (taōk).

Breadth, tepesin (tepesindo).

Break, iri (pr. oi-'ri-e, p.p. ka-a-'ri).
  iyei (pr. a-'yei-e, p.p. ka-a-'yei).
  (*break off*), ñget (pr. a-ñget-e, p.p. ka-a-ñget).
  (*pound*), tu-i (pr. a-tu-e, p.p. ka-a-tu-i).

(*tear*), pâch (pr. a-poch-e, p.p. ka-a-pâch).

Break through (*pierce*), rut (pr. a-rut-e, p.p. ka-a-rut).

Break wind, kwat (pr. a-kwot-e, p.p. ka-a-kwat).

Breast (*human beings*), teget (teget), pl. tegēt (tegētik).
  (*animals*), tagat (tagatet), pl. tagot (tagotik).
  Woman's breast, murungu (murungut), pl. murungus (murungusiek).

Breasts, kīna (kīnet), pl. kīnai (kīnaiik).

Breath, kapuso (kapuset).

Breathe, ipus (pr. a-pus-i, p.p. ka-a-'pus).

Breathe oneself, imuny. (See **Rest**.)

Brew (*beer, &c.*), riech (pr. a-riech-e, p.p. ka-a-riech).

Bridge, etio (etiet), pl. etiōs (etiōsiek).

be Brilliant, tilil (pr. a-tilil-i, p.p. ka-a-tilil).

Bring (*things only*), ip-u (pr. a-ip-u, p.p. kâ-ip-u).
  (*persons only*), imut-u (pr. a-'mut-u, p.p. ka-a-'mut-u).
  (*persons and things*), kōn-u (pr. a-kōn-u, p.p. ka-a-kōn-u).

Broad, tepes, pl. tepesen.

Broom, kapukio (kapukiot), pl. kapuken (kapukēnik).
  kweyo (kweyot), pl. kweōn (kweōnik).

Brother, ñget-ap-kamet, pl. akut-ñget-ip-kamet (*or* akut-ñget-ip-kametuak).
  tupcho (tupchet), pl. akut-tupchet (*or* tupchōsiek).

Thy brother, ñget-ap-komit, pl. akut-ñget-ip-komit (*or* akut-ñget-ip-komituak).

My brother, ñget-ap-eiyo, pl. akut-ñget-ip-eiyo; kitupche;

ENGLISH-NANDI VOCABULARY

Brother:
weiri ne-kitupche, pl. weirik che-kitupche.
(*word used by women*), tete, pl. akut-tete.
Brother-in-law (*wife's brother*), kâp-yukoi (kâp-yukoiit).
(*man's sister's husband*), sanyo (sandit).
(*husband's brother*), pamur (pamurto).
Bruise (act.), ichirimit (pr. a-'chirimit-i, p.p. ka-a-'chirimit).
(neut.), chirimit (pr. a-chirimit-e, p.p. ka-a-chirimit).
Buffalo, so (soet), pl. soen (soenik).
Bug, kololio (kololiot), pl. kolol (kololik).
Build, têch (pr. a-têch-e, p.p. ka-a-têch).
(*erect an enclosure*), ñgot (pr. a-ñgot-e, p.p. ka-a-ñgot).
Bull, kiruk (kirkit), pl. kiruk (kirukik).
Bullet, parpario (parpariot), pl. parpar (parparek).
koii. (See **Stone.**)
Bullock, ei (eito), pl. ein (einik).
Bully, usin (usindet), pl. us (usik).
(v.), inyalil (pr. a-'nyolil-i, p.p. ka-a-'nyalil).
us (pr. a-us-e, p.p. ka-a-us).
Bulrush, cherungu (cherungut), pl. cherungus (cherungusiek).
Burn (*be consumed*), lach (pr. a-loch-e, p.p. ka-a-lach).
(*consume*), iloch (pr. a-'loch-i, p.p. ka-a-'loch).
(*be on fire, scorch*), lal (pr. a-lol-e, p.p. ka-a-lal).
(*set on fire, make up a fire*), ilal (pr. a-'lol-i, p.p. ka-a-'lal).
(*apply fire to, bake, brand*), pel (pr. a-pel-e, p.p. ka-a-pel).
(*kindle*), inam (pr. a-'nom-i, p.p. ka-a-'nam).

(*burn the skin off*), ichur (pr. a-'chur-e, p.p. ka-a-'chur).
(*feed a fire*), iyuok-chi mat.
Burrow, ikut-u (pr. a-'kut-u, p.p. ka-a-'kut-u).
Burst (act.), pêt (pr. a-pêt-e, p.p. ka-a-pêt).
(neut.), pêt-ake (pr. a-pêt-at, p.p. ka-a-pêt-ake).
Bury, tup (pr. a-tup-e, p.p. ka-a-tup).
Place a corpse ready for the hyenas, ison (pr. a-'son-i, p.p. ka-a-'son); mwi (pr. a-mwi-e, p.p. ka-a-mwi).
Bush, ket (ketit), pl. ket (ketik).
Bustle (act.), iserserin (pr. a-'serserin-e, p.p. ka-a-'serserin).
Be in a bustle, serserin (pr. a-serserin-i, p.p. ka-a-serserin).
But, ako.
Butcher (*cattle*), par *or* tor kimutit (ap-teta).
(*sheep* or *goats*), iket. (See **Choke, Strangle.**)
Butter, mwait'-ap-cheko; mwait'-ap-tany-kīna.
Butterfly, tapurpur (tapurpuriet), pl. tapurpur (tapurpurik).
Buttock, kwetio (kwetiot), pl. kwetua (kwetuek).
Buy, al (pr. a-ol-e, p.p. kâ-al).
Buy for, al-chi (pr. a-ol-chi, p.p. kâ-al-chi).
Buyer, alin (alindet), pl. al (alik).
Buzz (*like a bee*), imut (pr. a-'mut-i, p.p. ka-a-'mut).
(*like a drone*), ite (pr. a-'te-i, p.p. ka-a-'te).

Calabash, sot (sotet), pl. sotōn (sotōnik).
(*small*), terga (terget), pl. tergoi (tergōk).

R 2

Calabash:
Half-calabash, sepet (septet), pl. sepetai (sepetaiik).
Wide-mouthed calabash (female), sotet ne-marīch-kut.
Narrow-mouthed calabash (male), sotet ne-para-kut.
Long-necked calabash, sotet ne-koi-kut.
Put a calabash to one's mouth, nyoput (pr. a-nyoput-i, p.p. ka-a-nyoput).
Stick for cleaning calabashes, sosio (sosiot), pl. sos (sosik).
Calabash fruit, tenderia (tenderiat), pl. tender (tenderik).
Calabash plant, silakwa (silakwet), pl. silakon (silakonik).
Calf, moi (moita), pl. moii (moiek).
Young calf, kiptoiyo *or* kiptoi (kiptoiyot *or* kiptoito), pl. kiptoiin (kiptoiīnik).
Call, kur (pr. a-kur-e, p.p. ka-a-kur).
(name), itar (pr. a-'tor-i, p.p. ka-a-'tar).
Call out to, iten-ji (pr. a-iten-ji-ni, p.p. ka-a-iten-ji).
Call out, shout, wach (pr. a-woch-e, p.p. ka-a-wach).
Camel, tombes (tombesiet), pl. tombes (tombesik).
Camp, kâp-ruon (kâp-ruondo).
Camp on the war-path, olpul (olpulit), pl. olpulis (olpulisiek).
Can, imuch (pr. a-'much-i, p.p. ka-a-'much).
Cap, chepkule (chepkulet), pl. chepkules (chepkulesiek).
Cape (*warriors'*), kororik. (See **Feathers.**)
Caravan, un (undo), pl. unwa (unwek).
(small), rutoi (rutoito), pl. rutoiua (rutoiuek).
Caravan porter, otuag. (See **Slave.**)

Carcase, musio (musiot), pl. musua (musuek).
Care, iro. (See irregular verbs, p. 224.)
Take care of, rīp (pr. a-rīp-e, p.p. ka-a-rīp).
I don't care; no matter, ror-chi ket; ma-uu kii.
Carry, ip (pr. a-ip-e, p.p. kâ-ip).
Carry for, ip-chi (pr. a-ip-chi-ni, p.p. kâ-ip-chi).
Carry hither (bring), ip-u (pr. a-ip-u, p.p. kâ-ip-u).
Carry something heavy, sut (pr. a-sut-i, p.p. ka-a-sut).
Carry on the back, la (pr. a-lo-e, p.p. ka-a-la).
Carry a child or load, kesen (pr. a-kesen-i, p.p. ka-a-kesen).
Cartridge, parpario (parpariot), pl. parpar (parparek).
Cast, met-te (pr. a-met-toi-i, p.p. ka-a-met-te).
Cast upon or at, met-yi (pr. a-met-yi-ni, p.p. ka-a-met-yi).
Cast one's eyes upon, kwer-te konda.
Cast a light on, ikweny (pr. a-'kweny-i, p.p. ka-a-'kweny).
Castor-oil plant, imanya (imanyat), pl. iman (imanek).
Castrate, lat (pr. a-lot-e, p.p. ka-a-lat).
Cat, kiptuswai (kiptuswet), pl. kiptusai (kiptusaiik).
simba (simbet), pl. simboi (simbōk).
L., semingor (semingoret), pl. semingorin (semingorīnik).
Cerval cat, cheptuino (cheptuinet), pl. cheptuinōs (cheptuinōsiek).
L., kesogoror (kesogororet), pl. kesogororōs (kesogororōsiek).
Catch, tal (pr. a-tol-e, p.p. ka-a-tal).
Catch hold! ee!

ENGLISH-NANDI VOCABULARY 245

Catch:
 Catch in a trap, tech (pr. a-tech-e, p.p. ka-a-tech).
 Catch rain-water, tâch. (See **Receive.**)
 Catch a disease (v. imp.), inam.
Caterpillar, cheput (cheputiet), pl. cheput (cheputik).
Cattle, tany. (See **Ox.**)
 Cattle-fold, pē (pēut), pl. pēus (pēusiek).
 Raided cattle, koiyo (koiyet), pl. koiyōs (koiyōsiek).
Cave, kepen (kepenet), pl. kepenōs (kepenōsiek).
Cease, ias (pr. ai-'os-i, p.p. kâ-'as).
 Cease talking, sis (pr. a-sis-i, p.p. ka-a-sis).
Ceiling, taput(taputet), pl. taputon (taputonik).
Centipede, kimorin (kimorinet), pl. kimorin (kimorīnik).
Chaff, metetia (metetiat), pl. metet (metetek).
Chain, sirim (sirimdo), pl. sirimwag (sirimwagik).
Chair, ñgecher (ñgecheret), pl. ñgecheroi (ñgecherōk).
Chalk, tartar (tartarik).
Chameleon, nyirit (nyiritiet), pl. nyiritoi (nyiritōk).
Change (act.), wal (pr. a-wol-e, p.p. ka-a-wal).
 (neut.), wal-ak-e (pr. a-wal-at, p.p. ka-a-wal-ak-e).
Charcoal, nesio (nesiot), pl. nes (nesek).
Charm. (See **Amulet.**)
 Charm against the evil eye, lapuon (lapuonik).
Chase, loko (loket).
Chase away, oon (pr. a-oon-e, p.p. ka-a-oon).
Chatter (*lies*), lembech (lembechet), pl. lembech (lembechek).
 (v.), iperiper-itu (pr. a-'periper, p.p. ka-a-'periper-itu).

Chatter (of the teeth), kutkūt (pr. a-kutkūt-i, p.p. ka-a-kutkūt).
Chatterer (m.), kiplembechwa (kiplembechwet), pl. kiplembechon (kiplembechonik).
 (f.), cheplembechwa.
Cheap, ma-ui, pl. ma-uen.
 To sell cheap, al-ok-e ko-mie.
Cheat, ken (pr. a-ken-e, p.p. ka-a-ken).
 iperiper (pr. a-'periper-i, p.p. ka-a-'periper).
Cheek, matañg (matanda), pl. matoñgwa (matoñgwek).
Chest (*human beings*), teget (teget), pl. tegēt (tegētik).
Chew, nye (pr. a-nye, p.p. ka-a-nye).
 Chew and spit out, mit (pr. a-mit-e, p.p. ka-a-mit).
 Chew whilst walking, sos-ate (pr. a-sos-oti, p.p. ka-a-sos-ate).
Chicken, lakwet-ap-ingokiet, pl. lakōk-ap-ingokiet.
Chief (*captain*), olaitorio (olaitoriot), pl. olaitorin (olaitorīnik).
 (*spokesman*), kiruogin (kiruogindet), pl. kiruog (kiruogik).
 (*head man*), chiit'-ap-metit. (adj.), oo, pl. echen.
Chief medicine man, orkoiyo (orkoiyot), pl. orkoi (orkoiik).
Child, lakwa (lakwet), pl. lakoi (lakōk).
Chin, tamna (tamnet), pl. tamnoi (tamnōk).
Choke, iket (pr. a-'ket-i, p.p. ka-a-'ket).
Choose, letye (pr. a-letye-i, p.p. ka-a-letye).
 kwe (pr. a-kwe, p.p. ka-a-kwe).
Chop, ep (pr. a-ep-e, p.p. ka-a-ep).
 Chop to a point, lit (pr. a-lit-e, p.p. ka-a-lit).
 Chop up small, murmur (pr. a-murmur-i, p.p. ka-a-murmur).

Churn milk, isach (pr. a-'soch-i, p.p. ka-a-'sach).
Circumcise, muratan (pr. a-muraton-i, p.p. ka-a-muratan). itum (pr. a-'tum-i, p.p. ka-a-'tum).
He has been circumcised, ka-ki-muratan; ki-kwa tum.
A person recently circumcised, or *one about to be circumcised,* tarusio (tarusiot), pl. tarus (tarusiek).
A circumcised man or woman, kipkelel (kipkeleldet), pl. kipkelelai (kipkelelaiik).
Circumcision ceremony, tum (tumdo), pl. tumwa (tumwek).
Clan, or. (See **Road.**)
Clap the hands, rapach (pr. a-rapoch-i, p.p. ka-a-rapach).
Clasp (*in the hand*), nam (pr. a-nom-e, p.p. ka-a-nam).
(*in the arms*), suup (pr. a-suup-e, p.p. ka-a-suup).
Claw, siiya (siiyet), pl. sioi (siōk).
(*talon*), silolio (siloliot), pl. silolēn (silolēnik).
(v.), sīl (pr. a-sīl-e, p.p. ka-a-sīl).
kut (pr. a-kut-e, p.p. ka-a-kut).
pach (pr. a-poch-e, p.p. ka-a-pach).
Clay (*red*), ñgario (ñgariet), pl. ñgarioi (ñgariōk).
(*white*), eorio (eoriot), pl. eor (eorik).
(*grey, yellow*), tartar (tartariet), pl. tartar (tartarik).
Clean, iun (pr. a-'un-i, p.p. ka-a-'un).
Clean the teeth, siit kelek.
Clear, tilil, pl. tililen.
(*open*), iseñgeñgat, pl. iseñgeñgot-in.
(*white*), lēl, pl. lelach.
Clear (at night), lapke, pl. lapkein.

Clear the ground preparatory to planting, tem (pr. a-tem-e, p.p. ka-a-tem).
Cleave, pêt. (See **Tear.**)
Clever, ñgom, pl. ñgomin.
Climb, lany (pr. a-lony-e, p.p. ka-a-lany).
Climb up, tokos (pr. a-tokos-i, p.p. ka-a-tokos).
Climb a tree without branches, sikop ketit.
Climb (e. g. *a hill*) *and descend again,* iñgir-te (pr. a-'ñgir-toi-i, p.p. ka-a-'ñgir-te).
Stick used to assist a climber, kombo (kombet), pl. kombes (kombesiek).
Close, isip-chi (pr. a-'sip-chi-ni, p.p. ka-a-'sip-chi).
iēn (pr. a-'ēn-i, p.p. ka-a-'ēn).
(*shut*), ker (pr. a-ker-e, p.p. ka-a-ker).
Close the eyes, inuch (pr. a-'nuch-i, p.p. ka-a-'nuch).
Close the fist, mumut ēut.
Cloth, anga (anget), pl. angas (angasiek).
Clothe, ilach (pr. a-'loch-i, p.p. ka-a-'lach).
Clothes. (See **Garment.**)
Cloud, poldo (poldet), pl. pol (polik).
Club, rungu (rungut), pl. rungus (rungusiek).
Old men's club, shari (sharit), pl. sharin (sharinik).
Handle of club, irumo (irumet), pl. irumai (irumaiik).
Head of club, metit-ap-rungut.
Coax, ken-ji (pr. a-ken-ji-ni, p.p. ka-a-ken-ji).
Cock, kipsoiyua (kipsoiyuet), pl. kipsoon (kipsoonik).
A cock's comb, soñgonyet-ap-kipsoiyuet.
A cock's spur, silolio (siloliot) pl. silolēn (silolēnik).

ENGLISH-NANDI VOCABULARY 247

Cock :
A cock's wattles, keneya (keneyat), pl. kene (keneek).
Cockroach, solopcho (solopchot), pl. solop (solopik).
Coition, engumisio (engumisiet).
Cold, koris (koristo).
I have a cold, am-a tuñgwek *or* ka-ker-a met. (adj.), kaitit, pl. koitit.
Collar-bone, malingot (malingotiet), pl. malingotai (malingotaiik).
kôwet-ap-malingotiet.
Collect, ium (pr. a-'um-i, p.p. ka-a-'um).
itui-ye (pr. a-'tui-tos-i, p.p. ka-a-'tui-ye).
Collect together goats, preparatory to driving them home, ision-u (pr. a-ision-u, p.p. kâ-ision-u).
Colour, chesoleyua (chesoleyuat), pl. chesole (chesoleyuek).
Black, tui, pl. tuen.
Black and white, pusien, pl. pusienen.
Blue, arus, pl. arusen.
Brown, mur *or* muruon, pl. muruonen.
Dark brown, omo, pl. omonen.
Green, nyalil, pl. nyalilen.
Khaki-coloured, grey, yellow, talelio, pl. talelion.
Many-coloured, samo, pl. samoen.
Red, pirir, pl. piriren.
Red-brown, sitye, pl. sityonen.
Red and white, mongorio, pl. mongorionin.
White, lēl, pl. lelach.
Come, nyo. (See irregular verbs, p 222.)
(*arrive*), it-u (pr. a-it-u, p.p. ka-a-it-u).
Come apart, ñget (pr. a-ñget-e, p.p. ka-a-ñget).
Come behind, let-u (pr. a-let-u, p.p. ka-a-let-u).
Come by, for, to, &c., nyon-ji (pr. a-nyon-ji-ni, p.p. ka-a-nyon-ji).
Come from, pun-u (pr. a-pun-u, p.p. ka-a-pun-u).
Come in, out, mañg-u (pr. a-moñg-u, p.p. ka-a-mañg-u).
Come in the morning, mus-u (pr. a-mus-u, p.p. ka-a-mus-u).
Come near, inak-u (pr. a-'nok-u, p.p. ka-a-'nak-u).
nēgit-yi (pr. a-nēgit-yi-ni, p.p. ka-a-nēgit-yi).
Come round, alak-u (pr. a-alak-u, p.p. kâ-alak-u).
Come silently, sis-anu (pr. a-sis-anu, p.p. ka-a-sis-anu).
Come upon (*meet with*), nyor-u (pr. a-nyor-u, p.p. ka-a-nyor-u).
Come with (*someone*), ire-u (pr. a-'re-u, p.p. ka-a-'re-u).
Comet, cheptapis (cheptapisiet), pl. cheptapisoi (cheptapisōk).
kipsarur (kipsaruriet).
Command, ñgat (pr. a-ñgot-e, p.p. ka-a-ñgat).
Companion, chorua (choruet), pl. choronai (choronōk).
Company (*of warriors*), poror (pororiet), pl. pororōs (pororōsiek).
(*parish*), sirit (siritiet), pl. siritai (siritaiik).
Complete, tukul.
Comprehend, nai. (See irregular verbs, pp. 223-4.)
Conceal, uny (pr. a-uny-e, p.p. ka-a-uny).
Conduct a person, imut (pr. a-'mut-i, p.p. ka-a-'mut).
Conquer, ipēl (pr. a-'pēl-i, p.p. ka-a-'pēl).
(*win*), lot (pr. a-lot-e, p.p. ka-a-lot).
Be too great a task for one, temene (pr. a-temene, p.p. ka-a-temene).
Consent, cham (pr. a-chom-e, p.p. ka-a-cham).

Consider, ipwat (pr. a-'pwot-i, p.p. ka-a-'pwat). kerer met.
Construct, têch (pr. a-têch-e, p.p. ka-a-têch).
Consult, iruoch (pr. a-'ruoch-i, p.p. ka-a-'ruoch).
Consultation, kiruog (kiruoget), pl. kiruogut (kiruogutik).
Consultation place (*large*), kâp-kiruog (kâp-kiruoget), pl. kâp-kiruogut (kâp-kiruogutik).
(*small*), kokwa (kokwet), pl. kokwan (kokwanik).
(*warriors'*), kâp-tui (kâp-tuiet), pl. kâp-tuion (kâp-tuionik).
Consume, am (pr. a-om-e, p.p. kâ-am).
Consume by fire, pel (pr. a-pel-e, p.p. ka-a-pel).
Contempt:
Make a noise with one's mouth to show contempt, isony (pr. a-'sony-i, p.p. ka-a-'sony).
Continue (*stay at work, &c.*), peni (pr. a-peni-e, p.p. ka-a-peni).
(*remain*), tepi (pr. a-tepi-e, p.p. ka-a-tepi).
Contract (*lessen*), iñgir-te (pr. a-'ñgir-toi-i, p.p. ka-a-'ñgir-te).
(*press together*), kwilil (pr. a-kwilil-i, p.p. ka-a-kwilil).
Cook, kaoin (kaoindet), pl. kaoi (kaoik).
(v.), ioi (pr. a-'oi-i, p.p. ka-a-'oi).
kwany (pr. a-kwany-e, p.p. ka-a-kwany).
Cook for, io-chi (pr. a-'o-chi-ni, p.p. ka-a-'o-chi).
Cook with fat, isus (pr. a-'sus-i, p.p. ka-a-'sus).
Boil, ikut-u (pr. a-'kut-u, p.p. ka-a-'kut-u).
Cooking-pot, ter. (See **Pot.**)
Stones for resting a cooking-pot on, koiik-am-ma.

Cool (*persons*), iur (pr. a-'ur-e, p.p. ka-a-'ur).
(*things*), ema (pr. a-ema-i, p.p. ka-a-ema).
(adj.), urot, pl. urotin.
Copulate, kum (pr. a-kum-i, p.p. ka-a-kum).
Cord, porowa (porowet), pl. poroon (poroonik).
(*used for building purposes*), tingwa (tingwet).
Cord of skin, anua (anuet), pl. anoi (anōk).
Corn:
Eleusine, paiyua (paiyuat), pl. pai (päk).
Indian corn, ipandia (ipandiat), pl. ipande (ipandek).
Millet, mosongio (mosongiot), pl. mosong (mosongek).
Seed grain, kesua (kesuot), pl. kesui (kesuek).
Corn-stalk, mopcho (mopchot), pl. mop (mopek).
Corner, tapan (tapanda), pl. tapanua (tapanuek).
Corpse, musio (musiot), pl. musua (musuek).
Cough, tuñgwo (tuñgwot), pl. tuñgwa (tuñgwek).
(v.), lâl (pr. a-lâl-e, p.p. ka-a-lâl).
Counsellor, kiruogin. (See **Adviser.**)
Count, iīt (pr. a-'īt-i, p.p. ka-a-'īt).
L., rar (pr. a-ror-e, p.p. ka-a-rar).
One who counts, koiītin (koiītindet), pl. koiīt (koiītik).
Countenance, tokoch (toket), pl. tokōch (tokōchik).
Country, em (emet), pl. emotinua (emotinuek).
(*district*), kor (koret), pl. korotinua (korotinuek).
Cousin (*paternal*), tupchet, pl. akut-tupchet.
(*maternal*), weirit-ap-lakwet-ap-chepto; imamet.

Cover, tuch (pr. a-tuch-e, p.p. ka-a-tuch).
(*shut*), ker (pr. a-ker-e, p.p. ka-a-ker).
Lid, kereyuo (kereyuot), pl. kere (kereyuek).
Cow (*any animal that has borne*), iyuog (iyuoget), pl. iyuog (iyuogik).
Coward, simba (simbet), pl. simboi (simbōk).
Cowardly, niokor, pl. niokoren. *To be cowardly,* niokor-itu (pr. a-niokor, p.p. ka-a-niokor-itu).
Cowry, sekerio (sekeriot), pl. seker (sekerek).
Crab, kiploñgon (kiploñgonit), pl. kiploñgonin (kiploñgonīnik).
Crawl, kuikuiot (pr. a-kuikuiot-i, p.p. ka-a-kuikuiot).
Crease, aruny (pr. a-aruny-i, p.p. kâ-aruny).
Crease for, &c., aruñg-ji (pr. a-aruñg-ji-ni, p.p. kâ-aruñg-ji).
Be creased, aruñg-ake (pr. a-aruñg-at, p.p. kâ-aruñg-ake).
Creep, kuikuiot (pr. a-kuikuiot-i, p.p. ka-a-kuikuiot).
Creeping-thing, kuikui (kuikuiet), pl. kuikui (kuikuiik).
Cricket, keteria (keteriat), pl. keterēn (keterēnik).
Cripple (m.), kimuguñg (kimuguñgit), pl. kimuguñgin (kimuguñgīnik).
(f.), chemuguñg.
Crocodile, tiñgoñgo (tiñgoñget), pl. tiñgoñgōs (tiñgoñgōsiek).
Cross (*a river*), oi-iye (pr. o-oitos-i, p.p. kâ-oi-iye).
lan-de (pr. a-lon-doi-i, p.p. ka-a-lan-de).
(*a road*), i̯mrok (pr. a-i̯mrok-e, p.p. ka-a-i̯mrok).
Crowd, tuiyo (tuiyot), pl. tuiyōs (tuiyōsiek).
Crumble (*with two hands*), pur (pr. a-pur-e, p.p. ka-a-pur).

(*with one hand*), pirir (pr. a-pirir-i, p.p. ka-a-pirir).
Crush, nyinyir (pr. a-nyinyir-i, p.p. ka-a-nyinyir).
Cry, riro (riret), pl. rirōs (rirōsiek).
(v.), rir (pr. a-rir-e, p.p. ka-a-rir).
Cry out with pain, ite (pr. a-'te-i, p.p. ka-a-'te).
Cultivate, ipat (pr. a-'pot-i, p.p. ka-a-'pat).
Cultivation (*work of cultivating*), kapato (kapatet), pl. kapatōs (kapatōsiek).
(*field*), imbar (imbaret), pl. imbaren (imbarēnik).
Land out of cultivation, ur (uret).
Be out of cultivation, ur (pr. a-ur-e, p.p. ka-a-ur).
Cunning, ñgom, pl. ñgomen.
To be cunning, ñgom-itu (pr. a-ñgom, p.p. ka-a-ñgom-itu).
Cup (*men's*), saiga (saiget), pl. saigoi (saigōk).
(*women's*), mwendo (mwendet), pl. mwendōs (mwendōsiek).
(v.), kul (pr. a-kul-e, p.p. ka-a-kul).
Cup slightly, wat (pr. a-wat-e, p.p. ka-a-wat).
(*bleed*), kwer (pr. a-kwer-e, p.p. ka-a-kwer).
Cupper, kulin (kulindet), pl. kul (kulik).
Cupping-horn, lal (lalet), pl. laloi (lalōk).
Curdled milk, mursi (mursiik).
Cure, isap (pr. a-'sop-i, p.p. ka-a-'sap).
Be cured, sap (pr. a-sop-e, p.p. ka-a-sap).
Current (*of a stream*), sororua (sororuet).
Curse (*abuse*), chup (pr. a-chup-e, p.p. ka-a-chup).

Custom, piiton (piitondo), pl. piitonua (piitonuek).
Cut, til (pr. a-til-e, p.p. ka-a-til).
(*chop*), ep (pr. a-ep-e, p.p. ka-a-ep).
(*slash*), iep (pr. oi-'ep-e, p.p. ka-a-'ep).
Cut for, til-chi (pr. a-til-chi-ni, p.p. ka-a-til-chi).
Cut to shreds, tilatil (pr. a-tilatil-i, p.p. ka-a-tilatil).
Cut up meat, firewood, &c., murmur (pr. a-murmur-i, p.p. ka-a-murmur).
Cut off joints of meat, sach (pr. a-soch-e, p.p. ka-a-sach).
Cut the skin (preparatory to skinning), kerer (pr. a-kerer-i, p.p. ka-a-kerer).
Cut a piece off a skin or garment, rar (pr. a-ror-e, p.p. ka-a-rar).
Cut to a point, lit (pr. a-lit-e, p.p. ka-a-lit).
Cut corn-stalks, kes (pr. a-kes-e, p.p. ka-a-kes).
Cut slightly, wat (pr. a-wot-e, p.p. ka-a-wat).
Cut trees and undergrowth, tem (pr. a-tem-e, p.p. ka-a-tem).
Cut branches off a tree, sabor (pr. a-sabor-i, p.p. ka-a-sabor).

Daily, katukul; kwekeny.
Dam (*a river*), tokom (pr. a-tokom-i, p.p. ka-a-tokom).
Damage, ñgem (pr. a-ñgem-e, p.p. ka-a-ñgem).
Dance, tien (tiendo), pl. tienwag (tienwagik).
(v.), tien (pr. a-tien-i, p.p. ka-a-tien).
(*play*) ureren (pr. a-ureren-i, p.p. ka-a-ureren).
Circumcision dances (men's), cheptile (cheptilet), pl. cheptiles (cheptilesiek); aiyuo (aiyuet); suiye (suiyet).
(*women's*), kipsergoi (kipsergoiit), pl. kipsergoiin (kipsergoiīnik).
Old men's dance, sondoiyo (sondoiyet), pl. sondoiyōs (sondoiyōsiek).
Warriors' dance, kambak (kambakta), pl. kambakwag (kambakwagik).
Dandy (m.), kipleleya (kipleleyat), pl. kiplelein (kipleleīnik).
(f.), chepleleya.
Dare, kany (pr. a-kony-e, p.p. ka-a-kany).
Dare to ask for something, itañgany (pr. a-'toñgony-i, p.p. ka-a-'tañgany).
Dark, ap-tuindo.
Darkness, tuin (tuindo).
(*no moon*), mesundei (mesundeito).
Darling, chaman (chamanet), pl. chaman (chamanik).
Daub (*plaster huts*), mal (pr. a-mol-e, p.p. ka-a-mal).
(*oil*), iil (pr. a-'il-e, p.p. ka-a-'il).
Daub clay or paint on the body, sir (pr. a-sir-e, p.p. ka-a-sir).
Daughter, tie (chepto), pl. tīpin (tīpīk).
lakwa (lakwet), pl. lakoi (lakōk).
Dawn, korirun (korirunet).
Day, êkon (êkonet), pl. êkones or êkōs (êkonesiek or êkōsiek).
All day, pēt koimen.
Another day, pesiet ake.
One day, pētun-ak; pētut-akenge.
Daylight, pēt (pētut).
Dazzle, lil (pr. a-lil-e, p.p. ka-a-lil).
Dead person (*whose name must not be mentioned*), kimaita (kimaitet).
Dead body, musio (musiot), pl. musua (musuek).
Deaf (m.), kimiñgat, pl. kimiñgotin.

ENGLISH-NANDI VOCABULARY 251

Deaf:
(f.), chemiñgat, pl. chemiñgotin.
Dear, ui, pl. uen; kīm, pl. kīmen.
Death, myat (myat).
Be near death, rik-te (pr. a-rik-toi-i, p.p. ka-a-rik-te).
Debt, pesen (pesendo), pl. pesenua (pesenuek).
Decay, pul (pr. a-pul-e, p.p. ka-a-pul).
Decease, me. (See irregular verbs, pp. 224–5.)
Deceive, iperiper (pr. a-'periper-i, p.p. ka-a-'periper).
Decrease (act.), iñgir-te (pr. a-'ñgir-toi-i, p.p. ka-a-'ñgir-te).
(neut.), ñgeriñg-itu (pr. a-ñgeriñg, p.p. ka-a-ñgeriñg-itu).
Deep water, tolil (tolilet), pl. tolilon (tolilonik).
Defend, rīp (pr. a-rīp-e, p.p. ka-a-rīp).
Deformed person, salua (saluet), pl. salus (salusiek).
salomua (salomuet), pl. salomus (salomusiek).
Delay (act.), ikaa (pr. a-'koo-i, p.p. ka-a-'kaa).
(neut.), ikaa-ke (pr. a-'kaa-i-ke, p.p. ka-a-'kaa-ke).
Delicacy (*nice dish*), kariseyuo (kariseyuot), pl. karise (kariseyuek).
Give delicacies to a sick person, karis (pr. a-koris-i, p.p. ka-a-karis).
Demolish, iyei (pr. a-'yei-e, p.p. ka-a-'yei).
ñgem (pr. a-ñgem-i, p.p. ka-a-ñgem).
Den, kepen (kepenet), pl. kepenōs (kepenōsiek).
Deny, ios-ie (pr. a-'os-tos-i, p.p. ka-a-'os-ie).
(*argue*), tii-ye (pr. a-tii-tos-i, p.p. ka-a-tii-ye).

(*refuse*), esie (pr. a-esie-i, p.p. ka-a-esie).
Depart, ui. (See irregular verbs, pp. 220–1.)
(*go out*), man-de (pr. a-mon-doi-i, p.p. ka-a-man-de).
Depart from me, is-te-ke eñgdaitan-nyō.
Deride (*laugh at*), rore-chi (pr. a-rore-chi-ni, p.p. ka-a-rore-chi).
Descend (*hither*), chor-u-ke (pr. a-chor-u-ke, p.p. ka-a-chor-u-ke); rek-u.
(*thither*), chor-te-ke (pr. a-chor-toi-i-ke, p.p. ka-a-chor-te-ke); rek-te.
Desert, pakak-te. (See **Forsake**.)
met-te. (See **Throw away**.)
Desert, kewo (kewet), pl. kewōs (kewōsiek).
Desire, mach (pr. a-moch-e, p.p. ka-a-mach).
cham (pr. a-chom-e, p.p. ka-a-cham).
Despise, mon-de (pr. a-mon-doi-i, p.p. ka-a-mon-de).
Destroy, ñgem (pr. a-ñgem-i, p.p. ka-a-ñgem).
(*break*), iyei (pr. a-'yei-e, p.p. ka-a-'yei).
Detain (*a person*), ikaa (pr. a-'koo-i, p.p. ka-a-'kaa).
(*a thing*), tep-te (pr. a-tep-toi-i, p.p. ka-a-tep-te).
Deter, ete (pr. a-ete, p.p. ka-a-ete).
Devil, musambwania (musambwaniat), pl. musambwan (musambwanik).
(*spirit of deceased*), oiin (oiindet), pl. oi (oiik).
One-legged devil, chemos (chemosit).
Devise, ai-te (pr. o-oi-toi-i, p.p. kâ-ai-te).
Dew, rewo (rewot).
Dewlap (*oxen*), takol (takolet), pl. takoles (takolesiek).

252 ENGLISH-NANDI VOCABULARY

Dewlap:
(*sheep* or *goats*), lakop (lakopet), pl. lakopōs (lakopōsiek).
Dialect, ñgal (ñgalek).
have Diarrhoea, kaiyuai (pr. a-koiyuoi-i, p.p. ka-a-kaiyuai). *Person* or *animal that has diarrhoea*, kipor (kiporto).
Die, me. (See irregular verbs, pp. 224–5.)
(*of an old man*), ilil (pr. a-'lil-i, p.p. ka-a-'lil).
Different, ake, pl. alak.
Difficult, ui, pl. uen.
Dig, pal (a-pol-e, p.p. ka-a-pal).
(*cultivate*), ipat (pr. a-'pot-i, p.p. ka-a-'pat).
Dig out, pal-u (pr. a-pal-u, p.p. ka-a-pal-u).
Dig easily (e.g. *in light soil*), pumbun (pr. a-pumbun-i, p.p. ka-a-pumbun).
Digging-stick (*large*), kipturur (kiptururit), pl. kiptururin (kiptururīnik).
(*small*), maīyo (maīyat), pl. maen (maēnik).
maipun (maipunit), pl. maipunin (maipunīnik).
Diminish (act.), iñgir-te (pr. a-'ñgir-toi-i, p.p. ka-a-'ñgir-te).
(neut.), ñgeriñg-itu (pr. a-ñgeriñg, p.p. ka-a-ñgeriñg-itu).
Dip, iroch (pr. a-'roch-i, p.p. ka-a-'roch).
Dip thither, irok-te (pr. a-'rok-toi-i, p.p. ka-a-'rok-te).
Dirt, sim (simdo), pl. simwag (simwagik).
Disagree (*make a noise*), pol (pr. a-pol-e, p.p. ka-a-pol).
(*argue*), tii-ye (pr. a-tii-tos-i, p.p. ka-a-tii-ye).
Disappear, ui. (See **Go.**)
(*of the moon*), ilingan (pr. a-'lingon-i, p.p. ka-a-'lingan).
Discuss, tii-ye (pr. a-tii-tos-i, p.p. ka-a-tii-ye).

Disease, mion. (See **Illness.**)
Disembowel, undur (pr. a-undur-i, p.p. ka-a-undur).
Dish, tapo (tapet), pl. tapoi (tapōk).
Dish up (*hither*), pal-u (pr. a-pol-u, p.p. ka-a-pal-u).
(*thither*), pal-de (pr. a-pol-doi-i, p.p. ka-a-pal-de).
Dislike, sos (pr. a-sos-e, p.p. ka-a-sos).
reny (pr. a-reny-e, p.p. ka-a-reny).
Distribute, chwe (pr. a-chwe, p.p. ka-a-chwe).
District, poror (pororiet), pl. pororōs (pororōsiek).
Ditch, kering (keringet), pl. keringon (keringonik).
Dive, ilis (pr. a-'lis-i, p.p. ka-a-'lis).
Divide, ịpche (pr. a-ịpche, p.p. ka-a-ịpche).
chwe (pr. a-chwe, p.p. ka-a-chwe).
Divine, ñgor (pr. a-ñgor-e, p.p. ka-a-ñgor).
Do, ai (pr. o-oi-e, p.p. kâ-ai).
Do again, nyil (pr. a-nyil-e, p.p. ka-a-nyil).
Don't do it again! ias!
How shall I do it? o-lio-chi ni?
I have done nothing, ma-ai-e kii.
It is done (*cooked*), ka-ko-rur; ka-ki-'o.
It is done (*finished*), ka-rok; ka-ka-rok.
What shall I do? o-oi-e ni?
Doctor, kipkericho (kipkerichot), pl. kipkerichin (kipkerichīnik).
Dog, sese (seset), pl. sesen (sesēnik).
Wild dog, suio (suiot), pl. sui (suik).
Donkey, sigirio (sigiriet), pl. sigiroi (sigirōk).
Door, kurkat (kurket), pl. kurkot (kurkotik).

ENGLISH-NANDI VOCABULARY

Door:
Door of cattle-fold, ormarīch (ormarīchet), pl. ormarīchoi (ormarīchōk).
Door of calves' house, soimo (soimōut), pl. soimōus (soimōusiek).
Front door of a house, kurketap-serem.
Back door of a house, kurketap-injor.
Door opening into back part of house, ñgotie (ñgotiēut), pl. ñgotiēus (ñgotiēusiek).
Door plank, musere (musereta), pl. musereua (musereuek).
Door-post, tukatuk (tukatukchet), pl. tukatuk (tukatukik).
Door-post of cattle-fold, ikēnio (ikēniot), pl. ikēn (ikēnik).
Wickerwork door, irpa (irpet), pl. irpoi (irpōk).
Gate of field, kisirua (kisiruet), pl. kisiron (kisironik).
Doze, pir-te met.
Drag, Draw, ichut (pr. a-'chut-i, p.p. ka-a-'chut).
Draw out (e.g. *string, entrails*), nīrnīr (pr. a-nīrnīr-i, p.p. ka-a-nīrnīr).
Draw water, sil pêk; ram pêk.
Dread, iyue (pr. a-'yue-i, p.p. ka-a-'yue).
Dream, iruoti-te (pr. a-'ruoti-toi-i, p.p. ka-a-'ruoti-te).
Dress, ingor (ingoriet), pl. ingorai (ingoraiik).
(v.), ilach (pr. a-'loch-i, p.p. ka-a-'lach).
Drink, ie (pr. oi-'e, p.p. ka-a-'e).
Drink milk, lu (pr. a-lu-e, p.p. ka-a-lu).
Give to drink, inak-e (pr. a-'nok-i, p.p. ka-a-'nak-e).
Drink greedily, ikuikuch (pr. a-'kuikuch-i, p.p. ka-a-'kuikuch).
Drinking-place for cattle, tapar (taparta), pl. taparuag (taparuagik).
Drip (*hither*), sa-u (pr. a-sa-u, p.p. ka-a-sa-u).
(*thither*), sa-te (pr. a-sa-toi-i, p.p. ka-a-sa-te).
Let drip, isa-u; isa-te.
Drive (*as a shepherd*), iak-e (pr. a-'ok-i, p.p. kâ-'ak-e).
Drive cattle or goats home, irot (pr. a-'rot-i, p.p. ka-a-'rot).
Drive cattle or goats home and separate the herds, kwe (pr. a-kwe, p.p. ka-a-kwe).
Drive away, oon (pr. a-oon-e, p.p. ka-a-oon).
(*of several things*), iuriet (pr. a-'uriet-i, p.p. ka-a-'uriet).
Push away, och (pr. a-och-e, p.p. ka-a-och).
Drop, soiitoi-pêk (*water*); soiitoicheko (*milk*); &c.
(v. act.), wir-te (pr. a-wir-toi-i, p.p. ka-a-wir-te).
(*throw*), met-te (pr. a-met-toi-i, p.p. ka-a-met-te).
(v. neut.), iput (pr. a-'put-i, p.p. ka-a-'put).
(*fall in drops*), sa-u (pr. a-sa-u, p.p. ka-a-sa-u).
Drown, me em-pêk; me-chi pêk.
(*sink*), lis (pr. a-lis-i, p.p. ka-a-lis).
Drum, sukut (sukutit), pl. sukutin (sukutīnik).
Friction drum, keto (see **Barrel**); ñgetūny (see **Lion**); cheplanga (see **Leopard**).
be **Drunk,** pôkit (pr. a-pôkit-i, p.p. ka-a-pôkit).
Drunkard, kipôkitio (kipôkitiot), pl. kipôkitin (kipôkitīnik).
Drunkard or a drunken crowd, kimaiyo (kimaiyot), pl. kimaiin (kimaiīnik).
Dry (neut.), yâm (pr. a-yom-e, p.p. ka-a-yâm).

254   ENGLISH-NANDI VOCABULARY

Dry:
(act.), iyâm (pr. a-'yom-i, p.p. ka-a-'yâm).
Put out to dry, ma (pr. a-mo-e, p.p. ka-a-ma).
Become dry or *hard (of fat)*, kor (pr. a-kor-e, p.p. ka-a-kor).
Dry, yâmat, pl. yâmotin.
Dry thing, kiptâm (kiptâmit).
Drying-place for grain, saina (sainet), pl. sainoi (sainōk).
Dumb (m.), kimotuek, pl. kimotuekin.
(f.), chemotuek.
Dung (*cattle*), ñgatatia (ñgatatiat), pl. ñgotot (ñgototek).
(*goats* or *sheep*), soroiyo (soroiyot), pl. soroi (soroiek).
Dunghill, kâp-ñgotot (kâp-ñgototek).
Dust, terit (tertit).
temburio (temburiot), pl. tembur (temburiek).
Dwarf, chiito ne-mining.
Dwell, tepi (pr. a-tepi-e, p.p. ka-a-tepi).
Dwelling-place, atep (atepet), pl. atepōs (atepōsiek).

Each, tukul.
Ear, iit (iitīt), pl. iitin (iitīk).
Ear-ring. (See **Ring.**)
Grass inserted in top part of ear, solio (soliot), pl. sol (solik).
Ear of corn, iitīt-ap-päk *or* iitīt-am-mosongek, &c.
Early, korirun.
Earth, em (emet), pl. emotinua (emotinuek).
(*world, universe*), kia (kiet), pl. kias (kiasiek).
(*sand*), ñguñgunya (ñguñgunyat), pl. ñguñguny (ñguñgunyek).
Ease oneself, pi (pr. a-pi-e, p.p. ka-a-pi).
Easy, wesis, pl. wisisin.
To do easily or *quickly,* chokchi.

Eat, am (pr. a-om-e, p.p. kâ-am).
Eat with someone, am-de (pr. a-om-doi-i, p.p. kâ-am-de).
Be eaten or *eatable,* am-ake.
Have eaten enough, piiy-e (pr. a-piiy-onyi, p.p. ka-a-piiy-e).
Overeat oneself, uiren (pr. a-uiren-i, p.p. ka-a-uiren).
Educate, inêt (pr. a-'nêt-i, p.p. ka-a-'nêt).
Egg, koii. (See **Stone.**)
make an Effort, inêt-ke kut.
Eight, sisiit.
Eighteen, taman ok sisiit.
Eighth, ap-sisiit.
Eighty, tomonuagik sisiit.
Either . . . or, annan.
Elbow, kutuñg (kutunda), pl. kutuñgwa (kutuñgwek).
kutunda-ap-ēut.
Elder (*old man*), poiyo (poiyot), pl. poiisio (poiisiek).
Elder *or* **Eldest,** oo, pl. echen.
Elephant, pēlio (pēliot), pl. pēl (pēlek).
Eleusine grain, paiyua (paiyuat), pl. pai (päk).
(*stalks of*), mopcho (mopchot), pl. mop (mopek).
Eleven, taman ak akenge.
Elsewhere, olt' ake.
Embrace, toroch (pr. a-toroch-i, p.p. ka-a-toroch).
Employment, poiisio (poiisiet), pl. poiision (poiisionik).
Empty (adj.), puch, pl. puch.
(v.), tar-te (pr. a-tor-toi-i, p.p. ka-a-tar-te).
(*spill*), tum-de (pr. a-tum-doi-i, p.p. ka-a-tum-de).
Pour from one receptacle into another, rañg-de (pr. a-roñg-doi-i, p.p. ka-a-rañg-de).
Enclosure, ñgotua (ñgotuet), pl. ñgotonoi (ñgotonōk).
toi (tōōt), pl. tōōs (tōōsiek).
(*for cattle*), sipaiya (sipaiyat), pl. sipaien (sipaiēnik).

ENGLISH-NANDI VOCABULARY 255

End (*the after part*), let (letut), pl. letus (letusiek).
End of a journey, letut-ap-panda.
It is finished, ka-ko-pek ; ka-ko-wonge.
Enemy, punyo (punyot), pl. pun (punik).
Enigma, tangoch (tangochet), pl. tongōch (tongōchik).
Enjoy, ikas-ke (pr. a-'kos-i-ke, p.p. ka-a-'kas-ke).
Enlarge, iet (oi-'et-i, p.p. ka-a-'et).
(*increase*), tes (pr. a-tes-e, p.p. ka-a-tes).
be Enough, yam (pr. a-yam-e, p.p. ka-a-yam).
Have enough food, piiy-e (pr. a-piiy-onyi, p.p. ka-a-piiy-e).
Enquire, tepe (pr. a-tepe, p.p. ka-a-tepe).
Ensnare, tech (pr. a-tech-e, p.p. ka-a-tech).
Enter (*hither*), mañg-u (pr. a-moñg-u, p.p. ka-a-mañg-u).
(*thither*), man-de (pr. a-mon-doi-i, p.p. ka-a-man-de).
Enter a hole, chut (pr. a-chut-e, p p. ka-a-chut).
Enter without leaving a trace behind, ikes-chi-ke (pr. a-'kes-chi-ni-ke, p.p. ka-a-'kes-chi-ke).
Entirely, mīsing ; kwe-keny.
Entrail, akutan (akutaniet), pl. akutan (akutanik).
kipsegetet (kipsegetetit), pl. kipsegetetoi (kipsegetetōk).
Entreat, som (pr. a-som-e, p.p. ka-a-som).
Equal (*in standing* or *in age*), ap-ipinda akenge.
be Equal to, ioiechin-e (pr. a-'oie-chin-dos-i, p.p. kâ-'oiechin-e).
Be equal to an undertaking, &c., imuch (pr. a-'much-i, p.p. ka-a-'much).
Be a match for, ikany (pr. a-'kony-e, p.p. ka-a-'kany).

Ergot (*horny spur of an ox*), segeiyo (segeiyot), pl. segei (segeik).
Err (*make a mistake*), lēl (pr. a-lēl-e, p.p. ka-a-lēl).
(*miss*), ichilil (pr. a-'chilil-i, p.p. ka-a-'chilil).
Error, kachililo (kachililet).
Escape, chilil (pr. a-chilil-e, p.p. ka-a-chilil).
(*run away*), lapat (pr. a-lopot-i, p.p. ka-a-lapat).
(*of many people*), o-rua (pr. kirua-i, p.p. ka-ki-rua).
Escort (*accompany*), iomis (pr. a-'omis-i, p.p. ka-a-'omis).
European, Asungio (Asungiot), pl. Asungu (Asunguk).
(*woman*), chemñgiñginzue ('cut at the waist').
Even, akut.
Even I, akut ane.
Evening, koskoling (koskolingut) ; imen (imenet) ; koimen.
Ever, kwe-keny.
For ever, akut keny.
Every, tukul.
Every man, chii tukul.
Everywhere, olto tukul ; ola tukul ; oii tukul.
Every time I go, or *whenever I go,* oii tukul ya-a-wendi.
Evil, ya, pl. yaach.
Evil eye, sakutin (sakutindet), pl. sakut (sakutik).
Exceed, sir-te. (See **Pass by.**)
Except, nem-u (pr. a-nem-u, p.p. ka-a-nem-u).
Exchange, wal (pr. a-wol-e, p.p. ka-a-wal).
Excrement (*human*), pie (piek).
Expect, iken (pr. a-'ken-i, p.p. ka-a-'ken).
Expel, oon (pr. a-oon-e, p.p. ka-a-oon).
Explain, mwo-chi (pr. a-mwo-chi-ni, p.p. ka-a-mwo-chi).

Explode, pêt-ak-e (pr. a-pêt-at, p.p. ka-a-pêt-ak-e).
Explode in the fire with a great noise, tiol (pr. a-tiol-i, p.p. ka-a-tiol).
Extinguish (*the fire*), par (mat); pakách (mat).
Pour water on the fire, tis (pr. a-tis-e, p.p. ka-a-tis).
To go out, me. (See irregular verbs, pp. 224–5.)
Eye, koñg (konda), pl. konyan (konyek).
Loss of an eye or *one-eyed* (m.), kipkoñgak; (f.), chepkoñgak.
Put something (e.g. *a finger*) *in the eye,* chul (pr. a-chul-e, p.p. ka-a-chul).
Eyebrow or **eyelash,** kororik-ap-konda.

Fable, kâpchemosin (kâpchemos-īnik).
Face, tokoch (toket), pl. tokōch (tokōchik).
Faint, tanui (pr. a-tonui, p.p. ka-a-tanui).
Fall, kaputo (kaputet).
(v.), iput (pr. a-'put-i, p.p. ka-a-'put).
Fall down with something, ipu-ite (pr. a-'put-itoi-i, p.p. ka-a-'put-ite).
Fall into, on to, &c., iput-yi (pr. a-'put-yi-ni, p.p. ka-a-'put-yi).
Make to fall, throw down, wir-te (pr. a-wir-toi-i, p.p. ka-a-wir-te).
Fall from a tree or *into a hole,* rorok-chi (pr. a-rorok-chi-ni, p.p. ka-a-rorok-chi).
Fall like rain, robon (pr. a-robon-i, p.p. ka-a-robon).
Tree falling by itself, lul (pr. a-lul-e, p.p. ka-a-lul).
To fell trees, ilul (pr. a-'lul-i, p.p. ka-a-'lul).

Fall sick, mian (pr. a-mion-i, p.p. ka-a-mian).
Falsehood, lembech (lembechet), pl. lembech (lembechek).
Family, or. (See **Road.**)
Husband's family, kâp-katun.
Wife's family, kâp-yukoi.
Famine, rub (rubet), pl. rubōs (rubōsiek).
Fan, kipkaliañg(kipkaliañgit), pl. kipkaliañgis (kipkaliañgisiek).
us (uset), pl. uso (usōsiek).
(v.), us (pr. a-us-e, p.p. ka-a-us).
Far or **far off,** loo.
Fast, mīban, pl. mīban.
Fasten, rat (pr. a-rot-e, p.p. ka-a-rat).
Fasten feathers on to an arrow, tar (pr. a-tar-e, p.p. ka-a-tar).
Fat, mwai (mwaita), pl. mwan (mwanik).
Fat used and thrown away, ma-mitia (mamitiat).
Fat person, nero (neret), pl. nerōs (nerōsiek).
(adj.), nyikis, pl. nyikisen; ne-rat, pl. nerotin.
To be fat, akwai-itu (pr. a-akwai, p.p. kâ-akwai-itu).
ner (pr. a-ner-i, p.p. ka-a-ner).
Fatten, iner (pr. a-'ner-e, p.p. ka-a-'ner).
Get fat, nerak-e (pr. a-ner-at, p.p. ka-a-ner-ak-e).
Father, kwan (kwanda), pl. akut-kwan (akut-kwanda *or* akut-kwanuak).
Own father (*child talking*), papa, pl. akut-papa.
(*man talking*), apoiyo, pl. akut-apoiyo.
(*woman talking*), pakwa, pl. angut-pakwa.
Thy father, kōn (kōnut), pl. akut-kōn (akut-kōnut *or* akut-kōnu-ak).
So-and-so's father, kwamba anum.

ENGLISH-NANDI VOCABULARY

Father-in-law(*man's*), kâp-yukoi (kâp-yukoiit).
(*woman's*), pamoñgo (pamoñget).
Own father-in-law (*man talking*), apoiyo.
(*woman talking*), pamoñgo.
be Fatigued, ñget (pr. a-ñget-e, p.p. ka-a-ñget).
Fault, kachililo (kachililet), pl. kachililōs (kachililōsiek).
Favourite, chaman (chamanet), pl. chaman (chamanik).
Fear, nyokorio (nyokoriet).
(v.), iyue (pr. a-'yue-i, p.p. ka-a-'yue).
Feast day, kambak. (See **Warriors' Dance.**)
Feather, kororia (kororiet), pl. yuot), koror (kororik).
Feather of arrow, tareyuo (tareyuot, pl. tare (tareyuek).
Ostrich feather, songolia (songoliet), pl. songol (songolik).
(v.), tar (pr. a-tar-e, p.p. ka-a-tar).
Be feathered, tar-ak-e (pr. a-tar-at, p.p. ka-a-tar-ak-e).
Feeble person, choriren (chorirenet), pl. choriren (chorirēnik).
Be feeble, nyelnyel-itu (pr. a-nyelnyel, p.p. ka-a-nyelnyel-itu).
Feed cattle (act.), iak-e (pr. a-'ok-i, p.p. kâ-'ak-e).
(neut.), ak-et-e (pr. a-ak-et-i, p.p. kâ-ak-et-e).
Feed a child, pai (pr. a-poi-e, p.p. ka-a-pai).
Feeder, koiokin. (See **Herdsman.**)
Feel, kas (pr. a-kos-e, p.p. ka-a-kas).
Feel one's way (e.g. *in the dark*), sapsap (pr. a-sopsop-i, p.p. ka-a-sapsap).
Fell (*trees*), ilul (pr. a-'lul-i, p.p. ka-a-'lul).
Female (*human beings*), korko (korket), pl. korusio (korusiek).
(*animals*), kôko (kôket), pl. kôkon (kôkōnik).
One that has borne, iyuog (iyuoget), pl. iyuog (iyuogik).
One that bears frequently, misekutio (misekutiot), pl. misekut (misekutik).
One that bears rarely, oïlio (oïliot), pl. oïl (oïlik).
One that does not bear, son. (See **Barren.**)
Immature female, suben (subendo), pl. subenwa (subenwek).
(adj.), chepaike, pl. chepaikein.
Fence, ñgotua. (See **Enclosure.**)
Fence in, ñgot (pr. a-ñgot-e, p.p. ka-a-ñgot).
Ferry, tapar (taparta), pl. taparuag (taparuagik).
Ferry over (neut.), oi-iye (pr. o-oi-tos-i, p.p. kâ-oi-iye).
(*hither*), lañg-u (pr. a-lañg-u, p.p. ka-a-lañg-u).
(*thither*), lan-de (pr. a-lon-doi-i, p.p. ka-a-lan-de).
(act.), ilañg-u; ilan-de.
Fetch, ip-u (pr. a-ip-u, p.p. kâ-ip-u).
Few, che-ñgeriñg.
Field, imbar (imbaret), pl. imbaren (imbarēnik).
Field in which nothing has been sown, kapatut (kapatut), pl. kapatut (kapatutik).
Field that has been harvested, ror (roret), pl. rorotinua (rorotinuek).
Fierce, korom, pl. koromen.
Fifteen, taman ak mut.
Fifth, ap-mut.
Fifty, onom.
Fight, porio (poriet), pl. poriōs (poriōsiek).
(v.), o-pir-ke (pr. ki-pir-i-ke, p.p. ka-ki-pir-ke).

Fight:
Fight with someone, por-ie (pr. a-por-tos-i, p.p. ka-a-por-ie).
Cause to fight with some one, iul-ie (pr. a-'ul-dos-i, p.p. ka-a-'ul-ie).
Fill, inyīt (pr. a-'nyīt-i, p.p. ka-a-'nyīt).
(*become full*), nyi (pr. a-nyi-e, p.p. ka-a-nyi).
(*abound with*), nyītat (pr. a-nyītat, p.p. ka-a-nyītat).
Fill in (a hole), tīm (pr. a-tīm-e, p.p. ka-a-tīm).
Fill with food, ipiiy-e (pr. a-'piiy-onye, p.p. ka-a-'piiy-e).
To be full, to have had enough to eat, piiy-e (pr. a-piiy-onyi, p.p. ka-a-piiy-e).
Filth, sim (simdo), pl. simuag (simuagik).
be Filthy, tinye simdo.
Find, iro. (See irregular verbs, p. 224.)
sich (pr. a-sich-e, p.p. ka-a-sich).
nyor-u (pr. a-nyor-u, p.p. ka-a-nyor-u).
Find out a crime, kin (pr. a-kin-e, p.p. ka-a-kin).
Person who finds out a crime, kinen (kinendet), pl. kin (kinik).
Fine, kararan. (See **Beautiful.**)
Fine for a murder, tuk'-am-met.
He has paid a fine for a murder, ka-ko-pas tuk'-am-met.
Finger, morna (mornet), pl. morin (morīk).
Thumb, mornet ne-oo.
Middle finger, mornet-ap-kwen.
Little finger, chepkildo (chepkildet).
Finish (act.), poroch (pr. a-poroch-i, p.p. ka-a-poroch).
tar (pr. a-tar-e, p.p. ka-a-tar).

kes-u (pr. a-kes-u, p.p. ka-a-kes-u).
iwoñg-u (pr. a-'woñg-u, p.p. ka-a-'woñg-u).
(neut.), rok (pr. a-rok-e, p.p. ka-a-rok).
pek-u (pr. a-pek-u, p.p. ka-a-pek-u).
pit-u (pr. a-pit-u, p.p. ka-a-pit-u).
Fire, ma (mat), pl. mostinua (mostinuek).
Firewood, kwendo (kwendet), pl. kwen (kwenik).
Twigs for firewood, sikorio (sikoriot), pl. sikor (sikorik).
Stones on which to set a pot over the fire, koiik-am-ma.
Bonfire, sacred fire, korosio (korosiot), pl. koros (korosek).
Place where bonfire is made, kâp-koros.
Set on fire, in-de mat; ilal.
Make fire by the use of fire-sticks, parpar mat.
Apply fire to, pel (pr. a-pel-e, p.p. ka-a-pel).
Fire a gun, mwog mat (pr. a-mwog-e mat, p.p. ka-a-mwog mat).
Fire-stick, piōn (piōnet), pl. piōn (piōnik).
First, tae; ko-rok; nepo-met; ne-indoï.
First of all, isi.
I shall go first of all, isi a-wend-i.
To go first, indoï (pr. a-'ndoï-i, p.p. ka-a-'ndoï).
Fish, injirio (injiriot), pl. injiren (injirēnik).
Fist, lukut (lukutiet), pl. lukut (lukutik).
Five, mut.
Fix, kwilil (pr. a-kwilil-i, p.p. ka-a-kwilil).
Fix the eyes upon, ichil-chi konda.
Flay, eny (pr. a-eny-e, p.p. ka-a-eny).

ENGLISH-NANDI VOCABULARY 259

Flea, kimitia (kimitiat), pl. kimit (kimitek).
Flee, lapat (pr. a-lopot-i, p.p. ka-a-lapat).
Flesh, peny (pendo), pl. pany (panyek).
Fling, met-te (pr. a-met-toi-i, p.p. ka-a-met-te).
Fling hither, met-u (pr. a-met-u, p.p. ka-a-met-u).
Flog, pir (pr. a-pir-e, p.p. ka-a-pir).
Floor, ingoiny (ingoinyut), pl. ingoinyus (ingoinyusiek).
Flour, pusio (pusiek).
Sand or earth resembling flour, lump of flour mixed with water, pusia (pusiat).
Flow (*of water*), root (pr. a-root-e, p.p. ka-a-root).
Flower, tapta (taptet), pl. taptoi (taptōk).
Fluently, mīsing.
Fly, kaliañg (kaliañget), pl. kaliañg (kaliañgik).
Gad-fly, sokorio (sokoriet), pl. sokor (sokorik).
Midge, kipcharkarario (kipcharkarariet), pl. kipcharkarar (kipcharkararik).
(v.), toriren (pr. a-toriren-i, p.p. ka-a-toriren).
Fly away, sakuren (pr. a-sakuren-i, p.p. ka-a-sakuren).
Foam, puka (pukat).
Fog, kipurienge (kipurienget).
Fold, arungut (arungutiet), pl. arungut (arungutik).
Cattle-fold, pe (pēut), pl. pēus (pēusiek).
(v.), aruny (pr. a-aruny-i, p.p. kâ-aruny).
Foliage, soko (sokot), pl. sok (sokek).
Follow, isup (pr. a-'sup-i, p.p. ka-a-'sup).
Follower, kasupin (kasupindet), pl. kasup (kasupik).

Food, omit (omdit), pl. omituag (omituagik).
Fool, aposan (aposanet), pl. aposan (aposanik).
You are a fool, pet-in met or mi-tinye met.
Foot, kel (keldo), pl. kelien (keliek).
Pad, mukung (mukunget), pl. mukungon (mukungonik).
Sole of the foot, kel-tepes (kel-tepesiet), pl. kel-tepesoi (kel-tepesōk).
Arch of the foot, mukuleld'-ap-keldo.
Heel, muk'-ap-ker.
Footprint, marandu (marandut), pl. marandus (marandusiek).
kereng (kerenget), pl. kereng-on (kerengonik).
kel (keldo), pl. kelien (keliek).
For (conj.), amu ne ; amu kalia.
(prep.), eñg. *For* is generally expressed by the use of the applied form of the verb.
(*in the place of*), olt'-ap.
Forbid, ete (pr. a-ete, p.p. ka-a-ete).
Force, kôwo. (See **Bone.**)
Ford, tapar (taparta), pl. taparuag (taparuagik).
Foreigner, too (toot *or* toondet), pl. toi (toiek).
Forest, tim (timdo), pl. timua (timuek).
Forge, kâp-kitany (kâp-kitanyit).
Forge iron, itany (pr. a-'tony-i, p.p. ka-a-'tany).
Forget, utie (pr. a-utie, p.p. ka-a-utie).
Don't forget, me-utie.
Fork (*agricultural implement*), kipkarich (kipkarichet), pl. kipkarichai (kipkarichaiik).
Former, ap-ole-kinye ; ap-ko-rok ; ap-keny.
Formerly, kinye ; ole-kinye ; keny.

s 2

Forsake, pakak-te (pr. a-pokok-toi-i, p.p. ka-a-pakak-te).
L., pakâch (pr. a-pokoch-i, p.p. ka-a-pakâch).
Fort, irim (irimet), pl. irimon (irimonik).
(*cave*), kering (keringet), pl. keringon (keringonik).
Forth, saañg.
To go forth, man-de (pr. a-mondoi-i, p.p. ka-a-man-de).
Forty, artam.
Forward, tae.
To go forward, ui tae.
Four, añgwan.
Fourteen, taman ak añgwan.
Fourth, ap-añgwan.
Free, itiach. (See **Loose.**)
Free man, chii-ap-ka; chii-paka.
Frequently, êkōsiek che-chañg.
Fresh, tuon, pl. tuonen.
Fresh water, pêk che-koitit.
Friend, chorua (choruet), pl. choronai (choronōk).
Friend! (salutation), Poiyondónni! (*old man*); Murenón-ni! (*warrior*); Weír-i! (*boy*).
Be on friendly terms with, kalian (pr. a-kolion-i, p.p. ka-a-kalian).
Frighten, iyue-chi (pr. a-'yue-chi-ni, p.p. ka-a-'yue-chi).
Frog, mororoch (mororochet), pl. mororoch (mororochik).
From. *From* is generally expressed by the use of the forms denoting motion from, or by the preposition *eñg.*
Since, akut keny.
From now on, akoi tun.
From here to there, nette yu ok yun.
Front, tae (taeta), pl. toiua (toiuek).
Froth, pukaa (pukaandet); puka (pukat).
Frown, siriny toket.

Fruit, *different kinds of :—*
Vangueria edulis, kimolua (kimoluet), pl. kimolon (kimolonik).
Ximenia Americana, lamaiya (lamaiyat), pl. lamai (lamaiek).
Ficus sp., mokoiyo (mokoiyot), pl. mokoi (mokoiek).
Fry, isus (pr. a-'sus-i, p.p. ka-a-'sus).
Fugitive, lapatin (lapatindet), pl. lapot (lapotik).
Fun, urerio (ureriet).
Further, ko-keny.
Further on, tae.

Gait, pan (panda), pl. ponua (ponuek).
Gallop, lapat (pr. a-lopot-i, p.p. ka-a-lapat).
Game, urerio (ureriet).
Gape, tangurur (pr. a-tangurur-i, p.p. ka-a-tangurur).
Garment (*of skin*), ingor (ingoriet), pl. ingorai (ingoraiik).
(*of cloth*), anga (anget), pl. angas (angasiek).
(*worn by old men, made of hyrax, antelope or monkey skin*), sambu (sambut), pl. sambun (sambunik).
(*made of goat-skin*), sumat (sumet), pl. sumot (sumotik).
(*worn by warriors, to cover the shoulders*), kipoia (kipoiet), pl. kipooi (kipoōk).
(*apron worn by warriors*), koroiisi (koroiisit), pl. koroiisin (koroiisinik).
L., ñgoiisi (ñgoiisit), pl. ñgoiisin (ñgoiisinik).
(*worn by women, to cover the upper limbs*), koliko (koliket), kolikai (kolikaiik).
(*to cover the lower limbs*), chepkawi (chepkawit), pl. chepkawis (chepkawisiek).
(*worn by girls to cover the shoulders*), ingoriet-ap-ko.

ENGLISH-NANDI VOCABULARY 261

Garment: (*apron worn by girls*), osio (osiek). (*women's wedding garment*), kiskis (kiskisto), pl. kiskisua (kiskisuek).
Gate, kisirua. (See **Door**.)
Gather, put (pr. a-put-e, p.p. ka-a-put). kes (pr. a-kes-i, p.p. ka-a-kes).
Gather together (act.), ium (pr. a-'um-i, p.p. ka-a-'um). (neut.), ium-ke (pr. a-'um-i-ke, p.p. ka-a-'um-ke).
Generation, ipin. (See **Age**.)
Gentle, wesis, pl. wisisin.
Gently, mutio.
Geographical division, poror (pororiet), pl. pororōs (pororōsiek).
Get, sich (pr. a-sich-e, p.p. ka-a-sich).
Get better, get well, sap (pr. a-sop-e, p.p. ka-a-sap).
Get drunk, pôkit (pr. a-pôkit-i, p.p. ka-a-pôkit).
Get dry, yâm (pr. a-yom-e, p.p. ka-a-yâm).
Get for, sik-chi (pr. a-sik-chi-ni, p.p. ka-a-sik-chi).
Get goods on credit, pesen (pr. a-pesen-i, p.p. ka-a-pesen).
Get into, chut (pr. a-chut-e, p.p. ka-a-chut).
Get out, man-de (pr. a-mon-doi-i, p.p. ka-a-man-de).
Get out of the way, is-te-ke (pr. a-is-toi-i-ke, p.p. kâ-is-te-ke).
Get palm-wine, par porokek.
Get ripe, rur (pr. a-rur-e, p.p. ka-a-rur).
Get up (rise), ñgêt (pr. a-ñgêt-e, p.p. ka-a-ñgêt).
Get up or upon, lany (pr. a-lony-i, p.p. ka-a-lany).
Ghost, oiin (oiindet), pl. oi (oiik). (*shadow of people*), tomirimir (tomirimiriet), pl. tomirimirai (tomirimiraiik). (*shadow of things*), urua (uruet), pl. uruondoi (uruondōk).
be Giddy, u met.
I am giddy, ka-u-a met.
Person made giddy by turning round, cheptombirir (cheptombiririet), pl. cheptombiriroi (cheptombirirŭk).
Gift, melek (melekto), pl. melekua (melekuek).
Giraffe, ingotio (ingotiot), pl. ingotin (ingotīnik).
Girl, tie (chepto), pl. tīpin (tīpīk). cheplemia (cheplemiat), pl. cheplemin (cheplemīnik). melia (meliat), pl. mel (melik). (*uncircumcised*), somnyo (somnyot), pl. some (somek).
Give, nem-u (pr. a-nem-u, p.p. ka-a-nem-u).
Give to, ikochi. (See irregular verbs, pp. 222–3.)
Give back, iwech (pr. a-'wech-i, p.p. ka-a-'wech).
Give to eat to, pai (pr. a-poi-e, p.p. ka-a-pai).
Give trouble, iim (pr. a-'im-i, p.p. ka-a-'im).
Glance, wir-te konda.
Gleam, lil (pr. a-lil-e, p.p. ka-a-lil).
Glide, ichapaii-te (pr. a-'chapoii-toi-i, p.p. ka-a-'chapaii-te).
Glutton, kipkeya (kipkeyat), pl. kipkein (kipkeīnik).
Gnaw (*meat*), ñgeny (pr. a-ñgeny-e, p.p. ka-a-ñgeny). (*vegetables*), ñgōm (pr. a-ñgōm-e, p.p. ka-a-ñgōm).
Go, ui. (See irregular verbs, pp. 220–1.)
(*follow*), isup (pr. a-'sup-i, p.p. ka-a-'sup).
Go alone (without help), we-chi-ke (pr. a-we-chi-ni-ke, p.p. ka-a-we-chi-ke).

Go:

Go *away from*, pakak-te (pr. a-pokok-toi-i, p.p. ka-a-pakak-te).
Go *away in the morning*, mus-te (pr. a-mus-toi-i, p.p. ka-a-muste).
Go *back*, ket-u-ke (pr. a-ket-u-ke, p.p. ka-a-ket-u-ke).
Go *backward*, we-e patai.
Go *bad*, pul (pr. a-pul-e, p.p. ka-a-pul).
Go *before*, indoï (pr. a-'ndoï-i, p.p. ka-a-'ndoï).
Go *behind* (*follow*), isup let.
Go *by*, sir-te (pr. a-sir-toi-i, p.p. ka-a-sir-te).
Go *down*, chor-te-ke (pr. a-chor-toi-i-ke, p.p. ka-a-chor-te-ke).
Go *for a walk*, wend-ote (pr. a-wend-oti, p.p. ka-a-wend-ote).
Go *in place of*, we-chi (pr. a-wechi-ni, p.p. ka-a-we-chi).
Go *into*, mañg-u (pr. a-mañg-u, p.p. ka-a-mañg-u).
Go *lame*, iñgwal-ate (pr. a-'ñgwol-oti, p.p. ka-a-'ñgwal-ate).
Go *near*, inak-te (pr. a-'nok-toi-i, p.p. ka-a-'nak-te).
Go *out*, man-de (pr. a-mon-doi-i, p.p. ka-a-man-de); (*like a fire*), me. (See irregular verbs, pp. 224–5.)
Go *over, across*, lan-de (pr. a-lon-doi-i, p.p. ka-a-lan-de).
Go *past*, sir-te (pr. a-sir-toi-i, p.p. ka-a-sir-te).
Go *round*, imūt (pr. a-'mūt-i, p.p. ka-a-'mūt).
Go *running*, ui lapat.
Go *silently*, sis-ate (pr. a-sis-oti, p.p. ka-a-sis-ate).
Go *through*, chut (pr. a-chut-e, p.p. ka-a-chut).
Go *to meet someone*, torok-te (pr. a-torok-toi-i, p.p. ka-a-torok-te).
Go *to the devil !* ror-chi ket.
Go *to war*, set luket.
Go *up*, lany (pr. a-lony-i, p.p. ka-a-lany).
Go *up and down*, iñgir-te (pr. a-'ñgir-toi-i, p.p. ka-a-'ñgir-te).
Go *up higher*, itoch (pr. a-'toch-i, p.p. ka-a-'toch).

Goat, ñgoror (ñgororiet), pl. ñgoror (ñgororek).
 ara (artet), pl. no (nêko).
Kid, aruwa (aruwet), pl. are (arek).
Young she-goat, suben (subendo), pl. subenua (subenuek).
She-goat that has borne, iyuog (iyuoget), pl. iyuog (iyuogik).
He-goat, kwe (kwesta), pl. kwes (kwesik).
Castrated goat, tesiim (tesiimiet), pl. tesiim (tesiimik).

God, Asis. (See **Sun**.)
Godfather or **godmother,** moterio (moteriot), pl. moteren (moterēnik).
Going, pan (panda), pl. ponua (ponuek).
Good, mie, pl. miach.
To be good, mie-itu (pr. a-mie, p.p. ka-a-mie-itu).
 iriñg-se (pr. a-'riñg-se-i, p.p. ka-a-'riñg-se).
Do one good, iis (pr. a-'is-i, p.p. ka-a-'is).
Make good (*strong*), iweit (pr. a-'weit-i, p.p. ka-a-'weit).
Make good (*sweet*), ianyiny (pr. a-'anyiny, p.p. kâ-'anyiny).
Good-bye, saisere.
Say good-bye, ikat saisere.
Goodness, miēno (miēnot).
Gourd, sot. (See **Calabash**.)
Granary, choke (choket), pl. choken (chokēnik).
The space underneath a granary, kureret-ap-choket.
Grandchild, machakoro (machakoret), pl. machakoron (machakoronik).
Grandfather, ingug (inguget).

ENGLISH-NANDI VOCABULARY

Grandfather:
Own grandfather, agwi, pl. akutagwi.
Grandmother, ingog (ingoget).
Own grandmother, koko, pl. angut-koko).
Grasp, nam (pr. a-nom-e, p.p. ka-a-nam).
Grass, susuo (susuot), pl. susua (susuek).
Burnt grass, ñgemia (ñgemiat), pl. ñgem (ñgemik).
Place on which grass has been burnt, iwas (iwasto). lalua (laluet).
Place on which new grass has grown, malel (maleliet).
Grasshopper, talamwa (talamwat), pl. talam (talamwek).
Different kinds of grasshoppers:—
chemonjorua (chemonjoruet), pl. chemonjoroi (chemonjorōk).
kimekwan (kimekwanit), pl. kimekwanin (kimekwanīnik).
cheptoldol (cheptoldoliet), pl. cheptoldoloi (cheptoldolōk).
chemundu (chemundut), pl. chemundun (chemundunik).
chemoliog (chemolioget), pl. chemoliogoi (chemoliogōk).
cheptomoto (cheptomotet), pl. cheptomoton (cheptomotonik).
tañgwerer (tañgwereriet), pl. tañgwerer (tañgwererik).
chepuka (chepukat), pl. chepukas (chepukasiek).
cheptany (cheptanyit), pl. cheptanyin (cheptanyīnik).
cheptirtir (cheptirtiriet), pl. cheptirtirai (cheptirtiraiik).
Gratis, puch.
Grazing ground, līmo (līmet), pl. līmōs (līmōsiek).
Grease, mwai (mwaita), pl. mwan (mwanik).
Grease-pot, chepkirau (chepkiraut), pl. chepkiraun (chepkiraunik).
Great, oo, pl. echen.
To be great, oo-itu (pr. a-oo, p.p. ka-a-oo-itu).
Great age, oïn (oïndo).
Greedy person, kipkeya (kipkeyat), pl. kipkein (kipkeīnik).
Greet, ikat (pr. a-'kot-i, p.p. ka-a-'kat).
toroch (pr. a-toroch-i, p.p. ka-a-toroch).
Grey hair, kalualia (kalualiat), pl. kalual (kalualek).
Grieve, arogen (pr. a-arogen-e, p.p. kâ-arogen).
Grime (*on a pot*), nesek (apteret).
Grind, ñga (pr. a-ñgo-i, p.p. ka-a-ñga).
Grind coarsely, pak-te (pr. a-pok-toi-i, p.p. ka-a-pak-te).
Grind the teeth, nye kelek.
Grindstone, koiit'-ap-pai.
Groan, tiken (pr. a-tiken-i, p.p. ka-a-tiken).
Groin, palia (paliet), pl. palioi (paliōk).
Grope, sapsap (pr. a-sopsop-i, p.p. ka-a-sapsap).
Ground, kor (koret), pl. korotinua (korotinuek).
Grow (*of persons* and *animals*), et-u (pr. a-et-u, p.p. ka-a-et-u).
(*of plants*), pīt (pr. a-pīt-e, p.p. ka-a-pīt).
Sprout (*of plants*), kun-u (pr. a-kun-u, p.p. ka-a-kun-u).
siek-u (pr. a-siek-u, p.p. ka-a-siek-u).
Shoot (*as plants*), iñgat (pr. a-'ñgot-i, p.p. ka-a-'ñgat).
Grow fat, ner (pr. a-ner-e, p.p. ka-a-ner).
Grow thin, sagit (pr. a-sogit-i, p.p. ka-a-sagit).
Growl, moror (pr. a-moror-i, p.p. ka-a-moror).

Grub of bee or **wasp,** aruwa (aruwet), pl. are (arek).
Gruel, musar (musarek).
Cook gruel, chul musarek.
Guard, rīpin (rīpindet), pl. rīp (rīpik).
kakunin (kakunindet), pl. kakun (kakunik).
(v.), rīp (pr. a-rīp-e, p.p. ka-a-rīp).
ikun (pr. a-'kun-i, p.p. ka-a-'kun).
(*cover*), tuch (pr. a-tuch-e, p.p. ka-a-tuch).
Guard yourself ! Look out ! Take care ! Rīp-ke !
Guess, ñgor (pr. a-ñgor-e, p.p. ka-a-ñgor).
Guide, kaparun (kaparundet). segein. (See **Soldier.**)
(v.), ipor-chi.
(*show the way*), ipor-chi oret.
Gullet, siin (siindo), pl. siinua (siinuek).
Gum (*of the teeth*), pend'-ap-kelek.
(*of babies* or *toothless old men*), mununua (mununuet).
(*of trees*), kipit (kipitiet), pl. kipitoi (kipitōk).
Gum arabic, manga (manget), pl. mangoi (mangōk).
Gun, ma. (See **Fire.**)
Gun without ammunition, kiptuli (kiptulit), pl. kiptulis (kiptulisiek).
Gunpowder, pusaru (pusaruk).
Gut, akutan (akutaniet), pl. akutan (akutanik).

Haft (*of sword, axe, &c.*), kunyuk (kungit), pl. kunyuk (kunyukik).
(*of spear*), iruma (irumet), pl. irumai (irumaiik).
Haggle (*over a price*), kīm (pr. a-kīm-e, p.p. ka-a-kīm).

Hail, koiiyo (koiiyot), pl. koiin (koiik).
(v.), robon koiin.
Hair, sumeyo (sumeyot), pl. sume (sumek).
Hair of the beard, kororik-aptamnet.
Hair of the eyebrows, kororik-apkonda.
Hair of the armpits, kororik-apkulkulta.
Hair of the pubes, kororik-apnyuset.
Band for binding warrior's hair, anuet-ap-sumek.
When a girl has lost her elder brother or sister, it is customary to leave on the head a ridge of hair called—songonyo (songonyet), pl. songonyai (songonyaiik).
Half, matua (matuet), pl. matuas (matuasiek).
(*portion*), kipeperia (kipeperiat), pl. kipeperua (kipeperuek).
Halt (*rest*), imuny (pr. a-'muny-i, p.p. ka-a-'muny).
(*stand*), tonon (pr. a-tonon-i, p.p. ka-a-tonon).
(*put down burdens*), itu (pr. a-'tu-i, p.p. ka-a-'tu).
Hammer, kirisua (kirisuet), pl. kirisōn (kirisōnik).
Hand, ē (ēut), pl. ēun (ēunek).
Palm of the hand, rubei (rubeito), pl. rubeiuag (rubeiuagik).
Handle, kunyuk (kungit), pl. kunyuk (kunyukik).
Handle of hoe, kikoro (kikoret), pl. kikores (kikoresiek).
Handle of knife, ketit-ap-rotuet.
Handsome, kararan, pl. kororon.
Hang, ikartat (pr. a-'kortot-i, p.p. ka-a-'kartat).
(*strangle*), iket (pr. a-'ket-i, p.p. ka-a-'ket).
Harass, iim (pr. a-'im-i, p.p. ka-a-'im).

ENGLISH-NANDI VOCABULARY 265

Hard, ui, pl. uen.
To make hard, iweit (pr. a-'weit-i, p.p. ka-a-'weit).
To run hard, ñgwek mīsing.
Hare, kiplengwa (kiplengwet), pl. kiplengonoi (kiplengonōk).
Haste, chokchino (chokchinet).
Hasten, chok-chi (pr. a-chok-chi-ni, p.p. ka-a-chok-chi). girgir (pr. a-girgir-i, p.p. ka-a-girgir).
Hasten hither, chok-u (pr. a-chok-u, p.p. ka-a-chok-u).
Hasten thither, chok-te (pr. a-chok-tοi-i, p.p. ka-a-chok-te).
Hatch, ikēny (pr. a-'kēny-i, p.p. ka-a-'kēny).
Hatchet, mor (morut), pl. morus (morusiek).
Hate, wech (pr. a-wech-e, p.p. ka-a-wech).
Have, tinye (pr. a-tinye, p.p. ka-a-tinye).
He, inendet; ine.
Head, met (metit), pl. metōa (metōek).
Be smooth-headed, kuluny met.
Head-dress:
(worn by girls), ñgishelio (ñgisheliot), pl. ñgisheli (ñgishelik).
(worn by boys who have been recently circumcised), kimaranguch (kimaranguchet), pl. kimoranguchai (kimoranguchaiik).
(worn by girls who have been recently circumcised), soiyuo (soiyuet), pl. soon (soonik).
(worn by old men), chepkule (chepkulet), pl. chepkules (chepkulesiek).
(worn by brides), nario (nariet), pl. narioi (nariōk).
Head-dress of ostrich feathers (warriors'), sombe (sombet), pl. sombenut (sombenutik).
Head-dress of lion-skin (warriors'), kutua (kutuet), pl. kutonoi (kutonōk).

Head-dress of ox-hide (warriors'), eur (eurto), pl. eurua (euruek).
Heal, isap (pr. a-'sop-i, p.p. ka-a-'sap).
Health, sapon (sapondo); chametap-ke; uio (uiet); uin (uindo).
Be in good health, cham-ke (pr. a-cham-i-ke, p.p. ka-a-cham-ke).
Healthy, mukul, pl. mukulen.
Heap, kaumut (kaumutiet), pl. kaumut (kaumutik). karurukut (karurukutiet), pl. karurukut (karurukutik).
Heap up, iruruch (pr. a-'ruruch-i, p.p. ka-a-'ruruch).
(collect), ium (pr. a-'um-i, p.p. ka-a-'um).
Hear, kas (pr. a-kos-e, p.p. ka-a-kas).
Heart, mukulel (mukuleldo), pl. mukulelua (mukuleluek).
Heat, ilalany (pr. a-'lolony-i, p.p. ka-a-'lalany).
To get hot, sich mat.
To be hot, lalañg-itu (pr. a-lalañg, p.p. ka-a-lalañg-itu).
Heaven, parak (parakut); tororo (tororot); em-polik *(in the clouds).*
Heavy, nyikis, pl. nyikisin.
Hedge, ñgotua (ñgotuet), pl. ñgotonoi (ñgotonōk).
Hedge round cattle enclosure, sipaiya (sipaiyat), pl. sipaien (sipaiēnik).
Make a hedge, ñgot (pr. a-ñgot-e, p.p. ka-a-ñgot).
Heel, muk'-ap-kor.
Heifer, ror (rorta), pl. rorua (roruek). rarewa (rarewat).
Help, imuñg-ji (pr. a-'muñg-ji-ni, p.p. ka-a-'muñg-ji). toret (pr. a-toret-i, p.p. ka-a-toret).
Hen, ingok (ingokiet), pl. ingokai (ingokaiik).
Her, inendet; ine.

Her:
(poss.), nyi, pl. chik.
hers (used absolutely), nenyi, pl. chechiget.
Herb, ingua (inguot), pl. ingui (inguek).
Herd (*of cattle*), akwot (akwet), pl. akwotis (akwotisiek).
Herd cattle, iak-e. (See **Feed.**)
Herdsman, mistōa (mistōat), pl. mistōe (mistōek).
    koiokin (koiokindet), pl. koiok (koiokik).
Here, yu; oli.
He is here, mi-i; mi-te yu.
I am here, ane yu.
Here and there, yu ok yun.
Hero, kiruk. (See **Bull.**)
Hiccough (v. imp.), iket.
I have hiccoughs, ki-iket-o.
(*of children*), riech (pr. a-riech-e, p.p. ka-a-riech).
Hide (*ox*), mui (muito), pl. muiua (muiuek).
Piece of ox-hide, iririo (iririot), pl. iriren (irirēnik).
Strip of ox-hide, anua (anuet), pl. anoi (anōk).
Strip of dressed ox-hide, ingiriren (ingirirenet), pl. ingiriren (ingirirēnik).
Goat-hide, makata (makatet), pl. makatai (makataiik).
Strip of goat-hide, tapsien (tapsienet), pl. tapsienai (tapsienaiik).
Hide, uny (pr. a-uny-e, p.p. ka-a-uny).
High, koi, pl. koiin.
Hill, legem (legemet), pl. legemōs (legemōsiek).
    tulua (tuluet), pl. tuluondoi (tuluondōk).
Hilt, kunyuk (kungit), pl. kunyuk (kunyukik).
Him, inendet; ine.
Hinder, rany (pr. a-rony-i, p.p. ka-a-rany).

Hip, ingorai (ingoraiet), pl. ingoraiin (ingoraiīnik).
Hippopotamus, makas (makasta), pl. makasua (makasuek).
L., makai (makaita), pl. mokoi (mokoiik).
His (poss.), nyi, pl. chik.
(used absolutely), nenyi, pl. chechiget.
Hit, pir (pr. a-pir-e, p.p. ka-a-pir).
(*with a spear* or *arrow*), mwog (pr. a-mwog-e, p.p. ka-a-mwog).
Hither, yu; akui yu.
Hither is generally expressed by the form of the verb denoting motion towards.
Hither and thither, yu ok yun.
Hitherto, akut nguni.
Hock (*of animals*), kôwet-ap-kwariot.
Hoe, mokombe (mokombet), pl. mokombai (mokombaiik).
Hoist, ichūt (pr. a-'chūt-i, p.p. ka-a-'chūt).
(*lift*), sut (pr. a-sut-e, p.p. ka-a-sut).
Hold, nam (pr. a-nom-e, p.p. ka-a-nam).
Hold something in the open hand, irop (pr. a-'rop-i, p.p. ka-a-'rop).
Hold something in the closed hand, mumut (pr. a-mumut-i, p.p. ka-a-mumut).
Hole, koñg (konda), pl. koñgin (koñgik).
Hole in the earth, kering (keringet), pl. keringon (keringonik).
Hole in the upper part of the ear, kond'-ap-solik.
Hollow (*in tree*), pondo (pondet), pl. pondai (pondaiik).
Home (*man talking*), kain-nyō, kain-ñguñg, &c. (*at my house, at thy house, &c.*).
(*woman* or *child talking*), koïn-nyō, koïn-ñguñg, &c.
Home-stayer, kiptep (kiptepit).

ENGLISH-NANDI VOCABULARY

Honey, kumia (kumiat), pl. kumin (kumīk).
Honey-barrel, moing (moinget), pl. moingon (moingonik).
Honey-comb, masamia (masamiat), pl. masam (masamek).
Honey-comb (with honey in it), pôk (pôkiet), pl. pôk (pôkik).
Honey-wine, kipketin (kipketīnik).
Honour, konyit (konyit).
(v.), ikochi konyit.
Hoof, siiya (siiyet), pl. sioi (siōk).
Hoof of young oxen or goats, putul (putuldo), pl. putulua (putuluek).
Hope, tak (followed by the subjunctive).
I hope I shall be able to go, tak a-moch a-wa.
Horn, kuina (kuinet), pl. kuinai (kuinaiik).
lal (lalet), pl. laloi (lalōk).
Hornet, kiprorog (kiproroget), pl. kiprorogin (kiprorogīnik).
Horse, olbartany (olbartanyit), pl. olbartanyis (olbartanyisiek).
Hot, am-ma (am-mat).
To be hot, lalañg-itu (pr. a-lalañg, p.p. ka-a-lalañg-itu).
I am hot, ka-a-lalañg-itu *or* ko-'ñget-yi-o kaotik.
House *(man speaking),* ka (kaita), pl. korin (korik).
(woman speaking), ko (kot), pl. korin (korik).
Kaita when used in conjunction with the genitive becomes *kâp.*
Kot when used in conjunction with the genitive becomes *kop* or *kot-ap.*
Part of house occupied by people, koiima (koiimaut), pl. koiimaus (koiimausiek).
Part of house occupied by sheep and goats, injor (injorut), pl. injorus (injorusiek).

Milk compartment, kâplengu (kâplengut), pl. kâplengun (kâplengunik).
In front of the house, serem (seremut), pl. seremus (seremusiek).
Warriors' house, sigiroin (sigiroinet), pl. sigiroinōs (sigiroinōsiek).
Club-house, kait'-am-murenik.
Stone house, kopokoii (kopokoiik).
Dwelling-house, kâp-sat, pl. korik-ap-sat.
House in cattle-kraal, chepkimalia (chepkimaliat), pl. chepkimalin (chepkimalīnik).
Live in a house, meny (pr. a-meny-i, p.p. ka-a-meny).
How, ne ; ni.
How are you ? I-cham-i-ke ?
How often? kosakta ata ? inyil' ata ?
How much ? how many ? ata ?
However, ako ; ako-i.
Human, ap-chii.
Hump *(of an ox),* uk (ukta), pl. ukwa (ukwek).
Humpback, mulua (muluet), pl. mulondoi (mulondōk).
Hundred, pokol.
Hunger, rub (rubet), pl. rubōs (rubōsiek).
I am hungry, am-a rubet.
Hunt (act.), mwog (pr. a-mwog-e, p.p. ka-a-mwog).
logotin (pr. a-logotin-i, p.p. ka-a-logotin).
(neut.), mwog-se (pr. a-mwog-se-i, p.p. ka-a-mwog-se).
Hunter, kiplogotio (kiplogotiot), pl. kiplogotin (kiplogotīnik).
Hurry, chokchino (chokchinet).
(v.), chok-chi (pr. a-chok-chi-ni, p.p. ka-a-chok-chi).
Hurt (v. imp.), am. (See **Ache.**)
Husband, manoñgotio (manoñg-

Husband: otiot), pl. manoñgot (manoñgotik).
Husband's brother after husband's death, kipkondii (kipkondiit), pl. kipkondiin (kipkondiinik).
Husk, morio (moriot), pl. mor (morik).
(v.), ipony (pr. a-'pony-i, p.p. ka-a-'pony).
Hut. (See **House.**)
Hut in the corn fields, kerio (keriet), pl. kerion (kerionik).
Hut in which warriors eat meat, ekor (ekorto), pl. ekorua (ekoruek).
Boys' circumcision hut, menjo (menjet), pl. menjōs (menjōsiek).
Hyena, kimaket (kimaketyet), pl. kimaketoi (kimaketōk).
  lel (lelda), pl. lelua (leluek).
  K., apei (apeiet), pl. apeioi (apeiōk).
Hyrax, kipkoris (kipkorisiet), pl. kipkorisoi (kipkorisōk).

I, ane.
Idle person, choriren (chorirenet), pl. choriren (chorirenik).
If, ingo-ngo, etc. (See p. 196.)
Ignorance, periperio (periperiet).
Ignorant, periper, pl. periperen.
be Ill, mian (pl. a-mion-e, p.p. ka-a-mian).
Be very ill, nyīt-ak-e (pr. a-nyīt-at, p.p. ka-a-nyīt-ak-e).
Be nearly dead, rum-ok-e (pr. a-rum-ot, p.p. ka-a-rum-ok-e).
Illness, mion (miondo), pl. mionwag (mionwagik).
  The names of some illnesses are given in the following list:—
Abscess, mô (môet), pl. môoi (môōk).
Boil, undir (undiriet), pl. undir (undirik).

Catarrh (*cold*), tuñgwa (tuñgwek).
Chicken-pox, kâpimperu (kâpimperuk).
Dropsy, puras (purasta).
Dysentery, chelole (cheloleit).
Gonorrhoea, kipnonog (kipnonoget).
Heartburn, kalut (kalut).
Liver or *spleen complaints,* ñgasat (ñgasatet).
Lung complaints, chepuon (chepuonet).
Malaria, es (eset).
Mumps, lupan (lupanik).
Pimples, tigoi (tigoiik).
  (*itch*), koiicha (koiichat), pl. koiich (koiichek).
  (*rash*), ingosen (ingosēnik).
Rheumatism, mokongio (mokongiot).
  (*lumbago*), cherapuny (cherapunyet).
Small-pox, konjurio (konjuriot).
  L., chesirun (chesirunik).
Sore throat, kipkamog (kipkamogit).
Swelling of the neck, terit (tertit).
Syphilis, takan (takanet).
Ulcer, chepsergech (chepsergechet).
  The people of Kâpwaren suffer from a disease which is characterized by a hardening of the skin and a swelling of the testicles. This disease the Nandi call *temer* (*temerik*), and the Lumbwa *sarsar* (*sarsariek*). It is said to be caused by the bite of a fly which is known as *kâpkikonjek.*
Ill-treat, inyalil (pr. a-'nyolil-i, p.p. ka-a-'nyalil).
Imitate, ile. (See irregular verbs, p. 225.)
Immature, mining, pl. mingech.
Immediately, nguni ; ngunito.

Immerse, ilis (pr. a-'lis-i, p.p. ka-a-'lis).
Implore, som (pr. a-som-e, p.p. ka-a-som).
Imprecate against, iosie-chi (pr. a-'osie-chi-ni, p.p. kâ-'osie-chi).
In, eñg.
In front, tae.
In order that, si (followed by the subjunctive).
In place of, olt'-ap.
In the middle, kwen.
In the morning, korirun.
In the evening, koimen.
Incline (act.), iñguruch (pr. a-'ñguruch-i, p.p. ka-a-'ñguruch). (neut.), iñguruk-e (pr. a-'ñguruk-at, p.p. ka-a-'ñguruk-e).
Increase, tes (pr. a-tes-e, p.p. ka-a-tes).
Indeed, po-many.
Inform, mwo-chi (pr. a-mwo-chi-ni, p.p. ka-a-mwo-chi).
Information, ñgolio (ñgoliot), pl. ñgal (ñgalek).
    lokoiyo (lokoiyot), pl. lokoi-yua (lokoiyuek).
Inhabit, tepi (pr. a-tepi-e, p.p. ka-a-tepi).
Insect, kut (kutiet), pl. kut (kutik).
Inside, oriit.
He is inside, mi-i oriit.
Instantly, nguni; nguní-to.
Instruct, inêt (pr. a-'nêt-i, p.p. ka-a-'nêt).
Insult, chupisio (chupisiet). (v.) chup (pr. a-chup-e, p.p. ka-a-chup).
Use insulting language to, tach (pr. a-toch-e, p.p. ka-a-tach).
Inter, tup (pr. a-tup-e, p.p. ka-a-tup).
Intercede for, som-chi (pr. a-som-chi-ni, p.p. ka-a-som-chi).
Intercept, rany (pr. a-rony-i, p.p. ka-a-rany).

Interrupt (*when speaking*), til ñgalek.
Intestines, mootinua (mootinuek).
Small intestine, akutan (akutanik).
Large intestine, pe (pēut).
become Intoxicated, pôkit (pr. a-pôkit-i, p.p. ka-a-pôkit).
Investigate (*a crime*), kin (pr. a-kin-e, p.p. ka-a-kin).
Iron, karna (karnet), pl. karin (karīk).
Iron ore, ñgoriamu (ñgoriamuk).
Refuse of iron-ore, tapungen (tapungenik).
Irritate, tach (pr. a-toch-e, p.p. ka-a-tach).
Issue from, pun-u (pr. a-pun-u, p.p. ka-a-pun-u).
It, inendet; ine.
Itch, koiicha (koiichat), pl. koiich (koiichek).
(v.), iutut (pr. a-'utut-i, p.p. ka-a-'utut).
Its (poss.), nyi, pl. chik.
(used absolutely), nenyi, pl. chechiget.
Ivory, kelda (keldet), pl. kelat (kelek).

Jackal, lelua (leluot), pl. lelue (leluek).
Jar, ter. (See **Pot.**)
Men's water-jar, saiga (saiget), pl. saigoi (saigōk).
Women's water-jar, mwendo (mwendet), pl. mwendoi (mwendōk).
Jaw, takilkil (takilkiliet), pl. takilkil (takilkilik).
Jealous person, lōmin (lōmindet), pl. lōm (lōmik).
Jigger, kut. (See **Insect.**)
Join, rop (pr. a-rop-e, p.p. ka-a-rop).
Join with, itui-e (pr. a-'tui-tos-i, p.p. ka-a-'tui-e).

Joining together, tuio. (See **Amalgamation.**)
Joint, mongwa (mongwet), pl. mongwōs (mongwōsiek).
Journey, pan (panda), pl. ponua (ponuek).
 rutoi (rutoito), pl. rutoiua (rutoiuek).
 Two days' journey, pand'-apêkōsiek oieñg.
Joy, kakaso (kakaset).
Jugular vein, kep (kepet), pl. kepon (keponik).
 Open the jugular vein of animals after death, un (pr. a-un-i, p.p. ka-a-un).
Juice, pei. (See **Water.**)
Juicy, tinye pêk ; ap-pêk.
Jump, toromben (pr. a-toromben-i, p.p. ka-a-toromben).
 Jump over something, sir (pr. a-sir-e, p.p. ka-a-sir).

Keep, konor (pr. a-konor-i, p.p. ka-a-konor).
 (*guard*), rīp (pr. a-rīp-e, p.p. ka-a-rīp).
 (*hold*), nam (pr. a-nom-e, p.p. ka-a-nam).
Kick, itiar (pr. a-'tiar-i, p.p. ka-a-'tiar).
 Kick frequently or violently, itiartiar (pr. a-'tiartiar-i, p.p. ka-a-'tiartiar).
Kid, aruwa (aruwet), pl. are (arek).
Kidney, soromya (soromyet), pl. soromoi (soromōk).
Kill, par (pr. a-por-e, p.p. ka-a-par).
 Kill a Nandi, rum (pr. a-rum-e, p.p. ka-a-rum).
 Kill by slashing with a sword, iep (pr. oi-'ep-e, p.p. ka-a-'ep).
 Kill by stabbing, tor (pr. a-tor-e, p.p. ka-a-tor).
 Kill for, por-chi (pr. a-por-chi-ni, p.p. ka-a-por-chi).
 Kill for food, eny (pr. a-eny-e, p.p. ka-a-eny).
 Kill with, par-e (pr. a-por-e, p.p. ka-a-par-e).
 Give a coup de grâce, pakach (pr. a-pokoch-i, p.p. ka-a-pakach).
Kind, mie, pl. miach.
Kindle, inam (pr. a-'nom-i, p.p. ka-a-'nam).
 ilal (pr. a-'lol-i, p.p. ka-a-'lal).
Kiss, ñgutut (pr. a-ñgutut-i, p.p. ka-a-ñgutut).
Kitchen (*cooking-place*), kâpkoii-ma.
Knead, imoi (pr. a-'moi-i, p.p. ka-a-'moi).
Knee, kutuñg (kutunda), pl. kutuñgwa (kutuñgwek).
 kutund'-ap-keldo.
 The rectus femoris muscle, kipser (kipserit), pl. kipseris (kipserisiek).
Kneel, kutuny (pr. a-kutuny-i, p.p. ka-a-kutuny).
Knife, chepkeswai (chepkeswet), pl. chepkesoi (chepkesōk).
 (*large*), rotua (rotuet), pl. rotoi (rotōk).
 (*used for tapping palms*), kesimor (kesimoret), pl. kesimorōs (kesimorōsiek).
 (*used for butchering cattle*), chambolua (chamboluet), pl. chambolōs (chambolōsiek).
 Boys' circumcision knife, kipōs (kipōsit), pl. kipōsin (kipōsīnik).
 Girls' circumcision knife, mwatin (mwatindet), pl. mwat (mwatik).
Knit (*the brows*), ingusuk toket.
Knock (*tap*), ikoñggony (pr. a-'koñggony-i, p.p. ka-a-'koñggony).
 (*strike*), pir (pr. a-pir-e, p.p. ka-a-pir).
 Knock down, tu-i (pr. a-tu-e, p.p. ka-a-tu-i).

Knock: *Seize a person in order to knock him down*, iñgir (pr. a-'ñgir-i, p.p. ka-a-'ñgir).
Knot, ukut (ukutiet), pl. ukut (ukutik).
(v.), ūch (pr. a-ūch-e, p.p. kâ-ūch).
Know, nai. (See irregular verbs, pp. 223–4.)
(*recognize*), inyit (pr. a-'nyit-e, p.p. ka-a-'nyit).
I don't know whether he will like it, Tos! cham-e.
Knowing, ñgom, pl. ñgomen.
Kraal, ka *or* ko. (See **House**.)
Cluster of huts, ñganasa (ñganaset), pl. ñganasoi (ñganasōk).
Deserted kraal, kipkupere (kipkuperet), pl. kipkuperai (kipkuperaiik).
Site of former kraal, karatia (karaita), pl. karatua (karatuek).
Cattle-kraal on the grazing grounds, kâp-tich (kâp-tugut), pl. kâp-tugun (kâp-tugunik).
Cattle-kraal near the dwelling huts, pe (pēut), pl. pēus (pēusiek).

Labour, poiisio (poiisiet), pl. poiision (poiisionik).
To labour at birth, temel (pr. a-temel-i, p.p. ka-a-temel).
Lake, nianja (nianjet), pl. nianjas (nianjasiek).
be **Lame,** iñgwal (pr. a-'ñgwol-i, p.p. ka-a-'ñgwal).
Walk lame thither, iñgwal-ate (pr. a-'ñgwal-oti, p.p. ka-a-'ñgwal-ate).
Walk lame hither, iñgwal-anu (pr. a-'ñgwal-anu, p.p. ka-a-'ñgwal-anu).
Land (*country*), em (emet), pl. emotinua (emotinuek).
(*district, soil*), kor (koret), pl. korotinua (korotinuek).

Language, ñgal (ñgalek).
Insulting language, chupisio (chupisiet).
Lap, kupes (kupesto).
Put in one's lap, tiny (pr. a-tiny-i, p.p. ka-a-tiny).
Large, oo, pl. echen.
Last, nepo-let; ole-poch.
At last, let.
be **Late,** ek-chi (pr. oi-ek-chi-ni, p.p. koi-ek-chi).
Lately, ya-kinye.
Laugh, rorio (roriet).
(v.), rori (pr. a-rori-e, p.p. ka-a-rori).
Laugh at, rore-chi (pr. a-rore-chi-ni, p.p. ka-a-rore-chi).
Lay, konor (pr. a-konor-i, p.p. ka-a-konor).
Lay eggs, kolok (pr. a-kolok-i, p.p. ka-a-kolok).
Lay hold of, nam (pr. a-nom-e, p.p. ka-a-nam).
Lay open, ñgany (pr. a-ñgony-i, p.p. ka-a-ñgany).
Lay (*something*) *on its back,* itarñgany (pr. a-'tarñgony-i, p.p. ka-a-'tarñgany).
Lay out, iit-te (pr. oi-'it-toi-i, p.p. kâ-'it-te).
Lay upon, in-de (pr. a-'n-doi-i, p.p. ka-a-'n-de).
Lay a wager, irot-ie (pr. a-'rot-tos-i, p.p. ka-a-'rot-te).
be **Lazy,** eku choriren.
Lead (*show*), iaror-chi (pr. a-'aror-chi-ni, p.p. kâ-'aror-chi).
(*take a person*), imut (pr. a-'mut-i, p.p. ka-a-'mut).
Leader, kamutin (kamutindet), pl. kamut (kamutik).
Leaf, soko (sokot *or* sokondet), pl. sok (sokek).
Leak, pun (pr. a-pun-e, p.p. ka-a-pun).
The house leaks, robon-u kot.
become **Lean,** sagit (pr. a-sogit-i, p.p. ka-a-sagit).

ENGLISH-NANDI VOCABULARY

Lean:
Make lean, isagit (pr. a-'sogit-e, p.p. ka-a-'sagit).
Lean against, itur (pr. a-'tur-i, p.p. ka-a-'tur).
Lean upon, ti (pr. a-ti-e, p.p. ka-a-ti).
Lean upon a staff, tepen (pr. a-tepen-i, p.p. ka-a-tepen).
Leap, toromben (pr. a-toromben-i, p.p. ka-a-toromben).
Learn, inêt-ke (pr. a-'nêt-i-ke, p.p. ka-a-'nêt-ke)
Leather (*ox-hide*), mui (muito), pl. muiua (muiuek).
(*goat-skin*), makata (makatet), pl. makatai (makataiik).
Leave (*go away*), man-de (pr. a-mon-doi-i, p.p. ka-a-man-de).
(*come away*), mañg-u (pr. a-moñg-u, p.p. ka-a-mañg-u).
(*leave alone*), pakak-te (pr. a-pokok-toi-i, p.p. ka-a-pakak-te).
L., pakâch (pr. a-pokoch-i, p.p. ka-a-pakâch).
(*leave alone for*), pokok-chi (pr. a-pokok-chi-ni, p.p. ka-a-pokok-chi).
(*throw away*), lak-te (pr. a-lak-toi-i, p.p. ka-a-lak-te).
met-te (pr. a-met-toi-i, p.p. ka-a-met-te).
(*let go*), un-de (pr. a-un-doi-i, p.p. ka-a-un-de).
Leave it alone! Let go! pakak-te! un-de!
Be left, ñgit-u (pr. a-ñgit-u, p.p. ka-a-ñgit-u).
Give leave, cham-chi ; ikochi panda.
Take leave of, ikat (pr. a-'kot-i, p.p. ka-a-'kat).
Leave a piece when cutting off something, ituch (pr. a-'tuch-i, p.p. ka-a-'tuch).
Leech, pinyiny (pinyinyet), pl. pinyiny (pinyinyik).
Left (*hand, &c.*), ap-katam.

Leg, kel (keldo), pl. kelien (keliek).
kereng (kerenget), pl. kerengon (kerengonik).
One-legged person (m.), kipkelok, (f.), chepkelok.
Calf of leg, ai (aita), pl. aïsai (aïsaiik).
Shin, korok (korokta), pl. korokwa (korokwek).
Thigh, kupes (kupesto), pl. kupesua (kupesuek).
Fore-leg, kus (kusto), pl. kusua (kusuek).
Hind-leg, chat (chatit), pl. chatin (chatik).
Legend, kâpchemosin (kâpchemosīnik).
Leglet (*warriors', worn below the knee*), mungen (mungeniet), pl. mungen (mungenik).
marikcho (marikchot), pl. marik (marikik).
(*warriors', worn above the knee*), kipkurkur (kipkurkuriet), pl. kipkurkurai (kipkurkuraiik).
(*girls'*), tapakwa (tapakwet), pl. tapakwon (tapakwonik).
(*of brass wire*), tae (taet), pl. taoi (taōk).
have **Leisure,** para-itu (pr. a-para, p p. ka-a-para-itu).
Length, koiin (koiindo).
Lengthen, ikoiit (pr. a-'koiit-i, p.p. ka-a-'koiit).
Leopard, cheplanga (cheplanget), pl. cheplangoi (cheplangōk).
L. and K., melil (melildo), pl. melilua (meliluek).
Lessen, iñgir-te (pr. a-'ñgir-toi-i, p.p. ka-a-'ñgir-te).
Let (*leave alone*), pakak-te (pr. a-pokok-toi-i, p.p. ka-a-pakak-te).
(*allow*), cham-chi ; ikochi panda.
Level (*a gun* or *spear*) **at,** ñgat (pr. a-ñgot-e, p.p. ka-a-ñgat).
Lick, mēl (pr. a-mēl-e, p.p. ka-a-mēl).

Lid, kereyuo (kereyuot), pl. kere, (kereyuek).
Lid of honey-barrel, keleñgeyuo (keleñgeyuot), pl. keleñge (keleñgeyuek).
Lie (falsehood), lembech (lembechet), pl. lembech (lembechek).
(v.), ken-u (pr. a-ken-u, p.p. ka-a-ken-u).
chombil (pr. a-chombil-i, p.p. ka-a-chombil).
Lie down, ru (pr. a-ru-e, p.p. ka-a-ru).
Lie across, įmrok (pr. a-įmrok-e, p.p. ka-a-įmrok).
Lie on the top of, siep (pr. a-siep-e, p.p. ka-a-siep).
Lie on the back, siep patai.
Lift, sut (pr. a-sut-e, p.p. ka-a-sut).
Lift up, keleny (pr. a-keleny-i, p.p. ka-a-keleny).
Lift up and look underneath, ñgany (pr. a-ñgony-e, p.p. ka-a-ñgany).
Light (*not dark*), lēl, pl. lelach.
(*not heavy*), wesis, pl. wisisin.
Light (*a fire*), ilal (pr. a-'lol-i, p.p. ka-a-'lal).
Commence to be light, irir (pr. a-'rir-i, p.p. ka-a-'rir).
Lightning, koliel (kolielet).
Like, cham. (See **Love.**)
Like (*as*), kuu ; ile ; kuu 'le ; nette ; te.
Do like this! ai ile!
Make it like this, ai-te nette ni.
be Like, uu (pr. a-uu-e, p.p. ka-a-uu).
Liken, ioiechin-e (pr. a-'oiechindos-i, p.p. kâ-'oiechin-e).
Line, ropo (ropet).
Line down the back of a beast, urer (ureryet), pl. urer (urerik).
Linger, ikaa-ke (pr. a-'kaa-i-ke, p.p. ka-a-'kaa-ke).
Lion, ñgetūny (ñgetundo), pl. ñgetuny (ñgetunyik).

Lip, iririot-ap-kutit.
Listen, kas (pr. a-koṣ-e, p.p. ka-a-kas).
iep-chi iit.
Little, mining, pl. mingech.
A little (*of one thing*), kitegin.
Bring a little meat, ip-u pendo kitegin.
A little (*of several things*), totegin. *Bring a little water,* ip-u pêk totegin.
Little by little, a little at a time, kitegin-kitegin.
Live, tepi (pr. a-tepi-e, p.p. ka-a-tepi).
Be alive, sap (pr. a-sop-e, p.p. ka-a-sap).
Live in a house, meny (pr. a-meny-e, p.p. ka-a-meny).
Liver, koi (koito), pl. koiwag (koiwagik).
Lizard (*house-lizard*), cheringis (cheringisiet), pl. cheringisai (cheringisaiik).
(*tree-lizard*), chepenet (chepenetiet), pl. chepenetin (chepenetīnik).
Locust, chereñgen (chereñgendet), pl. chereñgenyen (chereñgenyēnik).
Cloud of locusts, kipereñgen (kipereñgeṇdet), pl. kipereñgenyen (kipereñgenyēnik).
Cooked locust, tyolio (tyoliot), pl. tyolin (tyolīk).
Locust egg, mukenya (mukenyat), pl. muken (mukenik).
Log, suben (subenet), pl. subenai (subenaiik).
Loin, suwe (suwet), pl. suwenut (suwenutik).
Loiter, ikaa-ke (pr. a-'kaa-i-ke, p.p. ka-a-'kaa-ke).
Long, koi, pl. koiin.
Longing, roñg (roñget).
He longs for some meat, tinye roñget-ap-pendo.

Look, iro. (See irregular verbs, p. 224.)
 tapen (pr. a-topen-i, p.p. ka-a-tapen).
Look after (*guard*), rīp (pr. a-rīp-e, p.p. ka-a-rīp).
Look after, while doing other things, ikun (pr. a-'kun-i, p.p. ka-a-'kun).
Look behind, kus koñg.
Look down, ñgurur (pr. a-ñgurur-i, p.p. ka-a-ñgurur).
Look for, cheñg (pr. a-cheñg-e, p.p. ka-a-cheñg).
Look out for, sege (pr. a-sege-i, p.p. ka-a-sege).
Look up, inyal (pr. a-'nyol-i, p.p. ka-a-'nyal).
Loose, itiach (pr. a-'tioch-i, p.p. ka-a-'tiach).
Loosen, iturtur (pr. a-'turtur-i, p.p. ka-a-'turtur).
Lose, ipet (pr. a-'pet-i, p.p. ka-a-'pet).
Be lost to, pet (pr. a-pet-e, p.p. ka-a-pet).
I have lost my knife, ko-pet-en-o rotuet.
Take away and lose, ilus (pr. a-'lus-i, p.p. ka-a-'lus).
Louse, iseria (iseriat), pl. iser (iserek).
Love, cham (pr. a-chom-e, p.p. ka-a-cham).
Lover (*man*), saanya (saandet), pl. saan (saanik).
 (*girl*), murer (mureret), pl. mureren (murerēnik).
 (*woman*), kipaikeiyo (kipaikeiyot), pl. kipaikein (kipaikeīnik).
Lower (*hither*), irek-u (pr. a-'rek-u, p.p. ka-a-'rek-u).
 (*thither*), irek-te (pr. a-'rek-toi-i, p.p. ka-a-'rek-te).
Lower a load, itu (pr. a-'tu-i, p.p. ka-a-'tu).
Luck, keluno (kelunet); tokoch (toket).

It is lucky, mi-i keluno *or* mi-i tokoch.
Lump (*piece*), kipeperia (kipeperiat), pl. kipeperua (kipeperuek).
Lump on the body, mulua (muluet), pl. mulondoi (mulondōk).
Lung, puon (puondet), pl. puon (puonik).
Lurk, tech. (See **Trap**.)

be **Mad**, tinye iyuek.
Mad person, kipiyuo (kipiyuet), pl. kipiyuon (kipiyuonik).
Maggot, kut (kutiet), pl. kut (kutik).
Magic, chepkericho (chepkerichot), pl. chepkerichin (chepkerichīnik).
Make magic, pan (pr. a-pon-e, p.p. ka-a-pan).
Magician, ponin (ponindet), pl. pon (ponik).
Maize (*corn*), ipandia (ipandiat), pl. ipande (ipandek).
 (*plant*), mopcho (mopchot), pl. mop (mopek).
Make, ai-te (pr. o-oi-toi-i, p.p. kâ-ai-te).
Make equal, like, &c., ioiechin-e (pr. a-'oiechin-dos-i, p.p. kâ-'oiechin-e).
 ikerke (pr. a-'kerke-i, p.p. ka-a-'kerke).
Make for, ai-to-chi (pr. o-oi-to-chi-ni, p.p. kâ-ai-to-chi).
Make haste, chok-chi (pr. a-chok-chi-ni, p.p. ka-a-chok-chi).
Make metal things, itany (pr. a-'tony-i, p.p. ka-a-'tany).
Make to go up, itoke (pr. a-'toke, p.p. ka-a-'toke).
Make or *take up a little at a time*, mukut (pr. a-mukut-i, p.p. ka-a-mukut).
Make up a fire, iyuok-chi mat.
Make water, sukus (pr. a-sukus-i, p.p. ka-a-sukus).

Make:
Make well, isap (pr. a-'sop-i, p.p. ka-a-'sap).
Don't make a noise! sis!
Male, kiruk (kirkit), pl. kiruk (kirukik).
 muren (murenet), pl. muren (murenik).
Man, chii (chiito), pl. piich (piik).
(warrior), muren (murenet), pl. muren (murenik).
(old man), poiyo (poiyot), pl. poiisio (poiisiek).
Mane *(along the neck),* urer (ureryet), pl. urer (urerik).
(falling between the ears), songonyo (songonyet), pl. songonyai (songonyaiik).
Mantis, chepkoima (chepkoimet), pl. chepkoimoi (chepkoimōk).
Many, chañg *or* che-chañg.
Mark, tisia (tisiet).
 perut. (See **Scar.**)
Markings on a shield, siro (siret).
Markings on the sword, spear, and body of a warrior who has killed an enemy, kamaro (kamaret), pl. kamarōs (kamarōsiek).
Market-place, kâpwalio (kâpwaliot).
 kâpsīro (kâpsīret).
Place of meeting for trade purposes, kesimo (kesimet), pl. kesimōs (kesimōsiek).
Marrow, amsa (amset), pl. amsoi (amsōk).
 mwait'-ap-kôwet.
Marry, itun (pr. a-'tun-i, p.p. ka-a-'tun).
Massage, imoi (pr. a-'moi-i, p.p. ka-a-'moi).
Matter *(pus),* purut (purutek).
A matter, ñgolio (ñgoliot), pl. ñgal (ñgalek).
What is the matter? Mi-í ne?
Meal *(food),* omit (omdit), pl. omituag (omituagik).

(flour), pusia (pusiat), pl. pusio (pusiek).
Meaning:
What is the meaning of this? Amu-ne? Ne kii-i? Kii-i ne?
Measure, ikwa (pr. a-'kwa-i, p.p. ka-a-'kwa).
Meat, peny (pendo), pl. pany (panyek).
Medicine, kericho (kerichot), pl. kerich (kerichek).
Chief medicine man, orkoiyo (orkoiyot), pl. orkoi (orkoiik).
Lesser medicine man, kipsakeiyo (kipsakeiyot), pl. kipsakein (kipsakeīnik).
 kipungu (kipungut), pl. kipungun (kipungunik).
Meet, o-nyor-u-ke (pr. ki-nyor-u-ke, p.p. ka-ki-nyor-u-ke).
Meet with, nyor-u (pr. a-nyor-u, p.p. ka-a-nyor-u).
Meet together with, tui-ye (pr. a-tui-tos-i, p.p. ka-a-tui-ye).
Go to meet someone, torok-te (pr. a-torok-toi-i, p.p. ka-a-torok-te).
Melt (act.), irot (pr. a-'rot-i, p.p. ka-a-'rot).
 (neut.), chôt (pr. a-chôt-e, p.p. ka-a-chôt).
 rot (pr. a-rot-e, p.p. ka-a-rot).
Mend, ai-te (pr. o-oi-toi-i, p.p. kâ-ai-te).
Stop or *fill up a hole,* rich (pr. a-rich-e, p.p. ka-a-rich).
Sew, nap (pr. a-nop-e, p.p. ka-a-nap).
Mend by sewing a piece on, kin (pr. a-kin-e, p.p. ka-a-kin).
Menstruous person, sunon (sunonik).
Mention, itar (pr. a-'tor-i, p.p. ka-a-'tar).
Merchandise, olisio (olisiet).
Merchant, makorio (makoriot), pl. mokore (mokorek).
Merely, kitio.

Messenger, koioktoio (koioktoi-et), pl. koioktoi (koioktoiik).
Middle, kwen (kwenut), pl. kwenus (kwenusiek).
Midge, sogoria (sogoriet), pl. sogor (sogorik).
kipchakarario (kipchakarariet), pl. kipchakarar (kipchakararik).
Midwife, kork'-ap-sikisis.
Milk, che (cheko).
A little milk, cheiyot totegin.
Milk which has been allowed to stand, kasamot.
Curdled milk, mursi (mursiik).
(v.), ke (pr. a-ke, p.p. ka-a-ke).
Millet (*corn*), mosongio (mosongiot), pl. mosong (mosongek).
(*stalk*), tiañgia (tiañgiat), pl. tiañgin (tiañgīnik).
Millipede, chepchongo (chepchonget), pl. chepchonges (chepchongesiek).
Mind (*take care of*), iro. (See irregular verbs, p. 224.)
(*bear in mind*), ipwat (pr. a-'pwot-i, p.p. ka-a-'pwat).
Never mind! ma-uu kii!
Mind, mukulel. (See **Heart**.)
Mine, nanyō, pl. chachōget.
Mingle, itui-e (pr. a-'tui-tos-i, p.p. ka-a-'tui-e).
(*mingle together*), o-'tui-eke (pr. ki-itui-tos-i-eke, p.p. ka-ki-itui-eke).
(*mix*), puruch (pr. a-puruch-i, p.p. ka-a-puruch).
Be mingled (*mixed*), puruch-ke (pr. a-puruch-i-ke, p.p. ka-a-puruch-ke).
Miscarriage, ñgem moiet.
Mislead, ipet (pr. a-'pet-i, p.p. ka-a-'pet).
Miss what is aimed at, ichilil (pr. a-'chilil-i, p.p. ka-a-'chilil).
Mist, puret (pureto).
kipurienge (kipurienget).

Mistake, kachililo (kachililet), pl. kachililōs (kachililōsiek).
Make a mistake, lēl (pr. a-lēl-e, p.p. ka-a-lēl).
Mix, puruch (pr. a-puruch-i, p.p. ka-a-puruch).
Modesty, konyit (konyit).
Mole, puñguñgwa (puñguñgwet), pl. puñguñgōn (puñguñgōnik).
Money:
Rupee, rupia (rupiet), pl. rupies (rupiesiek).
Pice, pesaiya (pesaiyat), pl. pesaiin (pesaiīnik).
Cent, olkisoi (olkisoiyet), pl. olkisoiin (olkisoiīnik).
Mongoose, chepkusiro (chepkusiret), pl. chepkusirai (chepkusiraiik).
Monkey:
Baboon, moso (moset), pl. moson (mosonik).
Colobus guereza, koroiit (koroiityet), pl. koroiit (koroiitik).
Cercopithecus albigularis, tisia (tisiet), pl. tisoi (tisōk).
C. griseo-viridis, cherere (chereret), pl. chereren (chererēnik).
Month, arawa. (See **Moon**.)
Moon, arawa (arawet), pl. araa (arawek).
More. (See p. 182.)
Make more, give more, tes (pr. a-tes-e, p.p. ka-a-tes).
Give more beer, res (pr. a-res-e, p.p. ka-a-res).
To be more something (e.g. *strong*), tamne (pr. a-tamne, p.p. ka-a-tamne).
Moreover, ko-keny.
Morning (*early*), korirun (korirunet).
(*later*), pēt (pētut).
Every morning, mutai.
Mortar (*for pounding corn*), ken (kenut), pl. kenus (kenusiek).
Mosquito, tiñgwich (tiñgwichet), pl. tiñgwich (tiñgwichik).

Moss, kurongur (kuronguriet), pl. kuronguris (kurongurisiek).
Moth, tapurpur (tapurpuriet), pl. tapurpur (tapurpurik).
Mother, kamet *or* kametit, pl. angut-kamet *or* angut-kametuak.
Own mother (*woman or child speaking*), eiyo, pl. angut-eiyo.
(*man speaking*), korket, pl. angut-korket.
Thy mother, komit, pl. angut-komit *or* angut-komituak.
So and so's mother, kopot anum.
Mother-in-law (*man's*), karukin (karukinit).
(*woman's*), pôkir (pôkirto).
(*man's own*), karucho.
(*woman's own*), pôkir.
Mound (*in fields*), kâpsagun (kâpsagunik).
Mount, lany (pr. a-lony-i, p.p. ka-a-lany).
Mountain, tulua (tuluet), pl. tuluondoi (tuluondōk).
Mourn, arogen (pr. a-arogen-i, p.p. kâ-arogen).
People who mourn, or *a house of mourning,* kimnam-kut.
Mouse, kimñgoris (kimñgorisiet), pl. kimñgorisoi (kimñgorisōk).
Mouth, kut (kutit), pl. kutusua (kutusuek).
Move (*hither*), inok-u (pr. a-'nok-u, p.p. ka-a-'nok-u).
(*thither*), inak-te (pr. a-'nok-toi-i, p.p. ka-a-'nak-te).
(*change place of dwelling*), u (pr. a-u-e, p.p. ka-a-u).
Cause to remove, iu (pr. a-'u-i, p.p. ka-a-'u).
Much, mīsing ; che-chañg.
Very much, kut.
Mucus (*from the nose*), seper (seperik).
Mud, lapcha (lapchat).
(*of river*), ñgatatia (ñgatatiat), pl. ñgatat (ñgatatek).

Multiply, ichañgit (pr. a-'choñgit-i, p.p. ka-a-'chañgit).
(*increase*), tes (pr. a-tes-e, p.p. ka-a-tes).
Multitude, tuiyo (tuiyot), pl. tuiyōs (tuiyōsiek).
Murder, par (pr. a-por-e, p.p. ka-a-par).
Murderer, porin (porindet), pl. por (porik).
Murderer of a Nandi, rumin (rumindet), pl. rum (rumik).
Mushroom, popa (popat), pl. pop (popek).
Musical instruments:
Horn, kuina (kuinet), pl. kuinai (kuinaiik).
Greater kudu horn, ikondi (ikondit), pl. ikondis (ikondisiek).
Wooden horn, serengwa (serengwet), pl. serengon (serengonik).
indureru (indurerut), pl. indurerus (indurerusiek).
Bell, kipkurkur (kipkurkuriet), pl. kipkurkurai (kipkurkuraiik).
Lyre, kipokan (kipokandet), pl. kipokandin (kipokandīnik).
Must, tai (followed by the subjunctive).
I must go, tai a-wa.
Mutilate, til (pr. a-til-e, p.p. ka-a-til).
My, nyō, pl. chōk.

Nail (*of finger or toe*), siiya (siiyet), pl. sioi (siōk).
Naked, puch, pl. puch.
Name, kaina (kainet), pl. kainoi (kainōk).
(v.), itar (pr. a-'tor-i, p.p. ka-a-'tar).
(*call*), kur (pr. a-kur-e, p.p. ka-a-kur).
(*give a name to*), ikochi kainet.
What is my name ? ki-kur-en-ó ne ?
What is thy name ? ki-kur-en-ín ne ?

Name:
What is his (or *her*) *name ?* ki-kur-én ne ?
What is our name ? ki-kur-enéch ne ?
What is your name ? ki-kur-enók ne ?
What is their name ? ki-kur-én ne ?
Naming, kurso (kurset).
Nape (*of the neck*), kimut (kimutit), pl. kumutis (kimutisiek).
Narrow, tenden, pl. tendin.
Navel (*small*), serumb (serumbet), pl. serumbon (serumbonik).
(*large*), muk (muket), pl. mukes (mukesiek).
Near, nēgit.
Neck, kat (katit), pl. katusua (katusuek).
Nape of the neck, kimut (kimutit), pl. kimutis (kimutisiek).
Necklace (*of iron bound with small iron rings*), asingai (asingaiit), pl. asingaiin (asingaiīnik).
(*of chains*), sirimwagik. (See **Chain.**)
(*of beads*), anongoiīnik, &c. (See **Bead.**)
(*of chips of gourd*), sepet (sepetiet), pl. sepetai (sepetaiik).
Married women's necklace, merenget-ap-tamok ; muit'-ap-sonoi.
Need, mach (pr. a-moch-e, p.p. ka-a-mach).
Needle, kata (katet), pl. katoi (katōk).
Neglect, irōkut (pr. a-'rōkut-i, p.p. ka-a-'rōkut).
Neighbour, kokwa (kokwet), pl. kokwan (kokwanik).
Neither —nor, annan (with negative).
Nest, kot-ap-tarityet.
Net (*trap*), mesto (mestet), pl. mestoi (mestōk).

Neutral land, surkwen (surkwenet), pl. surkwenōs (surkwenōsiek).
Never, akut keny *or* kie-keny (with negative).
I shall never forget, m-a-utie ñga kie-keny *or* m-o-tiny kie-keny.
New, lēl, pl. lelach.
News, lokoiyo (lokoiyot), pl. lokoiyua (lokoiyuek).
ñgolio (ñgoliot), pl. ñgal (ñgalek).
Nibble, nye (pr. a-nye, p.p. ka-a-nye).
Nice, mie, pl. miach.
(*sweet*), anyiny, pl. onyinyin.
Night, kemboi (kembaut), pl. kembaus (kembausiek).
lakat (lakatut), pl. lakatus (lakatusiek).
All night, kemboi kut koiech ; kemboi koiech ; koiech.
Nine, sokol.
Nineteen, taman ok sokol.
Ninety, tomonuagik sokol.
Ninth, ap-sokol.
Nipple, kīna (kīnet), pl. kīnai (kīnaiik).
No, achecha.
Nobody:
There is nobody, ma-mi-i chii.
Nobody's, mo pa-chii tukul.
Noise, pol (polet), pl. polōs (polōsiek).
Great noise, polot (polotet).
Shout, waka (wakat).
Make a noise, pol (pr. a-pol-e, p.p. ka-a-pol).
Nonsense, perperio (perperiet); apusan (apusanet).
Nose, ser (serut), pl. serun (serunek).
Not, m (prefixed to the verb).
Not yet, tom ; toma.
Notice, iro. (See irregular verbs, p. 224.)
Nourish, iak-e (pr. a-'ok-i, p.p. kâ-'ak-e).

ENGLISH-NANDI VOCABULARY 279

Now, nguno; rani (*to-day*); nguni (*at once*).
Just now, a short while ago, atkai.
Nowadays, êkōsie-chu.
Nullah, marin (marinda), pl. marinua (marinuek).
Number, iīt (pr. a-'īt-i, p.p. ka-a-'īt).
Nurse, cheplakwa (cheplakwet), pl. cheplakoi (cheplakōk).
 (v.), tiny (pr. a-tiny-e, p.p. ka-a-tiny).
 (*feed*), pai (pr. a-poi-e, p.p. ka-a-pai).
Oath, mumia (mumiat), pl. muma (mumek).
Take an oath, make peace, try by ordeal, par mumek.
Obstinate, ui-met, pl. uen-met.
Obstinate man, kimnyonyiyo (kimnyonyiyot), pl. kimnyonyiin (kimnyonyiīnik).
Obstinate woman, chemnyonyiyo.
Obtain, sich (pr. a-sich-e, p.p. ka-a-sich).
Offspring, iio (iiot).
Often, êkōsiek che-chañg; kosakta che-chañg.
Oil, mwai (mwaita), pl. mwan (mwanik).
Old (*of persons or things*), os, pl. ōsen.
Old age, oïn (oïndo).
Old person (m.), poiyo (poiyot), pl. poiisio (poiisiek).
 (f.), chepioso (chepioset), pl. chepiosoi (chepiosōk).
Old thing, old cow, &c., os (osit), pl. osua (osuek).
Omen (*striking the foot against something*), kanōkut (kanōkut), pl. konōkut (konōkutik).
Lucky omen, tailil (taililiet), pl. taililoi (taililōk).
Unlucky omen, sigoran (sigoranet), pl. sigoranoi (sigoranōk).

turio (turiet), pl. turionoi (turionōk).
On, parak; eñg.
Once, petun-ak.
At once, nguni; ngunī-to.
One, akenge.
One by one, akenge-akenge.
One-sided, kimosak.
Only, ineke, &c. (See p. 187.) kitio.
Ooze, robon-u; pun; sa-u.
Open (*uncover*), ñgany (pr. a-ñgony-e, p.p. ka-a-ñgany).
 (*unfasten,* act.), yat (pr. a-yot-e, p.p. ka-a-yat).
 (neut.), yat-ak-e (pr. a-yot-ot, p.p. ka-a-yat-ak-e).
 (*make wide*), ipara (pr. a-'paro-i, p.p. ka-a-'para).
Open the eyes, ichil-u (pr. a-'chil-u, p.p. ka-a-'chil-u).
Open place, tilil (tililiet), pl. tililoi (tililōk).
 (adj.), iseñgeñgat, pl. iseñgeñgotin.
Oppress, inyalil (pr. a-'nyolil-i, p.p. ka-a-'nyalil).
Order (*command*), ñgat (pr. a-ñgot-e, p.p. ka-a-ñgat).
 (*threaten*), ker koñg.
Arrange in order, tet (pr. a-tet-e, p.p. ka-a-tet).
Put in good order, ai-te (pr. o-oi-toi-i, p.p. kâ-ai-te).
In order that, si (followed by the subjunctive).
Orderly, mutio.
Ostrich, nyirot (nyirotiet), pl. nyirotoi (nyirotōk).
 tiony-ap-songolik.
Ostrich feather, songolia (songoliat), pl. songol (songolik).
Ostrich feather head-dress, sombe (sombet), pl. sombenut (sombenutik).
Box for keeping ostrich feathers in, olgitoñg (olgitoñgit), pl. olgitoñgai (olgitoñgaiik).

Ostrich:
Box for keeping ostrich feathers in, kâp-songolik.
Other, ake, pl. alak.
The other (L.), ingo, pl. iko.
Ought to, cham si (followed by the subjunctive).
I ought to go, chom-e si a-wa.
Our, nyo, pl. chok.
Ours, nenyo, pl. chechok.
Out, saañg.
Outside, saañg (saañgut).
Outside the hut, saañgut-ap-kot *or* kot saañg.
Over, parak.
Over the mountain, tuluet parak.
Overcome, ipēl (pr. a-'pēl-i, p.p. ka-a-'pēl).
Overeat oneself, uiren (pr. a-uiren-i, p.p. ka-a-uiren).
Overfeed, iuiren (pr. a-'uiren-e, p.p. ka-a-'uiren).
Overlooker (*overseer*), konortoiin (konortoiindet), pl. konortoi (konortoiik).
Overturn, iwech (pr. a-'wech-i, p.p. ka-a-'wech).
Owner (m.), chiit'-ap-kopo, pl. piik-ap-kopo; chii-chepo. (f.), korket-ap-kopo, pl. korusiek-ap-kopo.
Be part owner, am-de. (See **Eat with**.)
Ox, tany (teta), pl. tich (tuka).
Ox-hide, mui (muito), pl. muiua (muiuek).
Ox with marks cut in its ears, (m.), ki-masas, (f.), che-parīt.
Ox with brand marks, (m.), kipserat, (f.), chep-serat.
Black, (m.), ki-mīso, (f.), che-mīso.
Black and white, koroiit.
Black with white markings on the sides, (m.), kip-kepe, (f.), chep-kepe.
Black with coloured head, motoimet.
White, (m.), kip-sirue, (f.), chep-sirue.
(m.), kip-lelyo, (f.), cheplelyo.
White with brown head, (m.), kipirir-met, (f.), pirir-met.
With white marks round the eyes, (m.), kim-naria, (f.), chem-naria; komarkoñg.
Red-brown, (m.), kip-sitye, (f.), chep-sitye.
Partially brown, (m.), ki-mukye, (f.), che-mukye.
Dapple grey, (m.), kipsamo, (f.), che-samo.
Light grey, (m.), ki-porus, (f.), che-porus.
Hornless, (m.), kip-karai, (f.), chep-karai.
With horns erect, (m.), kim-ñgati-met, (f.), chem-ñgati-met.
With horns pointing in front, (m.), ki-puruk, (f.), puruk.
With crumpled horns, (m.), kipseta, (f.), chep-seta.
(m.), kim-ñgele-met, (f.), ñgelech.
With horns that point inwards, (m.), kip-kuluny-met, (f.), ehepkuluny-met.
One-eyed, (m.), ki-makoñg, (f.), che-makoñg.
Shy, (m.), kim-ñgosos, (f.), chem-ñgosos.
Thin, (m.), kip-tenden, (f.), cheptenden.
Well-fed (*sleek*), sambu.
Cow whose calf has died, arak (araket).
Cow given for wife, che-mwai (che-mwaita), pl. che-mwan (che-mwanik).
Cow that has been ransomed, kelengeyuo (kelengeyuot), pl. kelenge (kelengeyuek).
Cow that has been looted in war, koiyo (koiyet), pl. koiyōs (koiyōsiek).

ENGLISH-NANDI VOCABULARY

Ox:
Cow paid by murderer, iri-ñgot (iri-ñgotit).
Old cow, os (osit), pl. osua (osuek).

Pack, maman (pr. a-momon-i, p.p. ka-a-maman).
(*fasten*), rat (pr. a-rot-e, p.p. ka-a-rat).

Pad (*of grass*), ingatia (ingatiet), pl. ingatai (ingataiik).

Pain, am. (See **Ache**.)

Paint (*brown*), ingaria (ingariet), pl. ingarioi (ingariōk).
(*white*), eorio (eoriot), pl. eor (eorik).
(*any colour, but especially red*), chesoleyua (chesoleyuat), pl. chesole (chesoleyuek).
(v.), sal (pr. a-sol-e, p.p. ka-a-sal).
sir ingariet; sir eoriot, &c.
Paint a shield, imar *or* sir loñget.

Palm (*of the hand*), rubei (rubei-to), pl. rubeiuag (rubeiuagik).

Palm. (See Appendix I.)
Fruit of palm, päk ap sosik; päk ap tironik, &c.

Palm wine, porok (porokek).

Pant, isieny (pr. a-'sieny-i, p.p. ka-a-'sieny).

Pare (*with the hands*), ipony (pr. a-'pony-i, p.p. ka-a-'pony).
ichur (pr. a-'chur-i, p.p. ka-a-'chur).
ichirmit (pr. a-'chirmit-i, p.p. ka-a-'chirmit).
(*with a knife*), iai (pr. a-'oi-e, p.p. kâ-'ai).

Parish, sirit (siritiet), pl. siritai (siritaiik).

Parry, têch (pr. a-têch-e, p.p. ka-a-têch).

Part (*portion*), kipeperia (kipeperiat), pl. kipeperua (kipeperuek).

Part out, ipche (pr. a-ipche, p.p. ka-a-ipche).
chwe (pr. a-chwe, p.p. ka-a-chwe).

Pass, pun (pr. a-pun-e, p.p. ka-a-pun).
Pass by, sir-te (pr. a-sir-toi-i, p.p. ka-a-sir-te).
Pass along, over, ichut-ke (pr. a-'chut-i-ke, p.p. ka-a-'chut-ke).
Pass over (*a river*), lan-de (pr. a-lon-doi-i, p.p. ka-a-lan-de).
Make to pass, ipun (pr. a-'pun-i, p.p. ka-a-'pun).

Pastoral people, poropcho (poropchot), pl. porop (poropek).

Pasture, iak-e (pr. a-'ok-i, p.p. kâ-'ak-e).

Path, or (oret), pl. ortinua (ortinuek).

Pay, mshaharen (mshaharēnik).
Pay thither, yak-te (pr. a-yok-toi-i, p.p. ka-a-yak-te).
Pay hither, yak-u (pr. a-yok-u, p.p. ka-a-yak-u).
Pay to or *for*, yok-chi (pr. a-yok-chi-ni, p.p. ka-a-yok-chi).
Pay a fine, pas (pr. a-pas-e, p.p. ka-a-pas).

Peace, tilia (tiliet), pl. tilionut (tilionutik).
Make peace, ai-te tiliet; par mumek.

be Peaceful, tala-itu (pr. a-tala, p.p. ka-a-tala-itu).

Pebble. (See **Stone**.)

Peel. (See **Pare**.)

Peep, iit (pr. a-'it-e, p.p. ka-a-'it).
Peep in, iit-u (pr. a-'it-u, p.p. ka-a-'it-u).

Peg (*for pegging out skins*), ket (ketit), pl. ket (ketik).
(*for hanging utensils on*), irēu (irēut), pl. irēus (irēusiek).

Pelt, wir-chi (pr. a-wir-chi-ni, p.p. ka-a-wir-chi).

Penetrate, chut (pr. a-chut-e, p.p. ka-a-chut).

Penis (*circumcised*), pirit (pirtit), pl. pirīt (pirītik).
(*uncircumcised*), monyis (monyiset), pl. monyisōs (monyisōsiek).
People, piich (piik).
Other people's, ap-piik.
People like us, (m.), akut-achek, (f.), angut-achek.
Perceive, iro. (See irregular verbs, p. 224.)
Perhaps, iiyo ; apere.
Perhaps it is thus, apere noto.
Permission, pan (panda).
Permit, cham-chi ; ikochi panda.
I permit him to go, a-cham-chini kwa *or* a-'kochi panda kwa.
Perpetually, kwe-keny.
Person, chii (chiito), pl. piich (piik).
A grown person, chiito ne-mukul.
Perspiration, kaot (kaotik).
Pestle, mosi (mosit), pl. mosin (mosīnik).
aruwet-ap-kenut.
Phlegm, ñgurureyuo (ñgurureyuot).
To bring up phlegm, ñgurur (pr. a-ñgurur-i, p.p. ka-a-ñgurur).
Physic, kericho (kerichot), pl. kerich (kerichek).
Physician, kipkericho (kipkerichot), pl. kipkerichin (kipkerichīnik).
Pick (*gather*), put (pr. a-put-e, p.p. ka-a-put).
Pick out, letye (pr. a-letye-i, p.p. ka-a-letye).
Pick up one thing, inem-u (pr. a-'nem-u, p.p. ka-a-'nem-u).
Pick up several things, one by one, kwe (pr. a-kwe, p.p. ka-a-kwe).
Pick up several things in a handful, samat (pr. a-samot-i, p.p. ka-a-samat).
(*lift*), sut (pr. a-sut-i, p.p. ka-a-sut).

Piece, kipeperia (kipeperiat), pl. kipeperua (kipeperuek).
Pierce, rut (pr. a-rut-e, p.p. ka-a-rut).
Pierce with a knife or spear, &c., tor (pr. a-tor-e, p.p. ka-a-tor).
Pierce the lobe of the ear, parpar (pr. a-porpor-i, p.p. ka-a-parpar).
Pig, tora (toret), pl. toroi (torōk).
Wart-hog, putie (putieto), pl. putieua *or* putiei (putieuek *or* putieik).
Giant pig, tum (tumda), pl. tumua (tumuek).
Pimple, tigoi (tigoiik).
(*itch*), koiicha (koiichat), pl. koiich (koiichek).
(*rash*), ingosen (ingosēnik).
Pinch, komot (pr. a-komot-i, p.p. ka-a-komot).
mokot (pr. a-mokot-i, p.p. ka-a-mokot).
Pipe (*tobacco*), teret-ap-tumatet.
Pipe-stem, rokor (rokoret), pl. rokorōs (rokorōsiek).
Pit, kering (keringet), pl. keringon (keringonik).
Place, oii (olto), pl. oltōs (oltōsiek).
(v.), konor (pr. a-konor-i, p.p. ka-a-konor).
Plain, oñgata (oñgatet).
(*valley*), otepwa (otepwet), pl. otepwōs (otepwōsiek).
Plan, lokoiyo (lokoiyot), pl. lokoiyua (lokoiyuek).
Plant, kol (pr. a-kol-e, p.p. ka-a-kol).
Plantain. (See **Banana**.)
Plantation, imbar (imbaret), pl. imbaren (imbarēnik).
Plaster (*huts*), mal (pr. a-mol-e, p.p. ka-a-mal).
Plate (*men's*), muit'-ap-kōk.
(*women's*), muit'-ap-koi.
Dish, tapo (tapet), pl. tapoi (tapōk).

Play, ureren (pr. a-ureren-i, p.p. ka-a-ureren).
Please (v. imp.), inyol-chi.
The thing has pleased me, ka-'nyol-cho kii.
Pleasure, kakaso (kakaset).
Plenty, chang.
Pluck (*gather*), put (pr. a-put-e, p.p. ka-a-put).
Pluck out feathers, cut off sheep's wool, &c., sul (pr. a-sul-e, p.p. ka-a-sul).
Plug, tīm (pr. a-tīm-e, p.p. ka-a-tīm).
Plug up a hole, rich (pr. a-rich-e, p.p. ka-a-rich).
Plunder, chor (pr. a-chor-e, p.p. ka-a-chor).
Pocket, lol (lolet), pl. lolotinua (lolotinuek).
Point, kiplitua (kiplituet), pl. kiplitoi (kiplitōk).
Cut to a point, lit (pr. a-lit-e, p.p. ka-a-lit).
Point at, ñgwerer (pr. a-ñgwerer-i, p.p. ka-a-ñgwerer).
Point out, ipor-chi (pr. a-'por-chi-ni, p.p. ka-a-'por-chi).
Pointed, ñgatip, pl. ñgotipen.
Poison, ñgwan (ñgwanet), pl. ñgwanōs (ñgwanōsiek).
(v.), ikochi ñgwanet.
Rub poison on an arrow, inyul (pr. a-'nyul-i, p.p. ka-a-'nyul).
Pole (*stout*), lumeyua (lumeyuot), pl. lume (lumeyuek).
(*slender*), roteyua (roteyuot), pl. rote (roteyuek).
(*stout and long, used for roofs of houses*), kureyua (kureyuot), pl. kure (kureyuek).
(*slender, used for roofs of houses*), chokeyua (chokeyuot), pl. choke (chokeyuek).
Central pole of a house, toloi (toloita), pl. toloiua (toloiuek).
Polish (*by rubbing*), ipuch (pr. a-'puch-i, p.p. ka-a-'puch).

(*by scraping with a knife*), ñgoiñgoi (pr. a-ñgoiñgoi-i, p.p. ka-a-ñgoiñgoi).
Pond, tolīl (tolīlet), pl. tolilon (tolīlonik).
kīnet-ap-nyanjet.
Cattle-pond, sukut (sukutek).
Ponder, kerer met (pr. a-kerer-i met, p.p. ka-a-kerer met).
Poor, panan, pl. ponon.
Poor man (*no relations and no property*), panan (pananet), pl. ponon (pononik).
(*no property*), kâpsuretin (kâpsuretindet), pl. kâpsuret (kâpsuretik).
Porcupine, chepswerer (chepswererit), pl. chepswereren (chepswererēnik).
Porcupine quill, sabitia (sabitiat), pl. sabiten (sabitēnik).
Porridge, kimnyio (kimnyiet), pl. kimoi (kimoiik).
Lump of porridge, kererut (kererutiet), pl. kererut (kererutik).
To stir porridge, kwany kimnyiet.
To cook porridge, chul kimnyiet.
Porter, otuag. (See **Slave.**)
Portion, kiperperia (kiperperiat), pl. kiperperua (kiperperuek).
(*half*), matua (matuet), pl. matuas (matuasiek).
Possessions, tukun (tukuk).
Possessor (m.), chiit'-ap-kopo, pl. piik-ap-kopo.
(f.), korket-ap-kopo, pl. korusiek-ap-kopo.
Possibly, iiyo ; apere.
Post, lumeyuo (lumeyuot), pl. lume (lumeyuek).
Pot (*cooking-pot, jar*), ter (teret), pl. teren (terēnik).
Bake pots, kwañg (pr. a-kwañg-e, p.p. ka-a-kwañg).
Potato, roboonio (robooniot), pl. roboon (roboonik).

Potato:
(*rotten*), metonga (metonget), pl. metongoi (metongōk).
Potsherd, rokcho (rokchet), pl. rokchonoi (rokchonōk).
Potter, chepterenio (cheptereniot), pl. chepterenin (chepterenīnik).
Potter's clay, men (menet).
Poultry, ingok (ingokiet), pl. ingokai (ingokaiik).
Pound (*clean corn by pounding*), tu-i (pr. a-tu-e, p.p. ka-a-tu-i).
Pour (*hither*), roñg-u (pr. a-roñg-u, p.p. ka-a-roñg-u).
(*thither*), ran-de (pr. a-ron-doi-i, p.p. ka-a-ran-de).
Pour for, roñg-ji (pr. a-roñg-ji-ni, p.p. ka-a-roñg-ji).
Pour away, tar-te (pr. a-tor-toi-i, p.p. ka-a-tar-te).
Pour away a little, iñgir-te (pr. a-'ñgir-toi-i, p.p. ka-a-'ñgir-te).
Pour out, apuk-te (pr. a-apuk-toi-i, p.p. kâ-apuk-te).
Pour water on a person's hands, kir-chi (pr. a-kir-chi-ni, p.p. ka-a-kir-chi).
Powder, pusio (pusiek).
Gunpowder, pusaru (pusaruk).
Power, kimnat (kimnatet).
Health, strength, uin (uindo).
Prairie, oñgata. (See **Plain**.)
Pray, som (pr. a-som-e, p.p. ka-a-som).
Beseech (act.), sa (pr. a-so-e, p.p. ka-a-sa).
(neut.), sa-ise (pr. a-so-ise-i, p.p. ka-a-sa-ise).
Beseech fervently, saisai (pr. a-soisoi-e, p.p. ka-a-saisai).
Prayer, somo (somet), pl. somōs (somōsiek).
samso (samset).
sao (saet).
Precede, indoï (pr. a-'ndoï-i, p.p. ka-a-'ndoï).

Prefer, cham (pr. a-chom-e, p.p. ka-a-cham).
be **Pregnant,** manach (pr. a-manoch-i, p.p. ka-a-manach).
Pregnant woman, tomono (tomonet), pl. tomonōs (tomonōsiek).
Pregnant girl, chesorpucho (chesorpuchot), pl. chesorpuchon (chesorpuchonik).
Prepare, ai-te (pr. o-oi-toi-e, p.p. kâ-ai-te).
Present, melek (melekto), pl. melekua (melekuek).
(v.), ikochi. (See irregular verbs, pp. 222–3.)
Presently, toma-kitegin.
Press, ikich (pr. a-'kich-i, p.p. ka-a-'kich).
Press out, iiny (pr. o-'iny-i, p.p. kâ-'iny).
Press heavily upon, irurun-ji (pr. a-'rurun-ji-ni, p.p. ka-a-'rurun-ji).
Prevent, rany (pr. a-rony-e, p.p. ka-a-rany).
(*refuse to*), imelel (pr. a-'melel-i, p.p. ka-a-'melel).
Prick, tor (pr. a-tor-e, p.p. ka-a-tor).
Prisoner of war, cheploñgio (cheploñgiot), pl. cheploñgin (cheploñgīnik).
Privy, kapia (kapiat).
To go to, pi (pr. a-pi-e, p.p. ka-a-pi).
Proceed, ui. (See irregular verbs, pp. 220–1).
Procure for, sik-chi (pr. a-sik-chi-ni, p.p. ka-a-sik-chi).
Prod, iur (pr. a-'ur-i, p.p. ka-a-'ur).
Prohibit, ete (pr. a-ete, p.p. ka-a-ete).
Prop up, ti (pr. a-ti-e, p.p. ka-a-ti).
Properly, ko-mie.
Property, tukun (tukuk).

Prophesy, | ñgor (pr. a-ñgor-e, p.p. ka-a-ñgor).
Prostitute, chepkumeio (chepkumeiot), pl. chepkumein (chepkumeīnik).
chemarat sainet; makerko kere kwet.
Protect, rīp (pr. a-rīp-e, p.p. ka-a-rīp).
iuit (pr. a-'uit-i, p.p. ka-a-'uit).
Proverb, atindio (atindiot), pl. atindon (atindonik).
aina. (See **River.**)
Puff, kut (pr. a-kut-e, p.p. ka-a-kut).
Be puffed up, men (pr. a-men-e, p.p. ka-a-men).
Pull, ichut (pr. a-'chut-i, p.p. ka-a-'chut).
Pull out, itut (pr. a-'tut-i, p.p. ka-a-'tut).
Pull out hairs, &c., put (pr. a-put-e, p.p. ka-a-put).
Pull or take out teeth, ot (pr. a-ot-e, p.p. ka-a-ot).
Pumpkin, chepololo (chepololet), pl. chepololin (chepololīnik).
Punishment, peluku (pelukut).
Punishment of God, ñgokis (ñgokisto).
Pure, tilil, pl. tililen.
Purgative, seketet (seketetik).
Purge, ikor-ke (pr. a-'kor-i-ke, p.p. ka-a-'kor-ke).
Purpose (*do on purpose*), kwet-yi (pr. a-kwet-yi-ni, p.p. ka-a-kwet-yi).
Pursue, isup (pr. a-'sup-i, p.p. ka-a-'sup).
(*hunt*), mwog (pr. a-mwog-e, p.p. ka-a-mwog).
(*seek for*), cheñg (pr. a-cheñg-e, p.p. ka-a-cheñg).
Pus, purut (purutek).
Push, riep (pr. a-riep-e, p.p. ka-a-riep).

Push away, och (pr. a-och-e, p.p. ka-a-och).
Put, konor (pr. a-konor-i, p.p. ka-a-konor).
Put across (*a river*), ilan-de (pr. a-'lon-doi-i, p.p. ka-a-'lande).
Put a pot on the fire, korkot (pr. a-korkot-i, p.p. ka-a-korkot).
Put a pot near the fire, kwany (pr. a-kwony-i, p.p. ka-a-kwany).
Put down (e. g. *a load*), itu (pr. a-'tu-i, p.p. ka-a-'tu).
Put down by oneself, itu-ke (pr. a-'tu-i-ke, p.p. ka-a-'tu-ke).
Put in a line (*join*), rop (pr. a-rop-e, p.p. ka-a-rop).
Put in a row, tet (pr. a-tet-e, p.p. ka-a-tet).
Put into, put on, in-de (pr. a-'n-doi-i, p.p. ka-a-'n-de).
Put in the sun, ma (pr. a-mo-i, p.p. ka-a-ma).
Put on clothes, ilach (pr. a-'loch-i, p.p. ka-a-'lach).
Put out, inem-u (pr. a-'nem-u, p.p. ka-a-'nem-u).
Put out fire, par (pr. a-por-e, p.p. ka-a-par).
Put out fire by water, tis (pr. a-tis-e, p.p. ka-a-tis).
Put thus, ile-chi (pr. a-'le-chi-ni, p.p. ka-a-'le-chi).
Put to (*shut*), is-chi (pr. a-is-chi-ni, p.p. ka-a-is-chi).
Put to flight, ilapat (pr. a-'lopot-i, p.p. ka-a-'lapat).
Put to rights, ai-te (pr. o-oi-toi-i, p.p. kâ-ai-te).
Put together, iom-e (pr. a-'omdos-i, p.p. kâ-'om-e).
Put up, itoke (pr. a-'toke, p.p. ka-a-'toke).
Put wood on a fire, iyuok-chi mat.

Quake, pôtan (pr. a-pôton-i, p.p. ka-a-pôtan).

Quarrel (*fight, battle*), porio (poriet), pl. poriōs (poriōsiek).
(*shouting, noise*), wakutio (wakutiet).
(v.), o-por-ie (pr. ki-por-tos-i, p.p. ka-ki-por-ie).
(*strike*), pir (pr. a-pir-e, p.p. ka-a-pir).
Cause to quarrel with, ipe (pr. a-'pe-i, p.p. ka-a-'pe).
iul-ie (pr. a-'ul-dos-i, p.p. ka-a-'ul-ie).
Don't quarrel! ket!
Quarrelsome, ap-wakutiet; aporiet.
Quell, isis (pr. a-'sis-i, p.p. ka-a-'sis).
Quench (*fire*), tis (pr. a-tis-e, p.p. ka-a-tis).
Question, tepo (tepet), pl. tepōs (tepɔsiek).
(v.), tep (pr. a-tep-e, p.p. ka-a-tep).
Question people to ascertain who has committed a crime, kin (pr. a-kin-e, p.p. ka-a-kin).
Questions, questioning, tepso (tepset).
be **Quick, do Quickly**, chokchi (pr. a-chok-chi-ni, p.p. ka-a-chok-chi).
Come quickly, chok-u (pr. a-chok-u, p.p. ka-a-chok-u).
Go quickly, chak-te (pr. a-choktoi-i, p.p. ka-a-chak-te).
Quiet, isis (pr. a-'sis-i, p.p. ka-a-'sis).
Become quiet, sis (pr. a-sis-e, p.p. ka-a-sis).
Quietly, mutio.
Quit, man-de (pr. a-mon-doi-i, p.p. ka-a-man-de).
Quite, kwe-keny.
Quiver (*full of arrows*), moot (mootiet), pl. mootoi (mootōk).
(*empty*), songo (songet), pl. songōs (songōsiek).

Quiver for the loñgnet *arrows*, kâploñgin (kâploñginit), pl. kaploñginin (kaploñginīnik).
To quiver, pôtan (pr. a-pôton-i, p.p. ka-a-pôtan).
Rabbit (*hare*), kiplengwai (kiplengwet), pl. kiplengonoi (kiplengonōk).
Race, o-maimai-ye (pr. ki-maimai-tos-i, p.p. ka-ki-maimai-ye).
Rafter, lumeyuo (lumeyuot), pl. lume (lumeyuek).
Rag, akwo (akwot), pl. akwai (akwek).
Raid, lug (luget), pl. lugōs (lugōsiek).
(v.), set (pr. a-set-i, p.p. ka-a-set).
Raider, kipset.
Rain, rob (robta), pl. robua (robuek).
(v.), robon.
It rains, robon-i *or* robon-i robta.
Cause to rain, irobon (pr. a-'robon-e, p.p. ka-a-'robon).
Rainbow (*inner*), chemñgisir (chemñgisiriet), pl. chemñgisiroi (chemñgisirōk).
(*outer*), kwapal (kwapaliet), pl. kwapaloi (kwapalōk).
Rainmaker, uin (uindet), pl. ui (uik).
Rainmaker's medicine, kiptakcha (kiptakchat), pl. kiptaken (kiptakēnik).
Raise, sut (pr. a-sut-e, p.p. ka-a-sut).
Make to rise, itoke (pr. a-'toke, p.p. ka-a-'toke).
Ransom, itiach (pr. a-'tiach-i, p.p. ka-a-'tiach).
keleny (pr. a-keleny-i, p.p. ka-a-keleny).
Rap (*with the knuckles*), ikoñgony (pr. a-'koñgony-i, p.p. ka-a-'koñggony).

ENGLISH-NANDI VOCABULARY 287

Rap:
luch (pr. a-luch-e, p.p. ka-a-luch).
Rash, ingosen (ingosēnik).
Rat, muria (muriat), pl. mur (murek).
There are several kinds of rats :—
House-rat, kipkoiyo (kipkoiyot), pl. kipkoiin (kipkoiīnik).
kipkēu (kipkēut), pl. kipkēun (kipkēunik).
(*mouse*), kimñgoris (kimñgorisiet), pl. kimñgorisoi (kimñgorisōk).
Field-rat, isundu (isundut), pl. isundus (isundusiek).
kipsukuchuchu (kipsukuchuchut), pl. kipsukuchuchun (kipsukuchuchunik).
masiroria (masiroriat), pl. masirorin (masirorīnik).
(*mole*), puñguñgwa (puñguñgwet), pl. puñguñgon (puñguñgonik).
Rather (*preferably*), kaikai.
Rations, omit (omdit), pl. omituag (omituagik).
Raw (*uncooked* or *inexperienced*), tuon, pl. tuonen.
Be made raw, ichur (pr. a-'chur-i, p.p. ka-a-'chur).
isindīt (pr. a-'sindīt-i, p.p. ka-a-'sindīt).
Be made raw by fire, tiol (pr. a-tiol-i, p.p. ka-a-tiol).
Razor, murunyo (murunyet), pl. murunyoi (murunyōk).
Reach (*arrive at*), it (pr. a-it-e, p.p. ka-a-it).
Reach a person, it-yi (pr. a-it-yi-ni, p.p. ka-a-it-yi).
Cause to reach, iit (pr. a-'it-i, p.p. ka-a-'it).
Ready. (See **Finish**.)
It is ready, ka-ko-rok.
I am ready, ka-a-pīt-u.

Reap, kes (pr. a-kes-e, p.p. ka-a-kes).
(*break off the heads of eleusine corn*), pâch (pr. a-poch-i, p.p. ka-a-pâch).
(*break off the heads of millet*), iri mosongek.
Rear (*a child*), tiny (pr. a-tiny-e, p.p. ka-a-tiny).
Rearguard, oltim (oltimdo), pl. oltimwag (oltimwagik).
Receive, tâch (pr. a-toch-e, p.p. ka-a-tâch).
(*take*), nam (pr. a-nom-e, p.p. ka-a-nam).
(*accept*), cham (pr. a-chom-e, p.p. ka-a-cham).
Receive for some one else, namchi (pr. a-nom-chi-ni, p.p. ka-a-nam-chi).
Reckon, iīt (pr. a-'īt-i, p.p. ka-a-'īt).
Recline, liel-de (pr. a-liel-dos-i, p.p. ka-a-liel-de).
(*rest*), imuny (pr. a-'muny-i, p.p. ka-a-'muny).
Recognize, inyit (pr. a-'nyit-i, p.p. ka-a-'nyit).
Recollect, ipwat (pr. a-'pwot-i, p.p. ka-a-'pwat).
Recover, sap (pr. a-sop-e, p.p. ka-a-sap).
Rectum, kimesto (kimestoet).
Red, pirir, pl. piriren.
Redeem, keleny (pr. a-keleny-i, p.p. ka-a-keleny).
Reduce, iñgir-te (pr. a-'ñgir-toi-i, p.p. ka-a-'ñgir-te).
(e.g. *to the ranks*), miniñg-itu (pr. a-miniñg, p.p. ka-a-miniñg-itu).
Reed, kirondo (kirondet), pl. kirondōs (kirondōsiek).
Bulrush, cherungu (cherungut), pl. cherungus (cherungusiek).
Reed used for drinking through, rogor (rogoret), pl. rogoron (rogoronik).

Reflect (*consider*), ipwat (pr. a-'pwot-i, p.p. ka-a-'pwat).
Reflect a glare, lil (pr. a-lil-e, p.p. ka-a-lil).
Refuse, esie (pr. a-esie-i, p.p. ka-a-esie).
Cause to refuse, iete (pr. a-'ete, p.p. ka-a-'ete).
(*deter, forbid*), ete (pr. a-ete, p.p. ka-a-ete).
(*prohibit*), ias (pr. a-'os-e, p.p. kâ-'as).
Refuse to (*withhold from*), imelel (pr. a-'melel-i, p.p. ka-a-'melel).
Refute, tii-ye (pr. a-tii-tos-i, p.p. ka-a-tii-ye).
Reject, esie (pr. a-esie-i, p.p. ka-a-esie).
Rejoice, ikas-ke (pr. a-'kos-i-ke, p.p. ka-a-'kas-ke).
Relate, mwa-chi (pr. a-mwo-chi-ni, p.p. ka-a-mwa-chi).
Relation, relative, tilia (tiliet), pl. tilionut (tilionutik).
be **Relaxed** (*loose, slack*), nyelnyel-itu (pr. a-nyelnyel, p.p. ka-a-nyelnyel-itu).
Relish, sutio (sutiot), pl. sut (sutek).
(v.), iro ñgw-anyiny.
Remain (*stay*), tepi (pr. a-tepi-e, p.p. ka-a-tepi).
(*stay for a time*), peni (pr. a-peni-e, p.p. ka-a-peni).
Be left, ñget-u (pr. a-ñget-u, p.p. ka-a-ñget-u).
Remain over, ituch (pr. a-'tuch-i, p.p. ka-a-'tuch).
Remainder, katukia (katukiat), pl. katuken (katukēnik).
Remember, ipwat (pr. a-'pwot-i, p.p. ka-a-'pwat).
Remind, ipwot-chi (pr. a-'pwot-chi-ni, p.p. ka-a-'pwot-chi).
Remorse, ndara (ndarait).
Remove, is-te (pr. a-is-toi-i, p.p. ka-a-is-te).

Rend, kerer (pr. a-kerer-i, p.p. ka-a-kerer).
murmur (pr. a-murmur-i, p.p. ka-a-murmur).
Repair, ai-te (pr. o-oi-toi-i, p.p. kâ-ai-te).
Repay, yak-te-chi (pr. a-yok-toi-i-chi-ni, p.p. ka-a-yak-te-chi).
Reply(*give an answer*),twek-u (pr. a-twek-u, p.p. ka-a-twek-u).
am lokoi.
Reply to, twek-chi (pr. a-twek-chi-ni, p.p. ka-a-twek-chi).
(*answer when called*), iten (pr. a-iten-i, p.p. kâ-iten).
Representative:
Chief medicine man's representative, maotio (maotiot), pl. maot (maotik).
People's representative, kiruog (kiruogindet), pl. kiruog (kiruogik).
Request (*wish*), mach (pr. a-moch-e, p.p. ka-a-mach).
(*pray*), som (pr. a-som-e, p.p. ka-a-som).
Resemble, ioiechin-e (pr. a-'oiechin-dos-i, p.p. kâ-'oiechin-e).
Reservoir, tokom (tokomda), pl. tokomwa (tokomwek).
Respire, ipus (pr. a-'pus-i, p.p. ka-a-'pus).
Rest (neut.),imuny(pr. a-'muny-i, p.p. ka-a-'muny).
(act.), imuny-ji (pr. a-'muny-ji-ni, p.p. ka-a-'muny-ji).
Rest, lât (lâtit).
Ten and the rest (i. 'e. *more than ten*), taman ak lâtit.
Retire (*go back*), ket-ite-ke (pr. a-ket-itoi-i-ke, p.p. ka-a-ket-ite-ke).
(*come back*), ket-u-ke (pr. a-ket-u-ke, p.p. ka-a-ket-u-ke).
Return (neut.), we-i-ke (pr. a-we-ch-i-ke, p.p. ka-a-we-i-ke).

ENGLISH-NANDI VOCABULARY

Return:
  wek-e (pr. a-wek-se-i, p.p. ka-a-wek-e).
  (*go alone and return*), we-chi-ke (pr. a-we-chi-ni-ke, p.p. ka-a-we-chi-ke).
  (act.), iwech (pr. a-'wech-i, p.p. ka-a-'wech).
  Return hither, ket-u (pr. a-ket-u, p.p. ka-a-ket-u).
  Return thither, ket-ite (pr. a-ketitoi-i, p.p. ka-a-ket-ite).
  Return cattle to their kraals, irot (pr. a-'rot-i, p.p. ka-a-'rot).
Reveal, ñgany. (See **Uncover.**)
Revenge, yak-u *or* yak-te. (See **Pay.**)
  iker-te (pr. a-'ker-toi-i, p.p. ka-a-'ker-te).
Reverse, iwech (pr. a-'wech-i, p.p. ka-a-'wech).
Rhinoceros, kipsirīch (kipsirīchet), pl. kipsirīchai (kipsirīchaiik).
Rib, karas (karasta), pl. korosua (korosuek).
Riches, tukun (tukuk); karin (karīk).
Rich man, makorio (makoriot), pl. mokore (mokorek).
Riddle, tangoch (tangochet), pl. tongōch (tongōchik).
Ride upon, lany (pr. a-lony-e, p.p. ka-a-lany).
Ridicule, ias-e (pr. ai-'os-e, p.p. kâ-'as-e).
Right (*hand, &c.*), ap-tai.
Rind, morio (moriot), pl. mor (morik).
Ring, tamokyo (tamokyet), pl. tamok (tamokik).
Ear-ring:
  Iron-wire ear-ring (old men's), kimeiteitio (kimeiteitiot), pl. kimeiteitin (kimeiteitīnik).
  Long iron-wire ear-ring (men's), injololio (injololiot), pl. injololen (injololēnik).
  Small iron slabs (men's), engosholai (engosholaiit), pl. engosholai (engosholaiik).
  Ear-ring worn by junior warriors, chepolungu (chepolungut), pl. chepolungus (chepolungusiek).
  Chain ear-ring, worn by senior warriors, sirim (sirimdo), pl. sirimwag (sirimwagik).
  Married women's ear-ring, tae (taet), pl. taoi (taōk).
  Old women's ear-ring, asuleyo (asuleyot), pl. asulein (asuleīnik).
  Wooden ear-ring, ketit-apiitīt.
  Boys' wooden ear-ring (ornamented), kipalpalio (kipalpaliot), pl. kipalpalin (kipalpalīnik).
  Bead-ring worn by women in the upper part of the ear, chepuchecho (chepuchechot), pl. chepuchechai (chepuchechaiik).
  Reed worn by boys in the upper part of the ear, solio (soliot), pl. sol (solik).
Ring a bell, isach twoliot.
Rip, pêt (pr. a-pêt-e, p.p. ka-a-pêt).
Ripe, rurot, pl. rurotin.
Ripen, rur (pr. a-rur-e, p.p. ka-a-rur).
Rise (*get up*), ñgêt (pr. a-ñgêt-e, p.p. ka-a-ñgêt).
  (*stand up*), tonon (pr. a-tonon-i, p.p. ka-a-tonon).
  (*of the sun*), iech (pr. a-'ech-i, p.p. ka-a-'ech).
  chor-u (pr. a-chor-u, p.p. ka-a-chor-u).
River, aina (ainet), pl. ainōs (ainōsiek).
Rivulet, kereru (kererut), pl. kererus (kererusiek).
Road, or (oret), pl. ortinua (ortinuek).
  Main road, kiboñgboñg (ki-

Road: boñgboñgit), pl. kiboñgboñgen (kiboñgboñgēnik).
Side road, path leading off the main road, kamasan (kamasanet), pl. kamasanoi (kamasanōk).
Roar, moror (pr. a-moror-e, p.p. ka-a-moror).
(of waters), imut (pr. a-'mut-i, p.p. ka-a-'mut).
(of waters at night time), isoi-ye (pr. a-'soi-tos-i, p.p. ka-a-'soi-ye).
Roast *(grain, meat, &c.),* isus (pr. a-'sus-i, p.p. ka-a-'sus).
Roast meat by a slow fire, watan (pr. a-waton-i, p.p. ka-a-watan).
Roast meat with the hair on, imel (pr. a-'mel-i, p.p. ka-a-'mel).
Roast fat, kor (pr. a-kor-e, p.p. ka-a-kor).
Bake meat, pel (pr. a-pel-e, p.p. ka-a-pel).
Make biltong, imerur (pr. a-'merur-i, p.p. ka-a-'merur).
Rob, chor (pr. a-chor-e, p.p. ka-a-chor).
(take by force), rep (pr. a-rep-e, p.p. ka-a-rep).
ipe (pr. a-ipe-i, p.p. ka-a-ipe).
Robber, chorin (chorindet), pl. chor (chorīk).
Roll up, maman (pr. a-momon-i, p.p. ka-a-maman).
Roof, kesiok (kesiokut), pl. kesiokun (kesiokunik).
(ceiling), taput (taputet), pl. taputon (taputonik).
Room *(apartment),* ko *or* ka. (See **House.**)
Is there room here? para yu?
Make room! o-para!
Root, tīkītio (tīkītiot), pl. tīkīt (tīkītik).
Root out, itut (pr. a-'tut-i, p.p. ka-a-'tut).

Rope, porowa (porowet), pl. poroon (poroonik).
Rot, pul (pr. a-pul-e, p.p. ka-a-pul).
nun (pr. a-nun-e, p.p. ka-a-nun).
Rotten, nunat, pl. nunotin; somsom, pl. somsomin; pulot, pl. pulotin; sames, pl. somis.
Be very rotten, nunanun (pr. a-nunanun-e, p.p. ka-a-nunanun).
Round, mukul, pl. mukulen.
Row *(put in row),* tet (pr. a-tet-e, p.p. ka-a-tet).
Rub, siny (pr. a-siny-e, p.p. ka-a-siny).
parpar (pr. a-porpor-i, p.p. ka-a-parpar).
Rub the skin off, isindīt (pr. a-'sindīt-i, p.p. ka-a-'sindīt).
ichur (pr. a-'chur-e, p.p. ka-a-'chur).
Rub on, inyul (pr. a-'nyul-i, p.p. ka-a-'nyul.)
Rub in ointment, iil (pr. a-'il-i, p.p. ka-a-'il).
Rub to pieces (e.g. *corn*), pur (pr. a-pur-e, p.p. ka-a-pur).
Rubbish, meketiwen (meketiwēnik).
pures (puresik).
Rump, sukulum (sukulumdo), pl. sukulumwag (sukulumwagik).
Run, lapat (pr. a-lopot-i, p.p. ka-a-lapat).
toromben (pr. a-toromben-i, p.p. ka-a-toromben).
Outstrip by running, ñgwen-itu (pr. a-ñgwen, p.p. ka-a-ñgwen-itu).
Run away, mwe (pr. a-mwe, p.p. ka-a-mwe).
(of several people), o-rua (pr. ki-rua-i, p.p. ka-ki-rua).
(escape), chilil (pr. a-chilil-e, p.p. ka-a-chilil).
Make to run away, ilapat (pr. a-'lopot-e, p.p. ka-a-'lapat).

ENGLISH-NANDI VOCABULARY

Run:
Run after, awen-ji (pr. a-awen-ji-ni, p.p. kâ-awen-ji).
(*seek after*), sor (pr. a-sor-e, p.p. ka-a-sor).
Run down (e. g. *like water*), chor-te-ke (pr. a-chor-toi-i-ke, p.p. ka-a-chor-te-ke).
Run hard, lapat mīsing; inem-u ñgwek; ñgwen-itu mīsing; mīban.
Runaway, lapatin (lapatindet), pl. lopot (lopotik).
Runner, chepchepin (chepchepindet), pl. chepchep (chepchepik).
ñgwenin (ñgwenindet), pl. ñgwen (ñgwenik).
Rupee, rupia (rupiet), pl. rupies (rupiesiek).
Rust, keruoti (keruotito).

Saliva, ñgul (ñgulek).
Salt, munyu (munyuk).
Salt for tobacco, makat (makatit), pl. makatin (makatīnik).
munyo (munyot), pl. muny (munyek).
(v.), kerech (pr. a-kerech-i, p.p. ka-a-kerech).
Cook without salt, itupan (pr. a-'tupon-i, p.p. ka-a-'tupan).
Salt-lick, ñgeñg (ñgenda), pl. ñgeñgwa (ñgeñgwek).
Salute, ikat (pr. a-'kot-i, p.p. ka-a-'kat).
(*embrace*), toroch (pr. a-toroch-i, p.p. ka-a-toroch).
Sand, ñguñgunya (ñguñgunyat), pl. ñguñguny (ñguñgunyek).
Sandal, kweyo (kweyot), pl. kweōn (kweōnik).
Sandfly, tiñgwich (tiñgwichet), pl. tiñgwich (tiñgwichik).
be Satisfied, mie-itu (pr. a-mie, p.p. ka-a-mie-itu).
Satisfy with food, ipiiy-e (pr. a-'piiy-onye, p.p. ka-a-'piiy-e).

Be satisfied with food, piiy-e (pr. a-piiy-onyi, p.p. ka-a-piiy-e).
Savage, korom, pl. koromen.
Save, sar-u (pr. a-sar-u, p.p. ka-a-sar-u).
Save up, pas (pr. a-pas-e, p.p. ka-a-pas).
Say, mwa (pr. a-mwo-i, p.p. ka-a-mwa).
ñgalal (pr. a-ñgolol-i, p.p. ka-a-ñgalal).
Say bad things of a person, chot (pr. a-chot-e, p.p. ka-a-chot).
Say to, mwa-chi (pr. a-mwa-chi-ni, p.p. ka-a-mwa-chi).
Say thus, ile. (See irregular verbs, p. 225.)
Say thus to, ile-chi (pr. a-'le-chi-ni, p.p. ka-a-'le-chi).
Scabbard. (See **Sheath.**)
Scald, pel (pr. a-pel-e, p.p. ka-a-pel).
Scar, perut (perutiet), pl. perut (perutik).
Scare, in-de nyokornan.
Scarify, wat (pr. a-wot-e, p.p. ka-a-wat).
Scatter, iser-te (pr. a-'ser-toi-i, p.p. ka-a-'ser-te).
Be scattered, iser (pr. a-'ser-i, p.p. ka-a-'ser).
iser-te-ke (pr. a-'ser-toi-i-ke, p.p. ka-a-'ser-te-ke).
Scatter about, iserser (pr. a-'ser-ser-i, p.p. ka-a-'serser).
Scorch, mel (pr. a-mel-i, p.p. ka-a-mel).
Scorch meat, imerur (pr. a-'merur-i, p.p. ka-a-'merur).
(*consume by scorching*), lach (pr. a-loch-e, p.p. ka-a-lach).
(*be on fire*), lal (pr. a-lol-i, p.p. ka-a-lal).
Scorpion, melmel (melmeldo), pl. melmeluag (melmeluagik).
Scour, siny (pr. a-siny-e, p.p. ka-a-siny).

Scout, ñgoror (ñgororet), pl. ñgororōs (ñgororōsiek).
(*spy*), ñgerṭimio (ñgertimiot), pl. ñgertimin (ñgertimīnik).
Scowl at, injurur (pr. a-'njurur-i, p.p. ka-a-'njurur).
Scrape, sīt (pr. a-sīt-e, p.p. ka-a-sīt).
Clean by scraping, ñgoiñgoi (pr. a-ñgoiñgoi-i, p.p. ka-a-ñgoiñgoi).
Scrape off (*husks*), porpor (pr. a-porpor-i, p.p. ka-a-porpor).
(*peel*) iai (pr. a-'oi-e, p.p. ka-'ai).
Scraps (*left after eating*), katukania (katukaniat), pl. katukan (katukanik).
(*left during circumcision*), toloñgia (toloñgiat), pl. toloñg (toloñgik).
Scratch, ingwar (pr. a-'ngwar-i, p.p. ka-a-'ngwar).
Scratch like a hen, was (pr. a-wos-e, p.p. ka-a-was).
Scratch with the claws, kut (pr. a-kut-e, p.p. ka-a-kut).
Scratch a cow (*similar to patting a horse*), ingô (pr. a-'ngô-i, p.p. ka-a-'ngô).
Scrotum, lato (latet), pl. latōs (latōsiek).
(*when castrated*), kâp-lat (kâp-latit), pl. kâp-latin (kâp-latīnik).
Scull, takungu (takungut), pl. takungus (takungusiek).
Sea, nianja. (See **Lake.**)
Search (*look for*), cheñg (pr. a-cheñg-e, p.p. ka-a-cheñg).
Search everywhere, cheñgcheñg (pr. a-cheñgcheñg-e, p.p. ka-a-cheñgcheñg).
Take a light to search for something in the dark, ikweny (pr. a-'kweny-i, p.p. ka-a-'kweny).
Season, oii (olto), pl. oltōs (oltōsiek).
The rainy season (*March to August*), olt'-ap-iwot *or* iwotet.

The dry season (*September to March*), olt'-ap-keme *or* kemēut.
Seat, atep (atepet), pl. atepōs (atepōsiek).
(*stool*), ñgecher (ñgecheret), pl. ñgecheroi (ñgecherōk).
Second, ap-oieñg.
Section (*of warriors*), sirit (siritiet), pl. siritai (siritaiik).
Seduce, sâch (pr. a-soch-e, p.p. ka-a-sâch).
See, iro. (See irregular verbs, p. 224.)
L., ker (pr. a-ker-e, p.p. ka-a-ker).
(*meet*), nyor-u (pr. a-nyor-u, p.p. ka-a-nyor-u).
See coming towards one, iañganu (pr. a-'añg-anu, p.p. kâ-'añg-anu).
See going away from one, iañgate (pr. a-'añg-ati, p.p. ka-'añg-ate).
Seed, kesua (kesuot), pl. kesui (kesuek).
Seek, mach (pr. a-moch-e, p.p. ka-a-mach).
Seek for, cheñg (pr. a-cheñg-e, p.p. ka-a-cheñg).
Seek out for, cheñg-ji (pr. a-cheñg-ji-ni, p.p. ka-a-cheñg-ji).
Seize, nam (pr. a-nom-e, p.p. ka-a-nam).
(*take by force*), ipe (pr. a-ipe-i, p.p. ka-a-ipe).
rep (pr. a-rep-e, p.p. ka-a-rep).
Select, letye (pr. a-letye-i, p.p. ka-a-letye).
Sell, al-te (pr. a-ol-toi-i, p.p. kâ-al-te).
Sell for, al-to-chi (pr. a-ol-to-chi-ni, p.p. kâ-al-to-chi).
Sell dear, kīm (pr. a-kīm-e, p.p. ka-a-kīm).
Seller, altoin (altoindet), pl. alto (altoik).

Send, imut (pr. a-'mut-i, p.p. ka-a-'mut).
Send to a person, ip-chi (pr. a-ip-chi-ni, p.p. kâ-ip-chi).
Send a person, iok-te (pr. a-'ok-toi-i, p.p. kâ-'ok-te).
Send a person to a person, iok-to-chi (pr. a-'ok-to-chi-ni, p.p. kâ-'ok-to-chi).
Send away, is-te (pr. a-is-toi-i, p.p. kâ-is-te).
Send away (*dismiss*), oon (pr. a-oon-e, p.p. ka-a-oon).
Send back, return, iwech (pr. a-'wech-i, p.p. ka-a-'wech).
Sense, met (metit); ñgomnot (ñgomnotet).
He has no sense, ma-tinye ñgomnot; ma-tinye met.
Sentry, rīpin (rīpindet), pl. rīp (rīpik).
Separate (*apart*), loo.
v. (*set far apart*), ilooit (pr. a-'looit-i, p.p. ka-a-'looit).
(*set apart*), ipes-ie (pr. a-'pes-tos-i, p.p. ka-a-'pes-ie).
Separate people who are fighting, ket (pr. a-ket-e, p.p. ka-a-ket).
Servant, otuag. (See **Slave.**)
Serve, poiisie-chi (pr. a-poiisie-chi-ni, p.p. ka-a-poiisie-chi).
ut (pr. a-ut-e, p.p. ka-a-ut).
Be a servant, poiisie (pr. a-poiisie-i, p.p. ka-a-poiisie).
Set, konor (pr. a-konor-i, p.p. ka-a-konor).
(*plant*), kol (pr. a-kol-e, p.p. ka-a-kol).
(*of the sun*), rorok-te (pr. a-rorok-toi-i, p.p. ka-a-rorok-te).
Set (e.g. *a dog*) *at somebody,* ipê (pr. a-'pê-i, p.p. ka-a-'pê).
Set a trap, tech (pr. a-tech-e, p.p. ka-a-tech).
Set fire to, in-de mat; ilal; inam.
Set in order, tet (pr. a-tet-e, p.p. ka-a-tet).
Set out on a journey, ru-te (pr. a-ru-toi-i, p.p. ka-a-ru-te).
Set up, itelel (pr. a-'telel-i, p.p. ka-a-'telel).
Seven, tisap.
Seventeen, taman ak tisap.
Seventh, ap-tisap.
Seventy, tomonuagik tisap.
Sew, nap (pr. a-nop-e, p.p. ka-a-nap).
Sew on, kin (pr. a-kin-e, p.p. ka-a-kin).
Shade, urua (uruet), pl. uruondoi (uruondōk).
(v.), in-de ururet.
Shadow (*of inanimate objects*), urua (uruet), pl. uruondoi (uruondōk).
(*of animate objects*), tomirimir (tomirimiriet), pl. tomirimirai (tomirimiraiik).
Shake, isach (pr. a-'soch-i, p.p. ka-a-'sach).
Shake out, lilich (pr. a-lilich-i, p.p. ka-a-lilich).
Shake trees, itumtum (pr. a-'tumtum-i, p.p. ka-a-'tumtum).
Shake milk to make butter, saisach (pr. a-saisach-e, p.p. ka-a-saisach).
Shake oneself (e.g. *like a sheep*), lele-ke (pr. a-lele-i-ke, p.p. ka-a-lele-ke).
Shame, in-de konyit.
Share, chwe (pr. a-chwe, p.p. ka-a-chwe).
Sharp, ñgatip, pl. ñgatipen.
Sharpen, lit (pr. a-lit-e, p.p. ka-a-lit).
Shave, inem-u (pr. a-'nem-u, p.p. ka-a-'nem-u).
Pull out the hairs, put (pr. a-put-e, p.p. ka-a-put).
She, inendet; ine.
Sheath (*with sword in*), chōk (chōket), pl. chōkon (chōkonik).
Empty sheath, arak (araket), pl. arakai (arakaiik).

Sheath-belt, piren (pirenet), pl. pirenai (pirenaiik).
    pireyuo (pireyuot), pl. pire (pireyuek).
Strap of sheath-belt, torogeyuo (torogeyuot), pl. toroge (torogeyuek).
Sheath of ox, sasai (sasaita), pl. sasaiua (sasaiuek).
Sheep, kechir (kechiriet), pl. kechīr (kechīrek).
    ara (artet), pl. no (nêko).
Ram, mengich (mengit), pl. mengīch (mengīchik).
Castrated sheep, tesiim (tesiimiet), pl. tesiim (tesiimik).
Spotted sheep, cheleke (chelekeit).
Lamb, aruwet-ap-kechir.
Shell (*of fish, snail, &c.*), chemuruag (chemuruaget), pl. chemuruag (chemuruagik).
Husk, morio (moriot), pl. mor (morik).
Shell (*beans, &c.*), ipuny (pr. a-'puny-i, p.p. ka-a-'puny).
Shelter, in-de uruet.
Small hut as shelter, kerio (keriet), pl. keriōn (keriōnik).
Take shelter, têk-u (pr. a-têk-u, p.p. ka-a-têk-u).
Shepherd, mistōa (mistōat), pl. mistōe (mistōek).
    koiokin (koiokindet), pl. koiok (koiokik).
Shield, loñg (loñget), pl. loñgotinua (loñgotinuek).
Outside edge of shield, saanya (saanyat), pl. saanyas (saanyasiek).
Midrib of shield, ketit-ap-loñget.
Raised portion on outside of shield, ketup (ketupet), pl. ketupōs (ketupōsiek).
Leather protection for the hand on midrib of shield, rarai (raraita), pl. raraiua (raraiuek).
Skin used for binding midrib on to shield, tikiseyuo (tikiseyuot), pl. tikise (tikiseyuek).

Kavirondo shield, torkoch (torkochet), pl. torkōch (torkōchik).
Shin, korok (korokta), pl. korokwa (korokwek).
Shine, lelit-u (pr. a-lelit-u, p.p. ka-a-lelit-u).
Shine on, lil (pr. a-lil-e, p.p. ka-a-'lil).
Shiver, pôtan (pr. a-pôton-i, p.p. ka-a-pôtan).
Shoot, mwog (pr. a-mwog-e, p.p. ka-a-mwog).
Shoot into the jugular vein, char (pr. a-chor-e, p.p. ka-a-char).
Shoot (e.g. *as a plant*), iñgat (pr. a-'ñgot-i, p.p. ka-a-'ñgat).
Short, nuach, pl. nuoken.
Be short, nuak-itu (pr. a-nuak, p.p. ka-a-nuak-itu).
Shorten, inuakit (pr. a-'nuakit-i, p.p. ka-a-'nuakit).
Shoulder (*human beings*), tikik (tikikiet), pl. tikikai (tikikaiik).
Shoulder (*animals*), **shoulder-blade** (*human beings*), laiya (laiyet), pl. laiyas (laiyasiek).
Shout, waka (wakat).
    (v.), wach (pr. a-woch-e, p.p. ka-a-wach).
Shout with pain, ite (pr. a-'te-i, p.p. ka-a-'te).
Show, ipor-chi (pr. a-'por-chi-ni, p.p. ka-a-'por-chi).
    iaror-chi (pr. a-'aror-chi-ni, p.p. kâ-'aror-chi).
Shower, kipines (kipinesit).
Shrewd, ñgom, pl. ñgomen.
Shrewd person, ñgomin (ñgomindo), pl. ñgominwag (ñgominwagik).
Shudder, pôtan (pr. a-pôton-i, p.p. ka-a-pôtan).
Shut, ker (pr. a-ker-e, p.p. ka-a-ker).
    (*close*), isip-chi (pr. a-'sip-chi-ni, p.p. ka-a-'sip-chi).

Sick, mioni, pl. miondōs.
Be sick or ill, mian (pr. a-mion-e, p.p. ka-a-mian).
Sickness, mion. (See **Illness.**)
Side (*of a river, &c.*), tapan (tapanda), pl. tapanuag (tapanuagik).
komas (komasto), pl. komasuag (komasuagik).
Near the water, pīt (pītit).
The other side, pītón-in.
Side of the body, karas (karasta), pl. korosua (korosuek).
Side by side, tapan-tapan.
One-sided, kimosak.
Sift grain (*by shaking*), ñga (pr. a-ñgo-i, p.p. ka-a-ñga).
(*by tossing*), ses (pr. a-ses-e, p.p. ka-a-ses).
Silence, isis (pr. a-'sis-e, p.p. ka-a-'sis).
Become silent, sis (pr. a-sis-i, p.p. ka-a-sis).
iep iit.
A silent person, siso (siset), pl. sis (sisek); kipsise (kipsise-it).
Silently, sison ; sisonsison.
Go silently, sis ate (pr. a-sis-ati, p.p. ka-a-sis-ate).
Come silently, sis-anu (pr. a-sis-anu, p.p. ka-a-sis-anu).
Sin, chaluog (chaluogto), pl. choluogwa (choluogwek).
(v.), chaluogen (pr. a-choluogen-i, p.p. ka-a-chaluogen).
Since, akut-keny.
Since then, otkote atkinye.
Sing, tien (pr. a-tien-i, p.p. ka-a-tien).
Sing to a child, isīch (pr. a-'sīch-i, p.p. ka-a-'sīch).
Sing a solo, kur-u (pr. a-kur-u, p.p. ka-a-kur-u).
Sink (act.), ilis (pr. a-'lis-i, p.p. ka-a-'lis).
(neut.), lis (pr. a-lis-e, p.p. ka-a-lis).

Sinner, chaluogin (chaluogindet), pl. choluog (choluogik).
Sister, tupcho (tupchet), pl. angut-tupchet (*or* tupchōsiek).
chep-kamet, pl. angut-chep-kamet (*or* angut-chep-kametuak).
My sister, chep-eiyo, pl. angut-chep-eiyo ; lakwán-ni, pl. lakóchu.
Thy sister, chep-komit, pl. angut-chep-komit (*or* angut-chep-komituak).
Sister-in-law (*wife's sister*), pamur (pamurto).
(*husband's sister*), kamati (kamatit).
Own sister-in-law (*man speaking*), pamuru.
(*woman speaking*), kamati.
Sit, tepi (pr. a-tepi-e, p.p. ka-a-tepi).
Sit upon (e.g. *a stool*), tepe (pr. a-tepe, p.p. ka-a-tepe).
Move along in a sitting posture, like a child unable to walk, yech (pr. a-yech-i, p.p. ka-a-yech).
Sit on eggs, &c., siep (pr. a-siep-e, p.p. ka-a-siep).
Six, illo ; kullo.
Sixteen, taman ak illo.
Sixth, ap-illo.
Sixty, tomonuagik illo.
Skeleton, kôwoi (kôwek).
Skin (*human beings*), iririo (iririot), pl. iriren (irirēnik).
Ox-skin, goat's skin. (See **Hide.**)
(v.), eny (pr. a-eny-e, p.p. ka-a-eny).
kiny (pr. a-kiny-e, p.p. ka-a-kiny).
To skin without cutting the hide, isindīt (pr. a-'sindīt-i, p.p. ka-a-'sindīt).
Sky, parak. (See **Heaven.**)
Sky-light, kutit-ap-taput.
Slap, irapach (pr. a-'rapoch-i, p.p. ka-a-'rapach).

ENGLISH-NANDI VOCABULARY

Slash (*with a knife*), iep (pr. oi-'ep-e, p.p. ka-a-'ep).
Slaughter, eny (pr. a-eny-i, p.p. ka-a-eny).
Slaughter-house, ekor (ekorto), pl. ekorua (ekoruek).
Slave, otuag (otuaget), pl. otuag (otuagik).
  Work as a slave, ut (pr. a-ut-e, p.p. ka-a-ut).
Sleek, akwai, pl. akwoien.
Sleep, ruon (ruondo).
  (v.), ru (pr. a-ru-e, p.p. ka-a-ru).
  Sleep well, ru ko-mie.
  Sleep hungry, rukut (pr. a-rukut-i, p.p. ka-a-rukut).
  Be sleepy, inuich (pr. a-'nuich-i, p.p. ka-a-'nuich).
  I am sleepy, a-'nuich-i or am-a ruondo.
  Doze, pir-te met.
  Sleep on the back, tarñgañg-se (pr. a-tarñgañg-se-i, p.p. ka-a-tarñgañg-se).
  Sleep in somebody else's house, ket (pr. a-ket-e, p.p. ka-a-ket).
  Be unable to sleep, kelel (pr. a-kelel-i, p.p. ka-a-kelel).
Sleeping-place, kâp-ruon (kâp-ruondo).
Sleeping-place (*camp*) *on the war-path*, olpul (olpulit), pl. olpulis (olpulisiek).
Slim, tenden, pl. tendin.
Slip, chapai (pr. a-chapoi-i, p.p. ka-a-chapai).
  Slip away, chilil (pr. a-chilil-i, p.p. ka-a-chilil).
  Slip out of the hand, chirkwin (pr. a-chirkwin-i, p.p. ka-a-chirkwin).
  Slip off, ichewit (pr. a-'chewit-i, p.p. ka-a-'chewit).
Slit, pêt (pr. a-pêt-e, p.p. ka-a-pêt).
Slowly, mutio.

Slug, kimñgeliek. (See **Snail**.)
Small, mining, pl. mingech.
  Be small, miniñg-itu (pr. a-miniñg, p.p. ka-a-miniñg-itu).
  Be very small, nyarat-itu (pr. a-nyarat, p.p. ka-a-nyarat-itu).
Smear on, iil (pr. a-'il-i, p.p. ka-a-'il).
Smell (act.), iñgu (pr. a-'ñgu-i, p.p. ka-a-'ñgu).
  (neut.), ñgu-u (pr. a-ñgu-u, p.p. ka-a-ñgu-u).
  ñgu-te (pr. a-ñgu-toi-i, p.p. ka-a-ñgu-te).
Smith, kitoñgin (kitoñgindet), pl. kitoñg (kitoñgik).
  kutin. (See **Tanner**.)
  Smith's house, kâp-kitoñgin (kâp-kitoñgindet), pl. kâp-kitoñg (kâp-kitoñgik).
Smithy, kâp-kitany (kâp-kitanyit).
Smoke, iyet (iyeto), pl. iyetwag (iyetwagik).
  (v.), moñg-u iyeto.
  Smoke tobacco, kul tumatet.
Smooth, tapulul, pl. tapululin.
  (v.), tapulul (pr. a-tapulul-i, p.p. ka-a-tapulul).
Snail, kimñgeliek (kimñgeliekut), pl. kimñgeliekus (kimñgeliekusiek).
Snake, eren (erenet), pl. erenoi (erenōk).
  Puff-adder, kipchuse (kipchuseit), pl. kipchusein (kipchuseīnik).
  Python, indara (indaret), pl. indaroi (indarōk).
  Other kinds, kâpseroiyo (kâpseroiyot), pl. kâpseroiin (kâpseroiīnik).
  kiptalelio (kiptaleliet), pl. kiptaleloi (kiptalelōk).
Snare, tech (pr. a-tech-e, p.p. ka-a-tech).

ENGLISH-NANDI VOCABULARY 297

Sneeze, irion (pr. a-'rion-i, p.p. ka-a-'rion).
Snore, tangurur (pr. a-tangurur-i, p.p. ka-a-tangurur).
Snort, iñgir (pr. a-'ñgir-i, p.p. ka-a-'ñgir).
(of oxen), tarar (pr. a-tarar-i, p.p. ka-a-tarar).
(of goats), ipir (pr. a-'pir-i, p.p. ka-a-'pir).
Snuff, chepkochut (chepkochut-it), pl. chepkochutin (chepkochutīnik).
Snuff-box, kiprau (kipraut), pl. kipraus (kiprausiek). chepkirau (chepkiraut), pl. chepkiraus (chepkirausiek).
Snuff-box for liquid snuff (L.), kironges (kirongesiet), pl. kirongesoi (kirongesōk).
Soak, inur (pr. a-'nur-i, p.p. ka-a-'nur).
Soft, tangus, pl. tangusin.
Soften, itangus (pr. a-'tangus-i, p.p. ka-a-'tangus).
Soften by putting into water, inūr (pr. a-'nūr-i, p.p. ka-a-'nūr).
Soldier, segein (segeindet), pl. sege (segeik).
    asikarin (asikarindet), pl. asikari (asikarik).
Sole *(of the foot),* keltepes (keltepesiet), pl. keltepesoi (keltepesōk).
    mukuleldo-ap-keldo.
Some, ake, pl. alak.
Somebody, chiit' ake.
Something, kiit' ake.
Sometimes, katukul.
Somewhere, olt' ake.
Son, lakwa (lakwet), pl. lakoi (lakōk).
    ñgeta (ñgetet), pl. ñget (ñgetik).
My son (man speaking), weír-i, lakwán-ni, *or* apoiyo.
My son (woman speaking), lakwán-ni.

Son-in-law, sandi (sandit).
Own son-in-law, sandanaa, pl. akut-sandanaa.
Song, tien (tiendo), pl. tienuag (tienuagik).
Soon, toma kitegin.
First of all, isi.
Soot, ñgetetio (ñgetetiot).
    nesio (nesiot), pl. nes (nesek).
Soothe, sis-chi (pr. a-sis-chi-ni, p.p. ka-a-sis-chi).
Sore, mô. (See **Abscess.**)
Touch a sore place, ioch (pr. a-'och-i, p.p. ka-a-'och).
be Sorry, arogen (pr. a-arogen-i, p.p. kâ-arogen).
Sough *(of the wind),* imut (pr. a-'mut-i, p.p. ka-a-'mut).
Soul, mukulel (mukuleldo), pl. mukuluâ (mukuleluek).
Sound, pol (polet), pl. polōs (polōsiek).
Sound *(whole),* mie, pl. miach; mugul, pl. mugulen.
(healthy), kīm, pl. kīmen.
Soup, sut (sutek).
Sour, ñgwan, pl. ñgwonin.
Sow seeds, kol (pr. a-kol-e, p.p. ka-a-kol).
Sow seeds by scattering, let-te (pr. a-let-toi-i, p.p. ka-a-let-te).
Space, para.
There is space here, para yu.
There is no space here, ma-rich.
Speak, mwa (pr. a-mwo-i, p.p. ka-a-mwa).
    ñgalal (pr. a-ñgolol-i, p.p. ka-a-ñgalal).
    ile. (See irregular verbs, p. 225.)
(of a dying man), twek-u (pr. a-twek-u, p.p. ka-a-twek-u).
Speak! Speak out! amu! mwa mīsing!
Not to speak, sis.
Speaker, mwain (mwaindet), pl. mwai (mwaiik).
Quick speaker, kiplepilep (kip-

Speaker:
lepilepit), pl. kiplepilepis (kiplepilepisiek).
Slow speaker, kipkones (kipkonesit), pl. kipkonesin (kipkonesīnik).
Spear, ñgot (ñgotit), pl. ñgotua (ñgotuek).
Long-shafted small-bladed spear, ndīri (ndīrit), pl. ndīris (ndīrisiek).
Old men's spear, ereñgatia (ereñgatiat), pl. ereñgatin (ereñgatīnik).
Blade, melei (meleito), pl. meleiua (meleiuek).
Ridge of blade, surio (suriot), pl. suriōs (suriōsiek).
Edge of blade, ñgotep (ñgotepto), pl. ñgotepua (ñgotepuek).
Handle, irumo (irumet), pl. irumai (irumaiik).
Where the blade is fixed on to the handle, ko. (See **House.**)
Iron butt, chileyuo (chileyuot), pl. chile (chileyuek).
Leather ring on butt, tikiseyuo (tikiseyuot), pl. tikise (tikiseyuek).
Spider, kiprorog (kiproroget), pl. kiprorogōs (kiprorogōsiek).
Spill, tum-de (pr. a-tum-doi-i, p.p. ka-a-tum-de).
Spinal column, oret-ap-patai.
Spit (*hither*), ñgut-u (pr. a-ñgut-u, p.p. ka-a-ñgut-u).
Spit thither, ñgut-u-te (pr. a-ñgut-u-toi-i, p.p. ka-a-ñgut-u-te).
Spit at, ñgut-yi (pr. a-ñgut-yi-ni, p.p. ka-a-ñgut-yi).
Spit out water or *honey-wine,* piit (pr. a-piit-e, p.p. ka-a-piit).
Spittle, ñgul (ñgulek).
Splash, was (pr. a-was-e, p.p. ka-a-was).
(*of rain*), imut (pr. a-'mut-i, p.p. ka-a-'mut).
Spleen, nuak (nuakta), pl. nuokoi (nuokōk).
Splice, rop (pr. a-rop-e, p.p. ka-a-rop).
Spoil, ñgem (pr. a-ñgem-e, p.p. ka-a-ñgem).
Spokesman, kiruogin. (See **Adviser.**)
Spoon, mukang (mukanget), pl. mukangan (mukanganik).
kutere (kuteret), pl. kuterai (kuteraiik).
seget (segetiet), pl. segetoi (segetōk).
Spoor (*footprints of animals*), mukung (mukunget), pl. mukungon (mukungonik).
Spotted, marmar, pl. mormor.
Spread (*a skin*), iit-te (pr. a-'it-toi-i, p.p. kâ-'it-te).
Spread out in the sun, ma (pr. a-mo-i, p.p. ka-a-ma).
Spring (*of water*), sukutia (sukutiat), pl. sukut (sukutek).
kond'-ap-pêk.
Hot spring, pêk che-lepilep.
Sprinkle, inak-e (pr. a-'nok-i, p.p. ka-a-'nak-e).
(*throw water on*), is (pr. a-is-e, p.p. ka-a-is).
Sprout, sororua (sororuet), pl. sororon (sororonik).
iñgat (pr. a-'ñgot-i, p.p. ka-a-'ñgat).
Spy (*scout*), ñgertimio (ñgertimiot), pl. ñgertimin (ñgertimīnik).
Squabble, o-agut-ie (pr. ki-aguttos-i, p.p. ki-agut-ie).
Cause to squabble with some one, iul-ie (pr. a-'ul-dos-i, p.p. ka-a-'ul-ie).
Squeeze, iiny (pr. o-'iny-i, p.p. ka-a-'iny).
Squirrel, kiplanget (kiplanget-

Squirrel:
iet), pl. kiplangetoi (kiplangetōk).
Stab, tor (pr. a-tor-e, p.p. ka-a-tor).
Stab in the jugular vein, un (pr. a-un-e, p.p. ka-a-un).
Stalk, mopcho (mopchot), pl. mop (mopek).
(*of millet*), tiañgia (tiañgiat), pl. tiañgin (tiañgīnik).
Stalk an animal, sap-chi (pr. a-sop-chi-ni, p.p. ka-a-sap-chi).
Stand, tonon (pr. a-tonon-i, p.p. ka-a-tonon).
telel (pr. a-telel-i, p.p. ka-a-telel).
Stand on something, tonon-e (pr. a-tonon-e, p.p. ka-a-tonon-e).
Make to stand, itonon (pr. a-'tonon-i, p.p. ka-a-'tonon).
Make to stand against, itur (pr. a-'tur-i, p.p. ka-a-'tur).
Stand on one side, yepen (pr. a-yepen-i, p.p. ka-a-yepen).
Stand upright! tonon ko-mie!
Star, kecheia (kecheiat), pl. kechei (kecheik).
The milky way, poit'-ap-kechei.
The evening star, kipokiot.
The morning star, tapoiyot.
The midnight star, kokeliet.
Orion's belt and sword, kakipsomok.
The Pleiades, koremerik.
Stare at, ichil-chi konda.
Start (neut.), yepen (pr. a-yepen-i, p.p. ka-a-yepen).
Startle, imu (pr. a-'mu-i, p.p. ka-a-'mu).
Starve, me eñg-rubet.
Stay, tepi (pr. a-tepi-e, p.p. ka-a-tepi.
(*wait*), kany (pr. a-kony-e, p.p. ka-a-kany).
(*loiter*), ikaa-ke; tepi keny.
Steal, chor (pr. a-chor-e, p.p. ka-a-chor).

Steal from, chor-chi (pr. a-chor-chi-ni, p.p. ka-a-chor-chi).
Stick, kiruk (kirukto), pl. kirukwa (kirukwek).
korok (korokto), pl. korokwa (korokwek).
Swizzle stick, purpo (purpet), pl. purpōs (purpōsiek).
Fire stick, piōn (piōnet), pl. piōn (piōnik).
Women's walking-stick, sigilgilio (sigilgiliot), pl. sigilgil (sigilgilik).
Still, ko-keny.
I am still following him, ta-a-'sup-i; ta-a-'sup-i ko-keny.
Sting, ut (pr. a-ut-e, p.p. ka-a-ut).
Stinging-nettle, siwo (siwot), pl. siwa (siwek).
Stink, samis-itu (pr. a-samis, p.p. ka-a-samis-itu).
A person who stinks, (m.), kipkopok; (f.), chepkopok.
Stir, korkoren (pr. a-korkoren-i, p.p. ka-a-korkoren).
Stir porridge, kwany (pr. a-kwony-i, p.p. ka-a-kwany).
Stomach, mo (moiet), pl. mootinua (mootinuek).
Second stomach, kipkonyan (kipkonyanit), pl. kipkonyanis (kipkonyanisiek).
Third stomach, kipsager (kipsageriet), pl. kipsagerai (kipsageraiik).
Fourth stomach, kiminyor (kiminyoriet), pl. kiminyorai (kiminyoraiik).
Water stomach, imbojo (imbojet), pl. imbojai (imbojaiik).
Stone, koii (koiita), pl. koiin (koiik).
A stone house, kot-ap-koiik; kopokoii.
Stones used for divining purposes, parpar (parparek).
Quartz, kiparkoii (kiparkoiita), pl. kiparkoiin (kiparkoiik).

Stone :
Obsidian, sengwet (sengwetiet), pl. sengwetai (sengwetaiik).
Stool, ñgecher (ñgecheret), pl. ñgecheroi (ñgecherōk).
Stoop, ripis (pr. a-ripiɛ-e, p.p. ka-a-ripis).
 iñguru-ke (pr. a-'ñguru-i-ke, p.p. ka-a-'ñguru-ke).
Stop (act.), rany (pr. a-rony-e, p.p. ka-a-rany).
 (neut.), telel (pr. a-telel-i, p.p. ka-a-telel).
 Stop up (a small hole, &c.), tīm (pr. a-tīm-e, p.p. ka-a-tīm).
 (a big hole, &c.), rich (pr. a-rich-e, p.p. ka-a-rich).
Stopper, muko (muket), pl. mukon (mukonik).
 kereyuo (kereyuot), pl. kere (kereyuek).
Story, kâpchemosin (kâpchemosīnik).
Stout, nyikis, pl. nyikisen; nerat, pl. nerotin.
Straighten, ilitit (pr. a-'litit-i, p.p. ka-a-'litit).
 (stretch), chul (pr. a-chul-e, p.p. ka-a-chul).
 (be straight), chul-ak-e (pr. a-chul-at, p.p. ka-a-chul-ak-e).
Stranger, too (toot *or* toondet), pl. toi (toiek).
Strangle, iket (pr. a-'ket-i, p.p. ka-a-'ket).
Stray, pet (pr. a-pet-e, p.p. ka-a-pet).
 An animal that has strayed, cheputio (cheputiot), pl. cheputin (cheputīnik).
Stream, aina (ainet), pl. ainōs (ainōsiek).
 kereru (kererut), pl. kererus (kererusiek).
Strength, kīmnon (kīmnonet), kīmnat (kīmnatet).
Stretch, chul (pr. a-chul-e, p.p. ka-a-chul).
Stretch oneself, chul-ke (pr. a-chul-i-ke, p.p. ka-a-chul-ke).
Stretch one's legs, iit-te keliek.
Stretch a skin, ui-te (pr. a-uitoi-i, p.p. ka-a-ui-te).
Strew, iser-chi (pr. a-'ser-chi-ni, p.p. ka-a-'ser-chi).
Strike, pir (pr. a-pir-e, p.p. ka-a-pir).
 Strike once with a stick, kwer (pr. a-kwer-e, p.p. ka-a-kwer).
 mas (pr. a-mos-e, p.p. ka-a-mas).
 Strike several times with a stick, kwerakwer (pr. a-kwerakwer-i, p.p. ka-a-kwerakwer).
 Strike a person who is not looking, luom (pr. a-luom-i, p.p. ka-a-luom).
 Strike a person who is not looking, with a view to stealing his property, ke-chi (pr. a-ke-chi-ni, p.p. ka-a-ke-chi).
 Strike the foot against something, inach (pr. a-'nach-i, p.p. ka-a-'nach).
 Strike with the fist, luch (pr. a-luch-e, p.p. ka-a-luch).
 Strike with the foot (kick), itiar (pr. a-'tiar-i, p.p. ka-a-'tiar).
String, porowa (porowet), pl. poroon (poroonik).
String *(beads, &c.)*, yua (pr. a-yua-i, p.p. ka-a-yua).
Strip off, ipony (pr. a-'pony-e, p.p. ka-a-'pony).
Strip off branches, leaves, &c., tur (pr. a-tur-e, p.p. ka-a-tur).
Stripe, siro (siret), pl. sireyua (sireyuek).
Striped, sirat, pl. sirotin.
Strive *(together)*, o-pir-ke (pr. ki-pir-i-ke, p.p. ka-ki-pir-ke).
 (make an effort), inêt-ke kut.
Stroke, sapsap (pr. a-sopsop-i, p.p. ka-a-sapsap).
Stroll about, wend-ote ola-tukul.
Strong, kīm, pl. kīmen.

Strongly, eṅg-gôwo; eṅg-gīmnon.
Stubble, ror (roret), pl. rorotinua (rorotinuek).
Stumble, teteri-ote (pr. a-teterioti, p.p. ka-a-teteri-ote).
Stupid, periper, pl. periperen.
(n.), apusan (apusanet), pl. apusan (apusanik).
Stutterer, kipuikut (kipuikutit), pl. kipuikutin (kipuikutīnik).
Subdue, ipēl (pr. a-'pēl-i, p.p. ka-a-'pēl).
Succeed (*follow*), isup (pr. a-'sup-i, p.p. ka-a-'sup).
Succeed in doing, sich (pr. a-sich-e, p.p. ka-a-sich).
Such and such (*people*), (piik) chette-chette.
Suck (*human beings*), chuchun (pr. a-chuchun-i, p.p. ka-a-chuchun).
(*animals*), reri (pr. a-reri-e, p.p. ka-a-reri).
Suck fruits with stones in them, ñgunñgul (pr. a-ñgunñgul-i, p.p. ka-a-ñgunñgul).
Suckle (*human beings*), chuchunji (pr. a-chuchun-ji-ni, p.p. ka-a-chuchun-ji).
(*animals*), reri-chi (pr. a-rerichi-ni, p.p. ka-a-reri-chi).
Suffice, yam (pr. a-yam-e, p.p. ka-a-yam).
Sugar (*honey*), kumia (kumiat), pl. kumin (kumīk).
sukaro (sukarōk).
Sugar-cane, mopcho (mopchot), pl. mop (mopek).
Suit, iam (pr. ai-'am-i, p.p. kâ-'am).
Summit, parak (parakut).
Sun, asis (asista), pl. asisua (asisuek).
Support, ti (pr. a-ti-e, p.p. ka-a-ti).
Suppose, apere noto.
Surpass, sir-te (pr. a-sir-toi-i, p.p. ka-a-sir-te).

oon (pr. a-oon-e, p.p. ka-a-oon).
Surprise, tañgany (pr. a-toñgony-i, p.p. ka-a-tañgany).
Surround, ikem (pr. a-'kem-i, p.p. ka-a-'kem).
(*go round*), imūt (pr. a-'mūt-i, p.p. ka-a-'mūt).
Swallow, lukui (pr. a-lukui-i, p.p. ka-a-lukui).
Swamp, tolīl (tolīlet), pl. tolīlon (tolīlonik).
Large swamp, rīro (rīret), pl. rīron (rīronik).
Sheet of water, peiyo (peiyot), pl. pei (pêk).
Swear, par mumek.
Swear at, chup (pr. a-chup-e, p.p. ka-a-chup).
Sweat, kaot (kaotik).
(v. imp.), iñget-yi kaot.
I have sweated, ka-'ñget-y-o kaot.
Sweep, ipūch (pr. a-'pūch-i, p.p. ka-a-'pūch).
Sweet, anyiny, pl. onyinyin.
Sweetheart (*man*), saanya (saandet), pl. saan (saanik).
(*girl*), murer (mureret), pl. mureren (murerēnik).
Sweet potato, roboonio (robooniot), pl. roboon (roboonik).
Swell, ipwan-e (pr. a-'pwan-i, p.p. ka-a-'pwan-e).
Swine, tora (toret), pl. toroi (torōk).
Switch, kiruk (kirukto), pl. kirukwa (kirukwek).
Sword, rotua (rotuet), pl. rotoi (rotōk); rotuet-ap-chōk.
Handle of sword, kungit-ap-rotuet.

Tail, katut (katutiet), pl. katutai (katutaiik).
Tail of sheep, sarur (saruriet), pl. sarurai (saruraiik).
Tail of an ewe, kiskis (kiskisto), pl. kiskisua (kiskisuek).

Tail:
End of a ram's tail, kipwal (kipwalit), pl. kipwalis (kipwalisiek).
Hair at the end of a tail, museyuo (museyuot), pl. muse (museyuek).
Tailor, napin (napindet), pl. nap (napīk).
Take, nam (pr. a-nom-e, p.p. ka-a-nam).
(receive), tâch (pr. a-toch-e, p.p. ka-a-tâch).
Take a person, imut (pr. a-'mut-i, p.p. ka-a-'mut).
Take to a person, ip-chi (pr. a-ip-chi-ni, p.p. kâ-ip-chi).
Take to a place, ip (pr. a-ip-e, p.p. kâ-ip).
Take a path, pun (pr. a-pun-e, p.p. ka-a-pun).
  ker-te (pr. a-ker-toi-i, p.p. ka-a-ker-te).
Take a walk, wend-ote (pr. a-wend-oti, p.p. ka-a-wend-ote).
Take across, ilan-de (pr. a-'londoi-i, p.p. ka-a-'lan-de).
Take as spoil, par-u (pr. a-par-u, p.p. ka-a-par-u).
Take away, is-te (pr. a-is-toi-i, p.p. kâ-is-te).
Take away cattle, ñgel (pr. a-ñgel-e, p.p. ka-a-ñgel).
Take beads off a string, chiruk-te (pr. a-chiruk-toi-i, p.p. ka-a-chiruk-te).
Take a load from a person, ituchi (pr. a-'tu-chi-ni, p.p. ka-a-'tu-chi).
Take from a person, inem-chi (pr. a-'nem-chi-ni, p.p. ka-a-'nem-chi).
Take by force, rep (pr. a-rep-e, p.p. ka-a-rep).
  ipe (pr. a-ipe-i, p.p. ka-a-ipe).
Take care, iro. (See irregular verbs, p. 224.)
Take care of, rīp (pr. a-rīp-e, p.p. ka-a-rīp).
  ikun (pr. a-'kun-i, p.p. ka-a-'kun).
Take down, irek-u (pr. a-'rek-u, p.p. ka-a-'rek-u).
Take leave of, ikat (pr. a-'kat-i, p.p. ka-a-'kat).
Take off (clothes, beads, &c.), irek-u (pr. a-'rek-u, p.p. ka-a-'rek-u).
Take off (the fire), sut-u (pr. a-sut-u, p.p. ka-a-sut-u).
Take one's revenge, yak-te; yak-u; yok-chi, &c.
Take out, inem-u (pr. a-'nem-u, p.p. ka-a-'nem-u).
Take out of a trap, itiach (pr. a-'tioch-i, p.p. ka-a-'tiach).
Take out of the sun or rain, inur (pr. a-'nur-i, p.p. ka-a-'nur).
Take out of the pot, pol-u (pr. a-pol-u, p.p. ka-a-pol-u).
Take to pieces, irarach (pr. a-'raroch-i, p.p. ka-a-'rarach).
Take up, inem-u (pr. a-'nem-u, p.p. ka-a-'nem-u).
Take up a load, sut (pr. a-sut-e, p.p. ka-a-sut).
Take up (e.g. grain) a little at a time, mukut (pr. a-mukut-i, p.p. ka-a-mukut).
Take up (e.g. grain) with both hands, ram (pr. a-ram-e, p.p. ka-a-ram).
Take up with the finger tips, suruch (pr. a-suruch-i, p.p. ka-a-suruch).
Take up a handful, samat (pr. a-somot-i, p.p. ka-a-samat).
Take up a handful of grain, irop (pr. a-'rop-i, p.p. ka-a-'rop).
Tale, kâpchemosin (kapchemosīnik).
Talk, mwa (pr. a-mwo-i, p.p. ka-a-mwa).
Talk about, at, of, &c., mwo-chi

Talk:
(pr. a-mwo-chi-ni, p.p. ka-a-mwo-chi).
Talk in one's sleep, be delirious, riewen (pr. a-riewen-i, p.p. ka-a-riewen).
Talk behind a person's back, châm (pr. a-chôm-e, p.p. ka-a-châm).
Tall, koi, pl. koiin.
Talon, silolio (siloliot), pl. silolen (silolēnik).
Tan (*skins*), kut (pr. a-kut-e, p.p. ka-a-kut).
Tanner, kutin (kutindet), pl. kut (kutik).
Tarry, tepi (pr. a-tepi-e, p.p. ka-a-tepi).
Taste, chamcham (pr. a-chom-chom-i, p.p. ka-a-chamcham).
Teach, inêt (pr. a-'nêt-i, p.p. ka-a-'nêt).
ñgat (pr. a-ñgot-e, p.p. ka-a-ñgat).
Tear, pêk-ap-koñg.
Tear, pêt (pr. a-pêt-e, p.p. ka-a-pêt).
pach (pr. a-poch-i, p.p. ka-a-pach).
kerer (pr. a-kerer-i, p.p. ka-a-kerer).
Tease, kwekwe (pr. a-kwekwe-i, p.p. ka-a-kwekwe).
Tell, mwo-chi (pr. a-mwo-chi-ni, p.p. ka-a-mwo-chi).
am-chi (pr. a-om-chi-ni, p.p. kâ-am-chi).
ñgalal-chi (pr. a-ñgolol-chi-ni, p.p. ka-a-ñgalal-chi).
Tell thus, ile-chi (pr. a-'le-chi-ni, p.p. ka-a-'le-chi).
Tell a tale, mwa kâpchemos-in.
Tell me! am-u!
Temper, atep (atepet).
Tempt, tiem (pr. a-tiem-e, p.p. ka-a-tiem).
Ten, taman.
(n.), taman (tamanut), pl. tomonuag (tomonuagik).
Tend (*sheep, &c.*), iak-e (pr. a-'ok-i, p.p. kâ-'ak-e).
Tender (*of meat*), tandus, pl. tandusen.
Tendon, kwario (leg *or* arm); met (back); segerua (neck); &c.
Terrify, iyue-chi (pr. a-'yue-chi-ni, p.p. ka-a-'yue-chi).
(*startle*), imu (pr. a-'mu-i, p.p. ka-a-'mu).
Testicles, mukuio (mukuiot), pl. mukui (mukuik).
Testicles of ox, ketio (ketiot), pl. ketin (ketik).
Tether, rat (pr. a-rot-e, p.p. ka-a-rat).
Thank, ile-chi kongoi.
Thank you, thanks, kongoi; asai.
That, nin *or* in.
Thatch, susuek-ap-kot.
(v.), siep kot.
The, def. article. (See p. 160.)
Thee, inye.
Theft, chorso (chorset).
Their, nywa, pl. chwak.
Theirs, nenywa, pl. chechwak.
Them, icheket; ichek.
There, yun.
Therefore, amu.
These, chu.
They, icheket; ichek.
Thick, nyikis, pl. nyikisin.
Thickness, nyikisin (nyikisindo).
Thief, chorin (chorindet), pl. chor (chorīk).
Cattle-thief, kipisoiyo (kipisoiyot), pl. kipisoiin (kipisoiīnik).
Person who steals Nandi cattle, koñgeldoin (koñgeldoindet), pl. koñgeldo (koñgeldoik).
Thigh, kupes (kupesto), pl. kupesua (kupesuek).
Thin, tenden, pl. tendin.

Thine, neñguñg, pl. chekuget.
Thing, kii (kiito), pl. tukun (tukuk).
Thing of no value, pures (puresto).
I have done nothing, mâ-ai kii.
Think (*consider, remember, think of*), ipwat (pr. a-'pwot-i, p.p. ka-a-'pwat).
(*suppose*), apere noto; ile.
Think deeply, iro-ke.
Thirst, melel (melelda).
I am thirsty, am-a melel.
Thirteen, taman ok somok.
Thirty, sosom; tomonuagik somok.
This, ni *or* i.
Thong, rīke (rīkeito), pl. rīkeyua (rīkeyuek).
Thorn, thorn-tree, kata (katet), pl. katoi (katōk).
Those, chun.
Thou, inye.
When calling a person (*male*), iñgwe!
When calling a person (*female*), inye!
Thousand, pokolaiik che-chañg; pokolaiik taman.
Thread, porowa (porowet), pl. poroon (poroonik).
Thread (*beads, &c.*), yua (pr. a-yua-i, p.p. ka-a-yua).
Threaten, ker koñg.
Three, somok.
Thresh (*corn*), pur (pr. a-pur-e, p.p. ka-a-pur).
Throat, mook (mookto), pl. mookwa (mookwek).
    cheporor (chepororet), pl. chepororōs (chepororōsiek).
Throb, itiar-u (pr. a-'tiar-u, p.p. ka-a-'tiar-u).
Throttle, iket (pr. a-'ket-i, p.p. ka-a-'ket).
Throw (*throw away*), met-te (pr. a-met-toi-i, p.p. ka-a-met-te).
    lak-te; wir-te; pakak-te.

Throw hither, met-u (pr. a-met-u, p.p. ka-a-met-u).
Throw down, wir-te (pr. a-wir-toi-i, p.p. ka-a-wir-te).
Throw down to, ser-chi (pr. a-ser-chi-ni, p.p. ka-a-ser-chi).
Throw at, wir-chi (pr. a-wir-chi-ni, p.p. ka-a-wir-chi).
Throw water at, is-chi (pr. a-is-chi-ni, p.p. ka-a-is-chi).
Throw in different places (*scatter*), iser-te (pr. a-'ser-toi-i, p.p. ka-a-'ser-te).
Throw a piece of wood as from a sling, tim (pr. a-tim-e, p.p. ka-a-tim).
Thumb, mornet ne-oo.
Thunder, īlat (īlet), pl. īlot (īlotik).
    (v.), che.
It thunders, che-i.
Thus, noto; kunoto; ko-parkio; ole; kule.
Thy, ñguñg, pl. kuk.
Tick (*small*), kerepes (kerepesiet), pl. kerepes (kerepesik).
    (*large*), talus (talusiet), pl. talus (talusik).
Tickle, kitkit (pr. a-kitkit-i, p.p. ka-a-kitkit).
Tie, rat (pr. a-rot-e, p.p. ka-a-rat).
Tie up an ox, rīch (pr. a-rīch-e, p.p. ka-a-rīch).
Tie a knot, uch (pr. a-uch-e, p.p. ka-a-uch).
Tighten, kwilil (pr. a-kwilil-i, p.p. ka-a-kwilil).
Till, kut; akut; oñg.
Till now, akut nguni; oñg ni; akora.
Time, oii (olto), pl. oltōs (oltōsiek).
What time is it? ti-a asis?
(*reply*), te asis, 'the sun is thus' (pointing to the sun).
be Tipsy, pôkit (pr. a-pôkit-i, p.p. ka-a-pôkit).

ENGLISH-NANDI VOCABULARY 305

be Tipsy :
Make tipsy, ipôkit (pr. a-'pôkit-e, p.p. ka-a-'pôkit).
be Tired, ñget (pr. a-ñget-e, p.p. ka-a-ñget).
To, eñg.
When *to* is used in English as the sign of the infinitive, the subjunctive or narrative is employed.
I want to go, a-moch-e a-wa.
Tell him to go, ile-chi kwa.
Tobacco, tumato (tumatet), pl. tumatoïn (tumatoïnik).
Tobacco for chewing, chepure (chepuret), pl. chepures (chepuresiek).
Cake of tobacco, mañgatia (mañgatiat), pl. mañgatin (mañgatīnik).
Large cake of tobacco, ipero (iperet), pl. iperai (iperaiik).
Tobacco-pouch (*made out of the scrotum of a goat*), olpesieny (olpesienyet), pl. olpesienyai (olpesienyaiik).
(*made out of the horn of an ox*), kiprau (kipraut), pl. kipraun (kipraunik).
To-day, rani.
Toe, mornet-ap-keldo.
Together, tukul; ak.
Both together, towae kwoieñg.
Be together, o-tet-ke (pr. ki-tet-i-ke, p.p. ka-ki-tet-ke).
Tomb (*dung-hill*), kâp-ñgotot.
To-morrow, mutai ; tun-mutai.
The day after to-morrow, tungwoiin.
Tongs, kanameyuo (kanameyuot), pl. kaname (kanameyuek).
Tongue, ñgelyep (ñgelyepta), pl. ñgelyepua (ñgelyepuek).
Tooth, kelda (keldet), pl. kelat (kelek).
Eye-tooth, keldet-ap-seset.
Middle incisor tooth, keldet-ap-kâp-rorio.

Back tooth, kipkermet (kipkermetiet), pl. kipkermetai (kipkermetaiik).
Hole where front teeth of lower row have been extracted, oto (otet) ; kâpioto (kâpiotet).
Hole where one or more of the middle incisor front teeth of the upper row have been knocked, or have fallen, out, kâpketioñg (kâpketioñget).
Hole where other teeth have been knocked out, mununua (mununuet).
Slit between two upper molars through which to spit, kâpsingil (kâpsingilit).
To extract the two middle incisors of the lower jaw, ot (pr. a-ot-e, p.p. ka-a-ot).
To extract other teeth, nem-u (pr. a-nem-u, p.p. ka-a-nem-u).
Tooth-stick for cleaning teeth, siito (siitet), pl. siitoi (siitōk).
Top, parak (parakut).
Tortoise, chepkoikoch (chepkoikochet), pl. chepkoikoches (chepkoikochesiek).
Toss (*of oxen, &c.*), lūch (pr. a-lūch-e, p.p. ka-a-lūch).
(*of sheep*), tirir (pr. a-tirir-i, p.p. ka-a-tirir).
Total, tukul.
Totally, kwekeny.
Totter, pôtan (pr. a-pôton-i, p.p. ka-a-pôtan).
Totter in one's walk, terteri-ote (pr. a-terteri-oti, p.p. ka-a-terteri-ote).
Touch, tua (pr. a-tua-i, p.p. ka-a-tua).
Touch gently, sapsap (pr. a-sopsop-i, p.p. ka-a-sapsap).
Town, ka *or* ko ; ñgasana, &c. (See **Kraal.**)
Track (*of one person or animal*), kel (keldo), pl. kelien (keliek).

ENGLISH-NANDI VOCABULARY

Track:
(*of several persons or animals*), marandu (marandut), pl. marandus (marandusiek).
(v.), isup marandut; isup keliek.
Trade, olisio (olisiet); olio (oliot).
Place of meeting for trade purposes, kesimo (kesimet), pl. kesimōs (kesimōsiek).
Trade, melekon (pr. a-melekon-i, p.p. ka-a-melekon).
ai-te olisiet.
Trample, tiech (pr. a-tiech-e, p.p. ka-a-tiech).
Trample under foot, tiechatiech (pr. a-tiechatiech-i, p.p. ka-a-tiechatiech).
be Transparent, sengelel (pr. a-sengelel-i, p.p. ka-a-sengelel).
Trap, mesto (mestet), pl. mestoi (mestōk).
Trap, tech (pr. a-tech-e, p.p. ka-a-tech).
Travel, ru-te (pr. a-ru-toi-i, p.p. ka-a-ru-te).
Travel in order to raid, set (pr. a-set-e, p.p. ka-a-set).
(*move*), u (pr. a-u-e, p.p. ka-a-u).
Traveller, unonio (unoniot), pl. unon (unonik).
(*visitor*), ruto (rutōet), pl. rutoi (rutoïk).
Tread, tiech (pr. a-tiech-e, p.p. ka-a-tiech).
Tread on (*crush*), nyinyir (pr. a-nyinyir-i, p.p. ka-a-nyinyir).
Tree, ket (ketit), pl. ket (ketik).
Stump of tree, musuk (musukiet), pl. musuk (musukik).
Tree marked to show ownership, kuketua (kuketuet), pl. kuketai (kuketaiik).
Tremble, pôtan (pr. a-pôton-i, p.p. ka-a-pôtan).
Tremble with cold, kutkut (pr. a-kutkut-i, p.p. ka-a-kutkut).
Tremble with fear, topot (pr. a-topot-i, p.p. ka-a-topot).

Tribe, em (emet), pl. emotinua (emotinuek).
Of what tribe are you? I chii ne inye? *or* Emen-ñguñg gwano?
Agricultural tribes, mee (meek).
Pastoral tribes, porop (poropek).
NAMES OF TRIBES.
Buret, Puretin (Puretindet), pl. Puret (Puretik).
Dorobo, Okio (Okiondet *or* Okiot), pl. Oki (Okiek).
Elgeyo, Keyo (Keyondet *or* Keyot), pl. Keyu (Keyek).
Elgonyi, Konyin (Konyindet), pl. Kony (Konyek).
European, Asungio (Asungiot), pl. Asungu (Asunguk).
Kamasia, Tukenin (Tukenindet), pl. Tuken (Tukenek).
Kamasyaïn (Kamasyaïndet), pl. Kamasya (Kamasyaek).
Kavirondo, Lemin (Lemindet), pl. Lem (Lemek). (See **Boy.**)
Lumbwa, Kipsikīsin (Kipsikīsindet), pl. Kipsikīs (Kipsikīsiek).
Marakwet, Merekwetin (Merekwetindet), pl. Merekwet (Merekwetek).
Masai, Ipuapcho (Ipuapchot), pl. Ipuap (Ipuapek).
Mâsaein (Mâsaeindet), pl. Mâsae (Mâsaeek).
Mbai, Mbaiin (Mbaiindet), pl. Mbai (Mbaiek).
Mutei, Mutein (Muteindet *or* Muteiyot), pl. Mutei (Muteik).
Nandi, Nandiin (Nandiindet), pl. Nandi (Nandiek).
(*old name*), Chemwalin (Chemwalindet), pl. Chemwal (Chemwalek).
Nyangori, Terikin (Terikindet), pl. Terik (Terikek).
Sabaut, Sabautin (Sabautindet), pl. Sabaut (Sabautik).
Save, Sapeinyin (Sapeinyindet), pl. Sapeiny (Sapeinyek).

ENGLISH-NANDI VOCABULARY 307

Tribe:
Sotik, Sootin (Sootindet), pl. Soot (Sootik).
Swahili (*man*), Chumbin (Chumbindet), pl. Chumba (Chumbek).
(*woman*), Chepchumbia (Chepchumbiat), pl. Chepchumbin (Chepchumbīnik).
Triumph, ipēl (pr. a-'pēl-i, p.p. ka-a-'pēl).
Trot, lapat (pr. a-lopot-i, p.p. ka-a-lapat).
Trouble, nyalil (nyalildo), pl. nyalilua (nyaliluek).
Trough (*for calves*), moing (moinget), pl. moingon (moingonik).
True, ap-iman.
Truly, iman.
Trunk (*of tree*), saborio (saboriot), pl. saborin (saborīnik).
The human trunk, por (porto), pl. porua (poruek).
Elephant's trunk, ē (ēut), pl. ēun (ēunek).
Truth, iman (imanet).
Try (*aim, endeavour*), imu-chi (pr. a-'mu-chi-ni, p.p. ka-a-'mu-chi).
(e. g. *a spear*), tiem (pr. a-tiem-e, p.p. ka-a-tiem).
Try by ordeal, par mumek.
Try by ordeal for theft, saise (pr. a-soise-i, p.p. ka-a-saise).
Tumble, iput (pr. a-'put-i, p.p. ka-a-'put).
Tumble into, iput-yi (pr. a-'put-yi-ni, p.p. ka-a-'put-yi).
Turf, tindinyo (tindinyot), pl. tindiny (tindinyek).
Turn, Turn over, (act.), iwech (pr. a-'wech-i, p.p. ka-a-'wech).
(neut.), we-ke (pr. a-we-i-ke, p.p. ka-a-we-ke).
Turn over from side to side, wewech-ke (pr. a-wewech-i-ke, p.p. ka-a-wewech-ke).

Turn out (e. g. *of a house*), iñget-te (pr. a-'ñget-toi-i, p.p. ka-a-'ñget-te).
Turn inside out, iluch (pr. a-'luch-i, p.p. ka-a-'luch).
Turn round something else, imūt (pr. a-'mūt-i, p.p. ka-a-'mūt).
Turn up, itoke (pr. a-'toke, p.p. ka-a-'toke).
Turtle, chepkoikochet-ap-pêk.
Twelve, taman ok oieñg.
Twenty, tiptem.
Twenty-one, tiptem ak akenge.
Twice, êkonēsiek oieñg; kosakt' oieñg ; ko-nyil oieñg.
Twig, sikorio (sikoriot), pl. sikor (sikorik).
simamia (simamiat), pl. simam (simamik).
Twin, saramia (saramiat), pl. saram (saramek).
Twist, iiny (pr. o-'iny-i, p.p. ka-a-'iny).
Twist two pieces of rope, &c., together, ilet (pr. a-'let-i, p.p. ka-a-'let).
Two, oieñg.

Udder, murungu (murungut), pl. murungus (murungusiek).
Ulcer, chepserkech (chepserkechet), pl. chepserkech (chepserkechik).
Umbilical cord, kâpwal (kâpwalda), pl. kâpwalua (kâpwaluek).
Umbrella (*native*), aoiyo (aoiyot), pl. aoin (aoinik).
(*European*), mwamvuli (mwamvulit).
Uncle (*father's brother*), netupche-ap-papa ; akut-chetupcho-ap-papa.
(*mother's brother*), imam (imamet).
Uncleanness, ñgwon (ñgwonik); ker (kerek); simwa (simwek).

x 2

Uncover, ñgany (pr. a-ñgony-i, p.p. ka-a-ñgany).
Uncover something heavy, keleny (pr. a-keleny-i, p.p. ka-a-keleny).
Under, inguny.
Under the house, kot inguny *or* ingunyut-ap-kot.
Underneath, inguny (ingunyut).
Underdone, tuon, pl. tuonen.
Understand, kas (pr. a-kos-e, p.p. ka-a-kas).
Understanding, met. (See **Head.**)
Undo, yat (pr. a-yot-e, p.p. ka-a-yat).
Untie a knot, itiach (pr. a-'tioch-i, p.p. ka-a-'tiach).
Undress, irek-u (pr. a-'rek-u, p.p. ka-a-'rek-u).
Unfasten, yat (pr. a-yot-e, p.p. ka-a-yat).
Unfasten cattle, itiach (pr. a-'tioch-i, p.p. ka-a-'tiach).
Unfold, iit-te (pr. a-'it-toi-i, p.p. ka-'it-te).
Unite, rop (pr. a-rop-e, p.p. ka-a-rop).
Unless, ngut-ko, followed by the negative.
Unless he does it, ngut-ko-ma-ai.
Unlucky omen, sigoran (sigoranet), pl. sigoranoi (sigoranōk).
Unripe, tuon, pl. tuonen.
Unsew, tur (pr. a-tur-e, p.p. ka-a-tur).
    tender (pr. a-tender-i, p.p. ka-a-tender).
Unthatch (*uncover*), ñgany (pr. a-ñgony-i, p.p. ka-a-ñgany).
Unthread, chiruk-u *or* chiruk-te.
Untie, yat (pr. a-yot-e, p.p. ka-a-yat).
Untie a knot, itiach (pr. a-'tioch-i, p.p. ka-a-'tiach).
Until, kut; akut; oñg.
Until now, akut nguni; oñg-ni.
Up, parak.

(*the upper part*), parak (parakut).
Uproar, polot (polotet).
Upset (*persons*), tu-i (pr. a-tu-e, p.p. ka-a-tu-i).
    (*things*), turur-te (pr. a-turur-toi-i, p.p. ka-a-turur-te).
Urinate, sukus (pr. a-sukus-i, p.p. ka-a-sukus).
    A person who urinates at night-time, or from fear, is called *poldamui.* Small children are frequently given the hoof of a young ox or goat (*putuldo*) to chew before going to bed.
Us, achek.
Use (*make use of*), am (pr. a-om-e, p.p. kâ-am).
    (*be of use*), mie-itu (pr. a-mie, p.p. ka-a-mie-itu).
Use (*accustom*), inai-te (pr. a-'noi-toi-i, p.p. ka-a-'nai-te).
    (*become used to*), nai-te (pr. a-noi-toi-i, p.p. ka-a-nai-te).
Utter, wal-u (pr. a-wal-u, p.p. ka-a-wal-u).
Utterly, kwekeny.

Vagina (*human beings*), mokol (mokolet), pl. mokolon (mokolonik).
    kusa (kuset), pl. kusas (kusasiek).
    (*animals*), let (letut), pl. letus (letusiek).
Vainly, puch.
Valley, otepwa (otepwet), pl. otepwōs (otepwōsiek).
    kulua (kuluet), pl. kulonoi (kulonōk).
Value:
What is it worth? Ti-a oliot?
It is worth an ox, ol-e teta.
Vanguard, ñgaimet (ñgaimetiet).
Vegetable, ingua (inguot), pl. ingui (inguek).
Veil. (See **Head-dress.**)
Venture, kany (pr. a-kony-e, p.p. ka-a-kany).

ENGLISH-NANDI VOCABULARY

Very, mīsing.
Vex, inerech (pr. a-'nerech-e, p.p. ka-a-'nerech).
Be vexed, nerech (pr. a-nerech-i, p.p. ka-a-nerech).
Vigorously, eñg-gôwa ; eñg-gimnon.
Village, ko *or* ka, &c. (See **Kraal.**)
Violence, kimnon (kimnonet).
With violence, eñg-gimnon.
Violent, kīm, pl. kīmen.
be a Virgin, iper-ke (pr. a-'per-e-ke, p.p. ka-a-'per-ke).
Visitor, ruto (rutōet), pl. rutoi (rutoïk).
Voice, twekuno (twekunet), pl. twekunōs (twekunōsiek).
Vomit, iñguñg-u (pr. a-'ñguñg-u, p.p. ka-a-'ñguñg-u).
Give a person medicine to cause vomiting, tap (pr. a-top-e, p.p. ka-a-tap).

Waist, suwe. (See **Loin.**)
Bind something round the waist, iu-ke (pr. a-'u-i-ke, p.p. ka-a-'u-ke).
Wait, wait for, kany (pr. a-kony-e, p.p. ka-a-kany).
Wait a little, kany ko-rok ; kany kitegin.
Wake (neut.), ñgêt (pr. a-ñgêt-e, p.p. ka-a-ñgêt).
(act.), iñgêt (pr. a-'ñgêt-i, p.p. ka-a-'ñgêt).
Wake in the night, iochi (pr. a-'ochi-i, p.p. ka-a-'ochi).
Wake with a start, sir-u (pr. a-sir-u, p.p. ka-a-sir-u).
Be awake, kas-u (pr. a-kos-u, p.p. ka-a-kas-u).
Walk (*gait*), pan (panda), pl. ponua (ponuek).
(v.), ui eñg-geliek.
Take a walk, wend-ote (pr. a-wend-oti, p.p. ka-a-wend-ote).

Walk lame, iñgwal (pr. a-'ñgwol-i, p.p. ka-a-'ñgwal).
Wall (*outer*), kiter (kiterut), pl. kiterus (kiterusiek).
(*inner*), inat (inatut), pl. inatun (inatunik).
Partition in huts, tōt (tōtet), pl. tōtōs (tōtōsiek).
Want, mach (pr. a-moch-e, p.p. ka-a-mach).
War, porio (poriot), pl. poriōs (poriōsiek).
(*raid*), luk (luket), pl. lukōs (lukōsiek).
Go to war, set luket.
Ward off, têch (pr. a-têch-e, p.p. ka-a-têch).
make Warm, ilalany (pr. a-'lalony-i, p.p. ka-a-'lalany).
Warmth, ma (mat).
Warn, ite-chi (pr. a-'te-chi-ni, p.p. ka-a-'te-chi).
Warner, kotein (koteindet), pl. kote (koteik).
Warrior, muren (murenet), pl. muren (murenik).
segein (segeindet), pl. sege (segeik).
Warrior who is poor and hunts, kiplagotio (kiplagotiot), pl. kiplagotin (kiplagotīnik).
Wart, kaimion (kaimionet), pl. kaimionoi (kaimionōk).
Wart-hog, putie (putieto), pl. putieua *or* putiei (putieuek *or* putieik).
Wash, iun (pr. a-'un-i, p.p. ka-a-'un).
Wash somebody (e.g. *a child*), tindiny (pr. a-tindiny-i, p.p. ka-a-tindiny).
Wash clothes (intr.), mwet-isie (pr. a-mwet-isie-i, p.p. ka-a-mwet-isie).
Wash by dabbing gently, mwet (pr. a-mwet-e, p.p. ka-a-mwet).
Wash the hands at circumcision, lap (pr. a-lop-i, p.p. ka-a-lap).

Wash:
(*soak*), inur (pr. a-'nur-e, p.p. ka-a-'nur).
Watch, kany (pr. a-kony-e, p.p. ka-a-kany).
Watch over, keep watch, rīp (pr. a-rīp-e, p.p. ka-a-rīp).
Water, pei (pêk).
Sheet of water, swamp, peiyo (peiyot), pl. pei (pêk).
Fresh or *cold water,* pêk chekoitit.
Hot water, pêk-am-ma.
Warm water, pêk che-lepilep.
Dirty water (i. e. *water stirred up by cattle*), turur (tururik).
Clean water, pêk che-tililin.
Water used at circumcision ceremonies to shave boys with, tanduio (tanduiet).
Water cattle, inak-e (pr. a-'nok-i, p.p. ka-a-'nak-e).
Water (*of the eyes*), toltol-u (pr. a-toltol-u, p.p. ka-a-toltol-u).
Make water, sukus (pr. a-sukus-i, p.p. ka-a-sukus).
Waterfall, asurur (asururiet), pl. asururai (asururaiik).
Water jar, ter, &c. (See **Jar**.)
Waver, moñgoñgen (pr. a-moñgoñgen-i, p.p. ka-a-moñgoñgen).
Wax, temen (temenyet), pl. temenai (temenaiik).
Way, or (oret), pl. ortinua (ortinuek).
The shortest way, oret ne-til-e.
Out of the way! is-te-ke!
We, achek.
Wealth, tukun (tukuk).
Weapon, karin. (See **Iron**.)
Wear, ilach (pr. a-'loch-i, p.p. ka-a-'lach).
    in-de-ke (pr. a-'n-doi-i-ke, p.p. ka-a-'n-de-ke).
be Weary, ñget (pr. a-ñget-i, p.p. ka-a-ñget).
Make weary, iñget (pr. a-'ñget-e, p.p. ka-a-'ñget).

Weather, oii (olto).
Weed, susuo (susuot), pl. susua (susuek).
Heap of dried weeds, rimborio (rimboriot), pl. rimboron (rimboronik).
To weed an eleusine field, put imbaret.
To weed a millet field, sember imbaret.
Weep, rir (pr. a-rir-e, p.p. ka-a-rir).
(*sob*), iñguiñguny (pr. a-'ñguiñguny-i, p.p. ka-a-'ñguiñguny).
Weigh, ker (pr. a-ker-e, p.p. ka-a-ker).
Try the weight of something, tiem (pr. a-tiem-e, p.p. ka-a-tiem).
Well (adv.), wei; ara.
Well (*healthy*), mukul, pl. mukulen.
Well-done (*cooked*), rurot, pl. rurotin.
be Well, cham-ke (pr. a-cham-i-ke, p.p. ka-a-cham-ke).
Wet, ap-pêk.
(v.), in-de pêk.
(*dip in water*), irok-te pêk.
What? ñgô? ne?
What do you want? i-mochí ne?
What tree is it? ne ket?
What man? chií ñgô? chií ne?
What sort of? añg?
When? au?
(adv.), ole.
Whence? ono?
(adv.), ole.
Where? ñgoro? pl. ñgocho?; ono?
Where is he? mi-i ono?
Where is the man? ñgoro chii-to?
Where are the men? ñgocho piik?
(adv.), ole.
Wherefore, amu; amú ne.
Wherever, ola-tukul.

ENGLISH-NANDI VOCABULARY 311

Whet, lit (pr. a-lit-e, p.p. ka-a-lit).
Whetstone, litei (liteito), pl. liteiua (liteiuek).
Which? ñgô?
Whisper, châm (pr. a-chôm-e, p.p. ka-a-châm).
Whistle, marian (pr. a-marion-i, p.p. ka-a-marian).
White, lēl, pl. lelach.
White ant, toiya (toiyat), pl. toi (toiik).
White ant in flying stage, kongaiya (kongaiyat), pl. kongai (kongaiek).
Whither? ono? (adv.), ole.
Who (rel. pron.), ne, pl. che. (See pp. 187-8.) (int. pron.), ñgô? pl. ñgô-ñgô? akut-ñgô? *or* angut-ñgô? (See pp. 188-9.)
Whole, mukul, pl. mukulen.
Whose? po-ñgô? pl. pakut-ñgô? *or* pangut-ñgô?
Why? kalia? amú-ne?
Wide, tepes, pl. tepesen ; marīch, pl. mariken.
Widow, mosog (mosoget), pl. mosogon (mosogonik).
Wife, kwany (kwando), pl. kwanyin (kwanyik).
Own wife, ka (kaita), pl. korusio (korusiek).
Co-wife, siyo (siyet), pl. siyon (siyonik).
Wild, ap-tim ; ap-tim-in.
Wild animal, tiony (tiondo), pl. tioñgin (tioñgik).
Wilderness, kewo (kewet), pl. kewōs (kewōsiek).
Will, mukulel (mukuleldo), pl. mukuleluag (mukuleluagik).
Win (*a wager*), lôt (pr. a-lôt-e, p.p. ka-a-lôt).
(*obtain*), sich (pr. a-sich-e, p.p. ka-a-sich).
Wind, usoon (usoonet), pl. usoonai (usoonaiik).

(*breeze*), chepusoon (chepusoonet), pl. chepusoonai (chepusoonaiik).
Wind-devil, kipchurchur (kipchurchuriet), pl. kipchurchurai (kipchurchuraiik).
Anything blown about by the wind, kimnyelnyel (kimnyelnyelit).
Wind-pipe, cheporor (chepororet), pl. chepororon (chepororonik).
Wing, kepep (kepepchet), pl. kepepai (kepepaiik).
Wink, ñgwech (pr. a-ñgwech-e, p.p. ka-a-ñgwech).
(*blink*), mismis (pr. a-mismis-i, p.p. ka-a-mismis).
Wipe, ipuch (pr. a-'puch-i, p.p. ka-a-'puch).
Wipe the nose, ipuch seperik.
Wish, mach (pr. a-moch-e, p.p. ka-a-mach).
Witch, ponin (ponindet), pl. pon (ponīk).
Witch's medicine, ponit (pondit).
Witchcraft, ponisio (ponisiet).
With, eñg.
Wither, res (pr. a-res-e, p.p. ka-a-res).
Withhold from, imelel (pr. a-'melel-i, p.p. ka-a-'melel).
Within, oriit.
Without, saañg.
Witness, paorio (paoriot), pl. paorin (paorīnik).
(v.), tiiye-chi (pr. a-tiiye-chi-ni, p.p. ka-a-tiiye-chi).
Wizard, ponin. (See **Witch.**)
Woman, korko (korket), pl. korusio (korusiek).
L., korko (korkot), pl. korusio (korusiek).
A young woman, melia (meliat), pl. melias (meliasiek).
A married woman, osotio (osotiot), pl. osot (osotik).

Woman:
An old woman, chepios (chepioset), pl. chepiosoi (chepiosōk).
Woman who gave birth to a child before marriage, chesorpucho (chesorpuchot), pl. chesorpuchon (chesorpuchonik).
Womb, ruand'-am-mo.
Wonder, tañgany (pr. a-toñgony-i, p.p. ka-a-tañgany).
Wood (*forest*), tim (timdo), pl. timuag (timuagik).
(*tree*), ket (ketit), pl. ket (ketik).
Dry wood, cheptamya (cheptamyat), pl. cheptam (cheptamik).
Firewood, kwendo (kwendet), pl. kwen (kwenik).
Word, ñgolio (ñgoliot), pl. ñgal (ñgalek).
Work, poiisio (poiisiet), pl. poiision (poiisionik).
(v.), ai poiisiet.
Work for, ōt (pr. a-ōt-e, p.p. ka-a-ōt).
Work in metal, itany (pr. a-'tony-i, p.p. ka-a-'tany).
World, kia (kiet), pl. kias (kiasiek).
Worry, iim (pr. a-'im-i, p.p. ka-a-'im).
Worth. (See **Value.**)
What is it worth ? ti-a ? ti-a oliot ?
Wound, mô. (See **Abscess.**)
Old wound, scar, perut (perutiet), pl. perut (perutik).
(v.), tor (*stab*); kwer (*strike*); iep (*slash*), &c.
Wrap (*fold*), aruny (pr. a-aruny-i, p.p. kâ-aruny).
Wrestle, o-kwet-ke (pr. ki-kwet-i-ke, p.p. ka-ki-kwet-ke).
Wriggle, yem-ak-e (pr. a-yem-at, p.p. ka-a-yem-ak-e).
Wring out (e.g. *water*), iiny (pr. o-'iny-i, p.p. ka-a-'iny).

Wrinkle, siriny (pr. a-siriny-i, p.p. ka-a-siriny).
Wrist, walel (waleldo), pl. waleluag (waleluagik).
(*word used by children*), kimnya (kimnyet), pl. kimoi (kimoiik).
Write, sir (pr. a-sir-e, p.p. ka-a-sir).
Writhe, nyulnyul-ke (pr. a-nyulnyul-i-ke, p.p. ka-a-nyulnyul-ke).
imelmel-ke (pr. a-'melmel-i-ke, p.p. ka-a-'melmel-ke).

Yam, akania (akaniat), pl. akan (akanek).
Yawn, ime (pr. a-'me-i, p.p. ka-a-'me).
Year, keny (kenyīt), pl. kenyīs (kenyīsiek).
This year, kenyīn nītok.
Next year, kenyīt-ap-tun.
Last year, kenyīt konye.
Year before last, kenyīt kinye.
Yearly, kenyīt ak kenyīt.
Yes, wei ; weis.
Yesterday, amut ; amt.
The day before yesterday, oiin.
You, okwek.
Young (*of goats, sheep,* &c.), aruwa (aruwet), pl. are (arek).
Younger, mining, pl. mingech.
Your, ñgwañg, pl. kwok.
Yours, neñgwañg, pl. chekwok.
Youth (*uncircumcised*), karemanin (karemanindet), pl. kareman (karemanik).
(*circumcised*), kipkelel (kipkeleldet), pl. kipkelelai (kipkelelaiik).

Zebra, oloitigo (oloitiget), pl. oloitigōs (oloitigōsiek).
sigirio-ap-tim (sigiriet-ap-tim), pl. sigiroi-ap-tim (sigirōk-ap-tim).

APPENDIX I
LIST OF NANDI TREES, GRASSES, ETC.

Malvaceae.
  sp., kerundu (kerundut), pl. kerundun (kerundunik).
  sp., motos (motosiet), pl. motōs (motōsik).
  Abutilon indicum, leltonge (leltonget), pl. leltonges (leltongesiek).
  Dombeya sp., silip (silipchet), pl. silipai (silipaiik).
  Hibiscus gossypinum, cheputio (cheputiot), pl. cheputin (cheputīnik).

Tiliaceae.
  sp., kipsepua (kipsepuet), pl. kipsepon (kipseponik).
  Grewia sp., nokiruo (nokiruet), pl. nokiron (nokironik).

Meliaceae.
  Turraea sp. (near *T. Mombasana*), sitiyo (sitiyot), pl. sitiin (sitiīnik).

Olacaceae.
  Ximenia americana, lamaiyuo (lamaiyuet), pl. lamaon (lamaonik).

Leguminosae.
  sp., koipeyo (koipeyot), pl. koipein (koipeīnik).
  Indigofera sp., nyonyoyo (nyonyoyot), pl. nyonyo (nyonyoek).
  Indigofera sp., menjeiyuo (menjeiyuet), pl. menjeon (menjeonik).
  Trifolium africanum, ndapipi (ndapipit), pl. ndapipin (ndapipīnik).
  Cassia didymobotrya, senetwo (senetwet), pl. seneton (senetonik).
  Acacia robusta, kata (katet), pl. katoi (katōk).
  Acacia sp., kâpkutuo (kâpkutuet), pl. kâpkuton (kâpkutonik).
  Erythrina tomentosa, kakorua (kakoruet), pl. kakoron (kakoronik).
  Bauhinia reticulata, kipsakcha (kipsakchat), pl. kipsaken (kipsakēnik).

Rosaceae.
  Rubus rigidus, momonio (momoniot), pl. momon (momonik).

Crassulaceae.
  Sedum sp., kuseruo (kuseruet), pl. kuseron (kuseronik).

Cucurbitaceae.
  Melothria sp., cheptendere (cheptenderet), pl. cheptenderai (cheptenderaiik).

Umbelliferae.
Foeniculum capillaceum, kirondo (kirondet), pl. kirondon (kirondonik).
Rubiaceae.
Vangueria edulis, kimoluo (kimoluet), pl. kimolon (kimolonik).
Compositae.
sp., chepturo (chepturot), pl. chepturon (chepturonik).
Vernonia sp., sekut (sekutiet), pl. sekut (sekutik).
Emilia integrifolia, tepengwa (tepengwet), pl. tepengon (tepengonik).
Senecio sp., kitungut (kitungutiet), pl. kitungutai (kitungutaiik).
Bidens pilosa, kipkole (kipkoleit), pl. kipkolein (kipkoleīnik).
Sonchus sp., kipkata (kipkatet), pl. kipkatoi (kipkatōk).
Myrsinaceae.
Ardisia sp., usuo (usuet), pl. uson (usonik).
Oleaceae.
Olea chrysophylla, emit (emdit), pl. emīt (emītik).
Apocynaceae.
Landolphia sp., ñgiñgich (ñgiñgichet), pl. ñgiñgichoi (ñgiñgichōk).
Carissa edulis, legetetuo (legetetuet), pl. legeteton (legetetonik).
Acokanthera Schimperi, kelio (keliot), pl. kelio (keliek).
Asclepiadaceae.
sp., chemñgombo (chemñgombet), pl. chemñgomboi (chemñgombōk).
Asclepias sp. (near *A. Kaessneri*), chepinoporokcho (chepinoporokchot), pl. chepinoporokchon (chepinoporokchonik).
Boraginaceae.
Myosotis abyssinica, cheserim (cheserimdo), pl. cheserimwag (cheserimwagik).
Solanaceae.
Solanum campylanthum, lapotuo (lapotuet), pl. lapoton (lapotonik).
Solanum sp., isocho (isochot), pl. isocho (isochek).
Orobancheae.
Orobanche minor, rungu-mistōe.
Bignoniaceae.
Dolichandrone platycalyx, mopo (mopet), pl. mopon (moponik).
Kigelia aethiopica, rotinuo (rotinuet), pl. rotinon (rotinonik).
Spathodea sp. (near *S. nilotica*), septa (septet), pl. septai (septaiik).

LIST OF NANDI TREES

Acanthaceae.
Acanthus arboreus, indakario (indakariot), pl. indakar (indakarek).

Verbenaceae.
Lantana salvifolia, pêk-ap-tarīt.
Lippia sp., mokio (mokiot), pl. mokin (mokīnik).
Lippia sp., chemosorio (chemosoriot), pl. chemosorin (chemosorīnik).
Clerodendron Neumayeri, kipsamis (kipsamisiet), pl. kipsamisoi (kipsamisōk).

Labiatae.
Ocimum suave, lumbeyo (lumebot), pl. lumbein (lumbeīnik).
Ocimum sp., chepkoicho (chepkoichot), pl. chepkoichin (chepkoichīnik).
Leonotis Elliottii, chuchunio (chuchuniot), pl. chuchun (chuchunek).
Ajuga bracteosa, kelyemoi (kelyemoit), pl. kelyemois (kelyemoisiek).

Chenopodiaceae.
Chenopodium sp., kipiros (kipirosit), pl. kipirosin (kipirosīnik).
Chenopodium sp., oroiyo (oroiyot), pl. oroi (oroiek).

Polygonaceae.
Polygonum senegalense, masirir (masiririet), pl. masiriroi (masirirōk).

Euphorbiaceae.
Euphorbia candelabrum, kures (kuresiet), pl. kuresoi (kuresōk).
Croton Elliottianus, chepkelel (chepkeleliet), pl. chepkelelai (chepkelelaiik).
Croton sp., tepeswa (tepeswet), pl. tepeson (tepesonik).
Ricinus communis, imanya (imanyat), pl. iman (imanek).

Urticaceae.
Ficus sp., mokoiyuo (mokoiyuet), pl. mokoon (mokoonik).
Ficus sp., sinende (sinendet), pl. sinendai (sinendaiik).
Ficus sp., teldo (teldet), pl. teldon (teldonik).
Ficus sp. (near *F. elegans*), simotua (somotuet), pl. simoton (simotonik).
Girardinia condensata, siwo (siwot), pl. siwa (siwek).

Amaryllidaceae.
Brunsvigia Kirkii, chemñgotioto (chemñgotiotet), pl. chemñgotiotoi (chemñgotiotōk).

Scitamineae.
Musa Ensete, sasur (sasuriet), pl. sasur (sasuret).
Liliaceae.
Scilla sp., sengolit (sengolitiet), pl. sengolit (sengolitik).
Asparagus sp., chasipaiyo (chasipaiyot), pl. chasipaiin (chasipaiīnik).
Aloë Schweinfurthii, tangarotuo (tangarotuet), pl. tangaroton (tangarotonik).
This aloe is also called mokol-am-mistōet.
Dracaena sp., lepekwa (lepekwet), pl. lepekon (lepekonik).
Commelinaceae.
Commelina zambesica, loblobit (loblobitiet), pl. loblobit (loblobitik).
Juncaceae.
Juncus sp., eseiyai (eseiyaiit), pl. eseiyaiin (eseiyaiīnik).
Palmae.
Phoenix reclinata, } sosio (sosiot), pl. sos (sosik).
Hyphaene thebaica, }
Borassus flabellifer, tir (tiret), pl. tiren (tirēnik).
Cyperaceae.
Carex sp., purpuret (purpuretiet), pl. purpuret (purpuretik).
Carex sp., saos (saoset), pl. saoson (saosonik).
Gramineae.
sp., pembia (pembiat), pl. pembin (pembīnik).
sp., kipriche (kipricheit), pl. kipricheis (kipricheisiek).
sp., mañguañg (mañguañgiet), pl. mañguañgai (mañguañgaiik).
sp., punyerio (punyeriot), pl. punyer (punyeriek).
sp., kipsaramat (kipsaramatiet), pl. kipsaramatai (kipsaramataiik).
sp., mbokcha (mbokchat), pl. mbok (mbokek).
Andropogon Sorghum, mosongio (mosongiot), pl. mosong (mosongek).
Pennisetum sp., kipcheio (kipcheiot), pl. kipchein (kipcheīnik).
Sporobolus sp. (near *Indicus*), segut (segutiet), pl. segut (segutik).
Chloris sp., chemoru (chemorut), pl. chemorus (chemorusiek).
Eleusine coracana, paiyua (paiyuat), pl. pai (päk).
Arundinaria alpina, teka (tekat), pl. tek (tekik).
Coniferae.
Juniperus procera, } tarakwa (tarakwet), pl. tarakon (tarakonik).
Podocarpus falcata, }

APPENDIX II

THE MEANINGS OF THE CLAN-NAMES.

ALL the clan-names mentioned on page 5 have meanings. A few of them are obvious, but they are mostly so obscure that my endeavour to work them out proved unsuccessful, and I was obliged to abandon the task.

The principal name of the clan is occasionally employed for the totem itself; thus, Kipamwi can be used for Cheptirgich, 'a duiker'; Tungo for Kimaket, 'a hyena'; Kipaa for Eren, 'a snake', &c. The three most obvious names are Kipkenda, Kipkōkōs, and Kipasiso, the totems being respectively Segemya ('bee'), Chepkōkōsio ('buzzard'), and Asis ('sun'). Toiyoi is used for 'thunder' (see pp. 9 and 99); Moi means 'calf', and doubtless has allusion to the clipping of the calves' ears as the distinctive mark of this clan (see p. 10); and Kipkoiitim, which means 'the stones of the forest', is equally applicable to the two totems, the elephant and the chameleon.

Of the names used by women, Kâpongen means 'the country of the person who knows', and may have reference to the elephant's superior knowledge, whilst Kiram-gel refers to the elephant's foot (kel). Maram-goñg refers to the bee's eye (koñg). Kami-pei means 'those who eat waters', in allusion to the habits of frogs. Kipya-kut and Tule-kut refer to the lion's jaws (kut = 'mouth'), and Pale-kut to the bush-pig's tusks. Rarewa means 'heifer', and is also used as a name for the crested crane (see p. 25, n. 2). Korapor has regard to the hyena's droppings (see also pp. 7 and 110), and Pale-pēt means 'those who retire in the morning', a suggestion of the hyena's habits. Koros is sometimes used for Koroiit ('Colobus monkey'), and Kâparakok means 'the country of those who live above', i.e. the sun.

INDEX

Adoption, 30; forbidden, 10.
Adultery, 76.
African pheasant, 25, 109.
Ages (social division), 11 sqq.; subdivision of ages into fires, 12, 62 sq., 69, 76, 77, 80.
Agreements, spitting at making of, 78 sq.
Agriculture, agricultural people (*see* also Corn and Harvest), 2 n. 1, 17 sqq., 126 pr. 17, 137 e. 20.
Amulets, 49, 68, 87.
Animals, sayings of, 109 sqq.
Ant, article of food, 24, 133 e. 3; totem, 5, 9.
Ant-hills, superstition regarding, 19, 78; at peace ceremony, 84.
Apron, warriors', 28; girls', 27; prohibition for men to wear, 27 n.
Arithmetic, 88 sq.
Arm-clamp, 28, 124 pr. 3.
Armlet (*see* Ornament).
Arrow, 25, 33 sq.; mentioned in folk-tales, 107, 108, 112, 123; mentioned in enigmas, 141 e. 38; for bleeding cattle, 22 sq., 30, 62, 65; word used for 'knife', 43.
Ashes, 19; used during thunderstorm, 9, 99.
Assault, 75.
Assemblies, places of assembly, 49, 76, 86, 149 e. 69.
Astonishment, spitting as sign of, 78.
Axe, kinds in use, 18; value of, 76; use of during thunderstorm, 9, 99; mentioned in enigmas, 139 e. 28.

Baboon (*see* Monkey).
Back-bone, 147 e. 60.

Bamboo, 49, 87.
Banana, 18; wild banana, 138 e. 22; leaves of, 26.
Banks of a river, 141 e. 37.
Bantu people, 1, 3, 84.
Barren women, 68; made fruitful, 49, 55, 87; inheritance of cattle lent to, 73.
Basket, 39; cut after death of owner, 72; mentioned in enigmas, 145 e. 50, 147 e. 57, 149 e. 67.
Beads, 27 sqq.; ceremony of the red bead, 84 sq.
Bean, 18.
Bed, description of, 15; during sickness, 69; broken after death, 72; superstition regarding snakes and women's beds, 90.
Bee, domestication of, 25; as totem, 5 sqq., 8; mentioned in enigmas, 135 e. 11 and 12.
Beehive, 25, 38, 79, 135 e. 12, 143 e. 44.
Beer, method of brewing, 25 sq.; superstitions regarding, 20; used as libation, 15, 43 sq., 48, 69 sq.; bride and bridegroom sprinkled with, 63; placed in the graves of old men, 72; mentioned in folk-tales, 98.
Beer-pots, 15 sq., 35.
Beeswax, 25.
Beetle, 102.
Bell, 87; warriors', 28; prohibition to wear in corn-fields, 20; worn by girls, 58, 88; mentioned in folk-tales, 106; mentioned in enigmas, 146 e. 54; calf bell worn by girls, 60, 62, 88.
Bellows, 37.
Belly, 134 e. 8, 135 e. 9.
Belt, warriors', 33; women's, 28, 64; knots tied in, 42; used at peace ceremony, 84; mentioned in enigmas, 138 e. 25.
Bhang, 26.
Biceps, 136 e. 14.
Bill-hook, 19.
Birds, as food, 25; as totems, 5, 8 sqq.; shot by boys during the circumcision ceremonies, 56; warriors referred to as birds, 43; charms against, 19, 86 sq.; sayings of, 109 sqq.; mentioned in folk-tales, 104, 105; mentioned in proverbs, 129 pr. 38; mentioned in enigmas, 135 e. 9, 142 e. 41, 146 e. 55, 151 e. 76.
Birth, 64 sqq.; deformed, unlucky and illegitimate children, 30, 68, 76; knots tied to facilitate delivery, 90; uncleanness of mother after birth, 65, 91 sq.
Blankets, 29 n.
Blessing, spitting as form of, 78 sq.
Blood, as food, 22, 52, 68, 116 sqq.; as libation, 22; as purifier, 24, 74; of person slain, 27; mentioned in folk-tales, 106, 110; mentioned in proverbs, 126 pr. 16, 127 pr. 19.
Blood-brotherhood, 84.
Blood-money, 51, 74 sq.
Blood-stains, how to be removed, 23, 27.
Bow, 23, 33 sq.; used in peace ceremonies, 78 n.; carried by boy recently circumcised, 56; mentioned in folk-tales, 107, 108, 112; mentioned in enigmas, 150 e. 73.
Bow-string, 84.
Bracelet, 27 sqq.; used as musical instrument, 26,

INDEX 319

40; mentioned in enigmas, 145 e. 49.
Branding of stock, 22; irons, 83.
Brass wire, 10, 28, 136 e. 16.
Bridge, 134 e. 5.
Broom, 134 e. 7.
Brother, girl's conception by, 9; part taken during sister's circumcision, 58; duty during sickness, 69; seized when a person is accused of witchcraft, 71; widows become property of, 73; greetings of, 91; names of, 92 sqq.
Buffalo, as totem, 5, 10; word used for 'cattle', 56; mentioned in folk-tales, 103, 108; mentioned in proverbs, 124 pr. 1.
Buffalo-hide, used for shields, 32.
Bull, Bullock (see Cattle).
Bull-roarer, 9, 40, 56 sq.
Buret tribe, 2.
Burial, 55, 72.
Bush, 19.
Bush-buck, 80; prohibition to wear skin as garment, 10.
Butter, 22, 116 sqq.
Buzzard, as totem, 5, 8; as bird of omen, 80.

Calabash, 21, 26, 36; method of cleansing, 21; used to eat from, 55, 59, 70, 92; used in marriage ceremonies, 62; used for washing the hands in, 66; used at peace ceremony, 84; mentioned in proverbs, 125 pr. 9; mentioned in enigmas, 134 e. 6, 137 e. 19, 143 e. 45, 149 e. 69.
Calabash-chips, used as ornament, 9, 29.
Calf, rearing, herding, &c., 21; compartment in houses for, 13, 16 sq.; mentioned in proverbs, 127 pr. 20.
Cannibalism, 27.
Cap (see Head-dress).
Carrion birds, prohibition to eat, 25.
Castor-oil leaves, use of, 69.

Cat, as totem, 5, 11; mentioned in folk-tales, 109.
Caterpillar, 127 pr. 22, 140 e. 33.
Cattle, herding and work in connexion with, 20 sqq., 45, 73; bleeding of, 9, 11, 22, 78 sq.; milking of, 21 sq.; branding and marking of, 10, 22; twisting horns of, 22; occasions when cattle are slaughtered, 12, 57, 64, 65, 71, 74 sqq., 80; method of butchering, 22, 75; distribution and inheritance of, 68, 72 sq.; distribution of raided cattle, 43 sq.; ceremonies performed when misfortune has befallen cattle, 45 sq.; when cattle are struck by lightning, 9, 99; seizure of criminal's cattle, 74 sqq.; superstition regarding grass and cattle, 77 sq.; counting cattle, 89; effect of the evil eye on cattle, 90; prohibition to mention cattle by name, 56; prohibition to go near cattle, 56, 60, 92; myth regarding origin of cattle, 98; mentioned in folk-tales, 101, 106, 107, 114 sq., 116 sqq., 123; mentioned in proverbs, 124 pr. 1, 125 pr. 8, 126 pr. 16, 130 pr. 45, 132 pr. 52 and 53; mentioned in enigmas, 134 e. 4, 136 e. 17, 141 e. 36, 150 e. 72 and 73.
Cattle-kraals, 10, 16 sq., 44, 134 e. 6; door of, 16, 47; prohibition to enter, 56, 60, 68, 74; burial of old people and children near, 72; halo likened to, 100.
Caves, 17.
Chains, as ornament, 26, 27 sq.
Chameleon, 79; as totem, 5, 8.
Charms, 87; for house or kraal, 16; at weddings, 11; in corn-fields, 19; to avert sickness and death, 29, 69; to avert the evil eye, 90; worn by twins, 29; worn by women when pregnant for the first time, 64; ring used as charm, 12, 46, 63, 87; claw or piece of hide used as charm, 29.
Chicken, when sick, 38.
Child, birth of, 64 sqq.; naming of, 66 sq.; dress of, 27; teeth of, 30; hair of, 29; instruction of, 6, 66, 125 pr. 7; burial of, 72; when sick, 38; charms against sickness, evil eye, &c., 29, 87, 90; spat on as sign of greeting and blessing, 78 sq.; fate of deformed, unlucky and illegitimate children, 30, 68, 76; prohibition for child and father to touch one another, 66; children permitted to do things which may not be done by others, 11, 23, 24, 56; mentioned in folk-tales, 102, 103, 105, 107, 116 sqq., 120 sq., 122, 123; mentioned in proverbs, 125 pr. 7 and 12, 131 pr. 50; mentioned in enigmas, 134 e. 6 and 7, 135 e. 10, 11, 12 and 13, 140 e. 34.
Cicatrice, 31.
Circumcision, of boys, 52 sqq.; of girls, 57 sqq.; *kireku leget* ceremony, 10; *kâponyony* ceremony, 53, 55; *kimusanyit* cage, 54; *kimasop* ceremony, 54; *lapat-ap-ēun* ceremony, 55, 59, 92; *kâpkiyai* ceremony, 11, 56, 60; *rīkset* ceremony, 9, 40, 56, 60; *kaandaet* songs, 56, 59; *kâpteriot* kraal, 59; *ñgetunot* feast, 57; *kirie korokon* feast, 57; prohibition to regard persons recently circumcised, 55, 59; prohibitions imposed on and ceremonial uncleanness of persons recently circumcised, 56, 60, 91 sq.; password of persons circumcised, 57; operator, 54, 59; knives, 53, 59; punishment of cowards, 55, 59; moral instruction given to per-

320 INDEX

sons recently circumcised, 57, 60; names used after circumcision, 67; ceremony termed 'branding' by children, 83; myth regarding origin of circumcision, 99.

Clans (Nandi), 5; intermarriage of, 6, 45, 61; prohibitions, peculiarities and traditions of, 7 sqq., 16, 36, 62, 66 n., 98, 99; marks for cattle, 22; murder of member of, 74.

Claw, used as charm, 29.

Clay, 33 n., 142 e. 41.

Cloth, used as dress, 28; spat at when seen, 79.

Club, warriors', 31, 33, 39; carried by girls, 58 sq.; old men's, 33; boys', 82; of rhinoceros horn, 33, 74; handed by chief medicine man to war-party, 49.

Colours, 33, 149 e. 67.

Comet, 79, 81, 100.

Cooking, methods of, 27.

Cooking-pots (see Pottery).

Cooking-stones, 143 e. 43.

Corn, kinds grown in Nandi, 18; work connected with sowing, harvesting, &c., 19 sq., 46; omens when sowing, 80; implements used in connexion with, 18 sq., 38 sq.; destruction by vermin of, 19; imitating grinding of in dances, 26; when considered unfit for use, 7, 11; when considered unfit for sowing, 20; prohibition to regard or approach, 17, 60, 76, 92; prohibition to plant millet, 8; eleusine grain used as offering, 46, 69; eleusine grain allowed to fall in fire, 46, 54, 70; use of millet stalks, 69; corn of criminal destroyed, 75 sq.; mentioned in folk-tales, 102, 105, 120 sqq.; mentioned in proverbs, 126 pr. 17, 128 pr. 29; mentioned in enigmas, 133 e. 1, 141 e. 38, 143 e. 42.

Corn-fields, houses built in or near, 13, 17; superstitions regarding, 20; prohibition to work in, 20; inheritance of, 73; mentioned in folk-tales, 102, 105, 120 sqq.; mentioned in proverbs, 132 pr. 57; mentioned in enigmas, 141 e. 35, 142 e. 40.

Corpse, disposal of, 70 sqq.; when not taken by hyenas, 11, 71; ceremonies to be observed by persons handling, 70 sq., 91 sq.

Counties, 4, 86; different implements and weapons used in, 18, 31; mentioned in enigmas, 145 e. 49, 147 e. 59.

Counting, 88 sq.

Cousin, maternal uncle's representative, 53; brother's representative, 71; punishment for intercourse with, 76; names of, 93 sq.

Cow (see Cattle).

Cow dung, used for building purposes, 13, 16 sq.; used at the *saket-ap-eito* ceremony, 12; used during the circumcision festivals, 54 sq.; used for cleansing house, 65, 92; placenta and umbilical cord buried in, 65; children buried in, 68, 72; old men and women buried in, 72; mentioned in enigmas, 149 e. 69.

Cow urine, use of, 21, 68.

Coward, during circumcision, 55 sq., 59 sq.

Cowry, used as ornament, 27 sq., 33, 36.

Crested crane, prohibition to eat, 25; as totem, 5, 10.

Crime (see Punishment).

Criminal, detection of, 51, 71.

Crops (see Corn).

Crow, 151 e. 76.

Crutch, used by devil, 41.

Cup, 36; chipped after death of owner, 72.

Cupping, 70.

Curses, 36, 37, 69, 85, 94.

Dances, during preparation of beer, 26; warriors' dances, 44, 47; circumcision dances, 53, 55 sq., 58; marriage dances, 62 sq.; old men's dance, 144 e. 46; prohibition to attend children's dances, 55.

Days, names of, 95 sq.; divisions of, 96 sq.

Death, 70 sqq.; of old people, 72, 123; steps taken to prevent death of children, 7, 29, 38; steps taken to prevent death of adults, 29, 55, 58 n. 3, 87; superstition regarding death and corn, 20; mysterious death attributed to witchcraft, 51, 71; myth regarding origin of death, 98; mentioned in proverbs, 129 pr. 34 and 36; mentioned in enigmas, 136 e. 18, 144 e. 48.

Devil (*Chemosit*), 41; mentioned in folk-tales, 106 sq.

Dew, 100.

Divination, methods employed, 49 sqq., 71, 81; mentioned in proverbs, 124 pr. 5.

Divorce, 68 sq.

Dogs, trained to hunt, 24; connected with bleeding of cattle, 22; omens connected with dogs, 80 sq.; at peace ceremony, 84; myth regarding origin of death, 98; mentioned in folk-tales, 109, 114 sq.

Donkeys, 22; prohibition to touch, 10; mentioned in folk-tales, 104.

Door (of hut), 39; prohibition to sit by, 17; omens connected with, 81.

Door-posts, embraced by children, 17; erected at harvest festival, 47.

Dorobo (people), 1 n. 2, 2, 17, 100; mentioned in folk-tales, 98, 107, 108 sq., 111 sqq.; (language), 2.

Dove, 109.

Draught (in houses), cause of, 16.

Dreams, 81 sq.; prayer after a bad dream, 41 sq.; interpretation by medicine men of, 49.

Dress (see Garments, Head-dress, Ornaments, &c.

INDEX 321

Drought, ceremonies observed during, 48.
Drum, 40; friction drum, 9, 40, 57, 60.
Drunkenness, 81 sq.; imitated by women and children, 26.
Duiker, as food, 8 sqq., 24; as totem, 5, 8; word used instead of 'goat', 56; mentioned in folk-tales, 108; mentioned in proverbs, 124 pr. 6.
Duiker-skin, as garment, 10, 28.

Eagle, 123.
Ear, boring of lobe, 73, 94; stretching of lobe, 27; hole in upper part of, 27.
Ear-rings, 27 sqq.; of married women, 28 n. 3, 62, 72.
Earth, myths regarding, 97 sq., 111 sqq.; as form of oath, 85; mentioned in enigmas, 141 e. 36.
Earthenware (*see* Pottery).
Earthquake, myth regarding, 100; superstition in connexion with corn, 20; superstition in connexion with people recently circumcised, 91.
East, the home of the Sun, 98; hair thrown towards, 30, 51, 53, 62, 65; teeth thrown towards, 30; spitting towards, 42 sq., 46, 56, 60, 78 sq.
Eggs, 25.
Eland-hide, shields of, 32.
Elephant, as food, 24; as totem, 5, 6, 8; mentioned in folk-tales, 98, 101, 111 sqq., 120 sqq.; mentioned in proverbs, 125 pr. 7, 131 pr. 48; mentioned in enigmas, 145 e. 49, 146 e. 56.
Eleusine grain (*see* Corn).
Elgeyo (Keyu) tribe, 2, 5, 39; prohibition to settle in country of, 9.
Elgon (Mount), 2, 5, 137 e. 21; tribes allied to the Nandi, 2.
Entrails (*see* Intestines).
Evil eye (*see* Eye).
Excrement (human), covered with grass, 51 sq., 78; thrown at an enemy as sign of submission, 74; in a house, 91.
Execution, methods of, 50, 74, 75.
Eye, watching a dying person's, 70; scrutinizing during the circumcision festival, 53; detection of criminals by regarding, 90; mentioned in enigmas, 145 e. 51; one-eyed person or cow, 80; evil eye, 87, 90.

Fainting, 82.
Families (Nandi), 6; intermarriage of, 6, 61; cattle marks of, 22.
Fat, eaten raw, 23; used for anointing, 47, 61, 70 sqq., 146 e. 56.
Father, prayer when sons have gone to the wars, 42 sq., 89; part played by during circumcision festivals, 52, 57 sq.; during marriage, 60 sqq.; father forbidden to touch his child, 66; name of father given to his son, 66, 68; mourning for, 71; inheritance from and of, 72 sq.; spitting on children as sign of blessing, 79; mentioned in folk-tales, 103; mentioned in enigmas, 140 e. 33, 151 e. 75.
Feasts (*see also* Circumcision, Dances, Marriage, &c.) held by men only, 12, 57, 64; held by women only, 63, 65 sq.
Feathers (*see also* Ostrich), 28, 34, 123, 132 pr. 53.
Fingers, used for counting, 88; mentioned in folk-tales, 107.
Fire (*see also* Ages), 85; sprinkling water on, 11; throwing grain on, 46, 54, 70; prohibition to go near, 60, 92; sacred fires, 44 sqq., 63, 85 sq.; mentioned in folk-tales, 106, 107, 120 sqq.; mentioned in proverbs, 127 pr. 23 and 25, 128 pr. 30, 129 pr. 39, 132 pr. 53.
Fire-sticks, 10, 33, 85; used for cauterizing wounds, 70.

Firewood, 86, 139 e. 28.
Fish, 24.
Flea, 137 e. 20, 144 e. 46.
Flies, 143 e. 44.
Folk-tales, 101 sqq.
Food, 22 sqq.; scarcity of, 17, 48; prohibition to eat certain foods, 8 sqq.; prohibition to eat food from broken pots, 36; prohibition to touch food, 55, 59, 65, 70, 92; prohibition to cook food, 82; disposal of food left by persons recently circumcised, 56; food placed in graves of old men, 72; mentioned in folk-tales, 101, 102, 105, 107, 108.
Foot, striking against stone, 79, 150 e. 70.
Footprints, people bewitched by, 51.
Forests, 17, 86; prohibition to build near, 9 sq.
Fowls, 25, 38.
Francolin (*see* Partridge).
Free love (*see* Sexual intercourse).
Frog, as totem, 5, 8; in games, 83.
Fruit, 127 pr. 24, 133 e. 2, 147 e. 58.

Gallas, 1.
Game, as food, 8, 24, 79; prohibition to drink milk after eating game, 11, 24 sq.
Game-pits (*see* Hunt).
Garment, 27 sqq.; prohibition to wear certain garments, 8 sqq.; occasions when garments are not worn, 45, 76; warriors' garment worn by girls, 58 sq.; women's garment worn by girls, 59 sq.; girls' garment worn by boys, 53; women's garment worn by boys, 55 sqq.; old men's garment worn by warriors, 13, 62; garment used to cover corpse, 70; garment worn inside out as sign of mourning, 71; garment exchanged with enemy as sign of submission, 75; garment tied on to sheep's

back, 48; omens connected with garments, 80; mentioned in proverbs, 127 pr. 22; mentioned in enigmas, 137 e. 22, 140 e. 33, 151 e. 76.
Garment-barrel, 40; used as friction drum, 40; used as divining box, 49.
Genealogical divisions (see Clan).
Generosity, 131 pr. 48.
Geographical divisions (see also Counties), 4, 47, 48 sq., 130 pr. 43; markings on shields of, 32; harvest festivals of, 46; land tenure of, 86.
Goats, 20 sq.; meat, milk, and blood taken as food, 22 sq.; method of butchering, 23; method of marking, 22; compartment in houses for, 13, 61, 69, 147 e. 57; occasions on which goats are slaughtered, 7, 8, 47, 56, 63, 65, 71, 75; anointing before slaughtering, 63, 65; punishment meted out to goats that steal, 75 sq.; goat castrated at peace ceremonies, 84; omens connected with goats, 20, 79 sqq., 89; myth re origin of goats, 98; mentioned in folk-tales, 102, 104; mentioned in proverbs, 132 pr. 52; mentioned in enigmas, 139 e. 27, 141 e. 35, 143 e. 43, 147 e. 57.
Goats' dung, teeth buried in, 30, 52; mentioned in folk-tales, 123.
Goat-skin, used as garment, 27 sq.; used for friction drum, 40; used as covering for bellows, 37; mentioned in proverbs, 125 pr. 9; mentioned in enigmas, 138 e. 25.
God (see Sun and Thunder).
Godfather, 52 sqq.
Godmother, 58 sqq., 61 sqq.
Gourd (see Calabash).
Government, 48.
Grain (see Corn).
Granary, 16; may not be looked into by woman who conceived before marriage, 17, 76; pebble placed in granary after harvest, 47; granary of thief burnt, 75; mentioned in folk-tales, 105.
Grandmother, at naming of children, 66; mentioned in games, 83; mentioned in enigmas, 139 e. 30, 147 e. 57, 149 e. 67.
Grass, roofs of houses made of, 13 sqq., 78; wet grass said to be good for cattle, 21; donkeys said to spoil grass, 22; considered sacred, 77 sq.; used as charm, 15, 62, 78, 89; hair, excrement, &c., hidden in grass, 30, 51 sq., 78; used to cover corpses, 70, 78; used when blood money is paid, 74; used at trial by ordeal, 77; as sign of peace, 74, 78; as form of oath, 85; thrown on ant mounds, 19, 78; used when cattle are bled, 78.
Grasshopper, 80.
Grazing grounds, 16, 20.
Grindstone, 143 e. 42.
Grubs, as food, 25.
Guardian (see Father).
Guinea fowl, 19, 110.

Hail, 20.
Hair, rules regarding wearing and disposal of, 29 sqq., 51; shaving as sign of mourning, 30, 70 sq.; shaving as sign of adoption and defeat, 30, 75; shaving during circumcision, 53, 58, 92; shaving during marriage ceremonies, 61 sq.; shaving of mother after birth, 65; cord used by warriors for binding hair, 87; mentioned in enigmas, 133 e. 1.
Halo, 100.
Hands, prohibition to eat with, 55, 59, 65, 70, 92; prohibition to touch body with, 92.
Handshaking, 80, 90 sq.; forbidden, 82.
Hare, mentioned in folk-tales, 101, 102 sq., 109; mentioned in proverbs, 125 pr. 7.
Harvest, work in connexion with, 19; ceremonies, 46; superstition regarding the Pleiades, 100.
Hawk, as totem, 5, 10; feather worn as ornament, 29.
Head, prohibition to strike, 9; of chief medicine man, 50, 83, 91; mentioned in enigmas, 151 e. 75.
Head-dress, of warriors, 28, 76, 150 e. 72; prohibition to wear, 9; of old men, 29; of persons recently circumcised, 56, 59 sq.; of brides, 58, 60, 61.
Heart, of person killed, 27; of animal killed, 23.
Herdsman, 20 sq., 61 sqq.; mentioned in enigmas, 150 e. 72 and 73.
Hiccoughs, 81.
Hide (see also Goat-skin and Thong), as dress, 27 sqq., 61 n. 4, 63, 141 e. 36; used at burial of old men, 72; piece of hide fastened on to gourds, 57; prohibition to sleep on new ox-hide, 25, 52; superstition regarding hides and corn-fields, 20; rings of hide, 12, 46, 63, 87.
Hill, feast held on top of, 47; Tindiret Hill, 48; Chepeloi Hill, 48; mentioned in enigmas, 146 e. 53.
Hoe, kinds in use, 18; value of, 76; superstition regarding breaking of, 20; mentioned in folk-tales, 102.
Homicide (see Murder).
Honey, as food, 25, 138 e. 24; prohibition to collect, 9.
Honey-barrel, 7, 25, 38, 86; value of, 76; used to eat from, 55; mentioned in folk-tales, 108.
Honey-bird, 25 n. 3, 111.
Honey-comb, 25, 137 e. 21.
Honey wine, method of preparing, 25.
Horn, used as musical in-

INDEX

strument, 33, 40; used by chief medicine man, 49; used during circumcision festivals, 55; hung in hut, 57; hung outside hut, 64; mentioned in enigmas, 151 e. 74.
Hornbill (ground), 104 sq., 111; prohibition to mention name of, 16.
Hornet, used during circumcision festival, 54.
Hornets' nest, 100.
Hospitality, 77, 125 pr. 10, 128 pr. 31 and 33, 130 pr. 40, 149 e. 68.
Houses, 13 sqq., 35, 37, 52 sqq., 61 sqq., 64 sqq., 69 sq.; furniture and central pole of, 14 sq., 72; partition between rooms, 13, 61, 69, 72, 150 e. 71; prohibitions regarding erection of, 8 sqq.; prohibition for women to enter, 16, 37; prohibition for men to enter, or to touch anything in, house, 35, 66, 74; prohibition for child to enter, 7; prohibition for mother of twins to enter, 68; prohibition for murderer to enter, 74; superstitions regarding interior of houses, 17, 61, 66, 68, 69 sqq., 140 e. 34; snakes in houses, 90; houses struck by lightning, 9, 100; charm for houses, 16; houses sprinkled with beer, 43; houses spat upon, 46; houses of thief destroyed, 75; omens connected with houses, 80 sq.; circumcision houses that catch fire, 91; mentioned in proverbs, 128 pr. 26; mentioned in enigmas, 145 e. 51, 147 e. 61.
Hunt, Nandi as hunters, 8 sqq., 17, 24, 120 sq., 125 pr. 11; dogs used for hunting, 24; superstitions of hunters, 24; hunter killed by wild animals, 72.
Hut (see House).
Hyena, as totem, 5, 7, 11; regarding killing of, 7, 80; punishment for imitating cry of, 7, 91; regarding droppings of, 7; flicking of ox-hide covers by women during howling of, 7, 11; prohibition for persons recently circumcised to be out of doors during howling of, 56, 60; called to eat corpse, 70; turning of corpse when not taken by, 11, 71; holding communication with spirits of the dead, 7; mentioned in folk-tales, 103, 104 sq., 109; mentioned in proverbs, 124 pr. 2, 128 pr. 28, 130 pr. 42 and 46; mentioned in enigmas, 139 e. 27.
Hyrax (skin), as garment, 8 sqq., 28.

Illness (see Sickness).
Incest, punishment for, 76.
Industries, 35 sqq.
Infanticide, 30, 68.
Inheritance, 72 sq.
Insects, sayings of, 111.
Intestines, eaten raw, 23; inspected, 45, 49, 63, 81; prayer for, 65.
Intoxication (see Drunkenness).
Iron, smelting and forging of, 36 sqq.; mentioned in proverbs, 127 pr. 25.
Iron wire, as ornament, 27 sqq.; used as payment, 71.

Jackal, as totem, 5, 8; mentioned in enigmas, 139 e. 27.
Judge, 11.
Jumping, 83.

Kamasia (Tuken) tribe, 2, 5, 7, 36, 52, 99, 134 e. 5; prohibition to go to or settle in country of, 8 sqq.
Kavirondo tribe, 24, 26 sq., 30, 50, 82, 139 e. 29; prohibition to go to or to settle in country of, 8 sqq.
Kidneys, eaten raw, 23.
Kikuyu tribe, 1 n. 2.
Kissing, 91.
Knives, 25; prohibition to mention by name, 43; bequeathed by father, 73; circumcision knives, 53, 59, 83; mentioned in proverbs, 129 pr. 35, 131 pr. 50; mentioned in enigmas, 142 e. 40.
Knot, 89 sq.; of feathers, 31; tied by mothers, 42, 89; prayer regarding, 43, 89; as record, 89.
Kosowa tribe, 5.
Kraal (see House and Cattle-kraal).

Land tenure, 86.
Lark, 111.
Laughing, at naming of children, 66.
Leglet, 27 sqq.; warriors' leglet worn by girls, 58 sq.
Leopard, tail worn by warriors, 28; claw worn as charm, 29; name for friction drum, 40; mentioned in folk-tales, 104.
Lightning, myths regarding, 99 sq., 111; huts struck by, 9, 100; cattle struck by, 9, 45, 99; trees struck by, 86 n. 5, 126 pr. 18; land struck by, 132 pr. 57; ceremonial uncleanness of person eating meat of animal struck by, 92, 99; may not be seen by women, 99.
Lion, as totem, 5, 9; claw or strip of skin worn as charm, 29; name for friction drum and bull roarer, 40; mentioned in folk-tales, 104, 109; mentioned in proverbs, 124 pr. 2.
Lion-skin head-dress, 28; prohibition to wear, 9; worn during the circumcision festivals, 54.
Liver, eaten raw, 23; mentioned in enigmas, 136 e. 15.
Lizard (tree), 111; (house), 140 e. 34.
Locusts, as food, 24, 92; charm against, 19, 86, 87; mentioned in folk-tales, 111.
Louse, 123, 137 e. 20, 139 e. 30.
Lumbwa (Kipsikīs) tribe,

INDEX

2, 5 ; prohibition to settle in country of, 8 sqq.; swords of, 33; liquid snuff used by, 26; chief medicine man of, 49, 64 n. 2 ; mentioned in enigmas, 145 e. 52.
Lyre, 39.

Madness, 81 sq., 106.
Magic, 51 sq., 71, 75, 132 pr. 52, 147 e. 61.
Magician, 51 sq., 71, 124 pr. 5.
Maize, 18.
Man, origin of, 98.
Manure, 19, 138 e. 26.
Marokor tribe, 5, 51.
Marriage, 60 sqq.; intermarriage of clans and families, 6, 8 sqq., 61; conception before marriage, 8 sqq., 17, 68, 76 ; marriage portion, 11, 61, 68, 69, 73 ; marriage by capture, 10 sq., 61 n. 2 ; marriage charm, 11, 62 sq.; slaughtering of goat at marriage, 8, 63; dress worn by bridegroom, 62 ; dress worn by bride, 61, 63; dress worn by women after marriage, 28 ; moral instruction given to bride and bridegroom, 62 ; consummation of marriage, 63 ; *eit'-ap-muket* ceremony, 64 ; hospitality to married people, 77; spitting when marriages are arranged, 79; superstition regarding stumbling of bride, 62, 91; mentioned in folk-tales, 105, 108, 114 sq.
Marrow, 116 sqq.
Masai tribe, 1 sqq., 5, 12 n. 2, 27, 29, 30, 31, 32, 41, 44, 48 n. 3, 88, 90 n., 106 ; Segella Masai, 5, 49 ; Uasin Gishu Masai, 36.
Meat, rules regarding eating of, 22 sq. ; mixing of meat and milk, 24, 55, 110; prohibition to eat certain meats, 25, 57, 64, 74 ; prohibition to eat alone, 43 ; ceremonial uncleanness after eating certain meats, 92; meat mentioned in games and folktales, 83, 101, 102.
Medicine, 24, 53, 58, 70, 74, 89, 92.
Medicine man (chief), 48 sqq. ; at *Saket-ap-eito* ceremony, 12 ; consulted before sowing corn, 19, 49; consulted before holding harvest festival, 47 ; consulted regarding war and welfare of warriors, 43, 49 sq. ; consulted by barren women, 68 ; donkeys of, 22 ; share of captured cattle, 43 sq. ; wives of, 51, 64 n. ; children of, 51, 83 ; representatives of, 43, 48 sqq., 86 ; methods of divining, 49, 82, 89 ; prohibition to touch head of, 50, 91 ; mentioned in folk-tales, 103, 104 sq.,108.
Medicine men (lesser), 51, 71 ; share of captured cattle, 44 ; methods of divining, 51, 89.
Menstruation, 82, 92.
Midwife, 64 sq.
Milk, as food, 22, 24, 68, 116 sqq. ; as libation, 15, 22, 44, 45, 69 ; used for anointing, 53, 58, 63, 65 ; mixing milk and meat, 24, 55, 110; mixing milk and game, 11, 24 sq. ; mixing milk and blood, 22, 52, 74 ; milking done by boys and girls, 21 ; milk compartment in houses, 14 sq.; milk given to the dying, 70 ; milk put in graves of old men, 72 ; goat's milk as purifier, 74 ; prohibition to drink milk, 70, 74 ; milk given to snakes, 90; milk given to dog, 98; mentioned in proverbs, 125 pr. 11; mentioned in enigmas, 137 e. 19, 149 e. 69.
Milk-vessel (*see* Calabash).
Millet (*see* Corn).
Miscarriage, superstitions regarding, 20, 90.
Mole, as food, 24 ; methods of trapping, 19 ; as totem, 5, 11; mentioned in enigmas, 146 e. 54.

Monkey (*Cercopithecus griseoviridis*), as totem, 5, 10.
(*Colobus guereza* var. *Caudatus*), as totem, 5, 11 ; skin used as dress or ornament, 28, 29 ; objection to killing, 80 ; mentioned in enigmas, 146 e. 55.
(Baboon), as food, 24 ; as totem, 5, 9.
Months, names of, 94 sq.
Moon, phases of, 95 sq. ; myths connected with, 97 sq. ; new moon, 79, 122 sq. ; eclipse of, 79, 100 ; halo round, 100 ; building poles cut during waning of, 15 ; mourning during waning of, 71 ; planting of corn during waxing of, 19 ; circumcision festivals started during waxing of, 52 ; marriage ceremonies during waxing of, 60 ; mentioned in enigmas, 151 e. 74.
Mortar, 38, 65 ; mentioned in folk-tales, 102.
Mother, prayer for absent warrior sons, 42 ; children of chief medicine man taken from, 51 ; duty during circumcision festivals, 52 sqq., 59 sq. ; part played during marriage,60sqq.; at birth, 64 sqq., 92 ; mourning for, 71 ; inheritance from, 73 ; answering greetings for children, 91 ; mentioned in folk-tales, 101 sq., 103, 107 ; mentioned in enigmas, 140 e. 31 and 32.
Mourning, 71 sq. ; prohibition to mourn, 56, 60.
Moving house or kraal, 10, 143 e. 43, 44 and 45, 144 e. 46 and 47.
Murder, 27, 73 sqq., 91 sq.
Mushroom, 146 e. 53.
Musical instruments, 39 sq.
Mutton, prohibition to eat, 25, 74.
Myths, 97 sqq.

Nail, 142 e. 40.
Nail-parings, 51.
Nakedness, shame regarding, 27, 132 pr. 55.
Names, 52 n. 3, 54 n., 55,

INDEX

57, 66 sqq., 85, 110 n. ; of twins, 68 ; naming of children of the Toiyoi and Kipasiso clans, 10 sq. ; prohibition to mention warriors by name, 43 ; prohibition for persons recently circumcised to call anybody by name, 56, 60 ; prohibition to mention dead person by name, 71.
Nandi tribe, history and origin of, 1 sqq., 5 ; old name for, 99 ; divisions of, 4 sq., 11 sq. ; tribal mark of, 27 ; representatives of, 48 sq., 86, 142 e. 39.
Nandi country, 1 ; old name for, 99 ; the *Saketap-eito* ceremony, 12 sq.
Neck, nape of, 22, 118 sq., 124 pr. 4.
Necklaces, 9, 27 sqq. ; girls' necklaces worn by boys during the circumcision ceremonies, 53, 55 ; necklaces worn to guard against the evil eye, 90.
Needle, 30, 33 ; teeth likened to and extracted by, 30.
Nettles (stinging), used during circumcision festival, 54, 57 ; used after marriage ceremony, 64 ; used to punish thieves, 75 sq.
Nile negroes, 1.
Nose, 148 e. 63.
Numbers, lucky and unlucky, 89.
Nurse, 61 sqq., 65, 101 sq.
Nyangori (Terik) tribe, 2, 5 n. 1, 111 n. 2 ; prohibition to settle in, 9 sq.

Oath, forms of, 85.
Obsidian, 138 e. 23.
Offal, used for purifying and cleansing, 7, 23, 65.
Offering (libation), 15, 22, 43, 47, 70 ; foreskins offered to God after circumcision, 55.
Oil (*see* Fat).
Omens, 23, 24, 36, 37, 38, 40, 45 sq., 62, 68, 70, 79 sqq., 81 sq., 150 e. 70 ; interpretation of, 49.
Ordeal, trial by, 76 sq.

Ornaments, 27 sqq. ; discarded or covered as sign of mourning, 71 ; inherited by daughters, 73 ; value of, 76 ; mentioned in folk-tales, 108.
Orphan, 52, 66.
Ostrich egg-shell beads, 28 sqq.
Ostrich-feather, head-dress, 28, 150 e. 72 ; as sign of peace, 78 n., 84.
Owl, 109 sq.
Ox (*see* Cattle).
Ox-pecker, 25, 129 pr. 38.

Paint, 33, 104.
Palm-wine, 26.
Parishes, 4, 48 ; captain of, 49.
Partridge, as food, 25 ; as totem, 5, 10 ; as bird of omen, 80 ; mentioned in folk-tales, 105, 110 sq.
Peace, 74, 78, 79, 84.
Pebbles, selected by women after the harvest festival, 47 ; used by medicine men for divining, 49, 71, 89.
Pegs, in houses, 15 ; broken after death, 72.
Pestle (*see* Mortar).
Pig, as totem, 5, 10 ; mentioned in proverbs, 128 pr. 29.
Pig-skin, shields of, 32.
Pigeon (green), 109.
Placenta, disposal of, 65.
Plaintain-eater, use of feathers of, 31.
Plantation (*see* Corn-fields).
Plants (*see* Trees).
Plate (of hide), 27 ; prohibition to use, 55.
Poison, methods of preparing, 25 n. ; ceremonial uncleanness connected with, 25, 92 ; poisoned arrows, 33 ; mentioned in folk-tales, 107 sq., 112 sq. ; mentioned in proverbs, 127 pr. 19.
Poles (of house), 15, 72, 135 e. 13, 142 e. 39.
Polygamy, 64.
Porcupine (quill), charm against vermin, 87.
Porridge, as food, 11, 22, 74 ; as offering, 46 ; mentioned in enigmas, 140 e. 31, 149 e. 67.
Pottery, 35 sq. ; as charm, 15, 69 ; used to eat with, 70 ; mentioned in enigmas, 145 e. 50.
Prayers, 15, 30, 35, 87, 41 sqq., 65, 78 sq., 81, 82, 123 ; attitude assumed whilst praying, 42 sqq. ; spitting before, 78.
Pregnant women, regarding food of, 23 ; *rutet-apkarik* ceremony, 64 ; prohibition to cohabit with, 66 ; superstitions connected with, 20, 90.
Pride, 130 pr. 43.
Prisoner of war, treatment of, 30, 75.
Products (agricultural), 17 sqq.
Prophecies, 49 sq.
Pumpkins, as food, 18 ; as drinking vessels, 36 ; mentioned in enigmas, 140 e. 32.
Punishment for crimes, 7, 24, 73 sqq., 131 pr. 51.

Quiver, 32 sq. ; value of, 76.

Rain, prayer for, 48 ; obtained by medicine men and rain-makers, 49, 52 ; as totem, 5, 9 ; prohibition to use rain water, 11 ; mentioned in enigmas, 148 e. 65.
Rainbow, 100, 149 e. 66.
Rain-makers, 52 ; share of captured cattle, 44.
Rain-medicine, 52.
Rat, as food, 24 ; method of trapping, 19 ; as totem, 5, 9 ; as good omen, 79 ; mentioned in folk-tales, 109 ; mentioned in proverbs, 132 pr. 54 ; mentioned in enigmas, 135 e. 10.
Record, how kept, 89.
Relationship, 92 sqq.
Relieving nature, 4?, 52, 78, 91.
Religious beliefs, 40 sqq.
Remorse, 128 pr. 32.
Rhinoceros, 6, 8, 24.
Ring, worn by old men,

326 INDEX

29; as charm, 12, 46, 63, 87.

River, huts built on banks of, 52, 74; bathing or washing in as method of lustration, 25, 44 sq., 56, 60, 65, 70, 82, 92; regarded as sanctuary, 74; mentioned in enigmas, 148 e. 64.

Road, prohibition to build near, 8; prohibition to relieve nature on the right side of, 43; mentioned in proverbs, 130 pr. 44; mentioned in enigmas, 148 e. 64.

Sacred animals (totem), 5, 6 sqq.; spitting at when seen, 79.

Salt, 21, 24; used as offering, 15, 19; used for anointing boys before circumcision, 53.

Salt-licks, 21, 46; mentioned in folk-tales, 108; mentioned in enigmas, 146 e. 56.

Salutations, 43, 90 sq.

Sandals, worn by warriors, 28, 79.

Scabbard, 32 sq.; of the sun, 98.

Scar, 31.

Scarifying the body, 70.

Seasons, 94.

Seed (see Corn).

Seminal emission, 92.

Senegal hartebeest, 24.

Serpent (see Snake).

Servants, of chief medicine man, 51.

Sexual intercourse, laws regulating, 6, 76, 91; before marriage, 6, 16, 82, 91; between guest and host's wife, 77, 125 pr. 10; prohibited, 15, 25, 26, 32, 52, 66, 74; ceremonial uncleanness after, 92.

Shadow, as embodying the soul, 41, 148 e. 62.

Shame, 27, 129 pr. 35, 132 pr. 55.

Shaving (see Hair).

Sheep, 20 sq.; compartment in houses for, 13; method of butchering, 23; branding, 22; bleeding, 22; slaughtering of pregnant sheep, 45 sq.; black sheep thrown in river during drought, 48; prohibition to eat flesh of, 25, 74; omens connected with, 80 sq.; myth re origin of, 98; mentioned in enigmas, 138 e. 26, 139 e. 27, 147 e. 57 and 58.

Shield, 31 sqq.; markings of, 32 sq.; beaten in lieu of drums, 40; of boys, 82.

Shoulder, cicatrices raised on, 31.

Sickness, 69 sq.; charms against, 29, 38, 87, 90; methods taken to ascertain cause of, 51; how diagnosis is made, 89; superstition connected with fire and sickness, 85; sickness of cattle, 45 sq., 81.

Sirikwa tribe, 2 sq.

Sister, salutations with brother, 91; guarded by brother after father's decease, 73; mentioned in enigmas, 130 e. 41.

Sitting down, prohibitions re, 36, 38.

Skins (see Hide and Garment).

Skull, used at trial by ordeal, 77.

Sky, myth regarding, 97 sq.; mentioned in enigmas, 141 e. 36.

Sleep, 81 sq., 144 e. 48; prohibited, 13, 54; turning over during, 98, 111 sqq.

Smiths, 36 sqq.; prohibition to associate with, 8; donkeys of, 22.

Snakes, 90; as totem, 5, 11; power of chief medicine man said to be derived from, 51; treatment of person bitten by, 70; omen connected with 79; charms against, 86, 87, mentioned in proverbs, 125 pr. 12; mentioned in enigmas, 138 e. 25.

Snare (see Trap).

Sneezing, 81; at naming of children, 66; forbidden, 43.

Snuff, 26.

Snuff-boxes, 26, 36.

Social divisions (see also Fire), 11.

Solanum fruit, as charm, 13; thrown on sacred fires, 45 sqq.; used by children as toys, 82.

Sorrow, shown at death, 70 sqq.

Sotik tribe, 2, 5.

Soul, 41, 70; departure of soul from body during sleep, 81.

Sparrow, 25, 111.

Speaking, 126 pr. 13, 128 pr. 27; prohibition to speak to chief medicine man, 50; prohibition to speak to pregnant girl, 76; prohibition to speak loudly, 72, 91 sq., 99.

Spear, different kinds of, 31; women forbidden to use, 31 n.; superstition connected with corn-fields, 20; of murderer, 74; value of, 76; striking or stepping over spear as form of oath, 85; boys' spears, 82 sq.; mentioned in folk-tales, 108; mentioned in enigmas, 151 e. 75.

Spider, 81.

Spirits of the dead, 41 sqq.; hyenas holding communication with, 7; persons holding communication with in dreams, 82; prayers addressed to, 41 sq., 51, 65; appeased by corn thrown into fire, 46, 70; invoked during the circumcision festivals, 54; believed to guard namesake, 66; held responsible for sickness, and propitiated, 69; believed to be responsible for earthquakes, 100; personified by snakes, 90; believed to set fire to grass, 100; fires and peep-holes of, 100; mentioned in enigmas, 133 e. 3, 150 e. 71.

Spitting, 37, 38, 78 sq., 81, 84; towards the east, 42, 43, 46, 56, 60; spitting out milk and beer, 47 sq.; prohibition to spit on the

INDEX

ground, 56; spitting by people possessed of the evil eye, 90.
Spittle, connected with witchcraft, 51, 147 e. 61.
Spokesman (*Kiruogindet*), 48 sq., 86, 142 e. 39.
Spoon, 59, 65, 92.
Spur-fowl (*see* Partridge).
Stars, 100; shooting stars, 79, 81.
Steam jets, 100.
Stepping over, spear or belt, 84 sq.; prohibition to step over various things, 23, 24, 36, 37, 38, 99.
Stick, carried by women, 28, 144 e. 47; carried by girls recently circumcised, 60; carried by herdsmen, 20, 73; notched as record, 89; used for cleansing milk vessels, 21, 62, 99; used for scratching the body, 92; prohibition to strike people and cattle with certain sticks, 86; mentioned in myth connected with origin of cattle, 98.
Stone (*see* also Pebble and Cooking-stones), 147 e. 59.
Stool, 12, 39, 63, 98; brought for stranger, 77; used at circumcision festival, 53; cut after death of owner, 72.
Straw for drinking through, 26, 98.
Striking people, prohibition regarding, 82.
Stumbling, omen of illluck, 62, 70, 91.
Suicide, 76.
Sun (*see* also East and West), myth *re*, 97 sq.; prayers and offerings to, 15, 22, 30, 35, 37, 42 sqq., 65; supposed not to be prayed to by chief medicine man, 51; *Ki-ingêt Asis* ceremony, 65, 66; as totem, 5, 11; mentioned in proverbs, 126 pr. 15 and 17; mentioned in enigmas, 136 e. 16; eclipse of, 79, 100; halo round, 100.
Surgery, 70.
Swahili, trading caravans of, 3; blood-brotherhood with, 84.
Sweet potatoes, 18 sq.
Sword, 31 sq.; women forbidden to gird on, 31 n.; value of, 76.

Tabu (*see* also Uncleanness), of clans, 8 sqq.
Tattoo, 30.
Teeth, 30, 51; extraction of two middle incisors of the lower jaw, 30, 72, 82, 94; burial of people who have no teeth, 72; mentioned in enigmas, 150 e. 71.
Tetanus, 30.
Theft, punishment for, 75 sq., 77; from potter, 36; from smith, 37; mentioned in proverbs, 130 pr. 40, 131 pr. 46 and 47.
Thigh, scars burnt on, 31.
Thong, 21, 57, 75, 139 e. 29.
Threshold, prohibition to sit on or touch, 17, 66; prohibition to cross, 68, 74.
Throbbing of the pulse, 81.
Thunder, myths *re*, 98, 99 sq., 111 sqq.
Thunder-gods, 41, 99 sq., 126 pr. 18, 132 pr. 57, 138 e. 24, 149 e. 66.
Thunder-storm, 9, 99.
Tick, 51, 83, 143 e. 45.
Time, divisions of, 94 sqq.
Tobacco, 18, 26; thrown in fire during thunderstorm, 99.
Tobacco pipes, 26.
Tobacco pouches, 26.
Toe, used for counting, 88 n.; omens connected with striking, 79; big toe, 69, 107.
Tongue, of animals, 23.
Tortoise, used at peace ceremony, 84.
Torture, during and after circumcision, 54, 57; after marriage, 64; of a thief, 75 sq.
Totem (*see* Sacred animals).
Town (*see* House).
Trade, 130 pr. 41.
Trance, 82.
Traps, for moles, rats, &c., 19; for game, 24; prohibition to make, 8 sqq.; superstition regarding stepping over a trap, 24.
Travellers, omens affecting, 79 sq.; hospitality accorded to, 77.
Trees, 86 sq.; sacred trees, 87; method of killing, 19; aversion to felling, 80, 87, 91; used for places of assembly, 49, 86; used for sacred fires, 45 sqq., 87; used as medicine, 24, 53, 58, 70, 74; foreskins buried at foot of, 55; used during the marriage ceremonies, 60 sqq.; planted on graves, 72; regarded as sanctuaries, 74; superstitious customs connected with, 86 sq.; struck by lightning, 86 n. 5, 126 pr. 18; mentioned in proverbs, 131 pr. 50 and 51; mentioned in enigmas, 142 e. 41, 145 e. 52, 147 e. 59.
Turf, used as manure, 19, 138 e. 26.
Twins, 68, 91; charm worn by, 29; mentioned in folk-tales, 103.

Uasin Gishu plateau, 1 sq.; former inhabitants of, 2, 36.
Uganda Railway, 1, 50 n. 2.
Umbilical cord, ceremony at cutting of, 65.
Uncle (maternal), 53, 58, 83, 94.
Uncleanness (ceremonial), 33, 91 sq.; methods of purification, 7, 25, 65, 68, 70, 72, 74, 91 sq.; unclean animals, 24; unclean birds, 25.

Vegetables, as food, 22, 133 e. 3.
Vermin in corn-fields, 19; charms against, 19, 86, 87.
Virgin, 58, 61 n. 5.
Vultures, cape made of feathers and worn by warriors, 28; feather worn as ornament, 29; mentioned in enigmas, 135 e. 9.

INDEX

War, 42 sqq.; positions held by the Talai and Tungo clans in, 9, 11; how warriors remind one another of, 31; officers responsible for the enrolment of troops, 49; chief medicine man's connexion with, 43, 49, 50 n. 1; omens connected with, 79 sq.; mentioned in folk-tales, 106, 114 sq., 120 sq.; mentioned in proverbs, 126 pr. 14; mentioned in enigmas, 139 e. 29.
War-horn, 33, 40.
Warriors, 12; houses of, 16, 128 pr. 26; duties of, 20; prohibition to till the ground, 78; prohibition to leave a house in the dark, 17; prohibitions during war, 43; superstition connected with pots, 36; superstition connected with gourds, 36; superstitions connected with the killing of an enemy, 27, 36, 74; superstitions connected with spitting, 78 sq.; superstitions connected with widows, 72; superstitions connected with the dead, 72; warriors' charms, 49, 87; dances, 44 sq., 47, 87; warriors who have been defeated, 44, 92; part taken by warriors in circumcision festivals, 53 sqq.; mentioned in folk-tales, 106 sq., 120 sqq.
Water, sprinkled on fire, 11; sprinkled on cattle, 45; prohibition to drink or wash the hands in, 52; purification by bathing or washing the hands in, 44, 55 sq., 59 sq., 65 sq., 70, 82, 92; purification by sprinkling water on the ground, 68; poured on the hands as sign of homage, 63, 77, 125 pr. 10, 128 pr. 33; mentioned in folk-tales, 106 sq.; mentioned in proverbs, 127 pr. 23, 129 pr. 39; mentioned in enigmas, 136 e. 17.
Waterbuck, 24.
Waterfall, 100.
Water-jar, 36; pebble placed in, 47.
Weaning, ceremonies connected with, 65 sq., 92.
Weapons, 31 sqq.; prohibition to carry, 50, 62; removal of at circumcision, 54; removal of at marriage, 63; left outside strangers' house, 77.
West, plants taken towards, 19; hair thrown towards, 30, 51, 71; corpses taken towards, 70.
Whetstone, 136 e. 15.
Whistling, to cattle, 20; to bees, 7; superstition regarding whistling in cornfields, 20.
Widows, treatment of, 71 sqq.; inherited by husband's brother, 73.
Wife (*see* also Barren and Marriage), rules regarding senior and junior wives, 8 sqq., 64; with child at the breast, 17, 66; maltreated by husband, 69; mentioned in folk-tales, 101 sq., 114 sq., 123; mentioned in enigmas, 141 e. 37.
Wild animal (*see* also Lion, Leopard, &c.), treatment of person mauled by, 70; ceremonies performed at death of persons killed by, 72.
Wind, superstition regarding, 20, 80; mentioned in enigmas, 150 e. 72.
Witchcraft (*see* Magic).
Woodpecker, prohibition to eat, 25; as bird of omen, 79 sq.
Work, woman's duty, 129 pr. 33; prohibition to, 20, 60, 64, 65, 100; wife's work performed by husband, 63.
Wrist, scars burnt on, 31.

Yawning, 81.

Zebra, 8, 24.

NANDI AND ALLIED TRIBES